Problems and Materials on Debtor and Creditor Law

ASPEN PUBLISHERS

Problems and Materials on Debtor and Creditor Law

Fourth Edition

Douglas J. Whaley
Emeritus Professor of Law
The Ohio State University

Jeffrey W. Morris
Samuel A. McCray Chair in Law
University of Dayton

Wolters Kluwer
Law & Business

AUSTIN   BOSTON   CHICAGO   NEW YORK   THE NETHERLANDS

Aspen Publishers
Attn: Permissions Department
76 Ninth Avenue, 7th Floor
New York, NY 10011-5201

To contact Customer Care, e-mail customer.care@aspenpublishers.com, call 1-800-234-1660, fax 1-800-901-9075, or mail correspondence to:

Aspen Publishers
Attn: Order Department
PO Box 990
Frederick, MD 21705

Printed in the United States of America.

1 2 3 4 5 6 7 8 9 0

ISBN 978-0-7355-7778-7

Library of Congress Cataloging-in-Publication Data

Whaley, Douglas J.
    Problems and materials on debtor and creditor law / Douglas J. Whaley, Jeffrey W. Morris — 4th ed.
        p. cm.
    Includes bibliographical references and index.
    ISBN 978-0-7355-7778-7 (alk. paper)
    1. Debtor and creditor — United States — Cases. 2. Bankruptcy — United States — Cases. I. Morris, Jeffrey W. II. Title. III. Title: Debtor and creditor law.

KF1501.W48 2006
343.7307′1 — dc22   2009032991

About Wolters Kluwer Law & Business

Wolters Kluwer Law & Business is a leading provider of research information and workflow solutions in key specialty areas. The strengths of the individual brands of Aspen Publishers, CCH, Kluwer Law International and Loislaw are aligned within Wolters Kluwer Law & Business to provide comprehensive, in-depth solutions and expert-authored content for the legal, professional and education markets.

CCH was founded in 1913 and has served more than four generations of business professionals and their clients. The CCH products in the Wolters Kluwer Law & Business group are highly regarded electronic and print resources for legal, securities, antitrust and trade regulation, government contracting, banking, pension, payroll, employment and labor, and healthcare reimbursement and compliance professionals.

Aspen Publishers is a leading information provider for attorneys, business professionals and law students. Written by preeminent authorities, Aspen products offer analytical and practical information in a range of specialty practice areas from securities law and intellectual property to mergers and acquisitions and pension/benefits. Aspen's trusted legal education resources provide professors and students with high-quality, up-to-date and effective resources for successful instruction and study in all areas of the law.

Kluwer Law International supplies the global business community with comprehensive English-language international legal information. Legal practitioners, corporate counsel and business executives around the world rely on the Kluwer Law International journals, loose-leafs, books and electronic products for authoritative information in many areas of international legal practice.

Loislaw is a premier provider of digitized legal content to small law firm practitioners of various specializations. Loislaw provides attorneys with the ability to quickly and efficiently find the necessary legal information they need, when and where they need it, by facilitating access to primary law as well as state-specific law, records, forms and treatises.

Wolters Kluwer Law & Business, a unit of Wolters Kluwer, is headquartered in New York and Riverwoods, Illinois. Wolters Kluwer is a leading multinational publisher and information services company.

Jeff Morris dedicates this book to C. David Butler, Esq., the Honorable W. Homer Drake, and the Honorable Joe Lee, who have provided him with many opportunities and invaluable guidance in learning about bankruptcy and its impact on people.

Douglas Whaley dedicates this book to his nephews, Adam Latek, Aaron Jeffrie, and Lee Matheson, with the sincere hope that they never need to know anything about bankruptcy.

SUMMARY OF CONTENTS

CONTENTS

Chapter 9. Reorganization in Chapter 11   **395**

Chapter 10. Family Farmer Reorganizations   **527**

Chapter 11. Jurisdiction   543

PREFACE

A knowledge of bankruptcy law is important not only to those attorneys who plan to become members of the bankruptcy bar, but for virtually everyone in legal practice. Whatever commercial plans are being made, the possibility that the various parties might end up in bankruptcy means that the careful advisor will consider what that will mean to the endeavor under consideration and will take steps to minimalize the impact a bankruptcy filing will have. Attorneys handling divorces must structure the divorce decree keeping in mind how the possible bankruptcy of one of the ex-spouses might affect the property division. Most attorneys will have clients who become ensnared in bankruptcy matters, even if the attorney him/herself manages to escape such difficulties.

The Bankruptcy Code is complicated, being much amended by Congress and subject to divergent interpretations by the courts. It is supplemented by the Bankruptcy Rules, and also by other federal statutes having to do with jurisdiction, bankruptcy crimes, etc. Outside of the federal bankruptcy arena, the states have enacted statutes dealing with debtor/creditor problems, and this book addresses many of the issues that arise from all of these things.

This fourth edition contains the major cases that address bankruptcy and related laws, and these cases deserve the careful study of anyone who would master this subject. However, the bulk of the rules and issues of this course are addressed through a series of Problems that the student must consider with statute book in hand, being ready to answer the Problems when called on by the instructor. We believe that the Problem method is the superior way to study statutory material and to understand why the statute is written the way it is. We hope you, the student, agree and finish the book with a confidence that the basics of this difficult subject have been covered so that you could practice law in this area feeling that the Bankruptcy Code and related statutes are not as mysterious as they certainly look to someone approaching them for the first time.

ACKNOWLEDGMENTS

Jeff Morris acknowledges the contributions of the following: my family, who once again endured in general good humor the limited patience I sometimes display during projects such as the writing of this book; my colleague, Charlie Hallinan, who has offered guidance on the widest range of legal issues (bankruptcy and otherwise) over the years; the members of the National Bankruptcy Conference who have allowed me to see lawyers working selflessly to improve the administration of the bankruptcy laws; the Chairs and members of the Advisory Committee on Bankruptcy Rules and the supporting staff from the Administrative Office of the United States Courts; Jeffrey Ferriell, who provided thoughtful and extensive comments on an earlier version of the text; and my students, who over the years have offered fresh perspectives on old and new issues and whose intellectual curiosity provides the spark that makes teaching prospective lawyers such a great job.

Douglas Whaley would like to thank the following: the late Pierre Loiseaux, Professor Emeritus at The University of California at Davis, who long ago taught him this subject when they were both at the University of Texas; Pamela Maggied, a bankruptcy specialist in Columbus who has answered many a query through the years; Elizabeth Warren and Jay Lawrence Westbrook; Jeffrey Ferriell of Capital University Law School, who bravely taught out of this book when it was still very rough and recommended many useful changes; and Jerry Bunge, who organized the material as the authors put it together. Finally, much thanks is owed to all the students who have studied this subject under him through the years, and who taught him as much about the law as he taught them, with a particular thanks to the Ohio State Debtor/Creditor class of the fall of 1996, who endured this book in embryonic form and made many useful suggestions.

Problems and Materials on
Debtor and Creditor Law

CHAPTER 1

Introduction to Debtor and Creditor Law

I. Overview of Bankruptcy Law

Bankruptcy is entirely a creation of federal law. Article 1, Section 8, Clause 4 of the U.S. Constitution provides that Congress "shall make uniform laws on the subject of bankruptcies throughout the United States." Over the years, Congress has acted a number of times to create a bankruptcy system. After a series of bankruptcy laws that were generally short-lived, Congress enacted what became our first truly permanent bankruptcy law system in 1898. Forty years later, during the Great Depression, Congress enacted substantial amendments to the bankruptcy system through the adoption of the Chandler Act, the passage of which greatly expanded the reorganization provisions of the bankruptcy laws.

Another forty years later, Congress passed the Bankruptcy Reform Act of 1978. This Act is commonly referred to as the Bankruptcy Code (to distinguish it from the Bankruptcy Act, as the prior law was known), and it became effective for all cases commenced on or after October 1, 1979. Congress has become a great deal more active in the area of bankruptcy legislation since the Bankruptcy Code was adopted. Rather than waiting another forty years for significant bankruptcy amendments, Congress enacted significant changes to the Code in 1984, 1986, 1990, and 1994. As we shall discuss in detail, in 2005 Congress made major amendments to the Bankruptcy Code, the chief aim of which was to make it more difficult for individuals to file a liquidation bankruptcy under Chapter 7, and therefore to force these people into repayment plans under Chapter 13. Congress also has authored a number of other amendments in between enactment of the more substantial revisions.

The Bankruptcy Code comprises the entirety of Title 11 of the United States Code. It is separated into eight chapters. Until 1986, all of the chapters had odd numbers: 1, 3, 5, 7, 9, 11, and 13. In 1986, Congress added Chapter 12, creating a new chapter for relief for family farmers. The arabic number designation of chapters also serves to distinguish the Bankruptcy Code from the Bankruptcy Act, whose chapters were designated by roman numerals. Therefore, you should be careful in reading older bankruptcy decisions involving Chapter XI or some other chapter identified by roman numerals. The concepts and policies included in those earlier decisions may still be part of the bankruptcy laws, but you must exercise caution in determining that the provisions of the Bankruptcy Code are consistent with the law being applied in cases under the Bankruptcy Act.

Bankruptcy law has two primary goals: It seeks the orderly and equitable repayment of claims for the benefit of creditors, and it offers an economic fresh start to the proverbial "honest but unfortunate debtor." *See* Local Loan Co. v. Hunt, 292 U.S. 234 (1934) (this is perhaps the most cited bankruptcy decision of the Supreme Court). In some ways, these goals conflict. The more assets we permit a debtor to keep, the "fresher" the debtor's start. On the other hand, the debtor's retention of the assets lessens the amount that creditors can recover in satisfaction of their claims. We will see a number of instances where this tension is evident.

As with most statutory schemes, definitions are vitally important. The Bankruptcy Code is no exception. Section 101 contains a lengthy list of definitions that apply generally throughout the Code. Specific provisions of the Code often contain their own definitions (*see, e.g.*, §547(a)), which you should become familiar with in addition to the listing of definitions in §101. In fact, it is always prudent to check back with §101's listing of definitions before offering advice or making an argument on a bankruptcy matter.

The provisions of Chapters 1, 3, and 5 apply generally in all bankruptcy cases except to the extent that specific provisions of the other operative chapters override the general provisions. For example, the automatic stay created under §362 applies in cases under Chapters 7, 11, and 13. By way of contrast, an objection to a Chapter 7 discharge under the terms of §727 would be inappropriate in a Chapter 13 case.

More than 1,590,000 bankruptcy cases were filed in the year 2004. In the bankruptcies filed by individuals, 55 percent were by women, and the average filer had 2.7 dependants to support. Many had had major medical difficulties in the period before filing, and had often lost their jobs and/or their homes. The median age of the filers was 41, and 54 percent had had some college education. Bankruptcy filings increased in 2005 to over 2,000,000 cases as debtors filed for relief in advance of the effective date of the substantial revisions to the Code that became effective on October 19, 2005. After the surge in filings, only 677,000 cases were filed in 2006. Problems with the economy have caused the filings to increase, and estimates are that approximately 1,700,000 cases will be filed in 2009. It seems that the rate of bankruptcy filings might ultimately be more closely correlated to economic factors than to legislative enactments.

There are two generic forms of bankruptcy relief, liquidation and reorganization, but debtors may proceed under five different chapters of the Bankruptcy Code to obtain that relief. Cases may be filed under Chapters 7, 9, 11, 12, or 13. Chapter 9 is available only to municipalities, and it is used only infrequently.[1] Chapter 12 relief is

---

1. The leading treatise on bankruptcy law of course treats the matter; *see* Collier on Bankruptcy Chapters 900-946 (15th ed. 1997); *see also* Michael W. McConnell & Randal C. Picker, When Cities Go Broke: A Conceptual Introduction to Municipal Bankruptcy, 60 U. Chi. L. Rev. 425 (1993).

limited to family farmers, and there are usually fewer than one thousand Chapter 12 cases commenced in any one year nationwide. The vast bulk of bankruptcy proceedings are brought under Chapter 7, Chapter 11, or Chapter 13.

The most common form of bankruptcy relief is under Chapter 7. In the typical case, the debtor files a petition for relief under Chapter 7 along with supporting documents setting out all of the debtor's assets and liabilities. The commencement of the case creates an automatic stay against creditor collection efforts (Bankruptcy Code §362), and it also operates to create a bankruptcy estate comprised, inter alia, of all of the debtor's interests in property as of the commencement of the case. Bankruptcy Code §541(a)(1). The creditors listed in the bankruptcy schedules soon receive notices from the court that the case has been filed. The creditors are given a limited amount of time in which to file objections to the debtor's discharge or to file complaints to have their individual claims excepted from the discharge. Simultaneously, a trustee is appointed or elected to represent the interests of the bankruptcy estate. The trustee may also object to the debtor's discharge, but his or her most regularly performed duty is to collect and liquidate the assets of the estate so they may be redistributed to creditors according to the priority established by the Bankruptcy Code. In evaluating the assets of the estate, the trustee will likely scrutinize the list of property the debtor claims as exempt from the estate. If the property is exempt, it is returned to the debtor free of most claims that creditors might assert. The trustee also will review the debtor's financial affairs to determine if the debtor improperly preferred one creditor over others or perhaps transferred property in a manner that remains vulnerable to attack by the trustee. If the trustee is successful in challenging those transactions, the property is returned to the estate and thereafter liquidated and distributed to the creditors. In that position, the trustee acts as a representative of the unsecured creditors of the debtor.

Obtaining a discharge of debts is the debtor's primary goal in seeking bankruptcy relief. The initial notice to creditors will inform them that they have a limited amount of time in which to object to the entry of a discharge for the debtor (or to make a motion to dismiss the case or convert it to another chapter per §707(b)). Additionally, there are a number of specific claims that might be excepted from the discharge. These include obligations for alimony and child support, taxes, and student loans. Debts from fraud, willful and malicious injuries inflicted by the debtor, and similar claims might also be excepted from the discharge. Once the property of the estate has been liquidated and distributed to the creditors, and either no objections to discharge are filed or all objections have been resolved, then the case is closed.

In most instances Chapter 7 cases are nominal or no asset cases involving very limited administration by a trustee. The cases pass through the system relatively expeditiously. That is especially important given that approximately 1,138,000 Chapter 7 cases were filed in 2004.

Cases under Chapters 11, 12, and 13 are fundamentally different from Chapter 7 cases. These reorganization chapters anticipate the payment of a debtor's obligations (in whole or in part) out of the debtor's future income. As indicated previously, Chapter 12 cases are available only to family farmers, and only individuals with regular income are eligible for Chapter 13 relief. Chapter 11, on the other hand, is much more generally available. Chapter 11 debtors include Enron, Kmart, Winn-Dixie, and a frightening number of major airlines. It has also been used by the singer James Taylor (no, not that one, but the James Taylor who was the lead singer in Kool and the Gang), as well as by individual debtors who are not engaged in business. Even the Catholic Dioceses of Tucson, Spokane, and Portland (Oregon) have filed for Chapter 11 relief. Nonetheless, it is primarily the chapter for business reorganizations. In 2009, even General Motors joined the ranks of Chapter 11 debtors with its filing.

In Chapter 11 cases, the debtor who initiates the case becomes a "debtor in possession," or DIP, and thus has all the rights and powers of a trustee and serves that function in the Chapter 11 case. Certainly, this creates difficulties in that the same people who were running the business unsuccessfully the day before bankruptcy are now continued in place to operate the debtor. During the pendency of the Chapter 11 case, the debtor continues to operate its business with a goal of increasing its profitability to generate the funds necessary to make the payments that may be called for in any plan. In some instances, it is possible to replace the debtor in possession with a trustee if appropriate cause is shown. The appointment of a trustee is a relatively drastic measure in a Chapter 11 case, and the norm is to retain the debtor in possession in order to avoid the additional expense of bringing in new management to operate the business, as would occur with the appointment of a trustee. In some cases, the court might appoint an examiner whose obligations do not entail operation of the debtor's business but instead are generally limited to investigation of the debtor's prebankruptcy financial affairs.

While the debtor in possession is operating the business, the automatic stay is holding off creditor collection efforts just as it does in Chapter 7 cases. In addition to operating the business, however, the debtor in possession also must begin to formulate a plan of reorganization that it will propose to creditors. The plan will classify creditors according to their interests in property or other legal status, and it will set out the means by which the debtor will accomplish or complete the plan. Generally speaking, the plan will offer the repayment of some or all of the debtor's outstanding obligations over a period of time. Creditors then vote on the plan, and if the requisite majorities in number and amount of creditors and claims accept the plan, the court may confirm it. Confirmation of the plan in Chapter 11 operates as a discharge of the debtor's past obligations. The new obligations set out in the plan are essentially substituted for the previously existing debts. While creditors may individually participate in the proceedings, unsecured creditors generally act through the medium of a creditors' committee appointed by the United States trustee.

Chapter 12 cases may only be commenced voluntarily, and only by family farmers (or family fishermen) with a regular income. This chapter of the Bankruptcy Code, added in 1986, was intended to meet the bankruptcy reorganization needs of the nation's family farmers, who faced severe financial crises in the mid-1980s. Bankruptcy relief under Chapter 11 was viewed as too cumbersome and expensive for family farmers, and the then-existing debt limits for Chapter 13 cases rendered many of those farmers ineligible for Chapter 13 relief. Thus Congress created Chapter 12, which permits the reorganization of a farming business but accomplishes it in a manner very similar to the process set out in Chapter 13. In fact, most of the provisions of Chapter 12 were taken directly from Chapter 13.

In Chapter 12 cases, the debtor proposes a repayment plan to creditors, but the creditors have no vote on that plan. Instead, the debtor must submit all of its disposable income to fund the plan for at least three years. Additionally, the value of the payments to be made to unsecured creditors over the life of the plan must be at least equal to what the creditors would receive in a Chapter 7 liquidation bankruptcy. Secured creditors must be paid an amount equal to the value of the secured claim. However, creditors do not have the ability to prevent confirmation of the debtor's Chapter 12 plan by virtue of their votes. Instead, creditors may object to confirmation of the plan on the grounds that it does not meet some requirements set out in the Bankruptcy Code.

If the plan is confirmed, then the provisions of that plan bind the debtor and all creditors. Unlike in Chapter 11, in a Chapter 12 case, the debtor does not receive a discharge until all of the payments required under the plan are made. If the debtor fails to make those payments, creditors may seek to have the case dismissed. Dismissal would operate to reinstate the obligations as if no bankruptcy had been filed.

Importantly, debtors can propose to repay secured claims over a lengthy period of time. Thus, debtors with large mortgages on their farmland can stretch those payments out over a very long period, thereby improving their cash flow in making the enterprise economically viable.

Chapter 13 cases are available only to individuals with a regular income whose unsecured debts do not exceed $336,900 and whose secured debts do not exceed $1,010,650. These figures are adjusted every three years, with the next adjustment to be made on April 1, 2010. Chapter 13 is available to individual debtors who operate businesses, as well as to consumers. The bulk of Chapter 13 cases are consumer bankruptcy proceedings. In Chapter 13 the debtor avoids the liquidation of assets that would occur in a Chapter 7 case. Instead, the debtor agrees to make payments on his or her various debts over a three- to five-year period. Unless the debtor is paying all claims in full, all of the debtor's income — after payment of the ordinary and necessary living expenses — must be devoted to the funding of the plan. This "disposable income" is usually turned over to the Chapter 13 trustee, who then distributes the funds to the creditors according to the terms of a confirmed plan. Creditors cannot vote on the debtor's plan, but instead are protected by the requirement that the debtor must pay all of his or her disposable income into the plan for at least three years, and by the requirement that the payments being made to creditors must equal at least what the creditors would receive in a Chapter 7 case.

Since Chapter 13 allows debtors to retain their nonexempt assets, they frequently use it to protect their interests in their principal residence. Many Chapter 13 cases are filed on the eve of (if not moments before) the foreclosure of a mortgage on their residence. The provisions of Chapter 13 allow the debtor to cure any defaults that may exist under the mortgage and reinstate their relationship with the creditor to their predefault status. As with Chapter 12 cases, the debtor does not receive a discharge until all of the payments called for under the plan have been made. If the debtor fails to complete the payments, then the case will be either dismissed or converted to Chapter 7 unless the debtor can demonstrate that the inability to make the payments is due to circumstances for which the debtor is not justly accountable and the payments that have already been made under the plan exceed the value that creditors would have received in the case had it proceeded to liquidation under Chapter 7. There are a number of prerequisites to confirmation of a debtor's Chapter 13 plan, but the most significant limitation on confirmation is the requirement that the court find that the plan is proposed in good faith. A substantial body of law has been created on this issue. Suffice it to say that the discretion provided to bankruptcy judges in determining whether a particular Chapter 13 plan is proposed in good faith is significant.

All of these issues are governed by Title 11 of the United States Code, the Bankruptcy Code, and most are decided by the bankruptcy court. The bankruptcy courts are established under Article I of the Constitution, and the judges who staff the court serve 14-year terms. Their salaries are not protected against reduction during the term, and they can be removed from office for less than impeachable grounds. Thus, they are not Article III courts under the Constitution, and their powers are limited.

In 1982, the Supreme Court decided Northern Pipeline Construction Co. v. Marathon Pipe Line Co., 458 U.S. 50 (1982). The Court held that the jurisdictional provisions governing the bankruptcy courts were unconstitutional because they placed excessive authority in an Article I court. After a lengthy period of congressional haggling, the current jurisdictional system was established in 1984. The "new" system may still suffer from the constitutional infirmities identified by the Supreme Court in *Marathon,* but it continues to operate, those questions notwithstanding.

The bankruptcy courts essentially exercise the jurisdiction of the district court pursuant to a referral of the cases by the district court to the bankruptcy judge. The bankruptcy judge can issue final orders in a variety of areas, and in other instances may submit proposed findings of fact and conclusions of law to the district court. Final orders issued by bankruptcy judges are appealable to the district court, or, in many circuits to a special Bankruptcy Appellate Panel ("BAP") made up of bankruptcy judges. In some cases, an appeal may go directly to the Circuit Court of Appeals. Thereafter, appeals follow the regular federal process to the courts of appeals and then to the Supreme Court.

As you work through these materials, keep in mind that the Bankruptcy Code offers several options for most debtors. They might seek relief under Chapter 7, Chapter 11, or Chapter 13. Similarly, creditor responses to those actions may vary. Be mindful of the significant time and expense limitations inherent in bankruptcy proceedings. Consider whether the solutions you propose to the problems presented are feasible, not just under the terms of the Bankruptcy Code, but also under the temporal and financial restraints presented by most bankruptcy cases.

II. Creditors and Their Liens

As mentioned above, creditors who have valid lien interests in a debtor's property are usually able to retrieve that property from the bankruptcy proceeding, a valuable right. A lien that the trustee in bankruptcy cannot attack is said to be "perfected," and it is the goal of every creditor to make sure his or her interest is perfected. With any luck you will have studied these issues in a course on secured transactions, but in any event, what follows is an overview of the matter.

A lien is a legal interest in the debtor's property awarded to a creditor to protect a credit extension. There are three basic kinds: consensual, judicial, and statutory.

A. *Consensual Liens*

With a consensual lien, the debtor voluntarily nominates some of his or her property as collateral to secure a loan. If the collateral is real property, the resulting lien is called a mortgage, with the debtor being the mortgagor and the creditor the mortgagee. The Statute of Frauds requires the mortgage to be in writing, and the mortgagee "perfects" its lien by filing it in the real property records, thus gaining priority over others such as buyers of the realty, different creditors, and the debtor's trustee in bankruptcy.

If the creditor wants a consensual lien in personal property (or fixtures), the resulting lien is called a *security interest,* and the process is governed by Article 9 of the Uniform Commercial Code. In Article 9 (entitled "Secured Transactions"), the creditor is called the "secured party," and certain steps are required before the creditor's security interest in the collateral is truly protected. The first of these is "attachment" of the security interest, a process that gives the creditor rights against the collateral that are valid between the creditor and the debtor. Attachment is described in §9-203 of the Uniform Commercial Code, but generally it requires that the secured party have given value, that the debtor have rights in the property nominated as collateral, and that the debtor sign a security agreement granting the creditor rights in certain described property. The secured party then *perfects* this security interest (makes it good against most of the rest of the world) in a number of possible different ways, the two most common being that the creditor takes physical possession of the collateral (called a "pledge"), or files a public notice (a "financing statement") alerting others to the creditor's security interest in the described collateral; *see* Uniform Commercial Code §§9-501 et seq. The financing statement is indexed under the debtor's name so that later creditors contemplating a loan to the same debtor can check the records and see what property of the debtor is already encumbered.

Generally, a perfected security interest in favor of a creditor prevails against later claimants to the collateral, particularly, for our purposes, the debtor's trustee in bankruptcy. However, if the secured party has failed to take the relevant steps to perfect his or her security interest — he or she has loaned the money and had the debtor sign a security agreement so "attachment" has occurred, but failed for some reason to file a financing statement, so that the security interest is still "unperfected" — the creditor will lose the collateral to others, most importantly the debtor's trustee in bankruptcy; *see* Uniform Commercial Code §§9-102(a)(52)(C) and 9-317(a)(2).

Article 9 of the Uniform Commercial Code also regulates many other facets of the secured transaction. The rules in the 9-600s of the Code regulate the repossession of the collateral in the event of default, allowing the secured party to seize the relevant property without going through a court proceeding — this is called self-help repossession — as long as this can be done without a breach of the peace (a creditor who breaches the peace while repossessing is guilty of conversion); *see* Uniform Commercial Code §9-609. Following repossession, the secured party may sometimes elect to keep the repossessed property and forget the rest of the debt (a "strict foreclosure" — *see* U.C.C. §9-620) or to hold a foreclosure sale, sell the property, and then pursue the debtor for any remaining deficiency; U.C.C. §9-608. If the collateral consists of consumer goods (the family car, the living room suite, etc.), state consumer laws often give the debtor special rights, and therefore must be consulted carefully before consumer goods are repossessed.

Other rules from Article 9 of the Uniform Commercial Code will be explored as they arise in a bankruptcy context later in this book.

B.   Judicial Liens

Comes the happy day when you, counselor at law, actually win a judgment in a lawsuit. Now what? All you currently have is a decree from a court that the judgment defendant owes your client a set amount of money. If the defendant is unwilling to pay up voluntarily, you must now take steps to *levy execution* of your judgment. The procedures vary from state to state, but generally this is done by sending out the sheriff or bailiff or other court official to seize property of the debtor, thus creating a judicial lien on that property, which is then sold by the sheriff and the proceeds applied against the judgment debt. (Sometimes, this process is done as a precautionary measure *before* trial, when the court can be convinced that otherwise the debtor will hide or destroy the property, in which case it is called "prejudgment attachment.") If the debtor has real property, the sheriff will subject it to the judgment by filing the writ of execution in the real property records (procedures vary from state to state — in some jurisdictions, the entry of judgment in the court records is enough by itself to impose the judicial lien on all of the debtor's property in the same county). In order to reach intangible rights of the debtor (for example, the debtor's equitable rights), the creditor files a "creditor's bill," which in most states, requires the debtor to appear and account, and in any event fixes a judicial lien on these intangible rights. In all states the laws provide for *proceedings supplemental* to a judgment by which the defendant may be made to appear and answer questions about his or her financial situation.

1.   Garnishment

If the debtor's property is in the hands of others (the debtor's employer may owe salary, for example, or a bank may carry an account for the debtor), it can be reached by a *garnishment* proceeding. Typically, this is a court proceeding ancillary to the original judgment by which a writ is issued to the person having the debtor's property (the garnishee defendant — *i.e.*, the employer or the bank), requiring this person to surrender to the court whatever property of the debtor he or she currently holds.

2.   Receivership

If the debtor's affairs are in a tangle or the debtor is misbehaving (hiding property, for example), creditors of all kinds may apply to a court and ask the judge to appoint a receiver, who will take charge of the debtor's property and make sure it is preserved. Again, the rules for a receivership vary widely from state to state, including the issue of whether a receivership creates a judicial lien of any kind on the property.

3.   Assignment for the Benefit of Creditors

Most states also have a statutory procedure whereby the debtor can go to court, make an "assignment for the benefit of creditors" (sometimes called an "ABC"), and have an assignee appointed. The assignee then takes control over all the debtor's property not already subject to perfected liens, and this typically creates a judicial lien over that property in favor of the unsecured creditors. The advantage to the debtor from an ABC is that the creditors have to stop hounding him or her, and from the moment of the assignment they are frozen in position, so that one cannot thereafter get an advantage over the other. The assignee will sell the debtor's property and make a mannered disposition of the proceeds to the creditors. The disadvantage to the debtor is that after the ABC is over, the debtor still owes the unpaid balance — there is no discharge of debts, as there is in a bankruptcy proceeding. For a discussion of the operation of one state's ABC system, *see* Joel B. Weinberg, California General Assignments: Still Alive, Kicking and Useful, 29 Cal. Bankr. J. 293 (2007).

On the other hand, while the ABC is in place, it may be possible for the debtor to accomplish a *workout* or, as it is sometimes called, a *composition of creditors*. This avoids entirely the need to have a lien of any kind, and is nothing more than a contract between the debtor and the creditors by which they agree to accept a portion of the monies owed them and forget the rest, and the rules here are simply those of basic contracts law. Such a workout is bounded only by the creativity of the parties involved in its negotiation.

PROBLEM 1-1

When her creditors' demands became so severe that she could no longer sleep nights, Portia Moot filed an Assignment for the Benefit of Creditors in the local court-house, and the judge appointed an assignee to take over her nonexempt property. The assignee sent notices to all of Portia's creditors, telling them that collection activities must cease and inviting them to a meeting at which Portia would appear and answer questions about her financial situation. When this meeting was held, Portia's attorney proposed a workout agreement by which all of the creditors would agree to accept half the monies owed them (payable over the next year) and forgo the rest, and Portia agreed that if they did this, she would forgo filing a petition in bankruptcy (where it was obvious they would get nothing and their debts would be discharged). One of these creditors was the electric company, and Joan Glass, the head of its credit department, comes to you, the attorney for the electric company, with the following dilemma. Portia owed the company $840, but in the workout the company agreed to accept $420, to be paid by Portia in 12 installments over a one-year period. All the other creditors also agreed to accept half in full satisfaction, but Joan has just learned that Portia made a secret agreement to pay her own mother in full the money Portia had borrowed years ago. Does this discovery void the composition agreement between the creditors? This could be important because Portia has recently secured a very high-paying job and can easily afford to pay her creditors more. The answer here should send you back to studying the basic course in contracts law. *See also* Hanover Natl. Bank v. Blake, 142 N.Y. 404, 37 N.E. 519 (1894); Comment, *Compositions With Creditors: Executed and Executory Secret Preferences,* 28 U. Pitt. L. Rev. 344 (1966).

C.   Statutory Liens

By statute, or by virtue of the common law, certain creditors are automatically given liens on the debtor's property to protect a credit extension. Statutory liens, like judicial liens, are involuntary, so that they in no way depend on the consent of the debtor before they arise. Every state has a wide variety of nonuniform statutes on point, but the most common kinds are mentioned below.

1.   Mechanics' Liens

Those who perform work on construction projects on real property ("mechanics") or those who supply materials to the jobsite ("materialmen") are entitled to file a lien on the realty in the real property records to secure the monies owed them from the construction project. These mechanics' liens can be claimed by the lowliest employee remaining unpaid. It does not matter that the owner of the realty paid the contractor in full; if the contractor did not pass this payment along to his or her employees, they can still file their mechanics' liens (though the statutes typically set up time periods in which to do so, say 60 days from the last day on which the mechanic performed any work). The idea here is to make the owner of the realty very interested in seeing that the payments are correctly applied so that all who worked on the project or supplied materials to it get paid.

2. Artisans' Liens

Similarly, those who perform work on *personal* property (the car repair shop, appliance repair departments, etc.) get an artisans' lien on any property repaired to the extent that the debtor does not make the required payments. Artisans' liens are usually *possessory* liens, meaning that the lien is lost if the artisan loses possession of the property, which is why the car dealership that has fixed your car won't give it back until you pay for the repairs.

3. Tax Liens

If you do not pay your taxes, the taxing entity will slap a tax lien on your property, seize it and sell it, and then come after you for any amount still due. The Federal Tax Lien, codified in the Internal Revenue Code, 26 U.S.C. §§6321-6323, is an awesome monster, reaching all of the debtor's property, real or personal, now owned or after-acquired, usually exempt from creditor process or not. Pay your taxes or the IRS literally has the ability to leave you standing in the middle of the street without even a barrel to hide your nakedness.

4. Many Others

Landlords, innkeepers, those caring for livestock ("agisters"), and a host of others are granted statutory liens by various laws. Attorneys — good news — also are the beneficiaries of statutory liens in their favor under the laws of most states, and these liens are typically of two types, both protecting the unpaid fees due the attorney: a *retaining* lien on any property of the client in the possession of the attorney, and a *charging* lien on any judgment obtained by the attorney's efforts.

III. Collection of Debts Outside of Bankruptcy

A. *Collection Torts*

The collection of debts is an ugly business in which the usage of trade seems to be outrageous conduct and a complete disregard for the rules of fair play. We are all familiar with the classic debtor dodge "the check is in the mail." Creditors feel little sympathy for the deadbeat debtor who is attempting to stiff his or her creditors, and they translate this lack of empathy into a license to do whatever comes to mind that will cause the debtor to cough up a payment or two. In the past, creditors have been known to play on people's worst fears. ("We'll throw you into involuntary bankruptcy if you can't pay," "A United States marshall is on his way to your house to arrest you for nonpayment of debt," "People who can't pay their debts lose their children and have to go to the poor house.") See Arthur Leff, Injury, Ignorance, and Spite — The Dynamics of Coercive Collection, 80 Yale L.J. 1 (1970), and the symposium thereon in 33 U. Pitt. L. Rev. 66 (1972).

Wholesale abuse of common decency shocked the courts when the debtors demonstrated the horrors inflicted upon them, and led to the development of a wide variety of torts designed to curb the more outrageous practices. These include obvious things like assault and battery, defamation (libel and slander — note, however, that truth is a defense here), and invasion of privacy. For the latter theory, the leading case is Housh v. Peth, 99 Ohio App. 485, 135 N.E.2d 440, aff'd, 165 Ohio St. 35, 133 N.E.2d 340 (1956), in which the creditor-defendant initiated a systematic campaign of harassment including numerous telephone calls at all hours for three weeks — calls made not only to the debtor but also to her employer, a school system, requiring her to be repeatedly pulled from the classroom to answer phone calls. The Ohio courts found this to be an invasion of privacy and allowed the plaintiff a recovery in spite of the fact that she really did owe the debt at issue. In Norris v. Moskin Stores, Inc., 132 So. 2d 321 (Ala. 1961), the court found an invasion of privacy where the creditor caused the debtor marital trouble by sending to his place of business a woman who pretended to be his paramour (promising to stop the pretense only if he paid the debt). The tort theory here was first developed in a famous law review article by Samuel D. Warren and Louis D. Brandeis, The Right to Privacy, 4 Harv. L. Rev. 193 (1890).

Other tort theories abound to protect debtors. Did the creditor take a postdated check drawn against a nonexistent account, telling the debtor who signed it that it was just "insurance" to ensure payment, and then have the debtor prosecuted for passing a bad check? The courts called this one abuse of process or malicious prosecution. Intentional infliction of mental distress has also been used when the creditor overreaches. Some states have created their own theories. Texas, for example, has a tort called "unreasonable collection efforts"; see, e.g., Southwestern Bell Co. v. Wilson, 768 S.W.2d 755 (Tex. App. 1988) (award of $5 million upheld!).

B.   Fair Debt Collection Practices Act

The federal government finally entered the field in 1978 by enacting a statute regulating debt collection and giving the injured debtor a civil remedy. The statute is the Fair Debt Collection Practices Act, 15 U.S.C. §1692, which is also Title VIII of the

Consumer Credit Protection Act (a broad consumer protection statute containing among others the Truth in Lending Act and the Fair Credit Reporting Act). Creditors covered by the statute are required to give certain mandatory notices to the debtor when collection is undertaken, and it is the failure to give these notices that is the most frequent violation of the statute.

Bartlett v. Heibl

United States Court of Appeals, Seventh Circuit, 1997
128 F.3d 497

POSNER, Chief Judge.

The Fair Debt Collection Practices Act, 15 U.S.C. §§1692-1692o, provides that within five days after a debt collector first duns a consumer debtor, the collector must send the debtor a written notice containing specified information. The required information includes the amount of the debt, the name of the creditor, and, of particular relevance here, a statement that unless the debtor "disputes the validity of the debt" within thirty days the debt collector will assume that the debt is valid but that if the debtor notifies the collector in writing within thirty days that he is disputing the debt, "the debt collector will obtain verification of the debt [from the creditor] . . . and a copy of [the] verification . . . will be mailed to the consumer." §§1692g(a)(1)-(4). A similar provision requires that the debtor be informed that upon his request the debt collector will give him the name and address of his original creditor, if the original creditor is different from the current one. §1692g(a)(5). If the debtor accepts the invitation tendered in the required notice, and requests from the debt collector either verification of the debt or the name and address of the original creditor, the debt collector must "cease collection of the debt . . . until the [requested information] is mailed to the consumer." §1692g(b). These provisions are intended for the case in which the debt collector, being a hireling of the creditor rather than the creditor itself, may lack first-hand knowledge of the debt.

If the statute is violated, the debtor is entitled to obtain from the debt collector, in addition to any actual damages that the debtor can prove, statutory damages not to exceed $1,000 per violation, plus a reasonable attorney's fee. §1692k(a).

A credit-card company hired lawyer John Heibl, the defendant in this case, to collect a consumer credit-card debt of some $1,700 from Curtis Bartlett, the plaintiff. Heibl sent Bartlett a letter, which Bartlett received but did not read, in which Heibl told him that "if you wish to resolve this matter before legal action is commenced, you must do one of two things within one week of the date of this letter": pay $316 toward the satisfaction of the debt, or get in touch with Micard (the creditor) "and make suitable arrangements for payment. If you do neither, it will be assumed that legal action will be necessary." Under Heibl's signature appears an accurate, virtually a literal, paraphrase of section 1692g(a), advising Bartlett that he has thirty days within which to dispute the debt, in which event Heibl will mail him a verification of it. At the end of the paraphrase Heibl adds: "suit may be commenced at any time before the expiration of this thirty (30) days." . . .

The letter is said to violate the statute by stating the required information about the debtor's rights in a confusing fashion. Finding nothing confusing about the letter, the district court rendered judgment for the defendant after a bench trial. The plaintiff contends that this finding is clearly erroneous. The defendant disagrees, of course, but also contends that even if the letter is confusing this is of no moment because Bartlett didn't read it. That would be a telling point if Bartlett were seeking actual damages, for example as a consequence of being misled by the letter into surrendering a legal defense against the credit-card company. He can't have suffered such damages as a result of the statutory violation, because he didn't read the letter. But he is not seeking actual damages. He is seeking only statutory damages, a penalty that does not depend on proof that the recipient of the letter was misled. *E.g.*, Tolentino v. Friedman, 46 F.3d 645, 651 (7th Cir. 1995); Harper v. Better Business Services, Inc., 961 F.2d 1561, 1563 (11th Cir. 1992); Clomon v. Jackson, 988 F.2d 1314, 1322 (2d Cir. 1993); Baker v. G.C. Services Corp., 677 F.2d 775, 780-81 (9th Cir. 1982). All that is required is proof that the statute was violated, although even then it is within the district court's discretion to decide whether, and if so how much, to award, up to the $1,000 ceiling. *E.g.*, Tolentino v. Friedman, *supra*, 46 F.3d at 651; Clomon v. Jackson, *supra*, 988 F.2d at 1322.

If reading were an element of the violation, then Bartlett would have to prove that he read the letter. But it is not. The statute, so far as material to this case, requires only that the debt collector "send the consumer a written notice containing" the required information. §1692g(a). It is unsettled whether "send" implies receipt or just mailing. *Compare, e.g.*, Bates v. C & S Adjusters, Inc., 980 F.2d 865, 868 (2d Cir. 1992) (receipt), *with, e.g.*, Maloy v. Phillips, 64 F.3d 607, 608 (11th Cir. 1995) (mailing). No matter; Bartlett did receive the letter. Sending a letter doesn't imply that the letter is read; there is no contradiction in saying, "I received your letter but I never read it." . . .

The main issue presented by the appeal is whether the district judge committed a clear error in finding that the letter was not confusing. The statute does not say in so many words that the disclosures required by it must be made in a nonconfusing manner. But the courts, our own included, have held, plausibly enough, that it is implicit that the debt collector may not defeat the statute's purpose by making the required disclosures in a form or within a context in which they are unlikely to be understood by the unsophisticated debtors who are the particular objects of the statute's solicitude. *E.g.*, Avila v. Rubin, 84 F.3d 222, 226 (7th Cir. 1996); Terran v. Kaplan, 109 F.3d 1428, 1431-34 (9th Cir. 1997); Russell v. Equifax A.R.S., 74 F.3d 30, 34-35 (2d Cir. 1996); Graziano v. Harrison, 950 F.2d 107, 111 (3d Cir. 1991); Miller v. Payco-General American Credits, Inc., 943 F.2d 482, 484 (4th Cir. 1991).

Most of the cases put it this way: the implied duty to avoid confusing the unsophisticated consumer can be violated by contradicting or "overshadowing" the required notice. *E.g.*, Chauncey v. JDR Recovery Corp., 118 F.3d 516, 518 (7th Cir. 1997); United States v. National Financial Services, Inc., 98 F.3d 131, 139 (4th Cir. 1996); Russell v. Equifax A.R.S., *supra*, 74 F.3d at 34; Graziano v. Harrison, *supra*, 950 F.2d at 111. This sounds like two separate tests, one for a statement that is logically inconsistent with the required notice and the other for a statement that while it doesn't actually contradict the required notice obscures it, in much the same way that static or cross-talk can make a telephone communication hard to understand even though the message is not being contradicted in any way. The required notice might be "overshadowed" just because it was in smaller or fainter print than the demand for payment. United States v. National Financial Services, Inc., *supra,* 98 F.3d at 139.

As with many legal formulas that get repeated from case to case without an effort at elaboration, "contradicting or overshadowing" is rather unilluminating — even, though we hesitate to use the word in this context, confusing. The cases that find the statute violated generally involve neither logical inconsistencies (that is, denials of the consumer rights that the dunning letter is required to disclose) nor the kind of literal "overshadowing" involved in a fine-print, or faint-print, or confusing-typeface case. In the typical case, the letter both demands payment within thirty days and explains the consumer's right to demand verification within thirty days. These rights are not inconsistent, but by failing to explain how they fit together the letter confuses. *E.g., id.;* Chauncey v. JDR Recovery Corp., *supra,* 118 F.3d at 518-19; Avila v. Rubin, *supra,* 84 F.3d at 226; Russell v. Equifax A.R.S., *supra,* 74 F.3d at 35; Miller v. Payco-General American Credits, Inc., *supra,* 943 F.2d at 484; Swanson v. Southern Oregon Credit Service, Inc., 869 F.2d 1222, 1225-26 (9th Cir. 1988) (per curiam).

It would be better if the courts just said that the unsophisticated consumer is to be protected against confusion, whatever form it takes. A contradiction is just one means of inducing confusion; "overshadowing" is just another; and the most common is a third, the failure to explain an apparent though not actual contradiction — as in this case, which is indistinguishable from our recent *Chauncey* decision, as well as from most of the other cases we have cited. On the one hand, Heibl's letter tells the debtor that if he doesn't pay within a week he's going to be sued. On the other hand, it tells him that he can contest the debt within thirty days. This leaves up in the air what happens if he is sued on the eighth day, say, and disputes the debt on the tenth day. He might well wonder what good it would do him to dispute the debt if he can't stave off a lawsuit. The net effect of the juxtaposition of the one-week and thirty-day crucial periods is to turn the required disclosure into legal gibberish. That's as bad as an outright contradiction.

Although the question whether a dunning letter violates the Fair Debt Collection Practices Act does not require evidence that the recipient was confused — or even, as we noted earlier, whether he read the letter — the issue of confusion is for the district judge to decide, subject to light review for "clear error." The cases, however, leave no room to doubt that the letter to Bartlett was confusing; nor as an original matter could we doubt that it was confusing — we found it so, and do not like to think of ourselves as your average unsophisticated consumer. So the judgment must be reversed. But we should not stop here. Judges too often tell defendants what the defendants cannot do without indicating what they can do, thus engendering legal uncertainty that foments further litigation. The plaintiff's lawyer takes the extreme, indeed the absurd, position — one that he acknowledged to us at argument, with a certain lawyerly relish, creates an anomaly in the statutory design — that the debt collector cannot in any way, shape, or form allude to his right to bring a lawsuit within thirty days. That enforced silence would be fine if the statute forbade suing so soon. But it does not. The debt collector is perfectly free to sue within thirty days; he just must cease his efforts at collection during the interval between being asked for verification of the debt and mailing the verification to the debtor. 15 U.S.C. §1692g(b). In effect the plaintiff is arguing that if the debt collector wants to sue within the first thirty days he must do so without advance warning. How this compelled surprise could be thought either required by the statute, however imaginatively elaborated with the aid of the concept of "overshadowing," or helpful to the statute's intended beneficiaries, eludes us.

The plaintiff's argument is in one sense overimaginative, and in another unimaginative — unimaginative in failing to see that it is possible to devise a form of words that will inform the debtor of the risk of his being sued without detracting from the statement of his statutory rights. We here set forth a redaction of Heibl's letter that complies with the statute without forcing the debt collector to conceal his intention of exploiting his right to resort to legal action before the thirty days are up. We are not rewriting the statute; that is not our business. Jang v. A. M. Miller & Associates, 122 F.3d 480, 484 (7th Cir. 1997). We are simply trying to provide some guidance to how to comply with it. We commend this redaction as a safe harbor for debt collectors who want to avoid liability for the kind of suit that Bartlett has brought and now won. The qualification "for the kind of suit that Bartlett has brought and now won" is important. We are not certifying our letter as proof against challenges based on other provisions of the statute; those provisions are not before us. With that caveat, here is our letter:

Dear Mr. Bartlett:

I have been retained by Micard Services to collect from you the entire balance, which as of September 25, 1995, was $1,656.90, that you owe Micard Services on your MasterCard Account No. 5414701617068749.

If you want to resolve this matter without a lawsuit, you must, within one week of the date of this letter, either pay Micard $316 against the balance that you owe (unless you've paid it since your last statement) or call Micard at 1-800-221-5920 ext. 6130 and work out arrangements for payment with it.

If you do neither of these things, I will be entitled to file a lawsuit against you, for the collection of this debt, when the week is over.

Federal law gives you thirty days after you receive this letter to dispute the validity of the debt or any part of it. If you don't dispute it within that period, I'll assume that it's valid. If you do dispute it — by notifying me in writing to that effect — I will, as required by the law, obtain and mail to you proof of the debt. And if, within the same period, you request in writing the name and address of your original creditor, if the original creditor is different from the current creditor (Micard Services), I will furnish you with that information too.

The law does not require me to wait until the end of the thirty-day period before suing you to collect this debt. If, however, you request proof of the debt or the name and address of the original creditor within the thirty-day period that begins with your receipt of this letter, the law requires me to suspend my efforts (through litigation or otherwise) to collect the debt until I mail the requested information to you.

Sincerely,

John A. Heibl

We cannot require debt collectors to use "our" form. But of course if they depart from it, they do so at their risk. Debt collectors who want to avoid suits by disgruntled debtors standing on their statutory rights would be well advised to stick close to the form that we have drafted. It will be a safe haven for them, at least in the Seventh Circuit.

The judgment is reversed and the case is remanded with instructions to enter judgment for the plaintiff and compute the statutory damages, costs, and attorneys' fees to which he is entitled.

REVERSED AND REMANDED.

A number of commentators have pointed out deficiencies in the letter Judge Posner proposes. For example, it does not contain the statement mandated by §807(11), which requires that all communications with the debtor disclose that the debt collector is attempting to collect a debt and that any information obtained will be used for that purpose.

There is one significant limitation on the scope of the Fair Debt Collection Practices Act: It does not apply to a creditor if that creditor is collecting its *own* debt. However, in 1986 the FDCPA was amended so that it did apply to any *attorney* engaged in the collection of debts. Nonetheless, years later there still are many attorneys blissfully collecting debts on behalf of clients, totally unaware that they are in violation of the statute.

Heintz v. Jenkins
United States Supreme Court, 1995
514 U.S. 291 (1995)

Justice BREYER delivered the opinion of the Court.

The issue before us is whether the term "debt collector" in the Fair Debt Collection Practices Act, 91 Stat. 874, 15 U.S.C. §§1692-1692o (1988 ed. and Supp. V), applies to a lawyer who "regularly," *through litigation,* tries to collect consumer debts. The Court of Appeals for the Seventh Circuit held that it does. We agree with the Seventh Circuit and we affirm its judgment.

The Fair Debt Collection Practices Act prohibits "debt collector[s]" from making false or misleading representations and from engaging in various abusive and unfair practices. The Act says, for example, that a "debt collector" may not use violence, obscenity, or repeated annoying phone calls, 15 U.S.C. §1692d; may not falsely represent "the character, amount, or legal status of any debt," §1692e(2)(A); and may not use various "unfair or unconscionable means to collect or attempt to collect" a consumer debt, §1692f. Among other things, the Act sets out rules that a debt collector must follow for "acquiring location information" about the debtor, §1692b; communicating about the debtor (and the debt) with third parties, §1692c(b); and bringing "[l]egal actions," §1692i. The Act imposes upon "debt collector[s]" who violate its provisions (specifically described) "[c]ivil liability" to those whom they, e.g., harass, mislead, or treat unfairly. §1692k. The Act also authorizes the Federal Trade Commission to enforce its provisions. §16921(a). The Act's definition of the term "debt collector" includes a person "who regularly collects or attempts to collect, directly or indirectly, debts owed [to] . . . another." §1692a(6). And, it limits "debt" to consumer debt, i.e., debts "arising out of . . . transaction[s]" that "are primarily for personal, family, or household purposes." §1692a(5).

The plaintiff in this case, Darlene Jenkins, borrowed money from the Gainer Bank in order to buy a car. She defaulted on her loan. The bank's law firm then sued Jenkins in state court to recover the balance due. As part of an effort to settle the suit, a lawyer with that law firm, George Heintz, wrote to Jenkins's lawyer. His letter, in listing the amount she owed under the loan agreement, included $4,173 owed for insurance, bought by the bank because she had not kept the car insured as she had promised to do.

Jenkins then brought this Fair Debt Collection Practices Act suit against Heintz and his firm. She claimed that Heintz's letter violated the Act's prohibitions against trying to collect an amount not "authorized by the agreement creating the debt," §1692f(1), and against making a "false representation of . . . the . . . amount . . . of any debt," §1692e(2)(A). The loan agreement, she conceded, required her to keep the car insured "against loss or damage" and permitted the bank to buy such insurance to protect the car should she fail to do so. App. to Pet. for Cert. 17. But, she said, the $4,137 substitute policy was not the kind of policy the loan agreement had in mind, for it insured the bank not only against "loss or damage" but also against her failure to repay the bank's car loan. Hence, Heintz's "representation" about the "amount" of her "debt" was "false"; amounted to an effort to collect an "amount" not "authorized" by the loan agreement; and thus violated the Act.

Pursuant to Rule 12(b)(6) of the Federal Rules of Civil Procedure, the District Court dismissed Jenkins's Fair Debt Collection lawsuit for failure to state a claim. The court held the Act does not apply to lawyers engaging in litigation. However, the Court of Appeals for the Seventh Circuit reversed the District Court's judgment, interpreting the Act to apply to litigating lawyers. Jenkins v. Heintz, 25 F.3d 536 (1994). The Seventh Circuit's view in this respect conflicts with that of the Sixth Circuit. See Green v. Hocking, 9 F.3d 18 (1993) (per curiam). We granted certiorari to resolve this conflict. 513 U.S. ____, 115 S. Ct. 416, 130 L. Ed. 2d 332 (1994). And, as we have said, we conclude that the Seventh Circuit is correct. The Act does apply to lawyers engaged in litigation.

There are two rather strong reasons for believing that the Act applies to the litigating activities of lawyers. First, the Act defines the "debt collector[s]" to whom it applies as including those who "regularly collec[t] or attemp[t] to collect, directly or indirectly, [consumer] debts owed or due or asserted to be owed or due another." §1692a(6). In ordinary English, a lawyer who regularly tries to obtain payment of consumer debts through legal proceedings is a lawyer who regularly "attempts" to "collect" those consumer debts. *See, e.g.*, Black's Law Dictionary 263 (6th ed. 1990) ("To collect a debt or claim is to obtain payment or liquidation of it, either by personal solicitation or legal proceedings").

Second, in 1977, Congress enacted an earlier version of this statute, which contained an express exemption for lawyers. That exemption said that the term "debt collector" did not include "any attorney-at-law collecting a debt as an attorney on behalf of and in the name of a client." Pub. L. 95-109, §803(6)(F), 91 Stat. 874, 875. In 1986, however, Congress repealed this exemption in its entirety, Pub. L. 99-361, 100 Stat. 768, without creating a narrower, litigation-related, exemption to fill the void. Without more, then, one would think that Congress intended that lawyers be subject to the Act whenever they meet the general "debt collector" definition.

Heintz argues that we should nonetheless read the statute as containing an implied exemption for those debt-collecting activities of lawyers that consist of litigating (including, he assumes, settlement efforts). He relies primarily on three arguments.

First, Heintz argues that many of the Act's requirements, if applied directly to litigating activities, will create harmfully anomalous results that Congress simply could not have intended. We address this argument in light of the fact that, when Congress first wrote the Act's substantive provisions, it had for the most part exempted litigating attorneys from the Act's coverage; that, when Congress later repealed the attorney exemption, it did not revisit the wording of these substantive provisions; and that, for these reasons, some awkwardness is understandable. Particularly when read in this light, we find Heintz's argument unconvincing.

Many of Heintz's "anomalies" are not particularly anomalous. For example, the Sixth Circuit pointed to §1692e(5), which forbids a "debt collector" to make any "threat to take action that cannot legally be taken." The court reasoned that, were the Act to apply to litigating activities, this provision automatically would make liable any litigating lawyer who brought, and then lost, a claim against a debtor. *Green, supra,* at 21. But, the Act says explicitly that a "debt collector" may not be held liable if he "shows by a preponderance of evidence that the violation was not intentional and resulted from a bona fide error notwithstanding the maintenance of procedures reasonably adapted to avoid any such error." §1692k(c). Thus, even if we were to assume that the suggested reading of §1692e(5) is correct, we would not find the result so absurd as to warrant implying an exemption for litigating lawyers. In any event, the assumption would seem unnecessary, for we do not see how the fact that a lawsuit turns out ultimately to be unsuccessful could, by itself, make the bringing of it an "action that cannot legally be taken."

The remaining significant "anomalies" similarly depend for their persuasive force upon readings that courts seem unlikely to endorse. For example, Heintz's strongest "anomaly" argument focuses upon the Act's provisions governing "[c]ommunication in connection with debt collection." §1692c. One of those provisions requires a "debt collector" not to "communicate further" with a consumer who "notifies" the "debt collector" that he or she "refuses to pay" or wishes the debt collector to "cease further communication." §1692c(c). In light of this provision, asks Heintz, how can an attorney file a lawsuit against (and thereby communicate with) a nonconsenting consumer or file a motion for summary judgment against that consumer?

We agree with Heintz that it would be odd if the Act empowered a debt-owing consumer to stop the "communications" inherent in an ordinary lawsuit and thereby cause an ordinary debt-collecting lawsuit to grind to a halt. But, it is not necessary to read §1692c(c) in that way—if only because that provision has exceptions that permit communications "to notify the consumer that the debt collector or creditor may invoke" or "intends to invoke" a "specified remedy" (of a kind "ordinarily invoked by [the] debt collector or creditor"). §§1692c(c)(2), (3). Courts can read these exceptions, plausibly, to imply that they authorize the actual invocation of the remedy that the collector "intends to invoke." The language permits such a reading, for an ordinary court-related document does, in fact, "notify" its recipient that the creditor may "invoke" a judicial remedy. Moreover, the interpretation is consistent with the statute's apparent objective of preserving creditors' judicial remedies. We need not authoritatively interpret the Act's conduct-regulating provisions now, however. Rather, we rest our conclusions upon the fact that it is easier to read §1692c(c) as containing some such additional, implicit, exception than to believe that Congress intended, silently and implicitly, to create a far broader exception, for all litigating attorneys, from the Act itself.

Second, Heintz points to a statement of Congressman Frank Annunzio, one of the sponsors of the 1986 amendment that removed from the Act the language creating a blanket exemption for lawyers. Representative Annunzio stated that, despite the exemption's removal, the Act still would not apply to lawyers' litigating activities. Representative Annunzio said that the Act "regulates debt collection, not the practice of law. Congress repealed the attorney exemption to the act, not because of attorney[s'] conduct in the courtroom, but because of their conduct in the backroom. Only collection activities, not legal activities, are covered by the act. . . . The act applies to attorneys when they are collecting debts, not when they are performing tasks of a legal nature. . . . The act only regulates the conduct of debt collectors, it does not prevent creditors, through their attorneys, from pursuing any legal remedies available to them." 132 Cong. Rec. 30842 (1986). This statement, however, does not persuade us.

For one thing, the plain language of the Act itself says nothing about retaining the exemption in respect to litigation. The line the statement seeks to draw between "legal" activities and "debt collection" activities was not necessarily apparent to those who debated the legislation, for litigating, at first blush, seems simply one way of collecting a debt. For another thing, when Congress considered the Act, other Congressmen expressed fear that repeal would limit lawyers' "ability to contact third parties in order to facilitate settlements" and "could very easily interfere with a client's right to pursue judicial remedies." H.R. Rep. No. 99-405, p. 11 (1985) (dissenting views of Rep. Hiler). They proposed alternative language designed to keep litigation activities outside the Act's scope, but that language was not enacted. Ibid. Further, Congressman Annunzio made his statement not during the legislative process, but after the statute became law. It therefore is not a statement upon which other legislators might have relied in voting for or against the Act, but it simply represents the views of one informed person on an issue about which others may (or may not) have thought differently.

Finally, Heintz points to a "Commentary" on the Act by the Federal Trade Commission's staff. It says: "Attorneys or law firms that engage in traditional debt collection activities (sending dunning letters, making collection calls to consumers) are covered by the [Act], but *those whose practice is limited to legal activities are not covered.*" Federal Trade Commission — Statements of General Policy or Interpretation Staff Commentary on the Fair Debt Collection Practices Act, 53 Fed. Reg. 50097, 50100 (1988) (emphasis added; footnote omitted). We cannot give conclusive weight to this statement. The Commentary of which this statement is a part says that it "is not binding on the Commission or the public." Id., at 50101. More importantly, we find nothing either in the Act or elsewhere indicating that Congress intended to authorize the FTC to create this exception from the Act's coverage — an exception that, for the reasons we have set forth above, falls outside the range of reasonable interpretations of the Act's express language. *See, e.g.,* Brown v. Gardner, 513 U.S. 115, ____, 115 S. Ct. 552, 555, 130 L. Ed. 2d 462 (1994) (slip op., at ____); *see also* Fox v. Citicorp Credit Servs., Inc., 15 F.3d 1507, 1513 (CA9 1994) (FTC staff's statement conflicts with Act's plain language and is therefore not entitled to deference); Scott v. Jones, 964 F.2d 314, 317 (CA4 1992) (same).

For these reasons, we agree with the Seventh Circuit that the Act applies to attorneys who "regularly" engage in consumer-debt-collection activity, even when that activity consists of litigation. Its judgment is therefore

Affirmed.

Following this decision, Congress amended the Fair Debt Collection Practices Act to address some of the statutory confusion highlighted by the Court in its opinion. Section 807(11), for example, now provides that formal pleadings made in connection with a legal action need not contain the usual statement that the debt collector is attempting to collect a debt.

IV. Fraudulent Transfers

When creditors start pressing, a common reaction of a harried debtor is to hide property or convey it to another, though our law has always condemned this sort of asset protection. In 1570, England's Parliament enacted the Statute of 13 Elizabeth, which voided all transfers of a debtor's property to another if the transfer was made with the intent to defraud creditors. The statute contained a proviso preserving these transfers if they were exchanged for a good consideration and were bona fide.

Since debtors are not stupid enough to take the witness stand and boldly confess that they transferred property intending to keep it from their creditors, courts soon established the so-called badges of fraud, meaning suspicious circumstances that led a court to infer the requisite intent. These badges of fraud included transfers to relatives or friends, transfers made in secret, transfers for no consideration, and transfers made when creditors commenced collection activity. In most jurisdictions, if one or more badges of fraud were found, the transfer was presumptively invalid, shifting the burden to the transferee to establish the bona fides of the transfer. The leading case interpreting the Statute of 13 Elizabeth follows.

Twyne's Case
Star Chamber, 1601
3 Coke 80b, 76 Eng. Rep. 809

In an information by Coke, the Queen's Attorney General, against Twyne of Hampshire, in the Star-Chamber, for making and publishing of a fraudulent gift of goods: the case on the stat. of 13 Eliz. cap. 5 was such; Pierce was indebted to Twyne in four hundred pounds, and was indebted also to C. in two hundred pounds. C. brought an action of debt against Pierce and pending the writ, Pierce being possessed of goods and chattels of the value of three hundred pounds, in secret made a general deed of gift of all his goods and chattels real and personal whatsoever to Twyne, in satisfaction of his debt; notwithstanding that Pierce continued in possession of the said goods, and some of them he sold; and he shore the sheep, and marked them with his own mark: and afterwards C. had judgment against Pierce, and had a *fieri facias*[2] directed to the Sheriff of Southhampton, who by force of the said writ came to make execution of the said goods; but divers persons, by the command of the said Twyne, did with force resist the said sheriff, claiming them to be the goods of the said Twyne by force of the said gift; and openly declared by the commandment of Twyne, that it was a good gift, and made on a good and lawful consideration. And whether this gift on whole matter was fraudulent and of no effect by the said Act of 13 Eliz. or not, was the question. And it was resolved by Sir Thomas Egerton, Lord Keeper of the Great Seal, and by the Chief Justice Popham and Anderson, and the whole Court of Star Chamber, that this gift was fraudulent, within the statute of 13 Eliz. And in this case divers points were resolved:

1st. This gift had the signs and marks of fraud, because the gift is general, without exception of his apparel, or any thing of necessity; for it is commonly said, *quod dolus versatur in generalibus.*[3]

2nd. The donor continued in possession and used them as his own; and by reason thereof he traded and trafficked with others, and defrauded and deceived them.

---

2. The common law writ of fieri facias is the basic writ issued to a sheriff directing the sheriff to seize the personal property of the debtor. The writ of levari facias was used to order the sheriff to attach real property.

3. "Fraud is cloaked in generalities."

3rd. It was made in secret, *et dona clandestina sunt semper suspiciosa.*[4]

4th. It was made pending the writ.

5th. Here was a trust between the parties, for the donor possessed all, and used them as his proper goods and fraud is always apparelled and clad with a trust, and a trust is the cover of fraud.

6th. The deed contains, that the gift was made honestly, truly, and *bona fide; et clausuloe insonsuet semper inducunt suspicionem.*[5]

Secondly, it was resolved, that notwithstanding here was a true debt due to Twyne, and a good consideration of the gift, yet it was not within the proviso of the said Act of 13 Eliz. by which it is provided, that the said Act shall not extend to any estate or interest in lands, &c. goods or chattels made on a good consideration and *bona fide,* for no gift shall be deemed to be *bona fide* within the said proviso which is accompanied with any trust; as if a man be indebted to five several persons, in the sums of twenty pounds, and hath goods of the value of twenty pounds, and makes a gift of all his goods to one of them in satisfaction of his debt, but there is a trust between them, that the donee shall deal favourably with him in regard of his poor estate, either to permit the donor, or some other for him, or for his benefit, to use or have possession of them, and is contented that he shall pay him his debt when he is able; this shall not be called *bona fide* within the said proviso; for the proviso saith on a good consideration, and *bona fide;* so a good consideration does not suffice, if it be not also *bona fide:* and therefore, reader, when any gift shall be to you in satisfaction of a debt, by one who is indebted to others also; 1st, Let it be made in a public manner, and before the neighbours, and not in private, for secrecy is a mark of fraud. 2nd, Let the goods and chattels be appraised by good people to the very value, and take a gift in particular in satisfaction of your debt. 3rd, Immediately after the gift, take the possession of them; for continuance of the possession in the donor, is a sign of trust. . . .

And because fraud and deceit abound in these days more than in former times, it was resolved in this case by the whole Court, that all statutes made against fraud should be liberally and beneficially expounded to suppress the fraud. Note, reader, according to their opinions, divers resolutions have been made.

PROBLEM 1-2

Annie was an orphan who had one valuable asset: Sandy, a prize-winning pure-bred dog. When she needed money to pay her many debts, she agreed to sell Sandy to her friend Oliver Warbucks, but they agreed to keep the sale secret and that Sandy would continue to live with Annie. When Annie failed to pay her debts, one of her creditors took a judgment against her and then had the sheriff levy execution on Sandy, at which point Warbucks presented his deed of sale and claimed a superior right to the dog. Who should prevail? See the following citation.

---

4. "Secret gifts are always suspicious."
5. "Unusual clauses always cause suspicion."

Uniform Commercial Code §2-402(2):

(2) A creditor of the seller may treat a sale or an identification of goods to a contract for sale as void if as against him a retention of possession by the seller is fraudulent under any rule of law of the state where the goods are situated, except that retention of possession in good faith and current course of trade by a merchant-seller for a commercially reasonable time after a sale or identification is not fraudulent.

PROBLEM 1-3

Assume that in the prior Problem Annie had given possession of Sandy to Warbucks with the understanding that when the heat was off, he would reconvey Sandy to her for the same price he had paid her. Now time has passed and Annie has settled all her debts with her creditors and tendered the relevant amount to Warbucks, but he has grown fond of the dog and refused to sell Sandy back to Annie. She is in your office crying her eyes out. Can she get specific performance here? *See* Seagirt Realty Corp. v. Chazanof, 13 N.Y.2d 282, 246 N.Y.S.2d 613, 196 N.E.2d 254 (1963); 21 A.L.R.2d 589.

The Statute of Elizabeth passed into the common law of most American jurisdictions, but because it was so vaguely worded and capriciously applied, about half the states adopted the Uniform Fraudulent Conveyances Act [UFCA], which gave more detail to the rules. The UFCA in turn has been replaced by the Uniform Fraudulent Transfer Act [UFTA], which should be in your statute book, and it has been widely adopted. Apply it to the following Problems.

PROBLEM 1-4

Paul Pious tricked many unwary investors into giving him money for a real estate venture that never materialized, and in doing so he lied to them constantly about what he was doing with their money. In reality he lost about half of it during the course of a wild weekend in Las Vegas at the gaming tables. He felt so guilty about this that he gave the other half, $600,000, to the Grapes of Wrath Church, which he had attended since he was a boy. The church immediately spent the money on missionary work. The investors discovered what had happened. Can they get their money back from the Las Vegas casino where Paul did most of his gambling? *See* UFTA §§5, 3, and 8 (in that order). Can the church be made to cough up the donation to it? *See* Scholes v. Lehmann, 56 F.3d 750 (7th Cir. 1995).

PROBLEM 1-5

Amelia Cloud was only slightly injured when she lost control of her private plane and crashed it into a suburban neighborhood, killing all the members of a family of five.

This led to a lawsuit against her. While the suit was in progress, Amelia's mother died, leaving a will in which she left half of her extensive property to Amelia and half to Amelia's children. Amelia immediately filed a document in the probate court renouncing her interest in her mother's estate (so that her children would get everything). The representative of the deceased family members objected to this, claiming that the renunciation was in fact a fraudulent transfer. How does this come out? *See* UFTA §§4 and 1(12); *compare* Stein v. Brown, 18 Ohio St. 3d 305, 480 N.E.2d 1121 (1985), *with* Frances Slocum Bank v. Estate of Martin, 666 N.E.2d 411 (Ind. App. 1996).

A leveraged buyout (LBO) is a controversial method of acquiring a corporation. Suppose you are a savvy investor who comes across an ailing corporation. You believe that if you could take over the corporation you could provide sufficient clever leadership so as to restructure it and make it profitable. You decide to purchase controlling stock in the corporation, but there is one difficulty: you have no money. Undaunted, you persuade the current owners of the stock and a local bank to cooperate in the following scheme: the bank will loan you the money to buy the stock from its current owners, with the bank taking a security interest in the assets of the corporation, which (after a vote by the current owners) will grant the bank such a security interest in the corporation's property. This is a classic LBO. Might existing creditors of the corporation object to this new encumbrance on the corporate assets? What value did the corporation get in return for the transfer of the security interest in its property? There has been a ferocious debate about whether LBOs are fraudulent transfers.

Bay Plastics, Inc. v. BT Commercial Corp.
(In re Bay Plastics, Inc.)

United States Bankruptcy Court, Central District of California, 1995
187 B.R. 315

SAMUEL L. BUFFORD, Bankruptcy Judge.

I. Introduction

The debtor has brought this adversary proceeding against the selling shareholders of a leveraged buyout ("LBO") to recover the funds that they received in the buyout transaction. While the action was also brought against the bank that financed the transaction, the bank has settled. The Court grants summary judgment to the debtor on the undisputed facts.

The Court holds that the transaction may be avoided as a constructive fraudulent transfer under the California version of the Uniform Fraudulent Transfer Act ("UFTA"), on which the debtor relies pursuant to Bankruptcy Code §544(b), and that in consequence the debtor is entitled to recover against the selling shareholders. The Court finds that the transaction rendered the debtor insolvent, and that the sellers did not act in good faith.

II. Facts

The Court finds that the following facts are undisputed. Defendants Bob Younger, Abner Smith and Paul Dodson ("the selling shareholders") formed debtor Bay Plastics, Inc. ("Bay Plastics") in 1979 to manufacture polyvinyl chloride ("PVC") plastic pipe for water well casings and turf irrigation. Bay Plastics filed this bankruptcy case on January 25, 1990.

A. The Buyout

Because they were nearing retirement, on October 31, 1988 (fifteen months before this bankruptcy filing) the selling shareholders sold their Bay Plastics stock to Milhous Corporation ("Milhous") for $3.5 million in cash plus $1.8 million in deferred payments. Milhous did not acquire the Bay Plastics stock directly. Instead, it caused its subsidiary Nicole Plastics to form its own subsidiary, BPI Acquisition Corp. ("BPI"), to take ownership of the Bay Plastics stock. Formally, the parties to the stock sale transaction were ultimately BPI and the selling share holders.

The sale was unexceptional. The difficulty lay in the financing of the purchase. Milhous put no money of its own, or even any money that it borrowed, into this transaction. Instead, it caused Bay Plastics to borrow approximately $3.95 million from defendant BT Commercial Corp. ("BT") (a subsidiary of Bankers Trust), and then caused Bay Plastics to direct that $3.5 million of the loan be disbursed to BPI. BPI in turn directed that the $3.5 million be paid directly to the selling shareholders in substantial payment for their stock. Thus, at the closing, $3.5 million of the funds paid into escrow by BT went directly to the selling shareholders.

As security for its $3.95 million loan, BT received a first priority security interest in essentially all of the assets of Bay Plastics. In consequence, BT has received all of the proceeds of debtor's assets in this bankruptcy case, and nothing is left for unsecured or even for administrative creditors.

The financing also provided a revolving credit facility for working capital, in addition to the payment for the LBO, up to a total loan of $7 million. A total of just over $4 million was owing to BT at the time of the bankruptcy filing, according to the debtor's schedules. Thus most of the debt (all but approximately $500,000) owing to BT at the time of the filing resulted from the LBO.

The selling shareholders were not in the dark about the financing. On October 25, 1988, they and their attorney met with Milhous representatives in Los Angeles to finalize the deal. While the Milhous representatives provided rather little information about the Milhous finances, they did disclose the details of the BT secured loan to Bay Plastics to finance the stock purchase. In addition, the selling shareholders received a projected post-transaction balance sheet, which showed a balance of $250,000 in equity only because of the addition to the asset side of the ledger the sum of $2,259,270 in goodwill. Both the selling shareholders and their attorney were experienced in LBOs, and the selling shareholders discussed this feature of the transaction, and their exposure on a fraudulent transfer claim, with their attorney on that date. With this information in hand, Younger, Smith and Dodson approved the terms of the sale.

In contrast to the selling shareholders, the industry did not know about the LBO character of the transaction until a number of months later. Shintech Corp., a creditor at the time of the transaction (and continuously thereafter), did not learn of it until ten months later, in August, 1989.

B.   The Shintech Debt

Some three months before the LBO, on July 22, 1988, Bay Plastics entered into a requirements contract with Shintech to supply PVC resin. Shintech agreed under the contract to supply up to 2.6 million pounds of PVC resin per month on payment terms of 30 days after shipment. To induce Shintech to enter into this contract, Bay Plastics granted Shintech a security interest in all its assets, and the shareholders gave personal guaranties. This arrangement stood in the way of the BT transaction.

In consequence, the selling shareholders, their attorney, and Milhous representatives met with Shintech in late October, 1988 (after Milhous had disclosed to the selling shareholders the terms of the LBO), to arrange a new deal with Shintech. The parties to the LBO persuaded Shintech of Milhous' good credit, and induced Shintech to release both its security interest and the guaranties. However, they did not disclose the LBO character of the transaction, and Shintech did not learn of this until ten months later.

The impact of this transaction on the balance sheet of Bay Plastics was dramatic. Immediately after the transaction, its balance sheet showed tangible assets of approximately $7 million, and liabilities of approximately $9 million. Only the addition of almost $2.26 million in goodwill, which had not appeared on prior balance sheets, and for which no explanation has been provided, permitted the balance sheet to show a modest shareholder equity of $250,000. But for the newly discovered goodwill, there would have been a net deficiency of some $2 million. In contrast, immediately before the transaction Bay Plastics had assets of $6.7 million and liabilities of $5.6 million, and a net equity of $1.1 million.

Bay Plastics was unable to service this overload of debt, and filed its bankruptcy petition fifteen months later. According to the debtor's schedules, at the time of filing its two principal creditors were BT and Shintech: it owed approximately $4 million in secured debt to BT, and $3.5 million in unsecured debt to Shintech. No other creditor was owed more than $20,000.

III.   Discussion

The Bankruptcy Code gives a trustee the power to avoid a variety of kinds of prepetition transactions. Such transactions include preferential payments to creditors (§547), fraudulent transfers (§548), the fixing of statutory liens (§545), and setoffs (§553). A debtor in possession in a chapter 11 case has all of the rights (except the right to compensation) and the powers of a trustee under chapter 11. This includes the right to exercise the avoiding powers. Bankruptcy Code §1107(a).

However, the debtor is unable to use the fraudulent transfer provision of the Bankruptcy Code (§548) in this case, because it is only applicable to transfers made or obligations incurred on or within one year before the date of the filing of the petition. 11 U.S.C.A. §548(a) (West 1993). Where state law provides a similar avoiding power to a creditor, on the other hand, Bankruptcy Code §544(b)[6] permits a trustee (or a debtor in possession) to stand in the shoes of the creditor and to assert the same cause of action. Kupetz v. Wolf, 845 F.2d 842, 845 (9th Cir. 1988). Trustees and debtors in possession routinely utilize this provision to make fraudulent transfer claims under applicable state law, which typically provides a statute of limitations of four to seven years. *See, e.g.*, Cal. Civ. Code §3439.09 (West Supp. 1995). Thus the debtor has brought this adversary proceeding under §544(b) and the UFTA as adopted in California.

A.   Fraudulent Transfer Law

The purpose of fraudulent transfer law is to prevent a debtor from transferring away valuable assets in exchange for less than adequate value, if the transfer leaves insufficient assets to compensate honest creditors. *See* 4 Collier on Bankruptcy ¶548.01 at 548-4 through 548-24 (Lawrence P. King ed., 15th ed. 1995); Pajaro Dunes Rental Agency v. Spitters (In re Pajaro Dunes Rental Agency), 174 B.R. 557, 571 (Bankr. N.D. Cal. 1994).

Modern fraudulent transfer law traces its origins to a statute of Elizabeth enacted in 1570. *See* 13 Eliz., ch. 5 (1570).[7] This statute provided that a conveyance made "to the End, Purpose and Intent to delay, hinder or defraud creditors" is voidable. Id., §1. Courts often relied on circumstantial "badges of fraud" to presume fraudulent intent. *See, e.g.*, Twyne's Case, 76 Eng. Rep. 809, 810-14 (1601). The English law of fraudulent conveyance passed into the common law in the United States. This law was revised and codified by the National Conference of Commissioners on Uniform State Laws ("NCCUSL") in 1918, when it promulgated the Uniform Fraudulent Conveyance Act ("UFCA"). 7A U.L.A. 427, 428 (1985). The UFCA was adopted by California in 1939, and by a number of other states on various dates.

The NCCUSL rewrote the UFCA and promulgated it as the UFTA in 1984. Id., at 639. California adopted its version of the UFTA, which is applicable in this case, in 1986. *See* Cal. Civ. Code §§3439-3439.12 (West Supp. 1995) (applicable to transfers made after January 1, 1987). Bankruptcy Code §548 contains a similar fraudulent transfer provision. U.S.C.A. §548 (West 1993).

---

6. Section 544(b) provides: The trustee may avoid any transfer of an interest of the debtor in property or any obligation incurred by the debtor that is voidable under applicable law by a creditor holding an unsecured claim. . . . 11 U.S.C.A. §544(b) (West 1993).

7. This statute is frequently referred to erroneously as the Statute of Elizabeth. In those times statutes were known according to the monarch under whom they were enacted. Thus every statute enacted during the reign of Queen Elizabeth I was a "statute of Elizabeth." The fraudulent conveyance statute was enacted during the thirteenth year of her reign (hence "13 Eliz."), and was the fifth statute enacted that year (hence "ch. 5"). A bankruptcy statute, England's second, was enacted the same year, and is found at 13 Eliz. ch. 7 (1570).

1. The Species of Fraudulent Transfer

A transfer or conveyance is fraudulent if it is (1) an intentional fraudulent transfer, i.e., a transfer made with the intent to defeat, hinder or delay creditors; or (2) a transfer that is constructively fraudulent because the debtor is in financial distress. There are three kinds of financial distress that make a transaction a fraudulent transfer: (a) a transfer while a debtor is insolvent or that renders a debtor insolvent; (b) a transfer that leaves a debtor undercapitalized or nearly insolvent (i.e., with insufficient assets to carry on its business); (c) a transfer when the debtor intends to incur debts beyond its ability to pay. See UFTA §§4, 5; UFCA §4; Bankruptcy Code §548(a). Constructive fraudulent transfer law applies without regard to intent (except the intent to incur debts in the last alternative). See, e.g., Moody v. Security Pacific Business Credit, Inc., 971 F.2d 1056, 1063 (3d Cir. 1992) (construing the UFCA).

In this adversary proceeding the debtor relies on the first two varieties of constructive fraudulent transfer, and is entitled to prevail if either cause of action is upheld. The Court addresses only the first (a transfer that renders the debtor insolvent), because it finds that the debtor is entitled to prevail on this cause of action.

2. Fraudulent Transfer Resulting in Insolvency

The UFTA, adopted in California effective for transactions after January 1, 1987, provides in relevant part: A transfer made or obligation incurred by a debtor is fraudulent as to a creditor whose claim arose before the transfer was made or the obligation was incurred if the debtor made the transfer or incurred the obligation without receiving a reasonably equivalent value in exchange for the transfer or obligation and the debtor was insolvent at the time or the debtor became insolvent as a result of the transfer or obligation. Cal. Civ. Code §3439.05 (West Supp. 1995).[8]

3. Application of Fraudulent Transfer Law to LBOs

a. General

The basic structure of an LBO involves a transfer of corporate ownership financed primarily by the assets of the corporation itself.[9] Typically the corporation borrows the funds, secured by the assets of the corporation, and advances them to the purchasers, who use the funds to pay the purchase price to the selling shareholders. Kathryn V. Smyser, Going Private and Going Under: Leveraged Buyouts and the Fraudulent Conveyance Problem, 63 Ind. L.J. 781, 784-85 (1988). LBOs have two essential features:

First, the purchaser acquires the funds necessary for the acquisition through borrowings secured directly or indirectly by the assets of the company being acquired. Second, the lender who provides such funds is looking primarily to the future

---

8. These provisions are identical to the corresponding parts of UFTA §5(a). 7A U.L.A. 652 (1985).

9. While LBOs have frequently been used by management to buy out existing shareholders and take over the ownership of a business, management is not an essential party to an LBO. Indeed, in this case the purchaser was an outside third party.

operating earnings of the acquired company and/or to the proceeds from future sales of assets of the company, rather than to any other assets of the purchasers, to repay the borrowings used to effect the acquisition. Id., at 785. LBO investors thus generally consider cash flow, the money available for working capital and debt service, as the most important factor in assessing a potential buyout candidate. Id., at 785 n.12.

The application of fraudulent transfer law to LBOs has generated considerable debate among courts and commentators.[10] LBOs were a popular form of consensual corporate takeover in the 1980's. They fell into disuse at the end of that decade for economic reasons. However, the use of the LBO as an acquisition device has recently become popular again. *See* Laura Jereski, "Recaps" Are Secret Fuel for Leveraged Buyouts, Wall St. J., July 25, 1995, at C1.

The LBO dates back long before the 1980's. In earlier years, it was known as a "bootstrap acquisition." Some of these transactions were invalidated as fraudulent conveyances. *See* Steph v. Branch, 255 F. Supp. 526 (E.D. Okla.), *aff'd,* 389 F.2d 233 (10th Cir. 1968); In re Process Manz Press, 236 F. Supp. 333 (N.D. Ill. 1964), *rev'd on juris. grounds,* 369 F.2d 513 (7th Cir. 1966), *cert. denied,* 386 U.S. 957, 87 S. Ct. 1022, 18 L. Ed. 2d 104 (1967); Diller v. Irving Trust Co. (In re College Chemists, Inc.), 62 F.2d 1058 (2d Cir. 1933); Smyser, *supra* note 12, at 788 & n.21.

b. Ninth Circuit Case Law

The Ninth Circuit has had difficulties with the application of fraudulent transfer law to LBOs. The Ninth Circuit case law is found in two opinions, Lippi v. City Bank, 955 F.2d 599 (9th Cir. 1992), which arose under Hawaii common law, and Kupetz v. Wolf, 845 F.2d 842 (9th Cir. 1988), which arose under the California version of the UFCA. The applicability of these precedents is complicated by the fact that each was based on a statute different from the California version of the UFTA involved in this case. . . .

B. Trustee's Prima Facie Case

After having explored the applicable statutes and governing case law, the Court is now in position to apply this law to the facts of the instant case.

The Court notes at the outset that this case is not determined by the Ninth Circuit case law as set forth in the *Lippi* and *Kupetz* cases. Those cases both involved a fraudulent transfer attack on behalf of subsequent creditors. This case, in contrast,

---

10. *See, e.g.*, 4 James F. Queenan, Jr. et al., Chapter 11 Theory and Practice: A Guide to Reorganization ch. 27 (1994); 3 William L. Norton, Jr., Norton Bankruptcy Law and Practice ch. 58A (2d ed. 1994); David Weinstein, From *Kupetz* to *Lippi* and Beyond: LBOs in the Ninth Circuit—Now What?, 21 Ca. Bankr. J. 169, (1993); 2 David G. Epstein et al., Bankruptcy §6-52 (1992); Emily L. Sherwin, Creditors' Rights Against Participants in a Leveraged Buyout, 72 Minn. L. Rev. 449 (1988); Kathryn V. Smyser, Going Private and Going Under: Leveraged Buyouts and the Fraudulent Conveyance Problem, 63 Ind. L.J. 781, 784-85 (1988); Kevin J. Liss, Note, Fraudulent Conveyance Law and Leveraged Buyouts, 87 Colum. L. Rev. 1491 (1987); Douglas G. Baird & Thomas H. Jackson, Fraudulent Conveyance Law and Its Proper Domain, 38 Vand. L. Rev. 829, 850-54 (1985).

is brought for the principal benefit of a creditor existing at the time of the transaction, which holds more than 99% of the outstanding unsecured debt.

We begin with the elements of the cause of action under the UFTA §5, as adopted in California, for a constructive fraudulent transfer rendering the debtor insolvent. The elements of a cause of action under this statute are as follows: the debtor (1) made a transfer or incurred an obligation, (2) without receiving a reasonably equivalent value in exchange, (3) which rendered the debtor insolvent (or the debtor was already insolvent), and (4) which is attacked by a pre-transaction creditor.

1. Transfer or Obligation

The selling shareholders do not dispute that, in making the BT loan, the debtor made a transfer or incurred an obligation. In fact, the debtor did both. The debtor undertook the $3.95 million obligation to BT, it transferred a security interest in essentially all of its assets to BT, and it transferred $3.5 million ultimately to the selling shareholders. Thus the first element of the cause of action is satisfied.

2. Lack of Reasonably Equivalent Value

The selling shareholders likewise do not contest whether the debtor received reasonably equivalent value for the BT loan. However, this element is not apparent on its face.

Nominally, BT's transaction was only with Bay Plastics. It lent the $3.95 million *to the debtor,* the debtor promised to repay the loan, and the debtor gave a first priority security interest in essentially all of its assets to secure the repayment. If this were the transaction, creditors likely would have no grounds for complaint, and it would not be vulnerable to fraudulent transfer attack.

However, the foregoing structure obscures the reality of the transaction. The selling shareholders' transaction was formally with Milhous, and eventually with BPI, the new owner of Bay Plastics. BPI purchased their stock, and arranged for their payment with funds that Bay Plastics borrowed from BT. Before Bay Plastics received the funds, it directed that $3.5 million be transferred to its incoming parent, BPI, and BPI in turn directed that the funds be paid out for the stock purchase. Thus in substance $3.5 million of the funds that Bay Plastics borrowed from BT went to pay for the stock of the selling shareholders, rather than to Bay Plastics.

This raises the question whether the Court should collapse the various transactions in this case into one integrated transaction. Under *Lippi* this turns on whether, from the perspective of the selling shareholders, the transaction appeared to be a straight sale without an LBO. *Lippi,* 955 F.2d at 612. If, in contrast, there is evidence that the parties knew or should have known that the transaction would deplete the assets of the company, the Court should look beyond the formal structure. Id. In *Kupetz* the Ninth Circuit found it improper to collapse the transactions where the selling shareholders had no knowledge of the LBO character of the transaction, and there were no pre-transaction creditors.

In this case, in contrast, the selling shareholders had full knowledge that this was an LBO. The Milhous representatives informed them of this at the October 25 meeting before the transaction was finalized, and it was disclosed in the financial projections provided at that time. In addition, the selling shareholders discussed this feature with their legal counsel on October 25, and specifically discussed their exposure to a fraudulent transfer claim. Both the selling shareholders and their legal counsel were familiar with leveraged buyouts, because they had done others previously, and they knew the fraudulent transfer risks. . . .

Thus, in this case the Court finds it appropriate to collapse the various pieces of this transaction into one integral transaction, in which the funds went to the selling shareholders, not to Bay Plastics or to its new parent BPI. The loan obligation, in contrast, was undertaken by Bay Plastics, which also provided the security for the loan.

Bay Plastics received no reasonably equivalent value for the security interest in all of its assets that it gave to BT in exchange for BT's funding of the stock sale. Under California law, reasonable equivalence must be determined from the standpoint of creditors. Hansen v. Cramer, 39 Cal. 2d 321, 245 P.2d 1059, 1061 (1952) (applying rule to "fair consideration" under predecessor statute); Patterson v. Missler, 238 Cal. App. 2d 759, 48 Cal. Rptr. 215, 221 (1965) (same). The Ninth Circuit has adopted the same view in interpreting the California version of the UFTA. [Citations omitted.] Payment of funds to a parent corporation prevents a transaction from satisfying the "reasonably equivalent value" requirement. *Pajaro Dunes, supra,* at 579. A financially healthy entity may give away its assets as it pleases so long as there remains enough to pay its debts. A financially distressed donor, however, may not be so generous. *Weinstein, supra* note 12, at 176.

From the debtor's perspective, it is apparent that the $450,000 that Bay Plastics presumably received (the $3.95 million loan less the $3.5 million paid to the selling shareholders) is not reasonably equivalent to the $3.95 million obligation that it undertook. *Cf.* Shape, Inc. v. Midwest Engineering (In re Shape, Inc.), 176 B.R. 1, 3 (Bankr. D. Me. 1994) (payment of $70,000 for stock worth more than $1.5 million lacks reasonably equivalent value). Thus Bay Plastics did not receive reasonably equivalent value for the loan obligation and security interest that it granted to BT.

3. Insolvency of the Debtor

The third element of the fraudulent transfer cause of action at issue in this litigation is that the transaction rendered the debtor insolvent, if it was not so already. In this case the Court finds the evidence undisputed that the LBO rendered the debtor insolvent. . . .

Indeed, this is exactly the type of transaction that poses the extreme risk of an LBO. No Milhous entity put any funds or assets at risk in the investment at all. In consequence of the structure of the transaction, all of the risks of the enterprise were placed on its creditors. Milhous retained only the right to reap the benefits if the business was sufficiently profitable to avoid bankruptcy.[11]

4. Attack by a Pre-Transaction Creditor

The final element of the cause of action for fraudulent transfer rendering a debtor insolvent is that the transaction must be attacked by a pre-transaction creditor. This element is satisfied in this case.

Shintech, the principal unsecured creditor in this case, which holds more than 99% of the unsecured debt, is the pre-existing creditor. It was secured until this transaction, and in addition it held guaranties from each of the selling shareholders. In this transaction the selling shareholders and Milhous induced it to relinquish its security and guaranties to permit the transaction to be consummated. Although knowing the LBO character of the transaction, both the selling shareholders and Milhous failed to disclose this feature to Shintech. . . .

C. Application of Fraudulent Transfer Law to LBOs

The Court finds it appropriate to apply fraudulent transfer law to an LBO. An LBO is different, not just in degree, but in character from the ordinary business and investment transactions engaged in by a corporation's management. An LBO is not a routine business transaction that should normally be given deference by the courts. It is not a corporate investment in a new venture, new equipment or property. Indeed, an LBO normally does not affect the business of the corporation at all; it only changes the ownership and adds a large layer of secured debt. Rather, an LBO is an investment of corporate assets, by borrowing against them, for the *personal* benefit of both old and new equity owners. Thus, the application of fraudulent transfer law to LBOs does not limit corporate entrepreneurial decisions.

Since an LBO reduces the availability of unencumbered assets, the buyout depletes estate assets available to pay creditors' claims. As the Ninth Circuit has stated:

> Existing unsecured creditors are vulnerable in [an LBO]. From their perspective, a pledge of the company's assets as collateral to finance the purchase of the company reduces the assets to which they can look for repayment.

Kupetz, 845 F.2d at 846; *accord,* Moody v. Security Pacific Business Credit, Inc., 971 F.2d 1056, 1073 (3d Cir. 1992). An LBO is attractive to the sellers, the buyers and the lender because it shifts most of the risk of loss to other creditors of the corporation. Mellon Bank v. Metro Communications, Inc., 945 F.2d 635 (3d Cir. 1991). The acquired corporation receives little or nothing in exchange for the debt that it incurs.

---

11. In such a transaction there is a danger that the selling shareholders will be paid more than their stock is worth. With nothing at risk if the business is not sufficiently profitable, the purchaser has less incentive to make sure that the price is not excessive. Absent fraudulent transfer law, there is nothing to deter the buyers, sellers and bank from imposing all of the risks of loss on the creditors, as they did in this case.

From a creditor's point of view, an LBO is indistinguishable from a distribution or a gift to shareholders. The harm is quite like the harm imposed on creditors by donative transfers to third parties, which is one of the most traditional kinds of fraudulent transfers.[12] If the value of the security interest given by the corporation does not exceed the shareholders' equity as shown on the balance sheet (after suitable revisions to mark the assets to market and to eliminate intangible assets of dubious value), there is usually no substantial harm to creditors. Indeed, typical corporate distribution statutes permit the payment of dividends in such circumstances, to the extent of the balance sheet equity. *See, e.g.*, Cal. Corp. Code §166 (West Supp. 1995). If the price paid to selling shareholders is higher, however, there may be insufficient assets remaining to satisfy creditors.

The vice of an LBO lies in the fact that the selling shareholders are paid indirectly with assets from the corporation itself, rather than by the purchasers. In effect, in an LBO the shareholders are paid with a corporate dividend or distribution. An LBO enables the selling shareholders to liquidate their equity interests, which are otherwise subordinate to general unsecured claims, without first paying creditors, which a normal liquidation would require. The selling shareholders in the transaction in effect disregard the status of the corporation as a separate entity for their benefit, but insist on respect of the corporation's separate status when it comes to creditors' claims (apart from those of the lender providing the funds for the transaction).

The possible detriment to creditors is exacerbated if the corporation's cash flow is not sufficient to service the loan. The bank eventually proceeds to foreclose on the corporation's assets and sells them at foreclosure prices, and leaves nothing for other creditors. Such foreclosure is frequently interrupted by the filing of a bankruptcy case. So it happened in this case.

Most courts that have considered the issue have decided that fraudulent transfer law should apply to LBOs. [Citations omitted.]

It does not follow, however, that the fraudulent transfer analysis of an LBO will result in a recovery for the benefit of the bankruptcy estate. In both *Moody* and *Mellon Bank* the Third Circuit upheld the transactions at issue against the fraudulent transfer attack. In *Lippi,* similarly, the Ninth Circuit ruled in favor of some of the defendants, and remanded for further consideration as to the remainder.

Should all LBOs be exposed to fraudulent transfer challenge? Certainly not. Under this Court's analysis, two kinds of LBOs ordinarily escape fraudulent transfer attack. This includes many, if not most, LBOs.

First, in a legitimate LBO, in which the assets mortgaged by a corporation to support an LBO do not exceed the net equity of the business (after appropriate adjustments), the transaction will not make the corporation insolvent, at least according to the balance sheet test.[13] If in addition it has sufficient projected cash flow to pay

---

12. David Epstein and his co-authors state: "[The creditors] are harmed just as much as if the debtor had given away the equity in its assets as a gift." Epstein, *supra* note 10, §6-52 at 69.

13. It makes sense to limit legitimate LBOs to transactions that do not leave a corporation insolvent. In a perfect world (as typically assumed by economists), an LBO would never run afoul of this rule, because the price paid for the stock would be the net equity in the firm. Baird & Jackson, supra note 10, at 851. Such an LBO would place the

its debts as they come due, the cash flow solvency test is met, also. This leaves an LBO exposed to fraudulent transfer attack only if the margin of equity is too thin to support the corporation's business.

A second kind of LBO also escapes fraudulent transfer attack, even though it leaves the subject corporation insolvent. If the cash flow is sufficient to make the debt payments, the transaction also is unassailable. This ordinarily turns on two factors: the degree of risk of default undertaken in the first instance, and the degree to which projected economic developments impacting the business are not overly optimistic. These LBOs escape fraudulent transfer attack either because of good financial projections or because of good luck: either factor is sufficient.

The Court's view of the proper application of fraudulent transfer law to LBOs does not make the selling shareholders the guarantors of the success of the LBO. A legitimate LBO, as described *supra,* shifts the risk of failure off their shoulders. As to subsequent creditors, they should not be required to shoulder the risk if the failure is caused by outside forces not reasonably foreseeable at the time of the transaction. Moody v. Security Pacific Business Credit, Inc., 971 F.2d 1056, 1073 (3d Cir. 1992) (failure caused by increased competition rather than lack of capital); Credit Managers Association v. Federal Co., 629 F. Supp. 175, 186-87 (C.D. Cal. 1985).

However, an LBO that is leveraged beyond the net worth of the business is a gamble. A highly leveraged business is much less able to weather temporary financial storms, because debt demands are less flexible than equity interest. The risks of this gamble should rest on the shoulders of the shareholders (old and new), not those of the creditors: the shareholders enjoy the benefits if the gamble is successful, and they should bear the burdens if it is not. This, after all, is the role of equity owners of a corporation. The application of fraudulent transfer law to LBOs shifts the risks of an LBO transaction from the creditors, who are not parties to the transaction, back to the old and new shareholders who bring about such transactions. As Sherwin states:

> These parties, who are directly involved as the principal engineers and beneficiaries of the buyout, should bear the risk of negative consequences if the transaction does not in fact comply with the standards for creditor protection set out in the fraudulent conveyance statutes. . . . They should be accountable to creditors for the benefits diverted from the corporation if they knew or should have known . . . of facts the court determines to establish a constructive fraud against creditors.

Sherwin, *supra* note 10, at 519.

How long should selling shareholders be exposed to the risk that an LBO will go bad? There is a traditional answer to this question: until the statute of limitations runs. Perhaps there should be a shorter statute of limitations for LBOs than the four to seven years that is common under the UFTA. This is a decision for the legislature to make.

---

corporation on the verge of insolvency, but not beyond. In the real world, some LBOs leave corporations insolvent, perhaps because of imperfect information about the value of the corporation's stock.

The Court perceives no unfairness in imposing the risks of an overleveraged LBO on the old and new shareholders who undertake the risks, rather [than] on the creditors who do not intend to do so. Indeed, it is the selling shareholders who are ordinarily least worthy of sympathy in an LBO. As Epstein states:

> In the beginning of the transaction they are below existing creditors. In the end, they "cash out" and march off over the heads of the existing creditors. It is a neat trick of legal magic that allows the shareholders to subordinate, unilaterally, the creditors' claims.

2 Epstein, *supra* note 10, at 74.

D. Good Faith Defense

The selling shareholders claim that they acted in good faith, and that this is a defense to the fraudulent transfer claim. From the earliest fraudulent transfer statutes, a good faith transferee for value has enjoyed an affirmative defense to the cause of action. *See, e.g.*, 13 Stat. Eliz. ch. 5, §6 (1570). However, this defense has been greatly restricted in recent statutes.

The UFTA, including California's version thereof, provides a complete defense to an intentional fraudulent transfer for a transferee who took "in good faith and for a reasonably equivalent value." UFTA §8(a); Cal. Civ. Code §3439.08(a) (West Supp. 1995). This defense is not available for a constructive fraudulent conveyance, and thus is not applicable in this adversary proceeding.

A second good faith provision is contained in UFTA §8(d) and the California Civil Code, which provide:

> Notwithstanding voidability of a transfer or an obligation under this chapter, a good faith transferee or obligee is entitled, *to the extent of the value given the debtor* for the transfer or obligation, to the following: (1) A lien on or a right to retain any interest in the asset transferred. (2) Enforcement of any obligation incurred. (3) A reduction in the amount of the liability on the judgment.

UFCA §8(d); Cal. Civ. Code §3439.08(d) (West Supp. 1995) (emphasis added).

In this case the selling shareholders gave up their shares of stock in the debtor in exchange for their payment of $3.5 million. However, this provision is not applicable in this case, because the shareholders did not transfer their shares or give any other value *to the debtor*. The shares went to BPI, the new parent corporation of Bay Plastics, and from there to Milhous. The debtor itself received neither shares nor money. This did not constitute "value given the debtor," within the meaning of UFTA §8(d) or California Civil Code §3439.08(d). Thus the good faith defense fails.

IV. *Conclusion*

Having found no triable issue of material fact, the Court concludes that the trustee is entitled to a summary judgment setting aside the constructive fraudulent transfer in this case to the selling shareholders. After having collapsed the series of transactions into a single transaction, the Court finds that in substance the selling shareholders received payment for their shares that was secured by the assets of debtor, and that this transaction defrauded an existing creditor. The payment to the selling shareholders is thus avoidable under UFTA §5, as adopted in California in California Civil Code §3439.05, which in turn is incorporated in Bankruptcy Code §544(b).

CHAPTER *2*

Commencement of the Case and Eligibility for Relief

Bankruptcy begins with the filing of a petition asking for relief. The petition can be filed in a number of different chapters of the Bankruptcy Code. In this chapter, we will consider both who can file such a petition, and in which of the various chapters the petition is to be filed.

I. Voluntary Proceedings

The vast majority of bankruptcy cases are commenced as voluntary proceedings under §301 of the Code. All it takes to commence a case is the filing with the bankruptcy court of a petition under a chapter of the Code for which the debtor is eligible for relief. Assuming eligibility, the filing of the petition "constitutes an order for relief" and has several other consequences. Most important, it creates the automatic stay (§362) and the bankruptcy estate (§541).

Although there has been a tremendous debate about the truth of this, Congress became concerned that bankruptcy has become a too easy method for those who could pay their debts to avoid them. The large increase in bankruptcy filings also signaled to Congress that many people were resorting to bankruptcy because of poor financial planning and/or irresponsible debt assumption. These factors (and others, such as the lobbying power of the credit card industry) led to the enactment of major amendments to the Bankruptcy Code in a law attractively entitled the "Bankruptcy Abuse Prevention and Consumer Protection Act of 2005," which President Bush promptly signed into law.

The new law is very complicated, making some 400 changes to the Bankruptcy Code, but some of its most important provisions relate to making Chapter 7 relief unavailable, so that individual debtors will file Chapter 13 repayment plans (thus repaying some of the debt owed to their creditors).

Other provisions restricting access to bankruptcy relief apply to all individual debtor cases. For example, §109(h) forbids the filing of any bankruptcy petition unless the debtor has undergone credit counseling from what the statute calls an "approved nonprofit budget and credit counseling agency." During the 180 days prior to the filing of the bankruptcy petition, the debtor must have received a briefing from such an agency (though this may be done over the telephone or via the Internet). This briefing must outline the opportunities for available credit counseling and assist the debtor in preforming a budget analysis. The United States trustee is to maintain a registry of approved credit counseling agencies, which must meet the standards set by §111(c), which you should now read.

PROBLEM 2-1

When Joe Btfsplk was diagnosed with AIDS his wife promptly left him and he became too ill to manage the cloud-seeding business he had run from years out of a local airport. Because of a severe depression he stopped opening his mail or answering the phone, and was shocked to learn one morning that the bank was going to hold a foreclosure sale on his home that afternoon at 3 P.M. His neighbor advised him that the filing of a bankruptcy petition would stop the sale, so Joe calls you, a bankruptcy attorney he found through the phone book. He has never been to a credit counseling agency. Will you be able to help him? See §109(h)(3). *Compare* In re Graham, 336 B.R. 292 (Bankr. W.D. Ky. 2005), *with* In re Talib, 335 B.R. 417 (Bankr. W.D. Mo. 2005). Suppose Joe had gone to an approved credit counseling agency but then tried to pay off his creditors. If it is now 182 days after his credit counseling briefing, does Joe have to go back to the agency for another briefing before filing a bankruptcy petition? *Compare* In re Giles, 361 B.R. 212 (Bankr. D. Utah 2007) (debtor ineligible for relief when he obtained counseling briefing 182 days prior to filing of petition), *with* In re Bricksin, 346 B.R. 497 (Bankr. N.D. Cal. 2006) (debtor's repayment efforts with the assistance of the credit counselor constituted ongoing counseling and debtor was eligible for relief even though initial briefing was more than 180 prior to filing of petition).

Congress wanted to make sure that everyone who goes into bankruptcy gets some financial training in order to avoid future bankruptcies. Thus whether the petition is filed in Chapter 7 or 13, the debtor will be denied a discharge unless he or she successfully completes an "instructional course concerning personal financial management" during the bankruptcy period; *see* §§727(a)(11) and 1328(g).

A. The "Means Test"

The second major hurdle that Congress requires the debtor to jump before filing a Chapter 7 petition is meeting the so-called "means test." The basic concept driving the following rules is that if the debtor has enough net income that he or she could repay a significant amount of debt under a Chapter 13 plan, the debtor should not be eligible to file for liquidation of these debts under Chapter 7. Thus, §707(b) states that the debtor is deemed to have "abused" the bankruptcy system, and the debtor will be barred from Chapter 7, if the debtor's monthly income (reduced by various allowed deductions) exceeds the median family income by a certain amount. Here are the rules:

The computations start with determining the debtor's "current monthly income," defined in §101(10A) to generally include the average of the debtor's income for the six months prior to the filing of the petition. The higher this amount the worse things are likely to go for the debtors in the tests that follow.

PROBLEM 2-2

Three months before she filed her petition, Alice Gown won $5000 in the lottery. She used these winnings to reduce some of her enormous bills, but finally decided that bankruptcy was her only recourse. Excluding the lottery winnings, her average monthly income was $3000, but those winnings will inflate the six-month average considerably. Is there anything she can do to keep it out of the calculations? See §§707(b)(2)(B)(i); 101(10A).

PROBLEM 2-3

Trevor Crespeen had a great job that paid him $6,000 per month. Unfortunately, Trevor had a $6,500 per month lifestyle. He had gotten by over the years by adding $500 per month to his credit card balance. Trevor has just been laid off and has not worked nor received any income for the past month. What is Trevor's current monthly income?

The second computation that comes into the picture compares the debtor's current monthly income (multiplied by 12 to reach an annual sum) with the Census Bureau's figures for the state's highest median income for a family household of comparable size to the debtor's household. Just as an example, the Ohio median income for a household of two persons in 2007 averaged around $51,400. If the debtor's income is *equal to or lower* than the state's median income, the "safe harbor" provisions of §707(b)(7) apply and the debtor may freely file a Chapter 7 petition. In that case, the means test, discussed next, is not relevant. You can see these income figures on the website of the Executive Office of United States Trustees, <www.usdoj.gov/ust/>.

If, however, the debtor's income exceeds the state's median income, the debtor must now enter the labyrinth called the "means test," and developed at length in §707. If the debtor flunks the means test, he or she is presumed to be abusing the bankruptcy system, and is forbidden to file a petition in Chapter 7 (but would still be eligible for relief in Chapter 13, where the debtor would have to try and repay creditors as much as possible over a five-year period).

Under the means test various adjustments are made to the debtor's current monthly income. First, it is reduced by deductions for expenses considered reasonable under §707(b)(2)(A)(ii), referencing those developed by the IRS, which has national and local standards for these living expenses. This section also allows some extra deductions, including those for support of elderly, ill, or disabled household or family members, plus some education expenses for children, and extra housing or utility expenses that the debtor can demonstrate are both reasonable and necessary. Finally, the section allows deduction for payments to secured and priority creditors stretched out over five years (60 months). So, if the debtor owes 12 monthly payments of $100 secured by a refrigerator, the means test deduction from the debtor's monthly income for that secured claim would be $20 ($1200 ÷ 60).

Once these calculations have been done, the amount remaining of the current monthly income is multiplied by 60 to see what income could be generated to fund a Chapter 13 plan for five years. The debtor will flunk the means test (and be barred from filing a Chapter 7 petition) if those payments exceed the *lesser* of either (1) $6,575 or 25 percent of nonpriority unsecured debt, whichever is greater, or (2) $10,950; see §707(b)(2)(A)(i) (keep in mind that these numbers are adjusted every three years). This can be reduced to a formula based on these "trigger points," as follows: First, the debtor does not flunk the means test if the adjusted monthly expenses are less than $109.58 a month ($6,575 divided by 60). Second, the debtor is barred from Chapter 7 if the adjusted month income is greater than $181.67 ($10,950 divided by 60). Finally, if the adjusted month amount is between $109.58 and $181.67, multiply it by 60 and determine whether it would then pay 25 percent of the nonpriority unsecured debt; if so, the debtor fails the means test and is barred from Chapter 7 because of a presumption of abuse of the bankruptcy system. There are a number of commercial products available that perform these calculations automatically once you enter some of the basic information such as the debtor's location, family size, and income. Enter the right information and bells go off and fireworks explode along with a message like "Congratulations, you just passed the means test!" Of course, if the calculations result in the debtor having too much disposable income, a grim reaper appears along with a message that you do not pass "Go" and that you cannot enter Chapter 7.

PROBLEM 2-4

After years of happy indulgence, once-wealthy Mame Dennis ended up in the offices of a bankruptcy attorney, who did the calculations just described. Mame's adjusted monthly income was $120, and her unsecured debt, mostly credit cards, was $20,000. Assuming that Mame's income is above the applicable state median income, will she be eligible for Chapter 7, or must she struggle for five years trying to pay off some of this debt under a Chapter 13 plan? Does your answer change if her credit card debts amount to $35,000?

PROBLEM 2-5

Assume that Mame from Problem 2-4 was concerned that she might not "pass" the means test. If her circumstances were the same as in the prior problem, but instead of owning a 2005 Ford Taurus on which she paid $350 per month, she owned a 2009 Mercedes for which the monthly payment was $800 per month, would she now "pass" the means test? Suppose Mame plans to surrender the Mercedes back to the secured creditor as a part of the bankruptcy case. Can she still deduct the $800 per month from her otherwise disposable income? See In re Ralston, 400 B.R. 854 (Bankr. M.D. Fla. 2009); Eugene R. Wedoff, Means Testing in the New §707(b), 79 Am. Bankr. L.J. 231, 275-76 (2005).

To make sure that the debtor reveals everything that is necessary to make all these calculations, the 2005 statute now requires the debtor, as of the time the petition is filed, to attach schedules detailing a great mass of information about his or her financial situation. This includes a list of creditors, assets and liabilities, and income (including payment stubs for the 60 days prior to the filing). Before the first meeting of creditors, the debtor must also produce a tax return for the past year, along with various certificates from the credit counseling agency. Read §521(a)(1), (b), (e)(2), and (h).

To "encourage" the debtor to compile and deliver the documents and information, §521(i) provides that if an individual debtor in a Chapter 7 or 13 case fails to file the required information, then "the case shall be automatically dismissed effective on the 46th day after the date of the filing of the petition." The concept of "automatic dismissal" is new to the Code and was added in 2005. Notwithstanding the "automatic" nature of the dismissal, there are some limitations on its operation. For example, under subsection (i)(3), the debtor can obtain additional time to provide the information if the debtor makes the request before the 45-day period expires, and the court "finds justification" for extending the time. Under subsection (i)(4), the trustee can also ask that the case not be dismissed if the request is made before the deadline passes and the court finds "that the debtor attempted in good faith to file all the information . . . and that the best interests of creditors would be served by the administration of the case." If the statute is truly automatic, does the court have to take any action for the case to be dismissed? If no action is taken, is the case dismissed, and how would anyone know in the absence of any entry on the court's docket?

The courts have not settled on an interpretation of the provision. Some have stated that the plain meaning rule removes any discretion from the courts in the matter and concluded that if the debtor has not filed some of the required information the case is dismissed. See, e.g., In re Brickey, 363 B.R. 59 (Bankr. N.D.N.Y. 2007); In re Fawson, 338 B.R. 505 (Bankr. D. Utah 2006). Other courts have rejected this view and concluded that the courts are not without authority to retain a case, particularly when the debtor has engaged in some behavior that would essentially be rewarded by a dismissal of the case. The First Circuit has rendered the first opinion in the courts of appeal on the issue.

In re Acosta-Rivera

United States Court of Appeals, First Circuit, 2009
557 F.3d 8

SELYA, Circuit Judge.

This appeal, which requires us to decide an issue of first impression at the federal appellate level, turns on the construction of a provision of the Bankruptcy Abuse Prevention and Consumer Protection Act of 2005 (BAPCPA or the Act), Pub. L. 109-8, 119 Stat. 23 (2005). Writ large, the provision in question expands the debtor's duties of financial disclosure to the extent that he or she must now file with the bankruptcy court, "unless the court orders otherwise," six traunches of financial information (including payment advices and an itemized statement of monthly net income). 11 U.S.C. §521(a)(1)(B)(iv), (v). The issue centers on whether the bankruptcy court may enter an order excusing non-disclosure *after* the time for filing the required information has expired. The bankruptcy court thought that it had the authority to enter such an order. It proceeded to exercise that power, thus avoiding dismissal of the debtors' petition under section 521(i)(1) (BAPCPA's so-called "automatic dismissal" provision). The district court construed the "orders otherwise" provision differently. Consequently, it determined that the order excusing the failure to file was beyond the scope of the bankruptcy court's authority. *See Rivera v. Miranda*, 376 B.R. 382, 386 (D.P.R. 2007).

We conclude that the bankruptcy court acted in consonance with the statutory scheme and within the realm of its discretion. Accordingly, we reverse the district court's order and remand for further proceedings.

The procedural background is uncomplicated. The debtors, Iván Acosta-Rivera and Aña Balseiro-Chacón, are married to each other. They originally filed a joint Chapter 13 petition and later converted that filing to a Chapter 7 petition. The debtors' estate included an unresolved employment discrimination suit brought by Acosta-Rivera against his quondam employer. In that suit, which had been pending for roughly eight years and had twice been appealed to the Supreme Court of Puerto Rico, Acosta-Rivera sought reinstatement, backpay, and compensatory damages.

At this point, the plot thickens. Although this chose in action was plainly an asset of the debtors' estate, it did not appear on their original bankruptcy schedules, their first amended schedules, or their second amended schedules.

Six months after the filing of the bankruptcy petition, the debtors revealed the existence of the chose in action, listing its value as "unknown," in their third amended set of schedules. Even then, they failed to disclose that the suit demanded pecuniary relief (e.g., backpay and money damages). After several further amendments (not material here), the debtors valued the chose in action at $2,700,000 and claimed an exemption of $350,000.

Eventually, the Chapter 7 trustee moved for leave to settle the suit for $200,000 (a sum that would have generated enough cash to pay all allowed claims and produce some surplus funds for the debtors). Balking at this proposal, the debtors moved under the automatic dismissal provision, 11 U.S.C. §521(i)(2), to confirm the dismissal of their petition. In support of their motion, they claimed not to have filed or otherwise provided the payment advices and statement of monthly net income required by BAPCPA. As their attorney acknowledged, the debtors wanted to dismiss the bankruptcy case so that they could "continue prosecuting the state court action" for damages.

We pause at this juncture to discuss the Act's "automatic dismissal" provision. When a debtor fails to file all the information required by section 521(a)(1)(B) within the prescribed period — that is, within forty-five days of the filing date of the bankruptcy petition — BAPCPA provides that "the case shall be automatically dismissed."[1] 11 U.S.C. §521(i)(1). The term "automatic dismissal" is something of a misnomer. Typically, dismissal under this provision takes place at the instance of a "party in interest." *Id.* §521(i)(2); *see, e.g., In re Spencer*, 388 B.R. 418, 421 (Bankr. D. D.C. 2008). Dismissal is, therefore, hardly "automatic."[2]

We return to what transpired below. In due season, the bankruptcy court denied the debtors' motion to dismiss, finding that "facts peculiar to this case do not require dismissal under section 521." In support, the court noted that the debtors' motion stemmed from their "disagreement with the proposed settlement." That was significant because the putative settlement would have satisfied all allowed claims; thus, neither the creditors nor the trustee needed the missing (undisclosed) information. Based on that reasoning, the court entered "an order nunc pro tunc . . . excusing the debtors from filing the payment advices mentioned in section 521(a)(1)(B)(iv)." In short, the court excused the detailed disclosure by ordering the debtors to do "otherwise" under section 521(a)(1)(B).

In a subsequent order, the court approved the trustee's revised recommendation to settle the discrimination case for $600,000, citing the likelihood of delay from further litigation, uncertainties surrounding collection, and the fact that Acosta-Rivera stood to receive nearly $400,000, less mortgage arrearages, after the allowed claims were paid.

The debtors appealed the denial of their motion to dismiss to the district court. The district judge ruled that the bankruptcy court lacked authority to excuse compliance with the disclosure requirement more than forty-five days after the debtors filed their bankruptcy petition. *See Rivera*, 376 B.R. at 386. In the judge's view, the strictures of the Act left the bankruptcy judge "with no discretion to fashion any reasonable or equitable solution." *Id.* at 386-87. The judge stated: " 'After the expiration of the specified period set forth in 11 U.S.C. §521(i)(1), there are no exceptions, no excuses, only dismissal and the consequences that flow therefrom.' " *Id.* at 386 (quoting *In re Ott*, 343 B.R. 264, 268 (Bankr. D. Colo. 2006)). This timely appeal followed.

Some preliminary pruning is in order. The Chapter 7 trustee devotes much of his brief to General Order 05-06 of the bankruptcy court, which directs debtors not to file

---

1. The automatic dismissal deadline can be extended by another forty-five days upon timely request. *See* 11 U.S.C. §521(i)(3). Moreover, the automatic dismissal provision is subject to an explicit statutory exception: a timely motion by the trustee to forestall dismissal based on the best interests of the creditors and the debtors' good-faith efforts to effect the required filing. *Id.* §521(i)(1), (4). That exception does not apply here.

2. A few courts have conceptualized dismissal under this section as a matter involving only the counting of the days. *See, e.g., In re Fawson*, 338 B.R. 505, 510 (Bankr. D. Utah 2006). To decide this case, we need not resolve that question.

the payment advices required by section 521(a)(1)(B)(iv), but, rather, to provide them to the trustee and interested creditors. The general order further provides that "[f]ailure of debtor to comply with the requirements of 11 U.S.C. §521(a)(1)(B)(iv)" — presumably as adjusted by the general order— "will result in automatic dismissal under section 521(i)(1)." This general order is standard fare: bankruptcy courts in numerous districts have adopted comparable orders. *See In re Brickey*, 363 B.R. 59, 64 & n. 4 (Bankr. N.D.N.Y. 2007).

Neither the bankruptcy court nor the district court mentioned General Order 05-06. Moreover, even if the debtors had complied with this general order — a circumstance that the record does not document and that the debtors deny — the statutory issue would persist. By its terms, the general order is limited to the payment advices required by section 521(a)(1)(B)(iv); it does not mitigate the debtors' duty to file the statement of monthly net income required by section 521(a)(1)(B)(v).

The trustee has yet another new argument. For the first time, he suggests that the debtors filed the functional equivalent of a monthly net income statement in the form of Schedule J. This is too little and too late.

Schedule J deals with a debtor's current expenditures. In the process, it responds to a different filing requirement, contained in 11 U.S.C. §521(a)(1)(B)(ii). Although line 20 of Schedule J is called a "Statement of Monthly Net Income" and the advisory committee note to the official bankruptcy forms states that this line was added to Schedule J in 2005 "as required by §521(a)(1)(B)(v)," there is no reason to think that Schedule J is a proxy for the statement of current monthly income required by section 521(a)(1)(B)(v). In fact, the case law suggests the opposite conclusion. *See, e.g., In re Turner*, 384 B.R. 852, 856 (Bankr. D. Colo. 2008) (holding that a Chapter 7 debtor's duty to file a section 521(a)(1)(B)(v) statement of monthly net income "can only be fulfilled by filing" Form B22A).

We need not probe this point too deeply. Whether Schedule J can ever serve double duty in a given case is not before us. Suffice it to say that, in this instance, we will not entertain the trustee's forfeited argument. *See Teamsters Union Local No. 59 v. Superline Transp. Co.*, 953 F.2d 17, 21 (1st Cir. 1992) ("If any principle is settled in this circuit, it is that, absent the most extraordinary circumstances, legal theories not squarely raised in the lower court cannot be broached for the first time on appeal.").

Having cleared away the underbrush, what remains is the question of the bankruptcy court's authority to waive the disclosure requirement after the expiration of the filing deadline. The statute provides that the debtor "shall . . . file" the required disclosures "unless the court orders otherwise." 11 U.S.C. §521(a)(1)(B). The grant of judicial power to "order[ ] otherwise" predated BAPCPA.[3] In overhauling section 521, Congress left this familiar language intact. We do not regard that as a mere fortuity. Nor do we think that a slip of the pen accounts for the fact that the

---

3. The pre-BAPCPA version of section 521(1) provided:

The Debtor shall . . . file a list of creditors, and unless the court orders otherwise, a schedule of assets and liabilities, a schedule of current income and current expenditures, and a statement of the debtor's financial affairs.

provision does not now contain an explicit deadline for ordering otherwise. In this context, we have a high regard for congressional silence.

Sharing this regard, a few courts have held that the bankruptcy court possesses authority to waive the disclosure requirement even after the forty-five-day filing deadline has expired. *See, e.g., In re Parker*, 351 B.R. 790, 801-02 (Bankr. N.D. Ga. 2006); *In re Jackson*, 348 B.R. 487, 499-500 (Bankr. S.D. Iowa 2006); *cf. In re Bonner*, 374 B.R. 62, 64-65 (Bankr. W.D.N.Y. 2007) (suggesting that "special circumstances can justify *nunc pro tunc* relief" under section 521(i)). Other courts, however, have taken the view that BAPCPA's new forty-five-day deadline applies to courts and debtors alike. *See, e.g., In re Spencer*, 388 B.R. at 422; *Warren v. Wirum*, 378 B.R. 640, 647 (N.D. Cal. 2007); *In re Hall*, 368 B.R. 595, 599 (Bankr. W.D. Tex. 2007); *In re Brickey*, 363 B.R. at 64-65 (Bankr. N.D.N.Y. 2007); *In re Calhoun*, 359 B.R. 738, 740 (Bankr. E.D. Mo. 2007). That view reads into the filing deadline a restriction on bankruptcy courts' authority gleaned by implication from the "automatic dismissal" provision.

Neither reading satisfies both head and heart in equal measure. The former (more flexible) reading honors the policy behind the Act by vesting bankruptcy courts with greater discretion to discourage bankruptcy abuse. Because any party in interest may request an order of automatic dismissal, debtors with something to hide are liable to treat dismissal as an escape hatch to be opened as needed. *See Parker*, 351 B.R. at 802; *see also Hall*, 368 B.R. at 602 (dismissing case on motion of debtor whom court describes as "the poster child for a bad faith debtor"). In such cases, the court has no occasion to address non-disclosure until long after the forty-five-day period has elapsed. That timetable rubs uneasily against the strictures of an inflexible reading — and bankruptcy courts are, after all, courts of equity.

But the story has another side. The stricter reading of the statute, though inflexible, gives sharper teeth to the automatic dismissal provision. It ensures that dismissal at a party's request is all but guaranteed once the forty-five days have passed. Given Congress's concern with "the recent escalation of consumer bankruptcy filings," H.R. Rep. No. 109-31, at 3-4, reprinted in 2005 U.S.C.C.A.N. 90, it can be argued that the stricter reading has some implicit support in the legislative history. *See, e.g., Warren*, 378 B.R. at 647; *see also Rivera*, 376 B.R. at 386 (voicing concern that retroactive relief from the filing requirement "would render the automatic dismissal provision in §521(i) meaningless").

This position has a certain superficial appeal. Still, we must caution against trying to stretch a morsel into a meal. The amendments to section 521 are part of an abuse-prevention package. With Congress's core purpose in mind, we are reluctant to read into the statute by implication a new limit on judicial discretion that would encourage rather than discourage bankruptcy abuse. It is safe to say that Congress, in enacting BAPCPA, was not bent on placing additional weapons in the hands of abusive debtors.[4]

---

4. By definition, such debtors are unfit for the "good faith" exception in section 521(i)(4). . . . Moreover, under 11 U.S.C. §707(a), a chapter 7 debtor has no absolute right to dismiss his petition but must instead show cause. *See In re Smith*, 507 F.3d 64, 72 (2d Cir. 2007).

In all events, we believe that it is possible to give effect to all of section 521, preserving the bankruptcy court's discretion to forgive compliance with disclosure requirements after the fact while at the same time preserving the authentic value of automatic dismissal. When a party moves under section 521(i)(2) for the entry of an order dismissing an incomplete petition, the court can do one of three things: dismiss the case, decline to dismiss the case if the good-faith exception for payment advices applies, *see supra* note 2; or determine, in its discretion, that the missing information is *not* "required under subsection (a)(1)." 11 U.S.C. §521(i)(1). In the last-mentioned event, the court can deny the motion to dismiss. Some courts in "strict" jurisdictions seem to assume that the second and third of these options cover the same ground. That thinking underlies the opinions construing the forty-five-day deadline for automatic dismissal as an implicit temporal limitation upon the court's authority to order otherwise. *See, e.g., Spencer,* 388 B.R. at 422; *Warren,* 378 B.R. at 646; *Hall,* 368 B.R. at 599; *Brickey,* 363 B.R. at 64-65; *Calhoun,* 359 B.R. at 740.

We find that mechanical reading unwise. While it may be textually plausible, it fails to harmonize the letter and purpose of the statute. There is another, equally plausible reading — a reading that avoids this vice.

The approach that we endorse recognizes that missing information may or may not be required, in a practical sense, depending upon what is deemed material by the court many months (or even years) after the bankruptcy petition has been filed. This would seem to be a likely reason for Congress to have entrusted the bankruptcy court with discretion to modify disclosure requirements on the fly. Where, as here, a previously hidden asset has more than enough value to cover the entire universe of creditors' claims, dollar for dollar, dispensing with the disclosure of statements reflecting payment advices and/or monthly net income is both pragmatic and reasonable. Common sense suggests that Congress never intended to strip the bankruptcy court of the flexibility needed to respond intelligently to the emergence of such a circumstance after the forty-five-day filing deadline has expired.

This intuition is reinforced by our certain knowledge that this degree of flexibility existed in the Bankruptcy Code prior to BAPCPA's passage. As we have said, BAPCPA did not expressly curtail this aspect of the bankruptcy court's authority and, given the practical realities, we are reluctant to step in where Congress has elected not to tread. Automatic dismissal may be a new twist, but the importance of the judiciary's ability to assess needs and respond to exigencies free of artificial constraints has not changed. In our view, Congress must have recognized that bankruptcy courts would still need a meaningful opportunity to gauge whether missing information is "required" in a particular case. We conclude, therefore, that when the missing information has become irrelevant or extraneous and the court, in lieu of dismissal on that account, "order[s] otherwise," section 521(i) does not compel dismissal of the case.

On the same reasoning, we also reject the assertion that the exceptions to automatic dismissal contained in section 521(i) [were] meant to supplant the bankruptcy court's discretion to order otherwise more than forty-five days after the filing date. Those exceptions apply when the court does not choose to waive the disclosure requirement either ex ante or ex post; they do not apply when the court does so elect. So understood, the exceptions operate within their own statutory ambit and do not cabin the bankruptcy court's discretion in other areas.

Let us be perfectly clear. We do not decide today whether bankruptcy courts possess unfettered discretion to waive the disclosure requirements ex post. Where, however, there is no continuing need for the information or a waiver is needed to prevent automatic dismissal from furthering a debtor's abusive conduct, the court has discretion to take such an action. This case is of that genre.

To sum up, the great divide in section 521 is between information that is required and information that is not. The Act allows courts to do the sifting suggested by that divide without rigid adherence to the forty-five-day deadline.

We need go no further. In this case the bankruptcy court, acting with care and restraint, was faithful to the evolving statutory scheme. Its order was, therefore, within the compass of its discretion.

The judgment of the district court is reversed and the matter is remanded for further proceedings consistent with this opinion.

But wait, there's more! The new statute also requires the debtor's attorney to certify that everything is in apple pie order. Before reading the following Problem, read Federal Rule of Bankruptcy Procedure 9011, which bankruptcy attorneys know well.

PROBLEM 2-6

Attorney Angelina Barth has practiced bankruptcy law for many years, primarily representing consumer debtors. The law has always required the debtor's attorney to sign the bankruptcy petition, and the Federal Rules of Bankruptcy Procedure have always provided in Rule 9011 for sanctions for an attorney who misleads the court. Barth was in astounded to learn that the 2005 amendments create liability in the attorney if the debtor's Chapter 7 petition is dismissed for abuse (as defined under that section, discussed above). Read §707(b)(4). Barth has traditionally filed around 150 Chapter 7 petitions a year, but that number is likely to be halved if she must do the work the new law suggests. How much investigation must she do of what her clients tell her? How will she do it? Her already sky-high premiums for malpractice insurance are likely to hit outer space. Should she raise her usual $750 fee for a simple Chapter 7 case? By how much? New §§526 and 527 also impose significant additional burdens on "debt relief agencies" (defined to include bankruptcy attorneys — see the next Problem) and this has further depressed her. Should she just retire?

Another concern for lawyers representing consumer debtors is the prohibition in §526(a)(4) of the Code against advising a client to incur more debt in contemplation of the client filing a bankruptcy case. Several suits were filed immediately upon the effective date of this 2005 amendment to the Code asserting that the provision improperly limits the First Amendment rights of the attorney, as well as otherwise being unconstitutional. That litigation is ongoing, and the Fifth Circuit has issued the first decision on the issue at the court of appeals level. It held that the statute could be construed in a manner that it is not unconstitutionally overbroad in that it would operate only when the attorney is offering advice that would result in an abuse of the bankruptcy system. Hersh v. U.S. ex rel. Mukasey, 553 F.3d 743 (5th Cir. 2008). Other courts have disagreed and concluded that the statute is an unconstitutional restriction on the attorneys' rights under the first amendment. *See, e.g.,* Conn. Bar Assn. v. U.S., 394 B.R. 274 (D. Conn. 2008); Milavetz, Gallop & Milavetz PA v. U.S., 355 B.R. 758 (D. Minn. 2006).

PROBLEM 2-7

BANKRUPTCY Я US is a nationwide for-profit corporation that advises debtors on how to restructure their debts by working out arrangements with their creditors, and, failing that, how to handle a bankruptcy proceeding without the need of consulting an attorney. Their advertising over the Internet, in newspapers and magazines, and on late night TV contained a prominent statement such as "Free Yourself From Your Creditors Legally!!!" For an average charge of $900, the company would counsel debtors about their various credit problems, explain how bankruptcy worked and how to file petitions, reaffirm debts, claim exemptions, and obtain a discharge. The company was careful never to advise the debtors to do any of these things, only explaining how they were to be done if the debtors wished to do them on their own. The company would also help the debtors fill out the schedules and other paperwork. Does this sound like the practice of law to you? *Compare* In re Moore, 290 B.R. 287 (Bankr. E.D.N.C. 2003), and In re Moore, 283 B.R. 852 (Bankr. E.D.N.C. 2002), *with* In re Leon, 317 B.R. 131 (Bankr. C.D. Cal. 2004). Is the company in violation of the Bankruptcy Code? See §§110, 526-528; the various relevant terms are defined in §§101(12A), (3), (4), and (4A). Note that attorneys are included within the definition of a "debt relief agency" and will also have to comply with these rules.

B. Other Matters

Joint Cases. In its only concession to romance, the Bankruptcy Code also provides for the filing of joint bankruptcy petitions by married couples. Under §302, an individual and that individual's spouse may file a joint bankruptcy petition, initiating a joint case, and the debtors will pay only one filing fee. Nevertheless, there are two bankruptcy estates, although consolidation of the estates is possible in appropriate circumstances. The courts have been strict in their interpretation of §302 and have refused to allow joint petitions filed by persons who are not spouses under the applicable state law. The court in In re Kandu, 315 B.R. 153 (Bankr. W.D. Wash. 2004), held that as a result of the Defense of Marriage Act (1 U.S.C. §7) a lesbian couple who had married in Canada were not eligible to file a joint petition under §302 of the Code. See also In re Malone, 50 B.R. 2 (Bankr. E.D. Mich. 1985) (unmarried heterosexual couple ineligible to file a joint petition notwithstanding long-term cohabitation); In re Buechler, 98 B.R. 965 (Bankr. W.D. Mo. 1988) (parent and minor child cannot commence joint bankruptcy case). Of course, the two debtors could file separate cases and pay two filing fees.

Foreign bankruptcies. A new Chapter 15 added in 2005 provides another form of bankruptcy relief that is a version of the Model Law on Cross-Border Insolvency; it governs cross-border and ancillary cases. *See* Bankruptcy Code §1501. Under the Chapter, the foreign representative of the debtor in a case pending in another country can petition a United States bankruptcy court for a recognition order. If the relief is granted (and it generally would be), a case ancillary to the foreign case would be initiated. This is not a case under one of the "substantive" chapters of the Code such as Chapter 7 or Chapter 11, although the foreign representative could initiate such a case. *See* Bankruptcy Code §1511. The chapter anticipates concurrent proceedings governing the debtor under the laws of more than one country, and the courts are directed to communicate and cooperate with the foreign representatives and foreign courts. *See* Bankruptcy Code §§1525-1527.

Filing fees. The 2005 reform legislation also includes an amendment to 28 U.S.C. §1930 regulating filing fees for bankruptcy cases. These fees are $220 for a Chapter 7 case, $150 for Chapter 13, and $1,000 for Chapter 11. There are other administrative fees that debtors must pay, but the 2005 Act added a provision authorizing the waiver of filing fees in appropriate circumstances. This overturns the infamous Supreme Court decision of United States v. Kras, 409 U.S. 434 (1973), which held that the inability to pay the filing fee barred a debtor from obtaining bankruptcy relief. Debtors also may pay the filing fee in installments. *See* Bankruptcy Rule 1006.

II. Involuntary Cases

PROBLEM 2-8

Simon Mustache, the most influential banker in your town, comes to your law office and tells you that Farmer Bean has once again defaulted on his many loans, and the bank has had enough. Simon, who has had a personal dislike for Farmer Bean for years, wants you to prepare an involuntary bankruptcy petition throwing Farmer Bean into bankruptcy. Will you do this? *See* Bankruptcy Code §303(a).

In one sense, most bankruptcy cases are involuntary. That is, debtors are often "pushed" into bankruptcy and file a petition in response to creditors' collection efforts, feeling that they have no choice but to seek bankruptcy relief. Although they could be described as being forced into bankruptcy, the cases they deliberately commence by filing a bankruptcy petition are described as "voluntary."

Involuntary cases, on the other hand, are a much nastier business, commenced either by creditors of the debtor or, in the case of a general partnership, by fewer than all of the general partners. Bankruptcy Code §303(b). Involuntary cases are available only under Chapters 7 and 11, and they may not be commenced against a "farmer, family farmer, or a corporation that is not a moneyed, business or commercial corporation." As with any petition, the debtor must be eligible for relief under the particular chapter of the Bankruptcy Code.

A.   Petitioning Creditors

Successful initiation of an involuntary bankruptcy case requires that the petitioner be an eligible creditor and that the alleged debtor either is not paying its debts or has already had a trustee or receiver appointed to take control of its property. The commencement of an involuntary bankruptcy case is similar to the initiation of any lawsuit. A complaint is filed, and the defendant, or in this case the alleged debtor, must respond to the complaint. If the debtor fails to file a response, the court is directed to "order relief against the debtor." Bankruptcy Code §303(h). Bankruptcy Rules 1010, 1011, and 1013 govern the procedure for the commencement and resolution of involuntary cases. Section 303(b) requires that at least three creditors join together to commence an involuntary bankruptcy case unless the debtor has fewer than 12 creditors. In that case, a single creditor can initiate an involuntary bankruptcy case. By requiring at least three creditors to commence cases in which the debtor has a larger number of creditors, §303 furthers the collective as opposed to individual creditor goals of bankruptcy law. If a petitioning creditor is found to be ineligible, other creditors may join the petition and cure the defective filing.

Section 303 also limits the category of eligible creditors to those who hold claims that are not contingent as to liability or the subject of a bona fide dispute. Additionally, the claims must aggregate at least $13,475 more than the value of any liens on property securing those claims. Again, involuntary bankruptcy generally is intended to protect the collective interests of unsecured creditors rather than the interests of secured creditors. Nevertheless, a secured creditor is an eligible creditor as long as the aggregate unsecured claim of the petitioning creditors exceeds $13,475. Paradise Hotel Corp. v. Bank of Nova Scotia, 842 F.2d 47 (3d Cir. 1988).

Section 303(b) excludes holders of "contingent claims" from the list of creditors eligible to commence an involuntary case, but the Bankruptcy Code contains no definition of contingent claims. Section 101(5) contains a lengthy list of modifiers to the definition of a "claim," including contingent status. That is, a right to payment is still a claim even though it is contingent. Generally, a claim is contingent if some additional act or occurrence must take place prior to the debtor becoming liable. For example, a parent corporation may guarantee the debt of a subsidiary to a creditor. Under the terms of most guarantee agreements, the creditor's claim against the parent corporation is contingent on the default by the subsidiary on its obligation to the creditor. Thus, the creditor is not eligible to commence an involuntary bankruptcy case against the parent corporation in the absence of the subsidiary's default on the underlying obligation. In re All Media Properties, Inc., 5 B.R. 126 (Bankr. S.D. Tex. 1980), *aff'd*, 646 F.2d 193 (5th Cir. 1981).

PROBLEM 2-9

Acme Construction, Inc., Consolidated Electric Corp., and Nightflyer Finance Co. filed an involuntary bankruptcy petition against Diamondback Steel, Inc., which has more than one hundred creditors. Nightflyer's claim was based on a fully secured promissory note with a balance due of $150,000, and Consolidated Electric was owed $46,000 for electricity it supplied to Diamondback. Acme's claim was based on an alleged breach of an implied warranty of fitness for a particular purpose. Acme purchased steel reinforcing bars for use in the construction of a building; during the construction a wall collapsed, delaying completion of the building and greatly increasing Acme's costs. Acme filed a complaint against Diamondback, the seller, denying that any implied warranty was given, and asserting that even if such a warranty existed, the goods conformed to the warranty. Diamondback also has now moved to dismiss the involuntary petition. Is Nightflyer an eligible petitioning creditor? Is Acme an eligible petitioning creditor? What additional information, if any, would you like to have to resolve these matters? Is there any other action that the petitioning creditors might take in response to Diamondback's motion to dismiss? *See* Bankruptcy Rule 1003(b).

PROBLEM 2-10

Rick Rowe responded to the slick advertising of Home Repair and Remodeling, Inc. [HRR], and met with a kitchen designer to discuss a remodeling project. Rick and the designer agreed to a design and signed a contract for the job. The price was $20,000; Rick paid $2,000 to HRR when the contract was signed. HRR failed to show up when work was to begin, and Rick eventually sued and got a judgment for $2,000 in compensatory damages and $20,000 in punitive damages. The trial court had found that HRR never intended to complete the job. Rick has filed an involuntary bankruptcy petition against HRR. HRR has moved to dismiss the petition on the grounds that it has 12 or more creditors. Included among the 14 creditors HRR has identified are Central Hardware, Inc., Contractors' Lumber Co., Hamilton Hardware Co., and Countywide Hardware and Lumber Co. Each of these creditors is owed less than $200 and each of their claims has been incurred within the last three weeks. HRR has an account with each of those suppliers, and payment is not due on any of those claims for another two weeks or so. HRR has moved to dismiss the petition. What response should Rick and his attorney offer? Suppose HRR proves that the nonpayment of some of the claims was the result of internal accounting procedures that have since been rectified? *See* In re Ramm Indus., Inc., 83 B.R. 815 (Bankr. M.D. Fla. 1988).

B.   Grounds for Involuntary Bankruptcy Relief

A key concept in bankruptcy law is the "order for relief," since many of the Code's provisions date their requirements in reference to it. In a voluntary case, the "order for relief" occurs at the moment of the filing of the petition; *see* §301. In an involuntary case, on the other hand, the debtor does not desire any relief, and the filing of an involuntary bankruptcy petition does not automatically constitute an order for relief. Section 303(h) sets out three ways in which an order may be entered. First, if the alleged debtor does not timely controvert the petition, an order for relief shall be entered. The alleged debtor has 20 days to respond to the petition. Bankruptcy Rule 1011(b). If the alleged debtor files a timely response to the involuntary petition, relief may be ordered against it only if it either is not paying its debts as they come due, or if a receiver has been appointed in the previous 120 days to take control of substantially all of the debtor's assets. Bankruptcy Code §303(h). These two grounds for the entry of an order for relief are very different. The assertion that a debtor is generally not paying its debts as they come due leaves a great deal of room for dispute. Whether a custodian has been appointed to take charge of substantially all the debtor's property within the 120 days prior to the commencement of the case, however, is intended to be a relatively straightforward determination.

Section 303(h)(1) authorizes the entry of an order for relief if "the debtor is *generally* not paying such debtor's debts as such debts become due *unless such debts are the subject of a bona fide dispute.*" The two highlighted portions of the statute create an opportunity for interpretive dispute. Claims that are the subject of a bona fide dispute are excluded from eligibility to commence an involuntary case; so, too, is the debtor's nonpayment of those claims excluded from a court's determination as to whether the debtor is paying the debtor's debts as they come due under §303(h)(1). Simply asserting a dispute, however, will not justify a debtor's failure to make payments on those claims. Instead, the claim is excluded only if there exists a substantial factual or legal dispute over the claim. In re Busick, 831 F.2d 1745 (7th Cir. 1987); Subway Equipment Leasing Corp. v. Sims (In re Sims), 994 F.2d 210 (5th Cir. 1993); *see also* B.D.W. Assoc, Inc. v. Busy Beaver Building Centers, Inc., 865 F.2d 65 (3d Cir. 1989).

In re Lough

United States Bankruptcy Court, Eastern District of Michigan, 1986
57 B.R. 993

STEVEN W. RHODES, Bankruptcy Judge.

The Peoples Bank & Trust of Alpena filed this involuntary petition against Bette Mae Lough pursuant to 11 U.S.C. §303 arising from two debts which the bank claims that Mrs. Lough owes to it. For the reasons stated in this memorandum opinion, the Court concludes that there is a bona fide dispute concerning the bank's claim, and that therefore the involuntary petition must be dismissed.

I.

The first debt upon which the bank claims liability arose from a joint note which Mrs. Lough signed with her husband on April 30, 1973; this note has a balance of approximately $75,000. The second debt allegedly arose from a guaranty which Mrs. Lough signed on November 30, 1967, relating to her husband's various sole obligations with the bank; these obligations were consolidated into one note executed by Mr. Lough on February 19, 1981, in the approximate amount of $135,000. Thus, the bank claims a total indebtedness by Mrs. Lough in the approximate amount of $210,000. In its petition, the bank alleged that there are fewer than twelve creditors and that Mrs. Lough was not generally paying her debts, especially the debt to the bank, as they became due.

In her amended answer, Mrs. Lough admitted signing the April 30, 1973, joint note but nevertheless denied any liability on that note. She claims that this note was secured by a mortgage on property held by her and her husband as tenants by the entirety; that this property was deeded to the bank in lieu of foreclosure; and that if the proceeds from the bank's sale of this property had been applied to this note, rather than to a note on which Mr. Lough was obligated on solely, as required, then the proceeds would have been sufficient to extinguish the joint note.

In her amended answer, Mrs. Lough further alleged that although she signed the November 30, 1967, guaranty, she has no further liability on it in regard to her husband's note of February 19, 1981. She claims she has no liability on it because in 1967 she did not intend to guaranty what arose some fourteen or fifteen years later as a $135,000 note. She also contends that there was no consideration for this guaranty and no reliance upon it by the bank.

Mrs. Lough contends that because there is a bona fide dispute about the bank's claim against her, the bank does not qualify under 11 U.S.C. §303 as a proper entity to file an involuntary petition in bankruptcy against her.

To this contention, the bank responds that there are no genuine issues of fact and that on the facts it is or would be entitled to a summary judgment against Mrs. Lough. Therefore, the bank argues, because there is no bona fide dispute, the bank is qualified to file this involuntary petition against Mrs. Lough.

II.

A.

11 U.S.C. §303(b) provides that an involuntary case against a person is commenced by the filing with the bankruptcy court of a petition, pursuant to either subparagraph (1), "by three or more entities, each of which is . . . a holder of a claim against such person that is not contingent as to liability or the subject [of] a bona fide dispute," or

subparagraph (2) if there are fewer than 12 such holders, excluding employees and insiders, "by one or more of such holders." The phrase "such holders" in subparagraph (2) refers to holders of claims which are "not contingent as to liability or the subject [of] a bona fide dispute." The Court notes that the phrase "bona fide dispute" also arises in subsection (h) of Section 303, which provides:

> If the petition is not timely controverted, the court shall order relief against the debtor in an involuntary case under the chapter under which the petition was filed. Otherwise, after trial the court shall order relief against the debtor in an involuntary case under the chapter under which the petition was filed only if — (1) the debtor is not generally paying such debtor's debts as such debts become due unless such debts are the subject of a bona fide dispute.

The parties cited three cases interpreting the phrase "bona fide dispute," and these cases are not entirely consistent.

In In re Johnson Hawks, Ltd., 49 B.R. 823 (Bankr. D. Hawaii 1985), the court noted that there had been a statutory change implemented by the Bankruptcy Amendments Act of 1984. After reviewing the pre-1984 law, the court noted that the 1984 amendments to the bankruptcy code made significant revisions regarding disputed claims. 49 B.R. at 830. First, the test for the standing of petitioning creditors was revised to provide that holders of claims which are subject to bona fide disputes are barred from being petitioning creditors. Second, debts which are subject to bona fide disputes were excluded from the test provided in section 303(h), which provides that the court shall order relief if the debtor is not paying debts as such debts become due. The court further stated:

> It is evident that under the 1984 amendments, creditors holding claims which are subject to bona fide disputes cannot be petitioning creditors under the threshold test of Section 303(b)(1). As stated in Colliers, "[t]his does not mean of course that the debtor can assert any defense to a claim and be successful. Presumably, there must be a 'bona fide dispute' which a bankruptcy judge must find either on a motion to dismiss or at trial." 2 Collier's on Bankruptcy ¶303.08(b) (1985). . . .
>
> A bona fide dispute is a conflict in which an assertion of a claim or right made in good faith and without fraud or deceit on one side is met by contrary claims or allegations made in good faith and without fraud or deceit on the other side.

49 B.R. at 830.

Then the court listed the following factors to determine whether the claims or defenses are subject to a bona fide dispute:

1. The nature of the dispute.
2. The nature and the extent of the evidence and allegations presented in support of the creditor's claim and in support of the debtor's contrary claims.
3. Whether the creditor's claim and the debtor's contrary claims are made in good faith and without fraud or deceit.
4. Whether on balance the interests of the creditor outweigh those of the debtor.

In re Henry, 52 B.R. 8 (Bankr. S.D. Ohio 1985), reviewed at length the legislative history relating to the addition of the "bona fide dispute" language to Sections 303(b) and 303(h). The Court stated:

> The reason for the introduction of this additional language in the statute was explained by its proponent as follows:
>
>> The problem can be explained simply. Some courts have interpreted section 303's language on a debtor's general failure to pay debts as allowing the filing of involuntary petitions and the granting of involuntary relief even when the debtor's reason for not paying is a legitimate and good-faith dispute over his or her liability. This interpretation allows creditors to use the Bankruptcy Code as a club against debtors who have bona fide questions about their liability, but who would rather pay up than suffer the stigma of involuntary bankruptcy proceedings.
>>
>> My amendment would correct this problem. Under my amendment, the original filing of an involuntary petition could not be based on debts that are the subject of a good-faith dispute between the debtor and his or her creditors. In the same vein, the granting of an order of relief could not be premised solely on the failure of a debtor to pay debts that were legitimately contested as to liability or amount.
>>
>> I believe this amendment, although a simple one, is necessary to protect the rights of debtors and to prevent misuse of the bankruptcy system as a tool of coercion. I also believe it corrects a judicial misinterpretation of existing law and congressional intent as to the proper basis for granting involuntary relief. 30 Cong. Rec. S7618 (June 19, 1984) (comments of Senator Baucus). 52 B.R. at 9-10.

In In re Stroop, 51 B.R. 210, 212 (Bankr. D. Colo. 1985), the court stated:

> This Court has concluded that an appropriate standard in determining whether a claim is subject to a bona fide dispute for purposes of 11 U.S.C. §303(b)(1) is that applicable on motions for summary judgment. If the defense of the alleged debtor to the claim of the petitioning creditor raises material issues of fact or law so that a summary judgment could not be rendered as a matter of law in favor of the creditor on a trial of the claim, the claim is subject to a bona fide dispute.

B.

This Court concludes that none of these standards for determining whether there is a bona fide dispute concerning a debt is entirely appropriate. The standard set forth in the *Johnston Hawks* case is unsatisfactory for two reasons. First, it improperly gives consideration to the balance of interests as between the creditor and the debtor. These considerations were carried forward from the pre-1984 Amendments Act cases, but there is no basis for this in the statute as amended.

Second, the inquiry into "good faith," "fraud," and "deceit," as mandated in *Johnston Hawks* involves subjective considerations as to the parties' respective intentions. For example, the *Johnston Hawks* test would disqualify a creditor when a debtor has a defense which he or she offers in subjective good faith but which objectively has little or no merit. This Court simply cannot conclude that Congress intended to invoke any such considerations in the language "bona fide dispute." Accordingly, the Court rejects the *Johnston Hawks* test.

Likewise, the Court rejects the test of In re Stroop. Under that test, if the alleged debtor's defense to the claim of the petitioning creditor raises material issues of fact so that a summary judgment could not be entered as a matter of law in favor of the creditor, the claim is subject to a bona fide dispute. The difficulty is that the test does not fully address a case where there is a substantial dispute as to the proper application of law but no substantial issue of fact. It might be argued that *Stroop* would then require the Court to resolve the question of law as if on a motion for summary judgment and simply determine whether the alleged debtor is liable to the creditor.

Yet, this Court concludes that, given the previously quoted legislative history, In re Henry, *supra*, if there is a bona fide dispute as to either the law or the facts, then the creditor does not qualify and the petition must be dismissed. The legislative history makes it clear that Congress intended to disqualify a creditor whenever there is any legitimate basis for the debtor not paying the debt, whether that basis is factual or legal. Congress plainly did not intend to require a debtor to pay a legitimately disputed debt simply to avoid the stigma of bankruptcy. Accordingly, if there is either a genuine issue of material fact that bears upon the debtor's liability, or a meritorious contention as to the application of law to undisputed facts, then the petition must be dismissed.

In this regard, the Court must emphasize that in deciding whether there is a bona fide dispute, it must not resolve any genuine issues of fact or law. If the Court concludes that there is a bona fide dispute on any issue of fact or law, this must not be interpreted as any indication of how the Court would resolve that issue of fact or law.

III.

A.

With regard to the joint 1973 note on which the bank claims liability against Mrs. Lough, the Court finds that the debtor's defenses do create a bona fide dispute and that therefore she should not be required as a result of that dispute to pay that debt in order to avoid bankruptcy. As noted, Mrs. Lough claims that the issue involves the application of the proceeds from the sale of jointly held property, which the bank undertook following a deed in lieu of foreclosure. It is reasonably clear that if these proceeds had been applied to the 1973 note rather than the subsequent 1981 note, then there would be no liability on the 1973 note.

The bank contends that in the absence of instructions from Mrs. Lough and her husband, the bank could apply the proceeds as it saw fit and therefore it was proper for it to apply these proceeds to the later sole note of Mr. Lough. Although the bank has cited numerous cases which hold to that effect, the Court concludes that there is substantial merit (without resolving the issue) in Mrs. Lough's argument that the proceeds should have been applied to the joint 1973 note. There is substantial merit in this position because the proceeds which came into the bank's possession were the result of the sale of a joint asset and thus Mrs. Lough could reasonably argue that therefore it should have been applied to the joint note rather than to her husband's sole note. In support, Mrs. Lough could reasonably argue that otherwise, there would have been no consideration to her for the deed in lieu of foreclosure which she executed in the bank's favor.

Moreover, there is a genuine issue of material fact as to whether the bank was given instructions as to how to apply the proceeds of that sale. The parties stipulated that if the Loughs' former attorney were called to testify, he would testify that in the time period prior to the deed in lieu of foreclosure, it was the Loughs' position that the proceeds from the sale should be applied to the joint 1973 note. This plainly raises an issue of fact about whether the bank was aware of the Loughs' intent as to the proceeds of this sale.

Finally, the Court finds that there is substantial merit in the Loughs' alternative position that as a matter of law the proceeds should have been applied on a pro rata basis between the two distinct obligations, the result of which would likewise extinguish Mrs. Lough's liability on the 1973 note.

The Court finds, therefore, that there are genuine issues of fact and substantial, non-frivolous arguments as to the applicable law. Therefore, the Court finds that there is a bona fide dispute as to Mrs. Lough's liability on the 1973 note.

B.

Likewise, the Court finds that there is a bona fide dispute as to her obligation on the guaranty. The bank has taken the position, and has cited case law, to the effect that this guaranty was an open-ended and continuing guaranty which, until revoked by Mrs. Lough, would apply to all obligations incurred by Mr. Lough after 1967. In response, however, Mrs. Lough has alleged that she simply never intended in 1967 when she signed this guaranty to guaranty her husband's debts for as long a period of time as fifteen years and to the extent of $135,000. The Court finds that there may be substantial merit to this position. It must be noted that on the day the guaranty was executed, Mr. Lough's only obligation was a rollover of an existing obligation in the amount of $20,000. In addition, credence is given to this argument by the fact that subsequently when the parties so intended, they entered into joint notes as to which then there would be no dispute about Mrs. Lough's obligation.

Perhaps most importantly, a legal issue arises as to whether there was consideration for the guaranty to the extent that the bank seeks to assert it now. In a guaranty circumstance, there is hardly ever, if ever, consideration which flows directly to the guarantor. In the circumstances of a guaranty, consideration most often consists of the reliance that the obligee, in this case the bank, places upon the guaranty. There is a substantial issue here about whether the bank relied upon this guaranty throughout this fourteen or fifteen year time period during which Mr. Lough continued to increase his borrowing for his business.

In this regard, the Court notes the testimony that the guaranty was buried in the files of the bank and apparently was located only in connection with preparation for this litigation. Thus, there is a substantial dispute about whether in February of 1981, when the note on which liability is now asserted was signed, the bank officers involved even knew about the guaranty. Finally, on Plaintiff's Exhibit 1, an account ledger card from this time period, the indication that there was a loan guaranty agreement signed by Mrs. Lough was crossed out; the question arises as to what inferences are to be drawn from that.

Therefore, the Court must conclude that there is a bona fide dispute as to whether Mrs. Lough is obligated on this guaranty.

IV.

Because there is a bona fide dispute concerning both of the bank's claims against Mrs. Lough, the bank is ineligible to file an involuntary petition against her. 11 U.S.C. §303(b).

Accordingly, the petition must be dismissed.

PROBLEM 2-11

Derek delivered pizzas to make a little extra money while he was in college. His parents owned the pizza parlor. One day on his way to a customer's home dealing with the surprise appearance of a bee in his car caused the vehicle to swerve onto the sidewalk and seriously injure Marie, a pedestrian who failed to jump in the right direction. Marie subsequently obtained a judgment against Derek for $1,000,000, but the insurance policy that covered the delivery drivers was limited to $100,000. Derek has no insurance, and he has no other assets to speak of. An insurance agency was supposed to obtain an "umbrella" policy for the pizza parlor that would have provided $1,000,000 in coverage, but it failed to do so. Other than the claim held by Marie, Derek owes only about $800 to a total of three other creditors, and he is current in his payments to them. Marie wants to initiate an involuntary bankruptcy proceeding against Derek in order to get a trustee appointed who will sue the insurance agency for failing to obtain the umbrella policy. Is Derek failing to pay his debts as they come due? Should the bankruptcy court abstain from the involuntary proceeding? *See* Paroline v. Doling, 116 B.R. 583 (Bankr. S.D. Ohio 1990).

PROBLEM 2-12

National Techtronics Corp. (NTC) intended to manufacture and market a telecommunications switching device. The device had generated some excitement when it was first announced because it promised to reduce telecommunications costs significantly. Unfortunately, the only switch that ever worked was the prototype. After a number of manufacturing setbacks, NTC's president and chief operating officer decided to close the business. The company had accumulated large debts, but it had raised significant capital from a wide range of investors. In the process of boosting shareholder morale, NTC had issued dividends to the shareholders about six months ago. The dividends were issued prior to deliveries of completed switches to customers, but a number of orders had been placed. Unfortunately, the manufacturing difficulties had prevented the company from paying any further dividends or even from paying all of its debts. Instead, the president of the company liquidated the business and distributed the funds generated through the sale of the company's assets to its creditors. At the conclusion of this distribution, creditors still were owed nearly $1 million. NTC was dissolved as a corporation according to the applicable state law. Nevertheless, three of its suppliers initiated an involuntary bankruptcy proceeding against the company. In its response, NTC asserted that since it has no assets and has paid all of its funds over to creditors, it is not generally failing to pay its debts as they come due. NTC also argued that the bankruptcy court should abstain from the case because all of the liquidation and distributional goals of bankruptcy had been met. The petitioning creditors argue, however, that the payment of dividends within the last six months might constitute either a fraudulent conveyance or other form of preferential transfer that could be recovered in a bankruptcy case (matters we will explore in a later chapter). Should the court grant the creditors' petition for involuntary bankruptcy relief against NTC? *See* In re Ethanol Pacific, Inc., 166 B.R. 928 (Bankr. D. Idaho 1994). *See also* In re Palace Oriental Rugs, Inc., 193 B.R. 126, 129 (Bankr. D. Conn. 1996) ("The Court must first undertake a rough calculus of the number and amount of the Alleged Debtor's delinquent and current debts on the Petition Date. The Court then utilizes the results of that calculus to determine if the ratio of delinquent to current debts is supportive of a pattern of 'generally not paying.' ").

Since bankruptcy is a collective form of relief, should involuntary petitions filed by a debtor's sole creditor be allowed? In In re Concrete Pumping Service Inc., 943 F.2d 627 (6th Cir. 1991), the alleged debtor had transferred its assets to an insider creditor, who then paid all of the debtor's obligations except the obligation to a single creditor. That creditor then sought to have an order for relief entered against the debtor so that the payments to the other creditors could be recovered as preferences and the property of the estate distributed according to the Bankruptcy Code. The court found that these purposes were sufficient to permit the entry for an order for relief even in the case where the debtor has only one creditor. The availability of preference recoveries and other avoiding powers of trustees in bankruptcy cases (explored in a later chapter) is often a reason for the commencement of involuntary bankruptcy proceedings. Individual creditors generally have little incentive to commence involuntary bankruptcy cases because they will have to share in any distribution of the bankruptcy estate's property with all other creditors. Outside of bankruptcy, the creditor could recover its entire claim even if that results in assets being unavailable to other creditors. Nevertheless, creditors sometimes seek involuntary bankruptcy relief against debtors in order to obtain greater control over the debtor's assets and financial affairs.

Even when a bankruptcy proceeding is properly commenced, either voluntarily or involuntarily, the court may still abstain from hearing a case. Under §305 of the Bankruptcy Code, the court may dismiss a case or suspend all proceedings in the case if the interests of creditors and the debtor would be better served by the dismissal or suspension of the proceedings. The legislative history supporting the Bankruptcy

Reform Act of 1978 suggested, for example, that dismissal or suspension of proceedings might be appropriate in the case where the debtor and creditors are working out a repayment proposal that does not prejudice the rights of creditors. If several recalcitrant creditors seek to undo the workout by commencing an involuntary case, the court might dismiss the case or suspend proceedings in the case under §305 to permit the nonbankruptcy workout to be completed. In re RAI Marketing Services, Inc., 20 B.R. 943 (Bankr. D. Kan. 1982).

The final limitation on creditor eligibility to initiate involuntary bankruptcy cases is that the claim held by that creditor must not be "the subject of a bona fide dispute." Again, consistent with the collective nature of bankruptcy proceedings, §303(b) excludes from eligibility those creditors whose claims are questionable. Permitting creditors whose claims are the subject of a bona fide dispute to obtain involuntary bankruptcy relief against the debtor arguably would grant those creditors too much leverage in their dealings with the debtor. Furthermore, resolving the underlying dispute between debtor and creditor might be a lengthy process. The Bankruptcy Code and Rules anticipate an expeditious resolution of these matters in involuntary cases. Even worse, keeping an alleged debtor in bankruptcy court for an extended period of time could damage the debtor's business to such a degree that the filing of the involuntary petition would become a self-fulfilling prophecy. More about that later.

PROBLEM 2-13

Harriet and Albert had guaranteed a variety of loans made to corporations they owned. Three of the bank lenders decided to initiate an involuntary bankruptcy proceeding against Harriet and Albert, who have defended by asserting that the banks had agreed orally to extend the repayment terms on the underlying obligations. The representative of each of the lenders has categorically denied that any such agreement was made. Albert and Harriet also aren't able to point to any documentary evidence to support their claim. Nonetheless, they assert that the claims are the subject of a bona fide dispute and that the creditors are ineligible to petition for involuntary bankruptcy relief. Assuming that the other requirements for the entry for an order for relief are present, are these creditors eligible to initiate the case? See In re Rimmell, 111 B.R. 250 (Bankr. E.D. Mo. 1990), aff'd, 946 F.2d 1363 (8th Cir. 1991), cert. denied, 112 S. Ct. 2275 (1992).

C.   Impact of Involuntary Petitions on the Debtor's Business

The filing of an involuntary petition against an alleged debtor can have devastating consequences for the debtor's business. Third parties will naturally become reluctant to continue their relationship with the debtor if it appears the debtor will be unable to perform its part of the bargain in the future. This is true even though the filing of an involuntary petition does not mean that an order for relief will be entered in the case. Consequently, §303 includes several safeguards to protect the debtor during the time between the filing of the involuntary petition and the court's resolution of the issue.

Section 303(f) provides that "any business of the debtor may continue to operate, and the debtor may continue to use, acquire, or dispose of property as if an involuntary case concerning the debtor had not been commenced" notwithstanding the filing of an involuntary petition. Moreover, §549(c) of the Bankruptcy Code protects those postpetition transfers against avoidance by the bankruptcy trustee. The claims created during the gap between the filing of the involuntary petition and the order for relief also occupy a special priority for repayment under §507(a)(2) of the Bankruptcy Code.

Of course, creditors who have gone so far as to initiate an involuntary bankruptcy proceeding against the debtor often are skeptical of the debtor's ability to operate a business. They may even be concerned about the debtor's integrity. In appropriate circumstances, the court can limit the debtor's ability to use, acquire, or dispose of the property. Furthermore, §303(g) authorizes the appointment of an interim trustee to take possession of the property of the estate and to operate the debtor's business. If the court authorizes the appointment of an interim trustee, the debtor still may reacquire the property, but to do so the debtor must post an appropriate bond. Thus, the Bankruptcy Code provides a mechanism for the continuation of an alleged debtor's business while concurrently protecting the interests of the creditors in the event that the debtor's business during the time between the filing of an involuntary petition and the entry for an order for relief suffers losses. The requirement of the bond is addressed squarely to the discretion of the court. *See, e.g.*, In re DiLorenzo, 161 B.R. 752 (Bankr. S.D.N.Y. 1993); In re Rush, 7 B.R. 579 (Bankr. N.D. Ala. 1980).

If the debtor is an individual and the bankruptcy court dismisses the involuntary petition, the court may enter an order prohibiting consumer credit reporting agencies from referring to this bankruptcy proceeding in subsequent consumer reports; §303(l)(2). And if the petition is deemed to contain false statements, the court may also seal the records of the proceeding so that these statements are not spread around to cause further mischief; §303(l)(1).

D.   Penalizing Petitioning Creditors

Not all petitions seeking involuntary bankruptcy relief will be granted. Nonetheless, the filing of the petition itself likely will have a significant effect on the debtor's business and financial affairs. Recognizing the power creditors can wield through the initiation of involuntary bankruptcy petitions, Congress enacted §303(i) to temper creditors' actions. That section provides generally that judgment may be entered against petitioning creditors for costs and attorneys' fees in the event the case is dismissed other than with the consent of the debtor. Moreover, if the court finds that the petitioner or petitioners acted in bad faith in filing the petition, they may also be liable for "(A) any damages proximately caused by such filings; or (B) punitive damages." Although the section separates the categories of potential recoveries with "or," the use of that term is not exclusive. Courts, in appropriate circumstances, can award both compensatory and punitive damages as well as costs and attorney's fees. In re Val W. Poterek & Sons, Inc., 169 B.R. 896 (Bankr. N.D. Ill. 1994); In re Wavelength, Inc., 61 B.R. 614 (Bankr. 9th Cir. 1986).

The award of damages under this section is directed to the discretion of the court. In re Nordbrock, 772 F.2d 397 (8th Cir. 1985); In re Fox, 171 B.R. 31 (Bankr. E.D. Va. 1994). In arriving at its conclusion whether to award judgment against the petitioning creditors, the court will evaluate the creditors' actions carefully. Nevertheless, petitioning creditors cannot avoid liability under this section simply by asserting that they honestly believed their actions were legal and proper. For example, in In re Atlas Machine and Ironworks, Inc., 190 B.R. 796 (Bankr. E.D. Va. 1995), the court rejected a creditor's assertion that a debtor had only six claims against it. The debtor had provided the creditor with a listing of its debts showing that it had more than 60 creditors. Nonetheless, the creditor argued that because only six or so of those obligations were past due, the debtor had fewer than 12 creditors. The creditor took this position on the advice of its counsel, who "admitted having done no research with regard to such distinction" between past due debts and other claims. The court held that this was sufficient grounds for finding that the creditor had acted in bad faith. The court ordered sanctions under Bankruptcy Rule 9011 against the petitioning creditor and its attorney, and also imposed punitive damages of $25,000 against the petitioning creditor under §303(i)(2)(B).

Only a very small number of bankruptcy cases are commenced by involuntary petitions. Certainly, the potential costs presented by §303(i) limit creditors' interest in seeking this form of relief. Furthermore, creditors often are more inclined simply to attempt collection of their claims in the state law system. After all, in that arena they do not have to share what they recover with other creditors. As with many "legal rights," the ability to threaten the filing of an involuntary bankruptcy petition is often more important than the actual ability to commence the case. In fact, debtors and creditors sometimes find themselves facing each other at the negotiating table, each side asserting that it will commence a bankruptcy case. All things considered, it appears that the small number of involuntary bankruptcy filings is not surprising, but may be somewhat misleading. A substantial percentage of the "voluntary filings" are in reality simply responses by debtors to creditors' collection efforts. Consequently, the balance established in §303 of the Bankruptcy Code seems appropriate. *See generally* Susan Block-Lieb, Why Creditors File So Few Involuntary Petitions and Why the Number Is Not Too Small, 57 Brook. L. Rev. 803 (1991).

III. Debtors Eligibility for Relief

Recall that although bankruptcy relief comes in two generic forms, liquidation and reorganization, it also comes in a variety of Chapters. Debtors may proceed under Chapters 7, 9, 11, 12, or 13. However, they may only proceed under those Chapters if they meet the statutorily defined eligibility requirements for the various Chapters. One might expect that the rules for eligibility would be found in the respective Chapters. Not so. Instead, §109 of the Bankruptcy Code lists the requirements for eligibility for debtors under each of these operative Chapters. Section 109 is not overly lengthy, and you should read it carefully now.

A. Municipalities and Chapter 9

Proceeding from the specific to the general, Chapter 9 relief is available only to insolvent municipalities that intend to adjust their debts under a plan. Furthermore, the municipality must be specifically authorized under the applicable state law to initiate the case. Until the recent past, very few Chapter 9 cases were filed. Additionally, those that were filed tended to be smaller governmental entities such as water districts. The relatively low profile of Chapter 9 changed in the 1980s, however, when Orange County, California, filed a petition to adjust its multibillion dollar debt, although Chapter 9 proceedings are still relatively quite rare.

B. Family Farmers and Fishermen and Chapter 12

Section 109(f) provides that "only a family farmer with regular annual income" may be a debtor under Chapter 12. This brief definition provides only the starting point for determining eligibility for Chapter 12 relief. It directs attention to "family" farmers and requires a consideration of "regular annual income" rather than some other measure of financial wherewithal. More importantly, §101(18)-(21) includes a variety of definitions that put the meat on the bones of §109(f)'s description of eligible Chapter 12 debtors. The 2005 amendments to the Bankruptcy Code added "family fishermen" to Chapter 12's rules.

Section 101(18) defines a family farmer according to aggregate indebtedness, which is not to exceed $3,237,000, and at least 50 percent of which (other than home mortgage debt) arises out of the farming operation.[5] Furthermore, more than 50 percent of the debtor's gross income for *any one* of the past three taxable years must arise

---

5. The numbers are slightly different for family fishermen; *see* §101(19A).

out of the farming operation. Recognizing that many "family farms" are owned in corporate or partnership form, the definition of "family farmer" includes those forms of ownership. In any event, an entity is eligible for Chapter 12 leave only if its income is sufficiently stable and regular to enable it to fund a plan. Section 101(19).

C.   Individuals and Chapter 13

Determining whether debtors are eligible for Chapter 13 relief requires analysis of §§109(e) and 101(30). Section 109(e) provides that Chapter 13 debtors must owe less than $307,675 of noncontingent, liquidated, unsecured debts and less than $922,975 of noncontingent, liquidated, secured debts. If spouses intend to commence a joint Chapter 13 case, their aggregate debts must fit under those same limitations. Bankruptcy Code §109(e). These debt limitations are subject to adjustment at three-year intervals. Bankruptcy Code §104(b). Under §109(e) a person whose debts fit under the limits may be a Chapter 13 debtor only if he or she is "an individual with regular income." That term is defined in §101(30) as "an individual whose income is sufficiently stable and regular to enable such individual to make payments under a plan under Chapter 13." Even if they otherwise comply with the eligibility requirements, neither stockbrokers nor commodity brokers can be Chapter 13 debtors. We will address Chapter 13 eligibility in greater detail later in this text.

D.   Most Everyone Else and Chapters 7 and 11

Finally, debtors may seek relief under either Chapter 7 or Chapter 11, where eligibility for relief is the least restricted. Chapter 7, which controls the liquidation of assets, is available to any person other than railroads, domestic insurance companies and banks, and foreign insurance companies and banks. Bankruptcy Code §109(b). Insolvencies involving insurance companies and banks are otherwise regulated by state or federal laws. Therefore, liquidation or reorganization of those entities under the Bankruptcy Code is unnecessary. Railroads are not left out because they are eligible to be debtors in a reorganization under Chapter 11. Any person that may be a Chapter 7 debtor may be a Chapter 11 debtor, with the exception of stockbrokers and commodities brokers, who are limited to relief under Chapter 7.

Some other categories of debtors are given special treatment in the Bankruptcy Code.

"Small business debtors" are persons engaged in commercial activities whose total noncontingent and liquidated debts do not exceed $2,000,000. The 2005 amendments to the Code introduce the term "small business case" (one involving a "small business debtor"). Bankruptcy Code §101(51C). Small business debtors have several options applicable only to them in Chapter 11 cases. We will look at those issues as we consider Chapter 11 in more detail later.

Another special category is the "single asset real estate" debtor. Under §101(51B), "single asset real estate" is a single property or project that generates substantially all of the debtor's income; residential properties with fewer than four units are excluded from the definition (as are family farmers). For this type of debtor, Chapter 11 cases include an expedited process for relief from the automatic stay in favor of lenders secured by "single asset real estate." Bankruptcy Code §362(d)(3). Again, we will address this matter in due course.

The 2005 amendments have added a newly defined type of debtor: health care businesses. Bankruptcy Code §101(27A). These debtors have special obligations to maintain the confidentiality of patient records and appropriate levels of care for the patients. These issues are addressed in §333 of the Code.

Eligibility for relief under Chapter 7 and Chapter 11 can be described algebraically as follows:

Chapter 7 = (All persons) – (*individuals who cannot pass the means test* + railroads + domestic insurance companies & banks + foreign insurance companies & banks)

Chapter 11 = All Chapter 7 debtors + railroads − (stockbrokers & commodity brokers)

Conspicuously absent from the eligibility requirements for bankruptcy relief is any need to make a showing of insolvency, and nothing prevents a solvent entity from filing a petition. *See, e.g.*, In re Keniston, 85 B.R. 202 (Bankr. D.N.H. 1988). Why would a solvent debtor resort to bankruptcy? Consider a company that has marketed a product that has injured people all over the United States, resulting in many lawsuits in the works. Bankruptcy might be the appropriate forum for resolving the corporate liability, and even if the company is solvent at the moment it files, that condition is not likely to last long. The absence of any requirement of insolvency for eligibility for relief under Chapter 7 or Chapter 11 is made more stark by comparing the requirements for eligibility for Chapter 9 relief. Under §109(c)(3), a municipality must be insolvent to obtain Chapter 9 relief. Clearly, Congress knew how to include a requirement of insolvency for a form of bankruptcy relief when it deemed it appropriate to do so.

PROBLEM 2-14

Use §§101 and 109 to determine whether the following are eligible for Chapter 7 and Chapter 11 relief. Consider also whether creditors can initiate an involuntary case against these debtors.

(1) Southwestern Health Corp., a health maintenance organization. *Compare* In re Family Health Services, Inc., 104 B.R. 279 (Bankr. C.D. Cal. 1989), *with* In re Beacon Health, Inc., 105 B.R. 178 (Bankr. D.N.H. 1989).

(2) Randy Consumer, a person whose name also describes his status. See Toibb v. Radloff, 501 U.S. 157 (1991).

(3) Moe, Larry, & Curly Co., a partnership.

(4) Trump Cards, the greeting card business of Ronald Trump.

(5) Multi Bank Holding Corp., the holding company of eight banks.

(6) Nicewill Rehabilitation Services, Inc., a charitable corporation that hires disabled persons to repair and renew items donated by the general public to NRS that are then resold, with the proceeds used to pay the employees and support other training programs for the disabled.

IV.   Limitations on Repeat Bankruptcy Filings

PROBLEM 2-15

Law student Joe Wheels was always behind in paying his debts, but taking the course in bankruptcy made him feel easier about his situation. He has confided his plan in you, a fellow student: If a creditor repossesses his car or other collateral, he'll simply file a bankruptcy petition, thereby invoking the automatic stay of creditor actions and getting the property back, at which point he'll dismiss the petition and pay off the creditor with money earned during the delay. If another creditor tries the same thing, he'll simply file another petition. You have been paying a bit more attention to your studies than Joe. Will this work? See Bankruptcy Code §109(g).

Section 109(g) renders debtors ineligible for bankruptcy relief for 180 days if the debtor's prior case was dismissed by the court for the willful failure of the debtor to follow court orders or properly prosecute the case, or if the debtor requested and obtained dismissal of the prior proceeding after a creditor had moved for relief from the automatic stay in the initial case. These two grounds for limiting access to bankruptcy relief address very different problems. Section 109(g)(1) is essentially punitive and provides basically that debtors who fail to play by the rules must take at least a 180-day breathing spell before they can obtain any form of bankruptcy relief again. Section 109(g)(2), on the other hand, is intended to prevent debtors from thwarting creditors' legitimate efforts to recover property subject to their claims. Consider these purposes as you read the following cases.

Montgomery v. Ryan (In re Montgomery)
United States Court of Appeals, Eighth Circuit, 1994
37 F.3d 413

BEAM, Circuit Judge.

George C. Montgomery appeals from an order of the district court affirming the section 109(g) dismissal of his second bankruptcy petition. We affirm.

I. Background

On March 24, 1992, Montgomery filed for bankruptcy protection under Chapter 13 of the Bankruptcy Code. The case was dismissed on June 8, 1992, because Montgomery did not attend a section 341 creditors meeting. On August 11, 1992, Montgomery filed a second Chapter 13 petition. Norah Ryan, a creditor, moved to dismiss the second petition, arguing that Montgomery was not eligible for bankruptcy relief because he was not a "debtor" within the meaning of 11 U.S.C. §109. After a hearing, the bankruptcy court granted Ryan's motion to dismiss and the district court affirmed.

II. Discussion

Under 11 U.S.C. §109(g)(1), no individual may be a "debtor" if he or she has been a debtor in the preceding 180 days and the previous case was dismissed for "willful failure . . . to abide by orders of the court. . . ." Failure to attend a creditors meeting is a failure to obey a court order within the meaning of section 109(g)(1). See, e.g., In re Pappalardo, 109 B.R. 622, 625 (Bankr. S.D.N.Y. 1990). Montgomery argues that dismissal of his second petition was not proper because the bankruptcy court, in its order dismissing the first petition, did not specifically find a "willful failure."[6] He also argues that the party moving for dismissal bears the burden of establishing such a "willful failure" and that Ryan has not done so. Like the district court, we review the bankruptcy court's legal conclusions de novo and its factual findings under the clearly erroneous standard. In re Commonwealth Cos., Inc., 913 F.2d 518, 521 (8th Cir. 1990).

Montgomery's first argument is without merit. No specific finding of willfulness was necessary in the order dismissing the first petition. Section 109(g) was not at issue until Ryan moved to dismiss the second petition. A finding of willfulness must be made when a sanction is imposed, but need not be made earlier. Here, a finding of willfulness was necessary only when the bankruptcy court dismissed the second petition.[7] Montgomery's arguments to the contrary amount to "no more than technical and/or semantic game playing." In re Ward, 78 B.R. 914, 916 (Bankr. E.D. Ark. 1987).

The remaining issue involves allocation of the burden of proving (or disproving) willfulness under section 109(g)(1). There is no evidence in the record (other than a copy of the first dismissal order of the bankruptcy court) regarding the circumstances of Montgomery's failure to attend the creditors meeting. Thus, the allocation issue is

---

6. The order of dismissal provided as follows:

Debtor(s) having failed to show cause, after notice, IT IS ORDERED AND YOU ARE HEREBY NOTIFIED THAT this Chapter 13 case is DISMISSED for Debtor(s) failure to appear for examination at the 11 U.S.C. §341 Creditors Meeting.. . .

7. This finding was made when the bankruptcy court found that "the facts herein warrant imposition of sanctions pursuant to 11 U.S.C. §109(g)." Though the term "willful" was not used, we agree with the district court that this language is properly read to constitute a finding of willfulness.

dispositive. If the burden is Montgomery's, his appeal fails. If the burden falls to Ryan, we must reverse.

The district court found that Montgomery bears the burden of showing that his failure to attend the creditors meeting was not willful.[8] We agree. The burden of establishing eligibility in bankruptcy lies with the party filing the bankruptcy petition. In In re Tim Wargo & Sons, Inc., 869 F.2d 1128, 1130 (8th Cir. 1989), we required the filing debtor to prove its eligibility for relief under Chapter 12. In Jenkins v. Petitioning Creditor — Ray E. Friedman & Co., 664 F.2d 184, 186 (8th Cir. 1981), a pre-Code case, we placed the burden of establishing eligibility on the creditor who filed the involuntary petition. Though this court has not previously addressed an eligibility issue specifically involving section 109(g), we believe our previous holdings are applicable here.

As Montgomery asserts, some lower courts have placed the burden on the creditor to show willfulness when the issue is raised by the creditor in a motion to dismiss. *See, e.g.*, In re Arena, 81 B.R. 851 (Bankr. E.D. Pa. 1988); In re Inesta Quinones, 73 B.R. 333, 336 (Bankr. D.P.R. 1987). They have done so without discussion, however, and are inconsistent with the precedent in this circuit. In Tim Wargo & Sons, Inc., we found the burden of establishing eligibility to fall on the filing debtor even though the issue was raised by the creditor. 869 F.2d at 1130.

Thus, we hold that where a section 109(g) issue is properly raised, the filing party must establish that the failure to obey a court order was not willful. This result is supported by policy considerations. Section 109(g) was enacted as part of a scheme to "curb abuses of the bankruptcy code and make its use truly a last resort." 130 Cong. Rec. 8894, reprinted in 1984 U.S.C.C.A.N. 576, 590, 598 (statement of Sen. Hatch). It would frustrate this purpose to require a creditor to prove a "willful failure" while a debtor who failed to comply with a court order stands silent.

In this case, the burden was on Montgomery to explain his failure to attend the creditors' meeting. Since he has offered no evidence on this point, the bankruptcy court's finding was not clearly erroneous.

III. Conclusion

For the foregoing reasons, the order of the district court is affirmed.

RICHARD S. ARNOLD, Chief Judge, concurring in the judgment.

I agree with the Court that, in the special circumstances of this case, it is fair to put the burden of proof on the filing debtor on the issue of fact of willfulness. I would limit this holding, however, to the burden of production, the burden of going forward initially with evidence.

---

8. Specifically, the district court held that Montgomery "bears the burden of demonstrating that jurisdiction in the bankruptcy court is proper." To the extent the district court characterized section 109(g)(1) as a jurisdictional provision, it was in error. We have held that 11 U.S.C. §109 is not meant to restrict the jurisdiction of the federal courts. Rudd v. Laughlin, 866 F.2d 1040, 1042 (8th Cir. 1989). See also In re Phillips, 844 F.2d 230, 235 n.2 (5th Cir. 1988) (discussing negative consequences of interpreting section 109(g) as a limit on subject matter jurisdiction of bankruptcy courts). Section 109 determines eligibility for bankruptcy relief, not jurisdiction.

Here, only the debtor knows why he did not attend the creditors' meeting at the time of the prior proceeding. He was given a chance to explain and did not take it. He has still offered no explanation for this violation of a court order. One suspects that the bankruptcy process is being abused. If the debtor had produced some evidence tending to show that his default was not willful, I would probably require the objecting creditor to go forward with rebutting evidence, and place the burden of persuasion on the creditor. But that did not happen here. We could require the creditor, I suppose, to depose the debtor and explore the reasons for the latter's default, but that seems to me to put too much of a burden on the one party in this case that we know to be innocent.

I therefore agree that the judgment should be affirmed.

QUESTIONS

Montgomery addresses the issue of which party has the burden of proof in §109(g) matters. The court apparently found that the debtor's failure to attend the §341 meeting of creditors violated the terms of §109(g)(1). The court did not address, however, the manner in which the debtor's absence from that meeting of creditors violated §109(g)(1). What court order did the debtor fail to follow? Is the failure to attend a meeting of creditors a failure "to appear before the court in proper prosecution of the case"? Under §341(a) and Bankruptcy Rule 2003, the meeting of creditors is called by the United States Trustee, who presides at the meeting. Moreover, under §341(c) the bankruptcy judge (i.e., the "court") is precluded from presiding at or even attending the meeting of creditors.

In re Sole
United States Bankruptcy Court, E.D. Virginia, 1998
233 B.R. 347

DAVID H. ADAMS, Bankruptcy Judge.

This matter comes before the Court on the Standing Chapter 13 Trustee's Motion for Dismissal pursuant to Section 109(g)(2) of the Bankruptcy Code. Having reviewed the pleadings and the competing legal interpretations of Section 109(g)(2), we reach the following factual findings and conclusions of law. This is a core proceeding and jurisdiction is proper. 28 U.S.C. §§157(b)(1), 1334.

Findings of Fact

The debtors, Wayne E. and Cynthia L. Sole, filed a Chapter 13 petition, case number 95-21014, on February 28, 1995. In that case, a Motion for Relief from the automatic stay was filed by Chemical Residential Mortgage Corporation in October 1995. That Motion was later resolved by consent with an Amended Order Granting Modification of the Stay entered on the Court's docket on March 21, 1996. On November 17, 1997, approximately 20 months after the filing of the motion for relief, this first Chapter 13 petition was dismissed pursuant to the debtors' request for dismissal. On November 20, 1997, three days following the voluntary dismissal of their earlier Chapter 13, the debtors filed their current Chapter 13 petition.

Conclusions of Law

The protections afforded by the Bankruptcy Code are generally available, with few exceptions, to all residents of the United States. One exception carved out by the Code is found in Section 109(g)(2), providing in part

> [N]o individual . . . may be a debtor under this title who has been a debtor in a case pending under this title at any time in the preceding 180 days if –
>
> (2) the debtor requested and obtained the voluntary dismissal of the case following the filing of a request for relief from the automatic stay provided by section 362 of this title.

11 U.S.C. §§109(g)(2).

Despite its apparent simplicity, Section 109(g)(2) has generated several competing interpretations and has not been addressed by the Fourth Circuit, nor has the matter been clarified by the District or Bankruptcy Courts for the Eastern District of Virginia. Generally, courts interpret Section 109(g)(2) in one of three manners. The first approach considers the equities of the situation, avoiding results that would lead to absurd, inequitable, or unfair results. The second approach is a strict application of Section 109(g)(2) using the plain meaning of the words of the statute. This line of cases asserts that Section 109(g)(2) is triggered anytime a voluntary dismissal follows the filing of a motion for relief. The last approach also applies the plain meaning of the statute, but conditions its application upon a causal connection between a motion for relief from the automatic stay and a debtor's voluntary dismissal of his case.[9]

1. Equitable Approach

We turn our attention first to the §109(g)(2) approach that balances the equities of each situation. Courts using this approach tend to fall in one of two camps. The first, as evidenced in In re Luna, defers to the equities of each situation because a strict application of the statute would lead to an "absurd, inequitable, or unfair result." 122 B.R. 575, 577 (9th Cir. BAP 1992). Other courts relying on concepts of equity cite Congressional intent and apply the statute in only a limited number of cases rather than effectuate the statute across the board. *See, e.g.,* In re Santana, 110 B.R. 819 (Bankr. W.D. Mich. 1990). In Luna, a creditor in her first case, Home Savings, requested and obtained relief from the automatic stay in order to sell previously foreclosed property. The debtor then filed a voluntary motion for dismissal and the judge granted her motion. Within 180 days of her voluntary dismissal, the debtor filed

---

9. *See generally* In re Richardson, 217 B.R. 479 (Bankr. M.D. La. 1998), for an exhaustive survey of the various approaches to Section 109(g)(2).

a second bankruptcy that should have prevented Home Savings from proceeding with the sale of the previously foreclosed property. Despite its knowledge of the second petition, however, Home Savings sold Luna's property three weeks after the second filing date. The court held that it would adopt a discretionary approach to §109(g)(2) because to do otherwise "would reward Home Savings for acting in bad faith [by willfully violating the automatic stay in the second case] and punish Luna for acting in good faith [by seeking to have the bankruptcy court resolve a dispute over possible redemption of the mortgaged property]." Luna, 122 B.R. at 577.

In Santana, on similar facts, the court concluded that the language of §109(g)(2) was unambiguous, and that, if applied as written, the statute dictated dismissal. However, the court went on to state that "to apply it literally to the facts now before me would produce, if not an absurd result, then certainly one which goes far beyond the scope of the abuse which it appears Congress was attempting to cure." Santana, 110 B.R. at 821. Consequently, the court declined to apply the statute as written, and denied the creditor's motion to dismiss.

Clearly bad facts make for bad law. In both instances, the Luna and Santana courts reached beyond their judicial roles to achieve a desired result. Neither Section 109(g)(2), while subject to various legitimate interpretations, nor the Bankruptcy Code provide for such extraordinary judicial discretion and interpretation. The Luna and Santana courts had other means with which to punish creditors for willful violations of the automatic stay. Both courts utilized Section 109(g)(2) to remedy a perceived wrong.

2. Strict Approach

The second approach is a strict application of Section 109(g)(2). Courts utilizing this approach hold that the meaning of Section 109(g)(2) is plain and unambiguous, and that the language of the statute dictates a broad rule of dismissal. See, e.g., In re Andersson, 209 B.R. 76 (6th Cir. BAP 1997); In re Keziah, 46 B.R. 551 (Bankr. W.D.N.C. 1985).

The rationale behind a strict interpretation is explained in the Keziah decision. There, the court held that even though one could interpret "the words 'following the filing' [to] mean[ ] 'in consequence of the filing' or 'as a result of the filing,' " the proper interpretation is that Section 109(g)(2) is activated any time a motion for relief from stay is filed earlier in time than the granting of a voluntary dismissal. Keziah, 46 B.R. at 555. The court added that Congress might have intended bankruptcy courts to look into debtor motivations when moving for a voluntary dismissal had the Section been placed in another part of the Code, such as sections 1112 or 1325. According to Keziah, however, the section is located in the eligibility provisions, setting the bounds of the court's interpretation. Id. at 554.

At the outset, we acknowledge that Section 109(g)(2) is written plainly. We note, however, that this strict approach begs the question of statutory ambiguity given the three general interpretations to the statute and their varied permutations. At the very least, the language of the statute is open to interpretation. While this strict approach does not vary from the letter of the statute, we disagree with the Keziah court to the extent that it does not read the words "following the filing" as necessitating some causal connection between the filing of a motion for relief and the subsequent voluntary dismissal of a debtor's case. Thus, as is the case with the equitable approach, we cannot agree with this particular interpretation and look elsewhere for construction of Section 109(g)(2).

3.   Causal Approach

The last approach to Section 109(g)(2) looks for a causal relationship between the voluntary motion to dismiss and the motion for relief from stay. *See* First Nat'l Bank of Rocky Mount v. Duncan (In re Duncan), 182 B.R. 156 (Bankr. W.D. Va. 1995); In re Patton, 49 B.R. 587 (Bankr. M.D. Ga. 1985). The court in *Patton* concluded that:

> [S]ection 109(f)(2) [now section 109(g) — Eds.] is intended to address the situation in which the debtor files a bankruptcy case to stay a foreclosure, and when the creditor seeks relief from the automatic stay, the case is then voluntarily dismissed by the debtor. The debtor then refiles prior to the creditor's completing his next attempt to foreclose, and through this scheme, the debtor can continually frustrate the creditor's attempts to foreclose.

49 B.R. at 589. Congress' justification for adding Section 109(g) to the Bankruptcy Code in 1984 is similar to the *Patton* court's analysis: "Subsection (f) adds a new paragraph to section 109. The purpose of the new paragraph is to provide the court with greater authority to control abusive multiple filings." S. Rep. No. 65, 98th Cong. 1st Sess. 74 (1983).

A similar rationale was adopted by Chief Judge Krumm in the *Duncan* matter. The court noted that by requiring that the debtor both "request" and "obtain" the dismissal after the request for relief, the statute requires a causal connection such that the request for relief triggers the dismissal. 182 B.R. at 159. "Absent a causal relationship, there is no abuse to curb and no purpose to be served by keeping the former debtor out [of] bankruptcy for 180 days." Id. The court concluded that the proper approach to Section 109(g)(2) is to examine the circumstances surrounding a creditor's motion for relief from stay and a debtor's subsequent motion to dismiss. If the examination reveals that the debtor was acting in response to the motion for relief from stay, then the debtor is barred by the terms of Section 109(g)(2) from being a debtor under Title 11 for 180 days. If, on the other hand, the examination reveals some other reason for the debtor's motion to dismiss, apart from an effort to thwart a creditor's valid exercise of its rights, then the Court should deny the creditor's motion to dismiss. Id.

We are convinced that this latter interpretation of Section 109(g)(2), rather than a strict interpretation, reflects both Congressional intent and the most natural and obvious reading of the statute. Indeed, the present case exemplifies the undesired result of a strict interpretation. Here, a creditor filed a motion for relief in October 1995 that was later resolved by consent with an Amended Order Granting Modification of the Stay entered on the Court's docket on March 21, 1996. Twenty months after the filing of the motion for relief, the debtors requested and received a voluntary dismissal of their case on November 17, 1997. Then, on November 20, 1997, three days after their dismissal, the debtors filed this second case that is the subject of the Trustee's Motion to Dismiss.

A strict interpretation of Section 109(g)(2) would have these debtors' case dismissed. In fact, any time a motion for relief is filed and then followed by a voluntary dismissal of a case, a strict interpretation of the statute would bar that debtor from refiling for 180 days regardless of the circumstances. That result goes beyond the fix intended by Congress and goes beyond even the simplest of logic. In the case at bar, there is no causal connection between the agreed relief from stay and the much later voluntary dismissal of the debtors' first case.

Thus, on a motion to dismiss based upon Section 109(g)(2) we will look for a causal connection between a motion for relief from the automatic stay and a debtor's subsequent request and receipt of a voluntary dismissal. Absent the causal connection, section 109(g)(2) is not triggered and a debtor is not barred from re-filing for 180 days.

Here, the Trustee failed to demonstrate any causal connection between Chemical Residential Mortgage's Motion for Relief and the debtors' subsequent voluntary dismissal. For those reasons, the Trustee's Motion to Dismiss pursuant to Section 109(g)(2) is denied.

It is so ORDERED.

PROBLEM 2-16

Marie filed for Chapter 13 relief; in response to her petition Acme Finance Co. moved for relief from the automatic stay so that it could repossess one of Marie's cars. Since she had two cars, Marie did not contest the creditor's motion, and the bankruptcy court granted relief to Acme. Two years later, Marie voluntarily dismissed her Chapter 13 case because she lost her job when her employer relocated the business. Two months after dismissing the case, Marie got another job and now wants to commence a new Chapter 13 case. Is she eligible?

PROBLEM 2-17

Dave Debtor was facing a foreclosure on his residence so he filed a Chapter 13 petition. Upon filing the case, Dave engaged in extensive negotiations with the mortgage holder, Nightflyer Finance, over the repayment of the past due amounts under the mortgage. The negotiations were going badly, and Nightflyer indicated that it intended to move for relief from the automatic stay in the case so that they could complete their foreclosure. Dave's response was to move to dismiss the Chapter 13 proceedings; under §1307(b) dismissal is essentially automatic. The case was dismissed, and Nightflyer followed that action by starting a new foreclosure proceeding. Just prior to the actual foreclosure sale, Dave again filed a Chapter 13 petition. The second Chapter 13 petition was filed 170 days after the dismissal of the first case. Nightflyer has objected to Dave's second case under §109(g)(2). Is Dave's second petition properly filed? In re Hicks, 138 B.R. 505 (Bankr. D. Md. 1992). What if Dave settles with a creditor who moves for relief, then dismisses his case for other reasons. Does the 180-day bar still apply?

The automatic stay of §362, which we will consider in detail in a later chapter, stops all creditor collection activity as of the moment the petition is filed. The 2005 amendments to the Bankruptcy Code have amended §362 in ways similar to the rules of §109(g) that you have just studied, with one difference. The new rules do not keep the debtor from filing a petition, they merely keep the automatic stay from coming into play. Thus the debtor who violates the new rules, as explored in the Problem that follows, can still proceed with the usual bankruptcy, but is not protected by a stay of creditor activity.

PROBLEM 2-18

Gladstone Gander filed a bankruptcy petition early in February 2007, but two days after the filing he won $2 million in the lottery, so he dismissed the petition and paid off all his creditors in full. However, his subsequent profligate spending of the new riches soon had him in financial disarray once more, so he filed a Chapter 7 petition in December of that same year. Will the automatic stay keep his creditors at bay while he goes through bankruptcy? See §362(c)(3). Does the stay become ineffective in 30 days as to property of the estate as opposed to property of the debtor and actions directly against the debtor? Compare In re Holcomb, 380 B.R. 813 (10th Cir. BAP 2008) (stay continues in effect as to property of the estate), with In re Curry, 362 B.R. 394 (Bankr. N.D. Ill. 2007) (automatic stay is ineffective as to property of the estate after 30 days after the commencement of the case). If Gander's new petition is dismissed because he was too drunk to fill out the necessary schedules, but he filed a third petition in early January of 2008, will the automatic stay go into effect at all? See §362(c)(4).

The Bankruptcy Code contains an additional limit on relief available to debtors. Section 727(a)(8) and (9) provides that debtors cannot obtain a discharge in a Chapter 7 case commenced within eight years of the commencement of a prior Chapter 7 case in which the debtor received a discharge. No subsequent Chapter 7 discharge is available for six years if the debtor received a discharge in a Chapter 12 or Chapter 13 case unless the debtor paid either all of the allowed unsecured claims in the prior proceeding or at least 70 percent of those claims, using his or her "best efforts" to do so. This limitation is truly only a limitation on the entry of a Chapter 7 discharge, as opposed to an eligibility limitation. Nevertheless, with no possibility for a discharge in Chapter 7, there is no real benefit to an individual debtor to initiate a Chapter 7 case. However, the debtor can still commence a Chapter 12 or Chapter 13 case if he or she is eligible.

CHAPTER 3

The Bankruptcy Estate

Bankruptcy debtors, like all economic entities, are evaluated on the basis of their assets and liabilities. In bankruptcy proceedings, we call those assets and liabilities "property of the estate" and "claims," respectively. In this chapter, we explore the limits of the concept of property of the estate. Determining what is property of the estate has consequences from the very beginning of the case right up to its conclusion. For example, the automatic stay that arises on commencement of the case protects property of the estate, and it is property of the estate, in Chapter 7 cases, that is distributed to creditors at the conclusion of the proceedings. Even in cases under other Chapters of the Bankruptcy Code, while the payment of claims may be from sources other than property of the estate, determining the amount of property of the estate is necessary to establish the minimum distribution to the creditors (under the "best interests of creditors" test that we shall explore later on).

"Property of the estate" is defined in Bankruptcy Code §541. That section provides, first, that property of the estate consists of "all legal and equitable interests of the debtor in property as of the commencement of the case." Bankruptcy Code §541(a)(1). Congress enacted this expansive definition to replace prior law, which it had described as "a complicated mélange of references to State law [that did] little to further the bankruptcy policy of distribution of the debtor's property to his creditors in satisfaction of his debts." H.R. Rep. No. 95-595 at 175 (1977). The courts have respected this congressional goal of expanding the concept of property of the estate. *See, e.g.*, Arango v. Third Natl. Bank (In re Arango), 992 F.2d 611 (6th Cir. 1993); Jim Walter Homes, Inc. v. Spears (In re Thompson), 894 F.2d 1227 (10th Cir. 1990); MacArthur Co. v. Johns-Manville Corp., 837 F.2d 89 (2d Cir.), *cert. denied,* 488 U.S. 868 (1988); In re Bagen, 186 B.R. 824 (Bankr. S.D.N.Y. 1995).

In the following case, United States v. Whiting Pools, Inc., the Supreme Court had its first opportunity to construe the definition of property of the estate under the Bankruptcy Code. In the case, the Chapter 11 debtor in possession sought the return of property (pool cleaning equipment) that the Internal Revenue Service had seized prior to the commencement of the bankruptcy proceedings. In fact, the debtor most likely filed its voluntary petition for bankruptcy relief in response to the IRS's action.

United States v. Whiting Pools, Inc.
United States Supreme Court, 1983
462 U.S. 198

Justice BLACKMUN delivered the opinion of the Court.

Promptly after the Internal Revenue Service (IRS or Service) seized respondent's property to satisfy a tax lien, respondent filed a petition for reorganization under the Bankruptcy Reform Act of 1978, hereinafter referred to as the "Bankruptcy Code." The issue before us is whether §542(a) of that Code authorized the Bankruptcy Court to subject the IRS to a turnover order with respect to the seized property.

I.

A.

Respondent Whiting Pools, Inc., a corporation, sells, installs, and services swimming pools and related equipment and supplies. As of January 1981, Whiting owed approximately $92,000 in Federal Insurance Contribution Act taxes and federal taxes withheld from its employees, but had failed to respond to assessments and demands for payment by the IRS. As a consequence, a tax lien in that amount attached to all of Whiting's property.

On January 14, 1981, the Service seized Whiting's tangible personal property — equipment, vehicles, inventory, and office supplies — pursuant to the levy and distraint provision of the Internal Revenue Code of 1954. According to uncontroverted findings, the estimated liquidation value of the property seized was, at most, $35,000, but its estimated going-concern value in Whiting's hands was $162,876. The very next day, January 15, Whiting filed a petition for reorganization, under the Bankruptcy Code's Chapter 11, 11 U.S.C. §§1101 et seq. (1976 ed., Supp. V), in the United States Bankruptcy Court for the Western District of New York. Whiting was continued as debtor-in-possession.

The United States, intending to proceed with a tax sale of the property, moved in the Bankruptcy Court for a declaration that the automatic stay provision of the Bankruptcy Code, §362(a), is inapplicable to the IRS or, in the alternative, for relief from the stay. Whiting counterclaimed for an order requiring the Service to turn the seized property over to the bankruptcy estate pursuant to §542(a) of the Bankruptcy Code. Whiting intended to use the property in its reorganized business.

B.

The Bankruptcy Court determined that the IRS was bound by the automatic stay provision. In re Whiting Pools, Inc., 10 B.R. 755 (Bkrtcy. 1981). Because it found that the seized property was essential to Whiting's reorganization effort, it refused to lift the stay. Acting under §543(b)(1) of the Bankruptcy Code, rather than under §542(a), the court directed the IRS to turn the property over to Whiting on the condition that Whiting provide the Service with specified protection for its interests. 10 B.R., at 760-761.

The United States District Court reversed, holding that a turnover order against the Service was not authorized by either §542(a) or §543(b)(1). App. to Pet. for Cert. 46a. The United States Court of Appeals for the Second Circuit, in turn, reversed the District Court. 674 F.2d 144 (1982). It held that a turnover order could issue against the Service under §542(a), and it remanded the case for reconsideration of the adequacy of the Bankruptcy Court's protection conditions. The Court of Appeals acknowledged that its ruling was contrary to that reached by the United States Court of Appeals for the Fourth Circuit in Cross Electric Co. v. United States, 664 F.2d 1218 (1981), and noted confusion on the issue among bankruptcy and district courts. 674 F.2d, at 145 and n.1. We granted certiorari to resolve this conflict in an important area of the law under the new Bankruptcy Code. 459 U.S. _____, 103 S. Ct. 442, 74 L. Ed. 2d 599 (1982).

II.

By virtue of its tax lien, the Service holds a secured interest in Whiting's property. We first examine whether §542(a) of the Bankruptcy Code generally authorizes the turnover of a debtor's property seized by a secured creditor prior to the commencement of reorganization proceedings. Section 542(a) requires an entity in possession of "property that the trustee may use, sell, or lease under §363" to deliver that property to the trustee. Subsections (b) and (c) of §363 authorize the trustee to use, sell, or lease any "property of the estate," subject to certain conditions for the protection of creditors with an interest in the property. Section 541(a)(1) defines the "estate" as "comprised of all the following property, wherever located: (1) . . . all legal or equitable interests of the debtor in property as of the commencement of the case." Although these statutes could be read to limit the estate to those "interests of the debtor in property" at the time of the filing of the petition, we view them as a definition of what is included in the estate, rather than as a limitation.

A.

In proceedings under the reorganization provisions of the Bankruptcy Code, a troubled enterprise may be restructured to enable it to operate successfully in the future. Until the business can be reorganized pursuant to a plan under 11 U.S.C. §§1121-1129 (1976 ed., Supp. V), the trustee or debtor-in-possession is authorized to manage the property of the estate and to continue the operation of the business. See §1108. By permitting reorganization, Congress anticipated that the business would continue to provide jobs, to satisfy creditors' claims, and to produce a return for its owners. H.R. Rep. No. 95-595, p.220 (1977), U.S. Code Cong. & Admin. News 1978, p.5787. Congress presumed that the assets of the debtor would be more valuable if used in a rehabilitated business than if "sold for scrap." Ibid. The reorganization effort would have small chance of success, however, if property essential to running the business were excluded from the estate. See 6 J. Moore & L. King, Collier on Bankruptcy ¶3.05, p.431 (14th ed. 1978). Thus, to facilitate the rehabilitation of the debtor's business, all the debtor's property must be included in the reorganization estate.

This authorization extends even to property of the estate in which a creditor has a secured interest. §363(b) and (c); *see* H.R. Rep. No. 95-595, p.182 (1977). Although Congress might have safeguarded the interests of secured creditors outright by excluding from the estate any property subject to a secured interest, it chose instead to include such property in the estate and to provide secured creditors with "adequate protection" for their interests. §363(e), quoted in n.7, *supra*. At the secured creditor's insistence, the bankruptcy court must place such limits or conditions on the trustee's power to sell, use, or lease property as are necessary to protect the creditor. The creditor with a secured interest in property included in the estate must look to this provision for protection, rather than to the nonbankruptcy remedy of possession.

Both the congressional goal of encouraging reorganizations and Congress' choice of methods to protect secured creditors suggest that Congress intended a broad range of property to be included in the estate.

B.

The statutory language reflects this view of the scope of the estate. As noted above, §541(a) provides that the "estate is comprised of all the following property, wherever located: . . . all legal or equitable interests of the debtor in property as of the commencement of the case." 11 U.S.C. §541(a)(1).[1] The House and Senate Reports on the Bankruptcy Code indicate that §541(a)(1)'s scope is broad.[2] Most important, in the context of this case, §541(a)(1) is intended to include in the estate any property made available to the estate by other provisions of the Bankruptcy Code. *See* H.R. Rep. No. 95-595, p.367 (1977). Several of these provisions bring into the estate property in which the debtor did not have a possessory interest at the time the bankruptcy proceedings commenced.

1. Section 541(a)(1) speaks in terms of the debtor's "interests . . . in property," rather than property in which the debtor has an interest, but this choice of language was not meant to limit the expansive scope of the section. The legislative history indicates that Congress intended to exclude from the estate property of others in which the debtor had some minor interest such as a lien or bare legal title. *See* 124 Cong. Rec. 32399, 32417 (1978) (remarks of Rep. Edwards); id., at 33999, 34016-34017 (remarks of Sen. DeConcini); cf. §541(d) (property in which debtor holds legal but not equitable title, such as a mortgage in which debtor retained legal title to service or to supervise servicing of mortgage, becomes part of estate only to extent of legal title); 124 Cong. Rec. 33999 (1978) (remarks of Sen. DeConcini) (§541(d) "reiterates the general principle that where the debtor holds bare legal title without any equitable interest, . . . the estate acquires bare legal title without any equitable interest in the property"). Similar statements to the effect that §541(a)(1) does not expand the rights of the debtor in the hands of the estate were made in the context of describing the principle that the estate succeeds to no more or greater causes of action against third parties than those held by the debtor. *See* H.R. Rep. No. 95-595, pp.367-368 (1977). These statements do not limit the ability of a trustee to regain possession of property in which the debtor had equitable as well as legal title.

2. "The scope of this paragraph [§541(a)(1)] is broad. It includes all kinds of property, including tangible or intangible property, causes of action (*see* Bankruptcy Act §70a(6)), and all other forms of property currently specified in section 70a of the Bankruptcy Act." H.R. Rep. No. 95-595, p.367 (1977); S. Rep. No. 95-989, p.82 (1978), U.S. Code Cong. & Admin. News 1978, pp.5868, 6323.

Section 542(a) is such a provision. It requires an entity (other than a custodian) holding any property of the debtor that the trustee can use under §363 to turn that property over to the trustee. Given the broad scope of the reorganization estate, property of the debtor repossessed by a secured creditor falls within this rule, and therefore may be drawn into the estate. While there are explicit limitations on the reach of §542(a), none requires that the debtor hold a possessory interest in the property at the commencement of the reorganization proceedings.

As does all bankruptcy law, §542(a) modifies the procedural rights available to creditors to protect and satisfy their liens. *See* Wright v. Union Central Life Ins. Co., 311 U.S. 273, 278-279, 61 S. Ct. 196, 199-200, 85 L. Ed. 184 (1940). *See generally* Nowak, Turnover Following Prepetition Levy of Distraint Under Bankruptcy Code §542, 55 Am. Bankr. L.J. 313, 332-333 (1981). In effect, §542(a) grants to the estate a possessory interest in certain property of the debtor that was not held by the debtor at the commencement of reorganization proceedings. The Bankruptcy Code provides secured creditors various rights, including the right to adequate protection, and these rights replace the protection afforded by possession.

C.

This interpretation of §542(a) is supported by the section's legislative history. Although the legislative reports are silent on the precise issue before us, the House and Senate hearings from which §542(a) emerged provide guidance. Several witnesses at those hearings noted, without contradiction, the need for a provision authorizing the turnover of property of the debtor in the possession of secured creditors. Section 542(a) first appeared in the proposed legislation shortly after these hearings. *See* H.R. 6, §542(a), 95th Cong., 1st Sess., introduced January 4, 1977. *See generally* Klee, Legislative History of the New Bankruptcy Code, 54 Am. Bankr. L.J. 275, 279-281 (1980). The section remained unchanged through subsequent versions of the legislation.

Moreover, this interpretation of §542 in the reorganization context is consistent with judicial precedent predating the Bankruptcy Code. Under Chapter X, the reorganization chapter of the Bankruptcy Act of 1878, as amended, §§101-276, 52 Stat. 883 (1938) (formerly codified as 11 U.S.C. §§501-676 (1976 ed.)), the bankruptcy court could order the turnover of collateral in the hands of a secured creditor. Reconstruction Finance Corp. v. Kaplan, 185 F.2d 791, 796 (CA1 1950); *see* In re Third Ave. Transit Corp., 198 F.2d 703, 706 (CA2 1952); 6A J. Moore & L. King, Collier on Bankruptcy ¶14.03, p.741-742 (14th ed. 1977); Murphy, Use of Collateral in Business Rehabilitations: A Suggested Redrafting of Section 7-203 of the Bankruptcy Reform Act, 63 Calif. L. Rev. 1483, 1492-1495 (1975). Nothing in the legislative history evinces a congressional intent to depart from that practice. Any other interpretation of §542(a) would deprive the bankruptcy estate of the assets and property essential to its rehabilitation effort and thereby would frustrate the congressional purpose behind the reorganization provisions.

We conclude that the reorganization estate includes property of the debtor that has been seized by a creditor prior to the filing of a petition for reorganization.

III.

A.

We see no reason why a different result should obtain when the IRS is the creditor. The Service is bound by §542(a) to the same extent as any other secured creditor. The Bankruptcy Code expressly states that the term "entity," used in §542(a), includes a governmental unit. §101(14). *See* Tr. of Oral Arg. 16. Moreover, Congress carefully considered the effect of the new Bankruptcy Code on tax collection, *see generally* S. Rep. No. 95-1106 (1978) (report of Senate Finance Committee), and decided to provide protection to tax collectors, such as the IRS, through grants of enhanced priorities for unsecured tax claims, §507(a)(6), and by the nondischarge of tax liabilities, §523(a)(1). S. Rep. No. 95-989, pp.14-15 (1978). Tax collectors also enjoy the generally applicable right under §363(e) to adequate protection forproperty subject to their liens. Nothing in the Bankruptcy Code or its legislative history indicates that Congress intended a special exception for the tax collector in the form of an exclusion from the estate of property seized to satisfy a tax lien.

B.

Of course, if a tax levy or seizure transfers to the IRS ownership of the property seized, §542(a) may not apply. The enforcement provisions of the Internal Revenue Code of 1954, 26 U.S.C. §§6321-6326 (1976 ed. and Supp. V), do grant to the Service powers to enforce its tax liens that are greater than those possessed by private secured creditors under state law. See United States v. Rodgers, ____U.S. ____, 103 S. Ct., ____, ____, 75 L. Ed. 2d ____ (1983) (slip op. 4); id., at ____, ____, n.7, 103 S. Ct. at ____, ____, n.7 (dissenting opinion) (slip op. 1, 6, n.7); United States v. Bess, 357 U.S. 51, 56-57, 78 S. Ct. 1054, 1057-1058, 2 L. Ed. 2d 1135 (1958). But those provisions do not transfer ownership of the property to the IRS.

The Service's interest in seized property is its lien on that property. The Internal Revenue Code's levy and seizure provisions, 26 U.S.C. §§6331 and 6332, are special procedural devices available to the IRS to protect and satisfy its liens, United States v. Sullivan, 333 F.2d 100, 116 (CA3 1964), and are analogous to the remedies available to private secured creditors. See Uniform Commercial Code §9-503, 3A U.L.A. 211-212 (1981); n.14, *supra*. They are provisional remedies that do not determine the Service's rights to the seized property, but merely bring the property into the Service's legal custody. *See* 4 B. Bittker, Federal Taxation of Income, Estates and Gifts P 111.5.5, p.111-108 (1981). *See generally* Plumb, Federal Tax Collection and Lien Problems, pt.1, 13 Tax L. Rev. 247, 272 (1958). At no point does the Service's interest in the property exceed the value of the lien. United States v. Rodgers, ____ U.S., at ____, ____, 103 S. Ct., at ____, ____ (slip op. 12); id., at ____, 103 S. Ct., at ____ (dissenting opinion) (slip op. 12); *see* United States v. Sullivan, 333 F.2d, at 116 ("the Commissioner acts pursuant to the collection process in the capacity of lienor as distinguished from owner"). The IRS is obligated to return to the debtor any surplus from a sale. 26 U.S.C. §6342(b). Ownership of the property is transferred only when the property is sold to a bona fide purchaser at a tax sale. *See* Bennett v. Hunter, 9 Wall. 326, 336, 19 L. Ed. 672 (1870); 26 U.S.C. §6339(a)(2); Plumb, 13 Tax. L. Rev., at 274-275. In fact, the tax sale provision itself refers to the debtor as the owner of the property after the seizure but prior to the sale. Until such a sale takes place, the property remains the debtor's and thus is subject to the turnover requirement of §542(a).

IV.

When property seized prior to the filing of a petition is drawn into the Chapter 11 reorganization estate, the Service's tax lien is not dissolved; nor is its status as a secured creditor destroyed. The IRS, under §363(e), remains entitled to adequate protection for its interests, to other rights enjoyed by secured creditors, and to the specific privileges accorded tax collectors. Section 542(a) simply requires the Service to seek protection of its interest according to the congressionally established bankruptcy procedures, rather than by withholding the seized property from the debtor's efforts to reorganize. The judgment of the Court of Appeals is affirmed.

It is so ordered.

The reach of §541(a)(1) is, of course, not unlimited. It separates interests of the debtor in property according to the time when the interest arises. If the interest comes into existence after the commencement of the case, it is not property of the estate under §541(a)(1). For example, if Dave Debtor files a bankruptcy petition on March 1, a gift he received from his mother on February 28 would be property of the bankruptcy estate, but a gift he received from his mother on March 2 would not be property of the estate.

The bulk of property of the estate questions are resolved under §541(a)(1) and usually concern either whether the debtor has any interest in a particular piece of property or whether the debtor's interest in the property existed as of the commencement of the case. Section 541(a)(5) operates to bring within the estate property in which the debtor's interest arose after the commencement of the case. Under that provision, any interest in property that the debtor acquires postbankruptcy by inheritance, through a property settlement or a divorce decree, or as a beneficiary of a life insurance policy is property of the estate as long as the debtor "acquires or becomes entitled to acquire" that property within 180 days after the commencement of the case.

Other "postbankruptcy" property can become property of the estate as well. Property that is recovered by the trustee for the benefit of the estate and the proceeds of the property of the estate also are included in the reach of §541. The most significant limitation on this postbankruptcy enlargement of the estate is set out in §541(a)(6). Under that section, "earnings from services performed by an individual debtor after the commencement of the case" are not property of the estate. This exclusion from property of the estate is a fundamental component of the debtor's fresh start. It can also be a difficult concept to apply in some circumstances.

PROBLEM 3-1

Race car driver Speed King got into financial trouble and filed a bankruptcy petition in early May, two weeks before he won the Indianapolis 500, the prize money for which was considerable. Can King's bankruptcy trustee get to this money? *See* Bankruptcy Code §541(a)(6).

PROBLEM 3-2

Redding Pools, Inc., sells, installs, and services swimming pools and related equipment and supplies. Although the company was scrupulous in its efforts to maintain current status on its tax obligations, it failed to make its last two monthly payments to Octopus National Bank. ONB had a properly perfected security interest in all of Redding's inventory, accounts receivable, and equipment. As a result of Redding's failure to make a timely payment, ONB declared Redding in default and repossessed the inventory and equipment. It also sent notices to Redding's customers directing that payments due to Redding be made directly to ONB. ONB notified Redding that it would be selling the inventory and equipment at a public auction two weeks hence, and it also provided Redding with a list of the 20 customers ONB had contacted to direct payment to it. Redding filed a Chapter 11 petition on the day before the scheduled public sale of the inventory and equipment. At that time, ONB had received payments from 10 of Redding's customers; another 10 customer accounts were still outstanding. Which, if any, of the foregoing assets are property of the estate under §541(a)(1) of the Bankruptcy Code? *See* In re Contractors Equipment Supply Co., 861 F.2d 241 (9th Cir. 1988).

PROBLEM 3-3

When Paul Penury's father died, he inherited Blackacre, but it came to him with a condition attached. The condition was that if he ever became insolvent and filed a bankruptcy petition, the property would revert to his mother, the prior owner. When Paul did file a Chapter 7 petition, his mother promptly moved onto the property and contended that it never became part of the bankruptcy estate. Is she right? *See* §541(c)(1).

Problem 3-3 contains a restriction on property that attempts to keep it out of the bankruptcy process by vesting it in someone else in the event of financial troubles. Restrictions like this are frequently thrown into contracts, deeds of property, security agreements, and the like, and are commonly called "bankruptcy clauses" (or "ipso facto" clauses, because on the happening of the triggering event, that is, insolvency, the property reverts "by the fact itself"). The Bankruptcy Code condemns such bankruptcy clauses and invalidates them in a number of different sections, of which §541(c)(1) is only the first example.

PROBLEM 3-4

Denise Debtor filed a Chapter 7 bankruptcy petition on March 12. She had only minimal assets, and the case was handled by the trustee relatively quickly. The trustee filed a "no-asset report" on May 6, and Denise received her discharge on June 25. On July 2, Denise's uncle passed away, leaving a will. Under the will, Denise inherited the house. Several of the heirs initiated a will contest action in state court, asserting a superior claim to the house. The state court litigation was concluded in Denise's favor the following year. The bankruptcy trustee now asserts a claim to the house. Is the house property of the estate? See §541(a)(5)(A); In re Elliott, 81 B.R. 460 (Bankr. N.D. Ill. 1987).

PROBLEM 3-5

Lucky Larry was certain that his financial fortunes were about to change. Of course, they couldn't get much worse. He owed lots of people lots of money. For some time, Larry played the lottery in hopes of solving his problems by being a clever number picker. He had never won in the past, although one time he did correctly choose three of the necessary six numbers. For that, of course, he got nothing. Finally, on April 11, he filed a Chapter 7 bankruptcy petition. On April 10 he had purchased a lottery ticket, and on April 12 the lottery numbers exactly matched the numbers on Larry's ticket. Is the $20 million lottery prize that Larry won property of the estate? §541(a)(1), (6) & (7). If you don't believe lottery winners file bankruptcy cases, see In re McNeill, 1996 WL 135330 (Bankr. E.D.N.Y. 1996); In re Brown, 86 B.R. 944 (N.D. Ind. 1988); In re Pizzi, 153 B.R. 357 (Bankr. S.D. Fla. 1993); In re Meyers, 139 B.R. 858 (Bankr. N.D. Ohio 1992); In re Dalton, 146 B.R. 460 (Bankr. D. Ariz. 1992); In re Skog, 144 B.R. 221 (Bankr. D.R.I. 1992). In fact, some debtors are so unlucky as to win the lottery while they are already in bankruptcy! In re Cook, 148 B.R. 273 (Bankr. W.D. Mich. 1992); In re Koonce, 54 B.R. 643 (Bankr. D.S.D. 1985).

The Court ordered the return of the pool cleaning equipment in Whiting Pools because the debtor had an interest in the property as of the commencement of the case. The debtor was not the only entity with an interest in the property. The IRS had a lien on the property, and the return of the property to the debtor did not extinguish that interest. Bankruptcy lawyers often describe this as the bankruptcy estate taking the debtor's property with both its benefits and its burdens. The classic example of this concept is the Supreme Court's decision in Chicago Board of Trade v. Johnson, 264 U.S. 1 (1924), in which the debtor held a seat on the Chicago Board of Trade when his bankruptcy case was commenced. He also owed a significant amount to other members of the Board. Under Board rules, a member's seat could not be transferred until all debts owed by the transferor to other members of the Board had been satisfied. The trustee in the bankruptcy sought to sell the seat, but the Supreme Court held that the transfer could not take place unless and until the outstanding debts owed to the Board members were paid. In this manner, the Court recognized that the estate takes the debtor's position with respect to property as to both its benefits and its burdens. Consider the application of that principle in the following case.

In re Chris-Don, Inc.

United States District Court, District of New Jersey, 2005
367 F. Supp. 2d 696

COOPER, District Judge.

This matter comes before the Court on appeal from the order of the United States Bankruptcy Court for the District of New Jersey ("Bankruptcy Court") dated April 30, 2004 ("4-30-04 Order"), granting summary judgment in favor of appellee, United Trust Bank ("United"). Appellants, the State of New Jersey Division of Taxation ("NJDOT") and the trustee, Daniel E. Straffi ("trustee"), are joined on this appeal by the intervening appellant, New Jersey Division of Alcoholic Beverage Control ("NJABC"). We have reviewed the papers filed in support of and in opposition to both appeals, and heard oral argument from the parties on March 21, 2005. For the reasons stated, we will reverse the 4-30-04 Order.

Background

The debtor in the underlying bankruptcy filed a voluntary petition for relief under Chapter 11 of the Bankruptcy Code, see 11 U.S.C. §1101 et seq., on May 29, 2001. (4-30-04 Op. at 3.) The corporate debtor operated a tavern located in Fanwood, New Jersey. (Id.) Mr. Straffi was appointed as Chapter 7 trustee, see 11 U.S.C. §701 et seq., after the Chapter 11 proceeding was converted to a Chapter 7 proceeding on motion by the United States Trustee. (Id.) One of the debtor's assets was a liquor license issued by the Borough of Fanwood ("the license"). (Id.) The trustee sold the license for a purchase price of $155,000, and held the proceeds pending a determination of the validity of liens attaching to the proceeds. (Id.)

The trustee filed an adversary complaint, seeking a determination of the extent, validity, and priority of any liens attaching to the proceeds from the sale of the license. (Id.) Three parties asserted liens on these proceeds: (1) United, (2) NJDOT, and (3) the State of New Jersey Department of Labor. (Id.)

United's lien stems from a loan of $300,000 it made to the debtor on December 8, 1995 ("the loan"). (Id.) The debtor granted United a security interest in its business assets, including its general intangibles, as collateral for the loan. (Id.) United filed a UCC-1 financing statement with the State of New Jersey on December 27, 1995 for the purpose of perfecting this security interest. (Id.; Appellee Br. at 4.) Before the Bankruptcy Court, United asserted that the debtor owed it $278,830.81 in principal and $83,707.63 in interest. (4-30-04 Op. at 3; Appellee Br. at 4.)

NJDOT obtained a judgment against the debtor in the amount of $33,980.55, and filed a Certificate of Debt based on this claim on April 17, 1997. (4-30-04 Op. at 4; NJDOT Br. at 4-5.)

United, NJDOT, and the trustee each moved for summary judgment before the Bankruptcy Court. (4-30-04 Op. at 4.) United argued that it was entitled to the proceeds of the sale of the license because it had a first-priority security interest in the proceeds. (Id.) The trustee and NJDOT argued that United's lien was not valid because state law precludes a licensee from granting a consensual security interest in a liquor license to a third party. (Id.) The Bankruptcy Court, in deciding the cross motions for summary judgment, was presented with the issue of whether certain revisions to the Uniform Commercial Code ("U.C.C.") negate the anti-alienation provisions of the New Jersey Alcoholic Beverage Control Statute, N.J.S.A. §33:1-1 et seq. ("ABC Law") (Id.)

I.   N.J.S.A. §33:1-26

The ABC Law, originally enacted by the New Jersey legislature in 1933, prevents a licensee from using a liquor license as collateral for a loan. N.J.S.A. §33:1-26 provides:

> Under no circumstances, however, shall a license, or rights thereunder, be deemed property, subject to inheritance, sale, pledge, lien, levy, attachment, execution, seizure for debts, or any other transfer or disposition whatsoever, except for payment of taxes, fees, interest and penalties imposed by any State tax law for which a lien may attach.

See also Butler Oak Tavern v. Div. of Alcoholic Beverage Control, 20 N.J. 373, 120 A.2d 24, 28 (1956) ("A license to sell intoxicating beverages is not a contract nor does it embody any property right. It is a temporary permit or privilege."). The purpose of N.J.S.A. §33:1-26 is "to protect the liquor license from any device which would subject it to the control of persons other than the licensee be it by pledge, lien, levy, attachment, execution, seizure for debts or the like." Boss Co. v. Bd. of Comm'rs of Atlantic City, 40 N.J. 379, 192 A.2d 584, 588 (1963) (citations omitted).

II.   N.J.S.A. §12A:9-408(c)

The New Jersey legislature enacted revised Article 9 of the U.C.C. in 2001. See N.J.S.A. §12A:9-101. Section 12A:9-408(c) provides:

> Legal restrictions on assignment generally ineffective. Except as provided in subsection (e), a rule of law, statute, or regulation that prohibits, restricts, or requires the consent of a government, governmental body or official, person obligated on a promissory note, or account debtor to the assignment or transfer of, or creation of a security interest in, a promissory note, health-care-insurance receivable, or general intangible, including a contract, permit, license, or franchise between an account debtor and a debtor, is ineffective to the extent that the rule of law, statute, or regulation:
>   (1) would impair the creation, attachment, or perfection of a security interest.

This section "allows the creation, attachment, and perfection of a security interest in a general intangible" and thus "enhances the ability of certain debtors to obtain credit." N.J.S.A. §12A:9-408 cmt. 2.

United argued before the Bankruptcy Court that N.J.S.A. §12A:9-408 overrides the anti-alienation provisions of N.J.S.A. §33:1-26. (4-30-04 Op. at 9.) NJDOT argued that N.J.S.A. §33:1-26 addresses liquor licenses specifically while N.J.S.A. §12A:9-408 addresses assignments generally, and therefore N.J.S.A. §33:1-26, as the more specific statute, controls when it conflicts with a more general statute like N.J.S.A. §12A:9-408. (Id.) The Bankruptcy Court agreed with United and found that N.J.S.A. §12A:9-408 overrides N.J.S.A.§33:1-26. . . .

We must determine whether a liquor license is a "general intangible" subject to N.J.S.A. §12A:9-408(c) such that a statute that impairs the creation of a security interest in the license, i.e. N.J.S.A. §33:1-26, would be ineffective under Article 9 of the U.C.C., as revised in 2001.

A "general intangible," under New Jersey law, is

> any personal property, including things in action, other than accounts, chattel paper, commercial tort claims, deposit accounts, documents, goods, instruments, investment property, letter-of-credit rights, letters of credit, money, and oil, gas, or other minerals before extraction. The term includes payment intangibles and software.

N.J.S.A. §12A:9-102(a)(42). For a liquor license to be a general intangible, then, it first must be found to be personal property. The revised U.C.C. Article 9, as enacted in New Jersey, does not define "personal property." "Neither this section nor any other provision of this Article determines whether a debtor has a property interest. . . . Other law determines whether a debtor has a property interest ('rights in the collateral') and the nature of that interest." N.J.S.A. §12A:9-408 cmt. 3.

NJDOT argues that N.J.S.A. §33:1-26 is the "other law" that determines whether the debtor has a property interest in the liquor license. (NJDOT Br. at 17.) We agree. Under N.J.S.A. §33:1-26, the "clear legislative pronouncement that liquor licenses are not property has been consistently supported by case law, all of the cases holding that a license to sell intoxicating liquor is not . . . a property right." Sea Girt Rest. & Tavern Owners Assoc. v. Borough of Sea Girt, 625 F. Supp. 1482, 1486 (D.N.J. 1986).

Courts have held that a liquor license may be considered property in certain specific contexts. See Sea Girt, 625 F Supp. at 1487-88 (finding liquor license to be interest in property for purposes of federal due process analysis); Boss, 192 A.2d at 586-88 (finding liquor license to be property for purposes of federal tax lien). However, such circumstances are limited. See Sea Girt, 625 F. Supp. at 1488 n. 4 (noting that the holding in Boss was limited specifically to the context of federal tax liens and stating similarly that "[t]his Court's holding that a license is property subject to federal due process protection in no way undermines the established state licensing scheme"); Boss, 192 A.2d at 588 ("The liquor license, although transferable, is still to be considered a temporary permit or privilege, and not property. Likewise, the vitality of N.J.S.A. [§]33:1-26 is in no way diminished."). While Sea Girt (a 1986 decision) and Boss (a 1963 decision) acknowledged federal law exceptions to the statutory determination that a liquor license is not property, both cases recognized N.J.S.A. §33:1-26 as the statute that defines the status of liquor licenses under New Jersey law, i.e. not property, and both noted the statute's continuing vitality.

The Bankruptcy Court, however, found that N.J.S.A. §33:1-26 was repealed specifically when the legislature enacted the Article 9 revisions in 2001. (4-30-04 Op. at 9.) N.J.S.A. §12A:9-408(e) provides:

> Section prevails over specified inconsistent law. Except to the extent otherwise provided in subsection (f), this section prevails over any inconsistent provision of an existing or future statute, rule or regulation of this State, unless the provision is contained in a statute of this State, refers expressly to this section and states that the provision prevails over this section.

N.J.S.A. §12A:9-408(e). Subsection (f) provides that subsection (c) does not apply to certain listed statutes that address workers' compensation claims, state winnings, and structured settlement agreements. N.J.S.A. §12A:9-408(f). The Bankruptcy Court found that the plain language of N.J.S.A. §12A:9-408 provides that it overrides N.J.S.A. §33:1-26 because N.J.S.A. §33:1-26 is an inconsistent statute not listed in N.J.S.A. §12A: 9-408(f)'s exceptions. (4-30-04 Op. at 9-10.)

We presume, in interpreting a statute, that the legislature was "familiar with its own enactments, with judicial declarations relating to them, and . . . passed or *preserved* cognate laws with the intention that they be construed to serve a useful and *consistent* purpose." State v. Greeley, 178 N.J. 38, 834 A.2d 1016, 1021 (2003) (emphasis in original) (citations omitted). When the legislature enacted N.J.S.A. §12A:9-408, the law regarding liquor licenses was clear: (1) N.J.S.A. §33:1-26 provided that liquor licenses were not to be deemed property, except for tax purposes and (2) with narrow exceptions, the "clear legislative pronouncement that liquor licenses are not property [had] been consistently supported by case law," *Sea Girt*, 625 F. Supp. at 1486. The legislature enacted Article 9, which by its own terms applies to personal property as such property is defined by other law, against a backdrop of New Jersey law that provides that a liquor license is not property except in regard to state and federal tax liens and federal due process requirements. *See Sea Girt*, 625 F. Supp. at 1487-88; *Boss*, 192 A.2d at 586-88.

N.J.S.A. §12A:9-408(c) renders ineffective statutes that restrict security interests in general intangibles. N.J.S.A. §12A:9-102(a)(42) defines "general intangible" to include personal property. But Article 9 of the U.C.C. deliberately does not define the term "personal property." *See* N.J.S.A. §12A:9-408 cmt. 3 (noting that Article 9 does not define personal property).[3] That definition is supplied, in the case of liquor licenses issued in New Jersey, by the ABC Law that expressly and emphatically defines such licenses as "not property." We hold, therefore, that Article 9 of the U.C.C., as amended in New Jersey in 2001, does not include a liquor license as a

---

3. We disagree with United's assertion that a liquor license is a general intangible. (*See* Appellee Br. at 12-13.) A liquor license may be considered a general intangible in other states, but as the Bankruptcy Court noted, "the courts holding that a liquor license is a general intangible did not have a state statute such as [N.J.S.A. §33:1-26] stating that a license is not property." (4-30-04 Op. at 13.) United cites First Pa. Bank, N.A. v. Wildwood Clam Co., 535 F. Supp. 266 (E.D. Pa. 1982), which compared clamming licenses and liquor licenses under New Jersey law. *Wildwood Clam* does not support United's conclusion because in that case the court (1) did not interpret the definition of "general intangible" found in the revised Article 9, and (2) did not find that a New Jersey liquor license was a general intangible that could be subject to a security interest. Id. at 268-69.

general intangible. Accordingly, a liquor license remains unavailable as collateral for a security interest under New Jersey's current statutory scheme. In so holding, we find that N.J.S.A. §12A:9-408(c) is not inconsistent with N.J.S.A. §33:1-26. We find also that N.J.S.A. §12A: 9-408(c) does not override or repeal N.J.S.A. §33:1-26.

United argues that we should "[look] behind the legislative 'labels' to evaluate whether a liquor license is property in a 'functional sense,' " as the court did in *Sea Girt*. (Appellee Br. at 16.) *See Sea Girt*, 625 F. Supp. at 1487-88. The *Sea Girt* court determined that a liquor license possesses attributes similar to property and therefore could be considered property for purposes of federal due process analysis. Id. We do not find a similar functional inquiry to be necessary here. Unlike the court in *Sea Girt*, we are asked to determine whether an allegedly inconsistent statute overrides the legislature's earlier pronouncement that a liquor license is not property. Read in conjunction, N.J.S.A. §33:1-26 and N.J.S.A. §12A:9-408 plainly provide that a liquor license is not property and therefore is not subject to Article 9.

III. Policy

The parties have advanced competing public policy arguments in connection with their opposing positions. Appellants argue that policy concerns support reversing the Bankruptcy Court's order. NJABC argues that it and 525 local license issuing authorities oversee approximately 12,500 licenses and they depend on N.J.S.A. §33:1-26 to prevent undisclosed interests from attaching to liquor licenses, e.g., to prevent criminals or other unregulated parties from infiltrating the alcoholic beverage industry. (Interven. Br. at 22-33.) United argues that the Bankruptcy Court's order will not disrupt the state's regulatory scheme for alcohol control; e.g., an otherwise unqualified person will not be able to obtain a security interest in a license. (Appellee Br. at 18-24.) We will not rely on such policy concerns to contradict the clear direction given by the legislature on this issue. The legislature may determine in the future that policy considerations support allowing third parties to hold security interests in liquor licenses. We merely hold that the legislature did not implement such a policy shift when it enacted the 2001 revisions to U.C.C. Article 9 in New Jersey.

Conclusion

For the reasons stated supra, we will reverse the Bankruptcy Court's order of April 30, 2004. We will issue a separate order and judgment.

NOTES AND QUESTIONS

Professor Thomas H. Jackson, a powerful name in bankruptcy commentaries, has forcefully argued that property restrictions outside of bankruptcy should remain valid in it; *see* Jackson, Statutory Liens and Constructive Trusts in Bankruptcy: Undoing the Confusion, 61 Am. Bankr. L.J. 287 (1987).

In In re Federal Communications Commission, 217 F.3d 125 (2d Cir. 2000), the court allowed the FCC, supposedly acting in its regulatory capacity, to do what most creditors could not do in bankruptcy: cancel a radio license when the licensee failed to make payments to the FCC pursuant to the amount due via the auction at which it procured the license, and then sell the license to others without the approval of the bankruptcy court. Does the concept of taking property with all of its "burdens" create circumstances in which the distributional goals of the Bankruptcy Code are frustrated? Can states enact legislation that will operate to exclude from bankruptcy estates valuable assets?

Another provision of the Bankruptcy Code, however, ultimately trumped the FCC's efforts to reacquire the licenses. The Second Circuit's decision left open the issue of whether the FCC had acted properly within the limits of its regulatory powers. The Supreme Court subsequently held in FCC v. Nextwave Personal Communications, Inc., 537 U.S. 293 (2003), that the FCC had attempted to cancel the leases solely on the basis of the debtor's attempt to obtain bankruptcy relief. Section 525 prohibits such action, and the Court concluded that Nextwave could retain the licenses in its Chapter 11 reorganization.

PROBLEM 3-6

WKRP struggled for a number of years as the No. 6 radio station in a "five-station market." Eventually the owners of the station decided they needed to make drastic changes in its operations. Their decision to switch from soft rock to "all Gregorian chants, all day" did not do the trick, and they filed a Chapter 11 petition. Their plan was to sell their broadcast license to a third party, Imus B. Sterne, Inc. (IBS). IBS was experiencing some difficulty in obtaining licenses because some of its disc jockeys in other cities had run afoul of FCC regulations in their broadcasts. The FCC had denied requests to transfer other radio broadcast licenses to IBS in the recent past, so IBS was willing to pay a premium for WKRP's license if it could side-step the FCC's scrutiny of a transfer. As expected, the FCC has objected to the proposed transfer from WKRP to IBS. IBS has argued that the license is property of the estate and could be transferred to it without FCC approval. Is the license transferrable over the objection of the FCC? *Compare* In re D.H. Overmyer Telecasting Co., Inc., 35 B.R. 400 (Bankr. N.D. Ohio 1984), *with* In re Central Arkansas Broadcasting Co., Inc., 170 B.R. 143 (Bankr. E.D. Ark. 1994).

More frequently, debtors seek to transfer liquor licenses to purchasers. The liquor license often is the only asset of value that can be used to generate money for the estate to satisfy claims. Many states' laws prohibit the transfer of liquor licenses until all delinquent tax liabilities owed to the state are satisfied. Satisfaction of these tax claims prior to the payment of other claims arguably is inconsistent with the distributional provisions of the Bankruptcy Code. Providing for the payment of these taxes in the absence of any lien on the liquor license transforms the taxing authority from an unsecured creditor (with perhaps a priority claim) to a secured creditor without meeting the requirements of providing public notice of any lien on the asset. On the other hand, enforcing the requirement that delinquent taxes be paid as a condition to transfer the license results in a consistent treatment of that claim both outside of bankruptcy and in a bankruptcy case.

I.   Postpetition Earnings from Personal Services

Section 541(a)(6) contains an important exclusion from property of the estate. Under that section, "earnings from services performed by an individual debtor after the commencement of the case" are not property of the bankruptcy estate. This exclusion of postpetition earnings from the estate is an essential component of the debtor's "fresh start." Generally, the debtor receives a discharge of all debts, and the debtor's postpetition earnings are free from the claims of those creditors.

This exclusion from the estate applies only in cases under Chapter 7. In cases, under Chapters 12 and 13, the debtor's postpetition earnings are property of the estate. Bankruptcy Code §§1207(a)(2), 1306(a)(2). In 2005, Congress amended Chapter 11 of the Code to provide that for individual debtors, postpetition earnings also become property of those bankruptcy estates; Bankruptcy Code §1115(a)(2). In Chapter 7 cases in which the debtor is a sole proprietor, the focus would be on whether payments that the debtor will receive after the commencement of the case are truly earnings attributable to prepetition activity of the debtor or result from the efforts of persons other than the debtor. As for debtors who are employees, if the debtor works for two weeks and files a Chapter 7 petition on the day before she is to be paid, she will receive her salary after the commencement of the case. Nevertheless, the payment is for services performed prior to the commencement of the bankruptcy proceeding. Therefore, her paycheck is property of the estate (unless she is able to exempt that asset under §522).

PROBLEM 3-7

Dr. Killdare owns and operates a thriving pediatric clinic. The clinic has five doctors in addition to Dr. Killdare, and more than a thousand patients. The other five physicians are employed by Killdare, and their salaries vary based on the number of patients they see and the total revenue generated by their efforts. Much of the patient base for the clinic derives from Dr. Killdare's reputation in the community, but a significant number of patients have come to the clinic either by referrals to the employee/physicians or through the Yellow Pages and sources other than Dr. Killdare. Total revenue from the clinic annually averages $6,000,000. Of this amount, Dr. Killdare generates $2,000,000 of the billings, while the other physicians generate the remaining $4,000,000. The clinic's operating expenses, including the salaries of the other physicians, are $3,500,000. Thus, Dr. Killdare's income tax return showed an income of $2,500,000.

Although Dr. Killdare was very successful in his medical practice, he was not so fortunate with his investments. His substantial losses from these caused him to file a Chapter 7 petition on March 12. The clinic has continued to operate during the case, and the revenues have continued in the same amounts as prior to the commencement of the case. To that end, the clinic is generating gross revenue of $500,000 per month with expenses (including physician/employee wages) totalling $275,000. Thus, the net monthly profits before any distribution to Dr. Killdare are $225,000. What portion, if any, of this amount is property of the estate? *See* §1115. *See* In re Cooley, 87 B.R. 432 (Bankr. S.D. Tex. 1988); In re Heberman, 122 B.R. 273 (W.D. Tex. 1990); In re Molina Y Vedia, 150 B.R. 393 (Bankr. S.D. Tex. 1992). Why do so many doctors in Texas end up in bankruptcy?

PROBLEM 3-8

Rosemary Forest has worked diligently for 18 years as a salesperson for Digital Controls, Inc. As a part of her job she sells computer software to businesses. She is paid a salary and commission for any sales she makes. She also receives a slightly lesser commission for any contract renewals and software upgrades agreed to by her customers. Furthermore, because Rosemary has been with the company for more than 10 years she is entitled to receive these renewal/upgrade commissions annually for each year she has worked for Digital in excess of 10 years. Consequently, she currently has a right to receive these commissions for 8 more years. These renewals/upgrades are frequently accomplished simply through correspondence from the main office of Digital to the specific customers. In most instances, sales personnel have little or no additional contact with customers, although that is not always the case. Personal financial problems have plagued her in the recent past, and Rosemary files a Chapter 7 bankruptcy petition. Are the commissions that accrue from renewals/upgrades after the commencement of the bankruptcy proceedings property of Rosemary's bankruptcy estate? *Compare* In re Kizis, 238 B.R. 89 (Bankr. M.D. Pa. 1999), *with* In re Rankin, 102 B.R. 439 (Bankr. W.D. Pa. 1989).

II. Limits on Property of the Estate

Section 541(d) of the Bankruptcy Code could be considered unnecessary. Under §541(a)(1), all of the debtor's legal and equitable interests in property become property of the estate. That section does not suggest in any way that something more than the debtor's interest comes into the estate. Nevertheless, §541(d) reminds us that if the debtor holds only legal title to property and has no equitable interest in the property, only the legal interest and not the equitable interest becomes property of the bankruptcy estate. This subsection also gives examples of its application. The debtor may be a mortgagee who holds legal title to the property but has no equitable interest in the property. In that case, the debtor's bankruptcy estate includes the legal title to the property, but it does not include the mortgagor's equitable interest of the real estate. *See, e.g.,* In re Alithicrome Corp., 53 B.R. 906 (Bankr. S.D.N.Y. 1985) (where debtor holds only legal title to property, the estate does not acquire any equitable interest in that property under §541); In re Hillcrest Foods, Inc., 31 B.R. 563 (Bankr. D. Me. 1983) (property held by debtor as trustee is subject to the interest of the trust beneficiaries, who have the burden of proving the existence of the trust and the identity of the property covered by the trust).

The more difficult issue presented by §541(d) is the extent to which its provisions apply to constructive or resulting trusts as compared to express trusts such as mortgages. Constructive and resulting trusts are essentially remedies imposed by courts on wrongdoers or others who have been unjustly enriched. These trusts are created to protect the injured party by establishing a claim in that party's favor in specific property of the debtor. This becomes problematic in bankruptcy because it removes from the estate property that would otherwise be available to satisfy the claims of all creditors on a pro rata basis and allocates it entirely to a specific creditor contrary to the usual bankruptcy distribution scheme.

In re Omegas Group, Inc.
United States Court of Appeals, Sixth Circuit, 1994
16 F.3d 1443

BATCHELDER, Circuit Judge.

Understandably, creditors of bankrupt debtors often feel like restaurant patrons who not only hate the food, but think the portions are too small. To press the analogy, they also don't like having to wait in line for a table, possibly being seated only to find out the kitchen has just closed. The bankruptcy court is a little like a soup kitchen, ladling out whatever is available in ratable portions to those standing in line; nonetheless, scarcity begets innovation in the hungry creditor's quest to get a little more than the next fellow. This case involves just such an effort. The creditor claimed the debtor defrauded it, and argued before the bankruptcy court, with partial success, that money paid to the debtor in the course of a business transaction was held in constructive trust since the debtor knew bankruptcy was imminent but assured the creditor otherwise. The district court agreed with this disposition. Since we hold that the bankruptcy court erred in applying the law of constructive trust to this bankruptcy situation, we reverse.

I.

While the parties do not generally dispute the underlying facts of this case, they do characterize them quite differently. Both parties, XL/Datacomp (Datacomp) and debtor Omegas (Debtor or Omegas) were "industry remarketers" (IRs) of "midrange" IBM computers. The companies had "IR contracts" with IBM that enabled them to purchase IBM hardware at a discount, custom-tailor software for an individual purchaser, and then sell the "value-added" system to the retail purchaser.

In early 1990, the two companies entered into a course of business dealings that Datacomp describes as a "unique relationship" and a "type of joint venture" and which the Debtor describes as a "clandestine relationship." Both parties agree that Omegas agreed to act as a middleman of sorts, ordering IBMs on behalf of Datacomp, taking a percentage down payment, ordering the computers, then taking the rest of the payment and sending full payment to IBM at the time of delivery. According to the Debtor, in early 1990, IBM paid Datacomp $8 million to terminate its IR agreement and sign on to a new IR agreement, which would eliminate the "competitive advantage which existed between the IRs and IBM's regular sales force." In order to come up with a new source of competitively priced IBMs, the Debtor explains, Datacomp approached Omegas (as well as other IRs still operating under the old IR agreements) and proposed that Omegas supply Datacomp with new IBM computers in exchange for a 4 percent of gross price commission. IBM would not know of this arrangement. Indeed, the Debtor claims that since Datacomp, as the purchaser from Omegas, the IR, would not be the "end-user" of the computers, this deal violated Omegas's IR agreement with IBM; for this reason, the Debtor points out, most of the transaction was arranged orally.

According to Datacomp, Omegas initially proposed this arrangement with Datacomp as a means to save itself from financial ruin. Datacomp explains that due to a misappropriation of funds within Omegas, Omegas owed IBM Credit Corp. (ICC) over $1.8 million. ICC declared the credit line to be in default on April 27, 1990. Omegas arranged a repayment schedule with ICC, but had to increase its volume of computer sales in order to make the payments. However, Omegas's order backlog with IBM had reached the limit IBM permitted it, some $1.5 million.

Datacomp stresses that while Omegas was initiating this deal with Datacomp, it at no time disclosed to Datacomp any of these goings-on with ICC. Datacomp describes Omegas's relationship to it as "fiduciary," with Datacomp relying on Omegas's trustworthiness and on the truth of its representations. The problems arose, Datacomp argues, because of Omegas's inability to convince IBM to lift or extend the firm ceiling on Omegas's credit line with ICC; without such an extension, Omegas could not process the orders Datacomp had placed. Omegas claims that ICC orally promised it a credit increase to $15 million at the time repayment was arranged, and that the Omegas principals/shareholders signed personal guarantees covering the $15 million credit line.

Between August 6 and 15, 1990, Datacomp sent Omegas orders for new IBM computers and down payments totalling $259,137. On August 29, Omegas sent Datacomp invoices totalling $618,759; Datacomp sent Omegas $587,763 by September 10. Shortly thereafter, Datacomp sent Omegas the balance due on the computers it had ordered; the total it paid reached $1,149,042. On September 12, Omegas's President, Jeffery Sanford, ordered the termination of all payments to IBM for computers on order. On September 19, representatives from the two companies met in Chicago; at the meeting Omegas informed Datacomp of its "financial problems," and that Omegas was considering the option of filing bankruptcy. At the meeting, Omegas suggested that Datacomp lend it $1.6 million, which loan would, according to Omegas, "remove the prospects of bankruptcy . . . and allow [it] to fulfill its contractual agreements with Datacomp." Datacomp describes this suggestion as being more of a demand: "Omegas was holding Datacomp's funds and would not pay IBM unless Datacomp loaned Omegas [the money]."

After the meeting, Datacomp's counsel sent Omegas a letter accusing Omegas of fraud and demanding the return of the money already paid. On October 15, without Datacomp's knowledge or consent, Omegas requested that IBM cancel all deliveries. Omegas claims that this cancellation was necessary to render IBM's 5 percent cancellation fee a prepetition debt. Omegas filed bankruptcy on October 16, 1990. Datacomp filed its complaint in this adversary proceeding in the bankruptcy court on October 26, 1990, seeking to recover the $1.1 million it paid Omegas by arguing that Omegas's fraud rendered all money it received pursuant to the deal subject to a constructive trust in Datacomp's favor, and thus not part of the bankruptcy estate, citing 11 U.S.C. §541(d).

After an expedited bench trial, the bankruptcy court held that Datacomp could recover $302,142 as held in a constructive trust by Omegas. In short, the bankruptcy court found that Datacomp entered into the agreement described above with Omegas, establishing a relationship which it characterized as "in a sense a joint venture," and that, while Omegas was having some difficulty sorting out its credit line with IBM, things went more or less according to plan for a while. The court found, however, that on September 12, 1990, Jeffery Sanford, the president of Omegas, "realized he was in serious financial straits with IBM" and that Omegas would not be able to complete the deal. The court found that "on September 12, [sic] 13th and/or 14th," Sanford terminated all further payments to IBM, but that after those dates Omegas continued to invoice Datacomp for the computers on order, and deposited a Datacomp check on September 17th. The court concluded that on September 12, "Sanford realized that Omegas was not going to be able to operate in its ordinary course of business with regard to its dealings with Datacomp," and that this development gave rise to an affirmative "duty to disclose its financial problems to Datacomp." The court therefore imposed a constructive trust on "all funds received [by Omegas] after September 12."

Datacomp moved to amend the judgment to recover the full amount it had paid; the court denied this motion on February 13, 1991. The parties cross-appealed, the debtor seeking reversal and Datacomp continuing to argue that the entire amount paid should be included in the constructive trust and excluded from the Debtor's estate. The district court affirmed on June 16, 1992. . . .

III.

A.

The bankruptcy court's disposition of Datacomp's action, and the district court's affirmance, left no one satisfied. On appeal, Datacomp defends the judgment of the bankruptcy court, but argues that the court should have imposed the constructive trust on the entire amount of funds it tendered to Omegas prior to Omegas's filing for bankruptcy. Under Kentucky law, Datacomp contends, money "wrongfully" appropriated from an innocent party does not become the property of the recipient, but is considered to be held in constructive trust for the benefit of the aggrieved party. Datacomp maintains that it did not have merely a debtor/creditor relationship with Omegas, but a joint venture arrangement that imposed fiduciary duties on Omegas, which Omegas breached. From the start, Omegas misrepresented its financial state and its ability to provide Datacomp with the computers it wanted; as its situation worsened and IBM made it crystal clear that no more computers would be forthcoming, Datacomp asserts, Omegas made no effort to inform Datacomp of the impending disaster, knowing all the while that Datacomp would continue in good faith to send its checks on time. Datacomp points out that the Bankruptcy Code provides that "[p]roperty in which the debtor holds . . . only legal title and not an equitable interest . . . becomes property of the estate . . . only to the extent of the debtor's legal title to such property, but not to the extent of any equitable interest in such property that the debtor does not hold." 11 U.S.C. §541(d). Datacomp argues that since by definition it has an equity interest in any funds held by Omegas in constructive trust, these funds are properly designated as remaining outside the bankrupt estate, and should therefore be returned to Datacomp rather than being incorporated into the estate and divided amongst the creditors.

Omegas, on the other hand, thinks its situation prior to bankruptcy was no different from that of the typical business threatened with insolvency. As Omegas tells the tale, its principals thought the deal with Datacomp would pull it out of financial danger. While the numbers seemed to work as the companies put the deal together, problems arose with getting IBM to process delivery of the computers Omegas ordered on behalf of Datacomp, and IBM Credit ultimately refused to permit Omegas to increase its credit line so this could be accomplished. By the time its principals recognized that Omegas was sinking faster than they could bail, Omegas could not return Datacomp's money or take other action to avoid immediate loss to its other creditors due to the Bankruptcy Code's prohibition of preferential transfers immediately prior to filing for bankruptcy. Omegas denies that its principals committed fraud on Datacomp; instead, it maintains that all its people did was to try, in good faith, to salvage the deal until the last possible moment, and only then take prudent measures, as advised by counsel, to prepare for bankruptcy. To characterize this as fraud giving rise to a constructive trust, Omegas argues, does not comport with the Bankruptcy Code's system of equitable and orderly distribution of the debtor's assets; Omegas claims that Datacomp is not materially different from any other disappointed creditor.

Omegas also argues that the fishy nature of Datacomp's attempt to keep getting IBM computers at a favorable rate through Omegas's still-valid IR agreement renders Datacomp's hands "unclean," thus preventing it from seeking the equitable remedy of constructive trust. Datacomp also knew about the straits Omegas was in, the Debtor contends; Datacomp took advantage of this knowledge in getting Omegas to agree to this "clandestine relationship," but also knowingly assumed the obvious risk that Omegas might fold before the deal was done.

B.

Nowhere in the Bankruptcy Code does it say, "property held by the debtor subject to a constructive trust is excluded from the debtor's estate." Title 11 U.S.C. §541 defines the estate in bankruptcy broadly, including "all legal or equitable interests of the debtor in property as of the commencement of the case," §541(a)(1), and "any interest in property preserved for the benefit of or ordered transferred to the estate under [the trustee's "strong-arm" or "avoiding" powers as provided in] section 510(c) or 551 of this title," §541(a)(4). However, §541(d) provides that

> [p]roperty in which the debtor holds, as of the commencement of the case, only legal title and not an equitable interest, such as a mortgage secured by real property . . . becomes property of the estate under subsection (a)(1) or (2) of this section only to the extent of the debtor's legal title to such property, but not to the extent of any equitable interest in such property that the debtor does not hold.

Courts, including the bankruptcy court in this case, which have excluded property from a debtor's estate as being subject to constructive trust, have done so on the authority of §541(d), usually over the protestations of trustees asserting their strongarm powers.

For example, in Vineyard v. McKenzie (In re Quality Holstein Leasing), 752 F.2d 1009 (5th Cir. 1985), Clayton McKenzie, the president and whole owner of a company, Quality Holstein Leasing (QHL), bought a private airplane, arranging the financing through Borg-Warner. McKenzie registered the plane in his own name. After two years, he decided he wanted a new plane, so he traded in the old one. Borg-Warner arranged to transfer its security interest to the new aircraft, but apparently botched this effort. By the time Borg-Warner got its act together, McKenzie had transferred title of the new plane to QHL, and QHL had filed for Chapter 11 reorganization.

When QHL's bankruptcy trustee sought to sell the plane, Borg-Warner informed the court that it had the right to recoup the value of its original lien from the sale proceeds. It argued that either McKenzie or QHL had defrauded it, and that therefore under applicable state law the new plane was subject to a constructive trust. Assets held in constructive trust, Borg-Warner argued, did not become incorporated into the debtor's estate. The *Quality Holstein Leasing* court ultimately held in favor of the trustee, since Borg-Warner could properly assert no rights to the aircraft or proceeds of its sale based on QHL's having defrauded McKenzie, a bizarre allegation the court was forced to deduce from the rather disorganized contentions put forth by Borg-Warner. "[A]ny fraud by QHL upon McKenzie conferred on Borg-Warner no [additional] rights." Id. at 1015.

In discussing Borg-Warner's constructive trust argument, the *Quality Holstein Leasing* court observed a conflict between the trustee's strongarm powers under 11 U.S.C. §544, and §541(d)'s exclusion of "equitable interest[s]" in the debtor's property from the debtor's estate. Id. at 1012. The court noted that a constructive trust is one such "equitable interest," and that under §541(d) constructive trusts are generally held to be superior in interest to the trustee, strongarm powers notwithstanding. Id. at 1013 ("Congress did not mean to authorize a bankruptcy estate to benefit from property that the debtor did not own."). The court "found" that the bankruptcy and district courts "erred in concluding that section 544 empowers a bankruptcy trustee to retain for the benefit of the estate property that the debtor obtained by fraud and upon which state law has imposed a valid constructive trust." Id. at 1015.

The problem with the Fifth Circuit's analysis in *Quality Holstein Leasing,* and with the analyses of the vast majority of courts that have addressed bankruptcy claims based on constructive trust, is that a constructive trust is not really a trust. A constructive trust is a legal fiction, a common-law remedy in equity that may only exist by the grace of judicial action. As Professor Sherwin writes,

> [t]he constructive trust remedy developed in equity, by analogy to the express trust arrangements in which one person holds legal title to property for the benefit of another. The same concept of separate legal and beneficial interests in property suggested a remedy for unjust enrichment: if, under principles of unjust enrichment, the defendant holds title to property that ought to belong to the plaintiff, the court will treat the defendant as a trustee, holding title for the plaintiff's benefit. At that point, however, the analogy to an express trust ends. The result of a constructive trust is a judicial decree ordering the defendant to convey the property to the plaintiff. . . . A constructive trust is merely a means by which the court can say that the defendant must relinquish to the plaintiff property that represents an unjust enrichment.

[Sherwin, Constructive Trusts in Bankruptcy, 1989 U. Ill. L. Rev. 297] at 301. The distribution of assets in a bankruptcy case is based on an identification of what assets and liabilities the debtor has "as of the commencement of the case," this being the exact moment the debtor files. Shirkey v. Leake, 715 F.2d 859, 863 (4th Cir. 1983). A debtor that served prior to bankruptcy as trustee of an express trust generally has no right to the assets kept in trust, and the trustee in bankruptcy must fork them over to the beneficiary. However, a claim filed in bankruptcy court asserting rights to certain assets "held" in "constructive trust" for the claimant is nothing more than that: a claim. Unless a court has already impressed a constructive trust upon certain assets or a legislature has created a specific statutory right to have particular kinds of funds held as if in trust, the claimant cannot properly represent to the bankruptcy court that he was, at the time of the commencement of the case, a beneficiary of a constructive trust held by the debtor.

Thus, the essence of the argument put forth by Borg-Warner and similarly situated claimants goes as follows: "Judge, due to debtor's fraud (or whatever), our property rights as beneficiaries of the constructive trust arose prepetition. Therefore, we stand not in the position of unsecured creditors, nor even equal to the trustee in the position of judgment creditors, but as the rightful owner of the res held in trust. Oh, and by the way, would you mind conferring on us these ownership rights and declaring that they arose prepetition?" This may seem silly phrased in this manner, but it is exactly the argument that most courts have accepted in holding that, due to some prepetition breach or bad act by the debtor, the claimed property or money is subject to a constructive trust and therefore "did not come into the bankruptcy estate and must be returned to the [debtor]." Sommer v. Vermont Real Estate Inv. Trust (In re Vermont Real Estate Inv. Trust), 25 B.R. 813, 817 (Bankr. D. Vt. 1982); *see also* City Natl. Bank of Miami v. General Coffee Corp. (In re General Coffee Corp.), 828 F.2d 699, 704 (11th Cir. 1987) ("[W]e agree with the district court that the constructive trust in favor of [claimant] came into existence before the bankruptcy proceedings began.").

Datacomp points out, correctly, that property rights in bankruptcy are determined only by reference to the state law of the jurisdiction. Datacomp further claims that under Kentucky law, Omegas's alleged fraud would give rise to a constructive trust imposed over all the money Omegas took unlawfully from Datacomp. What Datacomp, the bankruptcy court, the district court, and a number of other courts have failed to consider is that just because something is so under state law does not necessarily make it so under the Bankruptcy Code. As this court has previously noted, "[w]hile the nature and extent of the debtor's interest are determined by state law[,] 'once that determination is made, federal bankruptcy law dictates to what extent that interest is property of the estate.'" Bavely v. IRS (In re Terwilliger's Catering Plus, Inc.), 911 F.2d 1168, 1172 (6th Cir. 1990) (quoting N.S. Garrott & Sons v. Union Planters Natl. Bank of Memphis (In re N.S. Garrott & Sons), 772 F.2d 462, 466 (8th Cir. 1985)). Ultimately, "state law must be applied in a manner consistent with federal bankruptcy law." Torres v. Eastlick (In re North American Coin & Currency, Ltd.), 767 F.2d 1573, 1575 (9th Cir. 1985).

We cannot find a more succinct manner of making our point than did Judge Aspen of the Northern District of Illinois: "[A] constructive trust is fundamentally at odds with the general goals of the Bankruptcy Code." The Oxford Organisation, Ltd. v. Peterson (In re Stotler and Co.), 144 B.R. 385, 388 (1992). Quoting a Texas opinion, the judge explained:

> The reluctance of Bankruptcy Courts to impose constructive trusts without a substantial reason to do so stems from the recognition that each unsecured creditor desires to have his particular claim elevated above the others. Imposition of a constructive trust clearly thwarts the policy of ratable distribution and should not be impressed cavalierly.

Stotler, 144 B.R. at 388 (quoting Neochem Corp. v. Behring Intl., Inc. (In re Behring Intl., Inc.), 61 B.R. 896, 902 (Bankr. N.D. Tex. 1986)). We now see and raise Judge Aspen. We think that §541(d) simply does not permit a claimant in the position of Datacomp to persuade the bankruptcy court to impose the remedy of constructive trust for alleged fraud committed against it by the debtor in the course of their business dealings, and thus to take ahead of all creditors, and indeed, ahead of the trustee. Because a constructive trust, unlike an express trust, is a remedy, it does not exist until a plaintiff obtains a judicial decision finding him to be entitled to a judgment "impressing" defendant's property or assets with a constructive trust. Therefore, a creditor's claim of entitlement to a constructive trust is not an "equitable interest" in the debtor's estate existing prepetition, excluded from the estate under §541(d).

We do not address here property already impressed with a constructive trust by a court in a separate proceeding prepetition, in which case the claimant would be entitled to priority (although not superpriority to the trustee) as a secured creditor by virtue of the judgment. *See* 11 U.S.C. §506. Nor do we address property that a state by statute has declared to be held in trust for particular purposes, such as builders' trust funds created by statute in many states to remedy specific problems in the construction industry. *See* Selby v. Ford Motor Co., 590 F.2d 642 (6th Cir. 1979). We recognize that there is dicta in *Selby* noting that various courts have held that "[i]n the absence of statute . . . construction funds in the hands of a contractor are held subject to a constructive trust or an equitable assignment or an equitable lien." Id. at 648. However, the specific issue in *Selby* was how to treat a statutory state builders' trust under the Bankruptcy Act, and the cases cited to support the more general proposition that a constructive trust could be imposed in the absence of a state builders' statute are unique to the construction industry. The *Selby* case, and the cases cited therein, are limited in application to the specific exigencies of the construction industry.

Datacomp claims that Omegas defrauded it. If that be the case, then the Code already provides a remedy. The Code specifically excepts from discharge "any debt . . . for money, property, services, or an extension, renewal, or refinancing of credit, to the extent obtained by . . . false pretenses, a false representation, or actual fraud," 11 U.S.C. §523(a)(2)(A), as well as "any debt . . . for fraud or defalcation while acting in a fiduciary capacity, embezzlement, or larceny," id. §523(a)(4), and "any debt . . . for willful and malicious injury by the debtor to another entity or to the property of another entity," id. §523(a)(6). The purpose of §523(a)(2)(A), according to the leading treatise, is "to prevent the bankrupt from retaining the benefits of property acquired by fraudulent means." 3 Collier on Bankruptcy ¶523.08[1], at 523-46 (quoting Rudstrom v. Sheridan, 122 Minn. 262, 142 N.W. 313 (1913)). Section 523(a)(4) disallows the debtor from escaping liability for property it obtained through actual fraud, viz., "misrepresentation, falsehood, trick or deceit," or through "defalcation," which is "broader than 'embezzlement' and probably broader than 'misappropriation.' " Id. P 523.14[1][a-b], at pp.523-102-03. And §523(a)(6) preserves liability for debts resulting from the debtor's intentional torts, such as conversion, where the "wrongful act . . . necessarily produces harm and is without just cause or excuse." Id. at P 523.16[1].

So why would a creditor who thinks the debtor has defrauded him bother to base his claim on constructive trust? The answer is simple:

> it is harder to prevail by arguing that a debt is nondischargeable. For example, to prove an exception under §523(a)(2)(A), the creditor must prove that the debtor obtained money through a material misrepresentation that at the time the debtor knew was false or made with gross recklessness as to its truth. The creditor must also prove the debtor's intent to deceive. Moreover, the creditor must prove that it reasonably relied on the false representation and that its reliance was the proximate cause of loss.

In re Phillips, 804 F.2d 930, 932 (6th Cir. 1986). Although the creditor need only prove his reliance by a preponderance of the evidence, Grogan v. Garner, 498 U.S. 279, 111 S. Ct. 654, 112 L. Ed. 2d 755 (1991), the bankruptcy court must construe all exceptions to discharge "strictly," with the benefit of any doubt going to the debtor. In re Ward, 857 F.2d 1082, 1083 (6th Cir. 1988). A second, and certainly more compelling reason to avoid pursuing a claim under §523, is that the creditor who prevails in proving his debt to be nondischargeable comes away from the bankruptcy proceeding with only his debt intact; he has no more assurance than he did prepetition that the debtor, having reorganized or otherwise received its "fresh start," will ever pay him back. On the other hand, if the creditor successfully argues that he "owns" the money or property owed him since the debtor's fraud gave rise to a constructive trust, the creditor walks away with his debt fully satisfied, leaving the rest of the creditors to squabble over the remnants.

C.

The equities of bankruptcy are not the equities of the common law. Constructive trusts are anathema to the equities of bankruptcy since they take from the estate, and thus directly from competing creditors, not from the offending debtor. "Ratable distribution among all creditors" justifies the Code's placement of the trustee in the position of a first-in-line judgment creditor and bona fide purchaser for value, empowered to avoid certain competing interests (and even to nullify the debtor's "preferential" prepetition payments to otherwise entitled creditors) so as to maximize the value of the estate. To a party defrauded by the debtor, incorporating the proceeds of fraud in the debtor's estate may seem like allowing the "state to benefit from property that the debtor did not own." *Quality Holstein Leasing,* 752 F.2d at 1013. But as the Seventh Circuit has pointed out, "allowing the estate to 'benefit from property that the debtor did not own' is exactly what the strong-arm powers are about: they give the trustee the status of a bona fide purchaser for value, so that the estate contains interests to which the debtor lacked good title." Belisle v. Plunkett, 877 F.2d 512, 516 (7th Cir. 1989) (criticizing *Quality Holstein Leasing*). The Code recognizes that each creditor has suffered disappointed expectations at the hands of the debtor; for this reason, it makes maximization of the estate the primary concern and entitlement to shares of the estate secondary. Imposing a constructive trust on the debtor's estate impermissibly subordinates this primary concern to a single claim of entitlement.

Bankruptcy courts have believed themselves justified in imposing constructive trusts and ladling out portions of debtors' estates' assets because they are traditionally "courts of equity." *See, e.g., Quality Holstein Leasing,* 752 F.2d at 1012. However, "whatever equitable powers remain in the bankruptcy courts must and can only be exercised within the confines of the Bankruptcy Code." Norwest Bank Worthington v. Ahlers, 485 U.S. 197, 206, 108 S. Ct. 963, 969, 99 L. Ed. 2d 169 (1988); *see also* Childress v. Middleton Arms, L.P. (In re Middleton Arms, L.P.), 934 F.2d 723, 725 (6th Cir. 1991) (bankruptcy court's equitable powers "may only be used in furtherance of the goals of the Code"). As the Ninth Circuit noted in In re North American Coin & Currency, Ltd.:

> [w]e necessarily act very cautiously in exercising such a relatively undefined equitable power in favor of one group of potential creditors at the expense of other creditors, for ratable distribution among all creditors is one of the strongest policies behind the bankruptcy laws.

767 F.2d 1573, 1575 (1985). As we have endeavored to explain, §523 of the Code specifically provides the remedy of declaring nondischargeable debts arising from various types of fraud and deceit committed by the debtor. The Code endows the

trustee with generous powers to bring property of imperfect title or disputed ownership into the debtor's estate for distribution according to each creditor's ability to
prove its entitlement and priority in accordance with the dictates of the Code. To
permit a creditor, no matter how badly he was "had" by the debtor, to lop off a piece
of the estate under a constructive trust theory is to permit that creditor to circumvent
completely the Code's equitable system of distribution.

IV.

In light of these provisions and in light of the overall purposes of the Code,
§541(d) cannot properly be invoked as an equitable panacea whenever the bankruptcy
court thinks a claimant has been particularly burdened by a debtor's bad faith or bad
acts. Since the bankruptcy court here erred in doing so, the judgment of the district
court affirming the bankruptcy court's judgment is REVERSED.

PROBLEM 3-9

After months of sickness, it became clear that Mrs. Shoe would not live much
longer. She had two daughters: Mazie, who lived with her and had cared for her during
her illness, and Wanda, who had run away from home at age 16 and become an actor.
Mrs. Shoe's most valuable asset was a diamond necklace worth $300,000 that she
kept in a box under her pillow. Hearing that her mother was dying, and knowing about
the necklace, Wanda returned home one day when Mazie was out and went into her
mother's bedroom. Mrs. Shoe, now blind and quite hard of hearing, thought that
Wanda was Mazie, particularly because Wanda imitated Mazie's voice. Wanda
was very pleased when her mother gave her the necklace, and she got out of
there with it fast. The next day the mother and Mazie figured out what had happened,
and tracked Wanda down in her home in Los Angeles. Before they could take legal
action to retrieve the necklace, Wanda filed a bankruptcy petition. Is the necklace
property of the estate?

PROBLEM 3-10

For her sixteenth birthday Beth's grandparents bought her a car. They kept the title to
the car in their name, but it was truly Beth's car. When the first insurance premium came
due, however, the grandparents decided to look into some way to reduce the cost of the
insurance. They found out that if one of Beth's parents held title to the car, they could
include her in the "household" policy at a much lower rate than could be obtained if the
car were still titled in the grandparents' names. So title to the car was transferred from the
grandparents to their daughter, Beth's mother. Unfortunately, unrelated financial problems followed this transfer, and Beth's mother is now in bankruptcy. The trustee has
claimed the car as property of the estate, and the debtor, Beth, and the grandparents all
assert that the debtor holds the title in trust for Beth. Is this property excluded from the
estate under §541(d)? In re Smith, 73 B.R. 211 (Bankr. M.D. Fla. 1986). Would it make

any difference if the debtor had used the car as collateral for a loan? Tucker v. Jim's Pawn & Jewelry (In re Tucker) 181 B.R. 595 (Bankr. N.D. Ala. 1995).

III.   Exclusions from Property of the Estate

Certainly, Congress was most interested in expanding the concept of property of the estate in its enactment of the Bankruptcy Code in 1978. Nonetheless, it recognized that some types of property should be excluded from the estate. These exclusions are set out in §541(b) and (c). Among the more significant exclusions are powers that the debtor may exercise only for the benefit of another entity (for example, a power of appointment granted to the debtor by a testator's will), and any interest that a debtor may have as a lessee of a nonresidential lease that was properly terminated prior to the filing of the bankruptcy case. *See, e.g.*, In re Egyptian Bros. Donut, Inc., 190 B.R. 26 (D.N.J. 1995); Bear Valley Mutual Water Co. v. Prestige Point (In re Prestige Point), 113 B.R. 643 (Bankr. C.D. Cal. 1990).

While Congress viewed these items as appropriately excluded from the estate, it also recognized that parties may attempt to avoid the generally broad reach of §541(a)(1) by drafting provisions that would limit the access of a debtor's creditors to the property. Consequently, §541(c)(1) provides that these efforts to shelter property from becoming property of the estate will generally be ineffective. Nevertheless, §541(c)(2) provides that "a restriction on the transfer of a beneficial interest of the debtor in a trust that is enforceable under applicable nonbankruptcy law is enforceable in a (bankruptcy) case." The legislative history of the Bankruptcy Code notes that this provision will operate to exclude from the estate a debtor's beneficial interest in a spendthrift trust to the extent that those interests are beyond the reach of creditors under state law. H.R. Rep. No. 595, 95th Cong., 1st Sess. 369 (1977); S. Rep. No. 989, 95th Cong., 2d Sess. 83 (1978). A "spendthrift trust" is one created in such a fashion that neither the beneficiary of the trust nor his/her creditors can reach the property in the trust until distributions are made to the beneficiary (thus keeping so-called "spendthrifts" from dissipating their inheritances). Once the trustee hands the money over to the beneficiary, however, the trust's protection ceases and the beneficiary's creditors are free to try and realize on this new asset. *See* II Scott on Trusts §§151, 152.5 (W. Fratcher 1987). As you can see from the following case, however, the exclusion from property of the estate under §541(c)(2) reaches considerably more than just debtors' beneficial interests in spendthrift trusts.

Patterson v. Shumate
United States Supreme Court, 1992
504 U.S. 753

Justice BLACKMUN delivered the opinion of the Court.

The Bankruptcy Code excludes from the bankruptcy estate property of the debtor that is subject to a restriction on transfer enforceable under "applicable nonbankruptcy law." 11 U.S.C. §541(c)(2). We must decide in this case whether an anti-alienation provision contained in an ERISA-qualified pension plan constitutes a restriction on transfer enforceable under "applicable nonbankruptcy law," and whether, accordingly, a debtor may exclude his interest in such a plan from the property of the bankruptcy estate.

I.

Respondent Joseph B. Shumate, Jr., was employed for over 30 years by Coleman Furniture Corporation, where he ultimately attained the position of president and chairman of the board of directors. Shumate and approximately 400 other employees were participants in the Coleman Furniture Corporation Pension Plan (Plan). The Plan satisfied all applicable requirements of the Employee Retirement Income Security Act of 1974 (ERISA) and qualified for favorable tax treatment under the Internal Revenue Code. In particular, Article 16.1 of the Plan contained the anti-alienation provision required for qualification under §206(d)(1) of ERISA, 29 U.S.C. §1056(d)(1) ("Each pension plan shall provide that benefits provided under the plan may not be assigned or alienated"). App. 342. Shumate's interest in the plan was valued at $250,000. App. 93-94. In 1982, Coleman Furniture filed a petition for bankruptcy under Chapter 11 of the Bankruptcy Code. The case was converted to a Chapter 7 proceeding and a trustee, Roy V. Creasy, was appointed. Shumate himself encountered financial difficulties and filed a petition for bankruptcy in 1984. His case, too, was converted to a Chapter 7 proceeding, and petitioner John R. Patterson was appointed trustee.

Creasy terminated and liquidated the Plan, providing full distributions to all participants except Shumate. Patterson then filed an adversary proceeding against Creasy in the Bankruptcy Court for the Western District of Virginia to recover Shumate's interest in the Plan for the benefit of Shumate's bankruptcy estate. Shumate in turn asked the United States District Court for the Western District of Virginia, which already had jurisdiction over a related proceeding, to compel Creasy to pay Shumate's interest in the Plan directly to him. The bankruptcy proceeding subsequently was consolidated with the district court action. App. to Pet. for Cert. 53a-54a. The District Court rejected Shumate's contention that his interest in the Plan should be excluded from his bankruptcy estate. The court held that §541(c)(2)'s reference to "nonbankruptcy law" embraced only state law, not federal law such as ERISA. Creasy v. Coleman Furniture Corp., 83 B.R. 404, 406 (1988). Applying Virginia law, the court held that Shumate's interest in the Plan did not qualify for protection as a spendthrift trust. Id., at 406-409. The District Court also rejected Shumate's alternative argument that even if his interest in the Plan could not be excluded from the bankruptcy estate under §541(c)(2), he was entitled to an exemption under 11 U.S.C. §522(b)(2)(A), which allows a debtor to exempt from property of the estate "any property that is exempt under Federal law." Id., at 409-410. The District Court ordered Creasy to pay Shumate's interest in the Plan over to his bankruptcy estate. App. to Pet. for Cert. 54a-55a. The Court of Appeals for the Fourth

Circuit reversed. 943 F.2d 362 (1991). The court relied on its earlier decision in Anderson v. Raine (In re Moore), 907 F.2d 1476 (1990), in which another Fourth Circuit panel was described as holding, subsequent to the District Court's decision in the instant case, that "ERISA-qualified plans, which by definition have a non-alienation provision, constitute 'applicable nonbankruptcy law' and contain enforceable restrictions on the transfer of pension interests." 943 F.2d, at 365. Thus, the Court of Appeals held that Shumate's interest in the Plan should be excluded from the bankruptcy estate under §541(c)(2). Ibid. The court then declined to consider Shumate's alternative argument that his interest in the Plan qualified for exemption under §522(b). Id., at 365-366.

We granted certiorari, ____ U.S. ____, 112 S. Ct. 932, 117 L. Ed. 2d 104 (1992), to resolve the conflict among the Courts of Appeals as to whether an anti-alienation provision in an ERISA-qualified pension plan constitutes a restriction on transfer enforceable under "applicable nonbankruptcy law" for purposes of the §541(c)(2) exclusion of property from the debtor's bankruptcy estate.

II.

A.

In our view, the plain language of the Bankruptcy Code and ERISA is our determinant. *See* Toibb v. Radloff, 501 U.S. ____, ____, 111 S. Ct. 2197, 2199, 115 L. Ed. 2d 145 (1991). Section 541(c)(2) provides the following exclusion from the otherwise broad definition of "property of the estate" contained in §541(a)(1) of the Code: "A restriction on the transfer of a beneficial interest of the debtor in a trust that is enforceable under *applicable nonbankruptcy law* is enforceable in a case under this title." (Emphasis added).

The natural reading of the provision entitles a debtor to exclude from property of the estate any interest in a plan or trust that contains a transfer restriction enforceable under any relevant nonbankruptcy law. Nothing in §541 suggests that the phrase "applicable nonbankruptcy law" refers, as petitioner contends, exclusively to *state* law. The text contains no limitation on "applicable nonbankruptcy law" relating to the source of the law.

Reading the term "applicable nonbankruptcy law" in §541(c)(2) to include federal as well as state law comports with other references in the Bankruptcy Code to sources of law. The Code reveals, significantly, that Congress, when it desired to do so, knew how to restrict the scope of applicable law to "state law" and did so with some frequency. *See, e.g.*, 11 U.S.C. §109(c)(2) (entity may be a debtor under chapter 9 if authorized "by State law"); 11 U.S.C. §522(b)(1) (election of exemptions controlled by "the State law that is applicable to the debtor"); 11 U.S.C. §523(a)(5) (a debt for alimony, maintenance, or support determined "in accordance with State or territorial law" is not dischargeable); 11 U.S.C. §903(1) ("a State law prescribing a method of composition of indebtedness" of municipalities is not binding on nonconsenting creditors); *see also* 11 U.S.C. §§362(b)(12) and 1145(a).

Congress' decision to use the broader phrase "applicable nonbankruptcy law" in §541(c)(2) strongly suggests that it did not intend to restrict the provision in the manner that petitioner contends.[4]

The text of §541(c)(2) does not support petitioner's contention that "applicable nonbankruptcy law" is limited to state law. Plainly read, the provision encompasses any relevant nonbankruptcy law, including federal law such as ERISA. We must enforce the statute according to its terms. *See* United States v. Ron Pair Enterprises, Inc., 489 U.S. 235, 241, 109 S. Ct. 1026, 1030, 103 L. Ed. 2d 290 (1989).

B.

Having concluded that "applicable nonbankruptcy law" is not limited to state law, we next determine whether the anti-alienation provision contained in the ERISA-qualified plan at issue here satisfies the literal terms of §541(c)(2). Section 206(d)(1) of ERISA, which states that "[e]ach pension plan shall provide that benefits provided under the plan may not be assigned or alienated," 29 U.S.C. §1056(d)(1), clearly imposes a "restriction on the transfer" of a debtor's "beneficial interest" in the trust. The coordinate section of the Internal Revenue Code, 26 U.S.C. §401(a)(13), states as a general rule that "[a] trust shall not constitute a qualified trust under this section unless the plan of which such trust is a part provides that benefits provided under the plan may not be assigned or alienated," and thus contains similar restrictions. *See also* 26 CFR 1.401(a)-13(b)(1) (1991). Coleman Furniture's pension plan complied with these requirements. Article 16.1 of the Plan specifically stated: "No benefit, right or interest" of any participant "shall be subject to anticipation, alienation, sale, transfer, assignment, pledge, encumbrance or charge, seizure, attachment or other legal, equitable or other process." App. 342. Moreover, these transfer restrictions are "enforceable," as required by §541(c)(2). Plan trustees or fiduciaries are required under ERISA to discharge their duties "in accordance with the documents and instruments governing the plan." 29 U.S.C. §1104(a)(1)(D). A plan participant, beneficiary, or fiduciary, or the Secretary of Labor may file a civil action to "enjoin any act or practice" which violates ERISA or the terms of the plan. 29 U.S.C. §§1132(a)(3)

---

4. The phrase "applicable nonbankruptcy law" appears elsewhere in the Code, and courts have construed those references to include federal law.

See, e.g., 11 U.S.C. §1125(d) (adequacy of disclosure statement not governed by any "otherwise applicable nonbankruptcy law"); In re The Stanley Hotel, Inc., 13 B.R. 926, 931 (Bkrtcy. Ct. D. Colo. 1981) (§1125(d) includes federal securities law); 11 U.S.C. §108(a) (referring to statute of limitations fixed by "applicable nonbankruptcy law"); In re Ahead By a Length, Inc., 100 B.R. 157, 162-163 (Bkrtcy. Ct. SDNY 1989) (§108(a) includes Racketeer Influenced and Corrupt Organizations Act); Motor Carrier Audit & Collection Co. v. Lighting Products, Inc., 113 B.R. 424, 425-426 (N.D. Ill. 1989) (§108(a) includes Interstate Commerce Act); 11 U.S.C. §108(b) (referring to time for filing pleadings, notices, etc., fixed by "applicable nonbankruptcy law"); Eagle-Picher Industries, Inc. v. United States, 290 U.S. App. D.C. 307, 321-322; 937 F.2d 625, 639-640 (1991) (§108(b) includes Federal Tort Claims Act). Although we express no view on the correctness of these decisions, we note that our construction of §541(c)(2)'s reference to "applicable nonbankruptcy law" as including federal law accords with prevailing interpretations of that phrase as it appears elsewhere in the Code. *See* Morrison-Knudsen Constr. Co. v. Director, OWCP, 461 U.S. 624, 633, 103 S. Ct. 2045, 2050, 76 L. Ed. 2d 194 (1983) (recognizing principle "that a word is presumed to have the same meaning in all subsections of the same statute").

and (5). Indeed, this Court itself vigorously has enforced ERISA's prohibition on the assignment or alienation of pension benefits, declining to recognize any implied exceptions to the broad statutory bar. *See* Guidry v. Sheet Metal Workers Pension Fund, 493 U.S. 365, 110 S. Ct. 680, 107 L. Ed. 2d 782 (1990).

The anti-alienation provision required for ERISA qualification and contained in the Plan at issue in this case thus constitutes an enforceable transfer restriction for purposes of §541(c)(2)'s exclusion of property from the bankruptcy estate.

III.

Petitioner raises several challenges to this conclusion. Given the clarity of the statutory text, however, he bears an "exceptionally heavy" burden of persuading us that Congress intended to limit the §541(c)(2) exclusion to restrictions on transfer that are enforceable only under state spendthrift trust law. Union Bank v. Wolas, 502 U.S. ____, ____, 112 S. Ct. 527, 530, 116 L. Ed. 2d 514 (1991).

A.

Petitioner first contends that contemporaneous legislative materials demonstrate that §541(c)(2)'s exclusion of property from the bankruptcy estate should not extend to a debtor's interest in an ERISA-qualified pension plan. Although courts "appropriately may refer to a statute's legislative history to resolve statutory ambiguity," Toibb v. Radloff, 501 U.S., at ____, 111 S. Ct., at 2200, the clarity of the statutory language at issue in this case obviates the need for any such inquiry. *See* ibid.; United States v. Ron Pair Enterprises, Inc., 489 U.S., at 241, 109 S. Ct., at 1030; Davis v. Michigan Dept. of Treasury, 489 U.S. 803, 809, n.3, 109 S. Ct. 1500, 1504, n.3, 103 L. Ed. 2d 891 (1989). Those Courts of Appeals that have limited "applicable nonbankruptcy law" to state spendthrift trust law by ignoring the plain language of §541(c)(2) and relying on isolated excerpts from the legislative history thus have misconceived the appropriate analytical task. *See, e.g.*, Daniel v. Security Pacific Natl. Bank (In re Daniel), 771 F.2d, at 1359-1360; Lichstrahl v. Bankers Trust (In re Lichstrahl), 750 F.2d, at 1490; Samore v. Graham (In re Graham), 726 F.2d, at 1271-1272; Goff v. Taylor (In re Goff), 706 F.2d, at 581-582.

Even were we to consider the legislative materials to which petitioner refers, however, we could discern no "clearly expressed legislative intention" contrary to the result reached above. *See* Consumer Product Safety Commn. v. GTE Sylvania, Inc., 447 U.S. 102, 108, 100 S. Ct. 2051, 2056, 64 L. Ed. 2d 766 (1980). In his brief, petitioner quotes from House and Senate reports accompanying the Bankruptcy Reform Act of 1978 that purportedly reflect "unmistakable" congressional intent to limit §541(c)(2)'s exclusion to pension plans that qualify under state law as spendthrift trusts. Brief for Petitioner 38. Those reports contain only the briefest of discussions addressing §541(c)(2). The House Report states: "Paragraph (2) of subsection (c) . . . preserves restrictions on transfer of a spendthrift trust to the extent that the restriction is enforceable under applicable nonbankruptcy law." H.R. Rep.

No. 95-595, p.369 (1977); *see also* S. Rep. No. 95-989, p.83 (1978), U.S. Code Cong. & Admin. News 1978, pp.5787, 5869, 6325 (§541(c)(2) "preserves restrictions on a transfer of a spendthrift trust"). A general introductory section to the House Report contains the additional statement that the new law "continues over the exclusion from property of the estate of the debtor's interest in a spendthrift trust to the extent the trust is protected from creditors under applicable State law." H.R. Rep. No. 95-595, p.176, U.S. Code Cong. & Admin. News 1978, p.6136. These meager excerpts reflect at best congressional intent to include state spendthrift trust law within the meaning of Applicable nonbankruptcy law." By no means do they provide a sufficient basis for concluding, in derogation of the statute's clear language, that Congress intended to exclude other state and federal law from the provision's scope.

B.

Petitioner next contends that our construction of §541(c)(2), pursuant to which a debtor may exclude his interest in an ERISA-qualified pension plan from the bankruptcy estate, renders §522(d)(10)(E) of the Bankruptcy Code superfluous. Brief for Petitioner 24-33. Under §522(d)(10)(E), a debtor who elects the federal exemptions set forth in §522(d) may exempt from the bankruptcy estate his right to receive "a payment under a stock bonus, pension, profitsharing, annuity, or similar plan or contract . . . to the extent reasonably necessary for the support of the debtor and any dependent of the debtor." If a debtor's interest in a pension plan could be *excluded* in full from the bankruptcy estate, the argument goes, then there would have been no reason for Congress to create a limited *exemption* for such interests elsewhere in the statute.

Petitioner's surplusage argument fails, however, for the reason that §522(d)(10)(E) exempts from the bankruptcy estate a much broader category of interests than §541(c)(2) excludes. For example, pension plans established by governmental entities and churches need not comply with Subchapter I of ERISA, including the anti-alienation requirement of §206(d)(1). *See* 29 U.S.C. §§1003(b)(1) and (2); 26 CFR 1.401(a)-13(a) (1991). So, too, pension plans that qualify for preferential tax treatment under 26 U.S.C. §408 (individual retirement accounts) are specifically excepted from ERISA's anti-alienation requirement. *See* 29 U.S.C. §1051(6). Although a debtor's interest in these plans could not be excluded under §541(c)(2) because the plans lack transfer restrictions enforceable under "applicable nonbankruptcy law," that interest nevertheless could be exempted under §522(d)(10)(E). Once petitioner concedes that §522(d)(10)(E)'s exemption applies to more than ERISA-qualified plans containing anti-alienation provisions, *see* Tr. of Oral Arg. 10-11; Brief for Petitioner 31, his argument that our reading of §541(c)(2) renders the exemption provision superfluous must collapse.

C.

Finally, petitioner contends that our holding frustrates the Bankruptcy Code's policy of ensuring a broad inclusion of assets in the bankruptcy estate. *See* Brief for

Petitioner 37; 11 U.S.C. §541(a)(1) (estate comprised of "all legal and equitable interests of the debtor in property as of the commencement of the case"). As an initial matter, we think that petitioner mistakes an admittedly broad definition of includable property for a "policy" underlying the Code as a whole. In any event, to the extent that policy considerations are even relevant where the language of the statute is so clear, we believe that our construction of §541(c)(2) is preferable to the one petitioner urges upon us.

First, our decision today ensures that the treatment of pension benefits will not vary based on the beneficiary's bankruptcy status. *See* Butner v. United States, 440 U.S. 48, 55, 99 S. Ct. 914, 918, 59 L. Ed. 2d 136 (1978) (observing that "[u]niform treatment of property interests" prevents "a party from 'receiving a windfall merely by reason of the happenstance of bankruptcy,' " quoting Lewis v. Manufacturers National Bank, 364 U.S. 603, 609, 81 S. Ct. 347, 350, 5 L. Ed. 2d 323 (1961)). We previously have declined to recognize any exceptions to ERISA's anti-alienation provision outside the bankruptcy context. *See* Guidry v. Sheet Metal Workers Pension Fund, 493 U.S. 365, 110 S. Ct. 680, 107 L. Ed. 2d 782 (1990) (labor union may not impose constructive trust on pension benefits of union official who breached fiduciary duties and embezzled funds). Declining to recognize any exceptions to that provision within the bankruptcy context minimizes the possibility that creditors will engage in strategic manipulation of the bankruptcy laws in order to gain access to otherwise inaccessible funds. See Seiden, Chapter 7 Cases: Do ERISA and the Bankruptcy Code Conflict as to Whether a Debtor's Interest in or Rights Under a Qualified Plan Can be Used to Pay Claims?, 61 Am. Bankr. L.J. 301, 317 (1987) (noting inconsistency if "a creditor could not reach a debtor-participant's plan right or interest in a garnishment or other collection action outside of a bankruptcy case but indirectly could reach the plan right or interest by filing a petition . . . to place the debtor in bankruptcy involuntarily").

Our holding also gives full and appropriate effect to ERISA's goal of protecting pension benefits. *See* 29 U.S.C. §§1001(b) and (c). This Court has described that goal as one of ensuring that "if a worker has been promised a defined pension benefit upon retirement—and if he has fulfilled whatever conditions are required to obtain a vested benefit—he actually will receive it." Nachman Corp. v. Pension Benefit Guaranty Corp., 446 U.S. 359, 375, 100 S. Ct. 1723, 1733, 64 L. Ed. 2d 354 (1980). In furtherance of these principles, we recently declined in *Guidry,* notwithstanding strong equitable considerations to the contrary, to recognize an implied exception to ERISA's anti-alienation provision that would have allowed a labor union to impose a constructive trust on the pension benefits of a corrupt union official. We explained:

> "Section 206(d) reflects a considered congressional policy choice, a decision to safeguard a stream of income for pensioners (and their dependents, who may be, and perhaps usually are, blameless), even if that decision prevents others from securing relief for the wrongs done them. If exceptions to this policy are to be made, it is for Congress to undertake that task." 493 U.S., at 376, 110 S. Ct., at 687. These considerations apply with equal, if not greater, force in the present context.

Finally, our holding furthers another important policy underlying ERISA: uniform national treatment of pension benefits. *See* Fort Halifax Packing Co. v. Coyne, 482 U.S. 1, 9, 107 S. Ct. 2211, 2216, 96 L. Ed. 2d 1 (1987). Construing "applicable nonbankruptcy law" to include federal law ensures that the security of a debtor's pension benefits will be governed by ERISA, not left to the vagaries of state spendthrift trust law.

IV.

In light of our conclusion that a debtor's interest in an ERISA-qualified pension plan may be excluded from the property of the bankruptcy estate pursuant to §541(c)(2), we need not reach respondent's alternative argument that his interest in the Plan qualifies for exemption under §522(b)(2)(A). The judgment of the Court of Appeals is affirmed. It is so ordered.

Justice SCALIA, concurring.

The Court's opinion today, which I join, prompts several observations. When the phrase "applicable nonbankruptcy law" is considered in isolation, the phenomenon that three Courts of Appeals could have thought it a synonym for "state law" is mystifying. When the phrase is considered together with the rest of the Bankruptcy Code (in which Congress chose to refer to state law as, logically enough, "state law"), the phenomenon calls into question whether our legal culture has so far departed from attention to text, or is so lacking in agreed-upon methodology for creating and interpreting text, that it any longer makes sense to talk of "a government of laws, not of men. . . ."

NOTES

1. The Supreme Court's decision in Patterson v. Shumate created a new term of art. The Court held that the debtor's interest in an "ERISA-qualified" pension plan was excluded from the estate under §541(c)(2). Unfortunately, the term "ERISA-qualified" was not defined by the Court. Moreover, it has no meaning to professionals who create and administer pension and related retirement plans. This has created some confusion in the courts as they attempt to apply the holding in *Patterson* to circumstances slightly different from those presented in the case. *Compare* In re Watson, 161 F.3d 593 (9th Cir. 1998) (interest of self-employed physician in pension plan is not "ERISA-qualified" because he is not an employee, and interest is property of the estate notwithstanding anti-alienation), *with* In re Wilcox, 233 F.3d 417 (6th Cir. 2000) (debtor's interest in General Retirement System of Detroit is excluded from the estate even though it is not subject to ERISA nor did it comply with state spendthrift trust law).

2. The anti-alienation provisions of "ERISA-qualified" plans protect the debtor's entire interest in the plan. The tax benefits of these plans are varied. Among those

benefits is a right to defer income taxes that would otherwise be payable on the amounts that the employee earns but that are deposited into the plan. While these tax benefits are not unlimited, the debtor could fund the plan with amounts that exceed the amount that is tax deferred or deductible. He or she would still be liable for the current income tax due on the excess income over the amount deductible. The Ninth Circuit in In re Conner, 68 F.3d 227 (9th Cir. 1996), has held that the debtor's entire interest in the pension is excluded from the estate pursuant to §541(c)(2) and Patterson v. Shumate. The exclusion from the estate is not limited by the amount of pension plan funding for which income tax liability is deferred. This creates an incentive for debtors to "overfund" these pension plans in order to shelter those assets from their creditors. *See* In re Sewell, 180 F.3d 707 (5th Cir. 1999). Do you suppose that these contributions to the pension plans are subject to attack as fraudulent conveyances?

3. The Supreme Court also has held that the sole shareholder of a corporation is an "employee" for purposes of ERISA. In Raymond B. Yates, M.D. P.C., Profitsharing Plan v. Hendon, 541 U.S.1 (2004), the bankruptcy trustee argued that a sole shareholder could not also be an employee because that person was essentially the employer. The Court rejected that argument and concluded that the person was an employee. The decision resolved a conflict that had permitted some debtors to exclude their pension interests from the estate, while other courts had held to the contrary.

PROBLEM 3-11

Bob Herm (Fun Bob) was everybody's friend. Unfortunately, his social skills did not translate well to his employment situation, and Fun Bob found himself in serious financial difficulty. Fun Bob's mother, Prudence, is a great deal more cautious than her son. Fun Bob is her only living relative, and she loves him dearly. Her will currently provides that Fun Bob will inherit all of her property, which has a current net value of $1 million. Over the years, due to Bob's social largesse and bad investments, he has accumulated more than $400,000 of debt. Just to add to his troubles, Fun Bob recently caused an automobile accident, leaving another person partially disabled for the rest of her life. That matter is now in litigation, and it looks like the case will settle for $600,000. Unfortunately, Fun Bob's insurance will cover only the first $100,000 of that amount. He has come to you for assistance in obtaining bankruptcy relief. His mother has taken ill, and the long-term prognosis is not good. You have discussed the impact of a post-bankruptcy inheritance under §541(a)(5) with Fun Bob, and he is concerned that his entire inheritance will be lost to his creditors. Can you "suggest" to Prudence that she write a new will that would create a spendthrift trust that would exclude that interest from Bob's bankruptcy estate? *See, e.g.,* In re Davis, 110 B.R. 573 (Bankr. M.D. Fla. 1989). If Prudence lives longer than 180 days after the commencement of Bob's bankruptcy case, can you rewrite the will to return to its original terms? Do you have any ethical concerns about assisting Prudence and Bob in these matters? Consider DR 7-102(A)(7) of the Model Code of Professional Responsibility and Rule 1.2(d) of the Model Rules of Professional Conduct, each of which provides that a lawyer may not assist a client in conduct that is "criminal or fraudulent." Is this the kind of "fraudulent" conduct to which these ethics rules apply? Comment 9 to Model Rule 1.2 states that the Rule "applies whether or not the defrauded party is a party to the transaction. Hence, a lawyer should not participate in a sham transaction; for example, a transaction to effectuate criminal or fraudulent escape of tax liability."

IV. Exemptions and Lien Avoidance

Basic decency requires the law to protect some of the debtor's property from creditor process so that the hapless debtor is not left standing naked in the street sans even a barrel with shoulder straps. Both state and federal law have always exempted some minimal assets of debtors from the reach of creditors, and these exemption statutes must be given effect in the debtor's bankruptcy.

The bankruptcy laws have long recognized the vital role of exemptions in providing debtors with a fresh start. In conjunction with a discharge, the debtor's exempt property is intended to enable the debtor to become a productive person as quickly as possible. Moreover, exemptions serve the laudatory purpose of protecting the interests of the debtor's family. In fact, dependents of the debtor may claim exemptions on behalf of the debtor, should the debtor fail or refuse to do so. *See* Bankruptcy Rule 4003(a) ("If the debtor fails to claim exemptions [timely], a dependent of the debtor may file the list [of exempt property] within 30 days thereafter.").

Under the Bankruptcy Act of 1898, exemptions were purely a matter of state law. The exemptions in place in a particular state applied in the bankruptcy case. After studying the bankruptcy laws in the early 1970s, the Bankruptcy Commission proposed to Congress that federal exemptions be available to debtors in bankruptcy proceedings. Congress nearly accepted the proposal, but in the later stages of the legislative process, the compromise that is §522(b) emerged. Under that section, a debtor may claim as exempt either the property set out in §522(d) (i.e., the "federal exemptions") or "any property that is exempt under Federal law other than [§522](d), or [applicable] State or local law, and any interest in property in which the debtor had, immediately before the commencement of the case, an interest as a tenant by the entirety or joint tenancy to the extent that such interest . . . is exempt from process under applicable nonbankruptcy law." However, Congress provided further in §522(b)(1) that the "federal exemptions" are not available to debtors if the applicable state law "specifically does not so authorize" debtors to choose the exemptions set out in §522(d). This "opt-out" power was viewed as a way to prevent exemption levels that might be appropriate (or even stingy) for expensive urban areas to operate as windfalls for debtors in locations with significantly lower costs of living. More than 30 states have enacted "opt-out" legislation. Therefore, you must check your jurisdiction carefully to determine whether the federal exemptions are locally available.

This patchwork of exemptions might seem to violate the constitutional directive that "Congress shall make uniform laws on the subject of bankruptcies throughout the United States." U.S. Const. Art. I, Sec. 8, cl. 4. Nevertheless, this reference back to state law in bankruptcy cases is not unlike the practice that existed under the Bankruptcy Act of 1898. The Supreme Court in Hanover Natl. Bank v. Moyses, 186 U.S. 181 (1902), held that using applicable state exemption laws in bankruptcy cases satisfied the constitutional requirements of "geographical uniformity." The similar process employed under the Bankruptcy Code likewise has survived constitutional scrutiny. The Seventh Circuit in In re Sullivan, 680 F.2d 1131 (7th Cir. 1982), found that the "opt-out" system of Section 522(b) met the requirement of uniformity under the Constitution. Moreover, the courts have held that Section 522(b) does not constitute an improper delegation of congressional authority to the states.

While the majority of states have opted out of the federal exemption system, the enactment of the Bankruptcy Code in 1978 provided a ready opportunity for even those states to update their exemption statutes. Thus, in a sense, the efforts of the Bankruptcy Commission to update exemption law were successful, notwithstanding the massive opt-out.

Although many states have updated their exemptions, some have included within their newer exemption statutes provisions that apply only in bankruptcy proceedings. For example, Ohio Revised Code §2329.66(a)(18) provides that debtors may claim as exempt up to $400 in value of any property, but they may make such a claim only in a bankruptcy proceeding (which would seem to encourage Ohio debtors to prefer bankruptcy over state forms of debt relief, a result the Ohio legislature may not have considered). One might legitimately question whether the state has the authority to enact such a provision. After all, there is a difference between a state opting out of the federal exemption scheme and a state creating exemptions applicable only in a bankruptcy case. While the Ohio statute has withstood attack generally on this ground, In re Vasko, 6 B.R. 317 (Bankr. N.D. Ohio 1980), an Indiana exemption statute that purports to apply only in a bankruptcy case has been found to violate the Supremacy Clause of the Constitution. In re Cross, 255 B.R. 25 (Bankr. N.D. Ind. 2000). *See also* In re Regevig, 389 B.R. 736 (Bankr. D. Ariz. 2008) (California exemption law that applies only in bankruptcy violates supremacy clause); *but see* In re Morrell, 394 B.R. 405 (Bankr. N.D. W. Va. 2008) (West Virginia's bankruptcy specific exemption is consistent with Congressional intent allowing opt-out).

Many states that opted out not only took the opportunity to update their own exemptions, but actually patterned their new exemption systems on the scheme set out in §522(d) of the Bankruptcy Code. Typically, states followed the format of the federal exemptions, but provided for lesser amounts in value of exempt property in the categories set out in that section. Consequently, studying §522(d) can be very helpful even when it is not directly applicable to any particular debtor. Consider the categories of exempt property, as well as issues of valuation and entitlement to exemption, under that section to resolve the following Problems.

PROBLEM 3-12

Assume that the relevant state exemption law gives homeowners a $10,000 exemption for their homesteads. Few homes worth saving are worth only $10,000. Your client has a home worth $75,000, and it is subject to a $50,000 mortgage in favor of Last National Bank. What is going to happen to the home in bankruptcy?

PROBLEM 3-13

The State of Texas allows debtors an unlimited homestead exemption. Rancher Yosemite Sam has done well in the cattle business, and his lavish home west of Houston is worth $12,000,000. Bad investments, however, sent Sam into bankruptcy. Is Sam going to be able to exit from bankruptcy still living in this palace? Suppose the home had been worth $10,000,000 two years before bankruptcy, but in the six-month period before the filing of the petition, Sam saw the handwriting on the wall, and took all his spare cash and frantically used it on home improvements, so that now the house is worth $12,000,000. Is it all still exempt? *See* §522(o). Assume instead that Sam had no evil intent to hide money from creditors, but three years before the bankruptcy (and during a period when he had no money troubles), Sam built an addition to his home that raised its value by $600,000. May he still claim the entire home as exempt? *See* §522(p). Finally, assume that Sam has lived most of his life in the State of Wyoming, where the homestead exemption is only $10,000, but two years before he filed his bankruptcy petition he moved first to the State of Colorado ($30,000 homestead exemption), and then, two weeks before the bankruptcy to the State of Texas, where he used his assets to purchase a $100,000 home. Which state's exemption controls? *See* §522(b)(3)(A).

Problem 3-14 below involves in part a purchase money security interest, which means that the creditor having such an interest advanced the funds to enable the debtor to acquire the property. For example, if you buy a car on credit from the seller, the seller will take a purchase money interest in the vehicle to protect the rest of the purchase price. Similarly, if you borrow the money to buy the car from a credit union, the credit union will also get a purchase money security interest in the car. *See* Uniform Commercial Code §9-103(a). Since the debtor would not own the property but for the willingness of the creditor to make the loan, our law (both inside and outside of bankruptcy) typically gives greater rights to purchase money creditors than to others.

PROBLEM 3-14

Portia Moot, a first-year law student, rented an unfurnished apartment near campus and went to Plastic Furniture Mart to check out their wares. She picked out a living room suite that she much admired and bought it on time from Plastic Furniture Mart, granting the seller a purchase money security interest in the suite. The security agreement contained this clause: "Buyer also grants seller a security interest in all consumer goods that that buyer owns now or will acquire in the future, and buyer hereby waives the right to claim an exemption in said consumer goods against seller." When Portia's lavish lifestyle spiraled into bankruptcy, Plastic Furniture Mart claimed a security interest in both the living room suite and all other consumer goods Portia owned, and when she protested that these items were exempt under the relevant state law, Plastic Furniture pointed to the above clause in the security agreement. How will this come out? *See* §522(e). If Portia has two TV sets, one for the living room, one for her bedroom, will Plastic Furniture be able to keep its security interest in one of them? How about her DVD player? *See* §522(f)(4)(A).

PROBLEM 3-15

Assume that Portia Moot bought a new car and financed it with a loan from Octopus National Bank, which took a PMSI in the car. When Portia ran into financial difficulties, she went back to the bank and asked to refinance the loan and to borrow more money at the same time. The bank was willing to do this, and the new agreement between the parties specifically stated that the entire loan was still secured by the car. When Portia filed a bankruptcy petition shortly thereafter she claimed the car as exempt, and tried to strip away the bank's security interest by claiming that it had lost its PMSI status when the bank refinanced the original loan. Will this argument succeed? *See* In re Short, 170 B.R. 128 (Bankr. S.D. Ill. 1994).

Section 522 empowers a debtor to avoid some liens and security interests in otherwise exempt property. Section 522(f) was a significant addition to the Bankruptcy Code. It authorizes debtors to avoid the fixing of liens on an interest of the debtor in property to the extent that the lien impairs an exemption to which the debtor would have been entitled. Liens vulnerable to avoidance under §522(f) are judicial liens (other than judicial liens to secure alimony or support obligations), and non-possessory, non-purchase-money security interests in certain personal property.

PROBLEM 3-16

When Portia Moot, the law student from Problem 3-14, failed to pay the grocery bill she had run up at Mom & Pop's Grocery Store, the owners unpredictably turned mean and filed a small claims court action against her, securing a judgment, and sending the sheriff out to levy execution. The sheriff seized her dog, Lexis; panicked at losing him, Portia immediately filed a bankruptcy petition. Will §522(f) permit her to keep Lexis?

Congress authorized debtors to avoid the judicial liens and security interests described in §522(f) because it recognized the significant leverage available to creditors who held interests in the debtor's property. This was especially true with respect to non-purchase-money, nonpossessory security interests in the debtor's household goods. The creditors holding those security interests could threaten the repossession of the relatively worthless goods, and debtors would agree to reaffirm the debts owing to those creditors in order to retain possession of the collateral. The value of these goods was minimal, at best, but the "hostage value" provided to creditors asserting those secured claims was significant.

PROBLEM 3-17

Urban Finance Company made loans to people in a very poor part of town. It always took a security interest in all of their consumer goods, including clothing, furniture, appliances, jewelry, and pets. If these people did not repay the loan, Urban Finance would send goons to the debtors' homes, remove all the consumer goods subject to Urban Finance's security interest, and burn them in the street (pets were given away or turned over to the humane society). Urban found that this widely known method of debt collection was very effective in persuading all its debtors to pay their debts. If one of your clients has filed a bankruptcy petition and owes Urban money, can the client make use of §522(f) to free some consumer goods from Urban's grasp?

The Federal Trade Commission has promulgated a regulation called the "Credit Practices Rule" that, in part, also addresses this problem. It forbids creditors the ability to take a nonpossessory, non-purchase-money security interest in household goods (though the term "household goods" is given a restricted definition, and creditors have sometimes taken advantage of the technicalities here to get around the rule); see 12 C.F.R. Part 444.[5]

Congress rewrote §522(f) in 1994 to include a definition of impairment of an exemption under new §522(f)(2). Under that provision, "a lien shall be considered to impair an exemption to the extent that the sum of (i) the lien; (ii) all other liens on the property; and (iii) the amount of the exemption that the debtor could claim if there were no liens on the property; exceeds the value that the debtor's interest in the property would have in the absence of any liens." This recent addition to the Bankruptcy Code is an attempt at a codification of the Supreme Court's decision in Owen v. Owen, 500 U.S. 305 (1991). In that case, the Court construed the language in §522(f)(1) as requiring the courts to determine whether the debtor would have a right to an exemption if the lien asserted by a creditor did not exist. In other words, the courts should determine whether the debtor would have a right to exempt specific property if the debtor owned that property otherwise free and clear of liens. If that property would be exempt in the absence of a lien, then the lien impairs the debtor's exemption for purposes of §522(f) of the Bankruptcy Code.

The addition of §522(f)(2)(A) by the 1994 Amendments to the Bankruptcy Code provides additional clarification for the courts. The 1994 Amendments to §522(f)

---

5. The Federal Reserve Board has promulgated a similar rule covering banks; *see* 16 C.F.R. §227.13.

were intended, inter alia, to overturn the decisions of several courts of appeals regarding the avoidance of liens and security interests on otherwise exempt property. The commentary accompanying the enactment of the 1994 Amendments identified scenarios in which the courts had reached decisions that were viewed as inconsistent with Congress's intentions under the Bankruptcy Code. The first is a situation in which the consensual mortgages on the property equal or exceed the fair market value of the property and the debtor is seeking to avoid a junior judicial lien. Notwithstanding the absence of any "equity" in the property, the debtor would be able to avoid the judicial lien under the 1994 Amendment to §522(f). For example, if the debtor's home, worth $100,000, is subject to a first mortgage in the amount of $110,000, and then another creditor gets a $10,000 judicial lien on the home, the debtor could use §522(f) to avoid the judicial lien.

Similarly, the legislative history notes that a debtor may avoid a judicial lien where the amount of consensual mortgages with priority over the judicial lien does not exhaust the value of the property. For example, a $50,000 house subject to a $40,000 mortgage has $10,000 of "equity" that might be available to pay judicial liens. If a creditor has a judgment for $20,000, and the debtor's available exemption for the property is $10,000, the legislative history indicates that the entire lien could be avoided. This would overrule the Ninth Circuit's decision in In re Chabot, 992 F.2d 891 (9th Cir. 1992). By avoiding the judicial lien in its entirety, the commentary notes that the lienholder would not be able to assert a claim against the debtor's postpetition earnings by obtaining the benefit of the debtor's repayment of the senior mortgage. This is consistent with the prohibition against creditors reaching a debtor's postpetition earnings so as to support the longstanding policy of a fresh start in bankruptcy. Prior to the 1994 Amendments, decisions like *Chabot* had held that the lien was avoidable only to the extent of $10,000. The remaining portion of the lien was found not to "impair" the debtor's exemption, and so that portion of the lien was not subject to avoidance. The Amendment to §522(f) has been applied to reach the opposite conclusion. *See* In re Thomson, 181 B.R. 1013 (Bankr. M.D. Ga. 1995).

The final scenario identified in the legislative commentary as being changed by the application of the lien avoidance power is illustrated by the next Problem.

PROBLEM 3-18

At the time his bankruptcy petition was filed, Harold Suburbia had a home worth $80,000. It was subject to a first mortgage lien in the amount of $60,000, but the real property filing records then recorded a judicial lien Harold's unpaid doctor had acquired against the property in the amount of $5,000, followed by a $20,000 second mortgage. The state has opted out of the federal exemptions, but does allow debtors a household exemption of $5,000. Here's what Harold wants to do: avoid the doctor's judicial lien, use §522(i)(2) to "preserve" its priority position, claim that position as a household exemption, and thus come ahead of the second mort-gagee. Will this work?

PROBLEM 3-19

Nightflyer Finance Co. (NFC) obtained a judgment against Ray Gunn, and NFC promptly docketed the judgment according to applicable state law. Six months later, Ray purchased a home for $50,000. Six months after that, Ray filed a Chapter 7 bankruptcy and moved to avoid NFC's judicial lien under §522(f)(1)(A), claiming that it impaired his homestead exemption. Did NFC's lien affix to Ray's interest in the property? Is the lien avoidable? *See* In re Scarpino, 113 F.3d 338 (2d Cir. 1997).

Debtors cannot use the avoidance power of §522(f) to avoid a judicial lien that protects alimony, maintenance, or support obligations. For obvious policy reasons, Congress wanted such creditors to have many avenues available to them to protect these interests. If the lien protects a mere property settlement, however, it is avoidable under the language of that section. We will explore the difference between true alimony, maintenance or support obligations, and property settlements when we discuss the issue of discharge.

PROBLEM 3-20

Suppose that Luke Penury lives in Maine, which gives him a $12,500 exemption in his residence. He is married to Shelley, who also has a similar homestead exemption in the same home they both live in. The property has a current value of $185,000, and is subject to a mortgage they took out on the home on which they presently owe the bank $134,646, so they have an equity in the property of $50,354. When Luke failed to pay his stockbroker, the latter filed suit against him and obtained a judicial lien against the property for $24,000. Can this lien be avoided? If, at first glance, it looks like the stock-broker's lien will get something, consider the literal language of §522(f). According to Luke, the lien he seeks to avoid is in the amount of $24,000, "all other liens" total $134,626, and "the amount of the exemption" absent any liens is $12,500. The "sum" of these three figures ($171,126) exceeds "the debtor's interest in the property in the absence of any liens" — here, $92,500 (50% of $185,000) — by almost $80,000. Thus, Luke claims, the stockbroker's lien is impairing his exemption "to the extent" of this differential, which greatly exceeds the amount of the judicial lien, so he can avoid it in full. This issue, which comes up whenever the debtor owns the property jointly with another, has given the courts fits. *Compare* Nelson v. Scala, 192 F.3d 32 (1st Cir. 1999), and In re Lehman, 205 F.3d 1255 (11th Cir. 2000), *with* In re Piersol, 244 B.R. 309 (Bankr. E.D. Pa. 2000).

Finally, do not worry about the convoluted language of §522(f)(3). Its legislative history shows that it was enacted to deal with the peculiar wording of a Louisiana statute, and has no impact outside of that state; see the discussion of this in In re Zimmel, 185 B.R. 786 (Bankr. D. Minn. 1995).

PROBLEM 3-21

Dave Detter is a plumber. He, too, is "financially challenged." In addition to asking if you offer "family discounts" for bankruptcy representation, Dave has given you his list of assets and also wants to know what he will be able to keep without paying more for it under the federal exemption scheme. What difference would it make if Dave was married and co-owned the property with his wife, Teri?

Asset	Value	Lien
House	$147,000.00	$102,000.00 FirstBank/1st Mtg $18,000.00 Second Bank/ 2nd Mtg
2003 Ford Taurus	$9,000.00	$7,000.00 FMCC
1999 Ford van	$2,500.00	$10,500.00 Non-PMSI by Artisan's Natl. Bank
Plumbing tools	$6,000.00	"
Pipe and plumbing supplies	$900.00	"
Furniture (no item greater than $400)	$2,600.00	$0.00
Piano	$1,800.00	$1,250.00 Non-PMSI by Friendly Finance
Clothing	$400.00	$0.00
Golf Clubs	$500.00	$0.00
IRA	$6,750.00	$0.00
Patent #1012753 (basin wrench design)	Unknown	$0.00
First edition of *Tom Sawyer*	$1,500.00	$1,000.00 Pledge to Pete's Pawn Shop

In the event that the debtor is unable to avoid liens on property, the debtor either must surrender the property to the creditor, redeem the property under §722 of the Bankruptcy Code, or reaffirm the debt by entering into a new agreement with the creditor pursuant to §524. These are the options enumerated in §521(2) of the Bankruptcy Code. Some courts, however, have allowed debtors to retain the collateral if they were not in default on the loan at the time of the bankruptcy. We will explore these options in subsequent chapters.

V.   Claiming the Exemption

Section 522(l) directs the debtor to list the property that he or she claims as exempt. The section further provides that "unless a party in interest objects, the property claimed as exempt on such list is exempt." The Supreme Court addressed the meaning of this section in Taylor v. Freeland & Kronz, which follows.

Taylor v. Freeland & Kronz

United States Supreme Court, 1992
503 U.S. 638

Justice THOMAS delivered the opinion of the Court.

Section 522(l) of the Bankruptcy Code requires a debtor to file a list of the property that the debtor claims as statutorily exempt from distribution to creditors. Federal Rule of Bankruptcy Procedure 4003 affords creditors and the bankruptcy trustee 30 days to object to claimed exemptions. We must decide in this case whether the trustee may contest the validity of an exemption after the 30-day period if the debtor had no colorable basis for claiming the exemption.

I.

The debtor in this case, Emily Davis, declared bankruptcy while she was pursuing an employment discrimination claim in the state courts. The relevant proceedings began in 1978 when Davis filed a complaint with the Pittsburgh Commission on Human Relations. Davis alleged that her employer, Trans World Airlines (TWA), had denied her promotions on the basis of her race and sex. The Commission held for Davis as to liability but did not calculate the damages owed by TWA. The Pennsylvania Court of Common Pleas reversed the Commission, but the Pennsylvania Commonwealth Court reversed that court and reinstated the Commission's determination of liability. TWA next appealed to the Pennsylvania Supreme Court.

In October 1984, while that appeal was pending, Davis filed a Chapter 7 bankruptcy petition. Petitioner, Robert J. Taylor, became the trustee of Davis' bankruptcy estate. Respondents, Wendell G. Freeland, Richard F. Kronz, and their law firm, represented Davis in the discrimination suit. On a schedule filed with the Bankruptcy Court, Davis claimed as exempt property the money that she expected to win in her discrimination suit against TWA. She described this property as "Proceeds from lawsuit — [Davis] v. TWA" and "Claim for lost wages" and listed its value as "unknown." App. 18. Performing his duty as a trustee, Taylor held the required initial meeting of creditors in January 1985. See 11 U.S.C. §341; Fed. Rule Bkrtcy. Proc. 2003(a). At this meeting, respondents told Taylor that they estimated that Davis might win $90,000 in her suit against TWA. Several days after the meeting, Taylor wrote a letter to respondents telling them that he considered the potential proceeds of the lawsuit to be property of Davis' bankruptcy estate. He also asked respondents for more details about the suit. Respondents described the procedural posture of the case and expressed optimism that they might settle with TWA for $110,000.

Taylor decided not to object to the claimed exemption. The record reveals that Taylor doubted that the lawsuit had any value. Taylor at one point explained: "I have had past experience in examining debtors. . . . [.] [M]any of them . . . indicate they have potential lawsuits. . . . [M]any of them do not turn out to be advantageous and . . . many of them might wind up settling far within the exemption limitation." App. 52. Taylor also said that he thought Davis' discrimination claim against TWA might be a "nullity." Id., at 58.

Taylor proved mistaken. In October 1986, the Pennsylvania Supreme Court affirmed the Commonwealth Court's determination that TWA had discriminated against Davis. In a subsequent settlement of the issue of damages, TWA agreed to pay Davis a total of $110,000. TWA paid part of this amount by issuing a check made to both Davis and respondents for $71,000. Davis apparently signed this check over to respondents in payment of their fees. TWA paid the remainder of the $110,000 by other means. Upon learning of the settlement, Taylor filed a complaint against respondents in the Bankruptcy Court. He demanded that respondents turn over the money that they had received from Davis because he considered it property of Davis' bankruptcy estate. Respondents argued that they could keep the fees because Davis had claimed the proceeds of the lawsuit as exempt.

The Bankruptcy Court sided with Taylor. It concluded that Davis had "no statutory basis" for claiming the proceeds of the lawsuit as exempt and ordered respondents to "return" approximately $23,000 to Taylor, a sum sufficient to pay off all of Davis' unpaid creditors. In re Davis, 105 B.R. 288 (Bktcy. Ct. W.D. Pa. 1989). The District Court affirmed, In re Davis, 118 B.R. 272 (W.D. Pa. 1990), but the Court of Appeals for the Third Circuit reversed, 938 F.2d 420 (1991). The Court of Appeals held that the Bankruptcy Court could not require respondents to turn over the money because Davis had claimed it as exempt, and Taylor had failed to object to the claimed exemption in a timely manner. We granted certiorari, 502 U.S. 976, 112 S. Ct. 632, 116 L. Ed. 2d 602 (1991), and now affirm.

II.

When a debtor files a bankruptcy petition, all of his property becomes property of a bankruptcy estate. See 11 U.S.C. §541. The Code, however, allows the debtor to prevent the distribution of certain property by claiming it as exempt. Section 522(b) allowed Davis to choose the exemptions afforded by state law or the federal exemptions listed in §522(d). Section 522(l) states the procedure for claiming exemptions and objecting to claimed exemptions as follows:

> The debtor shall file a list of property that the debtor claims as exempt under subsection (b) of this section. . . . Unless a party in interest objects, the property claimed as exempt on such list is exempt.

Although §522(l) itself does not specify the time for objecting to a claimed exemption, Federal Rule of Bankruptcy Procedure 4003(b) provides in part:

> The trustee or any creditor may file objections to the list of property claimed as exempt within 30 days after the conclusion of the meeting of creditors held pursuant to Rule 2003(a) . . . unless, within such period, further time is granted by the court.

In this case, as noted, Davis claimed the proceeds from her employment discrimination lawsuit as exempt by listing them in the schedule that she filed under §522(*l*). The parties agree that Davis did not have a right to exempt more than a small portion of these proceeds either under state law or under the federal exemptions specified in §522(d). Davis in fact claimed the full amount as exempt. Taylor, as a result, apparently could have made a valid objection under §522(*l*) and Rule 4003 if he had acted promptly. We hold, however, that his failure to do so prevents him from challenging the validity of the exemption now.

A.

Taylor acknowledges that Rule 4003(b) establishes a 30-day period for objecting to exemptions and that §522(*l*) states that "[u]nless a party in interest objects, the property claimed as exempt . . . is exempt." He argues, nonetheless, that his failure to object does not preclude him from challenging the exemption at this time. In Taylor's view, §522(*l*) and Rule 4003(b) serve only to narrow judicial inquiry into the validity of an exemption after 30 days, not to preclude judicial inquiry altogether. In particular, he maintains that courts may invalidate a claimed exemption after expiration of the 30-day period if the debtor did not have a good-faith or reasonably disputable basis for claiming it. In this case, Taylor asserts, Davis did not have a colorable basis for claiming all of the lawsuit proceeds as exempt and thus lacked good faith.

Taylor justifies his interpretation of §522(*l*) by arguing that requiring debtors to file claims in good faith will discourage them from claiming meritless exemptions merely in hopes that no one will object. Taylor does not stand alone in this reading of §522(b). Several Courts of Appeals have adopted the same position upon similar reasoning. *See* In re Peterson, 920 F.2d 1389, 1393-1394 (CA8 1990); In re Dembs, 757 F.2d 777, 780 (CA6 1985); In re Sherk, 918 F.2d 1170, 1174 (CA5 1990).

We reject Taylor's argument. Davis claimed the lawsuit proceeds as exempt on a list filed with the Bankruptcy Court. Section 522(*l*), to repeat, says that "[u]nless a party in interest objects, the property claimed as exempt on such list is exempt." Rule 4003(b) gives the trustee and creditors 30 days from the initial creditors' meeting to object. By negative implication, the Rule indicates that creditors may not object after 30 days "unless, within such period, further time is granted by the court." The Bankruptcy Court did not extend the 30-day period. Section 522(*l*) therefore has made the property exempt. Taylor cannot contest the exemption at this time whether or not Davis had a colorable statutory basis for claiming it.

Deadlines may lead to unwelcome results, but they prompt parties to act and they produce finality. In this case, despite what respondents repeatedly told him, Taylor did not object to the claimed exemption. If Taylor did not know the value of the potential proceeds of the lawsuit, he could have sought a hearing on the issue, *see* Rule 4003(c), or he could have asked the Bankruptcy Court for an extension of time to object, *see* Rule 4003(b). Having done neither, Taylor cannot now seek to deprive Davis and respondents of the exemption.

Taylor suggests that our holding will create improper incentives. He asserts that it will lead debtors to claim property exempt on the chance that the trustee and creditors, for whatever reason, will fail to object to the claimed exemption on time. He asserts that only a requirement of good faith can prevent what the Eighth Circuit has termed "exemption by declaration." *Peterson, supra,* at 1393. This concern, however, does not cause us to alter our interpretation of §522(*l*). Debtors and their attorneys face penalties under various provisions for engaging in improper conduct in bankruptcy proceedings. *See, e.g.,* 11 U.S.C. §727(a)(4)(B) (authorizing denial of discharge for presenting fraudulent claims); Rule 1008 (requiring filings to "be verified or contain an unsworn declaration" of truthfulness under penalty of perjury); Rule 9011 (authorizing sanctions for signing certain documents not "well grounded in fact and . . . warranted by existing law or a good faith argument for the extension, modification, or reversal of existing law"); 18 U.S.C. §152 (imposing criminal penalties for fraud in bankruptcy cases). These provisions may limit bad-faith claims of exemptions by debtors. To the extent that they do not, Congress may enact comparable provisions to address the difficulties that Taylor predicts will follow our decision. We have no authority to limit the application of §522(*l*) to exemptions claimed in good faith.

B.

Taylor also asserts that courts may consider the validity of the exemption under a different provision of the Bankruptcy Code, 11 U.S.C. §105(a), despite his failure to object in a timely manner. That provision states:

> The court may issue any order, process, or judgment that is necessary or appropriate to carry out the provisions of this title. *No provision of this title providing for the raising of an issue by a party in interest shall be construed to preclude the court from, sua sponte, taking any action or* making any determination necessary or appropriate to enforce or implement court orders or rules, or *to prevent an abuse of process.* Ibid. (Emphasis added.)

Although Taylor stresses that he is not asserting that courts in bankruptcy have broad authorization to do equity in derogation of the Code and Rules, he maintains that §105 permits courts to disallow exemptions not claimed in good faith. Several courts have accepted this position. *See, e.g.,* Ragsdale v. Genesco, Inc., 674 F.2d 277, 278 (CA4 1982); In re Staniforth, 116 B.R. 127, 131 (Bktcy. Ct. W.D. Wis. 1990); In re Budinsky, No. 90-01099, 1991 WL 105640 (W.D. Pa., June 10, 1991).

We decline to consider §105(a) in this case because Taylor raised the argument for the first time in his opening brief on the merits. Our Rule 14.1(a) makes clear that "[o]nly the questions set forth in the petition [for certiorari], or fairly included therein, will be considered by the Court," and our Rule 24.1(a) states that a brief on the merits should not "raise additional questions or change the substance of the questions already presented" in the petition. *See* Yee v. Escondido, 503 U.S. 519, 535, 112 S. Ct. 1522, ____, ____ L. Ed. 2d ____ (1992). In addition, we have said that "[o]rdinarily, this Court does not decide questions not raised or resolved in the lower court[s]." Youakim v. Miller, 425 U.S. 231, 234, 96 S. Ct. 1399, 1401, 47 L. Ed. 2d 701 (1976) (per curiam). These principles help to maintain the integrity of the process of certiorari. *Cf.* Oklahoma City v. Tuttle, 471 U.S. 808, 816, 105 S. Ct. 2427, 2432, 85 L. Ed. 2d 791 (1985). The Court decides which questions to consider through well-established procedures; allowing the able counsel who argue before us to alter these questions or to devise additional questions at the last minute would thwart this system. We see no "unusual circumstances" that warrant addressing Taylor's §105(a) argument at this time. Berkemer v. McCarty, 468 U.S. 420, 443, n.38, 104 S. Ct. 3138, 3152, n.38, 82 L. Ed. 2d 317 (1984).

The judgment of the Court of Appeals is Affirmed.

PROBLEM 3-22

Mark "Hot Dog" Leister was an avid skier. As his nickname would suggest, he had a reputation for being a bit reckless on the slopes. On one of his ski trips, he suffered a rather ugly fall and injured his knee. The injury prevented Mark from working, and he fell behind on his financial obligations. Eventually, he was forced to seek relief under Chapter 7 of the Bankruptcy Code. Mark's assets were relatively limited, but they included his claim against Quik-Release, Inc., the manufacturer of the bindings on Mark's skis. Mark claimed that the bindings were defective, and he filed a lawsuit against Quik-Release claiming damages of $100,000. The civil action was in the early stages of discovery when Mark filed his bankruptcy petition. On his list of assets, Mark valued the claim as worth "$1." The bankruptcy trustee questioned Mark briefly about the cause of action, and the trustee also obtained information from Mark's personal injury lawyer. The personal injury lawyer indicated to the trustee that the insurance carrier for Quik-Release had refused to engage in any settlement negotiations once they found out about Mark's nickname. They also ascertained that Mark's injury occurred as he was skiing down a triple black diamond run named "The Widow Maker." Mark claimed the cause of action as exempt, and the trustee did not object to that claimed exemption. Approximately two months after the time to object to the exemption had expired, two other skiers were injured in unrelated accidents involving Quik-Release bindings. Quik-Release, in its efforts to settle all the claims quickly, offered Mark's personal injury lawyer $50,000. Mark agreed to settle the claim for that amount, and Quik-Release paid $50,000 to Mark's attorney. After taking his third, the attorney was about to send the balance to Mark when the bankruptcy trustee heard about the settlement. The trustee has claimed the balance of the settlement, and has filed an objection to Mark' exemption claim. Does Mark get to keep the balance of the settlement amount? Can he keep just $1? *See* §522(c). *Compare* Mercer v. Monczak, 53 F.3d 1 (1st Cir. 1995) (holding that exemption is limited to dollar amount stated by debtor), *with* In re Green, 31 F.3d 1098 (11th Cir. 1995) (holding that exemption claimed in "nominal amount of value for cause of action is exemption of entire cause of action"). The Supreme Court has agreed to resolve the issue. *See* In re Reilly, 534 F.3d 173 (3d Cir. 2008), *cert. granted*, 2009 WL 1107924 (April 27, 2009).

PROBLEM 3-23

Sparky was a real entrepreneur. She saw business opportunities where others saw folly. Sometimes, the others were right. Sparky decided that the American consumer was gullible enough to pay $1 for a bottle of tap water if the label on the tap water included a picture of a mountain spring. Initial sales were encouraging, but a news story identifying the product as tap water "dried up" the market. Sparky's house was worth $175,000. It was encumbered by a first mortgage in favor of Metropolis National Bank in the amount of $120,000. The applicable homestead exemption in the state where Sparky resided was $25,000. The state had opted out of the federal exemption system. Notwithstanding the $50,000 equity in her home, Sparky claimed the entire equity as exempt. In addition to the first mortgage, the house was subject to a judicial lien in favor of High Risk Finance Corp. High Risk had obtained a $35,000 judgment against Sparky eight months before she filed her bankruptcy petition. No objection was made to the exemption claim, and Sparky now seeks to avoid the judicial lien of High Risk under §522(f)(1)(A). High Risk, of course, objects to the avoidance of its judicial lien. Can Sparky have the judicial lien avoided? Is the exact wording of §522(f) a help or a hindrance here? *See* In re Chinosorn, 243 B.R. 688 (Bankr. N.D. Ill. 2000). Does the recent amendment to Bankruptcy Rule 4003(d) apply to this situation?

In re Drenttel

United States Court of Appeals, 2005
403 F.3d 611

HEANY, Circuit Judge.

Mary Jo A. Jensen-Carter, the trustee in bankruptcy (trustee) for the estate of Bradley and Mary Drenttel, appeals the Bankruptcy Appellate Panel's (BAP) reversal of the bankruptcy court, permitting the Drenttels to apply Minnesota's statutory $200,000 homestead exemption to their residence located in Arizona. The trustee contends that the Minnesota exemption should not be given extraterritorial effect. We affirm.

Background

The facts are undisputed. The Drenttels resided in Minnesota until June of 2003, when they sold their Minnesota residence and purchased a home in Arizona. On July 17, 2003, the Drenttels filed a Chapter 7 bankruptcy petition in the District of Minnesota. The Drenttels claimed their unencumbered Arizona property, valued at $181,682, was exempt from the bankruptcy estate under Minnesota's statutory homestead exemption. The trustee objected, claiming that the Minnesota homestead exemption may not be applied to real property located outside of Minnesota. The bankruptcy court sustained the objection. The Drenttels appealed to the BAP, which reversed. The trustee appeals.

Analysis

We review the legal conclusions of the BAP de novo. In re Wick, 276 F.3d 412, 415 (8th Cir. 2002). Debtors must file for bankruptcy protection under Title 11 in the district where the debtor's domicile was located for the longer portion of the 180-day period immediately preceding the filing. 28 U.S.C. §1408. As of July 17, 2003, the Drenttels' domicile for bankruptcy filing was Minnesota, because they had lived in Arizona fewer than 90 days.

> The Drenttels were permitted to exempt from the bankruptcy estate property that is exempt under
> Federal law . . . or State or local law that is applicable on the date of the filing of the petition at the
> place in which the debtor's domicile has been located for the 180 days immediately preceding the
> date of the filing of the petition, or for a longer portion of such 180-day period than in any other
> place.

11 U.S.C. §522(b)(2)(A). Therefore, only federal and Minnesota exemptions were available to the Drenttels when they filed for bankruptcy. Minnesota permits an exemption of up to $200,000 for the house owned and occupied by a debtor as the debtor's dwelling place, together with the land upon which it is situated. Minn. Stat. §§510.01-.02.

The trustee argues that the Minnesota exemption is unavailable to the Drenttels because their homestead is located outside of Minnesota, and states traditionally do not give extraterritorial effect to statutes relating to the ownership of real property. [Citing cases.] Bankruptcy courts are divided on this issue. *Compare* In re Sipka, 149 B.R. 181 (D. Kan. 1992) (refusing to exempt under Kansas law the proceeds of the involuntary sale of a Michigan residence), and In re Peters, 91 B.R. 401 (Bankr. W. D. Tex. 1988) (holding that the Texas homestead exemption, which was limited by statute to homesteads in the state, was not available to out-of-state residence), *with* In re Tanzi, 287 B.R. 557 (Bankr. W.D. Wash. 2002) (holding that either Washington or California exemptions applied to debtors' Florida residence), *and* In re Stratton, 269 B.R. 716 (Bankr. D. Or. 2001) (upholding debtor's claim of Oregon homestead exemption for property located in California). To reach this result, the trustee points not to the statutory language of Minnesota's homestead exemption, but to Minnesota choice-of-law principles. The phrase "the law that is applicable" as used in 11 U.S.C. §522(b)(2)(A) would therefore refer to the whole of Minnesota law. Following this approach, the bankruptcy court would determine what exemption to apply by asking whether Minnesota courts would apply the Minnesota homestead exemption, or another state's exemption, to the property.

We are not persuaded that Congress invoked state choice-of-law rules with this provision. References to state exemption statutes do not invoke the entire law of the state. Instead, Congress used state-defined exemptions as part of a federal bankruptcy scheme, while limiting the application of state policies that impair those exemptions. Owen v. Owen, 500 U.S. 305, 313, 111 S. Ct. 1833, 114 L. Ed. 2d 350 (1991) (finding no inconsistency in the policy of permitting state-defined exemptions while disfavoring waiver of exemptions and impingement of liens on exemptions); *cf.* Butner v.

United States, 440 U.S. 48, 55, 99 S. Ct. 914, 59 L. Ed. 2d 136 (1979) (acknowledging that property interests normally governed by state law could be analyzed differently if some federal interest requires a different result). The federal bankruptcy statute dictates the applicable exemptions, requiring the debtor to file in the designated district, and stating that the debtor is entitled to federal exemptions or the exemptions provided by the law of the state where the petition is filed. §522(b)(2)(A). "This is a federal choice of law in which the choice has been made. That choice is the applicable state exemption law, and in this case the exemption law is [Minnesota]'s statutory homestead exemption. Whatever [Minnesota]'s conflicts of law jurisprudence may be is simply irrelevant." In re Arrol, 170 F.3d 934, 936 (9th Cir. 1999) (citing In re Calhoun, 47 B.R. 119, 122 (Bankr. E.D. Va. 1985)).

Addition of state choice-of-law principles into the bankruptcy code would complicate and lengthen bankruptcy adjudications, while reducing the barriers to forum shopping by debtors. *Cf.* Butner, 440 U.S. at 55, 99 S. Ct. 914 (listing reducing uncertainty, discouraging forum shopping, and preventing windfalls as justifications for generally applying state law in bankruptcy cases). While the trustee suggests that its proposed rule is required to avoid forum shopping, the danger is increased, not decreased, if debtors reap an immediate benefit from the homestead exemptions in the state where they relocate. The application of state choice-of-law rules in these cases produces the very results the statute appears designed to avoid. *See, e.g.*, In re Tanzi, 287 B.R. at 558-60 (preventing debtors from applying Florida's homestead exemption to their Florida residence, valued at $985,000, because the debtors' domicile for bankruptcy purposes was either California or Washington). The trustee's construction would disrupt the federal scheme, which currently limits the ability of debtors to change their domicile[6] and would return to the process a measure of uncertainty removed by the federal statute.

We therefore look to the language of the Minnesota exemption, without reference to Minnesota choice of law, asking whether this exemption can be applied to an Arizona homestead. Minnesota courts have historically construed the homestead exemption liberally in favor of the debtor. [Citing cases.] The state's policy of protecting a debtor's homestead rests on the recognition that the state benefits from the sense of security and connection to the community nurtured in the home. *Jensen*, 11 N.W.2d at 799. The homestead exemption protects the debtor's family and helps to reduce the need for state services. *Denzer*, 126 N.W.2d at 443-44. The provision of the homestead exemption may even serve the long-term interests of creditors. "[E]xperience has taught that in the long run obligations are more likely to be fulfilled by those whose connections with the community are stabilized by a protected interest in a relatively permanent place of abode than by those not so anchored." Id. at 443. These

---

6. Under the current federal scheme, a debtor's domicile for bankruptcy purposes does not change immediately when the debtor relocates. Creditors may force a debtor into bankruptcy proceedings in the state they have moved from. If the trustee's interpretation were adopted, it is not clear why they would bother: the homestead exemption from the new residence would still apply.

policies are furthered by providing debtors a secure home protected from creditors; the location of the home is not relevant.

Permitting the exemption of the Arizona homestead is consistent with the general rule of liberal construction in favor of the debtor, and furthers the Minnesota policies underlying the exemption. The statute itself does not preclude use of the homestead exemption for an out-of-state property. *Accord* In re Arrol, 170 F.3d at 936 (noting that California's homestead exemption is not limited to in state dwellings). We therefore conclude that the Minnesota exemption can be applied to the Drenttels' Arizona homestead and affirm the decision of the BAP.

QUESTIONS

Is this case right in your opinion? How can the Minnesota legislature create an exemption covering real property in Arizona? How does a state exemption statute operate, and from whom or what is property exempt under those provisions? If your client lives in a state with a limited homestead exemption, what strategy does the case suggest?

Under §302, spouses may commence a joint bankruptcy case by filing a single petition. While this initiates a joint case, each debtor may individually claim exemptions under §522. Bankruptcy Code §522(m). While each debtor may claim property as exempt, §522(b) restricts the debtors to claiming exemptions either under the federal exemption scheme of §522(d) or the otherwise applicable nonbankruptcy exemptions. The debtors may not mix and match exemptions, with one spouse choosing exemptions under §522(d) while the other selects exemptions under the applicable nonbankruptcy law. When property is jointly owned, each debtor can claim its own interest as exempt up to the values provided under the applicable exemption provision. For example, §522(d)(2) exempts the debtor's interests in a motor vehicle up to $2,400 in value. If *H* and *W* jointly own an automobile worth $4,000, then the value of each interest in the automobile is $2,000 and can be claimed entirely exempt under §522(d)(2). If the automobile is owned only by *W*, however, *W*'s exemption in the automobile under §522(d)(2) would be limited to $2,400. *W* might be able to use the "spill-over" exemption of §522(d)(5) to protect the balance of her interest in the car.

CHAPTER *4*

The Automatic Stay

I. The Nature of the Stay

A major reason for the filing of a bankruptcy petition is to give the debtor breathing room in which to sort out financial affairs and figure out what should be paid to whom. It follows that all collection activity by creditors outside the bankruptcy forum must stop, and the Bankruptcy Code so provides. Under §362(a), the filing of the petition creates an automatic stay of any creditor collection activity (with the exceptions mentioned in subsection (b)), in effect an injunction making the creditors leave the debtor and the debtor's property alone. Applications for relief from the stay take the form of a motion under §362(d), (e), and (f). Read §362 and use it to answer the following Problems. As you read §362(a) be aware of the difference between "property of the estate" (the assets under the control of the trustee in bankruptcy pursuant to §541) and "property of the debtor" (exempt property or property acquired by the debtor postpetition).

PROBLEM 4-1

Ralph Debts, a lawyer, borrowed $5,000 from his neighbor, John Loans, and as collateral gave him a security interest in his valuable collection of lawn statuary. The two friends signed a security agreement in favor of John Loans, and Ralph gave him a financing statement, telling John he could perfect his security interest by filing the financing statement with the secretary of state's office (though John did not get around to doing this immediately). Two months later, Ralph was disbarred because of inattention to his clients' interests. His financial life in ruins, he filed a bankruptcy petition on October 1, a fact that he mentioned to John that same evening, when they happened to meet as they came home from their respective offices. "Does this mean I won't get paid?" John asked, and Ralph glumly nodded, whereupon John, furious, slugged Ralph in the face, knocking him to the ground. The next day John (a) filed the financing statement in the secretary of state's office, (b) took all the lawn statuary from in front of Ralph's house and put it in his own garage, and (c) posted a sign in front of his house saying "RALPH DEBTS STIFFS HIS FRIENDS!!!" When Ralph protested these actions and told John about the automatic stay, John replied that he had not received any formal notice that the bankruptcy petition had been filed and that Ralph could go to hell. Nonetheless, John was worried about this conversation, so he calls you, his regular attorney, and asks if he is in trouble. Tell him whether you think any of his actions violate the stay.

If John had waited until Ralph's debt to him had been discharged in the bankruptcy proceeding and the bankruptcy case closed to take these same actions, would he also be in trouble? *See* Bankruptcy Code §524(a)(2), and *see* In re Andrus, 184 B.R. 311 (Bankr. N.D. Ill. 1995) ("DEADBEAT" signs and threats postbankruptcy).

PROBLEM 4-2

In spite of the bankruptcy, could the state supreme court continue the disbarment proceedings against Ralph? If Ralph were living in California, a community property state, and his wife had sued for divorce, could the divorce trial proceed in spite of §362(a)? Could the divorce proceeding include the award of alimony and support? *See* §362(b)(2)(A)(ii).

PROBLEM 4-3

On May 1, the Oops Moving Company bought a new moving van on credit, using funds borrowed from Octopus National Bank, which took a security interest in the new van. State law requires creditors wishing a lien interest in motor vehicles to perfect that interest by getting the security interest noted on the certificate of title, giving the creditors a grace period of 20 days following the purchase in which to do so. On May 3, Oops Moving Company filed its Chapter 7 bankruptcy petition, and the following day, unaware of this, ONB applied for the certificate of title with its lien interest noted thereon. The title was issued two days later. When Oops failed to make the first payment on May 15, ONB, still unaware of the bankruptcy, repossessed the moving van. As ONB's attorney who has just learned all of this, answer the following questions:

(1)   Did the filing of the bankruptcy petition cut off the grace period that state law gives creditors in which to perfect their security interests? *See* Bankruptcy Code §§362(b)(3) and 546(b).

(2)   If the repossession was done without knowledge of the bankruptcy, does it still violate the automatic stay? If Oops Moving Company's manager had phoned the bank with the information that the bankruptcy petition had been filed, but the bank nonetheless repossessed the van, what relief is possible? *See* §362(k). The 2005 amendments to the Bankruptcy Code added §342(g); how does it affect the answer to this question?

(3)   Is a corporate debtor like Oops entitled to the relief in §362(k)? *See also* §105 and the next case.

PROBLEM 4-4

When Mazie Sloop's car was repossessed by Nightflyer Finance Company, which had a perfected security interest in the vehicle, she immediately filed a bankruptcy petition, and the trustee demanded that the finance company surrender the car or be deemed in violation of the automatic stay. Nightflyer Finance Company argued that once repossession occurred the car was no longer the "property of the estate" since title had passed to it on repossession. State law gives repossessing creditors the right to sell the collateral (subject to the debtor's right to redeem it by paying the amount due), and to get obtain a repossession certificate of title in order to do so. Thus Nightflyer contended that the automatic stay did not apply to it. How does this come out? *Compare* In re Kalter, 292 F.3d 1350 (11th Cir. 2002), *with* In re Rozier, 376 F.3d 1323 (11th Cir. 2004); *see also* Mitchell v. BankIllinois, 316 B.R. 891 (S.D. Tex. 2004).

In re Cordle

United States Bankruptcy Court, Northern District of California, 1995
187 B.R. 1

Leslie Tchaikovsky, Bankruptcy Judge.

The trustee of the above-captioned Chapter 7 estate ("Trustee") seeks sanctions against the Farmers Insurance Credit Union ("Credit Union") for willful violation of the automatic stay. For the reasons set forth below, the motion is granted.

Summary of Facts

Prior to the commencement of this bankruptcy case, the debtor (the "Debtor") sold insurance pursuant to a written contract (the "Appointment Contract") with the Farmers Insurance Group of Companies ("Farmers Insurance"). The Appointment Contract provided that, if the contract were terminated, certain amounts would be paid to the Debtor.

The Debtor borrowed approximately $50,000 from Credit Union (the "Loan"), which was affiliated with, but operated separately from, Farmers Insurance. As security for the Loan, the Debtor gave Credit Union a security interest in the Appointment Contract. Credit Union duly perfected its security interest in the Appointment Contract by filing a UCC-1 Financing Statement with the California Secretary of State's Office and by notifying Farmers Insurance of the security interest.

The Debtor commenced this bankruptcy case on March 30, 1995, by filing a voluntary petition seeking relief under Chapter 7 of the Bankruptcy Code. A few days later, without notice to the Trustee, the Debtor terminated the Appointment Contract with Farmers Insurance. He requested that the amounts due upon termination be paid to Credit Union to the extent necessary to satisfy the Loan and that the balance be paid to him. Farmers Insurance asked Credit Union for a payoff demand. In early June 1995, Farmers Insurance paid Credit Union approximately $47,000, the amount of the payoff demand. There is no evidence before the Court that Farmers Insurance knew of the Debtor's bankruptcy prior to making the payment to the Credit Union, and no wrongdoing on the part of Farmers Insurance is alleged at this time.

Credit Union admits receiving notice of the Debtor's bankruptcy prior to receiving the request for the payoff demand. However, at the hearing on the motion for sanctions, counsel for the Credit Union made an offer of proof — to which counsel for the Trustee did not object — that the request for the payoff demand did not alert it to the possibility that Farmers Insurance might be intending to pay any amount due to the Debtor to the Credit Union. Counsel represented that the Credit Union routinely received requests from Farmers Insurance for payoff demands, presumably to enable Farmers Insurance to keep their records current. In this instance, however, after providing the payoff demand, the Credit Union received the amount of the demand.

At about this time, the Trustee learned of the Debtor's termination of the Appointment Contract and of the monies paid to Credit Union. On June 9, 1995, counsel for the Trustee wrote to the Credit Union requesting that the Credit Union send the money received post-petition from Farmers Insurance to the Trustee. Counsel was apparently referred to the Credit Union's counsel. On June 13, 1995, counsel for the Trustee wrote to counsel for the Credit Union, memorializing a phone conversation, requesting the turnover of the money, and promising that "[t]he Credit Union's interest in the funds will not be adversely affected and will be recognized to the same extent and with the same validity and priority as if the funds had not been transferred in violation of the stay."

Counsel for the Credit Union wrote back on July 7, 1995. Her letter includes the following rationale for refusing to comply with the Trustee's turnover demand:

> . . . we see no benefit to anyone nor reason to remit the proceeds to the Trustee for safekeeping. The Credit Union instead has chosen to file a Motion for Relief from Automatic Stay to clarify that it has the right to accept the proceeds.

In fact, the Credit Union had filed a motion for relief on June 26, 1995. By the time of the hearing on the motion for relief, on August 4, 1995, the Trustee was satisfied that the Credit Union's security interest was duly perfected and consented to the Credit Union's motion for relief. However, the Trustee requested a determination by the Court that the Credit Union violated the automatic stay and for sanctions in the amount of any expense to the estate as a result of the Credit Union's violation.

Discussion

The Trustee does not appear to contend that the Credit Union violated the automatic stay by providing Farmers Insurance with a payoff demand or by accepting the funds paid over to it post-petition by Farmers Insurance. His contention that the Credit Union violated the automatic stay appears to be based solely on the Credit Union's refusal to pay the money received post-petition to the Trustee for safekeeping pending resolution of any issues concerning the validity of Credit Union's security interest.

The principal case upon which the Trustee relies is In re Abrams, 127 B.R. 239 (Bankr. 9th Cir. 1991). In *Abrams*, a secured creditor's agent repossessed the debtor's automobile post-petition but without knowledge of the bankruptcy. The debtor's attorney immediately informed both the secured creditor and its agent of the bankruptcy case and demanded the return of the vehicle. The vehicle was not returned. The trustee sought sanctions against the secured creditor pursuant to 11 U.S.C. §362(h) for willful violation of the automatic stay.

The trustee contended that, by refusing to turn over the vehicle, the creditor had "exercised control" over the vehicle in violation of the stay. Since the creditor knew of the bankruptcy case when it refused to turn the vehicle over, the violation was willful. The bankruptcy court found that the violation was not willful and denied sanctions. The Bankruptcy Appellate Panel reversed and remanded for a determination of the appropriate amount of sanctions. The Panel noted that:

> the duty to insure the post-petition return of property of the estate lies with the entity in possession of such property, and not with the debtor. A trustee or debtor-in-possession does have the ability to bring a motion to compel turnover under §542. However, the case law and the legislative history of §362 indicate that Congress did not intend to place the burden on the bankruptcy estate to absorb the expense of potentially multiple turnover actions, at least not without providing a means to recover damages sustained as a consequence thereof. Abrams, 127 B.R. at 243.

The Credit Union contends that *Abrams* and the other cases cited by the Trustee are distinguishable because the creditors in those cases obtained possession of the property in question through some affirmative act whereas the Credit Union simply accepted the payment. This distinction is not well taken. The *Abrams* court noted as persuasive In re Knaus, 889 F.2d 773 (8th Cir. 1989), a case in which, after a bankruptcy case was filed, a creditor refused to turn over property of the estate seized pre-petition. The court held the refusal to violate the automatic stay. In *Knaus*, although the property was obtained through an affirmative act, the act was not wrongful because there was no automatic stay in place at the time it occurred. *See* In re Abrams, 127 B.R. at 242 n.6.

Counsel for the Credit Union contends that its refusal to turn over the money did not violate the automatic stay because it filed a motion for relief from stay within a reasonable time. Counsel contends that it would have risked losing its security interest had it turned the funds over to the trustee because the perfection of its security interest depended upon its possession of the funds. In support of this theory, counsel cites In re Edgins, 36 B.R. 480 (9th Cir. BAP 1984). In *Edgins*, the Bankruptcy Appellate Panel held that a bank asserting a setoff right in funds in a deposit account did not violate the automatic stay by placing an administrative freeze on the account so that the debtor could not withdraw the funds provided it sought relief from the automatic stay within a reasonable period of time.

The Credit Union's argument is not persuasive. Its position is not analogous to that of a bank asserting a setoff right in funds in the debtor's deposit account at the time a bankruptcy case is filed. Despite the fact that one refers to funds being in a deposit account — as if the funds were tangible property — a positive balance in a deposit account constitutes nothing more than an obligation on the part of a bank to pay the amount previously deposited. Section 542(b) provides that:

> . . . an entity that owes a debt that is property of the estate and that is matured, payable on demand, or payable on order, shall pay such debt to, or on the order of, the trustee, *except to the extent that such debt may be offset under section 553 of this title against a claim against the debtor.* [Emphasis added.]

Thus, a bank asserting an offset claim is expressly excused from the general turnover requirement.

Unlike a bank asserting a setoff right with respect to a deposit account, by refusing to turn over the funds received from Farmers Insurance, the Credit Union was not declining to pay a matured debt to preserve its right of setoff. The Credit Union had actually received property of the estate post-petition from Farmers Insurance, had no right of setoff with respect to that property, and thus had no legitimate purpose in retaining the funds.

The Credit Union's contention that it would have lost its security interest had it turned the money over to the Trustee is unreasonable. The Credit Union had a duly perfected security interest in the Appointment Contract when the bankruptcy case was filed. The funds in question were the proceeds of that collateral, and the Credit Union's security interest continued in them. 11 U.S.C. §552(b)(1). Moreover, the Trustee's counsel stipulated in writing that the Credit Union's rights would be preserved notwithstanding the turnover. The Credit Union's suggestion that the Trustee's stipulation that the Credit Union's legal rights would not be adversely affected by the turnover might not be binding on the Trustee is nonsensical.

Section 362(h) provides that an individual injured by a willful violation of the automatic stay is entitled to damages. Moreover, if 11 U.S.C. §362(h) applies, sanctions are mandatory; a bankruptcy court does not have the discretion to decline to impose them. In re Taylor, 884 F.2d 478, 483 (9th Cir. 1989). A violation of the stay is willful if the creditor knew of the bankruptcy case and acted intentionally in such a way that the stay was violated. The fact that the creditor may have acted in good faith and reasonably believed that its conduct did not violate the stay does not make its conduct not willful. In re Bloom, 875 F.2d 224, 227 (9th Cir. 1989). The Credit Union's conduct clearly constituted a willful violation of the automatic stay.

However, 11 U.S.C. §362(h) only applies if the person aggrieved is an individual. In re Goodman, 991 F.2d 613, 619 (9th Cir. 1993).[1] In the instant case, the Trustee is moving for sanctions, not the debtor. Granted, the Trustee is an individual. However, he is moving on behalf of the bankruptcy estate, which is an artificial entity as is a corporation or partnership.

This precise issue was presented in In re Pace, 159 B.R. 890 (Bankr. 9th Cir. 1993). While all three judges on the Panel agreed that sanctions should be imposed in

---

1. There is also a split of authority on this issue. The Goodman court followed In re Chateaugay Corp., 920 F.2d 183, 184-87 (2d Cir. 1990) but noted that the Third and Fourth Circuits had held to the contrary. *See* In re Atlantic Business and Community Corp., 901 F.2d 325, 329 (3d Cir. 1990) and Budget Service Co. v. Better Homes of Virginia, Inc., 804 F.2d 289, 292 (4th Cir. 1986).

that case, only one of the three concluded that a trustee qualified as an individual within the meaning of 11 U.S.C. §362(h). *Pace*, 159 B.R. at 903-04. The other two judges held that the party aggrieved was the bankruptcy estate rather than the trustee. They held further that the estate was an artificial entity like a corporation or partnership and, thus, not an individual under 11 U.S.C. §362(h). *Pace*, 159 B.R. at 904-05.

Part of the basis for the majority's rationale was that looking to the trustee to satisfy the requirement of 11 U.S.C. §362(h) that the party aggrieved be an individual makes no sense because a trustee need not be an individual. Either a corporation or partnership may serve as a trustee. The majority could perceive no policy reason to explain why Congress might compel the imposition of sanctions under 11 U.S.C. §362(h) when the party aggrieved was an individual trustee while denying them when the party aggrieved was a corporate or partnership trustee.

In a similar vein, this Court also notes that, if an individual trustee may qualify as the individual injured by a violation of the stay, presumably, sanctions could be obtained pursuant to 11 U.S.C. §362(h) in a corporate or partnership chapter 11 case in which such a trustee had been appointed. By contrast, sanctions could not be obtained where the debtor remained a debtor-in-possession. Such a result would appear to be directly contrary to the intent of the statute.

All three judges in *Pace* agreed that sanctions should be imposed. The majority based its award of sanctions on 11 U.S.C. §105(a). Unlike sanctions under 11 U.S.C. §362(h), sanctions under §105(a) are discretionary rather than mandatory. In re Pace, 159 B.R. at 904. The Court concludes that the equities require the imposition of sanctions under these circumstances.

The Credit Union does not appear to have acted in bad faith. Counsel for the Credit Union may have sincerely believed that the Credit Union was entitled under the law to withhold the funds and to file a motion for relief from stay. However, her opinion was clearly mistaken. The result of her mistake was the estate was required to incur the expense of attempting to compel the turnover. The estate should be made whole for the amount of this expense.

The fact that the Trustee ultimately agreed that the Credit Union had a valid duly perfected security interest in the sums in question is irrelevant. At the time the Trustee requested that the sums be turned over, the Trustee was not in a position to make that determination. A Trustee has a duty to preserve the assets of the estate. The Trustee acted properly in attempting to obtain the funds for safekeeping, informally, in the first place, by offering to stipulate that the creditor would suffer no adverse effect and, when that failed, by filing a motion to compel the turnover. Unless the Credit Union is required to compensate the estate for those attorneys' fees and costs which would not have been incurred had the funds been turned over upon receipt of the June 13, 1995, letter, the other creditors of the estate will be required to bear this expense. Such a result would be inequitable.

Conclusion

The Credit Union willfully violated the automatic stay by refusing to turn over to the Trustee property of the estate when reasonably requested to do so. The fact that the

Credit Union did not take any affirmative action to obtain the funds, had a properly perfected security interest in the funds, and filed a motion for relief from stay a few weeks later does not excuse or justify the violation. Since the aggrieved party is the bankruptcy estate, which is an artificial entity rather than an individual, sanctions may not be imposed under 11 U.S.C. §362(h). However, sanctions may be imposed — and the Court concludes that they should be — under 11 U.S.C. §105(a).

Within 20 days from the date of service of this decision, counsel for the Trustee shall file a proposed form of order in accordance with this decision with a blank left for the amount of the sanctions. At the same time, counsel for the Trustee shall file a declaration identifying the time and charges which would not have been incurred by the Trustee had the Credit Union turned over the funds in response to the June 13, 1995, letter. Counsel for the Credit Union shall have 10 days from the date of service of the declaration to file an objection to the amounts requested. No reply will be entertained.

Parties that violate the automatic stay face not only the prospect of damages. Often, the courts will hold the entity that violates the stay in contempt. The stay is thus like any injunction, and ignoring its effect can lead to significant sanctions. For example, in one case a bankruptcy court was sufficiently outraged by the actions of a particular creditor that the court held the creditor in contempt and fined the creditor $1,000,000! The court suspended the fine on the condition that the creditor not violate the automatic stay in any other actions before the court for at least one year. The opinion was later withdrawn, but the message it sent was likely received.

A great deal of controversy has existed over the effect of actions taken in violation of the automatic stay. Traditionally, these actions were regarded as void rather than voidable. Section 362(d), however, allows the annulment of the stay, and this possible form of relief from the stay suggests that the stay is voidable rather than void. Read the following case, and consider the impact of a finding that actions in violation of the stay are voidable rather than void.

In re Siciliano
United States Court of Appeals for the Third Circuit, 1994
13 F.3d 748

Roth, Circuit Judge:

This appeal arises from a mortgage foreclosure sale that took place after the filing of debtor's second Chapter 13 petition in bankruptcy. The debtor, Leonard J. Siciliano, had repeatedly defaulted on mortgage payments owed to Prudential Savings and Loan Association (Prudential). After much maneuvering by both Siciliano and Prudential, the sheriff finally held a foreclosure sale three days after Siciliano had filed his second bankruptcy petition, without notifying either Prudential or the sheriff of this filing. Subsequently, Prudential sought relief from the automatic stay in order to validate the sale. The bankruptcy court refused to grant this relief and the district court affirmed. In this appeal, Prudential contends that the bankruptcy court should have granted retroactive relief from the automatic stay. For the reasons set forth below, we will reverse and remand this case to the bankruptcy court for further proceedings consistent with this opinion.

I.

Prudential is a savings and loan association with its principal office in Philadelphia, Pennsylvania. On September 4, 1984, Prudential secured a $17,000.00 loan to Siciliano with a mortgage on his residence located at 2027 South 24th Street, Philadelphia. Siciliano fell behind on his payments and on May 31, 1989, Prudential filed a complaint in the Philadelphia Court of Common Pleas to foreclose on the mortgaged property. In its complaint, Prudential alleged that Siciliano had failed to make his $169.00 monthly payments for the previous eight months. The debt and late charges amounted to $18,169.81. By order entered September 5, 1989, the state court awarded Prudential $19,838.99. A sheriff's sale of the property was scheduled for Monday, December 4, 1989.

On Friday, December 1, 1989, three days before the sheriff's sale, Siciliano filed the first Chapter 13 bankruptcy petition in the United States Bankruptcy Court for the Eastern District of Pennsylvania. Pursuant to the Bankruptcy Code, the petition triggered an automatic stay of all creditor proceedings. 11 U.S.C. §362(a). Thereafter, Siciliano failed to make several post-petition mortgage payments to Prudential.

On February 19, 1991, Prudential filed a motion for relief from the automatic stay. By order entered April 4, 1991, the bankruptcy court held that Prudential could proceed with its state foreclosure action if Siciliano should default again on his payments. As a prerequisite to foreclosure, Prudential had to provide Siciliano with notice and a five-day cure period. Siciliano, however, defaulted once more and by order entered June 20, 1991, the bankruptcy court granted Prudential relief from the automatic stay.

During this period, while Prudential was attempting to complete the foreclosure on the property, the United States Trustee had independently initiated steps to dismiss the bankruptcy proceeding because of Siciliano's failure to make the payments required by his Chapter 13 Plan. On October 4, 1991, the trustee filed a motion to dismiss the petition. A hearing on the trustee's motion was held on November 7, 1991, and the bankruptcy court granted the dismissal that same day.

Meanwhile, Prudential was still attempting to set up a sheriff's sale of the property. The sale was rescheduled for Monday, December 2, 1991. At that time, the mortgage debt amounted to $22,517.12. On Friday, November 29, 1991, once again just three days before the scheduled sale, Siciliano filed his second Chapter 13 bankruptcy petition. Despite this new filing, the December 2 foreclosure sale proceeded as scheduled. Prudential did not become aware of the second petition until December 4, when notice was published in a Philadelphia legal newspaper. Siciliano did not inform the sheriff of the second bankruptcy filing until December 5.

On December 23, 1991, Prudential filed a motion for relief from the automatic stay triggered by the November 29, 1991, petition. On January 6, 1992, while Prudential's motion was pending, the bankruptcy court dismissed Siciliano's second Chapter 13 petition because of Siciliano's failure to file the required documents. The court subsequently dismissed Prudential's motion for relief from the stay as moot.

On March 3, 1992, the bankruptcy court held a hearing to consider Siciliano's request for an opportunity to file a Chapter 7 petition, which the court construed as a motion to reconsider the January 6, 1992, dismissal of his second Chapter 13 petition. As a result of that hearing, the court entered an order on March 5, 1992, holding that any sale of the property on December 2, 1991, was void and that the dismissal of the bankruptcy petition would stand. Prudential filed a motion to reconsider the order and for retroactive relief from the automatic stay in order to validate the sheriff's sale of the mortgaged property. After a hearing, the court denied Prudential's motion. On appeal, the district court affirmed the bankruptcy court order. Prudential's timely appeal followed. Siciliano is appearing pro se in this appeal.

II.

. . . The bankruptcy court dismissed Prudential's motion for relief from the automatic stay as moot stating that, if a sale had occurred in violation of the stay, the sale was void ab initio. Moreover, it held that Siciliano did not exhibit any bad faith to warrant an annulment of the stay. The court questioned Prudential's good faith, noting that it had made no effort to remedy the consequences of the sheriff's sale.

On appeal, Prudential maintains that relief from the automatic stay could apply retroactively to validate the sheriff's sale. Furthermore, it submits that such relief is warranted because Siciliano has acted in bad faith in an attempt to frustrate the collection process. Because we find that authority for the bankruptcy court to validate the foreclosure sale was available under 11 U.S.C. §362(d), we do not go on to consider the issue of good faith.

After careful consideration of the relevant statutory provisions of the Bankruptcy Code, we find that the bankruptcy court erred when it dismissed Prudential's motion on the basis that the foreclosure sale was void, not merely voidable. While the court correctly articulated the general principle that any creditor action taken in violation of an automatic stay is void ab initio, *see* Maritime Electric Co. v. United Jersey Bank, 959 F.2d 1194, 1206 (3d Cir. 1991), we find that the instant case falls within an exception to that rule.

The Bankruptcy Code states that a bankruptcy petition operates as a stay of all enforcement proceedings against the debtor. 11 U.S.C. §362(a). The purpose of the automatic stay provision is to afford the debtor a "breathing spell" by halting the collection process. It enables the debtor to attempt a repayment or reorganization plan with an aim toward satisfying existing debt. Maritime Electric Co., 959 F.2d at 1204. *See also* H.R. Rep. No. 595, 95th Cong., 1st Sess. 340 (1978), reprinted in 1978 U.S.

Code Cong. & Admin. News 5787, 6296-97 (stating that the automatic stay is designed to relieve the debtor of "the financial pressures that drove him into bankruptcy").

It is undisputed that Prudential violated the automatic stay when it proceeded with the sheriff's sale of the mortgaged property after Siciliano filed his Chapter 13 petition. Prudential contends, however, that there is relief available to cure the violation.

Prudential relies on the portion of the Code which states:

> (d) On request of a party in interest and after notice and a hearing, the court shall grant relief from the stay provided under subsection (a) of this section, such as by terminating, annulling, modifying or conditioning such stay— . . .
> (2) with respect to a stay of an act against property under subsection (a) of this section, if—
>   (A) the debtor does not have an equity in such property, and
>   (B) such property is not necessary to an effective reorganization.

11 U.S.C. §362(d) (emphasis added). This provision clearly indicates that under the conditions prescribed in subsection (d)(2)(A) and (B), the bankruptcy court shall grant relief from the automatic stay, if requested to do so by a party in interest. Included in the relief available is the annulment of the stay. The issue we must address is whether such an annulment could effectively validate the December 2, 1991, sheriff's sale. While we have recognized the limited circumstances under which other Circuits have applied relief retroactively, this court has yet to directly address this issue. *See* Maritime Electric Co., 959 F.2d at 1207, n.11 (acknowledging that certain courts rely on section 362(d) to cure acts that are otherwise void under the automatic stay).

We agree with Prudential's contention that the inclusion of the word "annulling" in the statute indicates a legislative intent to apply certain types of relief retroactively and validate proceedings that would otherwise be void ab initio. As the Fifth Circuit has acknowledged, "[t]he power to annul authorizes the court to validate actions taken subsequent to the impressing of the section 362(a) stay."[2] Sikes v. Global Marine, Inc., 881 F.2d 176, 178 (5th Cir. 1989). *See also* In re Schwartz, 954 F.2d 569, 572 (9th Cir. 1992) (observing that "section 362 gives the bankruptcy court wide latitude in crafting relief from the automatic stay, including the power to grant retroactive relief from the stay"). We note that, if such relief did not apply retroactively, then "its inclusion next to 'terminating' would be superfluous." In re Albany Partners, Ltd., 749 F.2d 670, 675 (11th Cir. 1984). *See also* 2 Collier's Bankruptcy Manual ¶362.06 (3d ed. 1983) (stating that an order "annulling the stay could operate retroactively to the date of the filing the petition which gave

---

2. We find it significant that the Code expressly permits certain post-petition transactions that occur in violation of the automatic stay. Some transactions, for example, will be considered valid unless voided by the trustee. 11 U.S.C. §549. In addition, post-petition property transfers are valid when the parties act in good faith without knowledge that the debtor filed a bankruptcy petition. 11 U.S.C. §542(c). We agree with the Fifth Circuit's conclusion that "[i]f everything done post-petition were void in the strict sense of the word, these provisions would either be meaningless or inconsistent with the specific mandate of section 362(a)." Sikes, 881 F.2d at 179.

rise to the stay; . . . [while] an order terminating the stay would be operative only from the date of its entry").

Accordingly, we conclude that the bankruptcy court erred when it dismissed Prudential's motion for relief from the November 17, 1991, automatic stay as void, not voidable. Pursuant to section 362(d), the bankruptcy court had authority to grant an annulment of the stay. If it had done so, the post-petition sheriff's sale would have been validated as an exception to the void ab initio rule.

For the above reasons, we will remand this case to the bankruptcy court to determine whether this case meets the conditions of 11 U.S.C. §362(d)(2)(A) or (B). We note that, based on our review of the bankruptcy court hearing transcripts, there appears to be serious question whether Siciliano possessed equity in the mortgaged property. According to the hearing testimony, the estimated value of Siciliano's property was $22,000 and there were two outstanding mortgages with a total balance due of $37,500. *See* Bankruptcy Court Hearing Transcript, April 9, 1992, at 25. Thus, it appears that Siciliano lacked equity in the property when he filed his bankruptcy petition. Given these factors, upon Prudential's request for relief under §362(d), the bankruptcy court must consider whether Siciliano had an equity in the property and if not, grant appropriate relief to Prudential. For the reasons stated above, appropriate relief could include annulling the stay and validating the sheriff's sale.

Bank Accounts and the Automatic Stay. A setoff is nothing more than a subtraction of one debt from another. It arises whenever cross-obligations are compared. If, as a result of one transaction, I owe you $50 and, as a result of another transaction, you owe me $30, when you come to collect the $50 from me, I can set off the other debt and only pay you $20.

When someone deposits money in a bank, the law treats the deposit as a loan by the customer to the bank, so that the customer is the creditor and the bank is, to the amount of the deposit, a debtor. Say that the customer then borrows $1,000 for a home improvement from the same bank, but fails to repay it as agreed. If the bank takes the $1,000 out of the customer's checking account, this works as a setoff (which bankers, perversely, insist on calling an "offset"), the two debts being compared with one another. It is clear that this conduct done after the filing of the customer's bankruptcy petition would violate the automatic stay; *see* §362(a)(7).

Suppose that instead of a setoff of the home improvement loan against the bank account the following happens. When the bank learns of the filing of the bankruptcy petition, it freezes the account in the amount of $1,000 (not allowing the debtor access to this amount of the deposited funds, but not taking it for itself either — bankers sometimes call this an "administrative hold"). The bank also immediately files a motion under §362(d) to lift the stay so it can apply the frozen funds to the repayment of the home improvement debt. Would this conduct be the same thing as a setoff, and thus a violation of the automatic stay? The answer is no; an administrative hold on the

funds was held not a violation of the stay by the United States Supreme Court in
Citizens Bank of Maryland v. Strumpf, 516 U.S.16 (1995), in which the court reasoned that all the bank is doing here is preserving the status quo until given direction
by the bankruptcy court — hardly contemptuous activity.

Finally, it should be noted that the Truth in Lending Act, which regulates credit
cards, among other matters, flatly forbids a bank to set off consumer credit card debts
against the consumer's bank account without the cardholder's permission and provides severe penalties if the bank should do this (this is true whether or not a bankruptcy is involved). *See* TIL, 15 U.S.C. §1666h; the penalties are found at 15 U.S.C.
§1640.

In re Holford

United States Court of Appeals, Fifth Circuit, 1990
896 F.2d 176

Garza, Circuit Judge:

Alden Holford appeals contempt penalties imposed against him for violation of
the automatic stay in Powers' bankruptcy proceeding when he offset rents due against
damages in a state court fraud claim. Because we find that his actions constituted a
recoupment and not a setoff, we REVERSE the contempt holding.

Facts

In March of 1982, a Vice-President of M. Lane Powers Investment Builder
("Powers") negotiated a lease with Holford for 1000 square feet of office space at
$1,326.00 per month. Holford leased more space than he needed, as the vice-president
assured him that the extra space could be sublet with no problem; the extra space in
fact was never sublet despite Holford's efforts. The pro rata rental share of the extra,
unleased space was $600.00 per month.

Holford first brought up the issue of fraud in the negotiation of the lease in
January, 1983, in a letter to the vice-president who negotiated the lease with him
and told him he would have no problems leasing the extra space. Beginning in
February, 1983, Holford began noting on the monthly rental check that he was not
waiving any rights regarding the extra space. Upon learning of Powers' bankruptcy
proceedings in January of 1984, Holford began to send letters instead of rent checks,
recovering his fraud damages from the rental payments as they came due. No further
rent was paid through April 1985, when the lease terminated.

Powers sued for non-payment of rent in July, 1984, and Holford counter-claimed
for fraud damages. In his bankruptcy proceeding, Powers filed a Motion to Show
Cause why Holford should not be held in contempt for violating the automatic stay by
filing his fraud counterclaim. Powers' Bankruptcy Court held that Holford properly
filed the counterclaim, but was in violation of 11 U.S.C. §362(a)(7) by the setoff of
his fraud damages against rents due the post-petition Powers. The district court
below affirmed the finding and the award of $300.00 in attorneys' fees. This appeal
followed.

Discussion

Today we must determine not only whether Holford's actions constituted a recoupment and not a setoff, but also whether a recoupment is subject to the section 362(a) stay in a bankruptcy proceeding.

1.   Recoupment v. Setoff

"Recoupment allows a defendant to reduce the amount of a plaintiff's claim by asserting a claim against the plaintiff *which arose out of the same transaction* to arrive at a just and proper liability on the plaintiff's claim. Collier on Bankruptcy para. 553.03 (15th ed. 1984). In contrast, setoff involves a claim of the defendant against the plaintiff which arises out of a transaction which is different from that on which the plaintiff's claim is based. Id." In re Clowards, Inc., 42 B.R. 627, 628 (Bankr. D. Idaho 1984) (emphasis added).

Here, Holford used rental payments due under the lease to recoup losses caused by fraud in the inducement of that same lease; clearly, the two amounts arose out of the same transaction. Even so, the district court found that the transaction was a setoff because (1) there was no express contractual right in the lease to withhold the rental payments, and (2) the amount Powers may have ultimately owed to Holford could not be known until the resolution of the state court cause.

There need not have been any express contractual right to withhold payments for the transaction to be a recoupment. In In re B & L Oil Co., 782 F.2d 155, 159 (10th Cir. 1986), the court stated that application of the "equitable doctrine [of recoupment] should not depend on whether the parties expressly anticipated the problem," and allowed recoupment absent express contractual permission.

We also reject the district court's holding that the uncertainty of the fraud damages owed bars recoupment. Because most recoupment cases arise in adversarial proceedings in the bankruptcy court, the "amount to be recouped" is almost always in question. In In re Career Consultants, Inc., 84 B.R. 419, 426 (Bankr. E.D. Va. 1988), the court held that the recouping party's determination of the amount to be recouped was proper, subject to court oversight. As we have no evidence before us that Holford's pro rata determination of $600 per month was an improper amount of damages, we leave it intact.

Also, in *Clowards*, 42 B.R. at 628, the court did not directly address the issue of uncertain amounts of recoupment, but the result seems to do so. Contractors there were allowed to recoup their losses absent any certain determination of their damages.

Finally, recoupment is an equitable doctrine designed to "determine a just liability on the plaintiff's claim." Id. If Holford were required to pursue an adversarial proceeding to determine the final amount of his damages, and only then allowed to recoup those losses, the doctrine's purpose would be severely undermined. Indeed, the mere passage of time would take from Holford the opportunity to recoup the losses from their proper source: rents arising from the same transaction. And, the trustee would have been fully able to challenge those fraud damages and ultimately come to a "just liability" on the lease.

2. Recoupment and the Stay

The district court stated that, whether the actions constituted a recoupment or a setoff, the funds were the property of the bankruptcy estate and were subject to the section 362(a) automatic stay. We disagree. The trustee of a bankruptcy estate "takes the property subject to rights of recoupment." *Career Consultants*, 84 B.R. at 426. That is, "to the extent the damages equal or exceed the funds withheld, the debtor has no interest in the funds and, therefore, the stay has not been violated." Id. at 424. Further, in *B & L*, 782 F.2d at 158, the Tenth Circuit specifically allowed post-petition recoupment of damages against continuing payments.

Conclusion

Because we find that the transaction in question constituted a recoupment and not a setoff, and that a recoupment is not subject to the automatic stay of section 362(a), we REVERSE and RENDER the contempt order of the district court.

II. Lifting the Stay

Our law must play fair with all parties, and certainly in a bankruptcy proceeding the creditor is entitled to reach the collateral that was nominated by the debtor to encourage the credit extension. The automatic stay prevents the creditor from getting to that collateral, but the stay is always meant to be temporary until the bankruptcy court can sort out the various priorities. A creditor with a perfected security interest may make a motion for the trustee in bankruptcy to abandon the collateral to the creditor— *see* §554—which, at least in Chapter 7 cases, the trustee will not oppose if the bankruptcy estate has no equity in the property because the secured creditor's interest consumes the asset's economic value. In such a case, the property is surrendered to the creditor free of the interest of the bankruptcy estate and applied against the debt. If it does not pay it all, the creditor is, as to the remaining amount, an unsecured creditor.

Another tactic for the creditor is to make a motion under §362(d) or (f) for the bankruptcy court to lift the automatic stay and allow the creditor access to the collateral. First read the "irreparable damage" ground embodied in §362(f). There are some situations so dire (the collateral is rapidly losing value because of dramatic market collapse, for example), that immediate action is required or no action will be necessary. This is where the creditor's attorney will go in emergencies, but talking the court into granting §362(f) relief is reserved for obvious cases and/or talented attorneys. Easier, as relief, is the procedure described in §362(d) and (e). Read those subsections and apply them to the following Problem.

PROBLEM 4-5

William Wheels owned an automobile that he used to get to and from work. To finance the $18,000 purchase price of the vehicle, he had borrowed that amount from Nightflyer Finance Company, which made sure that its lien interest was noted on the certificate of title (thus perfecting its security interest in the car — Nightflyer will also keep possession of the certificate of title until it is paid in full). William made some payments on the car, but at the time he filed his Chapter 13 bankruptcy petition he still owed Nightflyer $12,500; the current retail value of the car is only $8,000. Nightflyer made a motion to lift the stay so that it could foreclose on the car. You are the bankruptcy judge who must decide whether to grant this motion.

(a) Does William have any "equity" in the car? This will be relevant under §362(d)(2)(A); see Stewart v. Gurley, 745 F.2d 1194 (9th Cir. 1984) ("equity" is the difference between the property value and the total amount of liens against it).

(b) If William needs the car to get to and from work, and needs the money from his job in order to fund his Chapter 13 plan, will you grant the motion? See §362(d)(2)(B).

(c) If William is a bad driver, forever getting drunk and smashing up the car (hence its rapid decline in value), will you now grant the motion under §362(d)(1)?

(d) If William gets property insurance on the car in an amount sufficient to make sure that Nightflyer will be paid, will this be "adequate protection" of Nightflyer's interest as that phrase is defined in §361?

(e) If you the judge do nothing for 45 days after Nightflyer files its motion, may it now repossess the car without having to get the court's permission, or would this be contemptuous activity? See §362(e). Suppose you hold a hearing in the matter, but no order is entered until 70 days after the filing of the motion for relief from the stay? Now what? See §362(e)(2).

As extensive as the automatic stay is, it is not without its limitations. Section 362(b) includes 28 situations to which the stay of subsection (a) does not apply. Some are almost so obvious that you would not think it is necessary to list them. For example, filing a bankruptcy petition will not stay a criminal action against the debtor. Some aspects of domestic relations actions are excepted from the stay, as are actions by governmental units to enforce their police and regulatory powers. In the 2005 amendments to the Bankruptcy Code, Congress gave landlords and mortgage holders some additional relief from the automatic stay under subsections (b)(2) to (24), so debtors with prior cases and those who have been sued for eviction from an apartment may not get the benefit of the automatic stay.

Generally, the primary focus of the court in a hearing on relief from the automatic stay is the value of the property subject to a creditor's claim. This valuation might be done on the assumption that the property will be liquidated, or the valuation could be set at a going concern value. For a description of the valuation process in a variety of contexts in bankruptcy proceedings, see Chaim J. Fortgang & Thomas M. Mayer, Valuation in Bankruptcy, 32 U.C.L.A. L. Rev. 1061 (1985). For a classic discussion of valuation that is still cited regularly by the courts and commentators, see J. Bonbright, Valuation of Property (1938). The following case also involves the issues and methods of valuation in bankruptcy proceedings. In 2005, §101(51B) of the Code was amended to expand the definition of single asset real estate cases. Prior to that time, single asset real estate was limited to entities with debts of no more than $4,000,000. The 2005 amendments deleted any debt limitation for single asset real estate, so the limitations in §362(d)(3) would now apply to the next case.

In re Indian Palms Associates, Ltd.

United States Court of Appeals, Third Circuit, 1995
61 F.3d 197

STAPLETON, Circuit Judge:

Creditor California Federal Bank ("CalFed"), holder of a first mortgage against the debtor partnership's primary asset ("the property"), seeks relief from the automatic stay in a Chapter 11 bankruptcy proceeding in order to initiate foreclosure proceedings. Nantucket Investors II ("Nantucket Investors"), who holds a second mortgage against the property, opposes the lifting of the stay.

The bankruptcy court granted CalFed relief from the stay under 11 U.S.C. §362(d)(1), finding that CalFed's interest in the property was not being adequately protected during the pendency of the bankruptcy proceedings. The district court reversed, finding that CalFed's current claim, having been reduced by post-petition payments, was less than the bankruptcy court had determined and was adequately protected. The district court also found that the debtor retained equity in the property and that relief from the automatic stay would therefore be unavailable under 11 U.S.C. §362(d)(2) as well. We will reverse the order of the district court and remand with instructions to return this matter to the bankruptcy court for further proceedings consistent with this opinion.

I.

Indian Palms Associates, the debtor partnership, was formed to acquire a 176-unit garden apartment complex located in Florida. The debtor purchased that property from Nantucket Investors in 1983, and it is the debtor's primary asset. In 1984 the debtor executed a promissory note of $3.9 million in favor of CalFed, and a mortgage and security agreement to secure payment of the note. Pursuant to the mortgage and note, CalFed also received an assignment of the property's leases, rents, and income.

On December 13, 1990, the debtor filed for relief under Chapter 11 of the Bankruptcy Code, triggering the automatic stay imposed by 11 U.S.C. §362(a). At that time, CalFed held a first mortgage against the property, which, with accrued interest and late charges, totalled approximately $4.5 million. Nantucket Investors held a second mortgage on the property of approximately $500,000, and a third mortgage was held by FEC Mortgage Company ("FEC") in the amount of $1.6 million. FEC was, and remains, an affiliate of the debtor. At the time of the bankruptcy filing, there was also a property tax lien against the property of between $92,000 and $300,000. The parties agree that the tax lien has priority over CalFed's first mortgage. At the time of the bankruptcy filing, the value of the property was between $4.65 and $5.25 million.

During the course of the bankruptcy proceedings, the debtor filed a series of plans of reorganization which were not confirmed. CalFed consented to both the second and third amended plans, but the debtor withdrew the third amended plan when CalFed refused to agree to certain amendments that were necessary to ensure the plan's confirmation. CalFed then moved for relief from the automatic stay under sections 362(d)(1) and (d)(2) of the Bankruptcy Code so that it could institute foreclosure proceedings against the property. In opposition to that motion, the debtor submitted a letter memorandum with a proposed fourth amended plan of reorganization.

The debtor's fourth amended plan proposed the following: (1) the continuance of CalFed's lien on the property in the full amount of its claim with annual interest payments based on an interest rate of 7.75%, plus payments of excess cash flow after the first two years, and a balloon payment for the remaining mortgage balance five years after confirmation, (2) the payment in full of all real estate taxes and arrearages, (3) an initial $50,000 payment to Nantucket Investors on its second mortgage with various payments to follow, and (4) the infusion of $425,000 in new capital by the debtor's partners for capital improvements on and maintenance of the property.

The bankruptcy court held a hearing on CalFed's motion to vacate the stay. At the hearing, Nantucket Investors joined the debtor in actively opposing the proposed lifting of the stay. The bankruptcy court granted CalFed's motion. In its oral ruling, the bankruptcy court explained that the debtor had failed to show that CalFed's interest in the property was adequately protected because the value of the property had been steadily declining since the bankruptcy petition was filed and the debtor had submitted no evidence to demonstrate that the value would not continue to decline if the stay were not lifted. The bankruptcy court thus found that the lifting of the stay could be granted under section 362(d)(1) which provides that "the court shall grant relief from the [automatic] stay . . . for cause, including the lack of adequate protection of an interest in property of such party in interest." 11 U.S.C. §362(d)(1).

Based on what it understood to be a concession by the debtor, the bankruptcy court determined that the $1.1 million in post-petition payments made by the debtor to CalFed had been interest payments rather than payments on the principal debt. Thus, in reaching the conclusion that CalFed was inadequately protected, the bankruptcy court did not reduce the principal debt by the amount of these post-petition payments and concluded that CalFed was owed just over $4.5 million. As a result, the debtor's secured indebtedness to CalFed was found to be slightly greater than the property's value at the time of the hearing, which was stipulated to be $4.5 million.

The bankruptcy court's discussion of the liens outstanding against the property led to an implicit finding that the total liens exceeded the current stipulated value of the property and that the debtor therefore had no equity in the property — a factor supporting relief from the stay under section 362(d)(2). Although the court noted that its resolution of the issues under section 362(d)(1) meant that it need not consider the factors necessary for relief from the stay under section 362(d)(2), the court went on to discuss the second section 362(d)(2) factor — whether the property is necessary to an effective reorganization. The court concluded that the proposed fourth plan would not be confirmable without CalFed's consent because it improperly extended the original maturity date of CalFed's loan. According to the bankruptcy court, section 362(d)(2) thus provided an alternate basis for granting relief from the automatic stay. The court entered an order lifting the stay and allowing CalFed to institute a foreclosure action against the debtor.

Nantucket Investors appealed to the district court. Thereafter, CalFed filed a motion to strike certain documents that Nantucket Investors had designated as part of the record on appeal. The district court denied CalFed's motion to strike the documents and reversed the bankruptcy court's order lifting the stay. . . .

As to Nantucket's appeal, the district court found clearly erroneous the bankruptcy court's finding of an agreement among the parties that the post-petition payments of $1.1 million represented interest payments. First, the district court noted that the debtor had argued to the contrary in the hearing before the bankruptcy court. Second, the district court determined that of the $1.1 million post-petition payments made by the debtor to CalFed, at least $955,000 should have been attributed to payments on principal rather than interest. Relying on United Savings Ass'n of Texas v. Timbers of Inwood Forest Assocs., Ltd., 484 U.S. 365, 108 S. Ct. 626, 98 L. Ed. 2d 740 (1988), the district court concluded that section 506(b) of the Bankruptcy Code limits post-petition interest to oversecured claims and only to the extent of their oversecurity at the time the bankruptcy petition is filed.[3] Based on the parties's appraisals, the district court estimated that the value of the property at the time of filing was approximately $4.75 million. It further found that CalFed's claim at that time was approximately $4.513 million subordinated to tax liens of $92,000.00. As a result, CalFed was only oversecured by approximately $145,000 and thus, under 11 U.S.C. §506(b), the full $1.1 million in post-petition payments could not have represented payments on interest. Rather, at most, only $145,000 of the post-petition payments were payments of interest. Allocating the balance of these payments to payments on principal left CalFed with a claim of approximately $3.558 million. Comparing this figure to the current value of the property (which for purposes of this motion the parties stipulated to be $4.5 million), less the outstanding value of the senior tax lien ($250,000), left CalFed with a $700,000 "equity cushion." The district court determined that this difference was sufficient to protect CalFed's interest, and held that CalFed was therefore not entitled to relief under section 362(d)(1).

The district court went on to determine whether relief could be granted under section 362(d)(2). The district court rejected the bankruptcy court's implicit comparison between the value of the property and the total liens against the property, and accepted Nantucket Investors's argument that only the difference between CalFed's claim and the property's current value (less the current value of the senior tax lien) should be considered. This left the debtor with an equity interest worth approximately $700,000. The court found this analysis appropriate under the circumstances because both junior lien holders, Nantucket Investors and the debtor's affiliate FEC, opposed the lifting of the stay and were willing to accept under the fourth plan of reorganization a drastic impairment of their claims, which the court found had the effect of

---

3. The Bankruptcy Code does not speak of secured and unsecured creditors, but of allowed secured and unsecured claims. 11 U.S.C. §506(a). An allowed claim is secured to the extent the value of the collateral equals the claim. To the extent a claim exceeds the value of the collateral securing it, it becomes an unsecured claim in the bankruptcy case. Thus, an undersecured claim becomes bifurcated under §506(a) into two claims, one secured and one unsecured. Because the bankruptcy court concluded that CalFed's claim was oversecured, its claim was considered a fully secured claim for purposes of determining the accrual of interest under §506(b).

increasing the debtor's interest in the property.[4] The district court found it equitable
under these circumstances to disregard their claims in determining whether the debtor
had equity in the property. The district court thus found that the stay could not be lifted
under section 362(d)(2).

The district court also reached the issue whether the property was necessary to an
effective reorganization, the second prerequisite to the granting of relief under section
362(d)(2). It rejected the bankruptcy court's view that a "cram down" which
extended the terms of a mortgage was unreasonable as a matter of law. The district
court stated that, if its ruling on the existence of equity were reversed on appeal, the
matter should be remanded to the bankruptcy court for a determination as to whether
the debtor had proposed an effective reorganization such that relief under §362(d)(2)
would be foreclosed. The district court entered an order remanding to the bankruptcy
court for entry of an order denying CalFed's motion and for further proceedings
consistent with its opinion. The "further proceedings" apparently referred to the
bankruptcy court's ability to determine the actual amount of the tax liens and the
actual value of the property as of the filing date. . . .

II.

Argo Loan Limited Partnership, as assignee of CalFed's claim, raises three issues
on appeal: (1) whether the district court erred in denying CalFed's motion to strike
documents not presented to or considered by the bankruptcy court in connection with
CalFed's motion to lift the stay; (2) whether the district court erred in determining
that the debtor had equity in the property for purposes of 11 U.S.C. §362(d)(2)(A),
and (3) whether the district court exceeded its scope of appellate review by making
factual findings with regard to the proper allocation of the $1.1 million post-petition
payments. . . .

We conclude that CalFed's motion to strike was properly denied because the
documents which CalFed sought to strike from the appellate record, having been
filed in the bankruptcy case record, were part of the relevant record in this contested
matter. However, we disagree with the district court's application of the standards for
determining the debtor's equity in the property and conclude that the debtor did not
have equity in the property under the correct legal standard. We will therefore reverse
and remand so that the bankruptcy court may determine whether relief from the
automatic stay should be granted under section 362(d)(2). We also conclude that

---

4. The debtor and Nantucket testified before the bankruptcy court regarding modifications to the fourth plan to
which the creditors had recently agreed. Under the revised fourth plan, Nantucket would get a payment of $50,000 upon
confirmation of the plan, and a $150,000 lien which would accrue interest at the rate of 8%, would be paid in full in five
years, and would be subordinated to CalFed's claim and the tax lien. The balance of its claim, $350,000, would accrue
at 8% and would be subordinated to the debtor's limited partners receiving four times its investment capital of
$425,000. App. 342-43. The FEC mortgage, held by the debtor's general partner, would be subordinated to all
other claims, including the unsecured claims and the equity interest holders receiving ten times the value of their
$425,000 new capital infusion. App. 343. The tax lien, which had been converted to a tax certificate and sold to another
party with whom the debtor negotiated a reduction in interest, would be reduced from $300,000 to $250,000 and accrue
interest at the negotiated rate of 10% instead of at the former 18% interest rate.

the district court did not engage in any impermissible factfinding in determining the proper allocation of the post-petition payments, but simply applied the law to the record developed before the bankruptcy court. . . .

IV.

When a debtor files for protection under Chapter 11 of the Bankruptcy Code, section 362(a) provides an automatic stay of most actions against the debtor's property, including actions to realize the value of collateral securing an obligation of the debtor. 11 U.S.C. §362(a). Because a secured creditor risks losing the benefit of its security interest if it is unable to foreclose against the property, the Bankruptcy Code permits a creditor to seek such relief by filing a motion for relief from the automatic stay under 11 U.S.C. §362(d) [which the court quoted]. Section 362(d) is thus intended to balance the interests of the creditors and the debtor.

CalFed sought relief from the automatic stay under both subsections (d)(1) and (d)(2) of section 362(d). We first review the district court's conclusion that the debtor retained equity in the property. We conclude that the district court committed an error of law.

A.

The classic test for determining equity under section 362(d)(2) focuses on a comparison between the total liens against the property and the property's current value citing cases. "All encumbrances are totalled to determine equity whether or not all lienholders have requested relief from the stay." Nazareth Nat'l Bank & Trust Co. v. Trina-Dee, Inc. (In re Trina-Dee, Inc.), 26 B.R. 152, 154 (Bankr. E.D. Pa. 1983), *aff'd*, 731 F.2d 170 (3d Cir. 1984). The district court chose not to apply this formula, finding it appropriate under the circumstances to exclude consideration of the junior secured claims held by Nantucket and FEC. Nantucket Investors argues that the district court properly excluded the interests of it and FEC because both agreed to compromise their interests in a subordination agreement in order to avoid foreclosure. We find that the following factors weigh against Nantucket Investors' position: (1) the plain language of section 362(d)(2)(A); (2) the legislative history and policies behind the Bankruptcy Code; and (3) the fact that the Code provides other means by which the interests of junior lienholders may be protected.

B.

The Bankruptcy Code does not define the term "equity" in section 362(d)(2)(A) or in any other section. Nor does the legislative history shine any direct light on the intended meaning of this term. When Congress enacted the present-day Bankruptcy Code, however, the generally understood meaning of equity interest was the value of a property above all secured liens. *See* Black's Law Dictionary 634 (4th ed. 1968) (defining equity for purposes of real estate transactions as: "The remaining interest belonging to one who has pledged or mortgaged his property, or the surplus of value which may remain after the property has been disposed of for the satisfaction of liens. The amount or value of a property above the total liens or charges."). We must assume that Congress was cognizant of this traditional meaning when it enacted section 362(d)(2)(A) without a controlling definition. *See* Walter E. Heller Western, Inc. v. Faires (In re Faires), 34 B. R. 549, 552 (Bankr. W.D. Wash. 1983).

Nantucket Investors argues that the term equity in section 362(d)(2) is ambiguous because equity is accorded a different meaning when the creditor's "equity cushion" is calculated in determining whether the creditor's interest is adequately protected under section 362(d)(1). The text of section 362(d)(1), which governs relief from the automatic stay for good cause including lack of adequate protection, does not contain the term "equity." However, in determining whether a secured creditor's interest is adequately protected, most courts engage in an analysis of the property's "equity cushion" — the value of the property after deducting the claim of the creditor seeking relief from the automatic stay and all senior claims. [citing cases]. Junior liens are disregarded for "equity cushion" analysis because the secured creditor is entitled to adequate protection only as to its claim; it may not claim protection for others. La Jolla Mortgage Fund, 18 B.R. at 289. In contrast, all liens are considered in calculating the equity retained by the debtor under section 362(d)(2), because the equity analysis in that section focuses on "the value, above all secured claims against the property, that can be realized from the sale of the property for the benefit of all unsecured creditors." Pistole v. Mellor (In re Mellor), 734 F.2d 1396, 1400 n.2 (9th Cir. 1984). Thus, the analysis of the creditor's "equity cushion" under section 362(d)(1) differs from a calculation of the debtor's equity under section 362(d)(2) and does not render the term "equity" ambiguous. *E.g., Mellor*, 734 F.2d at 1400 n.2 (noting that "equity cushion" differs from "equity" in that the former is concerned with the value of the property above the amount owed to the creditor with a secured claim and the latter is concerned with the value above all secured claims against the property); (citing cases).

C.

We recognize that some bankruptcy courts have rejected the standard definition of equity for purposes of section 362(d)(2) analysis when junior lienholders protest the lifting of the automatic stay to permit foreclosure [citing cases]. Nantucket Investors urges us to adopt that rule, but we decline to do so.

We find no hint in the language or legislative history of section 362(d), and the interests balancing it incorporates, that authorizes excluding the junior lienholders' claims from the equity calculation when their interests diverge from the senior lienholder's. As the Court of Appeals for the Ninth Circuit has explained:

> The language of the statute simply refers to the debtor's "equity," which has been defined as 'the amount or value of a property above the total liens or charges.' The statute does not refer to the debtor's equity as against the only plaintiff-lienholder seeking to lift the stay or persons holding

liens senior to that of the plaintiff-lienholder. The minority view improperly focuses upon the interests of junior lienholders. . . .[5]

Stewart v. Gurley, 745 F.2d at 1196 (quoting Walter E. Heller Western, Inc. v. Faires (In re Faires), 34 B.R. 549, 552 (Bankr. W.D. Wash. 1983)).

A definition of equity that requires consideration of all secured liens comports with the purpose of section 362(d)(2) analysis and strikes the proper balance among the secured creditors', the unsecured creditors', and the debtor's interests. The basic purpose behind Chapter 11 of the Bankruptcy Code is to offer protection to the insolvent debtor who seeks rehabilitation through a plan of reorganization. To the extent that property is of no benefit to the debtor, because the debtor retains no equity in it and the property is unnecessary to an effective reorganization, only the junior lienholders will benefit by avoiding foreclosure, at the expense of senior lienholders. *See* Stewart v. Gurley, 745 F.2d at 1196 ("Unless the debtor can demonstrate that the property is necessary to an effective reorganization, the property is of no value to him. Refusing to grant relief from the automatic stay under those circumstances would only promote the junior lienholders' interests over those of the senior lienholder.").

Furthermore, we note that the language of section 362(d)(2) is mandatory, when both factors necessary for relief under section 362(d)(2) are met "the court shall grant relief." 11 U.S.C. §362(d)(2). Excluding the claims of objecting junior lienholders from the equity calculation when the subsection (d)(2) factors are otherwise met would thus contravene the plain language of that provision.

D.

Our refusal to adopt Nantucket Investors' position does not prevent the bankruptcy court from otherwise considering the interests of objecting junior lienholders. On the contrary, when a senior lienholder successfully petitions the bankruptcy court for relief from the automatic stay in order to proceed with a foreclosure action, junior lienholders may protect their interests by bidding at foreclosure in order to retain their secured interest in the property. Additionally, it is appropriate for the bankruptcy court to consider the interests of junior lienholders in determining whether an effective reorganization is possible without the encumbered property. *See* In re Mellor, 734 F.2d at 1401; 2 Collier on Bankruptcy, §362.07[2], at 362-69 & n.15a (Lawrence P. King ed., 15th ed. 1994). Thus for example, in this case the bankruptcy court may properly consider the junior lienholders' subordination agreements in

---

5. To the extent we have located any legislative history that shines light on this issue, it appears that section 362(d)(2)(A) was intended to protect a creditor's right to foreclosure. In a joint explanatory statement prepared by the floor managers on the ultimately enacted compromise bill, it was noted that "section [362(d)(2)] is intended to solve the problem of real property mortgage foreclosures of property where the bankruptcy petition is filed on the eve of foreclosure." 124 Cong. Rec. H11047, H11092-93; 124 Cong. Rec. S17403, S17409. Excluding the junior lienholders' claims when they oppose foreclosure would not further this intent.

determining whether an effective reorganization is possible and whether the property is necessary to that end. Because we find that there are other means by which the bankruptcy court may consider the interests of junior lienholders in determining whether relief from the automatic stay is proper, we find no need to adopt a changeable definition of equity that excludes consideration of protesting junior lienholders' interests under certain circumstances.

We will therefore reverse the district court insofar as it determined that the debtor has equity in the property, and will remand with instructions to return this matter to the bankruptcy court so that it may consider the second factor necessary for relief under section 362(d)(2), namely whether the property is necessary to an effective reorganization. . . .[6]

VII.

We reverse the district court's determination that the debtor has equity in the property within the meaning of section 362(d)(2)(A) and remand with instructions to return this matter to the bankruptcy court so that it may determine whether the property is necessary to an effective reorganization, and thus whether relief from the automatic stay may be granted under section 362(d)(2). We affirm the district court's order in all other respects.

ROTH, Circuit Judge, concurring in part and dissenting in part.

Although I concur with the majority in Parts I-III, V and VI of their opinion, I cannot agree with their conclusion in Part IV that the debtor did not retain equity in the property. I must therefore respectfully dissent from the reversal of the district court's determination in that regard.

The majority adopts the "classic test" for determining equity under §362(d)(2): subtracting the value of all the secured liens on the property from the property's current value. They reject the district court's exclusion of the junior secured claims of Nantucket and FEC from the subtrahend of the calculation. However, if junior lienholders are willing to concede their secured position in such a way that the senior lienholder's interest is protected, the debtor may have actual, if not literal, equity in the property. I see no reason why that concession should not be permitted and "equity" be defined in a reorganization by the balance, reached by subtracting the security of concerned lienholders from the value of the property, rather than from a calculation of figures that do not represent the reality of the commercial situation. . . .

---

6. Under the proper equity calculation, the outstanding liens against the property exceed the current stipulated value of the property and the debtor thus retains no equity in the property.

PROBLEM 4-6

Fragrant Meadows Apartments, Ltd. (FMA) owned a 200-unit apartment complex. The project was only 70 percent occupied, and a number of the units were in need of significant repair. Nevertheless, the value of the project was generally agreed to be somewhere in the neighborhood of $7,000,000. FMA owed Investments Unlimited, Inc. $4,700,000, the amount that was secured by a first mortgage on the property. FMA was a couple of months behind in its payments on this mortgage, and it had also fallen behind on its required escrow payments for taxes on the property. FMA owed Local Savings and Loan Corp. $3,500,000, secured by a second mortgage on the same property, and it was also behind on payments to the S & L. These financial difficulties led to the filing of a Chapter 11 petition. Notwithstanding the problems with the project, its value has remained relatively stable over the last six months, and the debtor is currently seeking additional capital to complete the necessary repairs to the property. Investments Unlimited, however, is getting impatient and wants its money now. It has moved for relief from the automatic stay under §362(d). What options does FMA have now that a motion for relief from the stay has been filed? See §§101 (51B) and 362(d)(3).

The phrase "indubitable equivalent" in subsection (3) of §361 does not have an obvious meaning, but it was first used by the redoubtable Learned Hand, as explained in the following quotation from a Ninth Circuit opinion:

> Congress derived the term "indubitable equivalent" from Judge Learned Hand's opinion in In re Murel Holding Corp., 75 F.2d 941 (2d Cir. 1935). In *Murel*, Metropolitan Life Insurance Co. held a mortgage on an apartment house. When the apartment house owners defaulted on the mortgage, Metropolitan attempted to foreclose, but the owners obtained an ex parte stay after filing a petition for reorganization under section 77B of the Bankruptcy Act of 1898 (former 11 U.S.C. §207). The owners then proposed a plan of reorganization that required Metropolitan to forego amortization payments and extend the due date of the mortgage while the apartment house was renovated. Metropolitan would have received interest in the meantime. Metropolitan rejected the plan and moved to vacate the stay, but its motion was denied.
>
> On appeal Metropolitan argued that its interest was not adequately protected. Judge Hand, for the court, noted that the plan had little hope of success and the ability of the apartment house to satisfy Metropolitan's accruing claims was declining. 75 F.2d at 942. Judge Hand admitted, however, that the court had the power to confirm a plan over the objection of creditors if the plan provided "adequate protection for the realization by them of the full value of their interest, claims, or liens." Id. He then explained the concept of adequate protection:
>
> > In construing so vague a grant, we are to remember not only the underlying purposes of the section, but the constitutional limitations to which it must conform. It is plain that "adequate protection" must be completely compensatory; and that payment ten years hence is not generally the equivalent of payment now. Interest is indeed the common measure of the difference, but a credi tor who fears the safety of his principal will scarcely be content with that; he wishes to get his money or at least the property. We see no reason to suppose that the statute was intended to de prive him of that in the interest of junior holders, unless by a substitute of the most indubitable equivalence.

In re American Mariner Indus., Inc., 734 F.2d 426, 432-433 (9th Cir. 1984).

Making the debtor pay interest on the stayed obligation sounds fair, but the United States Supreme Court has forbidden the recovery of interest in Chapter 11 reorganizations during the pendency of the plan; *see* United Savings Assn. of Texas v. Timbers of Inwood Forest Associates, Ltd., 484 U.S. 365 (1988), although interest must be paid on the debt thereafter. In 1994, Congress amended the Bankruptcy Code to require the payment of interest in certain situations involving single asset real estate bankruptcies, *see* §362(d)(3)(B), a matter we shall explore in more detail when the issue comes up in Chapter 11 reorganizations.

CHAPTER 5

Claims

The two primary participants in bankruptcy cases are debtors and creditors. While there is only one debtor in a case (unless it is a joint case or several cases that have been consolidated), there usually are a number of creditors. The Bankruptcy Code, however, contains very few references to creditors. Section 101(10) defines a creditor as an "entity that has a claim against the debtor that arose at the time of or before the order for relief concerning the debtor." Creditors also include some holders of claims that arose after the commencement of the case, but only in limited circumstances. *See* Bankruptcy Code §101(10)(B).[1] Generally speaking, in the Bankruptcy Code the focus is on claims rather than on creditors. There are three types of claims with which you must become familiar: secured, priority, and unsecured claims.

When Congress enacted the Bankruptcy Code, one of its purposes was to expand the definition of "claims" to bring as many potential claims into the bankruptcy process as possible, an action that had two consequences. First, doing so increases the amount of claims that are eligible to receive a distribution out of the bankruptcy case. Second, it also increases the amount of claims that can be discharged through the bankruptcy process. To accomplish this expansion Congress enacted §101(5), which contains the definition of "claim," as a

> right to payment, whether or not such right is reduced to judgment, liquidated, unliquidated, fixed, contingent, matured, unmatured, disputed, undisputed, legal, equitable, secured, or unsecured; or . . . right to an equitable remedy for breach of performance if such breach gives rise to a right to payment, whether or not such right to an equitable remedy is reduced to judgment, fixed, contingent, matured, unmatured, disputed, undisputed, secured, or unsecured.

It is clear from the language of the section that Congress intended the definition of claim to be broadly construed. The Bankruptcy Code elsewhere limits the reach of the definition by choosing generally the date of the commencement of the case as a cutoff

---

1. Creditors also include entities that hold "community claim," a "claim that arose before the commencement of a case concerning the debtor for which property of the kind specified in §541(a)(2) of this title is liable, whether or not there is any such property at the time of the commencement of the case." Bankruptcy Code §101(7). Section 541(a)(2) consists of interest of the debtor and the debtor's spouse in community property.

point for the recognition of claims in the bankruptcy proceeding. There are several exceptions to this cutoff point, and they will be addressed later.

Within the definition of claims, the Bankruptcy Code provides different treatments for different types of claims. While most are discharged, some claims are excepted from the discharge. In this chapter, we will consider the rights of holders of claims to receive a distribution in bankruptcy proceedings. To that end, we must identify the claims as either secured, unsecured, or priority.

I.   Allowance of Claims Generally

When debtors commence bankruptcy cases, they must file schedules listing their assets and liabilities. Bankruptcy Code §521. In addition, they must provide a list of their creditors' names and addresses so that notice of the bankruptcy proceeding can be sent to those parties. Creditors can then participate to whatever extent they think is appropriate in the bankruptcy proceeding; however, creditors must submit proof of their claims against the debtor in order to share in the distribution of assets at the end of the case. The initial notice sent to the creditor will include a proof-of-claim form that the creditor can complete and file with the court. The notice will also identify the time in which the proof of claim must be filed. In Chapter 11 cases, the court will set a separate "bar date" for the filing of claims in those proceedings, after which a claim may not be filed. For Chapter 11 cases only, claims that are listed by the debtor as liquidated and undisputed are automatically allowed without the need for the filing of a proof of claim form by the creditor. Presumably this reduces paperwork for the clerk's office. In all other cases, including cases converted from Chapter 11 to another Chapter of the Bankruptcy Code, a proof of claim form must be filed.[2]

In the absence of an objection to the proof of claim the claim is allowed, meaning that the claimant may participate in the bankruptcy process. Bankruptcy Code §502(a). Section 502(b) contains a laundry list of potential objections to or limitations on claims, with subsections (b)(1) and (2) being the most significant. Under §502(b)(1), all of the nonbankruptcy defenses to claims are available in bankruptcy. For example, a creditor may file a proof of claim for the sale of realty to a debtor. If the debtor signed no writing evidencing the transaction, then the claim is objectionable under the statute of frauds. Section 502(b)(2) disallows any claim for unmatured interest. This is the provision that "cuts off" interest in bankruptcy cases. Note, however, that it cuts off only the interest, while the remaining unpaid principal of

---

2. Notwithstanding these general rules in many Chapter 7 cases, creditors are instructed that they need not file a proof of claim form. Most Chapter 7 cases are "no asset" and the clerk will notify creditors that there is no need to file a proof of claim form at that time. Instead, if significant assets are obtained and a distribution is likely to occur, the clerk will send out a supplement notice to the creditors stating that claims must be filed within a stated time. *See* Bankruptcy Rules 2002(e) and 3002(e)(5).

an installment debt is still fully allowed under §502. In fact, the definition of a claim in §101(5) specifically includes unmatured claims.

The definition of claim specifically includes equitable rights; however, it also limits claims to those equitable rights or remedies that give rise to a right to payment for breach of the debtor's required performance. For example, suppose the debtor has agreed to sell a baseball autographed by Babe Ruth. Upon the failure to turn over the baseball to the purchaser, the purchaser brought suit against the debtor and obtained an injunction directing the debtor to turn over the goods. After all, the baseball is a unique item, and specific performance would be available under UCC §2-716. Notwithstanding this right to force the debtor to turn over the property as a matter of state law, the equitable remedy of specific performance would be transformed into a claim for bankruptcy purposes. The creditor could assert a claim in the amount of the value of the item minus its cost to the creditor according to the terms of the original agreement, but the creditor could not get the ball, which would be property of the estate.

Other forms of equitable relief do not translate so well into claims. For example, assume that the debtor is the world's best quarterback. After signing an agreement to play exclusively for the New York Giants, he decides that he wants to play for the New York Jets. The Giants obtain an injunction against his playing for any other team. The debtor cannot commence a bankruptcy proceeding and discharge his obligation to the Giants by substituting a monetary claim for the right to enjoin him from playing for another team. The debtor may have other remedies with respect to this executory contract (which will be discussed later in this text), but he cannot rely on the claims allowance process to render him eligible to play football for the Jets.

Review §502 carefully and use it to solve the following Problems.

PROBLEM 5-1

Ven-Cap, Inc., a computer startup company, was booming with prospects when it signed a ten-year lease for an entire floor in The Glass Tower, the tallest building in town. The lease required monthly payments of $3,000 to the lessor, Tower Properties, but Ven-Cap, flowing with cash, was happy to agree to this amount. Two years later, when the lease had eight years left to run, Ven-Cap's fortunes had "tanked," and the company was forced to file a Chapter 7 bankruptcy petition. Tower Properties promptly filed a claim for $303,000. This consisted of five months of unpaid rent due as of the filing of the bankruptcy petition ($15,000) and eight years of future rent. What portion of this claim is allowable? *See* §502(b)(6). Why would Congress have placed such a "cap" on the amount landlords can recover? Are landlords less worthy than other creditors?

PROBLEM 5-2

Randy Blake's best friends were his credit cards. He took them with him wherever he went, and he used them frequently. This led to a substantial accumulation of debt, and eventually Randy visited Loans R Us to take out a consolidation loan to resolve his financial problems. The loan did consolidate his debts, but now he just owed one creditor rather than ten. Under the terms of the loan, Randy agreed to pay $397.25 per month to Loans R Us for seven years. Randy was able to make the payments for eight months, but then he was laid off from his job and has since been unable to find another job at the same pay. Four months later, and one year after he took out the consolidation loan, Randy filed a Chapter 7 bankruptcy petition. The original amount of the consolidation loan was $20,000, and interest was set at 16 percent per annum. The total amount of payments called for by the note was $33,369.00. The creditor has filed a claim for $29,191.00 ($397.25 × 76 months). What objection would the trustee raise to this claim? *See* §502(b)(2).

PROBLEM 5-3

About ten years ago Judith Taylor purchased a three-acre tract of land in a rural location. She had heard rumors that a new highway would be built close to that property, so she bought the land for $3,000 per acre, significantly in excess of the "pre-rumor" price of $800 per acre. Nonetheless, Judith thought she had made a very savvy purchase at the time. Unfortunately, the highway was redirected to another location that was coincidentally close to land holdings of a prominent state legislator. The legislator's good fortune was Judith's ill fortune, and Judith decided to sell the property. Unfortunately, she was unwilling to take a loss on the property and has held it ever since. She has never made any attempt to develop the property, nor has she paid any taxes on the property for those ten years. In fact, the back taxes total $4,000. Judith is now a Chapter 7 debtor, and the county taxing authority has filed a claim for the $4,000 in back taxes. Assuming the value of the property is $2,500, what is the maximum allowable claim for the county? *See* §502(b)(3).

PROBLEM 5-4

Advanced Software Corp. owed First Bank $100,000 on an unsecured basis. Eleanor Rigby, the president of the corporation, personally guaranteed that debt. The debt went unpaid, and Advanced filed a Chapter 7 bankruptcy petition. The assets of Advanced were liquidated, and after the payment of priority claims, the general unsecured creditors were to be paid ten cents on the dollar. First Bank filed a claim for $100,000, and Eleanor filed a claim for reimbursement in the amount of $90,000. The bank has also sued Eleanor in a separate state court action. How does all this work out? *See* §§502(e), 509. Suppose First Bank does not file a claim. What can Eleanor do? *See* §501(b).

II.   Estimation of Claims

The expansive definition of claims in §101(5) brings a number of rights to payment into the bankruptcy proceedings. Section 502(c) directs the bankruptcy court to estimate contingent and unliquidated claims if it would take too long to finally determine the value of those claims. For example, a creditor may assert an antitrust claim against the debtor that would require substantial and lengthy litigation to resolve. If the remaining issues in the bankruptcy case can be concluded rather quickly, the bankruptcy court is authorized to make its best guess as to the value of the creditor's claim against the debtor. The court can conduct a limited review of the claim in allowing the claim in an estimated amount. This permits the bankruptcy proceeding to go forward and be concluded in a timely fashion.

The estimation of both contingent and unliquidated claims requires a similar analysis by the court. Contingent claims are those that are not fixed unless some future event occurs. For example, suppose that Willie Loman has a right to receive a $10,000 bonus if the sales he generates for his employer exceed $1,000,000 during any calendar year. If Willie has sold $100,000 of widgets by February 15, when the company then filed a bankruptcy petition, he has no right to the bonus at the time of the commencement of the bankruptcy case. Nevertheless, if Willie is successful in selling an additional $900,000 of widgets he will have a right to the bonus. Determining the actual value of that claim could take as long as another 10½ months (the end of the year). The contingency might be met earlier if Willie's sales meet the $1,000,000 mark prior to that time. If, however, there is some reason for the proceedings to be concluded prior to that time, then the court could evaluate the likelihood that Willie will meet his sales goals. The percentage of that likelihood would then be multiplied by the amount of the bonus to reach the allowed amount of the estimated contingent claim.

The court will evaluate unliquidated claims in a similar fashion. For example, suppose that Willie was involved in an automobile accident while he was calling on one of his customers. The debtor, Willie's employer, is likely to be vicariously liable to the injured party for Willie's alleged negligence. Of course, there has been no determination that Willie's actions were negligent or that the injured party suffered damages in any particular amount. Normally, those determinations are made in the context of state court litigation between the injured party, Willie, and his employer. That litigation could take several years to complete. If the resolution of that issue would improperly delay the bankruptcy proceedings of the employer, the court can evaluate the quality of the injured party's case against the employer and estimate the claim for the purpose of allowing it in the bankruptcy case. Here again, the court would consider the likelihood of the injured party's success on the merits of the case as well as the full extent of the party's damages. Then the court would multiply the likelihood of success with the amount of damages to arrive at the estimated claim.

III. Secured Claims

In addition to allowed unsecured claims, most bankruptcy proceedings include allowed secured claims. A claim is secured if a creditor holds a lien on property in which the estate has an interest or if the creditor has a right of setoff against the debtor. The claim is secured to the extent of the lesser of the amount of the outstanding indebtedness or the value of the collateral. Suppose, for example, that Nightflyer Finance Co. has a security interest in the automobiles of two debtors. Each debtor owes Nightflyer $10,000. The value of debtor A's automobile is $6,000 and the value of debtor B's automobile is $15,000. Applying the definition of secured claims set out in §506(a) of the Bankruptcy Code, the creditor has a secured claim in debtor A's bankruptcy to the extent of $6,000, while the secured claim in debtor B's bankruptcy is $10,000. In each instance the secured claim is set at the lesser of the amount of the outstanding debt or the value of the collateral.

The creditor in debtor B's bankruptcy is generally referred to as "oversecured," while the creditor in debtor A's bankruptcy is "undersecured." Whether a creditor is oversecured or undersecured has significant consequences, as you have seen, with respect to the automatic stay. Another consequence of being undersecured is that no interest runs on that obligation during the bankruptcy. As you will recall, §502(b)(2) disallows claims to the extent that they are for unmatured interest. The general language of §502(b) would seem to suggest that interest would not run on the "oversecured" claim as well. However, §506(b) provides that "to the extent that an allowed secured claim is secured by property the value of which ... is greater than the amount of such claim, there shall be allowed to the holder of such claim, interest on such claim, and any reasonable fees, costs, or charges provided for under the agreement under which such claim arose." Thus, payment of interest and related fees is available on oversecured but not on undersecured claims in bankruptcy proceedings.

United States v. Ron Pair Enterprises, Inc.

United States Supreme Court, 1989
489 U.S. 235

Justice BLACKMUN delivered the opinion of the Court.

In this case we must decide the narrow statutory issue whether §506(b) of the Bankruptcy Code of 1978, 11 U.S.C. §506(b) (1982 ed., Supp. IV), entitles a creditor to receive postpetition interest on a nonconsensual oversecured claim allowed in a bankruptcy proceeding. We conclude that it does, and we therefore reverse the judgment of the Court of Appeals.

I.

Respondent Ron Pair Enterprises, Inc., filed a petition for reorganization under Chapter 11 of the Bankruptcy Code on May 1, 1984, in the United States Bankruptcy Court for the Eastern District of Michigan. The Government filed timely proof of a prepetition claim of $52,277.93, comprised of assessments for unpaid withholding and Social Security taxes, penalties, and prepetition interest. The claim was perfected through a tax lien on property owned by respondent. Respondent's First Amended

Plan of Reorganization, filed October 1, 1985, provided for full payment of the prepetition claim, but did not provide for postpetition interest on that claim. The Government filed a timely objection, claiming that §506(b) allowed recovery of postpetition interest, since the property securing the claim had a value greater than the amount of the principal debt. At the Bankruptcy Court hearing, the parties stipulated that the claim was oversecured, but the court subsequently overruled the Government's objection. The Government appealed to the United States District Court for the Eastern District of Michigan. That court reversed the Bankruptcy Court's judgment, concluding that the plain language of §506(b) entitled the Government to postpetition interest.

The United States Court of Appeals for the Sixth Circuit, in its turn, reversed the District Court. 828 F.2d 367 (1987). While not directly ruling that the language of §506(b) was ambiguous, the court reasoned that reference to pre-Code law was appropriate "in order to better understand the context in which the provision was drafted and therefore the language itself." Id., at 370. The court went on to note that under pre-Code law the general rule was that postpetition interest on an oversecured prepetition claim was allowable only where the lien was consensual in nature. In light of this practice, and of the lack of any legislative history evincing an intent to change the standard, the court held that §506(b) codified the pre-existing standard, and that postpetition interest was allowable only on consensual claims. Because this result was in direct conflict with the view of the Court of Appeals for the Fourth Circuit, *see* Best Repair Co. v. United States, 789 F.2d 1080 (1986), and with the views of other courts, we granted certiorari, 485 U.S. 958, 108 S. Ct. 1218, 99 L. Ed. 2d 420 (1988), to resolve the conflict.

II.

Section 506, enacted as part of the extensive 1978 revision of the bankruptcy laws, governs the definition and treatment of secured claims, i.e., claims by creditors against the estate that are secured by a lien on property in which the estate has an interest. Subsection (a) of §506 provides that a claim is secured only to the extent of the value of the property on which the lien is fixed; the remainder of that claim is considered unsecured. Subsection (b) is concerned specifically with oversecured claims, that is, any claim that is for an amount less than the value of the property securing it. Thus, if a $50,000 claim were secured by a lien on property having a value of $75,000, the claim would be oversecured, provided the trustee's costs of preserving or disposing of the property were less than $25,000. Section 506(b) allows a holder of an oversecured claim to recover, in addition to the prepetition amount of the claim, "interest on such claim, and any reasonable fees, costs, or charges provided for under the agreement under which such claim arose."

The question before us today arises because there are two types of secured claims: (1) voluntary (or consensual) secured claims, each created by agreement between the debtor and the creditor and called a "security interest" by the Code, 11 U.S.C.

§101(45) (1982 ed., Supp. IV), and (2) involuntary secured claims, such as a judicial or statutory lien, *see* 11 U.S.C. §§101(32) and (47) (1982 ed., Supp. IV), which are fixed by operation of law and do not require the consent of the debtor. The claim against respondent's estate was of this latter kind. Prior to the passage of the 1978 Code, some Courts of Appeals drew a distinction between the two types for purposes of determining postpetition interest. The question we must answer is whether the 1978 Code recognizes and enforces this distinction, or whether Congress intended that all oversecured claims be treated the same way for purposes of postpetition interest.

III.

Initially, it is worth recalling that Congress worked on the formulation of the Code for nearly a decade. It was intended to modernize the bankruptcy laws, see H.R. Rep. No. 95-595, p. 3 (1977) U.S. Code Cong. & Admin. News 1978 pp. 5787, 5963, 5964 (Report), and as a result made significant changes in both the substantive and procedural laws of bankruptcy. See Northern Pipeline Construction Co. v. Marathon Pipe Line Co., 458 U.S. 50, 52-53, 102 S. Ct. 2858, 2861-2862, 73 L. Ed. 2d 598 (1982) (plurality opinion). In particular, Congress intended "significant changes from current law in . . . the treatment of secured creditors and secured claims." Report, at 180. In such a substantial overhaul of the system, it is not appropriate or realistic to expect Congress to have explained with particularity each step it took. Rather, as long as the statutory scheme is coherent and consistent, there generally is no need for a court to inquire beyond the plain language of the statute.

A.

The task of resolving the dispute over the meaning of §506(b) begins where all such inquiries must begin: with the language of the statute itself. Landreth Timber Co. v. Landreth, 471 U.S. 681, 685, 105 S. Ct. 2297, 2301, 85 L. Ed. 2d 692 (1985). In this case it is also where the inquiry should end, for where, as here, the statute's language is plain, "the sole function of the courts is to enforce it according to its terms." Caminetti v. United States, 242 U.S. 470, 485, 37 S. Ct. 192, 194, 61 L. Ed. 442 (1917). The language before us expresses Congress' intent — that postpetition interest be available — with sufficient precision so that reference to legislative history and to pre-Code practice is hardly necessary.

The relevant phrase in §506(b) is: "[T]here shall be allowed to the holder of such claim, interest on such claim, and any reasonable fees, costs, or charges provided for under the agreement under which such claim arose." "Such claim" refers to an oversecured claim. The natural reading of the phrase entitles the holder of an oversecured claim to postpetition interest and, in addition, gives one having a secured claim created pursuant to an agreement the right to reasonable fees, costs, and charges provided for in that agreement. Recovery of postpetition interest is unqualified. Recovery of fees, costs, and charges, however, is allowed only if they are reasonable and provided for in the agreement under which the claim arose. Therefore, in the absence of an agreement, postpetition interest is the only added recovery available.

This reading is also mandated by the grammatical structure of the statute. The phrase "interest on such claim" is set aside by commas, and separated from the reference to fees, costs, and charges by the conjunctive words "and any." As a result, the phrase "interest on such claim" stands independent of the language that follows. "[I]nterest on such claim" is not part of the list made up of "fees, costs, or charges," nor is it joined to the following clause so that the final "provided for under the agreement" modifies it as well. *See* Best Repair Co. v. United States, 789 F.2d, at 1082. The language and punctuation Congress used cannot be read in any other way.[3] By the plain language of the statute, the two types of recovery are distinct.[4]

B.

The plain meaning of legislation should be conclusive, except in the "rare cases [in which] the literal application of a statute will produce a result demonstrably at odds with the intentions of its drafters." Griffin v. Oceanic Contractors, Inc., 458 U.S. 564, 571, 102 S. Ct. 3245, 3250, 73 L. Ed. 2d 973 (1982). In such cases, the intention of the drafters, rather than the strict language, controls. Ibid. It is clear that allowing postpetition interest on nonconsensual oversecured liens does not contravene the intent of the framers of the Code. Allowing such interest does not conflict with any other section of the Code, or with any important state or federal interest; nor is a contrary view suggested by the legislative history. Respondent has not articulated, nor can we discern, any significant reason why Congress would have intended, or any policy reason would compel, that the two types of secured claims be treated differently in allowing postpetition interest.

C.

Respondent urges that pre-Code practice drew a distinction between consensual and nonconsensual liens for the purpose of determining entitlement to postpetition

---

3. The United States Court of Appeals for the Fourth Circuit pointed out in Best Repair Co. that, had Congress intended to limit postpetition interest to consensual liens, §506(b) could have said: "there shall be allowed to the holder of such claim as provided for under the agreement under which such claim arose, interest on such claim and any reasonable fees, costs or charges." 789 F.2d, at 1082, n.2. A less clear way of stating this closer to the actual language would be: "there shall be allowed to the holder of such claim, interest on such claim and reasonable fees, costs, and charges provided for under the agreement under which such claim arose." Ibid.

4. It seems to us that the interpretation adopted by the Court of Appeals in this case not only requires that the statutory language be read in an unnatural way, but that it is inconsistent with the remainder of §506(b) and with terminology used throughout the Code. Adopting the Court of Appeals' view would mean that §506(b) is operative only in regard to consensual liens, i.e., that only a holder of an oversecured claim arising from an agreement is entitled to any added recovery. But the other portions of §506 make no distinction between consensual and nonconsensual liens. Moreover, had Congress intended §506(b) to apply only to consensual liens, it would have clarified its intent by using the specific phrase, "security interest," which the Code employs to refer to liens created by agreement. 11 U.S.C. §101(45) (1982 ed., Supp. IV). When Congress wanted to restrict the application of a particular provision of the Code to such liens, it used the term "security interest." See, e.g., 11 U.S.C. §§326(b)(12) and (13), 363(a), 547(c)(3)-(5), 552, 752(e), 1110(a), 1168(a), 1322(b)(2) (1982 ed. and Supp. IV).

interest, and that Congress' failure to repudiate that distinction requires us to enforce it. It is respondent's view, as it was the view of the Court of Appeals, that Midlantic National Bank v. New Jersey Dept. of Environmental Protection, 474 U.S. 494, 106 S. Ct. 755, 88 L. Ed. 2d 859 (1986), and Kelly v. Robinson, 479 U.S. 36, 107 S. Ct. 353, 93 L. Ed. 2d 216 (1986), so require. We disagree.

In *Midlantic* we held that §554(a) of the Code, 11 U.S.C. §554(a), which provides that "the trustee may abandon any property of the estate that is burdensome to the estate," does not give a trustee the authority to violate state health and safety laws by abandoning property containing hazardous wastes. 474 U.S., at 507, 106 S. Ct., at 762. In reaching that conclusion, we noted that according to pre-Code doctrine the trustee's authority to dispose of property could be limited in order "to protect legitimate state or federal interests." Id., at 500, 106 S. Ct., at 759. But we did not rest solely, or even primarily, on a presumption of continuity with pre-Code practice. Rather, we concluded that a contrary result would render abandonment doctrine inconsistent with other provisions of the Code itself, which embody the principle that "the trustee is not to have *carte blanche* to ignore nonbankruptcy law." Id., at 502, 106 S. Ct., at 760. We also recognized that the outcome sought would be not only a departure from pre-Code practice, but also "an extraordinary exemption from nonbankruptcy law," id., at 501, 106 S. Ct., at 759, requiring some clearer expression of congressional intent. We relied as well on Congress' repeated emphasis in environmental legislation "on its 'goal of protecting the environment against toxic pollution.'" Id., at 505, 106 S. Ct., at 762, quoting Chemical Manufacturers Assn. v. Natural Resources Defense Council, Inc., 470 U.S. 116, 143, 105 S. Ct. 1102, 1117, 84 L. Ed. 2d 90 (1985). To put it simply, we looked to pre-Code practice for interpretive assistance, because it appeared that a literal application of the statute would be "demonstrably at odds with the intentions of its drafters." Griffin v. Oceanic Contractors, Inc., 458 U.S., at 571, 102 S. Ct., at 3250.

A similar issue presented itself in Kelly v. Robinson, *supra*, where we held that a restitution obligation, imposed as part of a state criminal sentence, was not dischargeable in bankruptcy. We reached this conclusion by interpreting §523(a)(7) of the Code, 11 U.S.C. §523(a)(7), as "preserv[ing] from discharge any condition a state criminal court imposes as part of a criminal sentence." 479 U.S., at 50, 107 S. Ct., at 361. We noted that the Code provision was "subject to interpretation," ibid., and considered both legislative history and pre-Code practice in aid of that interpretation. But in determining that Congress had not intended to depart from pre-Code practice in this regard, we did not rely on a pale presumption to that effect. We concluded that the pre-Code practice had been animated by "a deep conviction that federal bankruptcy courts should not invalidate the results of state criminal proceedings," id., at 47, 107 S. Ct., at 360, which has its source in the basic principle of our federalism that "the States' interest in administering their criminal justice systems free from federal interference is one of the most powerful of the considerations that should influence a court considering equitable types of relief." Id., at 49, 107 S. Ct., at 361. In *Kelly*, as in *Midlantic*, pre-Code practice was significant because it reflected policy considerations of great longevity and importance.

Kelly and *Midlantic* make clear that, in an appropriate case, a court must determine whether Congress has expressed an intent to change the interpretation of a judicially created concept in enacting the Code. But *Midlantic* and *Kelly* suggest that there are limits to what may constitute an appropriate case. Both decisions concerned statutory language which, at least to some degree, was open to interpretation. Each involved a situation where bankruptcy law, under the proposed interpretation, was in clear conflict with state or federal laws of great importance. In the present case, in contrast, the language in question is clearer than the language at issue in *Midlantic* and *Kelly:* as written it directs that postpetition interest be paid on all oversecured claims. In addition, this natural interpretation of the statutory language does not conflict with any significant state or federal interest, nor with any other aspect of the Code. Although the payment of postpetition interest is arguably somewhat in tension with the desirability of paying all creditors as uniformly as practicable, Congress expressly chose to create that alleged tension. There is no reason to suspect that Congress did not mean what the language of the statute says. . . .

The judgment of the Court of Appeals is reversed.

PROBLEM 5-5

Wright Bros. Bicycles, Inc., decided to expand its business, so it borrowed $200,000 from Gem City Bank and granted a security interest in its equipment to the bank. Wright Bros. also agreed to use Gem City Bank for all of its banking needs and to maintain its operating accounts with the bank. After initial success, the company fell on hard times and was forced to file a Chapter 7 bankruptcy petition. At the time of the filing, the equipment was worth $150,000, and Wright Bros. had $17,000 in its bank account at Gem City. The outstanding balance on the obligation to the bank was $176,000. To what extent is the bank's claim a secured claim? An unsecured claim? *See* §506(a).

Secured claims receive significantly better treatment than unsecured claims in bankruptcy proceedings. Generally speaking, the holder of a secured claim is entitled to either a return of the collateral or the full payment of the secured claim. If that payment is to take place over time, then the "present value" of the payments to be received by the holder of the secured claim must equal the value of that secured claim. Any time the statute calls for the payment of "present value," it means that if the claim is not being paid in full immediately, interest must then be paid on the claim.

Since fully secured creditors must be paid their entire debt and may additionally have a right to interest and other charges on the outstanding amount, the determination of the value of collateral is an important part of most bankruptcy proceedings. Notwithstanding the lengthy list of definitions in §101, that section contains no definition of the word "value." Instead, §506(a) provides that "such value shall be determined in light of the purpose of the valuation and of the proposed disposition or use of" the collateral. Battles over valuation make or break bankruptcy proceedings.

In the 2005 amendments to the Code, Congress did give us some definite guidance for the meaning of "value" in individual cases under Chapters 7 and 13. Read new §506(a)(1) and apply it to the following Problem.

PROBLEM 5-6

In determining the value of a consumer's automobile, should the bankruptcy court consider all or any of the following evidence?

- Newspaper classified advertisements for similar cars;
- The debtor's personal opinion about the value of the car;
- The "Blue Book" values — wholesale and retail;
- The prices set on similar vehicles on an auto dealer's lot.

If bankruptcy had never occurred and the debtor's failure to pay resulted in the car being repossessed and sold at a dealer's auction (the usual method of disposition), would the creditor likely fare better or worse than the valuation of the vehicle in a bankruptcy proceeding?

Would your answers change if the asset being valued was a fleet of trucks owned by a trucking company that is a Chapter 11 debtor?

PROBLEM 5-7

Oliver and Lisa Douglas farm 60 acres just outside of Petticoat Junction. They were not farmers all of their lives, but they have been at it now for some 15 years. Between their occasionally successful harvests and their "nest egg," Oliver and Lisa have been able to make a go of it. Unfortunately, the last couple of years have been particularly difficult, and the nest egg is nearly gone. Nevertheless, Oliver and Lisa want to continue farming, so when the bank that held the mortgage on the farm commenced foreclosure proceeding, Oliver and Lisa filed a Chapter 12 petition. Chapter 12 allows family farmers to stretch out their mortgage payment to better meet their limited cash flow. Although they owe the bank $100,000, Oliver and Lisa assert that the value of the land is $1,000 per acre, for a total of $60,000. Therefore, they have proposed to pay the bank's $60,000 secured claim with interest at 9.5 percent and a monthly payment of $559.28 for 20 years. The bank has objected to this plan. It concedes that the value of this property as farmland is $60,000. However, the bank notes that other property in the area has recently been developed, and the urban sprawl of Hooterville has led to a significant increase in value in the property in Petticoat Junction. Their appraisal sets the value of Oliver and Lisa's real estate at $130,000. What value should the court fix? *See, e.g.*, In re Sherman, 157 B.R. 987 (Bankr. E.D. Tex. 1993).

PROBLEM 5-8

Octopus National Bank held a perfected security interest on all of the assets of Petting Zoo, Inc., a family attraction outside of Philadelphia. Hard times forced Petting Zoo to file a Chapter 7 bankruptcy petition, and an interim trustee was appointed to run the zoo for a short time prior to its liquidation. The trustee bought animal feed during this period from Farm Food, spending $600 for this purpose. When Octopus National Bank files its secured claim in the bankruptcy proceeding, can the trustee subtract the $600 spent on food from the allowed amount of the claim? *See* §506(c). If Farm Food has yet to be paid, can it use the same section to try to recover the $600 directly from the bank? *See* Hartford Underwriters Ins. Co. v. Union Planters Bank, 120 S. Ct. 1942 (2000).

IV.   Priority Claims

Holders of secured claims have a right to receive either their property or its value before any other distributions are made in the bankruptcy case. If there are any assets remaining after the satisfaction of secured claims, a distribution will be made to the holders of unsecured claims. In most instances, there is little or nothing available for the holders of unsecured claims. To the extent that any assets may be available, creditors would prefer to be first in line.

One might assume that since the equitable distribution of a debtor's assets is a fundamental goal of bankruptcy law ("equity is equality"), all creditors would share equally or pro rata in the debtor's assets. One would be wrong. The Bankruptcy Code creates priorities among unsecured creditors, mandating in §507 that some be paid before others. In most cases, the debtor's assets are insufficient to pay all claims, so having a right to go ahead of other creditors is extremely valuable. Section 507(a)(1) through (10) sets out the categories of claims that have priority over other unsecured claims. Not only do these ten categories of unsecured claims come ahead of other unsecured claims, but within the ten categories the order established by §507(a) is absolute. That is, all §507(a)(1) claims must be paid in full before §507(a)(2) claims receive anything, and so on down the line. One way to think about this distributional scheme is to consider a series of nine buckets representing the nine categories of priority claims. The buckets are situated one above another and the distribution of funds to these creditors begins with the pouring of the funds into bucket #1. When bucket #1 is full, any additional "funds" poured into bucket #1 overflow into bucket #2, and so on down the line.

In §507(a) Congress has made policy choices regarding the need for more favorable treatment for certain kinds of claims.

The 2005 amendments to the Bankruptcy Code moved domestic support obligations (alimony, child care, etc. — see the definition in §101(14)(A)) to the front of the line, reflecting a strong policy in favor of protecting those who suffer financially from the dissolution of a marriage; *see* §507(a)(1). As we shall see in Chapter 6, these alimony and support claims, along with the priority tax claims, are also nondischargeable under §523. Another important consequence of priority status, explored in Chapter 8, is that these claims must be paid *in full* in reorganization proceedings. The creditor may, but need not, accept less favorable treatment.

Next in priority, per §507(a)(2) are the expenses of the bankruptcy itself. Congress believed that unless the participants in the bankruptcy proceeding (the trustee, attorneys for the trustee or debtor in possession, and other professionals hired to assist the bankruptcy estate) are paid, or have some reasonable prospect for payment, they will not participate in the case. The third category of priority claims is the so-called 'involuntary gap' claims, which arise after the filing of an involuntary bankruptcy petition but before the entry of an order for relief. *See* Chapter 2 *supra*. The next two categories of priority claims protect the debtor's employees whose recent wages and benefits have not been paid. Other priority claims include the claims of farmers and fisherman against grain storage facilities and fish storage or processing facilities, consumer deposits (layaways), certain taxes, and the victims of drunken driving accidents.

In 2005, Congress indirectly expanded priority claims by amending §503(b) of the Code which defines administrative expenses. This expansion could result in an increase in claims having priority under §507(a)(2). Section 503(b)(9) includes within administrative expenses of a bankruptcy case any claim for the value of goods received by a debtor in the 20 days before the commencement of the case. This priority is available only if the goods were sold to the debtor in the ordinary course of the debtor's business. Because priority claims generally must be paid in full in Chapter 11 cases (see §1129(a)(9)(B)), a debtor's decision regarding when to file a voluntary petition may turn on the amount of goods received by the debtor in the immediate past. A delay in filing of just a few days can make a significant difference in the treatment of these claims.

Use §507 to determine whether and to what extent these claims have priority.

PROBLEM 5-9

(1) Maria sold medical supplies for American Surgical Devices Corp. She was paid $300 per week salary and also had a right to receive commissions to the extent that her sales exceeded $10,000 in any week. Maria was not paid for her last three week's work with the company, which is now in bankruptcy. She is also due $18,000 in unpaid commissions. How much, if any, of her $18,900 claim is entitled to priority? Section 507(a)(4).

(2) In addition to its failure to pay Maria, American Surgical Devices Corp. has neglected to fund its pension and profit sharing plan for its employees. The total obligation that was not funded at the time of the filing of the bankruptcy petition was $80,000. There were 45 employees covered by the pension plan, and Maria's claim for benefits totals $5,000. Is any or all of Maria's claim for the pension benefits entitled to priority? Section 507(a)(5).

(3) Steely Dan Corp. sold stainless steel to American Surgical Devices for many years. American Surgical usually purchased about 5,000 tons of stainless steel each

month, give or take 50 tons. Realizing it was headed for financial trouble, American Surgical called Steely Dan on August 19 and doubled its regular purchase to 10,000 tons of steel to be delivered on September 1. The steel was delivered on September 1, and American Surgical filed a Chapter 11 petition on September 14. Half of the steel has been used by American Surgical in its normal manufacturing, and the other half was still on hand at the time of the filing. Does Steely Dan have a priority claim? Sections 507(a)(2) and 503(b)(9). *See also* §546(c).

(4) Maria and her husband, Raymond, divorced last year after three years of marriage. They had no children, and the divorce was relatively amicable. Part of the divorce settlement provided that Maria would be paid $50,000 while Raymond retained ownership of an apartment building that he and Maria had purchased shortly after they were married. Raymond had other financial problems and so filed a bankruptcy proceeding. Is Maria's $50,000 claim entitled to priority? Section 507(a)(1).

(5) Joe Wyoming couldn't get to the Super Bowl, so he planned to invite a few close friends over to watch the game. In anticipation, he went to T.V. City to buy a mega-screen stereo television. He paid $2,750 for the unit, but he asked T.V. City to hold on to the television for a couple of months. He planned to have it installed a few days before the game. The day before the television was to be installed, T.V. City went bankrupt. Does Joe have a priority claim? Section 507(a)(7).

(6) When Portia Moot filed her bankruptcy petition on March 1, 2007, she owed income taxes to the federal government for the previous six years. She had always filed a return on February 15th of each year (though never paying in full). What taxes will be entitled to priority under the convoluted language of §507(a)(8)(A)(i) (where the trick is to understand that the filing of the bankruptcy petition does not stop the time analysis referred to in that subsection)?

PROBLEM 5-10

When Chapter 13 debtor William Wheels agreed to purchase property insurance sufficient to protect Nightflyer Finance Company's security interest in his car, the bankruptcy judge deemed this adequate protection of Nightflyer's interest and refused to lift the stay. Two months later, William Wheels stopped at a bar after work, had too much to drink, and then drove the car into the side of a bridge, destroying the vehicle, the bridge, and his left arm. At about the same time, the insurance company that had issued the property insurance policy itself went into receivership, unable to pay any claims. William Wheels was fired from his job, and the Chapter 13 plan was converted into a Chapter 7 liquidation. The bankruptcy estate has only enough money to pay some of the §507 priorities. If you are the attorney for Nightflyer Finance Company, is there anything you can do for your client? *See* §507(b).

V. Future Claims

Like stand-up comedy, in bankruptcy timing is everything. Section 502(b) directs the court to determine the amount of claims "as of the date of the filing of the petition." Suppose, for example, that Bobby Bankrupt files a Chapter 7 petition on September 22. The §341 meeting of creditors is scheduled to be held on October 27, and on his way to the meeting Bobby loses control of his car and damages two other vehicles. Bobby cannot amend his list of creditors to include the owners of the two damaged vehicles.

Much more troubling are those claims that have connections to both prior actions (or omissions) and future consequences. The circumstances can be as diverse as the negligent issuance of certified financial statements by an accounting firm that thereafter files for bankruptcy relief followed still later by the reliance of an institutional lender on those financial reports, and the discharge of hazardous wastes by a dry cleaner who then files a bankruptcy petition and is thereafter ordered to clean up the environmental hazard it created. Perhaps the most prominent examples of these kinds of claims are the mass tort claims. Tens of thousands of people injured by asbestos, the Dalkon Shield, and breast implants have been creditors in high-profile Chapter 11 cases. These creditors include persons whose injuries were manifested prior to the bankruptcy case and those who may potentially suffer the injuries much later. The courts have struggled with the proper treatment to be accorded to the various parties. To the extent that these "future claims" are included in the bankruptcy proceedings, the debts held by those "future claimants" will be subject to the bankruptcy discharge. On the other hand, if those creditors are excluded from the bankruptcy proceeding, the claim is not discharged, but the creditor could not share in any distribution that would be made in the bankruptcy case. Therefore, if the debtor is liquidated, no payments would be made to those persons who suffer injuries later in time.

In re UNR Industries, Inc.

United States Court of Appeals, Seventh Circuit, 1984
725 F.2d 1111

POSNER, Circuit Judge.

The district court in a bankruptcy proceeding refused to appoint a representative to file claims on behalf of individuals who may develop asbestosis or other lung diseases in the future from past exposure to asbestos manufactured and sold by the bankrupt, 29 Bkrtcy. 741 (N.D. Ill. 1983), and the bankrupt has appealed. The first and last issue we consider is the appealability of the judge's order.

In 1982 a group of affiliated corporations (collectively, UNR) petitioned under Chapter 11 of the Bankruptcy Code, 11 U.S.C. §§1101 et seq. The ground for the petition (as for Johns-Manville's, pending in the Southern District of New York, and Amatex's, pending in the Eastern District of Pennsylvania) is that UNR cannot satisfy its enormous tort liability, actual and potential, resulting from the thousands of asbestosis suits that have been or will be brought against it by shipyard workers and others who have inhaled fibers from asbestos that it manufactured. *See* Note, The Manville Bankruptcy: Treating Mass Tort Claims in Chapter 11 Proceedings, 96 Harv. L. Rev. 1121 (1983); Special Project, An Analysis of the Legal, Social, and Political Issues

Raised by Asbestos Litigation, 36 Vand. L. Rev. 573, 806-07, 845 (1983); Note, Manville: Good Faith Reorganization or "Insulated" Bankruptcy, 12 Hofstra L. Rev. §121 (1983).

Although UNR represents that it stopped manufacturing asbestos in 1970, some of its asbestos remained (and no doubt remains to this day) in shipyards and other places where people are exposed to airborne asbestos fibers; and in any event it is sometimes not until many years after last inhaling the fibers that one develops a diagnosable case of asbestosis (a term we use broadly to refer to any asbestos-related disease). Already a defendant in more than 17,000 asbestosis suits, UNR expects to be sued by 30,000 to 120,000 new asbestosis victims as their disease manifests itself and is diagnosed. *Compare* Walker et al., Projections of Asbestos-Related Disease 1980-2009, 25 J. Occupational Med. 409 (1983).

Believing that its ability to formulate a workable plan of reorganization might depend on its being able somehow to remove the enormous cloud of potential tort liability represented by the prospective suits, UNR in October 1982 filed in the bankruptcy court an "Application for the Appointment of a Legal Representative for Unknown Putative Asbestos-Related Claimants." UNR's hope was that if such a representative were appointed, he might, under the supervision of the bankruptcy court, negotiate with UNR some arrangement whereby all potential asbestosis claims could be fixed and discharged in the final plan of reorganization, along with the claims of UNR's existing asbestosis and other tort and contract creditors. *See* Note, Mass Tort Claims and the Corporate Tortfeasor: Bankruptcy Reorganization and Legislative Compensation Versus the Common-Law Tort System, 61 Tex. L. Rev. 1297, 1314 (1983). UNR might set up a revolving fund out of which the representative would pay possible future plaintiffs a fraction of their tort claims as they accrued, or it might purchase annuities for them. And it then could operate free of the threat to solvency posed by the prospective claims.

At about the same time that UNR's application was filed, the Supreme Court handed down its decision in Northern Pipeline Construction Co. v. Marathon Pipe Line Co., 458 U.S. 50, 102 S. Ct. 2858, 73 L. Ed. 2d 598 (1982), invalidating the provision of the Bankruptcy Reform Act of 1978, Pub. L. 95-598, that vests the exercise of the district courts' bankruptcy jurisdiction in bankruptcy judges who do not enjoy the guarantees of judicial independence in Article III of the Constitution. Interpreting the Supreme Court's decision as invalidating only the subsection of the new Act that provides, "The bankruptcy court . . . shall exercise all of the jurisdiction conferred by this section on the district courts," 28 U.S.C. §1471(c), and not the preceding subsections, 28 U.S.C. §§1471(a) and (b), which vest original jurisdiction over bankruptcy in the district courts, the United States District Court for the Northern District of Illinois, by direction of the Seventh Circuit Judicial Council acting pursuant to 28 U.S.C. §332(d)(1), adopted on December 20, 1982, as a General Order, a proposed rule drafted by the Judicial Conference of the United States under authority of 28 U.S.C. §331. The rule, so far as it bears on this case, allows the district court to hear any part of a bankruptcy case. (The rule is printed in 1 Collier on Bankruptcy, insert preceding ch. 3 (15th ed. 1983). The background of the rule is described, and its validity defended, in White Motor Corp. v. Citibank, N.A., 704 F.2d 254, 259-62 (6th Cir. 1983).) It was pursuant to the General Order that Judge Hart considered and denied UNR's application to appoint a representative. His ground for denial was that people who have not yet developed asbestosis do not have claims that can be proved in bankruptcy. *See* 11 U.S.C. §101(4)(A). . . .

We come at last to the heart of the appealability issue, which is whether Judge Hart's order was "final." There is an obvious sense in which it was not. It did not wind up the litigation before the district court; the bankruptcy reorganization goes on. But lack of finality in this sense is not fatal to the appeal. Orders disposing of claims filed against the bankrupt estate while the bankruptcy proceeding is pending are much more like final judgments in ordinary civil suits than like interlocutory orders in such suits. *See, e.g.,* In re Bestmann, 720 F.2d 484, 486 (8th Cir. 1983). If an asbestosis victim sues a solvent manufacturer of asbestos and the court dismisses the complaint, the dismissal is, of course, a final judgment. Under the former bankruptcy procedure, an asbestosis victim usually would sue a bankrupt asbestos manufacturer in just the same way; if he won he would file his judgment as a claim against the bankrupt in the bankruptcy proceeding, *see* 11 U.S.C. §103(a)(1) (1976 ed.); and if the claim was denied he could appeal the denial. *See* In re Saco Local Development Corp., *supra*, 711 F.2d at 444-45. But this was a cumbersome procedure, and a major change brought about by the Bankruptcy Reform Act of 1978 was to authorize the bankruptcy court to adjudicate claimants' rights under tort law, thus merging the tort determination with the claim determination. *See* H.R. Rep. No. 595, 95th Cong., 1st Sess. 445 (1977); S. Rep. No. 989, 95th Cong., 2d Sess. 18, 153 (1978), U.S. Code Cong. & Admin. News 1978, p.5787; Northern Pipeline Construction Co. v. Marathon Pipe Line Co., *supra*, 102 S. Ct. at 2862-63. (This expansion in the bankruptcy courts' power was a major reason why the Supreme Court held in *Marathon* that the new bankruptcy judges created by the Act were exercising powers reserved to Article III judges, and why in turn the General Order revested the bankruptcy judges' powers in the district judges.) When a claim is denied under the new procedure created by the Act, it is even clearer than under the former procedure that the denial is the equivalent of a final tort judgment and is therefore appealable consistently with conventional principles of finality.

UNR argues that in refusing to appoint the representative the district judge in effect denied the claims that the representative would have presented; and if this is right, the refusal would be appealable, as we have just seen. But we do not think it is right. Although the judge refused to make the appointment because he believed that such claims would have no status in bankruptcy, you cannot appeal from the implications of what a judge does as distinct from the actual order he enters. If a judge denied a plaintiff's request for a discovery order because he believed the plaintiff's case had no merit, the plaintiff could not appeal from that order; he would have to wait till the district judge dismissed the complaint. It is the same here. By denying the appointment of a representative on the ground he did the district judge telegraphed his punch; it is now highly predictable that when and if someone who has been exposed to asbestos manufactured by UNR but has not yet developed a diagnosable case of asbestosis files a claim against UNR in this bankruptcy proceeding the judge will deny the claim. But he has not done so yet.

Nor are we persuaded that his action is tantamount to denial because if no representative is appointed no member of the class sought to be represented will realize that he may have a claim and attempt to file it. Of the 30,000 to 120,000 people who UNR thinks may one day contract asbestosis and sue UNR for the damages resulting from their disease, some must already be aware that they may be ticking time bombs, and the very active plaintiffs' asbestosis bar will surely bend every effort to make the others aware. As a matter of fact a man named Robinson, who says he was exposed to asbestos sold by UNR but has not yet developed asbestosis, moved to intervene in the district court to oppose UNR's application for appointment of the representative. Robinson's motion was denied and he has not filed an appeal from the denial. His motion was not an attempt to file a claim and the denial of the motion was not the denial of a claim, but the motion shows that at least one member of the class of possible future asbestosis victims is aware of his situation and prepared to litigate in reference to it.

As we do not think the district judge's order has the effect of denying the claims of such victims, it is not a final order in a conventional bankruptcy sense, and is appealable if at all only under the "collateral order" doctrine created by the Supreme Court in Cohen v. Beneficial Industrial Loan Corp., *supra*. This doctrine allows orders that are not final in the sense of disposing of the entire lawsuit before the district court, but are final in the sense of irrevocably deciding the rights of a party, to be appealed under 28 U.S.C. §1291. . . .

For an order to be appealable under the *Cohen* doctrine its consequences for the appellant must be irreversible by subsequent proceedings. In re Continental Investment Corp., 637 F.2d 1, 5 (1st Cir. 1980). There is nothing irreversible, at least so far as the potential asbestosis plaintiffs themselves are concerned, about the district court's order refusing to appoint someone to represent them. Any such victim is free to file a claim with the district court, and if the claim is denied to appeal the denial to us as a final decision. And he can if he wants try to file a claim on behalf not only of himself but of others who have been exposed to asbestos sold by UNR but have not yet developed a diagnosable case of asbestosis. The judicial process will benefit from waiting for an actual claim to be filed. When that happens the district court — and, if it dismisses the claim and the dismissal is appealed, the court of appeals — will have before it a concrete claim and not merely speculation about potential claimants. This will create a more informative context for deciding whether the interests of potential victims of asbestosis can be dealt with — whether one-by-one or in gross — in this bankruptcy proceeding.

True, there is much learning that mass-disaster torts in general and asbestosis cases in particular are unsuitable for class-action treatment. *See, e.g.*, In re Northern District of California, Dalkon Shield IUD Products Liability Litigation, 693 F.2d 847, 852-54 (9th Cir. 1982); Yandle v. PPG Industries, Inc., 65 F.R.D. 566 (E.D. Tex. 1974); Williams, Mass Tort Class Actions: Going, Going, Gone?, 98 F.R.D. 323 (1983). We need not decide whether this learning would carry over to the bankruptcy context, whether it is entirely sound (a proposition questioned in Judge Williams' article), and whether in any event it is applicable to the unusual situation presented here, where each claim, because it is an estimate of a possible future harm rather than a definite past harm, will be smaller than the usual mass-disaster tort claim and therefore more needful of class treatment. These questions, too, would be presented in a more illuminating context if we had before us an actual claimant, not merely the bankrupt raising a procedural question before an actual claim has been filed.

Coopers & Lybrand v. Livesay, 437 U.S. 463, 98 S. Ct. 2454, 57 L. Ed. 2d 351 (1978), which held that orders refusing to certify suits as class actions under Rule 23 of the Federal Rules of Civil Procedure are not within the scope of the *Cohen* doctrine, bears directly on this case. When class certification is denied, many and sometimes all members of the class may be unable as a practical matter to get any relief against the defendant; their claims may be too small to make it worth their while to sue individually. Nevertheless the Court in *Livesay* refused to apply the *Cohen* doctrine and dismissed the appeal. The situation here is parallel. It may be that if no representative of potential victims of asbestosis is appointed many of those potential victims will not file claims against the bankrupt estate until too late. Yet the situation of the potential victims is actually better than that of members of a class when class certification is refused. Any member of the "class" that UNR wants a representative appointed for can, without incurring the cost of bringing an independent lawsuit, file a claim with the district court; and if the court denies his claim he can appeal immediately to us. If we decide on appeal that such claims are proper in bankruptcy the district judge will have to reexamine his refusal to appoint a representative for the potential claimants — the basis of his refusal (that the persons who would be represented have no rights in bankruptcy) having been destroyed.

Since some potential claimants might be discouraged by the fact that Judge Hart, in refusing to appoint a representative for them, expressed the view that they have no rights in bankruptcy, we emphasize that the correctness of his view (criticized in Roe, Bankruptcy and Tort: The Problem of Mass Disaster, 84 Colum. L. Rev. (1984)) is an open one in our minds. The practical difficulties of identifying, giving constitutionally adequate notice to, and attempting to estimate the damages of the thousands upon thousands of people who have been exposed to asbestos sold by UNR but have not yet developed asbestosis are formidable, and possibly insurmountable. Yet if any of them have already suffered a tort there would be no basis we can think of for not letting them file claims in this bankruptcy proceeding. And some, at least, probably have suffered a tort. The states differ on whether a cause of action in an asbestosis case accrues upon inhalation (*see, e.g.*, Steinhardt v. Johns-Manville Corp., 54 N.Y.2d 1008, 1010-11, 446 N.Y.S.2d 244, 246, 430 N.E.2d 1297, 1299 (1981); Braswell v. Flintkote Mines, Ltd., 723 F.2d 527 at 532-33 (7th Cir. 1983)) or not until there is palpable disease (*see, e.g.*, Nuebauer v. Owens-Corning Fiberglas Corp., 686 F.2d 570 (7th Cir. 1982)) or the disease is discovered (*see, e.g.*, Pauley v. Combustion Engineering, Inc., 528 F. Supp. 759, 764 (S.D. W. Va. 1981)). *See generally* Note, *supra*, 12 Hofstra L. Rev. at 138-39 and nn.118-27. Even in a "discovery" state the cause of action may "exist" before it "accrues" — that is, before the statute of limitations on bringing it begins to run. *See* Moore v. Jackson Park Hospital, 95 Ill. 2d 223, 232, 69 Ill. Dec. 191, 194-95, 447 N.E.2d 408, 411-12 (1983); *but see* Morrissy v. Eli Lilly & Co., 76 Ill. App. 3d 753, 761, 32 Ill. Dec. 30, 37, 394 N.E.2d 1369, 1376 (1979). These states postpone the date of accrual of the cause of action not in order to prevent the early filing of claims but in order to lift the bar of the statute of limitations to later filings. Since there is "medical evidence that the body incurs microscopic injury as asbestos fibers become lodged in the lungs and as the surrounding tissue reacts to the fibers thereafter," Keene Corp. v. Insurance Co. of North America, 667 F.2d 1034, 1042 (D.C. Cir. 1981), and since no particular amount of injury is necessary to create tort liability, courts in these states might hold that a tort claim arises as soon as asbestos fibers are inhaled, however much time the victim might have for bringing suit. In any event, some at least of the many thousands of workers who have been exposed to asbestos sold by UNR must have been exposed in states such as Indiana and New York where the cause of action accrues upon inhalation, and their claims against the bankrupt estate — accrued tort claims — would appear uncontroversially to be provable in bankruptcy.

Even in states where exposed workers are not injured in a tort sense till the disease manifests itself, and therefore do not have an accrued tort claim in any sense, and even assuming that an unaccrued tort claim cannot be a "claim" within the meaning of 11 U.S.C. §101(4)(A) (that is, a "right to payment, whether or not such right is reduced to judgment, liquidated, unliquidated, fixed, contingent, matured, unmatured, disputed, undisputed, legal, equitable, secured, or unsecured"), a bankruptcy court's equitable powers (on which *see, e.g.*, Pepper v. Litton, 308 U.S. 295, 304, 60 S. Ct. 238, 244, 84 L. Ed. 281 (1939); 1 Remington, A Treatise on the Bankruptcy Law of the United States §22 (Henderson 5th ed. 1950)) just might be broad enough to enable the court to make provision for future asbestosis claims against the bankrupt when it approved the final plan of reorganization. The date on which a person exposed to asbestos happens to develop a diagnosable case of asbestosis is arbitrary. Could it not be argued therefore that a bankruptcy court can and should use its equitable powers, which traditionally "have been invoked to the end that . . . substance will not give way to form, that technical considerations will not prevent substantial justice from being done," 308 U.S. at 305, 60 S. Ct. at 244 (especially, perhaps, in a reorganization case, *see* In re Michigan Brewing Co., 24 F. Supp. 430 (W.D. Mich. 1938)), to prevent the liquidation or discharge of the bankrupt before provision is made for such persons? And more than arbitrariness is involved. If future claims cannot be discharged before they ripen, UNR may not be able to emerge from bankruptcy with reasonable prospects for continued existence as a going concern. In that event, and assuming that UNR's going-concern value would exceed its liquidation value, both UNR (which is to say the creditors who will own UNR at the conclusion of the reorganization) and future plaintiffs would be made worse off, and UNR's current creditors would not necessarily be made better off, by the court's failure to act along the lines proposed by UNR.

But against all this it can be argued, returning to our first point, that it would be a quixotic undertaking far beyond the realistic boundaries of judicial competence to make sufficiently generous provision for upwards of a hundred thousand unidentified claimants to justify extinguishing their claims involuntarily; that even if only a small fraction of the claims were not extinguished the cloud of potential liability over UNR's head might still be too large for it to emerge from bankruptcy as a going concern with fair prospects of surviving in the long run; and that, as Judge Hart said, the solution to this problem must come from Congress.

Fortunately we need not decide these difficult and far-reaching questions here; their very difficulty, and far-reaching nature, are reasons for our refusing to decide them prematurely through a permissive interpretation of 28 U.S.C. §1291. We merely point out that they are substantial questions which the district court did not finally decide when it turned down the application to appoint a representative and on which the district court in any event does not have the final say.

We thus far have considered the question of irreversible consequences — the key to appealability under the *Cohen* doctrine — from the standpoint of possible future asbestosis victims, the people for whom UNR wanted the district judge to appoint a representative, rather than from the standpoint of UNR itself, though the motive for UNR's application was self-interest rather than altruism. It can be argued, and UNR does argue (though as a subordinate theme), that the denial of its application will, unless that denial is promptly reversed, have irreversible consequences for it; that by making it impossible for UNR to discharge potential as well as actual asbestosis claims Judge Hart has made it impossible for UNR to emerge successfully from the reorganization proceeding. But this argument confuses an interim procedural ruling with the terms of the final plan of reorganization. *Cf.* In re Kutner, 656 F.2d 1107, 1111 (5th Cir. 1981). When a final plan is approved (*see* 11 U.S.C. §§1126-1144) that makes no provision for possible future asbestosis victims, UNR will be able to appeal to us from the order adopting the plan, *see, e.g.*, In re Carbide Cutoff, Inc., 703 F.2d 259 (7th Cir. 1983); In re Fondiller, 707 F.2d 441, 442 n.1 (9th Cir. 1983), assuming it is not so hopelessly insolvent at that point that it is indifferent to the terms of the reorganization, *see* id. at 442. And it will be able to argue on appeal that the plan is defective because of the failure to make provision for potential asbestosis victims. If we agree and reverse, the district court will then appoint a representative or take whatever other steps may be necessary to comply with our instructions. And probably UNR will not have to wait that long. If one or more potential victims of asbestosis file or attempt to file a claim, the district court may decide to reconsider its refusal to appoint a representative for them. *Cf.* Coopers & Lybrand v. Livesay, *supra*, 437 U.S. at 469 and n.11, 98 S. Ct. at 2458 and n.11. And if it does not, and denies the claim, and is reversed and the matter remanded, the question whether to appoint such a representative will appear to it in a wholly new light.

We realize that reorganizations can be protracted and that the finality rule of section 1293(b) presupposes an opportunity for interlocutory appeals that *Marathon* has deprived the parties of. In the scheme of the 1978 Act, before *Marathon* knocked out key provisions of it, an order such as the district judge made in the present case would have been made by a bankruptcy judge, and though interlocutory his order would have been appealable either to a panel of three bankruptcy judges or to the district court, with the permission of either the panel or the court as the case may be. So there would have been some appellate review, if leave to appeal had been granted. There has been none here. But the confused situation created by the *Marathon* holding will be clarified by new legislation, and this proceeding returned in its entirety to a bankruptcy judge, long before a final plan of reorganization is confirmed. And if the bankruptcy judge issues the same order that the district judge has issued, and that order is appealed to the district court, the district court's order may be a final order appealable to us under the teaching of the *Marin* case. For all of these reasons the issue that UNR wants us to decide will probably come before us again before the final plan of reorganization is confirmed.

UNR asks us, if we dismiss the appeal, to mandamus the district judge to certify his order for an immediate appeal under 28 U.S.C. §1292(b). All other objections to the application aside, the prematurity of UNR's appeal would make us unwilling to entertain a discretionary appeal at this time.

APPEAL DISMISSED AND MANDAMUS DENIED.

NOTES

A more famous asbestos bankruptcy case involved the Johns-Manville Company. That case spawned substantial litigation. In order to address the problem of future claimants in that case, a plan of reorganization was proposed under which a trust was established through the transfer of substantially all of the common stock of the reorganized debtor. The trust assets were to be used to pay the claims of creditors as they arose in the future. An elaborate system was created to resolve those claims. Ultimately, the reorganization plan was upheld. Kane v. Johns-Manville Corp., 843 F.2d 686 (2d Cir. 1988). Similar solutions have been posed in other mass tort bankruptcy proceedings.

In 1994, Congress got into the act by amending §524 of the Bankruptcy Code to specifically authorize the type of plan approved in *Johns-Manville*. Section 524(g) provides generally that the courts may enforce "channeling injunctions" that require future claimants to assert their claims solely against a trust created for the purpose of paying those "future claims." These future claims are essentially "channeled" into the trust and away from the reorganized debtor. Congress went even further in the 1994 Amendments, adding §524(h), which retroactively authorizes these injunctions in cases concluded before the adoption of the Amendments.

Bankruptcy can intervene in much smaller matters than mass tort claims. Debtors' lives go on even as their financial circumstances deteriorate. The filing of a bankruptcy petition after a debtor engages in some action that might lead to the creation of a debt, but before the debt becomes final for state law purposes, requires the court to determine whether the claim exists for bankruptcy purposes even if it is not considered a debt under the non-bankruptcy law. Keep in mind that the definition of claim under §101(5) is intentionally broad. Use it to resolve the next Problem.

PROBLEM 5-11

The world of real estate ownership and development had provided Shari with a comfortable living for quite some time, but it ultimately proved her downfall. By 2008, Shari owned 28 different rental properties, and each one was subject to a mortgage that was equal to or greater than the value of the property. Many of the properties had fallen into disrepair and some were subject to housing department orders to demolish the buildings. Under the applicable ordinance, any person whose building is demolished is liable to the city for the cost of the demolition. If Shari files a Chapter 7 petition after she receives a notice that a building is condemned and no longer habitable, but before the building is actually demolished, will the city's claim against her for the subsequent demolition of the building be discharged in the Chapter 7 case? *See* In re Gray, 394 B.R. 900 (Bankr. C.D. Ill. 2008).

While there are some differences between mass tort claims and environmental claims, the similarities are substantial. Environmental claims may arise as soon as a debtor spills a toxic substance or otherwise violates environmental laws. The harm created by those acts, however, may not be identified until some time in the future. Once again, if the debtor is not able to establish the full extent of those claims, reorganization will become difficult, if not impossible. The policies underlying the environmental laws, however, may conflict with bankruptcy policy.

California Dept. of Health Services v. Jensen (In re Jensen)
United States Court of Appeals, Ninth Circuit, 1993
995 F.2d 925

Before ALDISERT, GOODWIN, and FLETCHER, Circuit Judges.
PER CURIAM:
The California Department of Health Services ("California DHS") appeals the decision of the Bankruptcy Appellate Panel that its claim against Robert Burns Jensen and Rosemary Tooker Jensen for cleanup of hazardous waste at the Jensens' former business property was discharged in the couple's bankruptcy. We have jurisdiction over California DHS's timely appeal pursuant to 28 U.S.C. §158(d) (1988). We affirm.

I. Facts

A decade ago, the Jensens owned a closely-held corporation called the Jensen Lumber Co. ("JLC") and briefly operated its lumber business. On December 2, 1983, JLC filed a voluntary Chapter 11 bankruptcy petition; the company had been in business only since May 1983.

Several weeks after the petition was filed, on January 25, 1984, an inspector from the California Regional Water Quality Control Board ("California Water Board") visited the inactive JLC site and noticed a large, cinder-block tank. The tank contained about 5,000 gallons of a lumber fungicide. JLC had used the "dip tank" and fungicide solution to treat the lumber it processed. The solution contained toxic chlorinated phenols (including pentachlorophenal, or "PCP").

By letter dated February 2, 1984, the California Water Board inspector expressed his concern to Robert Jensen that any release of the solution "through accident or vandalism . . . would probably cause a major fish kill in the South Fork Trinity River and could possibly affect the health of downstream water users." ER at 27. The inspector requested prompt action to prevent such a catastrophe, and advised Robert Jensen that he should either find another operating lumber mill that could use the fungicide, or contact an appropriate hazardous waste removal company.

The Jensens' attorney at the time responded by letter dated February 10, 1984. He advised the California Water Board that JLC would "almost certain[ly]" go completely out of business and that its bankruptcy case likely would be converted to a Chapter 7 proceeding. He also informed the California Water Board that JLC "has no funds available to dispose of the lumber fungicide." ER at 28. On February 13, 1984, the Jensens filed a Chapter 7 personal bankruptcy petition. On March 20, 1984, as predicted, JLC converted its pending corporate Chapter 11 proceedings to a Chapter 7 liquidation.

The California Water Board brought the California DHS in to assist in removing the fungicide on March 23, 1984. On May 18, 1984, a California DHS waste management specialist supervised the removal of the solution from the six foot by six foot by twenty foot dip tank. The California DHS specialist noticed spillage inside the building housing the tank, and evidence of leakage on the river side of the building. He took soil samples, which revealed varying concentrations of PCP contamination; the worst contamination seemed to be located, not surprisingly, in and around the dip tank. Initial estimates of the volume of fungicide in the tank had been about 3,000 gallons. In fact (as suggested above), about 5,000 gallons were pumped into the waste removal tanker, filling it to capacity.

The Jensens' personal bankruptcy case was closed on February 20, 1985. No assets were distributed to creditors. The JLC corporate bankruptcy proceedings closed March 18, 1987. On March 30, 1987, California DHS notified Robert Jensen that it considered him a responsible party liable for the cleanup of the hazardous waste at the JLC site. Rosemary Jensen was later named a potentially responsible party.

Eventually, having been unable to persuade the Jensens or other involved parties to undertake independently the cleanup operation, California DHS developed its own remedial action plan. California DHS has spent over $900,000 at the JLC site (including areas other than the dip tank). The Jensens, doing business as JLC, have been allocated ten percent financial responsibility for the cleanup.

On December 5, 1988, the Jensens' personal bankruptcy proceedings were reopened to permit them to list California DHS and the other parties to the JLC site cleanup as creditors. Their adversary proceeding complaint, dated April 24, 1989, sought a determination that their pro rata share of the cleanup expenses had been "discharged by the granting of the discharge to the debtors herein on July 23, 1984." ER at 7-8.

Ruling on cross-motions for summary judgment, the bankruptcy court determined that California DHS's cleanup recovery claim "arose postpetition and is not subject to discharge." In re Jensen, 114 B.R. 700, 707 (Bankr. E.D. Cal. 1990). The BAP reversed, finding that "[b]ecause . . . claims in bankruptcy arise based upon the debtor's conduct, . . . [California] DHS's claim arose in this case prepetition, and was therefore discharged in the Jensens' bankruptcy." In re Jensen, 127 B.R. 27, 33 (Bankr. 9th Cir. 1991). California DHS filed its notice of appeal from that decision on June 3, 1991.

II. Analysis

The BAP's decision is reviewed de novo. In re Dewalt, 961 F.2d 848, 850 (9th Cir. 1992). The bankruptcy court's conclusions of law are reviewed de novo, and its findings of fact are reviewed for clear error. Id.

The intersection of environmental cleanup laws and federal bankruptcy statutes is somewhat messy. The Comprehensive Environmental Response, Compensation, and Liability Act of 1980, 42 U.S.C.A. §§9601-9675 (1988 & Supp. 1993) ("CERCLA"), and similar state laws, like California's Carpenter-Presley-Tanner Hazardous Substance Account Act, Cal. Health & Safety Code §§25300-25395 (West 1992) ("HAS"), seek "to protect public health and the environment by facilitating the cleanup of environmental contamination and imposing costs on the parties responsible for the pollution." Kevin J. Saville, Note, Discharging CERCLA Liability in Bankruptcy: When Does a Claim Arise?, 76 Minn. L. Rev. 327, 327 (1991) [hereinafter Discharging CERCLA Liability in Bankruptcy].

By contrast, the Bankruptcy Reform Act of 1978, 11 U.S.C.A. §§101-1330 (1988 and Supp. 1993), is "designed to give a debtor a 'fresh start' by discharging as many of its 'debts' as possible." Arlene Elgart Mirsky et al., The Interface Between Bankruptcy and Environmental Laws, 46 Bus. Law. 626, 626 (1991) [hereinafter The Interface Between Bankruptcy and Environmental Law]. Consistent with this policy, a "claim" is defined at 11 U.S.C.A. §101(5) in these broad terms:

> (A) right to payment, whether or not such right is reduced to judgment, liquidated, unliquidated, fixed, contingent, matured, unmatured, disputed, undisputed, legal, equitable, secured, or unsecured; or
>
> (B) right to an equitable remedy for breach of performance if such breach gives rise to a right to payment, whether or not such right to an equitable remedy is reduced to judgment, fixed, contingent, matured, unmatured, disputed, undisputed, secured, or unsecured.

11 U.S.C.A. §101(5).

Conflict and confusion are almost inevitable. *See* In re Chicago, M., St. P. & P.R.R., 974 F.2d 775, 777 (7th Cir. 1992). For instance,

> [i]f a problem exists but has not been found or if a cleanup occurs at an identified site before liability is determined, can one of the potentially responsible parties ("PRPs") get a complete

discharge in bankruptcy? [And h]ow can a debtor get a fresh start if it is potentially subject to environmental liability, a large portion of which may be contingent . . . ?

The Interface Between Bankruptcy and Environmental Laws, 46 Bus. Law. at 627.

Notwithstanding what might be perceived to be diametrically opposed philosophies, the Supreme Court has indicated more than once that, if possible, these two conflicting objectives should be reconciled. Erman v. Lox Equip. Co., 142 B.R. 905, 907 (N.D. Cal. 1992) (citing, inter alia, Midlantic Natl. Bank v. New Jersey Dept. of Environmental Protection, 474 U.S. 494, 106 S. Ct. 755, 88 L. Ed. 2d 859 (1986); Ohio v. Kovacs, 469 U.S. 274, 105 S. Ct. 705, 83 L. Ed. 2d 649 (1985)); *see also* In re Natl. Gypsum Co., 139 B.R. 397, 404 (N.D. Tex. 1992) ("it is not a question of which statute should be accorded primacy over the other, but rather what interaction between the two statutes serves most faithfully the policy objectives embodied in the two separate enactments of Congress").

Courts considering when a claim for environmental response costs arose have employed somewhat varying approaches to the question. *See* In re Jensen, 127 B.R. at 30-33. Several courts, including the bankruptcy court below, have rejected the argument that a CERCLA claim arises upon the release or threatened release of hazardous waste, holding instead that each element of a CERCLA claim must be established, including the incurrence of response costs, before a dischargeable claim arises. United States v. Union Scrap & Metal, 123 B.R. 831, 838 (D. Minn. 1990) (citing In re Jensen, 114 B.R. at 706); *cf.* In re M. Frenville Co., 744 F.2d 332 (3d Cir. 1984) (defendant accounting firm in damages action filed by banks had "an unmatured, unliquidated, disputed claim" against debtor for indemnity and contribution when banks filed their action), *cert. denied*, 469 U.S. 1160, 105 S. Ct. 911, 83 L. Ed. 2d 925 (1985).

The BAP rejected this analysis as inconsistent with the broad statutory definition of a "claim" and with "the overriding goal of the Bankruptcy Code to provide a 'fresh start' for the debtor." In re Jensen, 127 B.R. at 31 (quoting Grogan v. Garner, 498 U.S. 279, 286-87, 111 S. Ct. 654, 659, 112 L. Ed. 2d 755 (1991)). Indeed, neither *Union Scrap* nor *Frenville* has had a substantial impact. The Minnesota district court, in an opinion subsequent to *Union Scrap*, disregarded the "response costs" rule and focused instead on when the party asserting the CERCLA claim had notice of the claim:

When the debtor has not disclosed its potential [CERCLA] liabilities in long-since closed bankruptcy proceedings, and the governmental agency has not had actual knowledge of the potential claim in sufficient time to file a claim in those proceedings, the potential [CERCLA] claim is not discharged.

Sylvester Bros. Dev. Co. v. Burlington N.R.R., 133 B.R. 648, 653 (D. Minn. 1991).

In a case following its decision in *Frenville*, the Third Circuit considered whether a contingent claim for contribution under CERCLA could arise before CERCLA was enacted. The court held, "[I]t was not until the passage of CERCLA that a legal relationship was created between the [parties] relevant to the petitioners' potential causes of action such that an interest could flow." In re Penn Cent. Transp. Co., 944 F.2d 164, 168 (3d Cir. 1991), *cert. denied*, _____ U.S. _____, 112 S. Ct. 1262, 117 L. Ed. 2d 491 (1992). The court did not cite *Frenville* but instead relied on Schweitzer v. Consolidated Rail Corp., 758 F.2d 936, 942 (3d Cir.) (claims of plaintiffs asserting tort causes of action under Federal Employers' Liability Act did not arise until plaintiffs suffered identifiable, compensable injuries), *cert. denied*, 474 U.S. 864, 106 S. Ct. 183, 88 L. Ed. 2d 152 (1985).

The Seventh Circuit has also considered this issue. In In re Chicago, Milwaukee, St. Paul & Pacific Railroad Co., 974 F.2d 775, the state of Washington took soil samples and conducted tests concerning possible contamination at a railyard formerly owned by the debtor in bankruptcy. Shortly before the consummation date, the test results were obtained, indicating that contamination had taken place. The state did not file a proof of claim before the relevant bar date. The court held:

> when a potential CERCLA claimant can tie the bankruptcy debtor to a known release of a hazardous substance which this potential claimant knows will lead to CERCLA response costs, and when this potential claimant has, in fact, conducted tests with regard to this contamination problem, then this potential claimant has, at least, a contingent CERCLA claim for purposes of Section 77.

Id. at 786.

A different approach — the one utilized by the BAP in reversing the bankruptcy court's decision in this case — counsels that the bankruptcy claim arises at the time of the debtor's conduct relating to the contamination. In re Jensen, 127 B.R. at 32-33. In other words, response costs expended by a California DHS or EPA are dischargeable where they result from pre-petition releases or threatened releases of hazardous substances. In re Chateaugay Corp., 944 F.2d 997, 1005 (2d Cir. 1991); In re Jensen, 127 B.R. at 33 ("a claim arises for purposes of discharge upon the actual or threatened release of hazardous waste by the debtor").

Another method for addressing the environmental/bankruptcy issue might be called the "relationship" test. *See* In re Edge, 60 B.R. 690 (Bankr. M.D. Tenn. 1986). This approach establishes the date of a bankruptcy claim "at the earliest point in the relationship between the debtor and the creditor." In re Jensen, 127 B.R. at 31. For example, although a debtor dentist's pre-petition negligence may escape detection until post-petition, a bankruptcy claim arises at the point of the dentist's negligent act. Id. at 31-32 (discussing In re Edge). A post-petition suit against the debtor dentist was prohibited by 11 U.S.C. §362's automatic stay. In re Edge, 60 B.R. at 705.

Not all of these analyses give adequate consideration to the policy goals of the environmental laws and the bankruptcy code. To hold that a claim for contribution arises only when there is an enforceable right to payment appears to ignore the breadth of the statutory definition of "claim." In relevant part, a claim is a "right to payment, whether or not such right is reduced to judgment, liquidated, unliquidated, fixed, contingent, matured, unmatured, disputed, undisputed, legal, equitable, secured, or unsecured." 11 U.S.C.A. §101(5)(A). This "broadest possible definition" of "claim" is designed to ensure that "all legal obligations of the debtor, no matter how remote or contingent, will be able to be dealt with in the bankruptcy case." H.R. Rep. No. 595, 95th Cong., 2d Sess. 1, 309 (1978), reprinted in 1978 U.S.C.C.A.N. 5963, 6266 (emphasis added); S. Rep. No. 598, 95th Cong., 2d Sess. 1, 22, reprinted in 1978 U.S.C.C.A.N. 5787, 5808 (same).

The breadth of the definition of "claim" is critical in effectuating the bankruptcy code's policy of giving the debtor a "fresh start." The Interface Between Bankruptcy and Environmental Laws, 46 Bus. Law. at 650. *Frenville*'s "right of payment" theory is "widely criticized" outside the Third Circuit, id. at 652, at least in part because it would appear to excise "contingent" and "unmatured" claims from §101(5)(A)'s list.

The debtor's conduct approach adopted by the BAP in this case is not immune from criticism, either. One commentator has noted that "[d]espite Congress's repeal of the 'provability' requirement and its broad definition of 'claim,' nothing in the legislative history or the Code suggests that Congress intended to discharge a creditor's rights before the creditor knew or should have known that its rights existed." Discharging CERCLA Liability in Bankruptcy, 76 Minn. L. Rev. at 348.

Moreover, "discharging liability solely because a release of hazardous substances occurred pre-petition may conflict with CERCLA's goal of cleaning up the environment quickly." Id. at 350. This drawback is, in a sense, the flipside of the "right to payment" approach, which ignores important bankruptcy concepts and objectives. Few would doubt that courts should not encourage the frustration of environmental cleanup efforts, just as courts should not override congressional attempts to legislate bankruptcy procedures and goals. The "relationship" approach, when defined as broadly as in In re Chateaugay, "undermine[s] the rationale for considering whether or not a relationship exists," namely "that a creditor with a relationship may anticipate its potential claim." Id. at 353. "When courts fail to limit the scope of the relationship to situations where some pre[-]petition interaction between the PRP and the EPA existed, this expansive relationship approach takes on the characteristics of and thus suffers from the same infirmities as the 'underlying acts' approach." Id.

The sometimes competing policy goals of environmental law and the bankruptcy code were carefully balanced by Judge Barefoot Sanders in In re National Gypsum, 139 B.R. at 409. What might be called the "fair contemplation" test provides that "all future response and natural resource damages cost based on pre-petition conduct that can be fairly contemplated by the parties at the time of [d]ebtors' bankruptcy are claims under the [Bankruptcy] Code." Id. This approach stems from the belief that

> [t]he only meaningful distinction that can be made regarding CERCLA claims in bankruptcy is one that distinguishes between costs associated with pre-petition conduct resulting in a release or threat of release that could have been "fairly" contemplated by the parties; and those that could not have been "fairly" contemplated by the parties.

Id. at 407-08.

In re National Gypsum spells out certain indicia of fair contemplation ("knowledge by the parties of a site in which a PRP may be liable, NPL ['National Priorities List'] listing, notification by EPA of PRP liability, commencement of investigation and cleanup activities, and incurrence of response costs," id. at 408), and emphasizes that it is "not meant to encourage or permit dilatory tactics on the part of EPA or any other relevant government agency." Id. The Seventh Circuit in In re Chicago, Milwaukee follows a kindred analysis. What Judge Sanders described as "fairly contemplated by the parties," the Seventh Circuit described as the contemplation of a potential CERCLA claimant. According to the Seventh Circuit, when a bankruptcy debtor can be tied to a known release of a dangerous substance and when a potential CERCLA claimant has conducted tests revealing a contamination problem, a contingent CERCLA claim arises.

In re Chateaugay "relationship" approach adopts "so broad a definition of claim so as to encompass costs that could not 'fairly' have been contemplated by the EPA or the debtor pre-petition." Id. at 407. In rejecting that approach, the court in In re National Gypsum remarked that

> conduct giving rise to release or threatened release of hazardous substances pre-petition should be the relevant inquiry in determining the existence of a claim in bankruptcy, [but] this Court is not willing to favor the Code's objective of a "fresh start" over CERCLA's objective of environmental cleanup to the extent exhibited by Chateaugay. . . . [T]here exists no distinction between debtor's conduct and the release or threatened release resulting from this conduct.

Id. (footnotes omitted).

Here, the California Water Board and California DHS are agencies of the same state, involved generally in many of the same capacities. An inspector from the California Water Board visited the inactive lumberyard on January 25, 1984, and observed the fungicide dip tank. The Board notified Robert Jensen of the problem by letter dated February 2, 1984. The letter demonstrates that the Board knew of the serious environmental hazard that existed at the site:

> If this cinder block tank were to be broken through accident or vandalism, the contents of the tank would reach the South Fork Trinity River via a small stream which runs behind the building. The volume of fungicide involved would probably cause a major fish kill in the South Fork Trinity River and could possibly affect the health of downstream water users.

ER at 27. We will impute the California Water Board's knowledge to California DHS. We conclude that the state had sufficient knowledge of the Jensens' potential liability to give rise to a contingent claim for cleanup costs before the Jensens filed their personal bankruptcy petition on February 13, 1984. The claim filed by California DHS against the Jensens therefore was discharged in the Jensens' bankruptcy.

AFFIRMED.

_____

The treatment of environmental claims in bankruptcy proceedings is so pervasive that there is even a book addressing just that issue. Kathryn R. Heidt, Environmental Obligations in Bankruptcy (Warren, Gorman and Lamont, 1993). Professor Heidt has also written a number of articles on the topic. *See, e.g.*, Kathryn R. Heidt, Environmental Obligations in Bankruptcy: A Fundamental Framework, 44 U. Fla. L. Rev. 153 (1992); Kathryn R. Heidt, The Automatic Stay in Environmental Bankruptcies, 67 Am. Bankr. L.J. 69 (1993); and Kathryn R. Heidt, Cleaning Up Your Act: Efficiency Considerations and the Battle for the Debtor's Assets in Toxic Waste Bankruptcies, 40 Rutgers L. Rev. 819 (1988).

The Third Circuit has addressed another issue that arises at the intersection of the environmental and bankruptcy laws. In Torwico Electronics, Inc. v. New Jersey (In re Torwico Electronics, Inc.), 8 F.3d 146 (3d Cir. 1993), the court held that a state environmental protection agency order for a debtor to clean up an existing hazardous waste site was not a claim. The court relied on the Supreme Court's decision in Ohio v. Kovacs, 469 U.S. 274 (1985). In *Kovacs*, Ohio had obtained an injunction against the individual debtor directing him to clean up hazardous waste on the property. Upon his failure to effect the clean-up, the state had a receiver appointed and directed the receiver to conduct the clean-up. The Supreme Court held that Ohio had a claim against the debtor that was discharged by the bankruptcy proceedings. In *Torwico Electronics*, on the other hand, the Third Circuit held that the state's interest was not in receiving payment, but rather was to cut off "an ongoing and continuing threat" to the health and safety of its citizens. While this result seems both reasonable and consistent with the goal of protecting the environment, one must keep in mind that the consequence of such a ruling is that if the debtor's assets are liquidated, none of those assets could be used to effect the clean-up. Only "creditors," that is, persons holding claims against the debtor, have a right to participate in the distribution of those assets in the bankruptcy case.

Similar concerns are presented when a manufacturer seeks bankruptcy relief and the manufacturer has put into the stream of commerce goods that may cause injury in the future. Exploding toasters, defective airplanes, and asbestos are just a few of the examples. It even seems possible that tobacco products could soon be included on the list. Once again, if persons who might be injured by these goods in the future are held not to have claims, then they cannot participate in the case. Of course, when their claims arise, they are not subject to the debtor's previous bankruptcy discharge. They can recover their claims in full from the debtor, if the debtor is still in existence. On the other hand, a Chapter 11 debtor that is trying to reorganize its business needs to have some idea of its future liability in order to exit successfully from the bankruptcy process. Therefore, the Chapter 11 debtors that manufacture airplanes need to be able to set their total liabilities so that they can be paid pursuant to a plan and the operation of the business of the debtor continued in the future. If the amount of these claims is unlimited, the debtor will not be likely to obtain financing for its business. Jobs will be lost, and the parties injured in the future will receive no payments in any event. Nonetheless, the language of the Bankruptcy Code presents some obstacles to the treatment of these claims. *See, e.g.* In re Piper Aircraft Corp., 58 F.3d 1573 (11th Cir. 1995).

The Bankruptcy Code was not written to resolve the problem of mass torts. Nevertheless, it has fallen to the bankruptcy courts and those professionals who work in the area to seek resolutions. Oftentimes, the solution requires the reconciliation of conflicting interests and policies, such as the protection of the environment and the reorganization of a company to save jobs. For a disturbing discussion of how judges manipulated bankruptcy rules while handling one famous mass tort case, see Richard B. Sobol, Bending the Law — The Story of the Dalkon Shield Bankruptcy (1991). In some instances Congress has provided an answer. For example, the automatic stay does not operate against criminal proceedings; *see* §362(b)(1). Yet there are a great many issues for which conflicts remain. Those areas provide opportunities for creative and careful lawyering.

CHAPTER 6

Discharge

I. Introduction

An individual filing for bankruptcy will expect relief on a number of different fronts. The debtor will want protection from creditor collection activity, a reasonable allocation of the debtor's assets between those creditors and the debtor him- or herself, and a forgiveness of the debts that cannot be repaid. In this chapter, we examine the latter form of relief: discharge of debts in bankruptcy.

The dischargeability of debts in a Chapter 7 liquidation is dealt with in two key sections: §523, on *exceptions* to discharge, and §727, on objections to the discharge itself. Discharge in other Chapters will be discussed as those Chapters come up later in the book. For now, it is important to appreciate the significance of a finding of nondischargeability under §523 as opposed to §727.

Section 727 is the "Global Denial of Discharge." If a party in interest successfully uses §727 to object to the debtor's discharge, the catastrophic effect on the debtor is a complete (sometimes called a "global" or "general") denial of discharge from *all* debts. This means that the debtor will have gone through bankruptcy all right, and will suffer the stigma, such as it is, of being a bankrupt individual and have been stripped of all his or her nonexempt property, and *still owe all the debts!* Bankruptcy for such a person will have been nothing more than a messy and time-consuming way of paying some of the debts, with those remaining unpaid still due and collectable from any property the debtor acquires thereafter. Since there will be few clients angrier at their attorneys than those to whom this happens, the debtor's attorney must take care from the outset to make sure that no §727 objections to discharge are going to occur; this necessitates both careful quizzing of and advice to that client early in the relationship.

Section 523 is "Exceptions to Discharge." A finding that a debt is nondischargeable under §523 is much less threatening to a debtor because it means that the debtor does get a discharge from most debts, but that those listed in §523 are not subject to the global discharge that usually occurs under §727 for most debts, and those lucky creditors can still pursue the debtor to collect the excepted debts. The debtor's attorney must also highlight these potential problems early in the relationship. If, for example, the debtor is seeking bankruptcy in order to get relief from tax debts, the client must be told that that is not likely to happen since most tax liabilities are excepted from the discharge.

II.   The Global Denial of Discharge

Section 727(a) starts with a presumption in favor of granting the debtor a discharge ("The court shall grant the debtor a discharge . . ."), and then goes on to list the situations in which the debtor will be denied a discharge and still owe all the original debts. The trustee, a creditor, or the United States trustee can object to the debtor's discharge, leading to a hearing on the issue; *see* §727(c). Since the presumption is in favor of the discharge, the person objecting to the discharge of course has the burden of proving the grounds for denial.

The first situation in which no discharge is granted occurs when the debtor is not an individual; §727(a)(1). In a Chapter 7 liquidation, corporations and other organizations die completely, and all of their assets are distributed to their creditors. They have no need of a discharge since they themselves will cease to be the legal fictions they once were. If a corporation wants a discharge and is planning to survive bankruptcy, it must proceed under another Chapter.

PROBLEM 6-1

Last August, when it became obvious he was going to have to file bankruptcy in the coming months, Dr. Ned Paine, a dentist, transferred the title to his house and BMW over to his wife, and now, in December, wants you, his attorney, to file his bankruptcy petition. He is willing to sign the oath on the schedules stating that he has fully disclosed all of his assets, though he does not list either the house or the car. If you know about all of this, what do you advise? See §727(a)(2) and (4). Will you sign his petition (Official Form 1) as his attorney even though you know the assets have been understated? *See* Rule 9011, which highlights some of the trouble you might be in. *See* Friedell v. Kauffman (In re Kauffman), 675 F.2d 127 (7th Cir. 1981).

PROBLEM 6-2

The state in which you practice bankruptcy law has a liberal exemption statute. It permits a debtor to keep as exempt household goods of any value and also, among other things, permits the debtor to exempt "one bull and one cow" of any value. Rancher Horace Drive, who is in major financial trouble, asks you for advice. He has numerous nonexempt assets. Would it be wise for him to sell those assets and take the resulting cash pool, putting some of it into buying a champion bull ($80,000) and cow ($50,000), and the rest into paying most of the mortgage on his home? Will this sort of financial planning for the indigent cause him any grief once he files his bankruptcy petition? *See* Lawrence Ponoroff & F. Stephen Knippenberg, Debtors Who

Convert Their Assets on the Eve of Bankruptcy: Villains or Victims of the Fresh Start?
70 N.Y.U. L. Rev. 235 (1995).

Norwest Bank Nebraska, N.A. v. Tveten
United States Court of Appeals, Eighth Circuit, 1988
848 F.2d 871

TIMBERS, Circuit Judge.

Appellant Omar A. Tveten, a physician who owed creditors almost $19,000,000, mostly in the form of personal guaranties on a number of investments whose value had deteriorated greatly, petitioned for Chapter 11 bankruptcy. He had converted almost all of his non-exempt property, with a value of about $700,000, into exempt property that could not be reached by his creditors. The bankruptcy court, on the basis of its findings of fact and conclusions of law, entered an order on February 27, 1987, denying a discharge in view of its finding that Tveten intended to defraud, delay, and hinder his creditors. The district court, in an order entered July 10, 1987, in the District of Minnesota, Diana E. Murphy, District Judge, affirmed the bankruptcy court's order. On appeal, Tveten asserts that his transfers merely constituted astute pre-bankruptcy planning. We hold that the bankruptcy court was not clearly erroneous in inferring fraudulent intent on the part of Tveten. We affirm.

I.

We shall summarize only those facts and prior proceedings believed necessary to an understanding of the issues raised on appeal.

Tveten is a 59 year old physician in general practice. He is the sole shareholder of Omar A. Tveten, P.A., a professional corporation. He has no dependents. He began investing in various real estate developments. These investments initially were quite successful. Various physician friends of Tveten joined him in organizing a corporation to invest in these ventures. These investments were highly leveraged. The physicians, including Tveten, personally had guaranteed the debt arising out of these investments. In mid-1985, Tveten's investments began to sour. He became personally liable for an amount close to $19,000,000 — well beyond his ability to pay. Appellees Norwest Bank Nebraska, N.A. ("Norwest Bank"), Business Development Corporation of Nebraska ("Business Development"), and Harold J. Panuska ("Panuska") as trustee of the Harold J. Panuska Profit Sharing Trust and the Harold J. Panuska Employee Trust Fund, became creditors of Tveten as a result of his various investment ventures.

Tveten filed a Chapter 11 petition on January 7, 1986. Meanwhile, several creditors already had commenced lawsuits against him. Panuska had obtained a $139,657 judgment against him on October 9, 1985. Norwest Bank and Business Development had commenced an action against him but had not obtained judgment when Tveten filed for bankruptcy. On the date the Chapter 11 petition was filed, Tveten owed his creditors close to $19,000,000.

Before filing for bankruptcy, Tveten consulted counsel. As part of his pre-bankruptcy planning, he liquidated almost all of his non-exempt property, converting it into exempt property worth approximately $700,000. This was accomplished through some seventeen separate transfers. The non-exempt property he liquidated included land sold to his parents and his brother, respectively, for $70,000 and $75,732 in cash; life insurance policies and annuities with a for-profit company with cash values totalling $96,307.58; his net salary and bonuses of $27,820.91; his KEOGH plan and individual retirement fund of $20,487.35; his corporation's profit-sharing plan worth $325,774.51; and a home sold for $50,000. All of the liquidated property was converted into life insurance or annuity contracts with the Lutheran Brotherhood, a fraternal benefit association, which, under Minnesota law, cannot be attached by creditors. Tveten concedes that the purpose of these transfers was to shield his assets from creditors. Minnesota law provides that creditors cannot attach any money or other benefits payable by a fraternal benefit association. Minn. Stat. §§550.37, 64B.18 (1986). Unlike most exemption provisions in other states, the Minnesota exemption has no monetary limit. Indeed, under this exemption, Tveten attempted to place $700,000 worth of his property out of his creditors' reach.

Tveten sought a discharge with respect to $18,920,000 of his debts. Appellees objected to Tveten's discharge. In its order of February 27, 1987, the bankruptcy court concluded that, although Tveten's conversion of non-exempt property to exempt property just before petitioning for bankruptcy, standing alone, would not justify denial of a discharge, his inferred intent to defraud would. The bankruptcy court held that, even if the exemptions were permissible, Tveten had abused the protections permitted a debtor under the Bankruptcy Code (the "Code"). His awareness of Panuska's judgment against him and of several pending lawsuits, his rapidly deteriorating business investments, and his exposure to extensive liability well beyond his ability to pay, all were cited by the court in its description of the circumstances under which Tveten converted his property. Moreover, the court concluded that Tveten intended to hinder and delay his creditors. Accordingly, the bankruptcy court denied Tveten a discharge.

Tveten appealed from the bankruptcy court order to the federal district court. In a memorandum opinion and order entered July 10, 1987, the district court affirmed the denial of a discharge, concluding that the bankruptcy court's finding as to Tveten's intent was not clearly erroneous.[1]

The instant appeal followed. Basically, Tveten asserts on appeal that as a matter of law we should reject the factors relied on by the bankruptcy court to infer that Tveten intended to delay, hinder and defraud creditors. We disagree. We affirm.

---

1. Before the district court entered its order, the Supreme Court of Minnesota held in a decision entered March 27, 1987, that annuities and life insurance contracts issued by a fraternal benefit society were exempt under Minnesota law, but that these statutory provisions violated the Minnesota Constitution. In re Tveten, 402 N.W. 2d 551 (Minn. 1987). Accordingly, Tveten no longer will be able to claim these exemptions. Following the opinion of the Supreme Court of Minnesota, Tveten claimed an exemption for his pension in the amount of approximately $200,000. He and his creditors settled this issue before the bankruptcy court. He will retain this property as exempt.

II.

The sole issue on appeal is whether Tveten properly was denied a discharge in view of the transfers alleged to have been in fraud of creditors.

At the outset, it is necessary to distinguish between (1) a debtor's right to exempt certain property from the claims of his creditors and (2) his right to a discharge of his debts. The Code permits a debtor to exempt property either pursuant to the provisions of the Code if not forbidden by state law, 11 U.S.C. §522(b) & (d) (1982 & Supp. IV 1986), or pursuant to the provisions of state law and federal law other than the minimum allowances in the Code. 11 U.S.C. §522(b)(2). When the debtor claims a state-created exemption, the scope of the claim is determined by state law. It is well established that under the Code the conversion of non-exempt to exempt property for the purpose of placing the property out of the reach of creditors, without more, will not deprive the debtor of the exemption to which he otherwise would be entitled. *E.g.*, Ford v. Poston, 773 F.2d 52, 54 (4th Cir. 1985); In re Lindberg, 735 F.2d 1087, 1090 (8th Cir.), *cert. denied sub nom.* Armstrong v. Lindberg, 469 U.S. 1073 (1984); In re Reed, 700 F.2d 986, 990 (5th Cir. 1983); 3 Collier on Bankruptcy ¶522.08[4], at 36-37 (15th ed. 1984). Both the House and Senate Reports regarding the debtor's right to claim exemptions state: "As under current law, the debtor will be permitted to convert nonexempt property into exempt property before filing a bankruptcy petition. The practice is not fraudulent as to creditors, and permits the debtor to make full use of the exemptions to which he is entitled under the law." H.R. Rep. No. 595, 95th Cong., 1st Sess. 361 (1977), reprinted in 1978 U.S. Code Cong. & Ad. News 5963, 6317; S. Rep. No. 989, 95th Cong., 2d Sess. 76 (1978), reprinted in 1978 U.S. Code Cong. & Ad. News 5787, 5862. The rationale behind this policy is that "[t]he result which would obtain if debtors were not allowed to convert property into allowable exempt property would be extremely harsh, especially in those jurisdictions where the exemption allowance is minimal." 3 Collier on Bankruptcy, *supra,* ¶522.08[4], at 40. This blanket approval of conversion is qualified, however, by denial of discharge if there was extrinsic evidence of the debtor's intent to defraud creditors. *E.g., Ford, supra,* 773 F.2d at 55; In re Reed, *supra*, 700 F.2d at 990.

A debtor's right to a discharge, however, unlike his right to an exemption, is determined by federal, not state, law. *Reed*, 700 F.2d at 991. The Code provides that a debtor may be denied a discharge under Chapter 7 if, among other things, he has transferred property "with intent to hinder, delay, or defraud a creditor" within one year before the date of the filing of the petition. 11 U.S.C. §727(a)(2) (1982 & Supp. IV 1986). Although Tveten filed for bankruptcy under Chapter 11, the proscription against discharging a debtor with fraudulent intent in a Chapter 7 proceeding is equally applicable against a debtor applying for a Chapter 11 discharge. The reason for this is that the Code provides that confirmation of a plan does not discharge a Chapter 11 debtor if "the debtor would be denied a discharge under section 727(a) of this title if the case were a case under Chapter 7 of this title." 11 U.S.C. §1141(d)(3)(C) (1982).

Although the determination as to whether a discharge should be granted or denied is governed by federal law, the standard applied consistently by the courts is the same as that used to determine whether an exemption is permissible, i.e., absent extrinsic evidence of fraud, mere conversion of non-exempt property to exempt property is not fraudulent as to creditors even if the motivation behind the conversion is to place those assets beyond the reach of creditors. *Ford, supra*, 773 F.2d at 55; In re Reed, *supra*, 700 F.2d at 990; Forsberg v. Security State Bank, 15 F.2d 499 (8th Cir. 1926).

As the bankruptcy court correctly found here, therefore, the issue in the instant case revolves around whether there was extrinsic evidence to demonstrate that Tveten transferred his property on the eve of bankruptcy with intent to defraud his creditors. The bankruptcy court's finding that there was such intent to defraud may be reversed by us only if clearly erroneous. McCormick v. Security State Bank, 822 F.2d 806, 808 (8th Cir. 1987); In re Reed, *supra,* 700 F.2d at 990; In re Cadarette, 601 F.2d 648, 650 (2d Cir. 1979).

There are a number of cases in which the debtor converted non-exempt property to exempt property on the eve of bankruptcy and was granted a discharge because there was no extrinsic evidence of the debtor's intent to defraud. In *Forsberg, supra*, an old decision of our Court, a debtor was granted a discharge despite his trade of non-exempt cattle for exempt hogs while insolvent and in contemplation of bankruptcy. Although we found that the trade was effected so that the debtor could increase his exemptions, the debtor "should [not] be penalized for merely doing what the law allows him to do." 15 F.2d at 501. We concluded that "before the existence of such fraudulent purpose can be properly found, there must appear in evidence some facts or circumstances which are extrinsic to the mere facts of conversion of nonexempt assets into exempt and which are indicative of such fraudulent purpose." Id. at 502. *Accord*, In re Adlman, 541 F.2d 999 (2d Cir. 1976); In re Ellingson, 63 B.R. 271 (N.D. Iowa 1986).

There also are a number of cases, however, in which the courts have denied discharges after concluding that there was extrinsic evidence of the debtor's fraudulent intent. In *Ford, supra*, the debtor had executed a deed of correction transferring a tract of land to himself and his wife as tenants by the entirety. The debtor had testified that his parents originally had conveyed the land to the debtor alone, and that this was a mistake that he corrected by executing a deed of correction. Under relevant state law, the debtor's action removed the property from the reach of his creditors who were not also creditors of his wife. The Fourth Circuit, in upholding the denial of a discharge, found significant the fact that this "mistake" in the original transfer of the property was "corrected" the day after an unsecured creditor obtained judgment against the debtor. 773 F.2d at 55. The Fourth Circuit held that the bankruptcy court, in denying a discharge, was not clearly erroneous in finding the requisite intent to defraud, after "[h]aving heard . . . [the debtor's] testimony at trial and having considered the circumstances surrounding the transfer." Id. In In re Reed, *supra*, shortly after the debtor had arranged with his creditors to be free from the payment obligations until the following year, he rapidly had converted non-exempt assets to extinguish one home mortgage and to reduce another four months before bankruptcy, and had diverted receipts from his business into an account not divulged to his creditors. The Fifth Circuit concluded that the debtor's "whole pattern of conduct evinces that intent." 700 F.2d at 991. The court went further and stated: "It would constitute a perversion of the purposes of the Bankruptcy Code to permit a debtor earning $180,000 a year to convert every one of his major nonexempt assets into sheltered property on the eve of bankruptcy with actual intent to defraud his creditors and then emerge washed clean of future obligation by carefully concocted immersion in bankruptcy waters." Id. at 992.

In most, if not all, cases determining whether discharge was properly granted or denied to a debtor who practiced "pre-bankruptcy planning," the point of reference has been the state exemptions if the debtor was claiming under them. Although discharge was not denied if the debtor merely converted his non-exempt property into exempt property as permitted under state law, the exemptions involved in these cases comported with federal policy to give the debtor a "fresh start" — by limiting the monetary value of the exemptions. This policy has been explicit, or at least implicit, in these cases. In *Forsberg, supra*, for example, we stated that it is not fraudulent for an individual who knows he is insolvent to convert non-exempt property into exempt property, thereby placing the property out of the reach of creditors "because the statutes granting exemptions have made no such exceptions, and because the policy of such statutes is to favor the debtors, at the expense of the creditors, in the limited amounts allowed to them, by preventing the forced loss of the home and of the necessities of subsistence, and because such statutes are construed liberally in favor of the exemption." *Forsberg, supra*, 15 F.2d at 501 (emphasis added). Similarly, in In re Ellingson, *supra*, 63 B.R. 271, in holding that the debtors' conversion of non-exempt cash and farm machinery did not provide grounds for denial of a discharge, the court relied on the social policies behind the exemptions. The court found that the debtors' improvement of their homestead was consistent with several of these policies, such as protecting the family unit from impoverishment, relieving society from the burden of supplying subsidized housing, and providing the debtors with a means to survive during the period following their bankruptcy filing when they might have little or no income. The court held that exemptions should further one or more of the following social policies: " '(1) To provide the debtor with property necessary for his physical survival; (2) To protect the dignity and the cultural and religious identity of the debtor; (3) To enable the debtor to rehabilitate himself financially and earn income in the future; (4) To protect the debtor's family from the adverse consequences of impoverishment; (5) To shift the burden of providing the debtor and his family with minimal financial support from society to the debtor's creditors.' " Id. at 277-78 (*quoting* Resnick, Prudent Planning or Fraudulent Transfer?, 31 Rutgers L.R. 615, 621); *see also* In re Adlman, *supra*, 541 F.2d at 1003; In re Zouhar, 10 B.R. 154, 156 (Bankr. D. N. Mex. 1981).

In the instant case, however, the state exemption relied on by Tveten was unlimited, with the potential for unlimited abuse. Indeed, this case presents a situation in which the debtor liquidated almost his entire net worth of $700,000 and converted it to non-exempt property in 17 transfers on the eve of bankruptcy while his creditors, to whom he owed close to $19,000,000, would be left to divide the little that remained in his estate.

Borrowing the phrase used by another court, Tveten "did not want a mere *fresh* start, he wanted a *head* start." In re Zouhar, *supra,* 10 B.R. at 156 (emphasis in original). His attempt to shield property worth approximately $700,000 goes well beyond the purpose for which exemptions are permitted. Tveten's reliance on his attorney's advice does not protect him here, since that protection applies only to the extent that the reliance was reasonable. In re Bateman, 646 F.2d 1220, 1224 (8th Cir. 1981).

The bankruptcy court, as affirmed by the district court, examined Tveten's entire pattern of conduct and found that he had demonstrated fraudulent intent. We agree. While state law governs the legitimacy of Tveten's exemptions, it is federal law that governs his discharge. Permitting Tveten, who earns over $60,000 annually, to convert all of his major non-exempt assets into sheltered property on the eve of bankruptcy with actual intent to defraud his creditors "would constitute a perversion of the purposes of the Bankruptcy Code." In re Reed, *supra,* 700 F.2d at 992. Tveten still is entitled to retain, free from creditors' claims, property rightfully exempt under relevant state law.

We distinguish our decision in Hanson v. First National Bank, 848 F.2d 866 (8th Cir. 1988), decided today. *Hanson* involves a creditor's objection to two of the debtors' claimed exemptions under South Dakota law, a matter governed by state law. The complaint centered on the Hansons' sale, while insolvent, of non-exempt property to family members for fair market value and their use of the proceeds to prepay their preexisting mortgage and to purchase life insurance policies in the limited amounts permissible under relevant state law. The bankruptcy court found no extrinsic evidence of fraud. The district court, in a memorandum opinion and order entered June 15, 1987, affirmed. We also affirmed, concluding that the case fell within the myriad of cases which have permitted such a conversion on the eve of bankruptcy.

III.

To summarize:

We hold that the bankruptcy court was not clearly erroneous in inferring fraudulent intent on the part of the debtor, rather than astute pre-bankruptcy planning, with respect to his transfers on the eve of bankruptcy which were intended to defraud, delay and hinder his creditors.

Affirmed.

ARNOLD, Circuit Judge, dissenting.

The Court reaches a result that appeals to one's general sense of righteousness. I believe, however, that it is contrary to clearly established law, and I therefore respectfully dissent.

Dr. Tveten has never made any bones about what he is doing, or trying to do, in this case. He deliberately set out to convert as much property as possible into a form exempt from attachment by creditors under Minnesota law. Such a design necessarily involves an attempt to delay or hinder creditors, in the ordinary, non-legal sense of those words, but, under long-standing principles embodied both in judicial decisions and in statute, such a purpose is not unlawful. The governing authority in this Court is Forsberg v. Security State Bank, 15 F.2d 499 (8th Cir. 1926). There we said:

> It is well settled that it is not a fraudulent act by an individual who knows he is insolvent to convert a part of his property which is not exempt into property which is exempt, for the purpose of claiming his exemptions therein, and of thereby placing it out of the reach of his creditors.

Id. at 501. Thus, under the controlling law of this Circuit, someone who is insolvent may convert property into exempt form for the very purpose of placing that property beyond the reach of his creditors.

A debtor's right to make full use of statutory exemptions is fundamental to bankruptcy law. To unsecured creditors, a debtor's conversion of his assets into exempt categories of property will always appear unfair, but this apparent unfairness is simply a consequence of the existence of exemptions under the jurisdiction's bankruptcy law. In an early case in this Circuit, Judge Walter H. Sanborn, one of the patriarchs of this Court, explained:

> An insolvent debtor may use with impunity any of his property that is free from the liens and equitable interests of his creditors to purchase a homestead. . . . If he takes property that is not exempt from judicial sale and applies it to this purpose, he merely avails himself of a plain provision of the constitution or the statute enacted for [his] benefit. . . . He takes nothing from the creditors by this action in which they have any vested right. The constitution or statute exempting the homestead from the judgments of creditors is in force when they extend the credit to him, and they do so in the face of the fact that he has this right. Nor can the use of property *that is not exempt from execution to procure a homestead be held to be a fraud upon the creditors* . . . , because that which the law expressly sanctions and permits cannot be a legal fraud.

First National Bank of Humboldt v. Glass, 79 F. 706, 707 (8th Cir. 1897) (emphasis added).

The same principle was confirmed by Congress when it enacted the Bankruptcy Code of 1978. The report of the House Judiciary Committee states as follows:

> As under current law, the debtor will be permitted to convert nonexempt property into exempt property before filing a bankruptcy petition. *See* Hearings, Pt. III, at 1355-58. The practice is not fraudulent as to creditors, and permits the debtor to make full use of the exemptions to which he is entitled under the law.

H.R. Rep. No. 595, 95th Cong., 2d Sess. 361, reprinted in 1978 U.S. Code Cong. & Admin. News 5963, 6317. The same language appears in S. Rep. No. 989, 95th Cong., 2d Sess. 76 (1978), reprinted in 1978 U.S. Code Cong. & Admin. News 5787, 5862. In the hearings referred to in the House Committee report, two federal judges, concerned about the "outrageous" implications of existing law, specifically urged Congress to incorporate provisions in the new Bankruptcy Code which would make pre-bankruptcy conversion of assets fraudulent as a matter of federal law. *See* Hearings on H.R. 31 and H.R. 32 Before the Subcomm. on Civil and Constitutional Rights of the House Comm. on the Judiciary, 94th Cong., 1st & 2nd Sess., ser. 27, pt. 3, pp. 1355-58 (1975-76). The fact that Congress declined to change existing law, when presented with the same objections to the propriety of debtor tactics like Tveten's that the Court now expresses, indicates that Congress did not intend §727(a)(2) to proscribe such conduct. The House Report's language plainly says that debtors may convert nonexempt property into exempt property, that doing so is not fraudulent, and that debtors may make "full use" of any applicable exemption. Recent cases in our Court have reiterated this principle. *E.g.*, In re Lindberg, 735 F.2d 1087, 1090 (8th Cir.), *cert. denied sub nom.* Armstrong v. Lindberg, 469 U.S. 1073, 105 S. Ct. 566, 83 L. Ed. 2d 507 (1984).

To be sure, if there is extrinsic evidence of fraud, or of a purpose to hinder or delay creditors, discharge may and should be denied, but "extrinsic," in this context, must mean something beyond the mere conversion of assets into exempt form for the purpose of putting them out of the reach of one's creditors. If Tveten had lied to his creditors, like the debtor in McCormick v. Security State Bank, 822 F.2d 806 (8th Cir. 1987), or misled them in some way, like the debtor in In re Reed, 700 F.2d 986 (5th Cir. 1983), or transferred property for less than fair value to a third party, like the debtor in Ford v. Poston, 773 F.2d 52 (4th Cir. 1985), we would have a very different case. There is absolutely no evidence of that sort of misconduct in this record, and the Court's opinion filed today cites none.

One is tempted to speculate what the result would have been in this case if the amount of assets converted had been $7,000, instead of $700,000. Indeed, the large amount of money involved is the only difference I can see between this case and *Forsberg*. It is true that the *Forsberg* opinion referred to "the limited amounts allowed to" debtors by exemptions, 15 F.2d at 501, but whether exemptions are limited in amount is a legislative question ordinarily to be decided by the people's elected representatives, in this case the Minnesota Legislature. Where courts punish debtors simply for claiming exemptions within statutory limits, troubling problems arise in separating judicial from legislative power. As Judge Kishel explained in his excellent opinion in In re Johnson, 80 B.R. 953 (Bankr. D. Minn. 1987):

> The legislative branch alone determines what is necessary . . . to meet a debtor's needs, by establishing the nature and value of the property subject to claims exemption. . . . To deny discharge for a debtor's non-fraudulent invocation of these protections is, overtly or covertly, to make a political and/or value judgment on these legislative determinations. To equate a non-fraudulent intent to "place assets beyond the reach of creditors" with an invidious intent to "hinder or delay creditors" is ultimately to frustrate statutory exemption rights by causing a chilling effect on the full exercise of those rights. A court which causes such a chilling effect is, in a very real sense, invading legislative prerogatives by substituting its own judgment for that of the legislature.

At 963 (footnote omitted).

If there ought to be a dollar limit, and I am inclined to think that there should be, and if practices such as those engaged in by the debtor here can become abusive, and I admit that they can, the problem is simply not one susceptible of a judicial solution according to manageable objective standards. A good statement of the kind of judicial reasoning that must underlie the result the Court reaches today appears in In re Zouhar, 10 B.R. 154 (Bankr. D.N.M. 1981), where the amount of assets converted was $130,000. The Bankruptcy Court denied discharge, stating, among other things, that " 'there is a principle of too much; phrased colloquially, when a pig becomes a hog it is slaughtered.' " Id. at 157. If I were a member of the Minnesota Legislature, I might well vote in favor of a bill to place an overall dollar maximum on any exemption.[2] But sitting as a judge, by what criteria do I determine when this pig becomes a hog? If $700,000 is too much, what about $70,000? Would it matter if the debtor were a farmer, as in Forsberg, rather than a physician? (I ask the question because the appellee creditor's brief mentions the debtor's profession, which ought to be legally irrelevant, several times.)

Debtors deserve more definite answers to these questions than the Court's opinion provides. In effect, the Court today leaves the distinction between permissible and impermissible claims of exemption to each bankruptcy judge's own sense of proportion. As a result, debtors will be unable to know in advance how far the federal courts will allow them to exercise their rights under state law.

Where state law creates an unlimited exemption, the result may be that wealthy debtors like Tveten enjoy a windfall that appears unconscionable, and contrary to the policy of the bankruptcy law. I fully agree with Judge Kishel, however, that [this] result . . . cannot be laid at [the] Debtor's feet; it must be laid at the feet of the state legislature. Debtor did nothing more than exercise a prerogative that was fully his under law. It cannot be said that his actions have so tainted him or his bankruptcy petition as to merit denial of discharge. *Johnson, supra,* at 963 (footnote omitted). I submit that Tveten did nothing more fraudulent than seek to take advantage of a state law of which the federal courts disapprove.

I would reverse this judgment and hold that the debtor's actions in converting property into exempt form do not bar a discharge in bankruptcy.

QUESTIONS

As a practical matter, where does this decision leave Dr. Tveten? Can he sue his bankruptcy attorney? If the debtor has fraudulently transferred property to creditors in the year prior to the filing of the petition in bankruptcy but, realizing this is a mistake, gets the property back before the petition is actually filed, should he or she be denied a discharge? *Compare* In re Adeeb, 787 F.2d 1339 (9th Cir. 1986) (debtor discharged since property no longer transferred in the year before bankruptcy), *with* In re Davis,

---

2. There is some irony in the fact that the exemption sought by the debtor in this case, that for benefits under annuities or life-insurance policies issued by fraternal associations, has been held unconstitutional under two provisions of the Minnesota Constitution. One such provision, Article 1, Section 12, provides that "[a] reasonable amount of property shall be exempt. . . ." The Supreme Court of Minnesota has held that the exemption statute involved in the present case is unconstitutional precisely because it contains no dollar limit. In re Tveten, 402 N.W. 2d 551, 556-58 (Minn. 1987). So the principle of limitation has been upheld, the debtor has in any event lost the exemption he sought, but he also loses his discharge under today's decision.

911 F.2d 560 (11th Cir. 1990) (no discharge since debtor has clearly violated the statute).

PROBLEM 6-3

Charles Bundle is a consumer who also wants you to file his bankruptcy petition, but he has absolutely no idea what he owes to whom, nor does he have any records or memory of what happened to all the money he has earned over the last few years in his various jobs as an itinerant carpenter. He explains to you that he has always been bad at keeping records (the tax authorities are after him for this very same reason), but that he desperately needs the relief that bankruptcy will bring. "If I were the sort of person who could keep records, I probably wouldn't have gotten into this financial mess in the first place," he tells you. How much trouble is he in? *See* §727(a)(3). Would it help or hurt him if he has a severe alcohol problem? If his records had been destroyed in a fire? If he has no education beyond the eighth grade?

PROBLEM 6-4

After years of bankruptcy practice you have trouble remembering most of your clients, but when Hazel Debts made an appointment you remembered her all too well. You filed a Chapter 7 bankruptcy for her just three years ago, and because her affairs were chaotic it took quite a bit of work to get her a discharge. Now she is back in your office and, predictably, her financial situation is as bad as ever. She wants you to file another bankruptcy petition for her and get her a discharge of the indebtedness she has piled up since her last discharge. Can you help her? *See* §727(a)(8).

Eight-Year Rule. One can only go bankrupt and receive a Chapter 7 discharge once every eight years. The period is measured from the filing of the original petition to the filing of the later petition. The policy is to keep people out of the bankruptcy courts more often than is reasonable. If the debtor has received a discharge under §727 in a previous case (or in a Chapter 11 proceeding), and then suffers a financial loss so severe as to require relief before eight years has passed, he or she can look to Chapter 11, Chapter 12, or Chapter 13 for relief, but cannot get a discharge in Chapter 7. This is not to say that such a debtor cannot file a Chapter 7 proceeding — he or she certainly may. It simply means that no discharge of debts will be forthcoming. A Chapter 7 filing might still be in order to take advantage of the automatic stay while seeking a mannered disposition of the debtor's assets, or the debtor may have no choice if an involuntary bankruptcy proceeding is commenced by the debtor's creditors, who certainly will be delighted by the fact that no discharge of the debts owed them will occur.

There is a major exception to the eight-year rule. Where the debtor has been granted a discharge under §1228 (family farmer reorganizations) or §1328 (wage earner plans) during the past six years and has either paid all of the unsecured claims in that proceeding or has paid 70 percent of them pursuant to a plan proposed in good faith as the debtor's best efforts, the debtor is still eligible for a §727 discharge no matter how short the period of time since the Chapter 12 or 13 discharge. The policy here is to reward those who tried to pay their debts in other Chapters, and who either did so or whose failure was at least a noble effort. Congress wanted to encourage the use of Chapters 12 and 13, under which creditors typically get more than they would glean in a Chapter 7 liquidation, so the time bar is waived in those circumstances.

PROBLEM 6-5

Deborah faced a series of financial setbacks and filed a Chapter 7 petition on April 22, 1999. She received her discharge in that case on July 7, 1999. That visit to the bankruptcy system proved insufficient for Deborah, and she filed a Chapter 13 petition on November 6, 2002. After two years in that Chapter 13 case, Deborah could not make the payments under her plan, and she voluntarily dismissed that case on December 9, 2004. Deborah was not through with the bankruptcy process, and she again filed a Chapter 13 petition on March 4, 2005. This Chapter 13 case was pending for almost three years, and it too was dismissed. In the meantime, Acme Auto Loans obtained a $5,000 judgment against Deborah on February 22, 2005. When Acme attempted to collect that judgment, Deborah filed another Chapter 13 petition on May 8, 2005. This case was pending until June 16, 2007, when it was dismissed. Acme then attempted to collect its judgment by garnishing Deborah's wages by a writ of garnishment filed on June 22, 2005. Deborah responded to that by filing a Chapter 7 petition on June 25, 2005, which stayed the garnishment action filed by Acme. Acme has objected to Deborah's discharge under §727(a)(8) arguing that because the intervening Chapter 13 cases stayed collection efforts the time between Chapter 7 discharges should be tolled. What do you think? *See* Tidewater Finance Co. v. Williams, 498 F.3d 249 (4th Cir. 2007).

The 2005 amendments to the Code created an important new ground for a global denial of discharge: failure to complete an instructional course in personal financial management (described in §111); *see* §727(a)(11). Congress wanted all those filing for bankruptcy to learn how to handle their finances better in the future, so it imposed this new barricade to a discharge of the old debts.

Bethea v. Robert J. Adams & Associates

United States Court of Appeals, Seventh Circuit, 2003
352 F.3d 1125

EASTERBROOK, Circuit Judge.

Three debtors in bankruptcy hired lawyers before filing their petitions. Each agreed to a retainer that would cover the legal services entailed in preparing and prosecuting the proceedings. Unlike most retainers, however, these were to be paid over time — some installments before the petition was filed, others thereafter. The lawyers performed as promised: all three debtors received their discharges, and the cases were closed. When the lawyers continued to collect the unpaid installments, the three debtors (with the assistance of new counsel) commenced adversary proceedings in which they asked the bankruptcy court to hold their former lawyers in contempt for violating the injunctions implementing the discharges. *See* 11 U.S.C. §524.

Bankruptcy Judge Barliant concluded that attorneys' fees "reasonable" under 11 U.S.C. §329(b) are not discharged. 275 B.R. 284 (Bankr. N.D. Ill. 2002). Section 329, which deals directly with attorneys' compensation, supersedes the more general reach of 11 U.S.C. §727, the discharge provision, the judge held, reasoning that any other conclusion would leave no work for §329(b) to do. Because statutes should not be read to make any section ineffectual, the bankruptcy court thought that §329(b) must be the only device for controlling debtors' legal fees. The debtors concede that the fees they had promised to pay their ex-attorneys are reasonable, so Judge Barliant dismissed the adversary proceedings. The district judge affirmed, substantially for the bankruptcy judge's reasons. 287 B.R. 906 (N.D. Ill. 2003).

Section 727(b) reads: "Except as provided in section 523 of this title, a discharge under subsection (a) of this section discharges the debtor from all debts that arose before the date of the order for relief under this chapter, and any liability on a claim that is determined under section 502 of this title as if such claim had arisen before the commencement of the case, whether or not a proof of claim based on any such debt or liability is filed under section 501 of this title, and whether or not a claim based on any such debt or liability is allowed under section 502 of this title." Attorneys' fees are not among the debts excepted from discharge by §523. The retainer is a pre-petition, liquidated debt; but even if it were an unliquidated "claim" for purposes of §502, that claim also would be covered. Unless §329 creates an unenumerated exception to §727(b), the debts to these attorneys were discharged.

Section 329(a) requires every attorney representing a debtor in bankruptcy to file with the court a statement of all compensation received during the preceding year, or to be received, in connection with the bankruptcy. This statement enables the court to determine whether the lawyer has received a preferential transfer. Debtors may not care who gets what money remains (if the attorney gets more, other creditors get less), and, when clients do not haggle over price, some attorneys will be tempted to divert the funds to themselves by charging excessive fees. Section 329(b) requires bankruptcy judges to use the information supplied under §329(a) to determine whether "such compensation exceeds the reasonable value of any such services." If it does, then "the court may cancel any such agreement, or order the return of any such payment, to the extent excessive." The bankruptcy and district judges believed that this power is exclusive of discharge under §727; otherwise, they stated, §329(b) would play no role in Chapter 7 cases even though 11 U.S.C. §103(a) declares that it (like the rest of Chapter 3) applies to Chapter 7 proceedings.

Our difficulty with this approach is that §329 has plenty to do in Chapter 7 cases, even if debts for legal fees are subject to discharge. First, prepaid fees exceeding the "reasonable" value of the legal services must be recouped for the benefit of other creditors. Second, the judge must ensure the reasonableness of any fees incurred during the proceeding itself, once more to protect other creditors. Third, if the debt is reaffirmed during the proceeding, yet again the judge must ensure reasonableness. Finally, if the debtor repudiates the executory portion of the agreement with counsel, and the estate rehires the same lawyer (an approach that gives administrative priority to ongoing legal fees), once again §329(b) requires the judge to review the fee agreement for reasonableness. Because grouping legal fees with other debts subject to discharge does not gut §329(b) for Chapter 7 cases, the structure of the Bankruptcy Code does not support treating §329 as an implicit exception to §727. We therefore agree with In re Biggar, 110 F.3d 685 (9th Cir. 1997), that pre-petition debts for legal fees are subject to discharge under §727. *See also* In re Sanchez, 241 F.3d 1148, 1150 (9th Cir. 2001). Although Biggar is the only appellate decision squarely in point, almost every bankruptcy judge and district judge who has considered the question has come to the same conclusion — essentially everyone other than the judges in this litigation.

The three lawyers contend that reading §727 this way would force the most destitute of debtors to forego legal assistance, because counsel neither could be paid in advance (the norm for Chapter 7 cases) nor could collect after the case ends. The bar therefore would shun these debtors, depriving them of the Code's benefits. That argument about what makes for good public policy should be directed to Congress; the judiciary's job is to enforce the law Congress enacted, not write a different one that judges think superior. *See* Barnhart v. Sigmon Coal Co., 534 U.S. 438, 460-62, 122 S. Ct. 941, 151 L. Ed. 2d 908 (2002). *Cf.* United States v. Kras, 409 U.S. 434, 93 S. Ct. 631, 34 L. Ed. 2d 626 (1973) (filing fee that makes it possible to be "too poor to go bankrupt" must be implemented). For what it may be worth, however, we do not share the view that taking §727(b) at face value necessarily injures deserving debtors. Those who cannot prepay in full can tender a smaller retainer for prepetition work and later hire and pay counsel once the proceeding begins — for a lawyer's aid is helpful in prosecuting the case as well as in filing it. Legal fees incurred after filing in such situations receive administrative priority; that prospect (plus some pre-filing retainer) should be enough to summon legal assistance. And debtors retain the ability to represent themselves, when legal aid cannot be found.

Bankruptcy Judge Barliant considered whether an intermediate position is possible, under which the portion of the retainer reflecting work done during the bankruptcy is immune from discharge, even if the portion of the retainer reflecting pre-filing work is discharged. In re Hines, 147 F.3d 1185 (9th Cir. 1998), adopted that position, limiting *Biggar* to fees for pre-filing work. The *Hines* majority wrote that it thought the Code as written (and as implemented in *Biggar*) is unsatisfactory as a matter of public policy, and it decided to do a little surgery under what it called a "doctrine of necessity." *See* 147 F.3d at 1190-91. Like Judge Barliant, who concluded that *Hines* is wrongly decided, we do not conceive revision of the Code as a proper part of the judicial job. The Bankruptcy Code is a complex compromise among debtors and different kinds of creditors; tilting it to help one of these interests is unwarranted. Attorneys compete with other creditors, such as banks, credit card issuers, supermarkets, auto dealers, colleges, spouses, and children; some of these have obtained protection under §523 and others have not. Judges are not entitled to override the legislative approach with a lawyer-centric public policy that puts members of their own social class higher in the priority list at the expense of other creditors, or of the debtors themselves.

Thus even though the debtors in this appeal have expressed willingness to accept the conclusion of *Hines*, we must determine whether that is a legally open middle ground. (Even when a litigant confesses error on a district court's conclusion, as these litigants effectively have done with respect to Judge Barliant's treatment of *Hines*, an appellate court must decide the issue independently. [Citing cases.] Failure to do so might lead to a remand with instructions to proceed in an unlawful manner.) Deciding whether to follow *Hines* is essential to the resolution of the appeal. Because both the bankruptcy judge and the district judge concluded that attorneys' fees are never discharged, the sums owed under the retainer have never been partitioned between pre- and post-filing work. We must either reverse outright (holding that the distinction is not legally material) or remand for apportionment; there is no way to duck.

Hines conceded that it was going against the Code's language. What is discharged is a claim to payment. One contract (the retainer) gives rise to one claim, meaning a "right to payment, whether or not such right is . . . fixed, contingent, matured [or] unmatured." 11 U.S.C. §101(5). *See* Pennsylvania Department of Public Welfare v. Davenport, 495 U.S. 552, 559, 110 S. Ct. 2126, 109 L. Ed. 2d 588 (1990). *Hines* shattered each retained agreement into multiple claims by holding that a "claim" does not accrue until the legal services are performed. Each month (potentially each day or hour) that the lawyer performs services for the estate then becomes a separate claim. That contradicts both the Code and the retainer agreement, which says that the fee is due whether or not the client uses the services. (That's the difference between a retainer and an hourly fee. Judge Tashima's concurrence in *Hines*, 147 F.3d at 1192-93, which rejected the majority's legislative approach but accepted the outcome, depends on dividing the retainer into hourly units — a step that avoids rewriting the Code by rewriting the contract instead.)

What is more, even the transformation of one retainer into many claims (using either the approach of the *Hines* majority or that of Judge Tashima) is not enough to support that decision's holding, which is that fees for post-petition work are not discharged. The most a court could do is give administrative priority to post-petition fees for work in the action's prosecution. Yet if the debtor's estate is insufficient to pay administrative claims, even those are discharged. Nothing in the Code permits a categorical exception for any kind of debt other than one listed in §523 — and legal fees are not on that list. Because this opinion creates a conflict with the ninth circuit's holding in *Hines* (though it follows the ninth circuit's original holding in *Biggar*), it was circulated before release to all active judges. *See* Circuit Rule 40(e). No judge favored a hearing en banc.

Counsel must repay the debtors any sums collected after the discharges were entered. If any sums were collected on account of the retainers during the bankruptcies in violation of the automatic stay, *see* 11 U.S.C. §362, these too must be refunded to the estates. Whether additional steps may be warranted is a question for the bankruptcy and district judges to consider in the first instance, and the cases are remanded for that purpose.

VACATED AND REMANDED.

NOTES AND QUESTIONS

In an omitted concurring opinion, Judge Richard Cudahy would have adopted the *Hines* result, while wondering if the omission of a provision for the payment of attorney's fees as part of the bankruptcy proceeding was truly Congress's intent. There have been major arguments that the changes made in the statute accidentally deleted such payments, but in Lamie v. U.S. Trustee, 540 U.S. 526 (2004), the Supreme Court stuck with the literal languages of the relevant statutory sections and held that the Code does not permit the payment of the debtor's attorney's fee as an administrative expense.

These decisions, and similar ones like them, have caused debtors' attorneys consternation. What can they do to avoid this problem? We will consider the reaffirmation possibility later in this chapter, but for now it is enough to know that it is optional with the debtor, and certainly no debtor's attorney would count on the possibility of a reaffirmation agreement to pay his or her bill. If you, future attorney, are representing a client who is asking you to file a bankruptcy petition on his or her behalf, what precautions can you take to make sure you get paid?

III. Exceptions to Discharge

PROBLEM 6-6

"Life would be great if only I could get the federal government off my back," distressed taxpayer Marvin Schedule tells you, his attorney. "The IRS has been hounding me about income taxes that are past due for the last five tax years. How about you file a bankruptcy petition for me and we'll wipe them off the slate?" Are you going to be able to promise Marvin much relief? *See* §523(a)(1), which refers you back to the priority payment rules of §507(a)(8). If Marvin's tax problems include a tax penalty for the income taxes due last year, can you at least get it discharged? *See* §523(a)(7) (one of the hardest statutes in the history of legislative enactments to decipher). On hearing your explanation of the law here, Marvin has another idea: He could borrow enough money to pay the tax debts and then discharge the loan in the bankruptcy proceeding. Will that work? *See* §523(a)(14) and In re Chrusz, 196 B.R. 221 (Bankr. D.N.H. 1996).

PROBLEM 6-7

Nightflyer Loan Company asks you, its attorney, to review its loan practices with a view to increasing its success in getting the debts owed it deemed nondischargeable in the bankruptcies of its customers. The chief loan officer shows you the application form potential borrowers fill out. The form is very short and only has room on it for listing three creditors to whom the consumer owes money. When you ask about this ("Won't your customers typically have more than three outstanding creditors?"), the loan officer smiles and replies that this is done deliberately — since the borrower will not have listed all of his or her creditors, he or she is therefore giving Nightflyer Loan Company a false financial statement, and thus the debt owed to them will survive the usual discharge. Is this right? *See* §523(a)(2)(B) and (D).

Field v. Mans
United States Supreme Court, 1995
516 U.S. 59

Justice SOUTER delivered the opinion of the Court.

The Bankruptcy Code's provisions for discharge stop short of certain debts resulting from "false pretenses, a false representation, or actual fraud." 11 U.S.C. §523(a)(2)(A). In this case we consider the level of a creditor's reliance on a fraudulent misrepresentation necessary to place a debt thus beyond release. While the Court of Appeals followed a rule requiring reasonable reliance on the statement, we hold the standard to be the less demanding one of justifiable reliance and accordingly vacate and remand.

I.

In June 1987 petitioners William and Norinne Field sold real estate for $462,500 to a corporation controlled by respondent Philip W. Mans, who supplied $275,000 toward the purchase price and personally guaranteed a promissory note for $187,500 secured by a second mortgage on the property. The mortgage deed had a clause calling for the Fields' consent to any conveyance of the encumbered real estate during the term of the secured indebtedness, failing which the entire unpaid balance on the note would become payable upon a sale unauthorized.

On October 8, 1987, Mans's corporation triggered application of the clause by conveying the property to a newly formed partnership without the Fields' knowledge or consent. The next day, Mans wrote to the Fields asking them not for consent to the conveyance but for a waiver of their rights under the due-on-sale clause, saying that he sought to avoid any claim that the clause might apply to arrangements to add a new principal to his land development organization. The letter failed to mention that Mans had already caused the property to be conveyed. The Fields responded with an offer to waive if Mans paid them $10,500. Mans answered with a lower bid, to pay only $500, and again failed to disclose the conveyance. There were no further written communications.

The ensuing years brought a precipitous drop in real estate prices, and on December 10, 1990, Mans petitioned the United States Bankruptcy Court for the District of New Hampshire for relief under Chapter 11 of the Bankruptcy Code. On the following February 6, the Fields learned of the October 1987 conveyance, which their lawyer had discovered at the registry of deeds. In their subsequent complaint in the bankruptcy proceeding, they argued that some $150,000 had become due upon the 1987 conveyance for which Mans had become liable as guarantor, and that his obligation should be excepted from discharge under §523(a)(2)(A) of the Bankruptcy Code, 11 U.S.C. §523(a)(2)(A), as a debt resulting from fraud.

The Bankruptcy Court found that Mans's letters constituted false representations on which petitioners had relied to their detriment in extending credit. The court followed Circuit precedent, however, *see* In re Burgess, 955 F.2d 134 (C.A.1 1992), in requiring the Fields to make a further showing of reasonable reliance, defined as "what would be reasonable for a prudent man to do under those circumstances." App. 43-44. The court held that a reasonable person would have checked for any conveyance after the exchange of letters, and that the Fields had unreasonably ignored further reason to investigate in 1988, when Mr. Field's boss told him of a third party claiming to be the owner of the property. Having found the Fields unreasonable in relying without further enquiry on Mans's implicit misrepresentation about the state of the title, the court held Mans's debt dischargeable.

The District Court affirmed, likewise following Circuit precedent in holding that §523(a)(2)(A) requires reasonable reliance to exempt a debt from discharge, and finding the Bankruptcy Court's judgment supported by adequate indication in the record that the Fields had relied without sufficient reason. The Court of Appeals for the First Circuit affirmed judgment for the Bankruptcy Court's reasons. Judgt. order reported at 36 F.3d 1089 (1994).

We granted certiorari, 514 U.S. ____, 115 S. Ct. 1821, 131 L. Ed. 2d 743 (1995), to resolve a conflict among the Circuits over the level of reliance that §523(a)(2)(A) requires a creditor to demonstrate.

II.

The provisions for discharge of a bankrupt's debts, 11 U.S.C. §§727, 1141, 1228, and 1328(b), are subject to exception under 11 U.S.C. §523(a), which carries 16 subsections setting out categories of nondischargeable debts. Two of these are debts traceable to falsity or fraud or to a materially false financial statement, as set out in §523(a)(2): "(a) A discharge under section 727, 1141, 1228(a), 1228(b), or 1328(b) of this title does not discharge an individual debtor from any debt — . . .

> "(2) for money, property, services, or an extension, renewal, or refinancing of credit, to the extent obtained by — "(A) false pretenses, a false representation, or actual fraud, other than a statement respecting the debtor's or an insider's financial condition; [or] "(B) use of a statement in writing — "(i) that is materially false; "(ii) respecting the debtor's or an insider's financial condition; "(iii) on which the creditor to whom the debtor is liable for such money, property, services, or credit reasonably relied; and "(iv) that the debtor caused to be made or published with intent to deceive."

These provisions were not innovations in their most recent codification, the Bankruptcy Reform Act of 1978 (Act), Pub. L. 95-598, 92 Stat. 2590, but had obvious antecedents in the Bankruptcy Act of 1898 (1898 Act), as amended, 30 Stat. 544. The precursor to §523(a)(2)(A) was created when §17(a)(2) of the 1898 Act was modified by an amendment in 1903, which provided that debts that were "liabilities for obtaining property by false pretenses or false representations" would not be affected by any discharge granted to a bankrupt, who would still be required to pay them. Act of Feb. 5, 1903, ch. 487, 32 Stat. 798. This language inserted in §17(a)(2) was changed only slightly between 1903 and 1978, at which time the section was recodified as §523(a)(2)(A) and amended to read as quoted above. Thus, since 1903 the statutory language at issue here merely progressed from "false pretenses or false representations" to "false pretenses, a false representation, or actual fraud, other than a statement respecting the debtor's or an insider's financial condition."

Section 523(a)(2)(B), however, is the product of more active evolution. The germ of its presently relevant language was also inserted into the 1898 Act by a 1903 amendment, which barred any discharge by a bankrupt who obtained property by use of a materially false statement in writing made for the purpose of obtaining the credit. Act of Feb. 5, 1903, ch. 487, 32 Stat. 797-798. The provision did not explicitly require an intent to deceive or set any level of reliance, but Congress modified its language in 1960 by adding the requirements that the debtor intend to deceive the creditor and that the creditor rely on the false statement, and by limiting its application to false financial statements. Act of July 12, 1960, Pub. L. 86-621, 74 Stat. 409. In 1978, Congress rewrote the provision as set out above and recodified it as §523(a)(2)(B). Though the forms of the 1960 and 1978 provisions are quite different, the only distinction relevant here is that the 1978 version added a new element of reasonable reliance.

The sum of all this history is two close statutory companions barring discharge. One applies expressly when the debt follows a transfer of value or extension of credit induced by falsity or fraud (not going to financial condition), the other when the debt follows a transfer or extension induced by a materially false and intentionally deceptive written statement of financial condition upon which the creditor reasonably relied.

III.

The question here is what, if any, level of justification a creditor needs to show above mere reliance in fact in order to exempt the debt from discharge under §523(a)(2)(A). The text that we have just reviewed does not say in so many words. While §523(a)(2)(A) speaks of debt for value "obtained by . . . false pretenses, a false representation, or actual fraud," it does not define those terms or so much as mention the creditor's reliance as such, let alone the level of reliance required. No one, of course, doubts that some degree of reliance is required to satisfy the element of causation inherent in the phrase "obtained by," but the Government, as amicus curiae (like petitioners in a portion of their brief), submits that the minimum level will do. It argues that when §523(a)(2)(A) is understood in its statutory context, it requires mere reliance in fact, not reliance that is reasonable under the circumstances. Both petitioners and the Government note that §523(a)(2)(B) expressly requires reasonable reliance, while §523(a)(2)(A) does not. They emphasize that the precursors to §§523(a)(2)(A) and (B) lacked any reasonableness requirement, and that Congress added an element of reasonable reliance to §523(a)(2)(B) in 1978, but not to §523(a)(2)(A). They contend that the addition to §523(a)(2)(B) alone supports an inference that, in §523(a)(2)(A), Congress did not intend to require reasonable reliance, over and above actual reliance. But this argument is unsound.

The argument relies on the apparent negative pregnant, under the rule of construction that an express statutory requirement here, contrasted with statutory silence there, shows an intent to confine the requirement to the specified instance. *See* Gozlon-Peretz v. United States, 498 U.S. 395, 404, 111 S. Ct. 840, 846-847, 112 L. Ed. 2d 919 (1991) (" '[W]here Congress includes particular language in one section of a statute but omits it in another section of the same Act, it is generally presumed that Congress acts intentionally and purposely in the disparate inclusion or exclusion' ") (quoting Russello v. United States, 464 U.S. 16, 23, 104 S. Ct. 296, 300, 78 L. Ed. 2d 17 (1983)). Thus the failure of §523(a)(2)(A) to require the reasonableness of reliance demanded by §523(a)(2)(B) shows that (A) lacks such a requirement. Without more, the inference might be a helpful one. But there is more here, showing why the negative pregnant argument should not be elevated to the level of interpretive trump card.

First, assuming the argument to be sound, the most it would prove is that the reasonableness standard was not intended. But our job does not end with rejecting reasonableness as the standard. We have to discover the correct standard, and where there are multiple contenders remaining (as there are here), the inference from the negative pregnant does not finish the job.

There is, however, a more fundamental objection to depending on a negative pregnant argument here, for in the present circumstances there is reason to reject its soundness even as far as it goes. Quite simply, if it proves anything here, it proves too much. If the negative pregnant is the reason that §523(a)(2)(A) has no reasonableness requirement, then the same reasoning will strip (A) of any requirement to establish a causal connection between the misrepresentation and the transfer of value or extension of credit, and it will eliminate scienter from the very notion of fraud. Section 523(a)(2)(B) expressly requires not only reasonable reliance but also reliance itself; and not only a representation but also one that is material; and not only one that is material but also one that is meant to deceive. Section 523(a)(2)(A) speaks in the language neither of reliance nor of materiality nor of intentionality. If the contrast is enough to preclude a reasonableness requirement, it will do as well to show that the debtor need not have misrepresented intentionally, the statement need not have been material, and the creditor need not have relied. But common sense would balk.[3]

---

3. The fact that §523(a)(2) uses the term "obtained by" does not avoid this problem, for two reasons. First, "obtained by" applies to both §§523(a)(2)(A) and (B); if it supplies the elements of materiality, intent to deceive, and actual reliance it renders §523(a)(2)(B)'s inclusion of materiality and intent to deceive redundant. More to the point, it

If Congress really had wished to bar discharge to a debtor who made unintentional and wholly immaterial misrepresentations having no effect on a creditor's decision, it could have provided that. It would, however, take a very clear provision to convince anyone of anything so odd, and nothing so odd has ever been apparent to the courts that have previously construed this statute, routinely requiring intent, reliance, and materiality before applying §523(a)(2)(A). *See, e.g.,* In re Phillips, 804 F.2d 930 (C.A.6 1986); In re Martin, 963 F.2d 809 (C.A.5 1992); In re Menna, 16 F.3d 7 (C.A.1 1994).

The attempt to draw an inference from the inclusion of reasonable reliance in §523(a)(2)(B), moreover, ignores the significance of a different and historically persistent textual difference between the substantive terms in §§523(a)(2)(A) and (B): the former refer to common-law torts, and the latter do not. The principal phrase in the predecessor of §523(a)(2)(B) was "obtained property . . . upon a materially false statement in writing," Act of Feb. 5, 1903, ch. 487, 32 Stat. 797; in the current §523(a)(2)(B) it is value "obtained by . . . use of a statement in writing." Neither phrase is apparently traceable to another context where it might have been construed to include elements that need not be set out separately. If other elements are to be added to "statement in writing," the statutory language must add them (and of course it would need to add them to keep this exception to dischargeability from swallowing most of the rule). The operative terms in §523(a)(2)(A), on the other hand, "false pretenses, a false representation, or actual fraud," carry the acquired meaning of terms of art. They are common-law terms, and, as we will shortly see in the case of "actual fraud," which concerns us here, they imply elements that the common law has defined them to include. *See* Durland v. United States, 161 U.S. 306, 312, 16 S. Ct. 508, 510, 40 L. Ed. 709 (1896); James-Dickinson Farm Mortgage Co. v. Harry, 273 U.S. 119, 121, 47 S. Ct. 308, 309, 71 L. Ed. 569 (1927). Congress could have enumerated their elements, but Congress's contrary drafting choice did not deprive them of a significance richer than the bare statement of their terms.

IV.

"It is . . . well established that '[w]here Congress uses terms that have accumulated settled meaning under . . . the common law, a court must infer, unless the statute otherwise dictates, that Congress means to incorporate the established meaning of these terms.' " Community for Creative Non-Violence v. Reid, 490 U.S. 730, 739, 109 S. Ct. 2166, 2172, 104 L. Ed. 2d 811 (1989) (quoting NLRB v. Amax Coal Co., 453 U.S. 322, 329, 101 S. Ct. 2789, 2794, 69 L. Ed. 2d 672 (1981)); see also Nationwide Mut. Ins. Co. v. Darden, 503 U.S. 318, 322, 112 S. Ct. 1344, 1347, 117 L. Ed. 2d 581 (1992). In this case, neither the structure of §523(a)(2) nor any explicit statement

---

renders Congress's addition of the requirements of actual reliance and intent to deceive to the precursor of §523(a)(2)(B) (§17(a)(2) of the 1898 Act) in 1960 nonsensical, since that provision also had the "obtained by" language. Second, it seems impossible to construe "obtained by" as encompassing a requirement of intent to deceive; one can obtain credit by a misrepresentation even if one has no intention of doing so (for example, by unintentionally writing that one has an annual income of $100,000, rather than $10,000, in applying for a loan).

in §523(a)(2)(A) reveals, let alone dictates, the particular level of reliance required by §523(a)(2)(A), and there is no reason to doubt Congress's intent to adopt a common-law understanding of the terms it used.

Since the District Court treated Mans's conduct as amounting to fraud, we will look to the concept of "actual fraud" as it was understood in 1978 when that language was added to §523(a)(2)(A). Then, as now, the most widely accepted distillation of the common law of torts was the Restatement (Second) of Torts (1976), published shortly before Congress passed the Act. The section on point dealing with fraudulent misrepresentation states that both actual and "justifiable" reliance are required. Id., §537. The Restatement expounds upon justifiable reliance by explaining that a person is justified in relying on a representation of fact "although he might have ascertained the falsity of the representation had he made an investigation." Id., §540. Significantly for our purposes, the illustration is given of a seller of land who says it is free of encumbrances; according to the Restatement, a buyer's reliance on this factual representation is justifiable, even if he could have "walk[ed] across the street to the office of the register of deeds in the courthouse" and easily have learned of an unsatisfied mortgage. Id., §540, Illustration 1. The point is otherwise made in a later section noting that contributory negligence is no bar to recovery because fraudulent misrepresentation is an intentional tort. Here a contrast between a justifiable and reasonable reliance is clear: "Although the plaintiff's reliance on the misrepresentation must be justifiable . . . this does not mean that his conduct must conform to the standard of the reasonable man. Justification is a matter of the qualities and characteristics of the particular plaintiff, and the circumstances of the particular case, rather than of the application of a community standard of conduct to all cases." Id., §545A, Comment b. Justifiability is not without some limits, however. As a comment to §541 explains, a person is

> "required to use his senses, and cannot recover if he blindly relies upon a misrepresentation the falsity of which would be patent to him if he had utilized his opportunity to make a cursory examination or investigation. Thus, if one induces another to buy a horse by representing it to be sound, the purchaser cannot recover even though the horse has but one eye, if the horse is shown to the purchaser before he buys it and the slightest inspection would have disclosed the defect. On the other hand, the rule stated in this Section applies only when the recipient of the misrepresentation is capable of appreciating its falsity at the time by the use of his senses. Thus a defect that any experienced horseman would at once recognize at first glance may not be patent to a person who has had no experience with horses."

Id., §541, Comment a. A missing eye in a "sound" horse is one thing; long teeth in a "young" one, perhaps, another.

Similarly, the edition of Prosser's Law of Torts available in 1978 (as well as its current successor) states that justifiable reliance is the standard applicable to a victim's conduct in cases of alleged misrepresentation and that "[i]t is only where, under the circumstances, the facts should be apparent to one of his knowledge and intelligence from a cursory glance, or he has discovered something which should serve as a warning that he is being deceived, that he is required to make an investigation of his own." W. Prosser, Law of Torts §108, p.718 (4th ed. 1971); *accord,* W. Keeton, D. Dobbs, R. Keeton, & D. Owen, Prosser and Keeton on Law of Torts §108, p.752 (5th ed. 1984) (Prosser & Keeton). Prosser represents common-law authority as rejecting the reasonable person standard here, stating that "the matter seems to turn upon an individual standard of the plaintiff's own capacity and the knowledge which he has, or which may fairly be charged against him from the facts within his observation in the light of his individual case." Prosser, *supra,* §108, at 717; *accord,* Prosser & Keeton, *supra,* §108, at 751; *see also* 1 F. Harper & F. James, Law of Torts §7.12, pp. 581-583 (1956) (rejecting reasonableness standard in misrepresentation cases in favor of justifiability and stating that "by the distinct tendency of modern cases, the plaintiff is entitled to rely upon representations of fact of such a character as to require some kind of investigation or examination on his part to discover their falsity, and a defendant who has been guilty of conscious misrepresentation cannot offer as a defense the plaintiff's failure to make the investigation or examination to verify the same") (footnote omitted); *accord,* 2 F. Harper, F. James, & O. Gray, Law of Torts §7.12, pp. 455-458 (2d ed. 1986).

These authoritative syntheses surely spoke (and speak today) for the prevailing view of the American common-law courts. Of the 46 States that, as of November 6, 1978 (the day the Act became law), had articulated the required level of reliance in a common-law fraud action, 5 required reasonable reliance, 5 required mere reliance in fact, and 36 required an intermediate level of reliance, most frequently referred to as justifiable reliance. Following our established practice of finding Congress's meaning in the generally shared common law when common-law terms are used without further specification, we hold that §523(a)(2)(A) requires justifiable, but not reasonable, reliance. *See* In re Vann, 67 F.3d 277 (C.A.11 1995); In re Kirsh, 973 F.2d 1454 (C.A.9 1992).

It should go without saying that our analysis does not relegate all reasoning from a negative pregnant to the rubbish heap, or render the reasonableness of reliance wholly irrelevant under §523(a)(2)(A). As for the rule of construction, of course it is not illegitimate, but merely limited. The more apparently deliberate the contrast, the stronger the inference, as applied, for example, to contrasting statutory sections originally enacted simultaneously in relevant respects, *see* Gozlon-Peretz v. United States, 498 U.S., at 404, 111 S. Ct., at 846 (noting that a single enactment created provisions with language that differed). Even then, of course, it may go no further than ruling out one of several possible readings as the wrong one. The rule is weakest when it suggests results strangely at odds with other textual pointers, like the common-law language at work in the statute here. *See* Alaska Airlines, Inc. v. Brock, 480 U.S. 678, 690-691, 107 S. Ct. 1476, 1482-1483, 94 L. Ed. 2d 661 (1987).

As for the reasonableness of reliance, our reading of the Act does not leave reasonableness irrelevant, for the greater the distance between the reliance claimed and the limits of the reasonable, the greater the doubt about reliance in fact. Naifs may recover, at common law and in bankruptcy, but lots of creditors are not at all naive.

The subjectiveness of justifiability cuts both ways, and reasonableness goes to the probability of actual reliance.

V.

There remains a fair question that ought to be faced. It makes sense to protect a creditor even if he was not quite reasonable in relying on a fraudulent representation; fraudulence weakens the debtor's claim to consideration. And yet, why should the rule be different when fraud is carried to the point of a written financial statement? Does it not count against our reading of the statute that a debtor who makes a mis-representation with the formality of a written financial statement may have less to bear than the debtor who commits his fraud by a statement, perhaps oral, about something other than his bank balance? One could answer that the question does have its force, but counter it by returning to the statutory history and asking why Congress failed to place a requirement of reasonable reliance in §523(a)(2)(A) if it meant all debtors to be in the same boat. But there may be a better answer, tied to the peculiar potential of financial statements to be misused not just by debtors, but by creditors who know this bankruptcy law. The House Report on the Act suggests that Congress wanted to moderate the burden on individuals who submitted false financial statements, not because lies about financial condition are less blameworthy than others, but because the relative equities might be affected by practices of consumer finance companies, which sometimes have encouraged such falsity by their borrowers for the very purpose of insulating their own claims from discharge.[4] The answer softens the ostensible anomaly.

VI.

In this case, the Bankruptcy Court applied a reasonable person test entailing a duty to investigate. The court stated that "the case law establishes an objective test, and that is what would be reasonable for a prudent man to do under those circum-stances. At a minimum, a prudent man, I think, would have asked his attorney, could he transfer it without my consent? And the answer would have to be yes, and then the next question would be, well, let's see if he's done it? And those questions simply were not asked, and I don't think on balance that was reasonable reliance." App. 43-44. Because the Bankruptcy Court's requirement of reasonableness clearly exceeds

---

4. "It is a frequent practice for consumer finance companies to take a list from each loan applicant of other loans or debts that the applicant has outstanding. While the consumer finance companies use these statements in evaluating the credit risk, very often the statements are used as a basis for a false financial statement exception to discharge. The forms that the applicant fills out often have too little space for a complete list of debts. Frequently, a loan applicant is instructed by a loan officer to list only a few or only the most important of his debts. Then, at the bottom of the form, the phrase 'I have no other debts' is either printed on the form, or the applicant is instructed to write the phrase in his own handwriting." H.R. Rep. No. 95-595, pp. 130-131, U.S. Code Cong. & Admin. News 1978, pp. 5787, 6091 (1977) (footnote omitted).

the demand of justifiable reliance that we hold to apply under §523(a)(2)(A), we vacate the judgment and remand the case for proceedings consistent with this opinion.

[The concurring opinion of Justice Ginsburg and the dissenting opinion of Justice Breyer, in which Justice Scalia joined, are omitted.]

If one of the exceptions to discharge applies, then the debtor usually exits from bankruptcy still owing the debt whether or not the bankruptcy court made a specific finding of nondischargeability, and suit can be brought on these debts in any later forum having jurisdiction over the matter. There are, however, major exceptions to this usual presumption. Section 523(c) lists the types of debts that must be deemed nondischargeable in the bankruptcy proceeding or they will not survive bankruptcy even though they fit exactly within the §523(a) categories. Track through the citations in that subsection, and as you do so ask yourself this question: Why would Congress have mandated that these matters be the subject of a mandatory bankruptcy hearing on point?

PROBLEM 6-8

The loan officer at Nightflyer has some other questions for you. First, if the debtor lies about his or her financial condition, and the lie will fit under either §523(a)(2) or §727(a)(3), which should Nightflyer use as the basis for its motion in the debtor's bankruptcy? The loan officer's next question is this: When a borrower files for bankruptcy and Nightflyer is fairly sure that the debt will survive discharge because it is based on a fraudulent financial statement, must it file any motions in the bankruptcy proceeding, or can it simply wait until the bankruptcy is over and then take its usual collection steps? See §523(c) and (d).

PROBLEM 6-9

You are in-house counsel for Octopus National Bank. The bank had issued a credit card to John and Mary Consumer; one month before they filed a joint petition in bankruptcy the Consumers took a trip to Mexico and ran up $5,000 in charges on the card. They have now scheduled this debt for discharge in the bankruptcy. Can you prevent this? See §523(a)(2)(C); cf. §523(c) and (d). If these charges were made more than 60 days prior to the commencement of the case, would the debt nevertheless be nondischargeable? What "representations" did John and Mary make: that they have the ability to pay the obligation in the ordinary course of their financial affairs, or that they have the present intention (as opposed to ability) to pay the debt? Did the creditor rely on the "representations" in extending the credit? Compare In re Alvi, 191 B.R. 724 (Bankr. N.D. Ill. 1996) (creditor has burden of demonstrating its actual reliance and that the reliance was justified, and passively extending credit does not meet this standard), *with* In re Hoyle, 183 B.R. 635 (Bankr. D. Kan. 1995) (when debtor uses credit card he impliedly represents that he has both the intent and the ability to repay the debt).

PROBLEM 6-10

Nancy Navin is one of those people who always seems to win door prizes, radio station contests, and poker. She had a few financial setbacks, but she figured that if she took her luck to the local casino, she could wipe out those recent losses and repay her debts in full. She used her three credit cards for cash advances in the amount of $26,500 and went to the casino several times over a four-month period. Alas, her cold streak continued, and she lost every penny of the cash advances. One week after the last unproductive visit to the casino, Nancy called her three credit card issuers and tried to settle up with them by agreeing to pay a total of $100 per month to the three creditors until she could get back on her feet. The minimum monthly payment on the debts according to the credit card agreements was $450. The credit card issuers were unwilling to accept her offer. Nancy responded by filing a Chapter 7 petition. Are these credit card charges excepted from the discharge under §523(a)(2)? *Compare* In re Anastas, 94 F.3d 1280 (9th Cir. 1996) (debt dischargeable if debtor had the intent to repay even if he did not have the ability to repay when the charges were made), *with* In re Nahas, 181 B.R. 930 (Bankr. S.D. Ind. 1994) (debtor's "hope" to repay credit card debt out of gambling winnings does not constitute the requisite intent to repay the debts). Should all legal gambling debts be nondischargeable? Should they all be dischargeable? Does it matter how the debt was incurred? For example, the debt could be a cash advance from a casino or from an ATM machine in a casino, or it could be a cash advance from an ATM machine at a bank with the cash then being used to place bets at a casino.

PROBLEM 6-11

When his boss discovered that corporate treasurer Eric Sociopath had been cooking the books and looting the corporation, he confronted Eric and demanded an explanation for the missing $832,496. Rather than explain, Eric pulled out a gun and shot the boss dead, and then left for lunch. He had five martinis and then totaled his car on the way home, running over three pedestrians in the process. Some other attorney is working on his criminal problems, but he wants you to put him through bankruptcy and wipe out the debts he owes the corporation, the estate of his boss, and the surviving but mutilated pedestrians. Assuming you can stomach him as a client, what relief will he find in bankruptcy? *See* §523(a)(4), (6), and (9).

The Bankruptcy Rules (4004(a) and 4007(c)) each set an initial deadline for filing an objection to discharge or a complaint to determine the dischargeability of a debt under §523(a)(2), (4), or (6), of 60 days after the first date set for the meeting of creditors. In Kontrick v. Ryan, 540 U.S. 443 (2004), the Supreme Court held that the deadlines set out in the rules were not jurisdictional, so the failure of a creditor to timely file a complaint to determine the dischargeability of a debt was not a bar to the action when the debtor did not raise the passing of the deadline as a defense to the action. Instead, the court characterized the rules as "claim-processing rules" which could not be used to limit the court's jurisdiction. The Court stated that "a debtor forfeits the right to rely on Rule 4004 if the debtor does not raise the Rule's time limitation before the bankruptcy court reaches the merits of the creditor's objection to discharge." 540 U.S. at 447.

Barrett v. Educational Credit Management Corp.

United States Court of Appeals, Sixth Circuit, 2007
487 F.3d 353

GRIFFIN, Circuit Judge.

Plaintiff-debtor Thomas Barrett filed a voluntary Chapter 7 bankruptcy petition on December 28, 2001, seeking the discharge of $302,342 in unsecured nonpriority debt. Among those claims are two student loans totaling $94,751. Defendant Educational Credit Management Corporation ("ECMC") appeals the judgment of the Sixth Circuit Bankruptcy Appellate Panel ("BAP"), 337 B.R. 896 (6th Cir. BAP 2006), affirming the bankruptcy court's order discharging Barrett's student loan debts on the basis of "undue hardship" pursuant to 11 U.S.C. §523(a). ECMC argues that Barrett was required to provide corroborating evidence in the form of expert medical proof to establish that the circumstances underlying his inability to repay the loans will likely continue for a substantial portion of the repayment period. ECMC contends further that Barrett failed to establish that he has made a good faith effort to repay his loans in light of his decision not to participate in the Income Contingent Repayment Plan. For the reasons set forth below, we affirm.

I.

Plaintiff-debtor Thomas Barrett incurred student loan debt totaling $94,751 while earning masters degrees in both Health Administration and Business Administration from Saint Louis University in 1999. Barrett has a long history of medical problems.[5] After receiving his graduate degrees, Barrett was diagnosed with Hodgkin's disease in the summer of 2000. Oncologists at the Cleveland Clinic discovered compromised lymph nodes in Barrett's neck, abdomen, spleen, lungs, and liver, and Barrett was

---

5. As the bankruptcy court noted, Barrett's health problems began when he was an undergraduate student at the University of Rhode Island ("URI") in 1989:

> [Barrett] was initially diagnosed with mononucleosis. In the fall of 1991, after he noticed that he had black spots in his field of vision, he was diagnosed with Pars Plinitus, a disease of the retina, which is also an autoimmune condition. During spring semester 1992, [Barrett] began to suffer high fevers, severe night sweats and loss of weight. His symptoms became so severe that he left [URI] and returned to his parents' home in Youngstown, Ohio, to seek treatment. Although he consulted a physician and had blood tests and a CAT scan, his symptoms subsided and the doctor was not able to make a diagnosis. Despite his health problems, [Barrett] returned to [URI], finished his undergraduate work and received his degree.

diagnosed as being at the "highest level" of Hodgkin's, stage IVB. He underwent intravenous chemotherapy treatment for over nine months, from August 2000 to April 2001. While Barrett received chemotherapy, his student loans became due. Barrett applied for, and received, an economic hardship deferment for his loans. While Barrett was recovering from chemotherapy, he was too weak to work and was unable to earn any income. Due to accumulated medical bills, Barrett filed for Chapter 7 bankruptcy on December 28, 2001.

In October 2002, Barrett began experiencing pain in his shoulders. He was diagnosed with avascular necrosis, a condition that causes the patient's bones to die due to lack of blood supply. Barrett testified that he experiences "massive pain" in his shoulders, hips, and knees. He was originally prescribed OxyContin pain medication, and later underwent surgery in April 2004 to repair the joint in his right shoulder. Following the surgery, Barrett continued to experience "a great deal of pain" in his shoulder. After arthroscopic surgery revealed that the shoulder cap's prosthetic was loose, a second surgery on the right shoulder was performed in August 2004. Due to the second surgery, Barrett was forced to wear a sling on his right shoulder at the trial before the bankruptcy court.

Barrett testified that he now takes forty milligrams of OxyContin three times per day, ten milligrams of Oxycodon four times per day, and two milligrams of hydromorphone four times per day, and that the pain in his right shoulder is so great that he "can't even hold a coffee cup with [his] right hand." Following a nine-month recovery period for each surgery, Barrett expects to undergo surgery to repair his left shoulder and both hips.

Due to the pain that he experiences, Barrett's work opportunities are limited. Barrett testified that he currently performs "computer networking jobs" on a word-of-mouth basis that require no more physical exertion than the movement of a computer mouse with his left hand. Barrett testified that he has attempted to find a job with a company but has been unable to secure employment because he "cannot work at a level that would have to be sustained to work at a full-time job." Because of the pain that he experiences, Barrett's ability to work "really depends on how [he] feel[s] that day, and that can be very bad or it can be somewhat bad." Moreover, Barrett testified that, in his experience, employers were not willing to hire someone in his condition, stating "if I bring up what I've — what's happened to me in the past, it seemed like they lose interest." Barrett testified that because his medical condition has worsened since he filed the Chapter 7 petition, he has incurred an additional $20,000 in medical bills and expenses. According to Barrett's Schedule J, his projected monthly income is $868 and his projected monthly expenses total $3,575.[6]

On November 23, 2004, the bankruptcy court conducted an adversary proceeding. Barrett was the sole witness. In addition to testimony from Barrett, the bankruptcy court also admitted Barrett's tax returns for the years 2000, 2002, and 2003,

---

6. At trial, Barrett testified that he earned approximately $2,000 per month, and that his average expenses per month totaled approximately $4,000. According to his 2003 income tax return, Barrett received $2,563 in wages and salary, $2,421 in business income, and $8,034 in unemployment compensation.

Barrett's Schedules I and J listing his current expenditures, a February 14, 2003, letter from Dr. Brad Pohlman, a print-out of a search performed on the Department of Education's Interactive Repayment Calculator, and a copy of the 2004 HHC Poverty Guidelines as originally published in the Federal Register on February 13, 2004. On December 14, 2004, the bankruptcy court issued a memorandum opinion stating that it found Barrett's testimony to be credible and concluding that Barrett had demonstrated that it would be an undue hardship if his student loans were excepted from his Chapter 7 discharge. On appeal, the BAP unanimously affirmed the bankruptcy court's determination. ECMC now timely appeals. . . .

III.

The Bankruptcy Code limits the discharge of student loans only to those circumstances where repayment "will impose an undue hardship on the debtor and the debtor's dependents." 11 U.S.C. §523(a)(8). As "undue hardship" is not defined in the Bankruptcy Code, we have joined most of our sister circuits in adopting the three-part *Brunner* test, named for the case in which it originated. *Oyler v. Educ. Credit Mgmt. Corp.,* 397 F.3d 382, 385 (6th Cir. 2005). The *Brunner* test requires the debtor to prove, by the preponderance of the evidence:

> (1) that the debtor cannot maintain, based on current income and expenses, a "minimal" standard of living for [himself] and [his] dependents if forced to repay the loans; (2) that additional circumstances exist indicating that this state of affairs is likely to persist for a significant portion of the repayment period of the student loans; and (3) that the debtor has made good faith efforts to repay the loans.

Id. (quoting *Brunner v. New York State Higher Educ. Serv. Corp.,* 831 F.2d 395, 396 (2d Cir. 1987)). To satisfy the second prong, Barrett must show that circumstances indicate a "certainty of hopelessness, not merely a present inability to fulfill financial commitment." *Id.* at 386 (quoting *In re Roberson,* 999 F.2d 1132, 1136 (7th Cir. 1993)); *see also In re Hornsby,* 144 F.3d 433, 438 (6th Cir. 1998) (observing that debtors "need not live in abject poverty before a discharge is forthcoming"). These circumstances may include, but are not limited to, "illness, disability, a lack of useable job skills, or the existence of a large number of dependents." *Id.* Ultimately, the most important factor in satisfying the second prong is that the "additional circumstances" must be "beyond the debtor's control, not borne of free choice." *Id.*

On appeal, ECMC does not challenge the bankruptcy court's finding that Barrett satisfied the first prong of the *Brunner* test: that Barrett cannot maintain, based on current income and expenses, a "minimal" standard of living if forced to repay the loans. Rather, ECMC argues that Barrett was required, and failed, to provide expert corroborating evidence to carry his burden of proof in satisfying the second prong. In particular, ECMC contends that Barrett could not competently testify to his prognosis or future health, and that expert medical evidence was necessary to competently project Barrett's future ability to repay his student loans.

In our prior interpretations of "undue hardship" under 11 U.S.C. §523(a)(8), we have not declared that expert medical evidence is necessary to corroborate a claim of "additional circumstances" premised on the debtor's health. In *Tirch,* the most recent Sixth Circuit case to apply the *Brunner* test to §523(a)(8), we held that a debtor's student loans are nondischargeable where the debtor fails to demonstrate how her physical condition prevented her from working. *Tirch,* 409 F.3d at 682. Despite ECMC's argument to the contrary, we did not hold that the debtor's claim was foreclosed by the lack of corroborating expert medical evidence. Rather, we emphasized repeatedly that the debtor's testimony by itself failed to meet the "undue hardship" standard. *See id.* at 681. In fact, we explicitly declined to consider whether expert corroboration was necessary to satisfy the second *Brunner* prong: "We have no occasion to delve into the BAP's holding that the bankruptcy court's assessment of the debtor's testimony regarding her mental and emotional health is sufficiently reliable to support the bankruptcy court's findings in that regard, without the necessity of expert corroboration, because the bankruptcy court made no such assessment." *Id.* at 681. Under *Tirch,* to satisfy *Brunner*'s second prong, Barrett must "precisely identify [his] problems and explain how [his] condition would impair [his] ability to work in the future." *Id.* at 681. *Tirch,* however, does not require Barrett to offer corroborating expert testimony to meet this burden.

Three other decisions by this court interpreting 11 U.S.C. §523(a)(8), cited by the parties, provide little guidance. In *Oyler,* this court formally adopted the *Brunner* test as the governing standard in an undue hardship analysis and held that a debtor's decision to accept a low-paying job — despite the fact that he was qualified for higher-paying work — did not constitute an undue hardship. *Oyler,* 397 F.3d at 386. In *In re Miller,* 377 F.3d 616, 622 (6th Cir. 2004), we held that a debtor seeking a partial, rather than total, discharge of student loans must nevertheless satisfy §523(a)(8)'s undue hardship standard. Neither *Oyler* nor *Miller* discuss the evidence a debtor must offer to support a finding that the debtor faces additional circumstances that indicate the debtor's state of affairs are likely to persist.

In *In re Cheesman,* 25 F.3d 356, 359 (6th Cir. 1994), we upheld a finding by the bankruptcy court that the debtors had satisfied the undue hardship standard. Because the *Cheesman* debtors did not claim "additional circumstances" due to their health, *Cheesman* is not on point. Nevertheless, we based our conclusion that the debtors had satisfied the "additional circumstances" requirement in part based on the debtors' employment history, which did "not indicate that the Cheesmans' financial condition would improve considerably if she obtained a position as a teacher's aide." *Id.* at 360. Thus, *Cheesman* suggests that a debtor's work history is a relevant and significant consideration in projecting whether a debtor's current state of affairs is likely to persist.

We decline to adopt here ECMC's position that Barrett was required to produce an expert witness to corroborate his health status, and instead concur with the BAP that "a requirement of corroborating evidence 'when Plaintiff is unable to afford expert testimony or documentation imposes an unnecessary and undue burden on

Plaintiff in establishing his burden of proof,' if corroborating evidence is understood to be limited to expert medical testimony." Even where some corroborating evidence of the debtor's claimed illness is required, the notion that only expert medical testimony would suffice has been rejected. *See, e.g., Burton v. Educ. Credit Mgmt. Corp. (In re Burton)*, 339 B.R. 856, 879 (Bankr. E.D. Va. 2006) ("This Court, in light of . . . the fact that other credible evidence often exists, does not suggest expert testimony is the only method of corroboration available to debtors."); *Swinney v. Academic Fin. Servs. (In re Swinney)*, 266 B.R. 800, 805 (Bankr. N.D. Ohio 2001) ("Although such [corroborating] evidence does not have to necessarily consist of extensive expert testimony, such evidence should consist of more than simply bare allegations; that is, whenever a debtor's health, whether mental or physical, is directly put at issue some corroborating evidence must be given supporting the proponent's position. . . . For example, if properly authenticated, letters from a treating physician could be utilized.").

We also find unpersuasive Barrett's position that, because of the expense involved with obtaining corroborating medical evidence, requiring such evidence creates a significant and unnecessary bar to debtors seeking discharge of student debt. At the adversary proceeding, Barrett argued that he was unable to submit his medical records or to obtain expert medical testimony because the cost to procure such evidence was prohibitive. ECMC disputes Barrett's contention, pointing to OHIO REV. CODE §3701.741, which limits a patient's copying costs for his medical records. OHIO REV. CODE §3701.741(B)(1) (limiting copying costs to two dollars and fifty cents per page for the first ten pages, fifty-one cents per page for pages eleven through fifty, and twenty cents per page for pages fifty-one and higher); *see also* 45 C.F.R. §164.524(c)(4) (requiring health care providers to impose "reasonable" copying costs in response to patient's request for medical records). We agree with ECMC that the copying costs of medical records are reasonable costs that a debtor may bear in order to substantiate his claim of undue hardship. In any event, we note that other forms of corroborating evidence may suffice — and, in this case, do suffice — to corroborate a debtor's claim of undue hardship based on illness. Medical bills, letters from treating physicians, and other indicia of medical treatment aside from medical records or expert medical testimony may corroborate a debtor's claim of undue hardship based on the debtor's health.

We hold that the evidence in the record is sufficient to support the bankruptcy court's finding that additional circumstances exist indicating that Barrett's current financial state is likely to persist for a significant portion of the repayment period. First, Barrett's petition was supported by his testimony, which detailed his medical history and current state of health. Because Barrett received a master's degree in health administration and attended medical school courses, Barrett testified informatively and cogently about his medical history. Barrett then testified about being diagnosed with avascular necrosis, describing with great detail the two surgeries performed on his right shoulder due to the avascular necrosis. Barrett explained how his condition affects his health and prevents him from working, stating that he is constantly in great pain and that movement in his right arm is limited to moving a computer mouse. The bankruptcy court found Barrett to be credible:

> Defendant does not challenge Plaintiff's testimony about his medical history and, indeed, Defendant's own exhibit, in the form of the letter from Dr. Pohlman, verifies that Plaintiff has been diagnosed and treated for stage IV Hodgkin lymphoma and received the ABVD chemotherapy treatment. There is also no doubt that Plaintiff actually underwent the two surgeries on his right shoulder earlier this year nor is there any challenge to the fact that Plaintiff is currently being prescribed heavy doses of pain medication. Based upon Plaintiff's physical demeanor, this Court finds it credible that Plaintiff is in a great deal of pain at all times. Even if Plaintiff is not required to have the five or more surgeries that he currently anticipates, which he stated would have a likely recovery period of nine months each, the pain that Plaintiff currently experiences is not likely to subside. As a consequence, this Court finds it credible that Plaintiff's current health problems will likely continue for a significant period into the future and that such problems not only prohibit him from working full time at this time, but will likely prohibit him from obtaining full-time employment into the foreseeable future.

The bankruptcy court, as the trier of fact, was competent to assess and credit Barrett's testimony, and such credibility determinations are traditionally afforded great weight. *See Otto v. Niles (In re Niles)*, 106 F.3d 1456, 1460 (9th Cir. 1997) ("The bankruptcy judge was, of course, entitled to assess the credibility of the witnesses and to accept [debtor's] testimony while rejecting [creditor's]."); *Faden v. Insurance Co. of N. Am. (In re Faden)*, 96 F.3d 792, 797 (5th Cir. 1996) ("When a bankruptcy judge, after listening to all of the testimony, finds that a debtor shirked his responsibility to provide notice to his creditors, this Court cannot then usurp the role of the bankruptcy judge and mandate its own equitable relief."). *See also Peveler v. United States*, 269 F.3d 693, 702 (6th Cir. 2001) ("We are generally reluctant to set aside credibility determinations made by the trier of fact, who has had the opportunity to view the witness on the stand and assess his demeanor.").

Nevertheless, ECMC argues that the bankruptcy court erred in allowing Barrett to testify about his avascular necrosis. We review the bankruptcy court's decision to admit Barrett's testimony for an abuse of discretion. *Gen. Elec. Co. v. Joiner*, 522 U.S. 136, 139, 118 S. Ct. 512, 139 L. Ed. 2d 508 (1997); *Sicherman v. Diamoncut, Inc. (In re Sol Bergman Estate Jewelers, Inc.)*, 208 F.3d 215, 2000 WL 263338, at *1-2, 2000 U.S. App. LEXIS 3357, at *4-5 (6th Cir. Feb. 29, 2000) (unpublished table decision). The bankruptcy court properly precluded Barrett from testifying about his prognosis and the cause of his current ailments. The court did, however, allow Barrett to testify concerning his diagnosis of avascular necrosis and how his health affects his life and limits his ability to work. We find no error in admitting this testimony. Indeed, a bankruptcy petitioner would have much difficulty in fulfilling our mandate as expressed in *Tirch* that the debtor "precisely identify [his] problems and explain how [his] condition would impair [his] ability to work in the future" if such testimony was prohibited. *Tirch*, 409 F.3d at 681.

In addition to Barrett's testimony, the bankruptcy court also considered evidence at the hearing that corroborated his testimony concerning his medical history. Barrett offered a letter from his treating physician, Dr. Pohlman, who confirmed that Barrett was diagnosed with stage IVB Hodgkin lymphoma in July 2000, and that Barrett received eight cycles of chemotherapy treatment in response. Dr. Pohlman also stated that Barrett "had vasculitis, which preceded the diagnosis of lymphoma and has required a gradually tapering dose of steroids since the completion of his therapy." Although Dr. Pohlman's letter was written before Barrett was diagnosed with avascular necrosis, and therefore does not discuss Barrett's prognosis with regard to that disease, it confirms Barrett's diagnosis of Hodgkin's and his rigorous chemotherapy treatment as a consequence.

In addition to Dr. Pohlman's letter and Barrett's testimony that described in significant detail his medical history and his diagnosis of avascular necrosis, the bankruptcy court also considered Barrett's tax returns for the years 2000, 2002, and 2003, which corroborate his testimony concerning his past ability to earn income due to his health problems since receiving his master's degree in 2000. Barrett's testimony concerning his past inability to work due to his health problems was further corroborated by Barrett's receipt of economic hardship deferments on his student loans in the years 2000, 2001, 2002, and 2003. Barrett's employment and salary history is a relevant and important consideration to determine whether it is likely that Barrett will be unable to maintain a minimal standard of living if forced to repay his student loans. *Cheesman,* 25 F.3d at 360. Moreover, Barrett also testified, and the bankruptcy court found credible, that his future ability to earn income was limited because — although he had actively sought work — employers would lose interest in his candidacy once they found out about his medical history.

We conclude that this evidence is sufficient to support the bankruptcy court's finding that Barrett is unlikely to be able to maintain a minimal standard of living if forced to repay his student debt. Unlike the debtor in *Tirch,* Barrett testified to how his past physical condition affects his ability to earn money. *Tirch,* 409 F.3d at 682. Moreover, unlike the debtor in *Oyler,* Barrett's financial woes are not the result of his own choice of profession, but rather are due to circumstances beyond his control. *Oyler,* 397 F.3d at 386 (noting that the "additional circumstances" under the *Brunner* test must be "beyond the debtor's control, not borne of free choice"). Barrett's long medical history and inability to work consistently indicate a "certainty of hopelessness" that satisfies the standards of 11 U.S.C. §523(a)(8), and it is apparent that this outlook is borne out of circumstances beyond his control.

Finally, we note that Barrett's account of his medical history and his current health status is uncontroverted. ECMC has offered neither evidence to contradict Barrett's description of his history of medical problems nor any proof to rebut Barrett's testimony concerning his diagnosis of avascular necrosis and its impact on his ability to work and repay his student debt. Rather, ECMC has declined the opportunity to subpoena Barrett's medical records, which it could have done if it genuinely disputed Barrett's testimony concerning his current health. *See* 5 U.S.C. §552a(b)(11) (permitting medical records to be disclosed "pursuant to the order of a court of competent jurisdiction"); 45 C.F.R. §164.512(e)(1) (providing that a "covered entity may disclose protected health information in the course of any judicial or administrative proceeding," including in response to a subpoena). Moreover, ECMC has not offered any challenge to Barrett's testimony concerning his current ability to work and likelihood to gain future employment. Where, as here, the debtor testifies credibly and without rebuttal about his medical history, his current health, his employment history, and his ability to perform work functions — and that testimony is corroborated in part by a letter from the debtor's treating physician and tax records — the debtor has offered proof sufficient to support a finding of undue hardship.

IV.

ECMC also argues that Barrett failed to satisfy the third prong of the *Brunner* test — that is, Barrett failed to show that he has made a good faith effort to repay his student loans — because he did not enroll in the Income Contingent Repayment Program ("ICRP"). ECMC contends that "Barrett's refusal to apply for the ICRP payment option was without factual and legal justification" and that this refusal demonstrates a lack of good faith under *Brunner.* We find ECMC's position unpersuasive.

As described by the bankruptcy court in *In re Korhonen,* 296 B.R. 492, 496 (Bankr. D. Minn. 2003), the ICRP:

> permits a student loan debtor to pay twenty percent of the difference between his adjusted gross income and the poverty level for his family size, or the amount the debtor would pay if the debt were repaid in twelve years, whichever is less. Under the program, the borrower's monthly repayment amount is adjusted each year to reflect any changes in these factors. The borrower's repayments may also be adjusted during the year based on special circumstances. *See* 34 C.F.R. §685.209(c)(3). At the end of the twenty five year payment period, any remaining loan balance would be cancelled by the Secretary of Education. However, the amount discharged would be considered taxable income.

See also Tirch, 409 F.3d at 682 (quoting *Korhonen*). Although ECMC doesn't state so explicitly, its position would create a per se rule requiring enrollment in the ICRP to satisfy the third *Brunner* prong and thus would, in effect, eliminate the discharge of student loans for undue hardship from the Bankruptcy Code.

We have already rejected ECMC's per se position. *See Tirch,* 409 F.3d at 682 (noting that a debtor's decision not to enroll in ICRP is "not a *per se* indication of a lack of good faith"). Moreover, Congress recently enacted "the most sweeping reform of bankruptcy law since the enactment of the Bankruptcy Code in 1978." Michael & Phelps, *supra,* at 77-78; *see also* Bankruptcy Abuse Prevention and Consumer Protection Act of 2005, Pub. L. No. 109-8, 119 Stat. 23 (codified in various sections of 11 U.S.C.). Yet Congress left §523(a)(8)'s "undue hardship" language intact. Had Congress intended participation in the ICRP — implemented in 1994 — to effectively repeal discharge under §523(a)(8), it could have done so. In addition, requiring enrollment in the ICRP runs counter to the Bankruptcy Code's aim in providing debtors a "fresh start." The debtor is encumbered with the debt for an additional twenty-five years, regardless of the length of the student loans. If, at the end of the twenty-five years, the debtor has been unable to repay all the student loans, the remaining debt is canceled and that discharge of indebtedness is treated as taxable income. *See* Michael & Phelps, *supra,* at 105. The result, as the bankruptcy court noted, would be that Barrett would "be trading one nondischargeable debt for another."

Although Barrett's decision to forgo the ICRP is not a per se indication of a lack of good faith, his decision "is probative of [his] intent to repay [his] loans." *Tirch,* 409 F.3d at 682. Nevertheless, we conclude that Barrett has demonstrated sufficient good faith to satisfy the third *Brunner* prong. Barrett testified that he looked into the ICRP, but declined to enroll in the program because the tax consequences would be too burdensome:

Q: Are you familiar with the Income Contingent Repayment format?
A: Yes, I am.
Q: Did you have occasion to visit a web site to see how it worked for you?
A: Yes, I did.
Q: And what web site did you visit?
A: It's WWW-dot-finaid-dot-org.

. . .

Q: What did you put in for your debt?
A: My debt was a hundred thousand dollars.
Q: And what did you put for your adjusted income?
A: Approximately $15,000.
Q: And what about income — the interest rate, what interest rate did you put in?
A: Four percent.
Q: What was the conclusion of that document as to the total balance you would still owe at the end of a 25-year period?
A: I would owe . . . two [hundred] sixty-eight thousand seven hundred and sixty-one dollars (sic) would be my final payment to the Government in the form of tax.
Q: I'm sorry. That would be the total amount that the Government would write off?
A: That's correct.

. . .

Q: And what — did you conclude what kind of tax impact that would have on you?
A: That would be huge. It would be like paying back more than the actual loan amount, so it doesn't really make any sense. This is not a viable alternative.

The bankruptcy court credited Barrett's testimony, concluding that Barrett "has used his best efforts to maximize financial potential; recognizing that his health has not permitted him to work full time, he still works part time to the best of his ability." In light of the significant tax consequences of enrolling in the ICRP due to his present and future inability to pay his student debt, Barrett's decision to forgo the ICRP was reasonable and is not grounds for finding bad faith.[7]

_____

7. ECMC argues that Barrett's tax concerns are overblown because Barrett would only be forced to pay those taxes if he became solvent. We disagree. If ECMC's position is accepted, then Barrett is faced with the following choice:

Although Barrett has made no payments on his student loans, no loan payments have come due; Barrett has received economic hardship deferments for each year since graduation due to his health. Even had payments become due, his inability to repay the loans was unlikely to evidence bad faith, as his monthly expenses exceed by double his monthly income. Despite his health problems that have prevented him from working full-time since graduation, Barrett has made repeated efforts to work as his health and opportunities have allowed, even as his physical capability has been limited to moving a computer mouse. Further, Barrett testified that but for the medical bills, he would not have filed his Chapter 7 petition.

In sum, we concur with the BAP's analysis of the third prong of the *Brunner* test:

> The Debtor in this case has reasonable expenses, yet continues to accrue debt for medical care. He has made efforts to increase his income within his ability. He has cooperated in providing information to his student loan creditors on an annual basis to obtain deferments. He has never had the ability to repay his student loans as evidenced by the deferments granted to him as the result of economic hardship. . . . Utilization of the ICRP would likely result in a substantial increase in his student loan debts over the repayment period. The Debtor has amply demonstrated his good faith.

V.

The BAP's judgment affirming the bankruptcy court's December 14, 2004, order discharging Barrett's student loan obligation to defendant ECMC is therefore affirmed.

In a later case, the Sixth Circuit approved the practice of ordering a "partial" discharge of educational loan debt. The court found that the bankruptcy courts have the equitable power to issue these orders under §105, the all writs section of the Bankruptcy Code. In re Hornsby, 144 F.3d 433 (6th Cir. 1998). Other courts have rejected this position noting that, unlike other subsections in §523(a), §523(a)(8) does not provide for the nondischargeability of debts "to the extent" of some action or omission. They have also noted that §105 should not be used to contravene a provision of the Code. *See, e.g.*, In re Taylor, 223 B.R. 747 (9th Cir. BAP 1998); In re Grigas, 252 B.R. 866 (Bankr. D. N.H. 2000).

Sovereign Immunity. The sovereign immunity of state lenders has become a fertile ground of litigation in §523(a)(8) matters. The Supreme Court has issued

---

resign himself to insolvency for the rest of his life or be forced to repay a student debt that is twice its current size. Moreover, ECMC's argument overlooks the psychological effect of having a significant debt remain, *see Balaski v. Educ. Credit Mgmt. Corp. (In re Balaski)*, 280 B.R. 395, 400 (Bankr. N.D. Ohio 2002) ("While defendant may believe holding debtor hostage for twenty-five years to debt and compounding interest is not an undue hardship, the court does not accept this view."); BAP op. 337 B.R. at 904 ("ECMC . . . fails to take account of the additional worry and anxiety that the Debtor is likely to suffer if he is compelled to watch his debt steadily increase knowing that he does not have the ability to repay it for reasons beyond his control"), and discards the central aim of the Bankruptcy Code — to provide the debtor a fresh start.

several sovereign immunity decisions that have formed the basis for defenses to actions by debtors seeking the discharge of their educational loans through adversary proceedings in the bankruptcy courts. Many courts have held that sovereign immunity protects the states from these actions. *See, e.g.*, In re Addison, 240 B.R. 7 (C.D. Cal. 1999); In re Seay, 244 B.R. 12 (Bankr. E.D. Tenn. 2000); In re Perkins, 228 B.R. 431 (Bankr. E.D. Mo. 1998). Other courts have attempted to limit the impact of the states' sovereign immunity claims. For example, the court in In re Innes, 184 F.3d 1275 (10th Cir. 1999), concluded that the state had waived its immunity through its participation in a federal student loan program. The program's regulations required the state to defend dischargeability actions in the bankruptcy courts, and the legislation authorizing the state university to participate in the program explicitly referred to those regulations. Consequently, the Court of Appeals found a waiver of the state's sovereign immunity.

The court in In re Bliemeister, 251 B.R. 383 (Bankr. D. Ariz. 2000), took a more direct route to conclude that states have no sovereign immunity from suits in bankruptcy cases. The debtor owed excise taxes and sought a determination that the taxes were dischargeable because they were more than three years old. In response to the state's assertion of sovereign immunity, the court held that the Eleventh Amendment does not provide that protection to states because the Constitution elsewhere grants to Congress the exclusive authority to act on the subject of bankruptcies. The bankruptcy court conducted an extensive analysis of the issue and found that the grant of authority to Congress in the Constitution to enact bankruptcy laws abrogated state sovereignty. This conclusion is much broader than the piecemeal waiver arguments that have been employed against the states in dischargeability litigation.

The Supreme Court has had an opportunity to consider whether states can assert their sovereign immunity in these situations. In Tennessee Student Assistance Corp. v. Hood, 541 U.S. 440 (2004), the Court held that a bankruptcy court's exercise of its in rem jurisdiction to discharge a state-held student loan does not infringe on state sovereignty, and thus a debtor's initiation of an adversary proceeding seeking a hardship determination is not a suit against a state under the Eleventh Amendment; Tennessee Student Assistance Corp. v. Hood, 541 U.S. 440 (2004). While the Court in *Hood* avoided deciding whether sovereign immunity applies in bankruptcy cases, it has granted certiorari in another case that should finally answer the question. Central Viginia Community College v. Katz, 125 S. Ct. 1727 (2005) (grant of certiorari). In that case, the trustee brought a preference action against several state colleges. The colleges asserted the defense of sovereign immunity, but the lower courts rejected the argument. The Sixth Circuit affirmed and allowed the trustee to assert a claim for affirmative relief against the state actors. 106 Fed. App. 341 (2004). Since the case does not involve a debtor's discharge, the Court's analysis in *Hood* would not seem applicable, and the Court will be left to decide whether sovereign immunity is an available defense to the states if they are sued in a bankruptcy case. For a discussion of these issues in greater detail, *see* Leonard H. Gerson, A Bankruptcy Exception to Eleventh Amendment Immunity: Limiting the Seminole Tribe Doctrine, 74 Am. Bankr. L. J. 1 (2000).

PROBLEM 6-12

When Henry and Alice Squabble finally decided to end their marriage, it was agreed that he would keep the house and she would get the three small children. He also agreed to pay her a substantial amount of money each month. You are the divorce lawyer representing Alice. Does it matter whether the parties call this a "support agreement" or a "property settlement," an issue that may be relevant if Henry were to file a petition in bankruptcy two days after the divorce is final. *See* §523(a)(5) and (15).

PROBLEM 6-13

Ned Nuptials was a busy divorce lawyer in Center City. He represented Randy Traviselli (the famous Italian country singer) in his divorce proceedings. Randy suffered financially in the divorce action, and he owes Ned $25,000 for unpaid fees from the divorce proceedings. Randy has now filed for bankruptcy relief, and Ned has come to you asking whether his claim against Randy is excepted from the discharge under §523(a)(15). *Compare* In re Soderlund, 197 B.R. 742 (Bankr. D. Mass. 1996) (debtor's divorce lawyer has standing under the plain language of §523(a)(15) to assert non-dischargeability of legal fees incurred in connection with divorce action), *with* In re Beach, 206 B.R. 676 (Bankr. N.D. Ill. 1997) (only debtor's spouse may assert non-dischargeability under §523(a)(15)).

IV.   Effect of Discharge

The discharge acts as an injunction against any action by creditors to collect or offset debts owing to them by the debtor. This limitation on creditors' rights applies equally to judicial efforts to collect the debt as well as to any other actions such as sending dunning letters to the debtor. The discharge also voids any judgments previously obtained against the debtor, but only to the extent that the judgment involves personal liability of the debtor. Creditors with preexisting liens or security interests in the debtor's property can still enforce those liens once either the automatic stay has expired (*see* §362(c)) or the court has granted relief from the stay. In a sense, the discharge injunction takes the place of the automatic stay by providing continuing protection for the debtor from the efforts of creditors to collect obligations personally from the debtor.

The discharge does not provide any protection for persons who are liable with or over to the debtor on the underlying obligation. *See* §524(e). For example, if the debtor negligently caused an automobile accident, the injured party has a claim against the debtor that would be discharged. The injured party nonetheless should be able to collect from the debtor's insurance company up to the extent of the insurance coverage. If the creditor has a $1,000,000 claim against a debtor who has $500,000 of insurance, the creditor will be able to collect $500,000 from the insurance company, but the remaining claim against the debtor would be discharged. Under §524(a), the creditor is enjoined from seeking any recovery from the debtor. This exclusion from the protection of the discharge also comes into play when a third party has guaranteed a debt of the debtor.

Obtaining a discharge prevents creditors from pursuing collection, but the debtor can voluntarily repay any obligation that has been discharged. *See* §524(f). This recognition of voluntary repayments might be important for debtors who have a particular interest in paying certain creditors such as family members and the debtor's employer, who may have advanced funds to the debtor. The debtor might also want to pay the orthodontist who is caring for the debtor's children's teeth, and might even want to pay back a creditor who was particularly patient with the debtor during hard financial times.

V.   Reaffirmation

Some scrupulous debtors might voluntarily pay debts that were discharged in a bankruptcy proceeding, but creditors of course cannot count on that. Instead, creditors want the debtor to enter into a *reaffirmation* agreement that will survive the bankruptcy discharge and be enforceable personally against the debtor in the future. The Code allows such agreements only if they comply with the requirements of §524(c) and (d) of the Bankruptcy Code.

When the Bankruptcy Code was first enacted in 1978, it provided that reaffirmation agreements had to be approved by a bankruptcy judge to be enforceable. The judges were often reluctant to approve the agreements, instead advising debtors that they could always "voluntarily" repay the debt without getting back on the hook for the entire indebtedness. In 1984, in response to complaints from the consumer credit industry, Congress removed the requirement that the court approve the agreements whenever the debtor was represented by an attorney in the course of the negotiation of the reaffirmation. The thought was that the debtor's attorney could provide sufficient guidance and advice to protect the debtor's interests. If the debtor was not represented by counsel, the court still would have to approve the agreement for it to be enforceable.

The 2005 amendments to the Code made the reaffirmation process even more cumbersome. New §524(k) creates a complicated form that the debtor must fill out, warning the debtor of the problems with reaffirmation, and requiring the debtor to demonstrate that his or her monthly income will be sufficient to service the reaffirmation agreement. If the debtor cannot do this, "undue hardship" is presumed, and the court will not approve the reaffirmation agreement. This "judicial protection" does not apply, however, if the creditor seeking the reaffirmation is a credit union. Bankruptcy Code §524(m)(2).

As you work through the following Problems, consider the options available to the debtor under the Bankruptcy Code. Are you (the debtor's attorney) potentially liable to the debtor's children if you "approve" a reaffirmation agreement that causes a debtor to be unable to support the children's educational needs a year or two after the bankruptcy case is over? *See* Thomas W. Rynard, Malpractice Exposure for Attorney Approval of Reaffirmation Agreements: Avoiding the Pitfalls of Amended §524(c), 3 Bankr. Dev. J. 545 (1986).

PROBLEM 6-14

When her small son desperately needed an operation to save his life, Tessa Palmieri borrowed $8,000 for that purpose from her brother Marco. The operation was a success, but other financial difficulties eventually forced her into bankruptcy, and she was granted a discharge from all her debts, including the one owed her brother. A year after her discharge she came into some money when she won the lottery. Marco, facing major financial problems himself, implored her to promise repayment of the debt she owed him so, feeling guilty, Tessa signed a promissory note for $8,000 in his favor. Now her son is ill again and she needs all the money she has, but Marco has been on her doorstep waving the promissory note and threatening suit. You handled the bankruptcy for Tessa, so she calls you for advice. Can you offer her any legal relief? *See* §524(c). If Marco sues her, what can she do? *See* §524(a)(2).

PROBLEM 6-15

Same facts as Problem 6-14, except Tessa explains all of the above to you at the time you are filing the original bankruptcy for her, and she tells you that she does not want to discharge the debt to Marco in the bankruptcy proceeding, she just wants to get rid of her other financial obligations. Her plan, which she has worked out with her brother, is this: She simply won't list the debt owed to Marco on her schedules, and that way he won't be involved in the bankruptcy at all. Will this work? *See* §523(a)(3); also note possible problems with §727(a)(4). After you explain this to her, she then begs for advice and you explain the reaffirmation procedure of §524(c) to her. She is all for doing this, and asks you if you will sign the attorney's affidavit of §524(c)(3). You are worried about this because Tessa has so little money, her son is still sick, and her infant daughter also appears to have a mysterious malady. Will you sign the affidavit? *See* §524(f).

PROBLEM 6-16

Attorneys are often in a delicate and unpleasant position when the client wants to reaffirm a debt and asks for the attorney's affidavit. Take Adam Goodheart, your newest client, for example. He owes $3,500 to his current employer, Robin Oakapple, who loaned him the money last year so Adam could visit his ailing mother, who lives in England. Now Adam needs to file a bankruptcy petition, and he wants to reaffirm this debt. Will you sign the §524(c)(3) affidavit even though Adam has no real prospects of paying the debt? He is afraid he will lose his job if he doesn't reaffirm the debt. *See* §525(b). Would it influence your answer if Adam tells you that another reason he wants to reaffirm the debt is because his mother is the surety on the debt he owes his employer, and she has even less money than he has? *See* §524(e) and In re Izzo, 197 B.R. 11 (Bankr. D.R.I. 1996) (court sanctions attorney for debtor for proposing a reaffirmation agreement); In re Brady, 171 B.R. 635 (Bankr. N.D. Ind. 1993) (court approves a reaffirmation agreement over the objections of the debtor's attorney).

If Adam tells you that his monthly income post-bankruptcy will be $3,000 and his monthly expenses are $2,900, will the court approve the reaffirmation agreement if it calls for payments of $100 a month until debt is paid? *See* §524(m)(1). What if Adam has gotten married to a wealthy woman shortly after he filed the bankruptcy and she has agreed to fund the repayments, does that affect what the court might do?

PROBLEM 6-17

Adam Goodheart owns a fancy automobile worth $35,000 that was subject to a purchase money security interest in favor of Ruddigore Credit Union, to whom he still owes $24,800. He needs the car to get to and from work. Will you sign the attorney's affidavit if he wants to reaffirm this debt? If the credit union is not interested in a reaffirmation and refuses to go along, can he force the reaffirmation through?

Assume the credit union is willing to enter into the reaffirmation agreement. Does §524(m) cause problems?

PROBLEM 6-18

Russell Johnson suffered a series of career setbacks and eventually obtained a Chapter 7 discharge in 1999. Among the debts he discharged was one owed to Actors Equity Credit Union in the amount of $6,000. In an effort to revive his career, Johnson decided to take some acting lessons and to have some elective plastic surgery in 2001. He borrowed the necessary $15,000 from Actors Equity Credit Union. The promissory note that the Credit Union required Johnson to sign provided that Johnson would repay $21,000 plus interest at the contract rate. Can the Credit Union recover any or all of the amount due under the note? Read §524(c) carefully.

Another circumstance under which debtors enter into reaffirmation agreements is the settlement of dischargeability litigation. Rather than incur the cost of defending the action, the debtor instead agrees to pay the creditor an amount that may nearly equal the amount of the outstanding indebtedness. This form of reaffirmation may put creditors in a particularly advantageous position against the debtor. The debtor usually cannot afford to defend the action, so the creditor can exercise significant leverage to obtain a reaffirmation agreement. Congress recognized this as a problem when it considered and enacted the Bankruptcy Reform Act in 1978. In that version of the Bankruptcy Code the court was required to sign off on reaffirmation agreements, an action that was intended to protect debtors from being taken advantage of in such situations. In 1984, the Code was amended to make reaffirmation agreements enforceable based on the premise that the debtor's attorney could adequately counsel and protect the debtor.

In negotiating a reaffirmation agreement, creditors may be viewed as taking action to collect a prepetition debt in violation of the automatic stay. Many courts have held that legitimate efforts to negotiate a reaffirmation agreement do not run afoul of the stay. Nonetheless, trouble still may lurk for some creditors. Consider the following case.

In re Jamo

United States Court of Appeals, First Circuit, 2002
283 F.3d 392

SELYA, Circuit Judge.

This bankruptcy appeal requires us to decide an issue of first impression at the circuit level: In a Chapter 7 case, may a lender who is owed both secured and unsecured debts insist upon reaffirmation of the latter as a condition to reaffirmation of the former? The bankruptcy court ruled that such an "all or nothing" negotiating posture amounted to a per se violation of the automatic stay, Jamo v. Katahdin Fed. Credit Union, 253 B.R. 115 (Bankr. D. Me. 2000) [*Jamo I*], and the bankruptcy appellate panel (the BAP) agreed, Katahdin Fed. Credit Union v. Jamo, 262 B.R. 159 (B.A.P. 1st Cir. 2001) [*Jamo II*]. We reverse.

I. Background

The critical facts are not in dispute. On March 18, 1999, the debtors, Stephen J. Jamo and Lynn M. Jamo (husband and wife), initiated proceedings under Chapter 7 of the Bankruptcy Code, 11 U.S.C. §§701-766. On the filing date, they owed $61,010 to Katahdin Federal Credit Union (the credit union). This indebtedness was composed of $37,079 owed on a promissory note secured by a first mortgage on their residence in Millinocket, Maine; $12,731 owed on unsecured personal loans; and $11,200 owed on credit cards.

In their bankruptcy petition, the debtors indicated that they desired to reaffirm the mortgage obligation. When their attorney inquired about reaffirmation, the credit union responded, through counsel, that it would not enter into a reaffirmation agreement unless the debtors also agreed to reaffirm their other indebtedness with the credit union. In taking this position, the credit union cited a "long-standing" policy that stated in relevant part:

> It shall be the policy of [the credit union] to allow members to reaffirm debts owed to the credit union. If members have more than one debt with [the credit union], all debts must be reaffirmed or re-written (post-petition). Reaffirmation will not be granted to members who wish to have some debts excused (discharged), and to reaffirm others.

Initially, the debtors' counsel tried to get the credit union to accept a reaffirmation of the secured indebtedness alone. When that effort failed, he signaled that the debtors would consider reaffirming all of their obligations to the credit union. The credit union then proposed a comprehensive reaffirmation package that bundled the debtors' outstanding obligations into two loans (each secured by a home mortgage) and dramatically reduced the debtors' total monthly payments. The debtors executed the papers presented by the credit union.

The deal came a cropper when the debtors' counsel balked. *See* 11 U.S.C. §524(c)(3)(A)-(B) (stipulating that, as a condition precedent to reaffirmation, counsel for a represented debtor must certify that the agreement "represents a fully informed and voluntary agreement by the debtor . . . [and] does not impose an undue hardship on the debtor"). In refusing to approve the arrangement, the lawyer singled out the proposed reaffirmation of the unsecured debts and questioned whether his clients were "succumbing to the extortion that is inherently present in the Credit Union's all or nothing approach to reaffirmation."

The "linked" reaffirmation agreements were filed with the bankruptcy court. Absent counsel's stamp of approval, however, the court had no choice but to reject them.

The debtors promptly notified the credit union that they remained willing to reaffirm the mortgage, shorn of any linkage to the unsecured debts. Further negotiations ensued. The credit union and the debtors reached a second accord, this time purposing to reaffirm the secured indebtedness on its original terms and to reaffirm the unsecured debts without interest. Despite these changes, the debtors' lawyer remained adamant in his refusal to endorse the arrangement.

Although the revised agreements lacked the imprimatur of the debtors' counsel, the debtors filed them with the bankruptcy court. The debtors then commenced an adversary proceeding charging the credit union with a violation of the automatic stay, 11 U.S.C. §362(a)(6), and seeking sanctions. After some skirmishing (not relevant here), the bankruptcy court concluded that the credit union's efforts to condition reaffirmation of the mortgage debt upon the simultaneous reaffirmation of other (unsecured) debts violated the automatic stay in two ways. *Jamo I*, 253 B.R. at 127-30. First, the credit union's insistence upon linkage constituted an impermissibly coercive attempt to "strong-arm" the debtors into reaffirming their separate, unsecured obligations. *Id.* at 127-29. Second, the credit union had engaged in prohibited conduct by threatening to foreclose on the debtors' home. *Id.* at 129-30.

Consistent with these conclusions, the court enjoined the credit union from (1) foreclosing on the mortgage for any bankruptcy-related reason, (2) calling the mortgage on account of an asserted payment default for at least one year, (3) collecting (or attempting to collect) any attorneys' fees or costs accruing prior to the effective date of the injunction, (4) conditioning any reaffirmation of the mortgage debt upon the debtors' reaffirmation of their unsecured obligations, and (5) withholding its consent to reaffirmation of the mortgage debt on the terms specified in the original loan documents. *Id.* at 130. Effectively, then, the bankruptcy court overrode the parties' agreement to reaffirm the unsecured debts and (as a sanction) compelled reaffirmation of the mortgage debt on its original terms. To cap matters, the court awarded attorneys' fees and costs to the debtors. *Id.* at 130-31.

The credit union appealed, but the BAP affirmed the judgment. *Jamo II*, 262 B.R. at 165-68. This further appeal ensued.

II.   The Merits

We traverse an analytical path that delineates the structure of, and the relationship between, two mainstays of the Bankruptcy Code: reaffirmation and the automatic stay. We turn then to the question of whether the credit union transgressed the automatic stay either by conditioning reaffirmation of the mortgage indebtedness upon the reaffirmation of separate, unsecured obligations, or by engaging in strong-arm tactics.

A.   The Statutory Interface

To put this case into perspective, it is necessary to understand how the practice of reaffirmation and the operation of the automatic stay implicate bankruptcy practice. We turn to that task.

Reaffirmation. Within thirty days of filing a bankruptcy petition, a Chapter 7 debtor must serve a statement of intention with respect to outstanding consumer debts that are secured by property of the bankrupt estate. 11 U.S.C. §521(2)(A). The debtor may, of course, surrender the collateral to the secured creditor. Id. To retain it, however, he must (a) demonstrate the applicability of a recognized bankruptcy exemption, (b) pay off the secured creditor in full (thereby redeeming the collateral), or (c) reaffirm the secured debt. Id. The focus here is on reaffirmation.

The reaffirmation option is spelled out in 11 U.S.C. §524(c). We recently explained that section 524(c) requires reaffirmation agreements to satisfy five general criteria. Such an agreement must

(i)   be executed before the [general] discharge has been granted;

(ii)   be in consideration for a dischargeable debt, whether or not the debtor waived discharge of the debt;

(iii)   include clear and conspicuous statements that the debtor may rescind the reaffirmation agreement at any time prior to the granting of the general discharge, or within sixty days after the execution of the reaffirmation agreement, whichever occurs later, and that reaffirmation is neither required by the Bankruptcy Code nor by nonbankruptcy law;

(iv)   be filed with the bankruptcy court; and

(v)   be accompanied by an affidavit of the debtor's attorney attesting that the debtor was fully advised of the legal consequences of the reaffirmation agreement, that the debtor executed the reaffirmation agreement knowingly and voluntarily, and that the reaffirmation agreement would not cause the debtor "undue [*e.g.*, financial] hardship."

Whitehouse v. LaRoche, 277 F.3d 568, 574 (1st Cir. 2002).

There is, however, an overarching requirement. Section 524(c) makes manifest that reaffirmation requires a meeting of the minds. The statutory text uses the word "agreement" no less than nineteen separate times, and this pervasive emphasis can only mean that Congress envisioned reaffirmations as consensual. In conventional legal parlance the essence of an agreement is the existence of mutual consent, *e.g.*, Black's Law Dict. 67 (7th ed. 1999); Restatement (Second) of Contracts §3 (1981), and the presumption is "that Congress knew and adopted the widely accepted legal definitions of meanings associated with the specific words enshrined in the statute," United States v. Nason, 269 F.3d 10, 16 (1st Cir. 2001).

We conclude, therefore, that section 524(c) envisions reaffirmation agreements as the product of fully voluntary negotiations by all parties. *Whitehouse*, 277 F.3d at 575; Gen. Motors Acceptance Corp. v. Bell (In re Bell), 700 F.2d 1053, 1056 (6th Cir. 1983). Two things follow from this conclusion. First, both the creditor and the debtor must consent to reaffirmation. *See* In re Turner, 156 F.3d 713, 718 (7th Cir. 1998); Home Owners Funding Corp. v. Belanger (In re Belanger), 962 F.2d 345, 348 (4th Cir. 1992); *see also* 4 Collier on Bankruptcy ¶524.04[1] (15th rev. ed. 2001) ("[T]o be an enforceable agreement, the reaffirmation agreement must . . . be one to which both the debtor and creditor agree."). Second, just as a debtor is not obliged to seek reaffirmation, so too a creditor retains the right to reject any and all reaffirmation proposals, for whatever reason. In re Turner, 156 F.3d at 718-19; Brown v. Pa. State Employees Credit Union (In re Brown), 851 F.2d 81, 85 (3d Cir. 1988); In re Bell, 700 F.2d at 1056.

We add a caveat. Although reaffirmation is consensual in nature, the myriad safeguards erected by Congress reflect its recognition that a debtor's decision to enter into a reaffirmation agreement is likely to be fraught with consequence. In point of fact, reaffirmation represents the only vehicle through which an otherwise dischargeable debt can survive the successful completion of Chapter 7 proceedings. Moreover, once a debt is reaffirmed, the creditor can proceed to enforce its rights as if bankruptcy had not intervened. Because reaffirmation constitutes a debtor-invoked exception to the tenet that underpins the bankruptcy system — the "fresh start" principle — a reaffirming debtor must be afforded some protection against his own (potentially) short-sighted decisions.

Section 524(c) reflects Congress's intent to provide this protection, thereby safeguarding debtors against unsound or unduly pressured judgments about whether to attempt to repay dischargeable debts. In re Duke, 79 F.3d 43, 44 (7th Cir. 1996); 4 Collier on Bankruptcy, *supra*, ¶524.04. To cloak debtors in this protective garb, courts generally have insisted that reaffirmation agreements strictly comply with the conditions enumerated in the statute. *E.g.*, *Whitehouse*, 277 F.3d at 575; DuBois v. Ford Motor Credit Co., 276 F.3d 1019, 1022 (8th Cir. 2002); Bessette v. Avco Fin. Servs., 230 F.3d 439, 444 (1st Cir. 2000), *cert. denied*, 532 U.S. 1048, 121 S. Ct. 2016, 149 L. Ed. 2d 1018 (2001). By like token, courts have insisted upon a showing that a reaffirmation agreement is not the product of abusive creditor practices. In re Duke, 79 F.3d at 44-45.

The Automatic Stay. The automatic stay is one of the fundamental protections that the Bankruptcy Code affords to debtors. As its name suggests, the stay springs into effect upon the filing of a bankruptcy petition. Sunshine Dev., Inc. v. FDIC, 33 F.3d 106, 113 (1st Cir. 1994). The stay effectively suspends all collection efforts (including foreclosures), thus giving the debtor breathing room. *See* Soares v. Brockton Credit Union (In re Soares), 107 F.3d 969, 975 (1st Cir. 1997); *see also* 11 U.S.C. §362(a)(6) (prohibiting "any act to collect, assess, or recover a claim against the debtor that arose before the commencement of the [bankruptcy proceeding]"). The automatic stay remains in effect unless and until a federal court either disposes of the underlying case, 11 U.S.C. §362(c)(2), or grants relief to a particular creditor, id. §362(d)-(f).

The Interplay. Congress's encouragement to creditors and debtors alike to move expeditiously to negotiate reaffirmation agreements is in some tension with the automatic stay. Although Congress has explicitly excepted a handful of actions from the purview of the stay, *see* id. §362(b)(1)-(18), this enumeration does not include the negotiation of reaffirmation agreements. Taken to an extreme, the automatic stay could be construed to prohibit all post-petition contact between creditors and debtors pertaining to dischargeable debts, including the negotiation of reaffirmation agreements. But the Bankruptcy Code should be read as a whole, with a view toward effectuating Congress's discerned intent. MSR Exploration, Ltd. v. Meridian Oil, Inc., 74 F.3d 910, 914 (9th Cir. 1996). Such a commonsense approach leads us to reject a reading of the automatic stay provision that would effectively preclude all post-petition negotiations anent reaffirmation. To read the automatic stay provision that expansively would emasculate section 524(c) and thwart Congress's evinced intent of allowing parties to reach arm's-length reaffirmation agreements without undue delay. As the Seventh Circuit astutely observed:

> The option of reaffirming would be empty if creditors were forbidden to engage in any communication whatsoever with debtors who have pre-petition obligations. If that were the rule, it is also hard to see what purpose the detailed rules governing enforceability of reaffirmation agreements contained in §524(c) would serve.

In re Duke, 79 F.3d at 45.

To be sure, there is a fine line between hard-nosed negotiations and predatory tactics — and if the automatic stay is to have any bite, it must forfend against the latter. Courts have labored long to plot this line. The most sensible rule — and one that we endorse — is that a creditor may discuss and negotiate terms for reaffirmation with a debtor without violating the automatic stay as long as the creditor refrains from coercion or harassment. Cox v. Zale Del., Inc., 239 F.3d 910, 912 (7th Cir. 2001); Pertuso v. Ford Motor Credit Co., 233 F.3d 417, 423 (6th Cir. 2000). We believe that this measured approach gives effect to all parts of the statutory scheme, affording all parties a reasonable opportunity to consummate binding reaffirmation agreements while at the same time shielding debtors from unseemly creditor practices. Accordingly, we hold that, while the automatic stay is in effect, a creditor may engage in post-petition negotiations pertaining to a bankruptcy-related reaffirmation agreement so long as the creditor does not engage in coercive or harassing tactics.

B. The Attempt at Linkage

This brings us to the question of linkage: whether a creditor's attempt to condition reaffirmation of a secured debt upon reaffirmation of separate, unsecured debts crosses the line and should be deemed coercive as a matter of law. Both the bankruptcy court, *Jamo I*, 253 B.R. at 127-29, and the BAP, *Jamo II*, 262 B.R. at 165-66, answered that question affirmatively. For purposes of our review, "we focus on the bankruptcy court's decision, scrutinize that court's findings of fact for clear error, and afford de novo review to its conclusions of law," without according any special deference to the BAP's pronouncements. Brandt v. Repco Printers & Litho., Inc. (In re Healthco Int'l, Inc.), 132 F.3d 104, 107 (1st Cir. 1997).

There are two different ways in which a debtor might prevail on the linkage issue. The first is if a per se rule applies, that is, if any and all efforts by creditors to construct such a tie are deemed inherently coercive (and, therefore, violative of the automatic stay). The second is fact-specific; even if an "all or nothing" negotiating posture is not per se coercive, a creditor still might violate the automatic stay by articulating or acting upon that policy in an inappropriate manner during the course of negotiations. We examine both alternatives.

The Per Se Rule. Both lower courts took the position that a creditor's refusal to reaffirm a secured debt unless the debtor simultaneously agrees to reaffirm additional, unsecured debts constitutes a per se violation of the automatic stay. *Jamo II*, 262 B.R. at 165-66; *Jamo I*, 253 B.R. at 127-29. This is an abstract legal proposition, and, as such, engenders de novo review. 229 Main St. Ltd. P'ship v. Mass. Dep't of Envtl. Prot. (In re 229 Main St. Ltd. P'ship), 262 F.3d 1, 3 (1st Cir. 2001); In re Soares, 107 F.3d at 973.

To some extent, we write on a pristine page: no federal court of appeals has spoken to the issue. There is, however, a smattering of apposite case law. The bankruptcy courts that have addressed the question mostly reject a per se rule. *See, e.g.*, In re Brady, 171 B.R. 635, 639-40 (Bankr. N.D. Ind. 1994); In re Briggs, 143 B.R. 438, 460 (Bankr. E.D. Mich. 1992); Schmidt v. Am. Fletcher Nat'l Bank & Trust Co. (In re Schmidt), 64 B.R. 226, 228-29 (Bankr. S.D. Ind. 1986); *but see* Green v. Nat'l Cash Register Co. CI Corp. Sys. (In re Green), 15 B.R. 75, 78 (Bankr. S.D. Ohio 1981) (holding that such an attempt at linkage is inherently coercive and, therefore, violates the automatic stay).

We too reject a per se rule. When an individual debtor voluntarily files for bankruptcy, he usually has the option of proceeding under either Chapter 7 or Chapter 13. Unlike Chapter 7, Chapter 13 contains a "cram down" provision, 11 U.S.C. §1325(a)(5)(B), which permits a debtor to retain the collateral underlying a secured obligation without the creditor's approval. Bank of Boston v. Burr (In re Burr), 160 F.3d 843, 848 (1st Cir. 1998). Even if a debtor belatedly decides that "cramming down" is in his best interest, a decision to file under Chapter 7 ordinarily is not irrevocable. The Bankruptcy Code, with only a few exceptions, *see* 11 U.S.C. §706(a), allows a debtor who initially has filed for Chapter 7 relief to jump midstream to Chapter 13.

Conversely, a debtor who persists in traveling the Chapter 7 route knows that reaffirmation depends entirely on his ability to come to terms with the secured creditor. He also knows (or, at least, has every reason to expect) that the creditor may drive a hard bargain. Hence, a debtor must bear some degree of responsibility for choosing to proceed under Chapter 7.

Perhaps more important, the Bankruptcy Code does not outlaw linkage as an element of reaffirmation negotiations. The absence of such a prohibition makes sense, for a secured creditor's insistence on linkage does not force a debtor to reaffirm unsecured obligations. As we have explained, reaffirmation agreements are consensual, and a debtor always has the option of walking away from an unattractive proposal.

Of course, a debtor whose home is at stake is in an unenviable position. But a Chapter 7 discharge is not a walk in the park; it is "a benefit that comes with certain costs." In re Burr, 160 F.3d at 848. Consequently, a Chapter 7 debtor is not innoculated against the necessity for making hard choices. If the debtor surrenders his home, he is entitled to erase all his debts (secured and unsecured) and start afresh. If, however, his paramount interest is in keeping his home and he cannot redeem the collateral, he must come to terms with the mortgagee. Bankruptcy, as life itself, is a series of tradeoffs.

The debtors argue for a per se rule on policy grounds, but we doubt the prophylactic effects of such a rule. Creditors, as a class, have a highly developed instinct for self-protection, and, as the amici point out, such a rule could open Pandora's jar and produce a distinctly unfavorable climate for debtors. Creditors might become more reluctant to extend both secured and unsecured loans to a particular debtor, or might insist upon cross-collateralization clauses in all loans, or might categorically decide that foreclosure is a more judicious option than reaffirmation negotiations restricted to a single secured debt. Then, too, a creditor intent on negotiating for a "linked" reaffirmation arrangement simply could petition for relief from the automatic stay and refuse to negotiate until such relief had been obtained. This would not only delay the Chapter 7 proceedings, but also increase the ultimate cost of reaffirmation to the debtor. For these reasons, we find the debtors' policy-based arguments lacking in force.

That ends this inquiry. Based on the foregoing analysis, we reject the proposition that a creditor's decision to withhold reaffirmation of a secured debt unless the debtor agrees to reaffirm other, unsecured debts amounts to a per se violation of the automatic stay.

The Credit Union's Conduct. Even if a creditor's attempt to condition reaffirmation of a secured debt upon reaffirmation of other, unsecured obligations does not constitute a per se violation of the automatic stay, the question remains whether the creditor's conduct in a particular instance amounts to a violation of the automatic stay. While we review the bankruptcy court's findings of fact for clear error, Boroff v. Tully (In re Tully), 818 F.2d 106, 108 (1st Cir. 1987), we afford plenary review to the question of whether the evidence is legally sufficient to support particular findings. Here, the bankruptcy court calumnized the credit union for improperly bringing "leverage" to bear on the debtors' reaffirmation decision and, relatedly, for menacing the debtors with threats of foreclosure. *Jamo I*, 253 B.R. at 129-30. To the extent that these are findings that the credit union engaged in impermissibly coercive conduct, they lack adequate record support. We explain briefly.

The bankruptcy court's condemnation of the credit union for using its leverage manifests a fundamental misunderstanding of a creditor's rights vis-à-vis a debtor. In and of itself, the act of filing a bankruptcy petition negates the original pre-bankruptcy bargain between debtor and creditor. In re Burr, 160 F.3d at 848 (explaining that Chapter 7 debtors have no right "to maintain with their secured creditors advantageous arrangements in place prior to filing"). Thus, subject only to the constraints imposed by section 524(c) or by other provisions of the Bankruptcy Code, the parties to a secured obligation are free to strike a new bargain.

So viewed, the bankruptcy court's condemnation of the credit union's use of leverage amounts to a variation of its per se rule — a rule that we already have rejected. *See supra* Part II(B)(1). A reaffirmation negotiation — like any other negotiation — contemplates give and take between the participants. The fact that one party has a superior bargaining position does not warrant a court in placing a thumb on the scales. *See* In re Burr, 160 F.3d at 848 (recognizing that an oversecured creditor may attempt to use its "superior bargaining power" to obtain creditor-favorable terms in negotiating reaffirmation agreements without violating the automatic stay); *see also* In re Briggs, 143 B.R. at 454 (declaring that it would be "absurd" to interpret the Bankruptcy Code as prohibiting a secured creditor from using its leverage in negotiating a reaffirmation agreement).

That leaves the so-called threats of foreclosure. In theory, threats of foreclosure or repossession might justify a finding that a secured creditor has violated the automatic stay. *See* In re Duke, 79 F.3d at 44-45; *see also* In re Brown, 851 F.2d at 86 (noting that the automatic stay continues to preclude creditor communications that "threat[en] immediate action by creditors, such as a foreclosure or a lawsuit"). The facts of this case, however, do not support such a finding.

The bankruptcy court focused on written, rather than oral, communications. In corresponding with the debtors (or, more precisely, with the debtors' counsel), the credit union sent a total of nine separate reaffirmation-related letters. In those letters, it referred three times to foreclosure. The question, then, is whether these references, read favorably to the bankruptcy court's finding, plausibly can be deemed coercive. We think not.

The first mention of foreclosure came in a response to the debtors' initial request for reaffirmation of the mortgage indebtedness. After outlining the credit union's "all or nothing" policy, its lawyer asked the debtors' counsel to ascertain whether the debtors "will be discharging all their obligations," and if so, whether "they would be amenable to a deed in lieu of foreclosure."

The second foreclosure reference transpired after the bankruptcy court rejected the initial reaffirmation proposal. At that point, the debtors' attorney declared that his clients were willing to reaffirm the mortgage indebtedness (but no other obligations) and vowed "to fully litigate any foreclosure action" instituted by the credit union. Responding to this vow, the credit union's counsel wrote that:

> [I]t was the Credit Union's desire that the Parties could have arrived at a mutually agreeable — resolution. As foreclosing was not on the Credit Union's agenda, it would be premature to extensively respond to your assertions. . . . Should the Credit Union eventually foreclose, however, the terms of the Jamos' note and mortgage are that the Jamos are liable for the Credit Union's costs and fees of enforcing the obligation, and therefore, should the Credit Union prevail, the amount due increases rapidly as a result of all this litigation. Of course, the Jamos are not personally exposed to this liability, but such sums are secured by the mortgage.

The third reference came in a letter to the debtors that limned the terms of the second reaffirmation proposal. In that epistle, the credit union's lawyer expressed his belief that the contemplated overall reduction in payments would "eliminat[e] the risks of future litigation, including foreclosure."

These references were unarguably benign. The first letter merely inquired whether the debtors, if they decided to discharge all their debts (including the mortgage indebtedness), would be willing to deliver a deed to the credit union in lieu of foreclosure. The next letter was nothing more than a temperate response to statements made by the debtors' counsel. Far from hanging the Damoclean sword of foreclosure over the debtors' heads, the credit union accurately delineated the debtors' foreclosure-related liability and made clear that foreclosure "was not on [its] agenda." The final reference to foreclosure was likewise innocuous; in context, it cannot reasonably be deemed tantamount to a threat.

To say more on this point would be supererogatory. Because the credit union's passing references to foreclosure cannot reasonably be construed as threatening "immediate action" against the debtors, In re Brown, 851 F.2d at 86, those references were not impermissibly coercive. Accordingly, the credit union did not violate the automatic stay.

III. *The Remedy*

The question of remedy remains. Although the bankruptcy court erred in finding a violation of the automatic stay, its disapproval of the linked reaffirmation agreements is supportable on an independent ground. The critical datum is that the debtors' attorney, believing that reaffirmation on the agreed terms was not in the debtors' best interest, refused to approve the arrangement. Absent counsel's approbation, no valid reaffirmation could occur. 11 U.S.C. §524(c)(3); *Whitehouse*, 277 F.3d at 575 (explaining that a represented debtor must strictly comport with section 524(c) criteria to effect a valid reaffirmation).

The bankruptcy court's granting of injunctive relief, attorneys' fees, and costs against the credit union is less easily defended. We review a bankruptcy court's imposition of sanctions for abuse of discretion. Schwartz v. Kujawa (In re Kujawa), 270 F.3d 578, 581 (8th Cir. 2001). Here, however, both the injunctive relief and the assessment of fees and costs rest squarely on the court's erroneous determination that the credit union violated the automatic stay. Thus, these aspects of the court's order cannot endure. *See Sunshine Dev.*, 33 F.3d at 117 (dissolving injunction that erroneously restrained FDIC from exercising its lawful powers); *see also* In re Grand Jury Subpoena, 138 F.3d 442, 444 (1st Cir. 1998) (explaining that "a court that predicates a discretionary ruling on an erroneous view of the law inevitably abuses its discretion").

In an attempt to keep the remedial order intact, the debtors rely upon 11 U.S.C. §105(a). Their reliance is mislaid. Section 105(a) — a statute that empowers bankruptcy courts to "issue any order, process, or judgment that is necessary or appropriate" to effectuate the provisions of the Bankruptcy Code — supplies a source of authority for the bankruptcy court's imposition of sanctions in an appropriate case. *See* Bessette, 230 F.3d at 445; Hardy v. United States ex rel. IRS (In re Hardy), 97 F.3d 1384, 1389-90 (11th Cir. 1996). But section 105(a) does not provide bankruptcy courts with a roving writ, much less a free hand. The authority bestowed thereunder may be invoked only if, and to the extent that, the equitable remedy dispensed by the court is necessary to preserve an identifiable right conferred elsewhere in the Bankruptcy Code. *See* Norwest

Bank Worthington v. Ahlers, 485 U.S. 197, 206, 108 S. Ct. 963, 99 L. Ed. 2d 169 (1988) (explaining that a bankruptcy court's equitable powers "can only be exercised within the confines of the Bankruptcy Code"); Noonan v. Sec'y of HHS (In re Ludlow Hosp. Soc'y, Inc.), 124 F.3d 22, 27 (1st Cir. 1997) (similar).

The relief ordered below falls short of this benchmark. The bankruptcy court's order was designed to implement the reaffirmation option limned in section 524(c). As said, *see supra* Part II(B), the order failed in this endeavor: forced to operate without much precedential guidance, the court misapprehended the interplay between section 524(c) and section 362(a), mischaracterized lawful conduct as impermissibly coercive, and issued a flawed order. Absent any antecedent violation either of the automatic stay or of some other independent provision of the Bankruptcy Code, the bankruptcy court lacked the power, section 105(a) notwithstanding, to modify the proposed reaffirmation arrangement, compel the credit union to enter into a judicially-crafted reaffirmation agreement, or award monetary sanctions in the form of attorneys' fees and costs.

IV. Conclusion

We need go no further. We neither underestimate the difficulty of the question presented nor disparage the lower courts' thoughtful attempts to resolve it. In the end, however, we see the matter differently. Consequently, we reverse the decision of the BAP and remand the case to that tribunal with directions to vacate the bankruptcy court's judgment and to remand the matter to the bankruptcy court for further proceedings consistent with this opinion.

Reversed.

If a creditor violates the provisions of §524, the debtor can defend against the reaffirmation agreement and avoid having to repay the obligation. The courts have split over whether the debtor has any private right of action against the creditor. The First Circuit in Bessette v. Avco Fin. Serv., Inc., 230 F.3d 439 (1st Cir. 2000), held that §105 of the Bankruptcy Code provides authority for the debtor to recover from creditors who fail to abide by the dictates of §524(c). The Sixth Circuit, however, rejected that position in Pertuso v. Ford Motor Credit Corp., 233 F.3d 417 (6th Cir. 2000).

VI.   Redemption

PROBLEM 6-19

Patience Grosvenor has an automobile that has a current value of $1,000 but that originally cost her $12,000, the amount she borrowed from Nightflyer Loan Company, which perfected its security interest in the car by getting its lien interest noted on the certificate of title for the vehicle. Patience still owes Nightflyer $3,000 on this debt at the time she files her petition in bankruptcy. State law allows a debtor to claim an exemption in one motor vehicle for the amount of $1,500 and Patience wants to use this exemption to free her car from the bankruptcy but Nightflyer, of course, wants her to pay the $3,000 still due. What can she do here? *See* §§722 and 506(a)(2). If she decides to use this procedure, can she make the payments in installments? Suppose Patience is current on her car payments at the time she filed her bankruptcy petition. Can she just keep making the payments and hang onto the car? *See* §521(a)(6).

VII.   Protecting the Discharge

Section 525 forbids discrimination against bankrupts in the granting of government entitlements and private employment, and §366 regulates rights between the debtor and utility services. Read these sections and apply them to the following Problems.

PROBLEM 6-20

Seven years and two days after leaving law school, attorney Sam Ambulance left Oregon and his failing law practice and moved to Idaho. If his dismal attempts at practicing law have been so unsuccessful that he wants to file for bankruptcy, in which jurisdiction should he file? *See* 28 U.S.C. §1408 (don't panic; this statute is in your bankruptcy statutes book under "Bankruptcy Provision in Title 28 of the United States Code, Chapter 87 — District Courts: Venue"). He discharged all his debts in the bankruptcy proceeding, including his student loans (*see* §523(a)(8)), and then applied for admission to the Idaho bar, and was promptly turned down because he had shown financial irresponsibility in filing for bankruptcy when in the opinion of the bar examiners he could have paid these debts (some of which were owed to former Oregon clients). Will §525 help Sam here? *See* In re Anonymous, 74 N.Y. 938, 549 N.E.2d 472 (1989). Compare F.C.C. v. NextWave Personal Communications Inc., 537 U.S. 293 (2003).

PROBLEM 6-21

After her bankruptcy Portia Moot was annoyed that her credit union refused to loan her any money simply because she had discharged $800 in debts she owed it, and when she applied for a job she was well qualified to hold the prospective employer told her that it never employed former bankrupts. She is in your office asking you to file two suits on her behalf. Will you take these cases? *See* Fiorani v. Caci, 192 B.R. 401 (E.D. Va. 1996) (employment).

PROBLEM 6-22

When Portia Moot filed her bankruptcy petition, scheduling among others a $400 electric bill debt owed to Edison Power Company, Edison immediately shut off her electricity and informed her that it wouldn't restore the power until she paid the amount due plus put down a deposit equal to three times her average bill in the past year. Can they do this to her? *See* §366.

PROBLEM 6-23

Long before she sought bankruptcy relief, Portia had been behind on a number of her obligations. In fact, one creditor, Unfriendly Finance Co., received a judgment against Portia and properly docketed the judgment about one year prior to her bankruptcy case. Consequently, it had a judicial lien on Portia's house. Portia listed Unfriendly as a creditor in the case, but she took no other action in the proceedings to deal with that debt. Now, one year after the bankruptcy case has concluded, Unfriendly is trying to have the house sold to pay the claim it has against Portia. What can Portia do? *See* §§524(a)(1), 350(b), and 522(f)(1)(A). If she is unable to remove the lien, does Portia have a claim against her attorney?

CHAPTER 7

Avoidance Powers

I. Lien-Stripping

PROBLEM 7-1

In the days when he was wealthy, Lex Cigar used a painting, "The Lure," by local artist Tom Buckeye, as collateral for a $10,000 loan from Octopus National Bank. Buckeye's works were then highly regarded, and his reputation was growing daily. A string of bad investments sent Cigar into a Chapter 7 bankruptcy proceeding, and the bank wants the painting (in which it had duly perfected its security interest). Lex tells you, his attorney, that on the current market the painting will only bring about $6,000, but that Tom Buckeye is ailing, rumored to be near death, and Cigar is sure that once Buckeye has passed on, all his paintings will rise dramatically in value. Here is what he wants to do (you'll need to look carefully at §506(a) and (d) to follow this): have the court value the painting at $6,000 and declare the bank secured to that amount only. Since he still owes the bank $9,000 on this debt, the bank would be unsecured to the tune of $3,000. Cigar can easily borrow $6,000 from other sources, so he can use §506(d) to strip away the unsecured portion of the debt from this piece of collateral, pay the estate $6,000 for it, and thus capture any appreciation value that the painting might have for him. Cigar also can move to compel the trustee to abandon any interest that the estate may have in the painting. Under §554(a), the trustee can abandon any property that is either burdensome to the estate or of inconsequential value. The bank protests that this is similar to the redemption rights of §722, but without the limitations of that section, so Congress could not have intended to allow this sort of "lien-stripping," no matter what §506(d) appears to say, and it wants the painting so that it, the bank, gets the benefit of whatever appreciation value the painting possesses. Look at the cited sections and decide whether Cigar can save the painting from the bankruptcy proceeding. Keep in mind that under §506(a)(2), the valuation of the painting is based on its replacement value because Tom is an individual debtor in a Chapter 7 case.

Dewsnup v. Timm

Unites States Supreme Court, 1992
502 U.S. 410

Justice BLACKMUN delivered the opinion of the Court.

We are confronted in this case with an issue concerning §506(d) of the Bankruptcy Code, 11 U.S.C. §506(d). May a debtor "strip down" a creditor's lien on real property to the value of the collateral, as judicially determined, when that value is less than the amount of the claim secured by the lien?

I.

On June 1, 1978, respondents loaned $119,000 to petitioner Aletha Dewsnup and her husband, T. LaMar Dewsnup, since deceased. The loan was accompanied by a Deed of Trust granting a lien on two parcels of Utah farmland owned by the Dewsnups.

Petitioner defaulted the following year. Under the terms of the Deed of Trust, respondents at that point could have proceeded against the real property collateral by accelerating the maturity of the loan, issuing a notice of default, and selling the land at a public foreclosure sale to satisfy the debt. . . .

Respondents did issue a notice of default in 1981. Before the foreclosure sale took place, however, petitioner sought reorganization under Chapter 11 of the Bankruptcy Code, 11 U.S.C. §1101 et seq. That bankruptcy petition was dismissed, as was a subsequent Chapter 11 petition. In June 1984, petitioner filed a petition seeking liquidation under Chapter 7 of the Code, 11 U.S.C. §701 et seq. Because of the pendency of these bankruptcy proceedings, respondents were not able to proceed to the foreclosure sale. *See* 11 U.S.C. §362 (1988 ed. and Supp. II).

In 1987, petitioner filed the present adversary proceeding in the Bankruptcy Court for the District of Utah seeking, pursuant to §506, to "avoid" a portion of respondents' lien. App. 3. Petitioner represented that the debt of approximately $120,000 then owed to respondents exceeded the fair market value of the land and that, therefore, the Bankruptcy Court should reduce the lien to that value. According to petitioner, this was compelled by the interrelationship of the security-reducing provision of §506(a) and the lien-voiding provision of §506(d). Under §506(a) ("An allowed claim of a creditor secured by a lien on property in which the estate has an interest . . . is a secured claim to the extent of the value of such creditor's interest in the estate's interest in such property"), respondents would have an "allowed secured claim" only to the extent of the judicially determined value of their collateral. And under §506(d) ("To the extent that a lien secures a claim against the debtor that is not an allowed secured claim, such lien is void"), the court would be required to void the lien as to the remaining portion of respondents' claim, because the remaining portion was not an "allowed secured claim" within the meaning of §506(a).

The Bankruptcy Court refused to grant this relief. In re Dewsnup, 87 B.R. 676 (1988). After a trial, it determined that the then value of the land subject to the Deed of Trust was $39,000. It indulged in the assumption that the property had been abandoned by the trustee pursuant to §554, and reasoned that once property was abandoned it no longer fell within the reach of §506(a), which applies only to "property in which the estate has an interest," and therefore was not covered by §506(d).

The United States District Court, without a supporting opinion, summarily affirmed the Bankruptcy Court's judgment of dismissal with prejudice. App. to Pet. for Cert. 12a.

The Court of Appeals for the Tenth Circuit, in its turn, also affirmed. In re Dewsnup, 908 F.2d 588 (1990). Starting from the "fundamental premise" of §506(a) that a claim is subject to reduction in security only when the estate has an interest in the property, the court reasoned that because the estate had no interest in abandoned property, §506(a) did not apply (nor, by implication, did §506(d)). Id., at 590-591. The court then noted that a contrary result would be inconsistent with §722 under which a debtor has a limited right to redeem certain personal property. Id., at 592.

Because the result reached by the Court of Appeals was at odds with that reached by the Third Circuit in Gaglia v. First Federal Savings & Loan Assn., 889 F.2d 1304, 1306-1311 (1989), and was expressly recognized by the Tenth Circuit as being in conflict, see 908 F.2d, at 591, we granted certiorari. 498 U.S. 1081, 111 S. Ct. 949, 112 L. Ed. 2d 1038 (1991).

II.

As we read their several submissions, the parties and their amici are not in agreement in their respective approaches to the problem of statutory interpretation that confronts us. Petitioner-debtor takes the position that §§506(a) and 506(d) are complementary and to be read together. Because, under §506(a), a claim is secured only to the extent of the judicially determined value of the real property on which the lien is fixed, a debtor can void a lien on the property pursuant to §506(d) to the extent the claim is no longer secured and thus is not "an allowed secured claim." In other words, §506(a) bifurcates classes of claims allowed under §502 into secured claims and unsecured claims; any portion of an allowed claim deemed to be unsecured under §506(a) is not an "allowed secured claim" within the lien-voiding scope of §506(d). Petitioner argues that there is no exception for unsecured property abandoned by the trustee.

Petitioner's *amicus* argues that the plain language of §506(d) dictates that the proper portion of an undersecured lien on property in a Chapter 7 case is void whether or not the property is abandoned by the trustee. It further argues that the rationale of the Court of Appeals would lead to evisceration of the debtor's right of redemption and the elimination of an undersecured creditor's ability to participate in the distribution of the estate's assets.

Respondents primarily assert that §506(d) is not, as petitioner would have it, "rigidly tied" to §506(a), Brief for Respondents 7. They argue that §506(a) performs the function of classifying claims by true secured status at the time of distribution of the estate to ensure fairness to unsecured claimants. In contrast, the lien-voiding §506(d) is directed to the time at which foreclosure is to take place, and, where the trustee has abandoned the property, no bankruptcy distributional purpose is served by voiding the lien.

In the alternative, respondents, joined by the United States as *amicus curiae*, argue more broadly that the words "allowed secured claim" in §506(d) need not be read as an indivisible term of art defined by reference to §506(a), which by its terms is not a definitional provision. Rather, the words should be read term-by-term to refer to any claim that is, first, allowed, and, second, secured. Because there is no question that the claim at issue here has been "allowed" pursuant to §502 of the Code and is secured by a lien with recourse to the underlying collateral, it does not come within the scope of §506(d), which voids only liens corresponding to claims that have not been allowed and secured. This reading of §506(d), according to respondents and the United States, gives the provision the simple and sensible function of voiding a lien whenever a claim secured by the lien itself has not been allowed. It ensures that the Code's determination not to allow the underlying claim against the debtor personally is given full effect by preventing its assertion against the debtor's property.

Respondents point out that pre-Code bankruptcy law preserved liens like respondents' and that there is nothing in the Code's legislative history that reflects any intent to alter that law. Moreover, according to respondents, the "fresh start" policy cannot justify an impairment of respondents' property rights, for the fresh start does not extend to an in rem claim against property but is limited to a discharge of personal liability.

III.

The foregoing recital of the contrasting positions of the respective parties and their amici demonstrates that §506 of the Bankruptcy Code and its relationship to other provisions of that Code do embrace some ambiguities. See 3 Collier on Bankruptcy, ch. 506 and, in particular, ¶506.07 (15th ed. 1991). Hypothetical applications that come to mind and those advanced at oral argument illustrate the difficulty of interpreting the statute in a single opinion that would apply to all possible fact situations. We therefore focus upon the case before us and allow other facts to await their legal resolution on another day.

We conclude that respondents' alternative position, espoused also by the United States, although not without its difficulty, generally is the better of the several approaches. Therefore, we hold that §506(d) does not allow petitioner to "strip down" respondents' lien, because respondents' claim is secured by a lien and has been fully allowed pursuant to §502. Were we writing on a clean slate, we might be inclined to agree with petitioner that the words "allowed secured claim" must take the same meaning in §506(d) as in §506(a).[1] But, given the ambiguity in the text, we are not convinced that Congress intended to depart from the pre-Code rule that liens pass through bankruptcy unaffected.

---

1. Accordingly, we express no opinion as to whether the words "allowed secured claim" have different meaning in other provisions of the Bankruptcy Code.

1.

The practical effect of petitioner's argument is to freeze the creditor's secured interest at the judicially determined valuation. By this approach, the creditor would lose the benefit of any increase in the value of the property by the time of the foreclosure sale. The increase would accrue to the benefit of the debtor, a result some of the parties describe as a "windfall."

We think, however, that the creditor's lien stays with the real property until the foreclosure. That is what was bargained for by the mortgagor and the mortgagee. The voidness language sensibly applies only to the security aspect of the lien and then only to the real deficiency in the security. Any increase over the judicially determined valuation during bankruptcy rightly accrues to the benefit of the creditor, not to the benefit of the debtor and not to the benefit of other unsecured creditors whose claims have been allowed and who had nothing to do with the mortgagor-mortgagee bargain.

Such surely would be the result had the lienholder stayed aloof from the bankruptcy proceeding (subject, of course, to the power of other persons or entities to pull him into the proceeding pursuant to §501), and we see no reason why his acquiescence in that proceeding should cause him to experience a forfeiture of the kind the debtor proposes. It is true that his participation in the bankruptcy results in his having the benefit of an allowed unsecured claim as well as his allowed secured claim, but that does not strike us as proper recompense for what petitioner proposes by way of the elimination of the remainder of the lien.

2.

This result appears to have been clearly established before the passage of the 1978 Act. Under the Bankruptcy Act of 1898, a lien on real property passed through bankruptcy unaffected. This Court recently acknowledged that this was so. *See* Farrey v. Sanderfoot, 500 U.S. 291, 297, 111 S. Ct. 1825, 1829, 114 L. Ed. 2d 337 (1991) ("Ordinarily, liens and other secured interests survive bankruptcy"); Johnson v. Home State Bank, 501 U.S. 78, 84, 111 S. Ct. 2150, 2154, 115 L. Ed. 2d 66 (1991) ("Rather, a bankruptcy discharge extinguishes only one mode of enforcing a claim — namely, an action against the debtor *in personam* — while leaving intact another — namely, an action against the debtor *in rem*").

3.

Apart from reorganization proceedings, *see* 11 U.S.C. §§616(1) and (10) (1976 ed.), no provision of the pre-Code statute permitted involuntary reduction of the amount of a creditor's lien for any reason other than payment on the debt. Our cases reveal the Court's concern about this. In Long v. Bullard, 117 U.S. 617, 620-621, 6 S. Ct. 917, 918, 29 L. Ed. 1004 (1886), the Court held that a discharge in bankruptcy does not release real estate of the debtor from the lien of a mortgage created by him before the bankruptcy. And in Louisville Joint Stock Land Bank v. Radford, 295 U.S. 555, 55 S. Ct. 854, 79 L. Ed. 1593 (1935), the Court considered additions to the Bankruptcy Act effected by the Frazier-Lemke Act, 48 Stat. 1289. There the Court noted that the latter Act's "avowed object is to take from the mortgagee rights in the specific property held as security; and to that end 'to scale down the indebtedness' to the present value of the property." 295 U.S., at 594, 55 S. Ct., at 865. The Court invalidated that statute under the Takings Clause. It further observed: "No instance has been found, except under the Frazier-Lemke Act, of either a statute or decision compelling the mortgagee to relinquish the property to the mortgagor free of the lien unless the debt was paid in full." Id., at 579, 55 S. Ct., at 858.

Congress must have enacted the Code with a full understanding of this practice. *See* H.R. Rep. No. 95-595, p.357 (1977), U.S. Code Cong. & Admin. News 1978, pp. 5787, 6313 ("Subsection (d) permits liens to pass through the bankruptcy case unaffected").

4.

When Congress amends the bankruptcy laws, it does not write "on a clean slate." *See* Emil v. Hanley, 318 U.S. 515, 521, 63 S. Ct. 687, 690-691, 87 L. Ed. 954 (1943). Furthermore, this Court has been reluctant to accept arguments that would interpret the Code, however vague the particular language under consideration might be, to effect a major change in pre-Code practice that is not the subject of at least some discussion in the legislative history. *See* United Savings Assn. of Texas v. Timbers of Inwood Forest Associates, Ltd., 484 U.S. 365, 380, 108 S. Ct. 626, 634, 98 L. Ed. 2d 740 (1988). *See also* Pennsylvania Dept. of Public Welfare v. Davenport, 495 U.S. 552, 563, 110 S. Ct. 2126, 2133, 109 L. Ed. 2d 588 (1990); United States v. Ron Pair Enterprises, Inc., 489 U.S. 235, 244-245, 109 S. Ct. 1026, 1032-1033, 103 L. Ed. 2d 290 (1989). Of course, where the language is unambiguous, silence in the legislative history cannot be controlling. But, given the ambiguity here, to attribute to Congress the intention to grant a debtor the broad new remedy against allowed claims to the extent that they become "unsecured" for purposes of §506(a) without the new remedy's being mentioned somewhere in the Code itself or in the annals of Congress is not plausible, in our view, and is contrary to basic bankruptcy principles.

The judgment of the Court of Appeals is affirmed.

It is so ordered.

Justice THOMAS took no part in the consideration or decision of this case.

Justice SCALIA, with whom Justice SOUTER joins, dissenting.

With exceptions not pertinent here, §506(d) of the Bankruptcy Code provides: "To the extent that a lien secures a claim against the debtor that is not an allowed secured claim, such lien is void. . . ." Read naturally and in accordance with other provisions of the statute, this automatically voids a lien to the extent the claim it secures is not both an "allowed claim" and a "secured claim" under the Code. In holding otherwise, the Court replaces what Congress said with what it thinks Congress ought to have said — and in the process disregards, and hence impairs for future use, well-established principles of statutory construction. I respectfully dissent.

I.

This case turns solely on the meaning of a single phrase found throughout the Bankruptcy Code: "allowed secured claim." Section 506(d) unambiguously provides that to the extent a lien does not secure such a claim it is (with certain exceptions) rendered void. See 11 U.S.C. §506(d). Congress did not leave the meaning of "allowed secured claim" to speculation. Section 506(a) says that an "allowed claim" (the meaning of which is obvious) is also a "secured claim" "to the extent of the value of [the] creditor's interest in the estate's interest in [the securing] property." (Emphasis added.) (This means, generally speaking, that an allowed claim "is secured only to the extent of the value of the property on which the lien is fixed; the remainder of that claim is considered unsecured." United States v. Ron Pair Enterprises, Inc., 489 U.S. 235, 239, 109 S. Ct. 1026, 1029, 103 L. Ed. 2d 290 (1989).) When §506(d) refers to an "allowed secured claim," it can only be referring to that allowed "secured claim" so carefully described two brief subsections earlier.

The phrase obviously bears the meaning set forth in §506(a) when it is used in the subsections of §506 other than §506(d) — for example, in §506(b), which addresses "allowed secured claim[s]" that are oversecured. Indeed, as respondents apparently concede, *see* Brief for Respondents 40; Tr. of Oral Arg. 29-30, even when the phrase appears outside of §506, it invariably means what §506(a) describes: the portion of a creditor's allowed claim that is secured after the calculations required by that provision have been performed. *See, e.g.,* 11 U.S.C. §722 (permitting a Chapter 7 debtor to redeem certain tangible personal property from certain liens "by paying the holder of such lien the amount of the *allowed secured claim* of such holder that is secured by such lien"); §1225(a)(5) (prescribing treatment of "*allowed secured claim*[s]" in family farmer's reorganization plan); §1325(a)(5) (same with respect to "*allowed secured claim*[s]" in individual reorganizations). (Emphases added.) The statute is similarly consistent in its use of the companion phrase "*allowed unsecured claim*" to describe (with respect to a claim supported by a lien) that portion of the claim that is treated as "unsecured" under §506(a). *See, e.g.,* 11 U.S.C. §507(a)(7) (fixing priority of "*allowed unsecured claims of governmental units*"); §726(a)(2) (providing for payment of "*allowed unsecured claim*[s]" in Chapter 7 liquidation); §1225(a)(4) (setting standard for treatment of "*allowed unsecured claim*[s]" in Chapter 12 plan); §1325(a)(4) (setting standard for treatment of "*allowed unsecured claim*[s]" in Chapter 13 plan). (Emphases added.) When, on the other hand, the Bankruptcy Code means to refer to a secured party's entire allowed claim, *i.e.,* to both the "secured" and "unsecured" portions under §506(a), it uses the term "*allowed claim*" — as in 11 U.S.C. §363(k), which refers to "a lien that secures an allowed claim." Given this clear and unmistakable pattern of usage, it seems to me impossible to hold, as the Court does, that "the words 'allowed secured claim' in §506(d) need not be read as an indivisible term of art defined by reference to

§506(a)." *Ante*, at 777; *see ante*, at 777-778. We have often invoked the " 'normal rule of statutory construction' that 'identical words used in different parts of the same act are intended to have the same meaning.' " [Citations omitted.] That rule must surely apply, a *fortiori*, to use of identical words in the *same section of the same enactment*.

The Court makes no attempt to establish a textual or structural basis for over-riding the plain meaning of §506(d), but rests its decision upon policy intuitions of a legislative character, and upon the principle that a text which is "ambiguous" (a status apparently achieved by being the subject of disagreement between self-interested litigants) cannot change pre-Code law without the *imprimatur* of "legislative history." Thus abandoning the normal and sensible principle that a term (and especially an artfully defined term such as "allowed secured claim") bears the same meaning throughout the statute, the Court adopts instead what might be called the one-subsection-at-a-time approach to statutory exegesis. "[W]e express no opinion," the Court amazingly says, "as to whether the words 'allowed secured claim' have different meaning in other provisions of the Bankruptcy Code." *Ante*, at 778, n.3. "We . . . focus upon the case before us and allow other facts to await their legal resolution on another day." *Ante*, at 778.

II.

. . . The distinctive feature of the United States' approach is that it seeks to avoid invalidation of the so-called "underwater" portion of the lien by focusing not upon the phrase "allowed secured claim" in §506(d), but upon the prior phrase "secures a claim." ("To the extent that a lien secures a claim against the debtor that is not an allowed secured claim, such lien is void." (Emphasis added.)) Under the Government's textual theory, this phrase can be read to refer not merely to the object of the security, but to its adequacy. That is to say, a lien only "secures" the claim in question up to the value of the security that is the object of the lien — and only up to that value is the lien subject to avoidance under §506(d). This interpretation succeeds in giving the phrase "allowed secured claim," which appears later in §506(d), a meaning compatible with that compelled by §506(a). But that is its only virtue.

To begin with, the interpretation renders some of the language in §506(d) sur-plusage. If the phrase "[t]o the extent that a lien *secures* a claim" describes only that portion of a claim that is secured by actual economic value, then the later phrase "is not an allowed secured claim" should instead have read simply "is not allowed." For the phrase "allowed *secured* claim" *itself* describes a claim that is *actually* secured in light of §506(a)'s calculations. Another reading of §506(d)'s opening passage is available, one that does not assume such clumsy draftsmanship — and that employs, to boot, a much more natural reading of the phrase "lien secures a claim." The latter ordinarily describes the relationship between a lien and a claim, not the relationship between the value of the property subject to the lien and the amount of the claim. One would say that a "mortgage secures the claim" for the purchase price of a house, even if the value of the house was inadequate to satisfy the full amount of the claim.

In other words, "[t]o the extent that a lien secures a claim" means in §506(d) what it ordinarily means: "to the extent a lien provides its holder with a right to retain property in full or partial satisfaction of a claim." It means that in §506(d) just as it means that in §506(a), *see* 11 U.S.C. §506(a) ("An allowed claim of a creditor *secured* by a lien . . . is a secured claim to the extent . . .") (emphasis added), and just as it means that elsewhere in the Bankruptcy Code, *see, e.g.,* §362(a)(5) ("to the extent that such lien *secures* a claim"); §363(k) ("lien that secures an allowed claim"). An unnatural meaning should be disfavored at any time, but particularly when it produces a redundancy. *See* Montclair v. Ramsdell, 107 U.S. 147, 152, 27 L. Ed. 431 (1883).

Of course *respondents'* interpretation also creates a redundancy in §506(d). If a "secured claim" means only a claim for which a lien has been given as security (whether or not the security is adequate), then the prologue of §506(d) can be reformulated as follows: "To the extent that a lien secures a claim against the debtor that is not an allowed claim secured by a lien, such lien is void. . . ." Quite obviously, the phrase "secured by a lien" in that reformulation is utterly redundant and absurd — as is (on respondents' interpretation) the word "secured," which bears the same meaning. In other words, both the United States' interpretation and respondents' interpretation create a redundancy: the former by making both parts of the §506(d) prologue refer to *adequate* security, and the latter by making both parts refer to *security plain-and-simple*. Only when one gives the words in the first part of the prologue ("[t]o the extent that a lien secures a claim") their natural meaning (as the Government does not) and gives the words in the second part of the prologue ("allowed secured claim") their previously established statutory meaning (as the respondents do not) does the provision make a point instead of a *redundancy*.

Moreover, the practical consequences of the United States' interpretation would be absurd. A secured creditor holding a lien on property that is completely worthless would not face lien avoidance under §506(d), *even if the claim secured by that lien were disallowed entirely*. The same would be true of a lien on property that has *some* value but is obviously inadequate to cover all of the disallowed claim: the lien would be voided only to the extent of the property's value at the time of the bankruptcy court's evaluation, and could be asserted against any increase in the value of the property that might later occur, in order to satisfy the disallowed claim. Unavoided liens (or more accurately, potentials of unavoided liens, since no one knows whether or when future evaluations of the relevant property will exceed that of the bankruptcy court) would impede the trustee's management and settlement of the estate. It would be difficult, for example, to sell overencumbered property subject to outstanding liens pursuant to 11 U.S.C. §363(b) or (c), since any postsale appreciation in the property could be levied upon by holders of disallowed secured claims. And in a sale of debtor property "free and clear" of the liens attached to it, *see* 11 U.S.C. §363(f)(3), the undisturbed portion of the disallowed claimant's lien might attach to the proceeds of that sale to the extent of the collateral's postpetition appreciation, preventing the trustee from distributing some or all of the sale proceeds to creditors holding allowed claims. If possible, we should avoid construing the statute in a way that produces such absurd results.

III.

Although the Court makes no effort to explain why petitioner's straightforward reading of §506(d) is textually or structurally incompatible with other portions of the statute, respondents and the United States do so. They point out, to begin with, that the two exceptions to §506(d)'s nullifying effect both pertain to the disallowance of claims, and not to the inadequacy of security, see 11 U.S.C. §§506(d)(1) and (2) — from which they conclude that the applicability of §506(d) turns only on the allowability of the underlying claim, and not on the extent to which the claim is a "secured claim" within the meaning of §506(a). But the fact that the statute makes no exceptions to invalidation by reason of inadequate security in no way establishes that such (plainly expressed) invalidation does not exist. The premise of the argument — that if a statute qualifies a noun with two adjectives ("allowed" and "secured"), and provides exceptions with respect to only one of the adjectives, then the other can be disregarded — is simply false. The most that can be said is that the two exceptions in §506(d) do not contradict the United States' and respondents' interpretation; but they in no way suggest or support it.

Respondents and the United States also identify supposed inconsistencies between petitioner's construction of §506(d) and other sections of the Bankruptcy Code; they are largely illusory. The principal source of concern is §722, which enables a Chapter 7 debtor to "redeem" narrow classes of exempt or abandoned personal property from "a lien securing a dischargeable consumer debt." The price of redemption is fixed as "the amount of the *allowed secured claim* of [the lienholder] that is secured by such lien." (Emphasis added.) This provision, we are told, would be largely superfluous if §506(d) automatically stripped liens securing undersecured claims to the value of the collateral, *i.e.*, to the value of the allowed secured claims.

This argument is greatly overstated. Section 722 is necessary, and not superfluous, because §506(d) is not a *redemption* provision. It reduces the value of a lienholder's equitable interest in a debtor's property to the property's liquidation value, but it does not insure the debtor an opportunity to "redeem" the property at that price, *i.e.*, to "free [the] property . . . from [the] mortgage or pledge by paying the debt for which it stood as security." Black's Law Dictionary 1278 (6th ed. 1990). Congress had good reason to be solicitous of the debtor's right to redeem personal property (the exclusive subject of §722), since state redemption laws are typically less generous for personalty than for real property. *Compare, e.g.*, Utah Code Ann. §57-1-31 (1990) *with* Uniform Commercial Code §9-506, 3A U.L.A. 370 (1981). The most that can be said regarding §722 is that petitioner's construction of §506(d) would permit a more concise formulation: Instead of describing the redemption price as "the amount of the allowed secured claim . . . that is secured by such lien" it would have been *possible* to say simply "the amount of the claim . . . that is secured by such lien" — since §506(d) would automatically have cut back the lien to the amount of the allowed secured claim. I would hardly call the more expansive formulation a redundancy — not when it is so far removed from the section that did the "cutting back" that the reader has likely forgotten it. . . .

It is even more instructive to compare today's opinion with our decision a few years ago in United States v. Ron Pair Enterprises, Inc., 489 U.S. 235, 109 S. Ct. 1026, 103 L. Ed. 2d 290 (1989), which involved another subsection of §506 itself. The issue was whether §506(b) made post-petition interest available even to those oversecured creditors whose liens were nonconsensual. The Court of Appeals had held that it did not, because such a disposition would alter the pre-Code rule and there was no "legislative history" to support the change. We disagreed. The opinion for the Court began "where all such inquiries must begin: with the language of the statute itself." Id., at 241, 109 S. Ct., at 1030. We did not recite the contentions of the parties and declare "ambiguity," but entered into our own careful consideration of "[t]he natural reading of the [relevant] phrase," the "grammatical structure of the statute," and the "terminology used throughout the Code." Id., at 241 and 242, n.5, 109 S. Ct., at 1030 and 1031, n.5. Having found a "natural interpretation of the statutory language [that] does not conflict with any significant state or federal interest, nor with any other aspect of the Code," id., at 245, 109 S. Ct., at 1032-1033, we deemed the pre-Code practice to be irrelevant. And whereas today's opinion announces the policy judgment that "[a]ny increase over the judicially determined valuation during bankruptcy rightly accrues to the benefit of the creditor," *ante*, at 778, in *Ron Pair* we were undeterred by the fact that our result was "arguably somewhat in tension with the desirability of paying all creditors as uniformly as practicable," 489 U.S., at 245-246, 109 S. Ct., at 1033. "Congress," we said, "expressly chose to create that alleged tension." Id., at 246, 109 S. Ct., at 1033. Almost point for point, today's opinion is the methodological antithesis of *Ron Pair* — and I have the greatest sympathy for the Courts of Appeals who must predict which manner of statutory construction we shall use for the next Bankruptcy Code case.

The principal harm caused by today's decision is not the misinterpretation of §506(d) of the Bankruptcy Code. The disposition that misinterpretation produces brings the Code closer to prior practice and is, as the Court irrelevantly observes, probably fairer from the standpoint of natural justice. (I say irrelevantly, because a bankruptcy law has little to do with natural justice.) The greater and more enduring damage of today's opinion consists in its destruction of predictability, in the Bankruptcy Code and elsewhere. By disregarding well-established and oft-repeated principles of statutory construction, it renders those principles less secure and the certainty they are designed to achieve less attainable. When a seemingly clear provision can be pronounced "ambiguous" sans textual and structural analysis, and when the assumption of uniform meaning is replaced by "one-subsection-at-a-time" interpretation, innumerable statutory texts become worth litigating. In the bankruptcy field alone, for example, unfortunate future litigants will have to pay the price for our expressed neutrality "as to whether the words 'allowed secured claim' have different meaning in other provisions of the Bankruptcy Code." *Ante*, at 778, n.3. Having taken this case to resolve uncertainty regarding one provision, we end by spawning confusion regarding scores of others. I respectfully dissent.

NOTE

Before the Court handed down this decision, lien-stripping had been widely used. There was much dismay at its demise in Chapter 7 proceedings, and *Dewsnup* was much criticized. *See, e.g.*, Mary Josephine Newborn, Undersecured Creditors in Bankruptcy, Dewsnup, Nobelman, and the Decline of Priority, 25 Ariz. St. L.J. 547 (1993). After *Dewsnup*, what possible function does §506(d) serve? We will return to the issue of lien-stripping in other chapters of the Bankruptcy Code later in this book.

PROBLEM 7-2

Gary and Cynthia Cooper took advantage of a strong economy to borrow money secured by a mortgage on their home. In fact, they borrowed 125 percent of the value of the residence and took a vacation, bought some expensive clothes, and invested in a dotcom venture that they hoped would go through the roof. Unfortunately, their investment was ill advised, they got sick on the vacation, and the clothes went out of style. They were unable to make their payments for several months, so they accumulated some significant late charges and accrued interest. They still owe $170,000 on the mortgage, but the house is only worth approximately $125,000. Gary and Cynthia filed a Chapter 7 bankruptcy petition and in due course received a discharge of their debts. They continued to live in the house, and over the next two years had made their $1,500 monthly mortgage payments. At that point, they had reduced the balance on the loan to $162,000, and the house had appreciated in value to $155,000 due to a general increase in property values and the $4,000 of landscaping that Gary and Cynthia had added to the property. When they missed a mortgage payment, however, the bank commenced a foreclosure action and wants to be paid its full balance on the mortgage. If the house sells at foreclosure for $155,000 (an unlikely occurrence), can the Coopers obtain any of that amount?

II.   The Strong Arm Clause

Subsection (a) of §544 is commonly called the "strong arm" clause because it gives the trustee in bankruptcy a powerful weapon for attacking creditors' rights if those rights might be vulnerable outside bankruptcy. Under this subsection, when a debtor goes bankrupt the debtor's bankruptcy trustee is given the status of a hypothetical ideal judicial lien creditor who acquired a lien on all of the debtor's property by levying on it as of the moment of the filing of the bankruptcy petition (subsections (a)(1) and (2)), and, for attacking interests in real property (other than fixtures), the trustee is imbued with whatever rights a bona fide purchaser of the realty would have (subsection (a)(3)).

Under Article 9 of the Uniform Commercial Code, a creditor taking a security interest in the debtor's property must make sure that that security interest has "attached" to the collateral in order to have rights against the debtor, and then the creditor must "perfect" that security interest (typically by the filing of a financing statement in the appropriate public office) in order to have priority over most of the rest of the world. According to §9-203, attachment occurs when three things coalesce (no matter the order): the debtor has rights in the collateral, the creditor gives value, and the debtor signs a security agreement describing the collateral. As soon as these have occurred, the collateral is subject to the creditor's security interest (and therefore could be repossessed if the debtor defaults). If attachment has happened, but the creditor has not yet taken the steps required by Article 9 for perfection of the security interest, the creditor is said to be "unperfected," a very risky state. Section §9-317 lists the entities who then might prevail over the creditor's unperfected security interest in this particular piece of the debtor's property:

(a) **Conflicting security interests and rights of lien creditors**. A security interest or agricultural lien is subordinate to the rights of:

(1) a person entitled to priority under Section 9-322; and

(2) except as otherwise provided in subsection (e), a person that becomes a lien creditor before the earlier of the time:

(A) the security interest or agricultural lien is perfected; or

(B) one of the conditions specified in Section 9-203(b)(3) is met and a financing statement covering the collateral is filed.

(b) **Buyers that receive delivery**. Except as otherwise provided in subsection (e), a buyer, other than a secured party, of tangible chattel paper, documents, goods, instruments, or a security certificate takes free of a security interest or agricultural lien if the buyer gives value and receives delivery of the collateral without knowledge of the security interest or agricultural lien and before it is perfected.

(c) **Lessees that receive delivery.** Except as otherwise provided in subsection (e), a lessee of goods takes free of a security interest or agricultural lien if the lessee gives value and receives delivery of the collateral without knowledge of the security interest or agricultural lien and before it is perfected.

(d) **Licensees and buyers of certain collateral.** A licensee of a general intangible or a buyer, other than a secured party, of accounts, electronic chattel paper, general intangibles, or investment property other than a certificated security takes free of a security interest if the licensee or buyer gives value without knowledge of the security interest and before it is perfected.

(e) **Purchase-money security interest.** Except as otherwise provided in Sections 9-320 and 9-321, if a person files a financing statement with respect to a purchase-money security interest before or within 20 days after the debtor receives delivery of the collateral, the security interest takes priority over the rights of a buyer, lessee, or lien creditor which arise between the time the security interest attaches and the time of filing.

SECTION 9-102(a)(52) "Lien creditor" means:

(A) a creditor that has acquired a lien on the property involved by attachment, levy, or the like;

(B) an assignee for the benefit of creditors from the time of assignment;

(C) a trustee in bankruptcy from the date of the filing of the petition; or

(D) a receiver in equity from the time of appointment.

PROBLEM 7-3

Night Owl Bookstores, Inc., signed a security agreement giving Octopus National Bank a security interest in the bookstore's inventory in return for a $50,000 loan from the bank — thus attachment of the bank's security interest has occurred under U.C.C. §9-203, described above. ONB then created a financing statement describing the collateral in the public records. ONB's attorney took the financing statement to his office, meaning to file it that afternoon, but forgot to do so; the financing statement got lost in the enormous stack of papers on and around his desk, where it remains to this day. Will ONB's attached security interest be senior or junior to the following entities?

1. Night Owl sold the entire bookstore to a new buyer (this is a "bulk transfer"), who bought without notice of the ONB transaction. *See* U.C.C. §9-317(b).

2. Night Owl made an assignment for the benefit of creditors (*see* Chapter 1 of this book) when its financial situation grew dire. The assignee wants to sell the books and distribute the proceeds to Night Owl's creditors. *See* U.C.C. §§9-317(a) and 9-102(a)(52)(B).

3. Night Owl's major supplier, WWW Books, to whom it owed $34,000 on a past due account, sued it in state court and recovered a judgment. It then sent the sheriff out to levy execution on the inventory. Is WWW's judicial lien superior to ONB's? *See* §9-317(a) and 9-102(a)(52)(A).

4. Night Owl filed a bankruptcy petition. *See* U.C.C. §§9-317(a)(2) and 9-102(a)(52)(C), and Bankruptcy Code §544(a)(1) and (2).

PROBLEM 7-4

When Portia Moot bought a new car, she financed its purchase price through a loan from Last National Bank, which advanced her $22,000 for this purpose. She bought the car on September 10 and filed a bankruptcy petition on September 15; the bank perfected its security interest in the car by getting its lien interest noted on the certificate of title on September 16. Does the trustee's strong arm clause wipe out the bank's security interest? *See* U.C.C. §9-317(e), above, and Bankruptcy Code §546(b).

Probasco v. Eads

United States Court of Appeals, Ninth Circuit, 1988
839 F.2d 1352

BOOCHEVER, Circuit Judge:

Appellant William R. Probasco (Probasco) appeals from the Bankruptcy Appellate Panel's order, 69 B.R. 730, affirming the bankruptcy court's judgment that Bill J. Eads (Eads), as debtor in possession, could assert 11 U.S.C. §544(a)(3) (Supp. IV 1986) to avoid Probasco's unrecorded one-half interest in Parcel 1 of the Quail Meadows development. The controlling issue on appeal is whether a debtor in possession holding record title to property had constructive notice of an interest in that property, which, because of a secretarial mistake, did not appear on record.

Probasco asserts that: (1) there was sufficient possession and use of Parcel 1 under California law to provide Eads, in his capacity as debtor in possession and bona fide purchaser under section 544(a)(3), with constructive notice of Probasco's interest in the property, (2) the bankruptcy court erred in failing to grant equitable relief to Probasco so as to defeat the claims of Eads to the entirety of Parcel 1, (3) as a debtor in possession exercising his avoidance powers under section 544(a), Eads received a preference which Probasco, as debtor in possession of Probasco's estate, had the power to avoid pursuant to 11 U.S.C. §§547(b) (1982 & Supp. IV 1986) and 548(a)(2) (Supp. IV 1986), and (4) the bankruptcy court did not have the authority to sell Probasco's interest in a sewer easement adjacent to Quail Meadows.

We hold that Probasco's use and possession of Quail Meadows was sufficient under California law to constitute constructive notice to Eads as a hypothetical bona fide purchaser. Probasco's assertion that the bankruptcy court did not have the authority to sell Probasco's interest in the sewer easement is without merit. We do not reach the other issues. We therefore affirm in part and reverse in part the judgment of the Bankruptcy Appellate Panel and the bankruptcy court.

Background

The facts are undisputed. In 1978, Eads purchased Quail Meadows, consisting of 76.61 acres of undeveloped land. Approximately seventy-five percent of the acreage is in Parcel 1 and the remaining twenty-five percent is in Parcels 2 and 3.

In 1981, Eads agreed to make Probasco a one-half owner of Quail Meadows in exchange for Probasco's agreement to execute jointly with the Eads, a $600,000 note secured by a trust deed encumbering Quail Meadows. In addition, Probasco agreed to make payments on the note. A deed was to have been recorded conveying a fifty percent undivided interest in Quail Meadows from the Eads to Probasco concurrently with the recordation of the trust deed securing the $600,000 note.

The documents were executed and recorded in August 1981. The escrow company that prepared the deed and the deed of trust failed to attach a legal description of Parcel 1 to either the deed or the deed of trust. Both documents contained descriptions of Parcels 2 and 3. The escrow company has since gone out of business.

After August 1981, Eads and Probasco proceeded with their plans to subdivide the Quail Meadows property. Engineers, surveyors, and attorneys were employed to secure a tentative subdivision map which was approved by the Madera County Board of Supervisors. In connection with securing the subdivision plans, Probasco paid $25,000 for a sewer easement through neighboring property.

In July 1982, Eads filed a voluntary petition for reorganization under Chapter 11 of the Bankruptcy Code, 11 U.S.C. §§1101-74 (1982 & Supp. IV 1986). In August 1982, Probasco also filed a voluntary petition for reorganization under Chapter 11. The omission of a description of Parcel 1 from the deed and the deed of trust was not discovered until after the filing of both petitions.

The underlying adversary proceedings were commenced by Eads in his capacity as debtor in possession. The parties seek a determination of the nature, extent, and validity of all liens and other interests in the Quail Meadows property. . . .

I.   The Strong Arm Clause

Title 11 U.S.C. §544(a) (Supp. IV 1986), "the strong arm clause," gives a bankruptcy trustee power to avoid certain transfers or liens against property in the bankruptcy estate. Section 544(a)(3) allows the trustee to avoid all obligations and transfers that would be avoidable by "a bona fide purchaser of real property . . . that obtains the status of a bona fide purchaser . . . at the time of the commencement of the [bankruptcy] case, whether or not such a purchaser exists." Section 544(a) grants the bankruptcy trustee this power "without regard to any knowledge of the trustee or of any creditor." The powers of a bona fide purchaser for purposes of section 544(a) are defined by state law. [Citations omitted.] A debtor in possession has the same rights, powers, functions, and duties, except the right to compensation, as a bankruptcy trustee. 11 U.S.C. §1107 (1982 & Supp. IV 1986).

II.   Constructive Notice

Probasco argues that under California law Eads could not take title to Quail Meadows as a bona fide purchaser because he had constructive notice of Probasco's ownership in the property. The law of California requires every conveyance of real property to be recorded in order to be valid against a subsequent purchaser or mortgagee of the same property, who in good faith and for valuable consideration records first.[2] Thus, under California law a bona fide purchaser who records prevails over a prior transferee who failed to record.

Actual or constructive notice of a prior unrecorded transfer removes a subsequent purchaser from the protection of the recording acts. Clear and open possession of real property constitutes constructive notice of the rights of the party in possession to subsequent purchasers. Such a prospective purchaser must inquire into the possessor's claimed interests, whether equitable or legal. [Citations omitted.] Therefore, a bona fide purchaser who records does not take priority over one in clear and open possession of real property.

Eads, by virtue of section 544(a)(3), has the rights of a hypothetical bona fide purchaser. The language of the section renders the trustee's or any creditor's knowledge irrelevant. It does not, however, make irrelevant notice constructively given by open possession any more than it would make irrelevant the constructive notice given

---

2. Cal. Civ. Code §1214 (West 1982) provides:

> Every conveyance of real property, other than a lease for a term not exceeding one year, is void as against any subsequent purchaser or mortgagee of the same property, or any part thereof, in good faith and for a valuable consideration, whose conveyance is first duly recorded, and as against any judgment affecting the title, unless such conveyance shall have been recorded prior to the record of notice of action.

by recorded instruments that might evidence a competing claim of title to the real property in question. [Citations omitted.]

Probasco argues that in July 1982, when Eads filed his bankruptcy petition, the undisputed evidence of the physical condition of the Quail Meadows property as well as the subdivision activity on the property was more than sufficient to give constructive notice of Probasco's interest in Parcel 1. The evidence consisted of (1) surveyor's stakes criss-crossing all three parcels, (2) a fence around the perimeter with no intervening fences dividing parcels, (3) roadways across the three parcels which were not fenced at parcel lines, (4) proximity of the parcels to freeways, shopping centers and other subdivisions indicating that the parcels were part of a subdivision, and (5) a tentative subdivision map filed with the Clerk of Madera County.

Constructive notice is defined by California Civil Code §19 (West 1982) as follows:

> Every person who has actual notice of circumstances sufficient to put a prudent man upon inquiry as to a particular fact, has constructive notice of the fact itself in all cases in which, by prosecuting such inquiry, he might have learned such fact.

Whether the circumstances are sufficient to put one on inquiry of another's interest in property is a question of fact. High Fidelity, 210 Cal. App. 2d at 281, 26 Cal. Rptr. at 655. Our review is therefore under the clearly erroneous standard. We must accept the bankruptcy court's finding that there was no constructive notice unless we are "left with the definite and firm conviction that a mistake has been committed." United States v. United States Gypsum Co., 333 U.S. 364, 395, 68 S. Ct. 525, 542, 92 L. Ed. 746 (1948); Dollar Rent a Car, Inc. v. Traveler's Indem. Co., 774 F.2d 1371, 1374 (9th Cir. 1985). We note, however, that there is no dispute over the historical facts in this case. Nor are there any findings based on credibility of witnesses. The decision of the bankruptcy court that there was no constructive notice is based on inferences from the undisputed facts. Although, unlike credibility determinations, an appellate court is equally capable of making those inferences, the dictates of judicial economy require application of the clearly erroneous standard. See Anderson v. Bessemer City, 470 U.S. 564, 574-75, 105 S. Ct. 1504, 1511-12, 84 L. Ed. 2d 518 (1985).

At issue is whether a prudent purchaser would have actual notice of circumstances giving rise to inquiry about the unity of ownership of all three parcels. The fact that Eads had an interest in all three parcels does not dispose of that issue. The question is whether a prudent person, observing the indicia of unity of ownership of all three parcels, and knowing that Probasco had a one-half interest in Parcels 2 and 3, would be placed on inquiry about his interest in the remainder of Quail Meadows. It is almost inconceivable that such a prudent person, knowing that Parcels 2 and 3 were jointly owned, and seeing a perimeter fence around all three parcels, no fence between the parcels, the staking of all three parcels, and roads traversing the entire property, would not inquire whether a one-half owner of Parcels 2 and 3 had an interest in Parcel 1.

The California Code applies the standard of a "prudent" person. "Prudent" is defined as "a: marked by wisdom or judiciousness b: shrewd in the management of practical affairs c: marked by circumspection." Webster's Ninth New Collegiate Dictionary (1984). A prudent purchaser inquiring as to the unity of ownership of all three parcels "might have learned" of Probasco's interest in Parcel 1. Cal. Civ. Code §19.

The bankruptcy court concluded that none of the conditions of the property at the commencement of the case or the fact of the filing of the subdivision map with the Clerk of Madera County were acts inconsistent with the record title to the property so as to raise a duty of inquiry in a prospective purchaser. The Eads in their brief to this court amplified that terse conclusion, stating:

> Appellants' brief noted the presence of a road across Parcel 1 to Parcels 2 and 3, of a fence around Parcels 1, 2 and 3 and of certain survey stakes as items which would have given a bona fide purchaser constructive notice of the Probascos' interest in Parcel 1. Even if these items constituted "possession, use or occupancy" of which a bona fide purchaser would be deemed to have knowledge, such possession, use and occupancy was joint between Probascos and Eads and, thus, not inconsistent with the record title.

The error in their argument and the bankruptcy court's conclusions is that the physical evidence indicated a unity of ownership of all three parcels and the record revealed that two of those parcels were owned jointly by Eads and Probasco. The indications of unity of ownership were such as to put a prudent person on inquiry as to whether Probasco also had an interest in Parcel 1. Such an interest in Parcel 1 was inconsistent with the record title indicating that the Eads were its sole owners. We are left with the definite and firm conviction that the bankruptcy court made a mistake in finding that there was no constructive notice and voiding Probasco's interest in Parcel 1. Upon remand the court should reform the deed from Eads to Probasco to include Parcel 1 in accordance with the undisputed intention of the parties. *See* Higgs v. United States, 546 F.2d 373, 375-76, 212 Ct. Cl. 146 (1976) (where parties intended that land involved in sales contract include two parcels and draftmanship error excluded one parcel, reformation appropriate to reflect parties' true intent). . . .

Eads, acting as debtor in possession under the strong arm powers of 11 U.S.C. §544(a)(3), had constructive notice placing him on inquiry which might have revealed Probasco's interest in Parcel 1. Eads therefore did not take Parcel 1 free of Probasco's interest. The bankruptcy court did not abuse its discretion in ordering the sale of the sewer easement. Because of our decision on these two issues, we need not address other contentions.

AFFIRMED in part, REVERSED in part, and REMANDED.

III. Preferences

One of the maxims of the common law is that one must be "just before being generous," and the law of preferences, which we explore next, reflects that same idea. The Bankruptcy Code forbids debtors the right to pay their favorite creditors

(Mom, for example) on the eve of bankruptcy so that such creditors are spared the trouble of having to file a claim in the bankruptcy proceeding and possibly getting nothing. Such creditors are said to be "preferred," and the trustee will sue them in the bankruptcy proceeding and make them cough up whatever they got, or, for preferential security interests, simply avoid them. Preference law has the further benefit of discouraging creditors from engaging in a feeding frenzy on the eve of bankruptcy: seizing assets, forcing payments, demanding collateral, and so forth, and thus may keep the creditors from the sort of rapacious practices that lead to the filing of a bankruptcy petition.

A preference is a transfer of the bankrupt's property (including the creation of a security interest therein) to a creditor to pay or secure an old debt made in the 90-day period prior to the filing of the bankruptcy petition (the period is one year where the transfer is to an "insider," such as a corporate officer or a relative of the bankrupt), made while the debtor was insolvent (which is presumed in the 90-day period), and that would enable the creditor to receive more than that creditor would have gotten in the usual bankruptcy distribution. The Bankruptcy Code section reaching this result is the much-litigated §547, and we will parse out its meaning part by part.

A. The Basic Definition

Read §547(b), defining a preference, and apply it to the following Problems.

PROBLEM 7-5

The day before she filed her bankruptcy petition, Ivana Hotel gave her favorite diamond brooch to her daughter Mazie. Can Ivana's bankruptcy trustee recover this transfer under §547? *See* §547(b)(1).

PROBLEM 7-6

Mr. Whipple was running low on essential household products, so he went to the store and purchased some paper goods products. He paid cash for the goods and immediately took them home. The next week, Whipple filed a bankruptcy petition. Can his bankruptcy trustee recover the transfer under §547? *See* §547(b)(2).

PROBLEM 7-7

Antitrust National Bank took a perfected security interest in the inventory of abacuses, slide rules, eight-track tapes, Beta video machines, and other items that

Luddite Technologies kept in its warehouse. The day before it filed a bankruptcy petition Luddite made a $10,000 payment to ANB, which had been pressing it for collection for months. On the day of the payment the outstanding debt to ANB was $300,000 and the inventory, amazingly, was worth $500,000. Will Luddite's bankruptcy trustee be able to recover the $10,000 from ANB? Before answering, look carefully at §547(b)(5), and consider what ANB will be able to recover in the usual Chapter 7 distribution.

PROBLEM 7-8

When racecar driver Speed Track's much-loved, award-winning favorite racecar, The Brute, was seized by the local county sheriff after Speed failed to pay a judgment taken against him by his vindictive mother, to whom he owed much money as a consequence of the many loans made by her to finance his racing activities, Speed filed a bankruptcy petition that same day. Will his mother's judicial lien on the racecar be effective in bankruptcy? See §101(54). Assume that instead of filing a bankruptcy petition when the sheriff took the racecar, Speed had recovered the vehicle by posting a bond with the court equal to the value of the racecar. Speed obtained the bond from Bonds R Us, which protected itself by having Speed grant it a security interest in his valuable collection of automobile repair equipment. As we shall see below, §547(c)(1) ("contemporaneous exchanges") would ordinarily exempt from attack as a preference the security transfer made between Speed and Bonds R Us. If Speed now files his bankruptcy petition within a month after he gets The Brute back, what will happen to Bonds R Us's security interest in Speed's tools, et al.? See §547(d). Does Bonds R Us still owe the bond?

PROBLEM 7-9

Last National Bank gave lawyer Portia Moot a loan of $80,000 to finance the start of her law practice, taking a security interest in the monies she would receive in the future from her clients. She signed a security agreement with the bank to this effect, and also a financing statement covering this collateral, on April 1. The bank's attorney, careless as usual, didn't get around to filing the financing statement until May 25, the same day Portia, a heavy smoker, negligently started a fire that burned down much of the city in which she lived. Portia filed a bankruptcy petition on June 30. Did the bank receive a preferential transfer of an interest in Portia's property? Would the same result obtain if the bank had filed on April 9? See §547(e), explained in the next paragraph.

The Moment of "Transfer." Sometimes it is obvious when a transfer of the debtor's property occurs (the debtor gives a diamond ring to a creditor on Monday at 3:00 P.M., for example), but where the transfer is accomplished by creating a security interest in the property, when does it occur? Section 547(e) has rules concerning this. For real property (other than fixtures), the transfer is said to happen when a bona fide purchaser could no longer prevail over the creditor, which in almost all cases is the moment of the filing in the real property records. See §547(e)(1)(A). For personal property and fixtures, §547(e)(1)(B) chooses the moment when a judicial lien creditor could not achieve priority over the creditor, which under §9-317 (reprinted above as part of the discussion of the "strong arm" clause) is the moment of perfection (usually the filing of a financing statement). However, even here the Bankruptcy Code gives the creditor a break that state law may not because it creates a 30-day grace period from the moment of attachment (the "time such transfer takes effect between the transferor and the transferee"); if perfection is had in this grace period, a relation back occurs to protect the transfer from attack. *See* §547(e)(2)(A). If the creditor perfects after this period, as in Problem 7-9, §547(e)(2)(B) controls; if the creditor never gets around to perfecting the security interest, §547(e)(2)(C) engages in the fiction that the transfer occurred on the eve of bankruptcy so as to bring it within the preference period and thus condemn it.

When a payment is made in cash, the transfer occurs when the debtor physically turns over the cash to the creditor. However, since payments are often made by check, does the transfer of the debtor's property occur when the debtor sends the check to the creditor, when the creditor deposits the check at its bank, or not until the check clears at the debtor's bank? This issue could, of course, make all the difference if the preference period begins running in between these events. In Barnhill v. Johnson, 503 U.S 393 (1992), the U.S. Supreme Court used the rules of the Uniform Commercial Code to decide that, for purposes of §547(b), payment by check does not occur until the check clears through the drawee bank (until that moment the drawer/debtor could stop payment on it), so that that moment is the date of the transfer of the debtor's property.

PROBLEM 7-10

The Oops Moving Company owed $30,000 in unsecured debt to Ralph's Pads, which supplied the company with packing materials used in its business. When this debt was long overdue Ralph's Pads pushed for payment, so Oops borrowed $30,000, also unsecured, from Last National Bank and had Last National send the money directly to Ralph's Pads. Oops filed a bankruptcy petition two weeks later. Has Ralph's Pads received a preference? Consider §547(b)(5) carefully. Would it affect your answer if the bank handed the money over to Oops, which then sent it along to Ralph's? *See* In re Bohlen Enterprises, Ltd., 859 F.2d 561 (8th Cir. 1988), describing the so-called "earmarking doctrine" (which the court then declined to adopt), as follows:

> In every earmarking situation there are three necessary dramatis personae. They are the "old creditor" (the pre-existing creditor who is paid off within the 90-day period prior to bankruptcy), the "new creditor" or "new lender," who supplies the funds to pay off the old creditor, and the debtor.
>
> When new funds are provided by the new creditor to or for the benefit of the debtor for the purpose of paying the obligation owed to the old creditor, the funds are said to be "earmarked" and the payment is held not to be a voidable preference.

To answer upcoming Problem 7-11 you need to know something about letters of credit (which are regulated by Article 5 of the Uniform Commercial Code). Suppose you are the buyer of goods and you wish to order them from a seller in a remote location. The seller doesn't want to expend the effort and expense to send them to you and then have you not pay for them when they arrive. In this case the seller may make you agree to substitute a bank in your place as buyer so the seller can send the goods to the bank, which in turn will give them to you under whatever terms you and the bank have agreed to. To accomplish this you persuade your bank to issue a letter of credit to the seller. A letter of credit is just what it sounds like: a letter from the bank to the seller (called the "beneficiary") in which the bank agrees to pay the seller when the goods are sent, accompanied by various documents showing that the goods have been shipped as agreed. Of course, the bank will not do this for you (the "applicant") unless the bank is assured that you will repay it.

PROBLEM 7-11

Wonder Circus happened upon the chance to buy an elephant from Exotic Animal Imports of New York for $24,000 but the seller, to whom Wonder Circus already owed $15,000 in past due debts, demanded that the circus get a letter of credit for $39,000 in favor of Exotic Animal Imports. Wonder Circus went to its bank, Octopus National, and applied for a loan sufficient to cover this. ONB agreed to issue the letter of credit to Exotic Animal but required Wonder Circus to grant it a security interest in its circus equipment to secure the debt, which Wonder Circus did, and the bank promptly perfected its security interest by filing a financing statement in the appropriate place on the same day it sent the letter of credit to Exotic Animal. In the letter, the bank agreed to honor a draft drawn on it by Exotic Animal in the amount of $39,000 if the draft were accompanied by a bill of lading showing the shipment of the elephant in question to Wonder Circus. If the circus files for bankruptcy a few weeks later, is the transaction creating the security interest between the bank and the circus a preference? *See* §547(c)(1). When Exotic Animal delivers the elephant, presents the draft for $39,000 to the bank, and is paid, does it receive a preference? The payment, after all, was made by the bank out of the funds of the bank. Study the wording of §547(b) carefully; *see also* §550(a)(1); In re Compton Corp., 831 F.2d 586 (5th Cir. 1987).

PROBLEM 7-12

When World Wide Wickets, Inc., borrowed $200,000 from Finch National Bank, CEO J. B. Biggley himself guaranteed the repayment of this amount to the bank. When the company got into financial trouble, Biggley was worried about his personal liability on this debt, so he made sure that the company used its remaining meager assets to pay Finch National in full four months before World Wide Wickets filed its bankruptcy petition. The trustee in bankruptcy then attacked the payment as a preference using the following argument: Biggley is an insider (§101(31)) and is a creditor of World Wide Wickets by virtue of his rights of subrogation and reimbursement as a guarantor of the Finch debt. Therefore, the payment to Finch was "for the benefit of a creditor," the first requirement for a preference in §547(b)(1), allowing the trustee to recover any payments made that benefited Biggley in the year before the filing of the petition. Is this right? *See* §§547(i) and §550(c). Who is liable here?

B.   The Exceptions

Certain transactions would meet the definition of a preference even though they have nothing to do with the evil conduct that preference law was meant to undo. Thus subsection (c) of §547 lists nine transactions that are legislatively excused from attack as preferences. We next explore those exceptions.

PROBLEM 7-13

His financial life in ruin, Harold Debts went to the law offices of Angelina Barth and engaged her services to file his bankruptcy petition, agreeing to pay her $800 for handling his case. She insisted on payment up front, and he told her he could borrow that amount from his brother and have it in her hands the next day. That same day the two of them sat in her office and filled out the schedules using the computer program she had devised for this purpose, though he was missing certain records that he had failed to bring with him. The next day he brought in those records, along with a check for $800, and she finished filling out his schedules. The petition was filed later that afternoon, immediately after she had cashed his check. On learning this, Harold's trustee in bankruptcy wanted Angelina to cough up the $800, on the theory that she had received a preference. Is the trustee right? *See* §547(c)(1).

PROBLEM 7-14

In the three months before he filed his bankruptcy petition, Harold Debts paid his usual bills for electricity, credit cards, and the like. Are these payments preferences? *See* §547(c)(2).

PROBLEM 7-15

ZZZZ Best Co. borrowed $7 million from Union Bank and signed a long-term promissory note for that amount. ZZZZ made regular payments on that amount for several years, including the monthly payments for October through December of 2007. On January 3, 2008, ZZZZ filed a bankruptcy petition. The trustee has sued Union seeking to recover the payments it received from ZZZZ during the 90 days prior to the filing of the bankruptcy petition. Union is relying on the §547(c)(2) exception. Is that defense available for repayments on long-term loans? See the following case.

Union Bank v. Wolas

United States Supreme Court, 1991
502 U.S. 151

Justice STEVENS delivered the opinion of the Court.

Section 547(b) of the Bankruptcy Code, 11 U.S.C. §547(b), authorizes a trustee to avoid certain property transfers made by a debtor within 90 days before bankruptcy. The Code makes an exception, however, for transfers made in the ordinary course of business, §547(c)(2). The question presented is whether payments on long-term debt may qualify for that exception.

On December 17, 1986, ZZZZ Best Co., Inc. (Debtor), borrowed $7 million from petitioner, Union Bank (Bank).[3] On July 8, 1987, the Debtor filed a voluntary petition under Chapter 7 of the Bankruptcy Code. During the preceding 90-day period, the Debtor had made two interest payments totaling approximately $100,000 and had paid a loan commitment fee of about $2,500 to the Bank. After his appointment as trustee of the Debtor's estate, respondent filed a complaint against the Bank to recover those payments pursuant to §547(b).

The Bankruptcy Court found that the loans had been made "in the ordinary course of business or financial affairs" of both the Debtor and the Bank, and that both interest payments as well as the payment of the loan commitment fee had been made according to ordinary business terms and in the ordinary course of business. As a matter of law, the Bankruptcy Court concluded that the payments satisfied the requirements of §547(c)(2) and therefore were not avoidable by the trustee. The District Court affirmed the Bankruptcy Court's summary judgment in favor of the Bank.

Shortly thereafter, in another case, the Court of Appeals held that the ordinary course of business exception to avoidance of preferential transfers was not available to long-term creditors. In re CHG Intl., Inc., 897 F.2d 1479 (CA9 1990). In reaching that conclusion, the Court of Appeals relied primarily on the policies underlying the voidable preference provisions and the state of the law prior to the enactment of the 1978 Bankruptcy Code and its amendment in 1984. Thus, the Ninth Circuit concluded, its holding in CHG Intl., Inc., dictated a reversal in this case. 921 F.2d 968, 969 (1990). The importance of the question of law decided by the Ninth Circuit, coupled with the fact that the Sixth Circuit had interpreted §547(c)(2) in a contrary manner, In re Finn, 909 F.2d 903 (1990), persuaded us to grant the Bank's petition for certiorari. 500 U.S. 915, 111 S. Ct. 2009, 114 L. Ed. 2d 97 (1991).

---

3. The Bankruptcy Court found that the Bank and Debtor executed a revolving credit agreement on December 16, 1986, in which the Bank agreed to lend the Debtor $7 million in accordance with the terms of a promissory note to be executed and delivered by the Debtor. No. 87-13692 (Bkrtcy. Ct. C.D. Cal., Aug. 22, 1988), App. to Pet. for Cert. 12a. On December 17, 1986, the Debtor executed and delivered to the Bank a promissory note in the principal sum of $7 million. The promissory note provided that interest would be payable on a monthly basis and would accrue on the principal balance at a rate of 0.65 percent per annum in excess of the Bank's reference rate. Ibid.

I.

We shall discuss the history and policy of §547 after examining its text. In subsection (b), Congress broadly authorized bankruptcy trustees to "avoid any transfer of an interest of the debtor in property" if five conditions are satisfied and unless one of seven exceptions defined in subsection (c) is applicable. In brief, the five characteristics of a voidable preference are that it (1) benefit a creditor; (2) be on account of antecedent debt; (3) be made while the debtor was insolvent; (4) be made within 90 days before bankruptcy; and (5) enable the creditor to receive a larger share of the estate than if the transfer had not been made. Section 547 also provides that the debtor is presumed to have been insolvent during the 90-day period preceding bankruptcy. §547(f). In this case, it is undisputed that all five of the foregoing conditions were satisfied and that the interest and loan commitment fee payments were voidable preferences unless excepted by subsection (c)(2).

The most significant feature of subsection (c)(2) that is relevant to this case is the absence of any language distinguishing between long-term debt and short-term debt.

> The trustee may not avoid under this section a transfer —
>   . . . (2) to the extent that such transfer was —
>   (A) in payment of a debt incurred by the debtor in the ordinary course of business or financial affairs of the debtor and the transferee;
>   (B) made in the ordinary course of business or financial affairs of the debtor and the transferee; and
>   (C) made according to ordinary business terms.

Instead of focusing on the term of the debt for which the transfer was made, subsection (c)(2) focuses on whether the debt was incurred, and payment made, in the "ordinary course of business or financial affairs" of the debtor and transferee. Thus, the text provides no support for respondent's contention that §547(c)(2)'s coverage is limited to short-term debt, such as commercial paper or trade debt. Given the clarity of the statutory text, respondent's burden of persuading us that Congress intended to create or to preserve a special rule for long-term debt is exceptionally heavy. United States v. Ron Pair Enterprises, Inc., 489 U.S. 235, 241-242, 109 S. Ct. 1026, 1030-1031, 103 L. Ed. 2d 290 (1989). As did the Ninth Circuit, respondent relies on the history and the policies underlying the preference provision.

II.

The relevant history of §547 contains two chapters, one of which clearly supports, and the second of which is not inconsistent with, the Bank's literal reading of the statute. Section 547 was enacted in 1978 when Congress overhauled the Nation's bankruptcy laws. The section was amended in 1984. For purposes of the question presented in this case, the original version of §547 differed in one significant respect from the current version: it contained a provision that the ordinary course of business exception did not apply unless the payment was made within 45 days of the date the debt was incurred.[4] That provision presumably excluded most payments on long-term debt from the exception. In 1984 Congress repealed the 45-day limitation but did not substitute a comparable limitation. See Bankruptcy Amendments and Federal Judgeship Act of 1984, Pub. L. 98-353, §462(c), 98 Stat. 378.

Respondent contends that this amendment was intended to satisfy complaints by issuers of commercial paper and by trade creditors that regularly extended credit for periods of more than 45 days. Furthermore, respondent continues, there is no evidence in the legislative history that Congress intended to make the ordinary course of business exception available to conventional long-term lenders. Therefore, respondent argues, we should follow the analysis of the Ninth Circuit and read §547(c)(2) as protecting only short-term debt payments. *Cf.* In re CHG Intl., 897 F.2d, at 1484.

We need not dispute the accuracy of respondent's description of the legislative history of the 1984 amendment in order to reject his conclusion. For even if Congress adopted the 1984 amendment to redress particular problems of specific short-term creditors, it remains true that Congress redressed those problems by entirely deleting the time limitation in §547(c)(2). The fact that Congress may not have foreseen all of the consequences of a statutory enactment is not a sufficient reason for refusing to give effect to its plain meaning. Toibb v. Radloff, 501 U.S. 157, 164, 111 S. Ct. 2197, 2201, 115 L. Ed. 2d 145 (1991).

Respondent also relies on the history of voidable preferences prior to the enactment of the 1978 Bankruptcy Code. The text of the preference provision in the earlier Bankruptcy Act did not specifically include an exception for payments made in the ordinary course of business. The courts had, however, developed what is sometimes described as the "current expense" rule to cover situations in which a debtor's payments on the eve of bankruptcy did not diminish the net estate because tangible assets were obtained in exchange for the payment. *See* Marshall v. Florida Natl. Bank of Jacksonville, 112 F.2d 380, 382 (CA5 1940); 3 Collier on Bankruptcy ¶60.23, p. 873 (14th ed. 1977). Without such an exception, trade creditors and other suppliers of necessary goods and services might have been reluctant to extend even short-term credit and might have required advance payment instead, thus making it difficult for many companies in temporary distress to have remained in business. Respondent argues that Congress enacted §547(c)(2) in 1978 to codify that exception, and

---

4. As enacted in 1978, §547(c) provided, in relevant part:

> The trustee may not avoid under this section a transfer — . . .
> (2) to the extent that such transfer was —
> > (A) in payment of a debt incurred in the ordinary course of business or financial affairs of the debtor and the transferee;
> > (B) *made not later than 45 days after such debt was incurred*;
> > (C) made in the ordinary course of business or financial affairs of the debtor and the transferee; and
> > (D) made according to ordinary business terms.

92 Stat. 2598 (emphasis added).

therefore the Court should construe §547(c)(2) as limited to the confines of the current expense rule.

This argument is not compelling for several reasons. First, it is by no means clear that §547(c)(2) should be construed as the statutory analogue of the judicially crafted current expense rule because there are other exceptions in §547(c) that explicitly cover contemporaneous exchanges for new value. Those provisions occupy some (if not all) of the territory previously covered by the current expense rule. Nor has respondent directed our attention to any extrinsic evidence suggesting that Congress intended to codify the current expense rule in §547(c)(2).

The current expense rule developed when the statutory preference provision was significantly narrower than it is today. To establish a preference under the Bankruptcy Act, the trustee had to prove that the challenged payment was made at a time when the creditor had "reasonable cause to believe that the debtor [was] insolvent." 11 U.S.C. §96(b) (1976 ed.). When Congress rewrote the preference provision in the 1978 Bankruptcy Code, it substantially enlarged the trustee's power to avoid preferential transfers by eliminating the reasonable cause to believe requirement for transfers made within 90 days of bankruptcy and creating a presumption of insolvency during that period. *See* 11 U.S.C. §§547(b), (c)(2), (f); H.R. Rep. No. 95-595, p. 178 (1977), U.S. Code Cong. & Admin. News 1978, pp. 5787, 6138. At the same time, Congress created a new exception for transfers made in the ordinary course of business, 11 U.S.C. §547(c)(2). This exception was intended to "leave undisturbed normal financial relations, because it does not detract from the general policy of the preference section to discourage unusual action by either the debtor or his creditors during the debtor's slide into bankruptcy." H.R. Rep. No. 95-595, at 373, U.S. Code Cong. & Admin. News 1978, p. 6329.

In light of these substantial changes in the preference provision, there is no reason to assume that the justification for narrowly confining the "current expense" exception to trade creditors before 1978 should apply to the ordinary course of business exception under the 1978 Code. Instead, the fact that Congress carefully reexamined and entirely rewrote the preference provision in 1978 supports the conclusion that the text of §547(c)(2) as enacted reflects the deliberate choice of Congress.

III.

The Bank and the trustee agree that §547 is intended to serve two basic policies that are fairly described in the House Committee Report. The Committee explained:

> A preference is a transfer that enables a creditor to receive payment of a greater percentage of his claim against the debtor than he would have received if the transfer had not been made and he had participated in the distribution of the assets of the bankrupt estate. The purpose of the preference section is two-fold. First, by permitting the trustee to avoid prebankruptcy transfers that occur within a short period before bankruptcy, creditors are discouraged from racing to the courthouse to dismember the debtor during his slide into bankruptcy. The protection thus afforded the debtor often enables him to work his way out of a difficult financial situation through cooperation with all of his creditors. Second, and more important, the preference provisions facilitate

the prime bankruptcy policy of equality of distribution among creditors of the debtor. Any creditor that received a greater payment than others of his class is required to disgorge so that all may share equally. The operation of the preference section to deter "the race of diligence" of creditors to dismember the debtor before bankruptcy furthers the second goal of the preference section — that of equality of distribution.

Id., at 177-178, U.S. Code Cong. & Admin. News 1978, pp. 6137, 6138.

As this comment demonstrates, the two policies are not entirely independent. On the one hand, any exception for a payment on account of an antecedent debt tends to favor the payee over other creditors and therefore may conflict with the policy of equal treatment. On the other hand, the ordinary course of business exception may benefit all creditors by deterring the "race to the courthouse" and enabling the struggling debtor to continue operating its business.

Respondent places primary emphasis, as did the Court of Appeals, on the interest in equal distribution. *See* In re CHG Intl., 897 F.2d, at 1483-1485. When a debtor is insolvent, a transfer to one creditor necessarily impairs the claims of the debtor's other unsecured and undersecured creditors. By authorizing the avoidance of such preferential transfers, §547(b) empowers the trustee to restore equal status to all creditors. Respondent thus contends that the ordinary course of business exception should be limited to short-term debt so the trustee may order that preferential long-term debt payments be returned to the estate to be distributed among all of the creditors.

But the statutory text — which makes no distinction between short-term debt and long-term debt — precludes an analysis that divorces the policy of favoring equal distribution from the policy of discouraging creditors from racing to the courthouse to dismember the debtor. Long-term creditors, as well as trade creditors, may seek a head start in that race. Thus, even if we accept the Court of Appeals' conclusion that the availability of the ordinary business exception to long-term creditors does not directly further the policy of equal treatment, we must recognize that it does further the policy of deterring the race to the courthouse and, as the House Report recognized, may indirectly further the goal of equal distribution as well. Whether Congress has wisely balanced the sometimes conflicting policies underlying §547 is not a question that we are authorized to decide.

IV.

In sum, we hold that payments on long-term debt, as well as payments on short-term debt, may qualify for the ordinary course of business exception to the trustee's power to avoid preferential transfers. We express no opinion, however, on the question whether the Bankruptcy Court correctly concluded that the Debtor's payments of interest and the loan commitment fee qualify for the ordinary course of business exception, §547(c)(2). In particular, we do not decide whether the loan involved in this case was incurred in the ordinary course of the Debtor's business and of the Bank's business, whether the payments were made in the ordinary course of business, or whether the payments were made according to ordinary business terms. These questions remain open for the Court of Appeals on remand.

The judgment of the Court of Appeals is reversed, and the case is remanded for further proceedings consistent with this opinion.

It is so ordered.

Justice SCALIA, concurring.

I join the opinion of the Court, including Parts II and III, which respond persuasively to legislative-history and policy arguments made by respondent. It is regrettable that we have a legal culture in which such arguments have to be addressed (and are indeed credited by a Court of Appeals), with respect to a statute utterly devoid of language that could remotely be thought to distinguish between long-term and short-term debt. Since there was here no contention of a "scrivener's error" producing an absurd result, the plain text of the statute should have made this litigation unnecessary and unmaintainable.

PROBLEM 7-16

As Luddite Technologies fell on harder and harder times it had increasing trouble paying its bills, including creditors, payroll, and the IRS. Its creditors came to accept the fact that Luddite would make payments 10 to 20 days late as a routine matter. This went on for years before Luddite finally filed its bankruptcy petition. When its trustee in bankruptcy demanded the return of the payments made within 90 days of the filing of the petition, the routine creditors took refuge in §547(c)(2), only to be hit with the argument that *late* payments are hardly in the *ordinary* course of business. What will be the result? *See* In re Grand Chevrolet, Inc., 25 F.3d 728 (9th Cir. 1994); In re Tennessee Chemical Corp., 112 F.3d 234 (6th Cir. 1997).

In re Tolona Pizza Products Corp.

United States Court of Appeals, Seventh Circuit, 1993
3 F.3d 1029

POSNER, Circuit Judge.

When, within 90 days before declaring bankruptcy, the debtor makes a payment to an unsecured creditor, the payment is a "preference," and the trustee in bankruptcy can recover it and thus make the creditor take pot luck with the rest of the debtor's unsecured creditors. 11 U.S.C. §547. But there is an exception if the creditor can show that the debt had been incurred in the ordinary course of the business of both the debtor and the creditor, §547(c)(2)(A); that the payment, too, had been made and received in the ordinary course of their businesses, §547(c)(2)(B); and that the payment had been "made according to ordinary business terms." §547(c)(2)(C). The first two requirements are easy to understand: of course to defeat the inference of preferential treatment the debt must have been incurred in the ordinary course of business of both debtor and creditor and the payment on account of the debt must have been in the ordinary course as well. But what does the third requirement — that the payment have been "made according to ordinary business terms" — add? And in particular does it refer to what is "ordinary" between this debtor and this creditor, or what is ordinary in the market or industry in which they operate? The circuits are divided on this question, *compare* In re Fred Hawes Organization, Inc., 957 F.2d 239, 243-44 (6th Cir. 1992), and WJM, Inc. v. Massachusetts Dept. of Public Welfare, 840 F.2d 996, 1011 (1st Cir. 1988), *with* Lovett v. St. Johnsbury Trucking, 931 F.2d 494, 499 (8th Cir. 1991); J.P. Fyfe, Inc. v. Bradco Supply Corp., 891 F.2d 66, 71 n.5 (3d Cir. 1989), *and* In re Craig Oil Co., 785 F.2d 1563, 1565 (11th Cir. 1986) (per curiam), the scholarly literature inconclusive, 4 Collier on Bankruptcy ¶547.10 at p. 547-50 (Lawrence P. King 15th ed. 1993); Vern Countryman, The Concept of a Voidable Preference in Bankruptcy, 38 Vand. L. Rev. 713, 772-73 (1985); David J. DeSimone, Section 547(c)(2) of the Bankruptcy Code: The Ordinary Course of Business Exception Without the 45 Day Rule, 20 Akron L. Rev. 95, 123-28 (1986); Lissa Lamkin Broome, Payments on Long-Term Debt as Voidable Preferences: The Impact of the 1984 Bankruptcy Amendments, 1987 Duke L.J. 78, 86, our court undecided, In re Xonics Imaging, Inc., 837 F.2d 763, 766 (7th Cir. 1988); In re Excello Press, Inc., 967 F.2d 1109, 1114 (7th Cir. 1992), the bankruptcy judges divided. Id.

Tolona, a maker of pizza, issued eight checks to Rose, its sausage supplier, within 90 days before being thrown into bankruptcy by its creditors. The checks, which totaled a shade under $46,000, cleared and as a result Tolona's debts to Rose were paid in full. Tolona's other major trade creditors stand to receive only 13 cents on the dollar under the plan approved by the bankruptcy court, if the preferential treatment of Rose is allowed to stand. Tolona, as debtor in possession, brought an adversary proceeding against Rose to recover the eight payments as voidable preferences. The bankruptcy judge entered judgment for Tolona. The district judge reversed. He thought that Rose did not, in order to comply with section 547(c)(2)(C), have to prove that the terms on which it had extended credit to Tolona were standard terms in the industry, but that if this was wrong the testimony of Rose's executive vice-president, Stiehl, did prove it. The parties agree that the other requirements of section 547(c)(2) were satisfied.

Rose's invoices recited "net 7 days," meaning that payment was due within seven days. For years preceding the preference period, however, Tolona rarely paid within seven days; nor did Rose's other customers. Most paid within 21 days, and if they paid later than 28 or 30 days Rose would usually withhold future shipments until payment was received. Tolona, however, as an old and valued customer (Rose had been selling to it for fifteen years), was permitted to make payments beyond the 21-day period and even beyond the 28-day or 30-day period. The eight payments at issue were made between 12 and 32 days after Rose had invoiced Tolona, for an average of 22 days; but this actually was an improvement. In the 34 months before the preference period, the average time for which Rose's invoices to Tolona were outstanding was 26 days and the longest time was 46 days. Rose consistently treated Tolona with a degree of leniency that made Tolona (Stiehl conceded on cross-examination) one of a "sort of exceptional group of customers of Rose . . . fall[ing] outside the common industry practice and standards."

It may seem odd that paying a debt late would ever be regarded as a preference to the creditor thus paid belatedly. But it is all relative. A debtor who has entered the preference period — who is therefore only 90 days, or fewer, away from plunging into bankruptcy — is typically unable to pay all his outstanding debts in full as they come due. If he pays one and not the others, as happened here, the payment though late is still a preference to that creditor, and is avoidable unless the conditions of section 547(c)(2) are met. One condition is that payment be in the ordinary course of both the debtor's and the creditor's business. A late payment normally will not be. It will therefore be an avoidable preference.

This is not a dryly syllogistic conclusion. The purpose of the preference statute is to prevent the debtor during his slide toward bankruptcy from trying to stave off the evil day by giving preferential treatment to his most importunate creditors, who may sometimes be those who have been waiting longest to be paid. Unless the favoring of particular creditors is outlawed, the mass of creditors of a shaky firm will be nervous, fearing that one or a few of their number are going to walk away with all the firm's assets; and this fear may precipitate debtors into bankruptcy earlier than is socially desirable. In re Xonics Imaging, Inc., *supra*, 837 F.2d at 765; In re Fred Hawes Organization, Inc., *supra*, 957 F.2d at 243 n.5.

From this standpoint, however, the most important thing is not that the dealings between the debtor and the allegedly favored creditor conform to some industry norm but that they conform to the norm established by the debtor and the creditor in the period before, preferably well before, the preference period. That condition is satisfied here — if anything, Rose treated Tolona more favorably (and hence Tolona treated Rose less preferentially) before the preference period than during it.

But if this is all that the third subsection of 547(c)(2) requires, it might seem to add nothing to the first two subsections, which require that both the debt and the payment be within the ordinary course of business of both the debtor and the creditor. For, provided these conditions are fulfilled, a "late" payment really isn't late if the parties have established a practice that deviates from the strict terms of their written contract. But we hesitate to conclude that the third subsection, requiring conformity to "ordinary business terms," has no function in the statute. We can think of two functions that it might have. One is evidentiary. In re Loretto Winery, Ltd., 107 B.R. 707, 710 (9th Cir. BAP 1989); In re Morren Meat & Poultry Co., 92 B.R. 737, 740-41 (W.D. Mich. 1988); DeSimone, *supra*, at 127-28. If the debtor and creditor dealt on terms that the creditor testifies were normal for them but that are wholly unknown in the industry, this casts some doubt on his (self-serving) testimony. Preferences are disfavored, and subsection C makes them more difficult to prove. The second possible function of the subsection is to allay the concerns of creditors that one or more of their number may have worked out a special deal with the debtor, before the preference period, designed to put that creditor ahead of the others in the event of bankruptcy. It may seem odd that allowing late payments from a debtor would be a way for a creditor to make himself more rather than less assured of repayment. But such a creditor does have an advantage during the preference period, because he can receive late payments then and they will still be in the ordinary course of business for him and his debtor.

The functions that we have identified, combined with a natural reluctance to cut out and throw away one-third of an important provision of the Bankruptcy Code, persuade us that the creditor must show that the payment he received was made in accordance with the ordinary business terms in the industry. But this does not mean that the creditor must establish the existence of some single, uniform set of business terms, as Tolona argues. DeSimone, *supra*, at 127. Not only is it difficult to identify the industry whose norm shall govern (is it, here, the sale of sausages to makers of pizza? The sale of sausages to anyone? The sale of anything to makers of pizza?), but there can be great variance in billing practices within an industry. Apparently there is in this industry, whatever exactly "this industry" is; for while it is plain that neither Rose nor its competitors enforce payment within seven days, it is unclear that there is a standard outer limit of forbearance. It seems that 21 days is a goal but that payment as late as 30 days is generally tolerated and that for good customers even longer delays are allowed. The average period between Rose's invoice and Tolona's payment during the preference period was only 22 days, which seems well within the industry norm, whatever exactly it is. The law should not push businessmen to agree upon a single set of billing practices; antitrust objections to one side, the relevant business and financial considerations vary widely among firms on both the buying and the selling side of the market.

We conclude that "ordinary business terms" refers to the *range* of terms that encompasses the practices in which firms similar in some general way to the creditor in question engage, and that only dealings so idiosyncratic as to fall outside that broad range should be deemed extraordinary and therefore outside the scope of subsection C. In re SPW Corp., 96 B.R. 676, 681-82 (Bankr. N.D. Tex. 1989); In re White, 64 B.R. 843, 850 (Bankr. E.D. Tenn. 1986); In re Economy Milling Co., 37 B.R. 914, 922 (D.S.C. 1983). Stiehl's testimony brought the case within the scope of "ordinary business terms" as just defined. Rose and its competitors pay little or no attention to the terms stated on their invoices, allow most customers to take up to 30 days to pay, and allow certain favored customers to take even more time. There is no single set of terms on which the members of the industry have coalesced; instead there is a broad range and the district judge plausibly situated the dealings between Rose and Tolona within it. These dealings are conceded to have been within the normal course of dealings between the two firms, a course established long before the preference period, and there is no hint either that the dealings were designed to put Rose ahead of other creditors of Tolona or that other creditors of Tolona would have been surprised to learn that Rose had been so forbearing in its dealings with Tolona.

Tolona might have argued that the district judge gave insufficient deference to the bankruptcy judge's contrary finding. The district judge, and we, are required to accept the bankruptcy judge's findings on questions of fact as long as they are not clearly erroneous. Fed. R. Bankr. P. 8013; In re Bonnett, 895 F.2d 1155, 1157 (7th Cir. 1989). But since Tolona did not argue that the district judge had applied an incorrect standard of review, we need not decide whether the district judge overstepped the bounds. Which is not to say that he did. While he did not intone the magic words "clear error," he may well have believed that the record as a whole left no doubt that Tolona's dealings with Rose were within the broad band of accepted practices in the industry. It is true that Stiehl testified that Tolona was one of an exceptional group of Rose's customers with whom Rose's dealings fell outside common industry practice. But the undisputed evidence concerning those dealings and the practices of the industry demonstrates that payment within 30 days is within the outer limits of normal industry practices, and the payments at issue in this case were made on average in a significantly shorter time.

The judgment reversing the bankruptcy judge and dismissing the adversary proceeding is AFFIRMED.

[The dissenting opinion of Judge Flaum, disagreeing with the majority's reading of the facts, is omitted.]

QUESTION

The 2005 amendments make the §547(c)(2) elements disjunctive. Would that change Judge Posner's analysis in any significant way?

Purchase Money Security Interests. Our law has always struggled to protect a purchase money creditor, one whose credit advance permits the debtor to acquire the property (i.e., the seller on credit or the lender who advances the purchase price to the buyer — *see* U.C.C. §9-103). Article 9 of the Uniform Commercial Code gives such a creditor a 20-day grace period from the debtor's first possession of the collateral in which to perfect a purchase money security interest and have a relation back to the moment of the debtor's possession so as to beat out other creditors; *see* U.C.C. §§9-317(e) and 9-324(a). In §547(c)(3), the Bankruptcy Code grants similar relief to purchase money creditors who would otherwise be deemed to have received a preference, though it expands the period to 30 days.

PROBLEM 7-17

The Happy Earwig Motel needed to buy 50 new beds, and it arranged to borrow the $15,000 it needed for this purpose from Security State Bank. The parties signed a security agreement and financing statement using the beds themselves as collateral for the loan. The bank loaned the motel the $15,000 on October 1, and Happy Earwig bought the beds six weeks later on November 11. The bank filed its financing statement in the appropriate place on November 12, and Happy Earwig filed its bankruptcy petition two weeks after that. If §547(c)(3) were not relevant, would the bank's perfection on November 12 have been a preference?

Subsequent advance rule. Under the now-replaced Bankruptcy Act, many courts recognized a "net result rule" which operated to reduce the amount of preferences by the amount of any other value given to the debtor by the preferred creditor during the preference period. The Bankruptcy Code carries this principle forward in a limited fashion under §547(c)(4). Rather than adopting the "net result rule," however, §547(c)(4) creates a "subsequent advance" rule. This protection is more limited than the protection available under the net result rule because it only offers protection to the extent that the new value was given to the debtor *after* the creditor received the preferential transfer. The subsequent transfer essentially replenishes the debtor's estate by eliminating some of the previous preferential transfer. *See* In re Fulghum Constr. Corp., 706 F.2d 171 (6th Cir. 1983).

PROBLEM 7-18

When Last National Bank, an unsecured creditor, pressed a debtor, Pestle Drugstore, for payment of the store's outstanding $75,000 debt, Pestle sent the bank a check for $30,000 on August 1. Encouraged by this, Last National loaned the debtor $10,000 on August 15, which amount the debtor repaid on September 1. On September 15, the drugstore borrowed $15,000 more from the bank, granting the bank a security interest in its inventory, though the bank never got around to filing its financing statement covering this transaction before the drugstore filed a Chapter 7 petition on October 2. Assume that the only part of subsection (c) in §547 that can help the bank here is §547(c)(4). What amount can the trustee recover from the bank? *Cf.* §544(a).

In re Roberds, Inc.

United States Bankruptcy Court, Southern District of Ohio, 2004
315 B.R. 443

THOMAS F. WALDRON, Chief Judge.

Background

On December 26, 2001, Roberds, Inc., the Debtor and Debtor in Possession (Debtor), filed a complaint against Broyhill Furniture (Creditor) to recover thirty-two allegedly preferential transfers totaling $2,797,806.71. (Doc. 1) Count I sought to avoid these transfers pursuant to 11 U.S.C. §547(b); Count II sought to avoid these transfers pursuant to Ohio law ("11 U.S.C. §544(b) and O.R.C. §1313.56 et seq."); Count III sought recovery of the transfers pursuant to 11 U.S.C. §550; and Count IV sought to disallow, pursuant to 11 U.S.C. §502(d), any claim of the Creditor until all preferential transfers were recovered. On May 6, 2002, the Creditor filed an answer generally denying the transfers were preferential and asserting affirmative defenses. (Doc. 7) After an Initial Status Conference, extensive discovery and a series of subsequent pretrial conferences, the trial in this adversary proceeding was scheduled for August 30, 2004. (Doc. 31) On July 23, 2004, the Creditor filed a Motion For Partial Summary Judgment (Doc. 55), which sought to dismiss Count II of the Debtor's Complaint-seeking recovery "under 11 U.S.C. §544(b), Ohio Revised Code §§1313.56 and 1313.57 and other applicable law." The Motion was granted resulting in a dismissal of the state law claim. Roberds, Inc. v. Broyhill Furniture (In re Roberds, Inc.), 313 B.R. 732 (Bankr. S.D. Ohio 2004). . . .

III. The Subsequent New Value Issue

Under 11 U.S.C. §547(c)(4), can the Creditor assert, as a defense to a preference payment, subsequent new value when: (1) the subsequent new value was given to the Debtor (prior to the filing of the bankruptcy and subsequent to a preference payment); (2) the subsequent new value given to the Debtor was repaid by the Debtor to the Creditor; and (3) the Debtor's repayment of the subsequent new value can ultimately be avoided (is not ultimately found to be "otherwise unavoidable") by the Debtor?

11 U.S.C. §547(c)(4) states that:

> The trustee may not avoid under this section a transfer to or for the benefit of a creditor, to the extent that, after such transfer, such creditor gave new value to or for the benefit of the debtor —
>> (A) not secured by an otherwise unavoidable security interest; and
>> (B) on account of which new value the debtor did not make an otherwise unavoidable transfer to or for the benefit of such creditor[.]

The Creditor has asserted the defense of subsequent new value. This affirmative defense is based on the premise that if a creditor receives a preference, but subsequently supplies new value (in this adversary proceeding, furniture) to the debtor, this subsequent new value should be a defense to the preference. The policy is that the creditor, having replenished the debtor's estate so that there has been no overall diminution in the estate, has not, in reality, been preferred by the debtor.

The reported decisions establish that this arguably simple policy has proven less than simple in application. The text of 11 U.S.C. §547(c)(4)(B) contains a double-negative and it has been noted this may have contributed to confusion in interpreting the statutory language. *See* Boyd v. The Water Doctor (In re Check Reporting Srvs., Inc.), 140 B.R. 425, 434 (Bankr. W.D. Mich. 1992). Two distinct methods of determining the appropriate amount of subsequent new value exist in the current case law. Depending on the facts of a particular adversary proceeding, the methodology utilized can produce dramatically different results. The Sixth Circuit Court of Appeals has not addressed, nor has this court ruled on, this question of statutory interpretation.

Before reviewing the two methodologies, it is important to note the binding requirement that this court must apply the plain meaning of the statutory language, unless it is the rare instance in which a "literal application of the statute will produce a result demonstrably at odds with the intentions of its drafters." United States v. Ron Pair Enters., Inc., 489 U.S. 235, 242, 109 S. Ct. 1026, 1031, 103 L. Ed. 2d 290 (1989). In those rare instances, the intention of the drafters is paramount. Id.

The Debtor argued that "paid" new value cannot be allowed as an affirmative defense to a preferential transfer. This argument asserts that if a creditor received a transfer determined to be a preference, then subsequently provides new value, if, after the creditor has provided this subsequent new value, the creditor receives an additional transfer from the debtor, that additional transfer reduces the subsequent new value defense to the original preference, because, in the nomenclature of this position in the case law, the new value provided by the creditor has been "paid" by the debtor. It, of course, must be recognized the word "paid" is not present in the text of the statute.

The Creditor argued that paid new value may be an affirmative defense to a preference if, in the text of the statute, the debtor, in the repayment of the subsequent new value, did not make "an otherwise unavoidable transfer." Under the line of cases the Creditor advances, the key question (without the confusing double-negative in the statute) is simply: Did the Debtor, in repaying the subsequent new value provided by the Creditor, repay with a transfer that ultimately can be avoided by the Debtor? If that repayment by the Debtor ultimately can be avoided, the Creditor argues the subsequent new value provided should still be allowed as a defense. As will be further explained, the court agrees with the line of cases which adopt this view.

The difference in the parties' positions, reflecting the two opposing lines of authority, can be illustrated by a simple example:

- The debtor pays the creditor $50 on an open account
- Subsequently, the creditor advances the Debtor $20 worth of goods
- Thereafter, the debtor pays the creditor $20 on the open account
- Subsequently, the creditor advances the debtor $30 worth of goods
- The debtor files bankruptcy

Under the Debtor's position, a creditor can provide subsequent new value, but the subsequent new value must remain unpaid and, in the above example, the first $20 advance by the creditor was repaid, so it is not considered subsequent new value. The second advance by the creditor remains unpaid so it is considered subsequent new value. Accordingly, the net preference total is $70 ($50, plus $20, paid by the debtor on the open account), minus $30 in subsequent new value paid to the debtor by the creditor, for a net total preference of $40.

Under the Creditor's position, a creditor can assert subsequent new value as a defense, even if it is paid by the debtor, as long as that payment can be ultimately avoided (typically, recoverable as a preference because it meets the elements of §547(b) and is not subject to any of the other §547(c) defenses) by the debtor. Again, in the above example, the $20 advance by the creditor has been repaid; but, if that repayment to the creditor is ultimately avoided by the debtor (again, typically because the repayment is recoverable as a preference because it meets the elements of §547(b) and is not subject to any of the other §547(c) defenses), the paid subsequent new value must be counted as subsequent new value. Thus, the $70 ($50, plus $20) in preference payments is offset by $50 in advances by the creditor (the $30 unpaid advance and also the $20 advance, which was paid by the Debtor, but can ultimately be avoided by the debtor) and the net total preference amount subject to recovery is $20, not $40.

The position that "new value must remain unpaid" is followed by the Third, Seventh and Eleventh Circuits. The position that new value which, restated without the double-negative, is "otherwise avoidable" is a proper affirmative defense under the language of 11 U.S.C. §547(c)(4)(B) is followed by the Fifth, Eighth and Ninth Circuits. See also Check Reporting Svcs., 140 B.R. at 430-44.

In Mosier v. Ever-Fresh Food Co. (In re IRFM, Inc.), 52 F.3d 228 (9th Cir. 1995), the court reviewed the two competing analyses of the 11 U.S.C. §547(c)(4)(B):

> Courts and commentators agree that the exception contains two key elements. First, the creditor must give unsecured new value and, second, this new value must be given after the preferential transfer. See In re Fulghum Constr. Corp., 706 F.2d 171, 172 (6th Cir.) cert. denied, 464 U.S. 935, 104 S. Ct. 342, 343, 78 L. Ed. 2d 310 (1983). The majority of courts have also adopted a short hand approach to section 547(c)(4)(B) and hold that section 547(c)(4) contains a third element, that the new value must remain unpaid. The Eighth Circuit recently followed this approach in In re Kroh Bros. Dev. Co., 930 F.2d 648, 653 (8th Cir. 1991) (creditor who has been paid for the new value by the debtor may not assert a new value defense). See also In re New York City Shoes, Inc., 880 F.2d 679, 680 (3d Cir. 1989); In re Jet Florida Sys., Inc., 841 F.2d 1082, 1083 (11th Cir. 1988); In the Matter of Prescott, 805 F.2d 719, 731 (7th Cir. 1986).
>
> The rationale for this position is (1) if new value has been repaid by the debtor, the estate has not been replenished and; (2) the creditor is permitted the double benefit of a new value defense and the repayment of the new value. See Kroh Bros., 930 F.2d at 652. However, focusing only on the issue of whether the new value is unpaid may lead to some absurd results, as Mosier's position demonstrates. As a result, an emerging trend has developed where a few courts have reached the contrary result and hold that new value need not remain unpaid. See In re Ladera Heights Comm. Hosp., Inc., 152 B.R. 964, 968 (Bankr. C.D. Cal. 1993).
>
> However, an even more recent trend has developed where courts and commentators have rejected the shorthand approach and have undertaken a more thorough analysis of the language of section 547(c)(4)(B). These cases reason that the numerous decisions focusing on the narrow issue of whether the new value remains unpaid are incomplete and inaccurate. In the Matter of Toyota of Jefferson, Inc., 14 F.3d 1088, 1093 n.2 (5th Cir.1994); In re PNP Holdings Corp., 167 B.R. 619, 629 (Bankr. W.D. Wash. 1994); In re Check Reporting Servs., Inc., 140 B.R. 425, 431-34 (Bankr. W.D. Mich. 1992).
>
> According to this view, the proper inquiry directed by section 547(c)(4)(B) is whether the new value has been paid for by "an otherwise unavoidable transfer." In the Matter of Toyota of Jefferson, 14 F.3d at 1093 n.2. This inquiry follows the *Kroh Bros.* rationale that a creditor should not get double credit for an advance of new value. However, instead of barring the new value defense altogether anytime new value has been repaid, this approach allows the new value defense if the trustee can recover the repayment by some other means.
>
> This analysis fully comports with the statute's plain language. While the phrase "the debtor did not make an otherwise unavoidable transfer" is complicated, it is not ambiguous and its meaning is easily discernible. See Check Reporting Servs., 140 B.R. at 434-36 (conducting an exhaustive analysis of the phrase "did not make an otherwise unavoidable transfer"). As one commentator has explained:
>
>> If the debtor has made payments for goods or services that the creditor supplied on unsecured credit after an earlier preference, *and if these subsequent payments are themselves voidable as preferences* (or on any other ground), then under section 547(c)(4)(B) the creditor should be able to invoke those unsecured credit extensions as a defense to the recovery of the earlier voidable preference. On the other hand, the debtor's subsequent payments might not be voidable on any other ground and not voidable under section 547, because the goods and services were given C.O.D. rather than on a credit, or because the creditor has a defense under

section 547(c)(1), (2), or (3). In this situation, the creditor may keep his payments but has no section 547(c)(4) defense to the trustee's action to recover the earlier preference. In either event, the creditor gets credit only once for goods and services later supplied.

Vern Countryman, The Concept of a Voidable Preference in Bankruptcy, 38 Vand. L. Rev. 713, 788 (1985) (emphasis added and footnotes omitted) (quoted in In the Matter of Toyota of Jefferson, Inc., 14 F.3d at 1092-93).

We agree with this analysis and hold that a new value defense is permitted unless the debtor repays the new value by a transfer which is otherwise unavoidable.

Id. at 231-32. Similarly, the Eighth Circuit has stated:

Section 547(c)(4)(B) defines subsequent new value as value not offset by "an *otherwise unavoidable transfer*" to the creditor. Here, [the creditor] received weekly payments made after employees provided subsequent new value, but those payments were "otherwise *avoidable*" and therefore cannot deprive [the creditor] of §547(c)(4) protection." (emphasis in original)

Jones Truck Lines, Inc v. Central States (In re Jones Truck Lines, Inc.), 130 F.3d 323, 329 (8th Cir. 1997).

The Fifth Circuit adopted this text based approach and noted that the axiom "subsequent new value must remain unpaid," restated in earlier circuit decisions, does not accurately describe the plain meaning of the statute:

Some of our sister circuits have, in dicta, described §547(c)(4)(B) as requiring the subsequent advance to go "unpaid." *See* In re Kroh Brothers, 930 F.2d at 652; New York City Shoes, Inc. v. Bentley Int'l, Inc. (In re New York City Shoes, Inc.), 880 F.2d 679, 680 (3d Cir. 1989); Charisma Inv. Co., N.V. v. Airport Sys., Inc. (In re Jet Florida Sys., Inc.), 841 F.2d 1082, 1083 (11th Cir. 1988); In re Prescott, 805 F.2d 719, 731 (7th Cir. 1986). Although this description may be an adequate shorthand description of §547(c)(4)(B), a more complete statement of the (c)(4) exception would be that a creditor who raises it has the burden of proving that (1) new value was extended after the preferential payment sought to be avoided, (2) the new value is not secured with an otherwise unavoidable security interest, and (3) the new value has not been repaid with an otherwise unavoidable transfer. *Cf.* In re Prescott, 805 F.2d at 731 ("The creditor that raises a 'subsequent advance' defense has the burden of establishing that new value was extended, which remains unsecured and unpaid after the preferential transfer.").

Laker v. Vallette (In re Toyota of Jefferson, Inc.), 14 F.3d 1088, 1093, fn. 2 (5th Cir. 1994); *Accord* Norton Bankruptcy Law and Practice 2d, §57.20, Page 57-112-14 (June 2004) ("There is a split of authority whether [the 547(c)(4)] exception requires that new value remain unpaid. . . . The resolution of this conflict is found in the Code itself. . . . The focus of the inquiry is on the avoidability of the debtor's subsequent payments, and not on whether the new value remains unpaid."; (footnotes omitted)); *See also* Deborah Thorne and Jesus E. Batista, Are All Creditor "Animals" Equal: Treatment of New Value Under §547, 23 APR Am. Bankr. Inst. J. 22 (April 2004); Robert H. Bowmar, The New Value Exception To The Trustee's Preference Avoidance Power: Getting The Computation Straight, 69 Am. Bankr. L.J. 65 (Winter 1995); Harris Quinn, The Subsequent New Value Exception Under Section 547(c)(4) of the Bankruptcy Code — Judicial Gloss Is Creditors' Loss, 22 Mem. State L. Rev. 667

(Summer 1994) (All three articles concluding that the "new value must remain unpaid" axiom does not comport with the plain meaning of §547(c)(4)).

In reviewing the circuit decisions relied on by the Debtor, this court notes these decisions state the axiom "new value must remain unpaid" as a shorthand, in dicta, or, to the extent these decisions represent the holdings of particular circuits, without an application of the plain meaning of the statutory language. *See* New York City Shoes, Inc. v. Bentley Int'l, Inc. (In re New York Shoes, Inc.), 880 F.2d 679 (3rd Cir. 1989); Charisma Inv. Co. v. Airport Sys., Inc. (In re Jet Florida Sys., Inc.), 841 F.2d 1082 (11th Cir. 1988) (new value must remain unpaid); In re Prescott, 805 F.2d 719 (7th Cir. 1986) (new value must remain unpaid). Without exhaustively reviewing all the lower court cases discussing this issue, the court determines that very few recent lower court decisions, which are clearly not bound by a particular circuit's ruling, have followed the "new value must remain unpaid" axiom. *See*, e.g., Claybrook v. SOL Bldg. Materials Corp. (In re U.S. Wood Products, Inc.), 2004 WL 870830, *3 (Bankr. D. Del. Apr. 22, 2004) (Bankruptcy court followed the *New York Shoes* decision.)

The court adopts the legal interpretation of 11 U.S.C. §547(c)(4)(B) that "paid" subsequent new value may be an affirmative defense to a preferential transfer if the subsequent new value is, stated without the double-negative, "otherwise avoidable" by the debtor. The court finds this approach follows the plain meaning of the statutory language and also meets the policy objective of Congress when the affirmative defense was enacted. *See* Chrysler Credit Corp. v. Hall, 312 B.R. 797, 805 (E.D. Va. 2004) (Court finding the "otherwise avoidable" approach is supported by the plain meaning of the statutory language and the policy of §547(c)(4)).

The court notes that any valid subsequent new value payment [as long as it is pre-petition — *See* TennOhio Transp. Co. v. Felco Comm. Servs. (In re TennOhio Transp. Co.), 255 B.R. 307, 310 (Bankr. S.D. Ohio 2000)] can reduce any prior preference payment; it need not be the immediate prior preference. It has been persuasively rejected that new value can only offset the immediately preceding preference. This analysis, usually referred to as the Leathers approach [*See* Leathers v. Prime Leather Finishes Co., 40 B.R. 248 (D. Me. 1984)], has been rejected in favor of a better reasoned approach, which allows new value to be carried over to any prior preference, rather than only the immediately preceding one. *See* Thomas W. Garland, Inc. v. Union Elec. Co. (In re Thomas W. Garland, Inc.), 19 B.R. 920 (Bankr. E.D. Mo. 1982). The *Leathers* approach appears to have almost no viability left in the case law. *See* Slone-Stiver v. Clemens Oil (In re Tower Metal Alloy Co.), 193 B.R. 273, 275-76 (Bankr. S.D. Ohio 1996).

It is important to recognize, under the analysis this court adopts, a creditor cannot receive a windfall or double benefit. If subsequent new value given by a creditor is paid with a subsequent advance from the debtor and this payment is subject to another affirmative defense (such as ordinary course of business, for example) which would make the payment "otherwise unavoidable," then the paid new value given cannot be used as an affirmative defense to any prior preferential transfer.

The Debtor argued that counting paid new value is unfair to debtors because it allows new value to be counted where the new value provided is no longer an unpaid receivable on its books. *See* Iannacone v. Klement Sausage Co., Inc. (In re Hancock-Nelson Mercantile Co., Inc.), 122 B.R. 1006, 1016-17 (Bankr. D. Minn. 1991). This argument ignores the plain meaning of the statutory language. Even if such a policy argument could be considered, it views new value analysis as a static formula that can be determined without regard to whether the paid new value will ultimately be returned to the debtor. *See* Official Cmte. of Unsecured Creditors v. American Sterilizer (In re Comptronix Corp.), 239 B.R. 357, 363 (Bankr. M.D. Tenn. 1999). The statutory language does not allow the new value exception without consideration of the viability of other defenses to preferential transfers. It is also true, as the Debtor notes, this approach is somewhat more complex because it requires the court to analyze other available defenses to paid new value first; however, this policy argument, valid or not, is not an acceptable reason to avoid applying the plain meaning of the statutory language.

In this instance, the court has determined that the checks dated from December 6, 1999 until December 29, 1999 are otherwise unavoidable — that is, these payments are not subject to any other affirmative defenses. Therefore, considering the remaining transfers as preferential, but subject to the subsequent new value defense, the following chart represents the net preference:

Invoice Ship Date	Subsequent Net Value Amount	Check Number	Check Date	Check Amount	Payment Received at the Lockbox	Net Preference
		118797	12/6/99	$42,466,12	12/13/99	$42,406.12
12/10/99	$76,845.00					0
12/11/99	$9,825.00					0
12/13/99	$13,513.00					0
		118966	12/8/99	$110,242.80	12/13/99	$110,242.86
12/14/99	$19,165.00					$91,077.86
12/15/99	$3,665.00					$87,412.86
12/16/99	$765.00					$86,647.86
		119194	12/10/99	$2,594.34	12/16/99	$89,242.20
		119337	12/13/99	$186,046.38	12/16/99	$275,288.58
12/18/99	$990.00					$274,298.58
		119482	12/15/99	$35,380.51	12/20/99	$309,679.09
12/21/99	$122.00					$309,557.09
		119557	12/17/99	$104,439.05	12/21/99	$413,996.14
		119751	12/20/99	$98,601.91	12/23/99	$512,598.05
12/27/99	$520.00					$512,078.05
		119934	12/23/99	$10,743.12	12/27/99	$522,821.17

Invoice Ship Date	Subsequent Net Value Amount	Check Number	Check Date	Check Amount	Payment Received at the Lockbox	Net Preference
12/29/99	$30,104.00					$492,717.17
12/30/99	$19,165.00					$462,181.17
12/31/99	$19,165.00					$336,032.17
11/1/99	$19,165.00					$267,000.17
		120202	12/27/99	$71,360.05	1/1/00	$339,260.22
1/3/00	$33,975.00					$305,285.22
		120410	12/29/99	$70,866.34	1/3/00	$376,171.56
1/4/00	$1,300.00					$374,171.56
1/5/00	$165.00					$374,706.56
1/10/00	$255.00					$374,451.56
1/12/00	$1,920.00					$372,531.56

Accordingly, the total amount of preferential transfers which may be recovered, net of the affirmative §547(c) defenses, is $372,531.56. . . .

An order in accordance with this decision will be simultaneously entered.

Floating Liens. Under the Uniform Commercial Code, lenders can advance money in return for a security interest in the sort of collateral that "turns over" routinely: inventory, accounts receivable, farm products, standard equipment, etc. Such a lien "floats" over the collateral even as it changes from day to day. However, floating liens like this can cause problems with the law of preferences, since they attach to some portions of the collateral for the first time during the preference period.

PROBLEM 7-19

Octopus National Bank had a perfected security interest in the inventory of Owl Bookstore. On January 1 the bookstore's inventory was worth $700,000 and the bank was owed $900,000 as a result of various loans. On April 1, the date on which the bookstore filed its bankruptcy petition, as a result of various payments and the receipt of new inventory yet unsold the inventory was worth $800,000 and the bank was owed $850,000. Is there a preference here? See the discussion below.

Whenever the debtor gives a lender a security interest in either inventory or accounts receivable, the security interest attaches to the existing inventory/accounts receivable immediately, but cannot attach to new similar collateral later becoming property of the debtor until the debtor actually acquires it (has "rights in it," in the language U.C.C. Article 9 uses when discussing attachment in §9-203). Even if the lender has filed a financing statement covering this collateral, perfection as to *after-acquired* inventory or accounts receivable must be postponed until the debtor actually does acquire the later-arriving collateral (per U.C.C. §9-308(a)) perfection is necessarily delayed until attachment has occurred). Bankruptcy Code §547(e)(3) reflects this same understanding: a transfer of an interest of the debtor in property cannot take place until the debtor acquires that property.

This causes problems in bankruptcy because it means that after-acquired inventory or accounts receivable that the debtor receives during the preference period is in effect feeding the debt owed to the security creditor in a manner that looks preferential. Prior to the adoption of the Bankruptcy Code, the courts used various devices to protect the lender in this situation, at least where the lender was not encouraging a build-up of collateral in this period in order to better protect its interest, *see* Grain Merchants of Indiana, Inc. v. Union Bank & Sav. Co., 408 F.2d 209, 6 U.C.C. Rep. Serv. 1 (7th Cir. 1960), but the matter is now resolved by Bankruptcy Code §547(c)(5), which is not as imposing as it at first looks. It requires the bankruptcy court to examine the collateral/debt amounts at two points: at the start of the preference period and at the moment of the filing of the petition, and condemns a security interest as preferential to the extent that the lender has improved its position between those two dates. (Note that if the lender first makes the loan during the preference period, that date is used as the first measuring moment.) Use that formula to resolve Problem 7-19, and then try to adapt the language of §547(c)(5) to the following.

PROBLEM 7-20

Octopus National Bank loaned Owl Bookstore $50,000 on December 1, taking a security interest on that date in the store's inventory, then worth $50,000. Brisk Christmas sales reduced the inventory to $10,000 as of January 1, when Owl still owed the bank $50,000. By April 1 the inventory has built back up and is now worth $45,000; Owl still owes the bank $50,000. Owl's owner calls the bank and asks for another loan, saying without it she will have to file a bankruptcy petition that very afternoon. You are the attorney for the bank. Is it wise to make the loan?

PROBLEM 7-21

Aristides Stables used its racehorses as collateral for a $60,000 loan from Day Star Bank at a time when all agreed that the horses were worth $40,000. Ninety days later, at the time Aristides filed its Chapter 7 petition, the racehorses were worth $60,000. No new horses had been bought or sold in this period — the increase in value was due solely to the fact that the horses had all been winning lately. Has the bank received a preference? *See* In re Nivens, 22 B.R. 287 (Bankr. N.D. Tex. 1982).

PROBLEM 7-22

Five days before he filed his Chapter 7 petition, Charles Condomine suddenly paid his ex-wife Ruth the $32,000 he had long owed her for child support. Did Ruth receive a preference? *See* §547(c)(7).

PROBLEM 7-23

Assume that the relevant state exemption law allows debtors to exempt $400 in cash. Two weeks before Charles Condomine filed for bankruptcy, his car was repossessed by Arcati Finance Company because he had not been paying the company, which had a purchase money security interest in the car. To get the car back, Charles did cough up $500. Now he wants to get back $400 of that and claim it as exempt. Can he do this? *See* §§522(h) and (i), and 547(c)(8). Suppose Charles made two payments of $400 each during the preference period. Does §547 (c)(8) insulate these transfers? *See* In re Hailes, 77 F.3d 873 (5th Cir. 1996). If Charles were a business debtor, are his small preferential payments also insulated from attack? *See* §547(c)(9).

PROBLEM 7-24

Robots of Tomorrow gave Antitrust National Bank a security interest in its inventory of robots on April 2 in return for a loan of $50,000, but ANB failed to record its financing statement until May 10 of that year. On May 13, Robots of Tomorrow, for a loan of $30,000, granted Octopus National Bank a security interest in the same robots, which ONB perfected by filing its financing statement that same day. On June 1, Robots of Tomorrow filed its Chapter 7 petition. The trustee hires you as his attorney. The robot inventory is worth $70,000. Who gets what? *See* §§547(b) and 551.

IV.   Setoff

The concept of setoff, discussed in earlier chapters, permits the subtraction of mutual debts between mutual debtors. Thus, if I owe you $500 and, as a result of another transaction, you owe me $200, the debts can be netted out against one another so that the end result is I only owe you $300; *see* Studley v. Boylston Natl. Bank, 229 U.S. 523 (1913) (setoff reflects the "absurdity" of making A pay B when B owes A). The most common example of a setoff occurs with bank accounts. As we have seen, a deposit of money in an account is a *loan* of that money to the bank, and to that extent makes the bank a debtor. If the customer then borrows money from the bank, the bank can exercise its right of setoff and pay the debt by deducting the amount due from the bank account. A bank that is lending money to one of its depositors is then very much in the same position as a secured creditor — it has easy access to a source of repayment — and Bankruptcy Code §506(a) treats a right of setoff the same as a security interest in collateral.

Section 553 of the Bankruptcy Code also treats a creditor with a right of setoff much like a creditor with a perfected security interest, and generally allows the creditor to exercise the right of setoff on getting relief from the automatic stay. Both the creditor's claim and the debt owed by the bankrupt must have arisen before the petition in bankruptcy was filed, and the claim must be allowable before the setoff is valid. If the creditor first acquired the claim in the 90 days before the filing of the petition (or after the petition is filed), while the debtor was insolvent and from someone other than the debtor, then the setoff is not allowed. This rule prevents creditors from "trading in claims" so as to improve their position. For example, suppose Debtor Industries, Inc., is on a fast slide into bankruptcy, and it owes an unsecured debt to Transnational Bank of $50,000. Assume further that Acme Widgets Co. owes Debtor Industries $80,000 for goods previously delivered to it by Debtor. Transnational is facing a limited recovery of its claim against Debtor, so it "sells" its $50,000 claim against Debtor to Acme for $10,000. Acme might then try to use that $50,000 claim as a setoff against the $80,000 it would otherwise owe to Debtor, reducing its obligation to only $30,000. Were this permitted, as it is not, Acme would have been able to purchase $80,000 of goods for $40,000 (the $10,000 it paid to Transnational and the $30,000 still due after the setoff). Section 553(a)(2) prevents this from happening.

Similarly, if the debt owed by the bankrupt was incurred during the same period, while the debtor was insolvent, and for the purpose of creating the right of setoff, no setoff is permitted. In effect this means that the creditor cannot artificially create the setoff situation on the eve of bankruptcy in order to better its position, just as a creditor cannot secure an old debt in the 90 days before bankruptcy without being subject to a preference attack.

Setoffs avoiding these pitfalls are valid, and are not subject to avoidance under other theories (such as preferences).

Congress wanted creditors with control over the debtor's fortunes to avoid precipitous action as the debtor's financial situation deteriorates before the bankruptcy petition is filed. Thus, the Bankruptcy Code condemns preferences and fraudulent conveyances and *ipso facto* clauses (those terminating rights on insolvency, etc.). Section 553(b) has a similar major limitation on the right of setoff. If the creditor (very typically the bank where the debtor banks) exercises the right of setoff before the petition is filed, the setoff is not valid to the extent that the creditor improved its position compared with the debt/claim ratio 90 days before the filing of the petition.

PROBLEM 7-25

As the result of a loan, Mom & Pop's Diner owed Last National Bank $10,000 as of July 1, at which point the checking account the diner maintained at the bank held $2,000. Five days before the filing of the diner's bankruptcy petition on September 25, the bank pulled the plug on the debtor by taking the $5,000 that was then in the bank account (the debt owed to the bank still being $10,000), and that caused the filing of the petition, at which time the numbers had not changed. What will happen to the bank? Would the bank have been better off waiting until after the petition was filed to try and get the money in the account? What is the downside of waiting?

PROBLEM 7-26

William (aka "Buck") Aye was the sole shareholder of Buck Aye Concrete Corp. The corporation owed First State Bank $150,000, and it maintained its bank accounts with First State. Buck had personally guaranteed the debt owed by the corporation to the bank. Ninety days prior to the bankruptcy filing by the corporation it had $95,000 in its account at the bank. It used the bulk of that money to pay both labor and materials expenses, so that one week later the account held only $6,000. The account stayed at approximately that level for the next 60 days or so, with only minimal deposits and withdrawals. During the three weeks before the bankruptcy filing, however, the corporation deposited $70,000 into its account and paid out only $5,000. This left a balance in the account of $71,000, which the bank set off just three days prior to the commencement of the bankruptcy proceedings. Is the setoff vulnerable to attack by the trustee? *See* §§553(a)(3) and 553(b).

In re Elcona Homes Corp.

United States Court of Appeals, Seventh Circuit, 1988
863 F.2d 483

Posner, Circuit Judge.

This appeal requires us to examine the Bankruptcy Code's provision on set offs, which states that the Code "does not affect any right of a creditor to offset a [prebankruptcy] mutual debt owing by such creditor to the debtor . . . against a [prebankruptcy] claim of such creditor against the debtor." 11 U.S.C. §553(a). The debtor, Elcona Homes Corporation, was (and still is, for this is a reorganization case) a manufacturer of mobile homes. Shortly before it went broke, Linda Markle had ordered a mobile home from one of its dealers, Monro Homes, Inc. The price was $36,700. Markle paid $14,000 down, and Elcona agreed to sell the home to Monro for $22,700. This was, of course, the difference between the retail price and the amount of the down payment; so the latter amount represented Monro's profit.

Payment of the balance was to be due when Monro delivered the home to Markle and set it up for her. Green Tree Acceptance, Inc., the creditor in the case, agreed to finance Markle's purchase by giving Monro $22,700 in exchange for an assignment of the installment contract that Monro had signed with Markle. So instead of making her monthly payments to Monro, Markle would make them to Green Tree, and Green Tree's profit would come from the interest it charged Markle. Upon receipt of the $22,700 from Green Tree, Monro would remit an equal amount to Elcona to pay for the mobile home. The parties refer to the type of arrangement by which Green Tree financed Monro's business as "retail proceeds" financing. It bears a family resemblance to the more common "floor-planning" system of dealer financing, but there the lender takes a security interest in the goods before the dealer sells them and here it was afterward.

This was not the first time that Green Tree had financed Monro's sales of Elcona homes; and a practice had developed of Green Tree's paying Elcona directly rather than paying Monro for remittance to Elcona. This meant that instead of Green Tree's paying Monro $22,700 for the installment contract and Monro's then turning around and paying Elcona $22,700 for the mobile home, Green Tree would be expected simply to pay $22,700 to Elcona. Elcona preferred this arrangement, since it protected it (how far we shall see) against the risk of Monro's defaulting. This was not only the practice between the parties but also, they have stipulated, the practice generally followed in the mobile home industry.

Elcona's bankruptcy occurred after the sale to Markle but before Green Tree had paid Elcona. Now it happened that Elcona owed Green Tree $16,000 (more or less) on an earlier transaction. Green Tree decided to set off this debt against the $22,700 that normally it would have sent directly to Elcona, and therefore sent Elcona only the difference between $22,700 and $16,000 (actually somewhat less, but like the exact amount owed Green Tree in the earlier transaction, that is a detail of no importance to this appeal). The bankruptcy judge did not consider this a proper set off. Since the $22,700 was not a debt that Green Tree owed Elcona but a debt it owed Monro, there was no mutual indebtedness between Elcona and Green Tree, as the statute requires. (Elcona adds that Green Tree was really just an escrow agent of Monro, Elcona's real debtor.) The district judge (after a procedural bobble recounted in In re Elcona Homes Corp., 810 F.2d 136 (7th Cir. 1987)) reversed the bankruptcy judge. He thought the evidence showed "a mutuality of obligations between Green Tree and Elcona and vice versa because it was both the industry practice and the practice between the parties for the lender (Green Tree) to pay the manufacturer (Elcona) directly the amount due the manufacturer from the dealer. That being the case, Green Tree was entitled to setoff the debt owed it by Elcona." Elcona appeals.

The set-off provision in the Bankruptcy Code seems at first glance inconsistent with the usual result in bankruptcy, which is that all unsecured creditors are treated alike ("equity is equality"). But it is no more than the usual result precisely because the principle that unsecured creditors shall be treated alike is riddled with exceptions. There are all sorts of preferences (for the Internal Revenue Service, for employees having wage claims, for persons who extend credit to the debtor after the petition for bankruptcy is filed, etc.) and discriminations (e.g., against creditors treated preferentially on the eve of bankruptcy). And it might be more accurate to say not that there is a principle (however qualified) of equal treatment among creditors but that bankruptcy provides a mechanism for enforcing pre-bankruptcy entitlements given by state or federal law, with some exceptions. But the idea of equal treatment is a useful as well as a persistent one. An important purpose of bankruptcy law is to prevent individual creditors from starting a "run" on the debtor by assuring them that they will be treated equally if the debtor is precipitated into bankruptcy, rather than being given either preferential treatment for having jumped the gun or disadvantageous treatment for having hung back.

The principle is not absolute, as we have stressed, but its exceptions generally are intelligible; and we will be helped in determining the scope of the set-off exception — which on its face is arbitrary — if we can understand its rationale, too.

Setoffs outside of bankruptcy are in no wise anomalous or problematic; no third party's rights comparable to those of unsecured creditors in bankruptcy are affected, and circuitous proceedings are avoided. But in bankruptcy an unsecured creditor fortunate enough to owe his debtor as much as or more than the debtor owes him can, by setting off his debt against the debtor's, in effect receive 100 cents on the dollar, while the other unsecured creditors, who have nothing to set off against the debtor, might be lucky to collect 10 cents on the dollar. The difference in treatment seems based on a fortuitous difference among the unsecured creditors, and therefore arbitrary. Let us inquire further.

Although the right of set off has been a part of Anglo-American bankruptcy law since 1705, *see* Act of 4 Anne, ch. 17, §11, its rationale has never been made clear. To say that it "recognize[s] the possible injustice in compelling a creditor to file its claim in full and accepting possible dividends thereon, while at the same time paying in full its indebtedness to the estate," 4 Collier on Bankruptcy ¶553.02, at p. 553-10 (King 15th ed. 1988) (footnote omitted), is to say very little; for why is it not an equal or greater injustice to advance one unsecured creditor over another merely because the first happens also to owe money to their common debtor? Nor is it helpful to point out that "it is only the balance which is the real and just sum owing by or to the bankrupt," Prudential Ins. Co. v. Nelson, 101 F.2d 441, 443 (6th Cir. 1939), for if the set off is allowed, the other unsecured creditors will not receive "the real and just sum owing" to them.

The only sense we can make of the rule is that it recognizes that the creditor who owes his debtor money is like a secured creditor; indeed, the mutual debts, to the extent equal, secure each party against the other's default. This reasoning figured in Congress's decision to retain the right of set off in the 1978 overhaul of bankruptcy law. See the useful discussion in Comment, Setoff in Bankruptcy: Is the Creditor Preferred or Secured?, 50 U. Colo. L. Rev. 511, 519-23 (1979). The reasoning may seem circular, however, for it is only by virtue of the Bankruptcy Code's preserving the right of set off that the creditor has, in the event of his debtor's bankruptcy, a form of security for the debt he is owed. (But of course not all defaulting debtors are bankrupt.) And one might suppose that if the theory of the set off is that it provides the creditor with security, the creditor would have to prove that the parties had intended a right of set off as a means of securing the creditor — that is, would have to prove that the creditor had been counting on the right in extending credit to the debtor on the terms he did. *See* Columbia Aircraft Co. v. United States, 163 F. Supp. 932, 934 (S.D.N.Y. 1958) (L. Hand, J.). But such proof is not in fact required.

Banks argue that the right to set off deposits (a bank deposit is a debt of the bank to the depositor) against the depositor's debts to the bank facilitates the provision of bank credit and lowers the rate of interest, by giving the bank security in the event of the depositor's going broke. But the more secure the bank is, the less secure the depositor's other creditors will be, so they will charge higher interest rates. This, however, is a general characteristic of secured lending. The secured lender faces a lower risk of loss in the event of default and therefore will lend at a lower interest rate, but unsecured lenders, facing a higher risk of loss because fewer assets will be available to satisfy their claims in the event of default, will charge higher interest rates. Nevertheless secured financing is so firmly established a commercial practice that it is hard to believe it does not serve important commercial purposes, and it is apparent what they might be: lenders differ in their ability to monitor their borrowers (in order to prevent the borrower from increasing the riskiness of its activities) and to bear risk, and thus a combination of secured and unsecured financing enables a borrower to appeal to the different capabilities and preferences of different lenders.

Yet if deposits are intended to secure the bank's loans, why not treat the bank as a secured creditor rather than creating a general right in all creditors to set off their debts against the bankrupt's debts to them? Maybe the answer is simply that set offs are just another form of secured financing that the Bankruptcy Code has decided to recognize, though under a different name and with different restrictions. But the underlying rights of creditors which are asserted in bankruptcy proceedings are the creation of state law, not of the Bankruptcy Code; for the general principle *see* Butner v. United States, 440 U.S. 48, 54-57, 99 S. Ct. 914, 917-19, 59 L. Ed. 2d 136 (1979), and for its application to set offs *see* Boston & Maine Corp. v. Chicago Pacific Corp., 785 F.2d 562, 565 (7th Cir. 1986). Maybe the right question to ask, therefore, is not why the Code allows set offs (for it also allows secured creditors to withdraw their collateral from the pool available to other creditors), but why it places restrictions on them. Against this view of set offs as a species of secured financing, however, it can be argued that, apart perhaps from such special situations as that of banks dealing with their depositor-borrowers, set offs are recognized in state law for their procedural convenience — the consolidation of offsetting claims in the same suit — and that this convenience should receive little weight in bankruptcy. Professor Gilmore thought the express exemption of set offs from the filing requirements in Article 9 (secured financing) of the Uniform Commercial Code, *see* §9-104(i), absurd: "Of course a right of setoff is not a security interest and has never been confused with one: the statute might as appropriately exclude fan dancing." 1 Gilmore, Security Interests in Personal Property §10.7, at pp. 315-16 (1965). This view seems extreme and has been questioned, see Clark, The Law of Bank Deposits, Collections and Credit Cards ¶11.3 (rev. ed. 1981); *see also* id., ¶1.8[9]; 4 Collier on Bankruptcy, *supra*, ¶553.15[1], but certainly there is no evidence here that the existence of mutual debts (if that is what they were) between Elcona and Green Tree reflected a desire by the parties to secure each other's obligations; it appears to have been an accident.

But we need not resolve these questions, or press our inquiry into the rationale for the Bankruptcy Code's treatment of set offs further, in order to decide this case. Whether that treatment reflects a felt tension between the right of set off and the normal practice in bankruptcy of treating unsecured creditors equally, or whether one denies the tension, points out that the recognition by state law of a right of set off makes the set off a form of secured financing, and argues (contrary to our earlier point) that there really is no policy of treating unsecured creditors in bankruptcy equally, the statute itself speaks of "a *mutual* debt" (emphasis ours), see 4 Collier on Bankruptcy, *supra*, ¶¶553.04[1], [2], and therefore precludes "triangular" set offs. *See, e.g.*, In re Berger Steel Co., 327 F.2d 401 (7th Cir. 1964); Depositors Trust Co. v. Frati Enterprises, Inc., 590 F.2d 377, 379 (1st Cir. 1979); In re Virginia Block Co., 16 B.R. 771 (Bankr. W.D. Va. 1982).

Two recurrent cases should be noted. In the first and easier, illustrated by In re Southern Industrial Banking Corp., 809 F.2d 329 (6th Cir. 1987), the creditor of a bankrupt buys a debt owed by someone else to the debtor in order to offset the debt that the bankrupt debtor owes him and so gain an advantage over the other unsecured creditors. This is plainly evasive and easily rebuffed. Indeed, it will normally violate 11 U.S.C. §553(a)(3), which was added in 1978 to close a loophole that had allowed preferences in the form of set offs, and which forbids a set off where the debt was incurred within 90 days before bankruptcy, while the debtor was insolvent, and for the purpose of obtaining a set off against him. *See* In re Prescott, 805 F.2d 719, 730 (7th Cir. 1986); In re Dayton Circuit Courts No. 2, 80 B.R. 434, 439-40 (Bankr. S.D. Ohio 1987).

In the second case, illustrated by both *Berger Steel* and *Depositors Trust*, a subsidiary or other affiliate of the creditor owes money to the bankrupt and the two affiliates ask that they be treated as a single entity. This is rebuffed by pointing out that, save in exceptional circumstances, corporate and commercial law treat affiliated corporations as separate enterprises. *See, e.g.*, In re Xonics Photochemical, Inc., 841 F.2d 198, 201 (7th Cir. 1988); In re Kaiser, 791 F.2d 73, 75 (7th Cir. 1986).

Our case follows neither of these familiar patterns. It is neither a transaction in contemplation of bankruptcy (the timing suggests it may be but Elcona does not argue the point, and it is therefore waived) nor an attempt by affiliated corporations to lift the corporate veil that separates them. Nevertheless there can be no set off unless the $22,700 was in fact a debt owed by Green Tree to Elcona. *See, e.g.*, In re Fasano/Harriss Pie Co., 43 B.R. 864, 870-71 (Bankr. W.D. Mich. 1984), *aff'd*, 70 B.R. 285 (W.D. Mich. 1987), *aff'd without opinion*, 848 F.2d 190 (6th Cir. 1988); Bloor v. Shapiro, 32 B.R. 993, 1001-02 (S.D.N.Y. 1983).

The district court's opinion does not deal satisfactorily with this issue. The court inferred the existence of a mutual debt from the practice of the parties and of the industry; indeed, he equated obligation to practice. He said, "there was a mutuality of obligation between Green Tree and Elcona and vice versa *because* it was both the industry practice and the practice between the parties for the lender (Green Tree) to pay the manufacturer (Elcona) directly the amount due the manufacturer from the dealer. *That being the case*, Green Tree was entitled to setoff the debt owed it by Elcona." (Emphasis added.) In other words, a practice equals or creates an obligation. It does not. *See, e.g.*, In re Virginia Block Co., *supra*, 16 B.R. at 774. Suppose the practice of a landlord is to accept late payment from his tenant. That practice does not entitle the tenant to pay late; it does not modify the contract. If every forbearance to enforce a contract to its hilt operated to modify the contract against the party exercising forbearance, such forbearance would become rare; promisees would always insist on exact performance of the promisor's obligation, and defaults and litigation would become more frequent. *See* In re Xonics Imaging, Inc., 837 F.2d 763, 767 (7th Cir. 1988). A practice may be evidence of an obligation, may give meaning to vague terms, and so on; but it is not the equivalent of it. See UCC §1-205; Farnsworth, Contracts §7.13 (1982).

The question can be put this way: if, instead of remitting $22,700 directly to Elcona, Green Tree had remitted the money to Monro, and Monro had absconded with the money without paying Elcona, could Elcona have sued Green Tree? Possibly so, since as we said the practice of Green Tree in remitting directly to Elcona provided both parties with security against a default by the dealer, and the security would be less if the contract were interpreted to allow either party to disregard the practice. Maybe, then, the practice was also an implied term of the contract. If so — and if, therefore, Elcona could have sued Green Tree (and won) in our hypothetical case — this would show that Green Tree was indeed indebted to Elcona, and then the debts were mutual and could be offset. The case must be remanded for a determination whether there was not only a practice of direct payment from the finance company to the manufacturer but an obligation to make such payments.

The reader may be wondering about the possibility that Elcona was a third-party beneficiary of the contract between Green Tree and Monro. If so, this would show that Green Tree had indeed been indebted to Elcona for the $22,700 and thus that there were offsetting debts. Such at least is the holding of In re Bacigalupi, Inc., 60 B.R. 442, 446 (9th Cir. Bank. App. Panel 1986). But In re J.A. Clark Mechanical, Inc., 80 B.R. 430, 433 (Bankr. N.D. Ohio 1987), holds that third-party beneficiary status cannot give rise to a right to set off in bankruptcy. These decisions give no reasons for their opposed conclusions, and we can find no other decisions on the question. We need not take sides; Green Tree does not argue to us that Elcona was a third-party beneficiary, and we shall leave it to the district court to decide (at least in the first instance) whether the argument has been waived below and if not whether it is a valid argument. Nor need we at this stage determine the limits on a bankruptcy court's discretion to disallow a set off that is within the terms of the statute; possibly it extends no further than to disallow a set off acquired for the purpose of stealing a march on other creditors, for as Judge Friendly has reminded us "the rule allowing setoff, both before and after bankruptcy, is not one that courts are free to ignore when they think application would be 'unjust.' " In re Applied Logic Corp., 576 F.2d 952, 957 (2d Cir. 1978). *See generally* Gardner v. Chicago Title & Trust Co., 261 U.S. 453, 43 S. Ct. 424, 67 L. Ed. 741 (1923); United States on Behalf of Internal Revenue Service v. Norton, 717 F.2d 767, 772 (3d Cir. 1983); In re Southern Industrial Banking Corp., *supra*, 809 F.2d at 332; In re Elsinore Shore Associates, 67 B.R. 926, 946 (Bankr. D.N.J. 1986). . . .

The decision of the district court is vacated and the case remanded for further proceedings consistent with this opinion.

WILL, Senior District Judge, dissenting.

While I agree with much of the majority opinion, I do not agree that the case in the words of the majority opinion "must be remanded for a determination whether there was not only a practice of direct payment from the finance company to the manufacturer but an obligation to make such payments." With all due respect, Judge Lee has already done just that. In his opinion he said:

> In this court's view, the stipulations differentiate the facts in this case from those presented in either *Virginia Block* or *Inland Steel*, even apart from the fact that in this case the court is not dealing with debts of subsidiary corporations. Here, unlike in In re Virginia Block, the practice was not "occasional" or "sporadic at best" nor was the arrangement here superseded by a "written blanket" agreement as it was in *Inland Steel*. Rather, the evidence in the record and the parties' stipulation clearly shows that there was a *mutuality of obligations* between Green Tree and Elcona and vice versa *because it was both the industry practice and the practices between the parties for the lender* (Green Tree) to pay the manufacturer (Elcona) directly the amount due the manufacturer from the dealer. That being the case, Green Tree was entitled to setoff the debt owed it by Elcona.

District Court Opinion at 9-10 (emphasis added).

I am not clear what more the majority would have him say. . . .

Since the facts as stipulated by the parties and found by Judge Lee support his legal conclusion that there was an obligation on Green Tree's part to remit directly to Elcona, his ultimate conclusion that there were mutual debts under 11 U.S.C. §553(a) was correct. Accordingly, I would affirm his decision rather than remanding for him to adumbrate in greater detail the conclusion he has already correctly reached.

V. Statutory Liens

Statutory liens are those "arising solely by force of a statute on specified circumstances or conditions." Bankruptcy Code §101(53). Among these liens are the federal tax lien and state mechanics' lien statutes. Of course, there are many others. The effect of these statutes is to grant to specific creditors an interest in some or all of a debtor's property. Having a lien on the property puts that creditor ahead of other creditors. It is a way to grant a special priority to the protected creditor. These "priorities" can completely undo the distributional priorities set out in the Bankruptcy Code. They are also often the result of political sway in the state legislature held by the soon-to-be-protected class. Section 545 of the Bankruptcy Code serves as a check on the state legislatures and Congress to prevent them from creating these special categories of lien claimants who would otherwise receive more favorable treatment than the Bankruptcy Code provides.

PROBLEM 7-27

The State of Ohio was concerned that dairy farmers were not getting paid for milk they delivered to milk processing plants when the plants went bankrupt before honoring the checks given to the farmers. It therefore passed a statute stating that if a milk processing plant became insolvent or filed a petition in bankruptcy, as of that moment the unpaid dairy farmers would have a lien on the inventory of the milk processing plant for the amount remaining unpaid on milk delivered. Is this lien a preference? *See* §547(c)(6). Is it valid in bankruptcy? *See* §545(1). Suppose the state changes the statute so that it provides that the lien in favor of the farmer is automatic on delivery of the milk and lasts until payment (whether or not the milk processing plant is insolvent), but that the lien is not effective against a bona fide purchaser of the milk in the inventory. Now what? *See* §545(2). What can the legislature do to protect the dairy farmers?

PROBLEM 7-28

Under the laws of most states, unpaid landlords have a lien on the property of their tenants and may refuse to surrender possession until the outstanding rent is satisfied. If the tenant files a bankruptcy petition, what can the landlord do? *See* §545(3) and (4).

VI.   Fraudulent Transfers

In Chapter 1, we considered fraudulent transfers outside bankruptcy under the Uniform Fraudulent Transfer Act and the common law. There we saw that if the debtor made a transfer with *actual* intent to defraud creditors, all future creditors could undo the transfer (at least until the rights of an innocent party intervened). Under the strong arm clause, §544(a), the trustee is such a future creditor, and could use this theory to attack the transfer. The UFTA also provides that transfers made by an insolvent for less than equivalent value were only void as to *existing* creditors, and here the strong arm clause would not help the trustee. However, §548 of the Bankruptcy Code has an independent condemnation of fraudulent transfers of both kinds and allows the trustee a one-year period following them in which to attack.

Congress amended §544 in 1998 to limit the trustee's ability to avoid fraudulent transfers under state law to the extent that they involve limited transfers to charitable organizations. *See* §544(b)(2), which includes a cross reference to the limitations on recovery of fraudulent transfers by trustees under §548 of the Bankruptcy Code. Those provisions protect transfers by individual debtors to charitable entities as long as the transfers do not exceed 15 percent of the debtor's annual income or are otherwise consistent with prior contribution patterns.

PROBLEM 7-29

Knowing that his creditors were soon going to try to seize his ancestral home, on November 3 Marmaduke Poindexter sold his house for half its true value to his son Alexis, who promptly moved onto the property and, at an expense of $8,000, had the house repainted. When Marmaduke filed a bankruptcy petition in late December the trustee demanded the house back. What are Alexis's rights here? *See* §§548(c) and 550(e).

Rupp v. Markgraf[5]

United States Court of Appeals, Tenth Circuit, 1996
95 F.3d 936

EBEL, Circuit Judge.

Stephen W. Rupp, the Chapter 7 bankruptcy trustee of Cowboy Enterprises, Inc. ("Cowboy"), appeals the district court's dismissal of an adversary proceeding to avoid and recover a fraudulent conveyance of Cowboy's property from appellees Edwin and Mary Markgraf under §§544(b) and 550 of the Bankruptcy Code, 11 U.S.C. §§544(b) & 550. We exercise jurisdiction under 28 U.S.C. §§158(d) & 1291 and remand for further proceedings consistent with this opinion.

Background

The events that give rise to this action began in 1988, when the Markgrafs became judgment creditors of Forrest Wood "Woody" Davis in the amount of $391,688. By December 1989, Mr. Davis and his wife, Mary, had become principal stockholders and officers in Cowboy. In December 1989, Mr. Davis agreed to pay the Markgrafs $100,000 in exchange for a pickup truck valued at $15,000 and satisfaction of the Markgrafs' judgment against him.

On December 13, 1989, Mrs. Davis instructed First Interstate Bank of Nevada to issue a cashier's check in the amount of $100,000 made payable to Edwin and Mary Markgraf. The cashier's check was purchased using Cowboy funds and it stated on its face that it was purchased by Cowboy Enterprises. Mrs. Davis instructed First Interstate to send the cashier's check "by over night or Fed Ex to: Cowboy Enterprises, Inc. 3535 E. Little Cottonwood Lane, Sandy Utah 84092." This address was not Cowboy's business address, but rather the address where Mr. Davis was living at the time. Subsequently, on December 19, 1989, the cashier's check was delivered to the Markgrafs, and the Markgrafs delivered a satisfaction of judgment and the pickup truck to the Davises.

In 1992, Cowboy filed for Chapter 11 bankruptcy protection, which was later converted to a Chapter 7 liquidation. The trustee brought this adversary proceeding in 1993 alleging that the transfer was fraudulent and seeking its avoidance and recovery against the Markgrafs under 11 U.S.C. §§544(b) & 550. The Markgrafs moved for judgment as a matter of law at the close of the trustee's case. The district court granted the Markgrafs' motion and dismissed the action on the grounds that the bank, and not the Markgrafs, was the "initial transferee" of Cowboy's funds under §550. Having considered the parties' arguments, we hold that the Markgrafs are liable as initial transferees, and that Forest Wood Davis is liable as the person for whose benefit the

---

5. [This case is a fraudulent transfer case, but the trustee uses §544(b) (state fraudulent transfer law) as the grounds for attack, §548 being unavailable since the fraudulent transfer occurred more than one year before the filing of the petition. State fraudulent transfer law has a longer statute of limitations. Section 544(b), discussed following the case, allows the trustee to use the rights of any actual creditor who could attack fraudulent transfers.]—EDS.

transfer was made. The issue of whether or not the transfer was fraudulent is not before us, and we therefore do not address it.

Discussion

The parties agree that this appeal presents a purely legal issue involving the interpretation and application of §550 of the Bankruptcy Code, a question that we review de novo. Jobin v. McKay (In re M & L Business Mach. Co.), 84 F.3d 1330, 1334-35 (10th Cir. 1996). Under §550 of the Bankruptcy Code, when a transfer is avoided under §544 of the Code, the trustee may recover the transferred property for the benefit of the estate. Section 550(a) provides that the trustee may recover from: (1) the initial transferee of such transfer or the entity for whose benefit such transfer was made; or (2) any immediate or mediate transferee of such initial transferee. 11 U.S.C. §550(a). However, the trustee's power to recover is limited by §550(b), which prevents recovery from immediate or mediate transferees of the initial transferee under §550(a)(2) who "take[] for value . . . , in good faith, and without knowledge of the voidability of the transfer avoided." 11 U.S.C. §550(b)(1). No such good faith defense is available to the initial transferee or the "entity for whose benefit such transfer was made" under §550(a)(1); the trustee may always recover from the initial transferee regardless of good faith, value, or lack of knowledge of the voidability of the transfer. Therefore, the central issue in this appeal becomes the determination of which party is the initial transferee of Cowboy's fraudulently transferred funds. If the Markgrafs are the initial transferee, the trustee can recover; if not, the trustee must attempt to recover from the Markgrafs as immediate or mediate transferees, and the Markgrafs may utilize the good faith defense of §550(b)(1). We hold that the Markgrafs are initial transferees under §550 of the Bankruptcy Code.

A.

The district court held that the initial transferee of Cowboy's funds was First Interstate Bank of Nevada. The court concluded that the "initial transfer, occurred when Mary Davis said, 'Bank, take Cowboy money and issue to us in return for Cowboy money, cashier's checks.' " Aplt. App. doc. 1 at 6. The court therefore ruled that "[w]here a bank issues a cashier's check, it is an initial transferee of the funds used to purchase the check." Id. at 8. We disagree.

In Bonded Fin. Servs., Inc. v. European Am. Bank, 838 F.2d 890 (7th Cir. 1988), the Seventh Circuit enunciated what is commonly referred to as the "conduit" theory for determining whether an intermediary, such as a bank, is an "initial transferee" for purposes of §550. In that case, the debtor (Bonded) sent a check to the bank payable to the bank's order, along with instructions to deposit the money into the account of a third party (Ryan), who was a principal of Bonded. Even though Ryan eventually used those funds to reduce his own indebtedness to the bank, the court held that the bank was not the initial transferee because it had no dominion over the money at the time it initially received the check from Bonded. Id. at 894. As the court reasoned, "[a]s the

Bank saw the transaction on January 21, it was Ryan's agent for the purpose of collecting a check from Bonded's bank. . . . The Bank had no dominion over the $200,000 until January 31, when Ryan instructed the Bank to debit the account to reduce the loan." Id. at 893-94 (citation omitted).

We adopted the *Bonded* approach in Malloy v. Citizens Bank of Sapulpa (In re First Sec. Mortgage Co.), 33 F.3d 42 (10th Cir. 1994), holding that " 'the minimum requirement of status as a "transferee" is dominion over the money or other asset, the right to put the money to one's own purposes.' " Id. at 43-44 (quoting *Bonded*, 838 F.2d at 893). In that case, the debtor's funds were fraudulently transferred to the defendant bank with instructions to deposit them in the account of Mr. Hobbs. We held that the bank was not the initial transferee because it "was obligated to make the funds available to Mr. Hobbs upon demand and, therefore, it acted only as a financial intermediary." Id. at 44. Moreover, the fact that in both *Bonded* and *Malloy* the funds were sent to the bank via an ordinary check rather than a cashier's check does not affect the bank's status as a conduit as opposed to a transferee. *See* Ross v. United States (In re Auto-Pak, Inc.), 73 B.R. 52, 54 (D.D.C. 1987) (bank was not the initial transferee where principal of debtor converted a check of the debtor into a cashier's check made payable to the IRS).

B.

If the bank merely acted as a conduit, and exercised no dominion and control over Cowboy's funds, then the initial transferee must be either Mr. Davis or the Markgrafs. We conclude that the language and underlying policy of 11 U.S.C. §§544(b) & 550, the law of this circuit, as well as persuasive authority from other jurisdictions, supports the conclusion that the Markgrafs are the initial transferees, and Davis is the person "for whose benefit such transfer was made."

Our decision in *Malloy*, adopting the approach taken by the Seventh Circuit in *Bonded*, indicates that we must apply the dominion and control test to determine the initial transferee of Cowboy's funds. *See Malloy*, 33 F.3d at 43-44; *Bonded*, 838 F.2d at 893-94. In doing so we must consider whether Davis exercised the requisite dominion and control over the funds either (1) by the mere act of causing the corporate debtor (Cowboy) to make a fraudulent transfer through his role as a principal of the corporate debtor, or (2) by conduct other than that stemming from his role as a principal of Cowboy. We conclude that Davis did not, through his capacity as principal or otherwise, exercise the type of dominion and control over the funds required in *Bonded* and *Malloy*.

Because we have adopted the Seventh Circuit's approach in *Bonded*, our analysis begins there. As discussed above, in *Bonded* the debtor corporation (Bonded) sent a check to the bank of its principal, Michael Ryan, with a note directing the bank to " 'deposit this check into [Ryan]'s account.' " *Bonded*, 838 F.2d at 891 (alteration in original). Ten days later, Ryan instructed the bank to debit this account in order to reduce an outstanding balance on a loan he *personally* had with the bank. Id. The court concluded that the bank acted as a mere financial intermediary and that it was not the initial transferee under §550. Id. at 893. In *Bonded*, the principal had the debtor's funds in his personal account for 10 days before he transferred the funds to a third party (the bank) in satisfaction of a personal debt owed to the bank. Thus, the principal clearly had the "right to put the money to [his] own purposes" for 10 days. Id. at 893. He could have paid the loan, as he did, or "invest[ed] the whole [amount] in lottery tickets or uranium stocks." Id. at 894.

After concluding that, under these circumstances, the bank was not the initial transferee, the court in *Bonded* went on to state hypothetically, "If the note accompanying Bonded's check had said: 'use this check to reduce Ryan's loan' instead of 'deposit this check into [Ryan]'s account,' §550(a)(1) *would provide a ready answer. The Bank would be the 'initial transferee' and Ryan would be the 'entity for whose benefit [the] transfer was made.'*" Id. at 892; *see also* Id. at 895. The distinction between the actual facts in *Bonded* and the contrasting hypothetical discussed by the court indicates that the *Bonded* court distinguishes between a one-step transaction in which the debtor's check is paid directly to its principal's creditor, and a two-step transaction in which the debtor's check is paid to the principal, who then pays his own creditor. In the first case, the creditor is the initial transferee, and the principal is the entity for whose benefit the transfer was made. In the second case, the principal is the initial transferee, and the creditor is the subsequent transferee. Schafer v. Las Vegas Hilton (In re Video Depot, Ltd.), 186 B.R. 126, 132 (Bankr. W.D. Wash. 1995). The facts of the case before us fit into the category of one-step transactions discussed in *Video Depot*, and the hypothetical situation discussed in *Bonded*. Cowboy had a cashier's check issued to the Markgrafs, which was made payable to the Markgrafs and listed Cowboy as remitter. The funds were never deposited into any personal account controlled by Davis and Davis never had dominion or control over the funds. Because he was neither payee nor remitter, Davis could not personally access the funds represented by the cashier's check. He was, at most, a mere courier of the cashier's check from Cowboy to the Markgrafs. As was the case in the *Bonded* hypothetical, the funds in this case were transferred directly from the debtor (Cowboy) to the principal's creditor (the Markgrafs). Thus, under the *Bonded* approach, which we have adopted, the Markgrafs are the initial transferees of Cowboy's funds and Davis is the entity for whose benefit the transaction was made.

It is clear that the *Bonded* court's discussion of dominion and control refers to dominion and control over the *funds* after the disputed *transfer*, not dominion and control over the transferor before the transfer. This point is illustrated by the fact that the court in *Bonded* presented two sets of contrasting facts, the actual facts before the court and a hypothetical situation. As discussed above, the court concluded that the result would be different in each case. Yet in both cases the principal exercised control over the transferor prior to the transfer of funds and caused the transferor to make transfer. Thus, the court's reasoning in *Bonded* could not have turned on any evaluation of the principal's control over the debtor. . . .

In this case, the only "control" Davis exercised over the funds after the check was issued was that he delivered the check to the Markgrafs, thus acting as a courier or agent for Cowboy. However, the court in *Bonded* clearly indicates that those who act as mere "financial intermediaries" or "couriers" are not initial transferees under §550. *See Bonded*, 838 F.2d at 893. The term "transferee" "must mean something different from 'possessor' or 'holder' or 'agent,'" or "anyone who touches the money." Id. at 894. Here, Davis, as courier, could only have *prevented* the Markgrafs from exercising dominion and control over the funds if he chose to be an unfaithful courier (much like a mailman can prevent a payee of a check mailed to the payee from ever exercising dominion over the funds represented by the check if the mailman decides never to deliver that piece of mail). However, because the check was made payable to the Markgrafs, this control amounts to nothing more than the ability to defeat the Markgrafs' "right to put the money . . . to [their] own purposes." Id. at 893. All couriers have this type of control. In contrast, the dominion and control test from *Bonded* requires control over the funds and the right to put those funds to *one's own purpose*, not merely the ability to prevent someone else from doing so. The contrary view, that a courier assumes dominion and control over funds entrusted to the courier, would transform the United States Postal Service into the initial transferee under §550 in innumerable instances merely by virtue of having been given the right to deliver financial instruments. The Postal Service would be shocked, no doubt, to learn of the potentially staggering financial liability it was assuming for the price of a thirty-two cent stamp. Furthermore, the fact that the money was being used by the Markgrafs to pay Davis' debt, without more, simply makes Davis the "entity for whose benefit [the] transfer was made." *See Bonded*, 838 F.2d at 895 ("The paradigm 'entity for whose benefit such transfer was made' is a guarantor or debtor — someone who receives the benefit but not the money.").

The Markgrafs argue that Davis' dominion and control began when he directed Cowboy, as principal, to make the transfer in the first place (i.e., they argued that a "transfer" to Davis occurred when he misappropriated Cowboy's funds by causing Cowboy to direct those funds to his own benefit through payment to the Markgrafs). This argument, however, proves too much. Many principals presumably exercise de facto control over the funds of the corporations they manage. They can choose to cause their corporations to use those funds appropriately or inappropriately. The distinction is only relevant to the question whether the principal's conduct amounted to a breach of duty to the corporation. However, that question is not before us. The issue under §550 is to what extent the principal, or anyone else for that matter, exercised control over the disputed funds after the funds left the debtor. Determining the *initial transferee* of a transaction is necessarily a temporal inquiry; there must be a transfer before there can be a transferee. The extent to which a principal has de facto control over the debtor before the funds are transferred from the debtor, and the extent to which the principal uses this control for his or her own benefit in causing the debtor to make a transfer, are not relevant considerations in determining the initial transferee under §550. *See Nordberg*, 904 F.2d at 598 ("[T]he extent of [the principal's] control over [the debtor] generally, and over [the debtor's] actions in transferring the disputed funds to [the creditor] in particular, is entirely irrelevant to the 'initial transferee' issue."); *but see* IRS v. Nordic Village, Inc. (In re Nordic Village, Inc.), 915 F.2d 1049, 1055 & n.3 (6th Cir. 1990) (indicating that the creditor in that case could either be the initial transferee or an immediate transferee, and without deciding, stating in dictum that there is "support for the conclusion that when a corporate officer takes checks drawn from corporate funds to pay personal debts, the corporate officer, and not the payee on the check is the initial transferee"), *rev'd on other grounds*, 503 U.S. 30, 112 S. Ct. 1011, 117 L. Ed. 2d 181 (1992).

In Richardson v. FDIC (In re M. Blackburn Mitchell Inc.), 164 B.R. 117 (Bankr. N.D. Cal. 1994), the court squarely addressed the issue the Markgrafs raise here: "whether a principal who directs and benefits from a fraudulent transfer of funds from a debtor to a third party is *ipso facto* the initial transferee within the meaning of §550 even though the debtor's funds moved directly to the third party; and if not, . . . whether merely by directing the debtor to use a cashier's check to effectuate the transfer, the principal becomes the initial transferee." 164 B.R. at 124. In *Richardson*, the FDIC obtained a judgment against Martha Mitchell, the sole share-holder of the corporation. Id. at 121. Mitchell caused the corporation to purchase from the corporation's bank a cashier's check payable to the FDIC in the amount that Mitchell owed the FDIC. Id. The trustee of the corporation in *Richardson* argued that the FDIC was the initial transferee, and the FDIC claimed (as the Markgrafs claim) that because Mitchell had directed the corporation to pay her personal debt, Mitchell was the initial transferee. The court rejected the FDIC's argument and held that [t]he FDIC obtained full dominion and control over the funds with the right to put the money to its own purposes; it was not holding those funds in trust, or as an agent, for any other party. Therefore, applying the rationale of *Bonded* to the case *sub judice*, the FDIC is the "initial transferee," and Ms. Mitchell would be the entity "for whose benefit [the] transfer was made." Id. at 125 (citation omitted, second alteration in original).

We find that *Richardson*'s interpretation of *Bonded* under these circumstances is persuasive. The court provided the following discussion in support of its interpreta-tion of *Bonded* and its ultimate conclusion that Ms. Mitchell was not the initial transferee:

> The Court believes that the proper focus when analyzing who is a transferee, is the flow of funds. In order to be an initial transferee, one must be a transferee in the ordinary sense of the word. A transfer that may be avoided under applicable sections of the Bankruptcy Code takes place from the debtor to some entity. Thus, receipt of the transferred property is a necessary element for that entity to be a transferee under §550. Simply directing a transfer, i.e., such as by directing a debtor to transfer its funds, is not enough. . . . This Court does not disagree that in order to be a transferee one must obtain dominion and control over funds. But that does not mean that merely because one has dominion and control of funds (as principals of companies ordinarily do) that one is also a transferee. Rather, in order for there to be a transfer of the debtor's funds, the debtor must dispose of or part with them, that is, such funds must actually leave the debtor. In order to be a transferee of the debtor's funds, one must (1) actually receive the funds, and (2) have full dominion and control over them for one's own account, as opposed to receiving them in trust or as agent for someone else. . . . The Court concludes that the mere fact that a debtor's fraudulent transfer was directed by a principal of the debtor does not *ipso facto* transmute that principal into being the "initial trans-feree" within the meaning of §550. Reaching the contrary conclusion in order to protect an "innocent" recipient of the transferred funds, is contrary to policy considerations underlying the Bankruptcy Code. A non-individual debtor such as a corporation or partnership almost always

effects a fraudulent transfer through the actions of its principals, or through the principals of its parent corporation, or other similar entity. . . . Turning every unscrupulous principal into the initial transferee does extreme disservice to §550, and twists the word "transferee" beyond recognition. It violates the statutory language and purpose and severely and unfairly limits the ability of a trustee to recover misappropriated estate property so as to effect a pro rata distribution among a debtor's creditors who have been defrauded. It would, as a practical matter, operate to block trustees from being able to recover funds fraudulently transferred from debtor's estates in numerous bankruptcy cases. Rendering the principal an initial transferee to insulate the entity that actually received the money, also gives too much power to an unscrupulous insider to effect a fraudulent transfer (e.g., to satisfy a personal obligation as was the case here) without allowing a trustee to have the means for avoiding the transfer for the benefit of the debtor's creditors.

Id. at 126-28. . . .

Concluding here, as we do, that Davis is the person for whose benefit the transfer was made and that the Markgrafs are the initial transferees permits the trustee in this case to recover under §550 from either party. Thus, the trustee has a greater chance of recovering the funds for the benefit of the estate. Section 550 expressly allows the trustee to recover from either party, indicating that, as a matter of policy, the option should be preserved where possible. If we were to conclude that Davis was the initial transferee, the Markgrafs would become "subsequent" transferees, and they would not then be regarded as the persons for whose benefit the transfer was made. *Bonded*, 838 F.2d at 895 ("[A] subsequent transferee cannot be the 'entity for whose benefit' the initial transfer was made.").

Our decision here is also consistent with considerations of equity and fairness. In most, if not all, bankruptcy cases someone is going to be injured. This is especially true when there has been a fraudulent transfer of the debtor's funds. However, Congress has already balanced the equitable considerations under §550 by distinguishing between initial transferees, who are strictly liable, and subsequent transferees, who are not strictly liable. Initial transferees are in the best position to monitor fraudulent transfers from the debtor. *Bonded*, 838 F.2d at 892-93 ("The initial transferee is the best monitor; subsequent transferees usually do not know where the assets came from and would be ineffectual monitors if they did."). "[Section] 550(b) leaves with the initial transferee the burden of inquiry and the risk if the conveyance is fraudulent." Id. at 892. The fairness of this approach is illustrated by the case before us. The Markgrafs, as initial transferees of Cowboy's funds, were in the best position to bear the risk of receiving a fraudulent transfer. They received a check purchased by one entity (Cowboy) for the purpose of paying a debt owed to them by another entity (Davis). However, the check clearly showed Cowboy as remitter. Thus, the Markgrafs had inquiry notice that they potentially were receiving funds to which they were not entitled. They could have protected themselves by making adequate inquiry or requiring Davis to issue them a check from his own account. However innocent the Markgrafs may have been, they presumably were no less innocent than the other creditors of the Cowboy estate who have been injured by this fraudulent transfer of funds from the Cowboy estate. Yet the Markgrafs, as initial transferees, were in a better position to investigate and determine the fraudulent nature of this transfer.

By receiving these funds without further investigation or without structuring the payment to make sure the funds came through Davis, the Markgrafs received funds to which they were not entitled. We do not think it is inequitable, under these facts, to make the Markgrafs bear the risk of the fraudulent nature of this transaction rather than Cowboy's other creditors in bankruptcy. In any event, Congress has made its own judgment of who should bear the risk of loss under these situations when it enacted Section 550, and we are bound to accept that judgment.

Conclusion

Based upon the foregoing discussion, we REVERSE the district court order dismissing this case, and REMAND the case for further proceedings not inconsistent with this opinion.

PAUL KELLY, Jr., Circuit Judge, dissenting.

I cannot agree with the Court that Mr. Davis is not a transferee of Cowboy's funds. I do agree that the bank was merely a conduit; the fact that the funds flowed through the bank is immaterial to the central issue, which is the bank's lack of dominion and control over the funds. The Court similarly strays from the central issue by analyzing the flow of funds through various accounts rather than asking if Mr. Davis, in fact, exercised dominion and control over the funds as required by the test established in Bonded Fin. Serv., Inc. v. European Am. Bank, 838 F.2d 890 (7th Cir. 1988), and adopted by us in Malloy v. Citizens Bank of Sapulpa (In re First Sec. Mortgage Co.), 33 F.3d 42 (10th Cir. 1994). I believe that the most persuasive case law as well as the concerns of equity and fairness support finding Mr. Davis to be the initial transferee and the Markgrafs to be subsequent transferees.

As the Court begins its analysis with the Seventh Circuit's decision in *Bonded*, so do I. Both *Bonded* and our decision in *Malloy* held that a bank which acted as a conduit of funds was not an initial transferee under §550 because the bank did not exercise dominion and control over those funds. *Malloy*, 33 F.3d at 44; *Bonded*, 838 F.2d at 893-94. Neither case directly answered the question of who, if not the bank, is the initial transferee. However, those decisions do indicate that we must apply the dominion and control test to determine whether Mr. Davis or the Markgrafs is the initial transferee of Cowboy's funds. *See Malloy*, 33 F.3d at 43-44; *Bonded*, 838 F.2d at 893-94. In IRS v. Nordic Village, Inc. (In re Nordic Village, Inc.), 915 F.2d 1049 (6th Cir. 1990), *rev'd on other grounds*, 503 U.S. 30, 112 S. Ct. 1011, 117 L. Ed. 2d 181 (1992), the Sixth Circuit confronted a similar factual situation. In that case, Joseph Lah, an officer and shareholder of the debtor, drew a check on the corporate account made payable to a bank, which in turn issued several cashier's checks to Lah. The cashier's check at issue was made payable to the IRS, and bore the notation "REMITTER: SWISS HAUS, INC.," under which name the debtor was doing business at the time. Id. at 1050. The court held that the IRS was liable, but it did so on the grounds that the IRS did not demonstrate that it took the cashier's check for value, in good faith, and without knowledge of the fraud, without reaching the "initial transferee" issue. Id. at 1055-56 & n.3. In a line of reasoning that is applicable to the case before us, the court stated in dictum:

> If Lah is viewed as acting for Nordic, then the IRS is the "initial transferee." If Lah is viewed as having taken money illegally from Nordic, he is the "initial transferee" and the delivery of the cashier's check to the IRS makes the IRS an "immediate transferee" of Lah, the "initial transferee." If the IRS is considered as an "immediate transferee" of Lah, the IRS can prevail if the IRS shows that it took for value, in good faith, and without knowledge of the voidability of the transfer.

Id. at 1055 (footnote omitted).

Based on this reasoning, it seems clear that Mr. Davis is the initial transferee of Cowboy's funds. The Davises purchased the cashier's check using Cowboy funds, and then used it to satisfy Mr. Davis's personal indebtedness to the Markgrafs. Surely, under these circumstances, Mr. Davis must be viewed as having taken Cowboy's money illegally, *see Nordic*, 915 F.2d at 1055, making him the initial transferee of the fraudulent conveyance. . . .

PROBLEM 7-30

Bernie Bundle made off with a lot of people's money. He had promised high rates of return (20 percent every 3 months) with low risk, and he actually repaid a number of his investors over a three-year period. His method for making these payments was to entice new investors to contribute to the enterprise and to use that new investment money to pay the dividends to the earlier investors. The talk of high returns and the repayments with interest to the early investors made participating in Bernie's investment pool very exciting. Unfortunately, it came crashing to a halt when a retired accounting professor started looking more closely into Bernie's methods. Bernie was indicted, and a bankruptcy case ensued. The trustee has sued a number of investors under §548(a) and asserts that all of the payments they received in the past two years must be returned. What result? *See* In re Lake States Commodities, Inc., 253 B.R. 866 (Bankr. N.D. Ill. 2000); Jobin v. McKay (In re M & L Business Machine Co.), 84 F.3d 1330, 1341-42 (10th Cir. 1996) ("*McKay*"); Merrill v. Abbott (In re Independent Clearing House Co.), 77 B.R. 843, 857 (D. Utah 1987). For an interesting discussion of the "original" Ponzi scheme perpetrated by Charles Ponzi, see Mary Darby, In Ponzi We Tru$t, Smithsonian Magazine, 135-49 (Dec. 1998), and for a book describing Ponzi's life and machinations, see Mitchell Zuckoff, Ponzi's Scheme, The True Story of a Financial Legend (2005).

VII.   Trustee as Successor to Actual Creditor

Subsection (a) of §544 is the strong arm clause discussed earlier in this chapter. Subsection (b) has nothing to do with that issue. Instead, it gives the trustee the rights of any actual unsecured creditor filing an allowable claim in the bankruptcy proceeding. This subsection has a complicated history. In the cryptic case of Moore v. Bay, 284 U.S. 4 (1931), the United States Supreme Court construed the predecessor of this statute to mean that the trustee could step into the shoes of said actual creditor, recover as if the trustee were such a creditor, pay the amount recovered into the bankruptcy estate (*i.e.*, it was not paid to the creditor him- or herself), and — here is the big part — the trustee was in no way limited by the size of the represented creditor's claim, but could squeeze all the debts owed to the estate into this position. The legislative history of §544(b) clearly states that it was meant to continue the rule of Moore v. Bay. *See* Douglas Whaley, The Dangerous Doctrine of Moore v. Bay, 82 Tex. L. Rev. 73 (2003).

PROBLEM 7-31

In a state the Uniform Fraudulent Transfer Act, sensing financial disaster on the horizon, Ralph Debts sold his valuable stamp collection for a fraction of its value to his nephew Donald, who was unaware of its true value. The only unsecured creditor that Ralph had at this moment was Dr. Paine, his dentist, to whom he owed $800 for some expensive dental work. Three years later, Ralph filed a bankruptcy petition, in which Dr. Paine filed a claim. Ralph scheduled debts amounting to $60,000. Can the trustee use §548(a)(2) to recover the stamp collection (now worth $1,200)? Under UFTA §9 the statute of limitations for attacking fraudulent transfers is four years. Does §544(b) help here?

PROBLEM 7-32

The State of Ohio was concerned that dairy farmers were not getting paid for milk they delivered to milk processing plants when the plants went bankrupt before honoring the checks given to the farmers. It passed a statute, Ohio Revised Code §1311.55 (Agricultural Product Lien), stating that unpaid dairy farmers would be given lien as follows:

> An agricultural producer who delivers an agricultural product under an express or implied contract to an agricultural product handler, or an agricultural product handler who delivers an agricultural product under an express or implied contract to another agricultural product handler, has a lien to secure the payment for all of the agricultural product delivered under that contract.

And a later section contained this priority rule:

> An agricultural producer or handler who perfects his lien within sixty days after the date of delivery, or first delivery if there was a series of deliveries under the contract, of the agricultural product has priority over secured creditors who have security interests under Chapter 1309 of the Revised Code, and has priority over all other liens, claims, or

encumbrances except wage and salary claims of workers who have no ownership interest in the business of the agricultural product handler, warehouseman's liens as provided in §1307.14 of the Revised Code, and amounts owed by the lienholder to the handler that are subject to setoff.

Assume that an Ohio milk processing plant files for bankruptcy while owing the following debts: a perfected lien in favor of Octopus National Bank (who is owed $100,000) all its inventory, a dairy farmer who delivered milk in return for a bounced $8,000 check, and the janitorial staff of the plant, who is owed back wages of $300. How does §544(b) fit into this picture?

PROBLEM 7-33

Luddite Technologies had one major asset: a building in downtown Manhattan worth $82,000,000. The building was subject to a first mortgage in favor of First Mortgage Bank for $42,000,000, a judicial lien in favor of Future Shock, Inc., in the amount of $30,000, and a second mortgage of $49,000,000 given to Second Mortgage Bank. Assume that both of the mortgages have been perfected by proper filings in the real property records, but that the judicial lien is subject to avoidance as a preference. Luddite's trustee in bankruptcy has hired you as the trustee's legal counsel. If it attacks the $30,000 judicial lien as a preference, wipes it out, but preserves its priority position over the second mortgage by using §551, can it then use §544(b) and the rule of Moore v. Bay to expand the $30,000 position and turn Second Mortgage Bank into an unsecured creditor?

VIII.   Postpetition Transfers

PROBLEM 7-34

The day after she filed her bankruptcy petition, Portia Moot gave her engagement ring to her mother as a gift. Is this a fraudulent transfer under §548? Can the trustee recover the ring? *See* §549(a).

PROBLEM 7-35

John Ross made a valiant — but ultimately unsuccessful — attempt to operate a dude ranch. He tried to cut his losses by selling the property, but after six months he gave up trying to find a buyer and filed a Chapter 7 petition. Two weeks later, Donald Harrumph offered to buy the property from John for $20,000 more than the outstanding mortgage on the property. John and Donald had spoken previously about the property, but those talks had broken off two months earlier. John was happy to hear about Donald's renewed interest in the property and promptly agreed to the sale, closing the deal four weeks after the bankruptcy case was commenced. The trustee is now seeking to recover the property from Donald. What result? *See* §549(c).

PROBLEM 7-36

Portia Moot banked at Octopus National Bank. For two days after she filed her petition the bank, unaware of this event, paid checks she had drawn on her account. The checks totaled $600. Is the bank in trouble here? *See* §542(c).

The 1999 revision of Article 9 has for the first time made a filed financing statement good against a judicial lien creditors even though attachment of the security interest has not yet occurred (which could happen if the creditor files before loaning the money to the debtor or before having the debtor sign the security agreement); *see* §9-317(a)(2) and Official Comment 4 thereto. Since the strong arm clause of the Bankruptcy Code in §544(a) gives the bankruptcy trustee the status of such a creditor, this creates the interesting question of whether a filed but unperfected security interest is also good against the trustee. The next Problem addresses that issue.

PROBLEM 7-37

Octopus National Bank agreed to loan Luddite Technologies $100,000, taking a security interest in Luddite's extensive inventory, and the parties signed a security agreement to this effect. The bank immediately filed a financing statement in the appropriate place. The next day, unknown to the bank, Luddite filed a Chapter 7 bankruptcy petition, and later that day received from the bank the bank's check for $100,000, which Luddite deposited in its bank account at another bank. Since perfection cannot occur until attachment (*see* §9-308(a)), and attachment is necessarily postponed until the bank gives value (which let's assume happened when the check was received by Luddite), does the bank have a perfected security interest in Luddite's inventory? If not, can the bank get its $100,000 back?

IX.   Avoidance and Postponement of Certain Liens

PROBLEM 7-38

Attorney Sam Ambulance was caught stealing the funds of his wealthiest client, Maude Riches, and she sued him for fraud and conversion, recovering a judgment for $300,000 in actual damages plus $100,000 in punitive damages. She had the sheriff execute this judgment by seizing all of Sam's property, and four months later he filed a Chapter 7 bankruptcy petition. Can the trustee avoid all or any part of Maude's lien? *See* §724(a).

The priority statute, §507, reflects the hierarchy that Congress thought most important in the payment of claims. Note that under that section tax claims get paid last of all the priority claims. However, in many bankruptcies the IRS has often filed a federal tax lien against the taxpayer's property, thus making it a secured creditor who would take off the top, defeating those who would otherwise get a superior §507 priority, were the IRS unsecured. To preserve the priorities established by §507 Congress enacted §724(b), (c), and (d), which establishes the so-called "postponement" principle. Use it to solve this last Problem.

PROBLEM 7-39

The taxpayer had one asset: a parcel of realty worth $900,000. It was subject to a perfected mortgage in favor of Octopus National Bank in the amount of $600,000, when the IRS filed a federal tax lien against the property. The taxpayer owed the federal government $200,000 in back taxes. After the tax lien was filed, Maude Riches sued the taxpayer, got a judgment for $80,000 against him, and filed a judicial lien against the property to secure this debt. Five months later the taxpayer filed a Chapter 7 petition. The §507 priorities, other than tax debts, amounted to $30,000, and the taxpayer had other unsecured, nonpriority debts of $400,000. Use §724 to decide who gets what.

CHAPTER *8*

Chapter 13 Cases

Open up the Yellow Pages of any larger city's phone book to "Attorneys" and you will find advertisements focusing on the wonders of Chapter 13 relief, with statements such as: "Go Bankrupt and Keep All Your Property!" "Consolidate Debts to One Affordable Payment!" and "Chapter 13: A Dignified, Honorable Way to Pay Your Debts!" Some bankruptcy judges are very fond of Chapter 13 plans, so much so that they seriously discourage debtors from choosing a Chapter 7 liquidation in consumer cases if they believe the debtors could pay any portion of their debts in a 13; other bankruptcy judges pooh-pooh the whole idea behind a Chapter 13 ("The reason these people are in bankruptcy in the first place is because they can't keep to a budget"), and rarely confirm proposed Chapter 13 plans. As you thread your way through these materials, make up your own mind whether Chapter 13 is panacea or Pandora's box.

In cases under Chapter 7, the debtor's nonexempt assets are liquidated and the funds distributed to creditors. In Chapter 13, on the other hand, the debtor keeps all of his or her nonexempt property. Instead of liquidating the property, the debtor agrees to pay the trustee an amount set out in the debtor's plan over a stated period of time. The trustee then redistributes that money to the debtor's creditors.

Chapter 13 offers a number of benefits not available under Chapter 7. For example, in Chapter 13 the debtor proposes a plan that, if confirmed by the court, permits the debtor to retain possession of all property, while paying some or all of the creditors' claims. Moreover, the debtor is even able to keep property that is subject to enforceable liens. Unlike the need to pay off those claims in full by way of redemption in a Chapter 7 case *(see* §722), in Chapter 13 the debtor can cram down secured claims by paying the value of the secured claim to the creditor over the length of the plan. If the value of the collateral equals or exceeds the amount of the claim, the debtor might consider curing any prepetition defaults and reinstating the underlying contract with the creditor. If the payments will extend beyond the life of the plan, the obligation remaining at the end of the plan will be excerpted from the Chapter 13 discharge. In the meantime, however, the debtor retains the property. This is particularly important for debtors trying to protect their homes from pending foreclosure proceedings.

Chapter 13 also provides for a stay in favor of *codebtors*. Family members, coworkers, and friends may be particularly appreciative of a debtor who seeks relief under Chapter 13 rather than under Chapter 7 because they may be protected against creditor collection efforts that would otherwise be undertaken against them.

In this chapter we will look at these and other issues peculiar to Chapter 13 cases. As you read these materials, consider whether debtors facing the problems presented are better served by seeking Chapter 13 relief rather than relief under Chapter 7.

I. Eligibility for Relief

The essence of Chapter 13 is demonstrated by the fact that only voluntary Chapter 13 cases are allowed. A creditor cannot file an involuntary Chapter 13 petition against a debtor.

To be a Chapter 13 debtor, one must be an individual with regular income. Section 101(30), in connection with §101(41), provides that only natural persons whose income is sufficiently stable and regular to make payments under a Chapter 13 plan may obtain Chapter 13 relief.[1] Section 109(e) also limits access to Chapter 13. Chapter 13 debtors must owe noncontingent, liquidated, unsecured debts of less than $336,900 and noncontingent, liquidated, secured debts of less than $1,010,650 in order to be eligible for relief. If spouses seek to commence a joint Chapter 13 case, then the aggregate amount of their debts must likewise fit under these same limitations. The debt limits are *not* doubled for them if they file a joint case. *See* Bankruptcy Code §302.

Two other issues arise with respect to the debt limits. First, the debts are determined as of the date of the filing of the petition; and second, contingent and unliquidated claims are excluded from the calculation for eligibility purposes. If you compare §109(e) with §303(b)(1), however, you will notice that disputed claims are not excluded explicitly from the §109 debt limits, but they are excluded from the category of claims that can commence an involuntary bankruptcy case. Congress knows how to exclude disputed claims when it wants to, and it certainly has not excluded disputed claims from the eligibility calculation in §109(e). Consequently, simply asserting a dispute over a particular claim will not cause that claim to be subtracted from the debtor's outstanding obligations to reduce them below the maximum allowed amounts in Chapter 13.

Just like individual debtors in Chapter 7 cases, Chapter 13 debtors also must complete a credit counseling briefing prior to filing their Chapter 13 petitions.

---

1. Individuals who are stockbrokers or commodity brokers are not eligible for Chapter 13 relief. Bankruptcy Code §101(30).

Bankruptcy Code §109(h)(1). The same exceptions to this requirement apply as in Chapter 7 cases. *See* Bankruptcy Code §109(h)(2) and (3).

Determine whether the following debtors are eligible for Chapter 13 relief.

PROBLEM 8-1

Phast Talker was an aluminum siding salesman. He was famous among "tin men" for his salesmanship. He became so famous that the state consumer protection agency came looking for him. Phast had a number of other debts that he owed, so he decided to file a Chapter 13 petition. He scheduled unsecured debts of $210,000 and secured debts of $175,000. At the time he filed the petition, the state consumer protection agency had brought an action against him for violations of state law and sought sanctions of $50,000. The state obtained relief from the automatic stay to continue to pursue the action, and four months later the consumer protection agency obtained a $150,000 judgment against Phast. In the meantime, both the Chapter 13 trustee and the state consumer protection agency had moved to dismiss Phast's Chapter 13 case on eligibility grounds. Is Phast Talker eligible for Chapter 13 relief? In re Hughes, 98 B.R. 784 (Bankr. S.D. Ohio 1989).

PROBLEM 8-2

Cosmo Palmer loved to acquire assets. He found that it was relatively easy to do if he was willing to grant sellers a security interest in the assets he purchased. Through these means, Cosmo was able to purchase a palatial residence, several beautiful automobiles, and a great deal of furniture. All told, the purchase price of these assets exceeded $1 million. Within eight months it became clear that Cosmo could not afford to make the payments required to retain these assets. The mortgage company had commenced foreclosure proceedings, and Cosmo was receiving increasingly nasty correspondence from his other creditors. Cosmo estimated the current value of the property he had purchased at $600,000. The outstanding balance he owed on the debts secured by those assets was $950,000. Assuming that Cosmo has no other indebtedness, is he eligible for Chapter 13 relief? In re Ficken, 2 F.3d 299 (8th Cir. 1993).

PROBLEM 8-3

Jody owned and operated Camp Armstrong. To run the camp, Jody had to purchase a significant amount of playground and other recreational equipment. She also incurred significant additional indebtedness for insurance, salaries, and a variety of other expenses incident to the operation of the camp. She purchased the equipment from Park Recreational Equipment Company for $300,000. However, Park failed to file a financing statement in the appropriate place so that its security interest was unperfected. Jody's other debts are unsecured and equal $150,000. Is she eligible for Chapter 13 relief? Section 544(a), §502(h); In re Toronto, 165 B.R. 746 (Bankr. D. Conn. 1994).

The unsecured/secured debt limitations in §109(e) are subject to periodic revision. The debt limits as of April 1, 2004, are $307,675 of noncontingent, liquidated unsecured debts, and $922,975 of noncontingent, liquidated secured debts. Under §104 of the Bankruptcy Code, these amounts are adjusted every three years. The periodic adjustments protect against any erosion in the availability of Chapter 13 relief both for consumer and business debtors. Keep in mind, however, that Chapter 13 remains available only to individuals. Corporations are not eligible for Chapter 13 relief. Can an individual who owns all the stock of a corporation dissolve the corporation, assume all the debts of the corporation, acquire its assets, and seek Chapter 13 relief?

A. Source and Sufficiency of Income

The other side of the coin from the amount and character of liabilities is the source and sufficiency of the debtor's income. Under §109(e) the debtor's income must be "sufficiently stable and regular to enable [the debtor] to make payments under a plan under Chapter 13." By making Chapter 13 relief available to individuals with regular income, Congress substantially expanded the pool of debtors eligible to proceed under Chapter 13, as compared to the more restricted definition of wage earners for whom Chapter XIII was available under the former Bankruptcy Act. Under current Chapter 13 wage earners, worm farmers, and welfare recipients are all eligible for relief. The source of the income is less important than the sufficiency and regularity of the income. Apply §§109(e) and 101(30) to the following individuals. Are they eligible for Chapter 13 relief?

PROBLEM 8-4

(a) Ward Cleaver had been laid off from his position as a mid-level manager with a large computer company. His unemployment benefits have run out, and he has no other source of income. Nevertheless, Ward has sought Chapter 13 relief and asserts that he can fund a plan through a monthly stipend from his wife, June. In re Cregut, 69 B.R. 21 (Bankr. D. Ariz. 1986).

(b) Jack and Jill were husband and wife. They operated a moving company, and in the course of their business, each suffered personal injuries that forced them to reduce their work activities. They filed a joint Chapter 13 petition and had proposed to fund a plan by borrowing $6,000 from Jack's parents. Are Jack and Jill eligible for Chapter 13 relief? In re Safka, 18 B.R. 196 (Bankr. D. Vt. 1982).

(c) Steve sold computers on commission. His business was up and down. Sometimes the computers sold like hotcakes, while at other times they seemed like rotten apples. During a good month Steve would net $6,000, while in a bad month he might take home only $500. Is Steve eligible for Chapter 13?

II. The Codebtor Stay

PROBLEM 8-5

When Donald filed his Chapter 13 petition he owed $8,000 to Huey State Bank on a vacation loan that had been guaranteed by Donald's Uncle Scrooge. The bank immediately contacted Scrooge and demanded repayment of this debt.

(a) Can the bank do this? *See* §1301(a). Could the bank do this if Donald had filed a Chapter 7 petition?

(b) If Uncle Scrooge is in the business of being a surety, does §1301 protect him?

(c) Does §1301 protect Scrooge if the loan had been made to help Donald run his comic book store? What if the debt was owed to the I.R.S. for taxes? As to this last issue, *see* In re Westberry, 215 F.3d 589 (6th Cir. 2000).

(d) Suppose the money for the loan had been given by Donald to Uncle Scrooge, who is the one who actually took the vacation. Would §1301 then protect Scrooge in Donald's Chapter 13 proceeding? *See* §1301(c)(1).

(e) Huey State Bank contacts you, its attorney. It has heard rumors that Scrooge is moving all his considerable assets to South America and is said to be packing his bags for a permanent move south. What can you do? *See* §1301(c) and (d).

The filing of a Chapter 13 petition operates as a stay of creditor actions against the debtor and the debtor's property pursuant to §362, but it also creates a codebtor stay, one of the major benefits of a Chapter 13 filing. The codebtor stay was enacted in response to problems that existed under the former Chapter XIII. In those cases, creditors who had third parties cosign the debtor's obligations were able to obtain more favorable treatment than other creditors. The cosigners frequently were friends, relatives, or coworkers of the debtor. Many times they agreed to help out the debtor at the insistence of the creditor. The relationship between debtor and cosigners created additional pressure for the debtor to ensure that the creditor holding the cosigned claim was paid in full. Section 1301 of the Bankruptcy Code is intended to operate to reduce that pressure by permitting the debtor to address those claims in a more systematic fashion. Together with the authorization in §1322(b)(1) to treat these codebtor claims more favorably, Chapter 13 debtors are now more able to reorganize their financial affairs while the codebtors retain some protection against collection activities during the Chapter 13 proceedings.

The codebtor stay does not entirely stymie creditors. If the debtor's plan does not propose to pay the codebtor claim in full, or if the creditor's ability to collect on the codebtor claim will be irreparably harmed, the court can grant relief from the codebtor stay to permit the creditor to take action directly against the codebtor. *See, e.g.,* In re Case, 148 B.R. 901 (Bankr. W.D. Mo. 1992).

PROBLEM 8-6

Hamlet's loan to Elsinore Credit Union was guaranteed by his mother, Gertrude. He filed his Chapter 13 petition, but Elsinore negligently failed to file a claim in the proceeding, thus losing its unsecured claim per §502(b)(9). Without an allowed claim, Elsinore has no right to receive payments under the plan. Since it is not receiving any payments from the debtor, it would like to commence a collection action against the Gertrude. Can Hamlet prevent this? *See* Abraham & Strauss v. Francis, 15 B.R. 998 (Bankr. E.D.N.Y. 1981). Could Elsinore seek relief under §1301(c)(3) if it could show irreparable harm?

The codebtor stay terminates by operation of law once the Chapter 13 case is closed, dismissed, or converted to a case under Chapter 7 or Chapter 11. At that point, the creditor could initiate action against the codebtor to collect any unpaid amounts. The claim against the debtor, on the other hand, would be discharged if the debtor had made all payments under the Chapter 13 plan.

III.   The Chapter 13 Plan

Further underscoring the voluntary nature of Chapter 13 proceedings, §1321 provides that only the debtor may file a plan. Under Rule 3015(b) the debtor is directed to file his or her plan either with the petition or within 15 days thereafter. In most instances, debtors meet the deadline. The creditors will receive a summary of the plan that will describe generally the proposed repayment terms. Under the 2005 amendments to the Bankruptcy Code, a debtor whose income is above the state median for a household of comparable size must commit his or her disposable income to the plan for five years under §1325(b)(1)(B) and (b)(4). That disposable income will be determined under the means test formula set out in §707(b). Debtors with a lower income will continue to be eligible to file plans without a specific duration, but if the trustee or a creditor objects, the plan will have to last for at least three years.

A.   *Mandatory Plan Provisions*

Section 1322 sets out the mandatory and permissive provisions for Chapter 13 plans. Under §1322(a), the debtor's plan must provide for the submission of future earnings or income sufficient to fund the plan, it must provide for the full payment, over time, of priority claims (unless the priority creditor agrees to less favorable treatment), and, if the debtor's plan classifies claims (as every plan does), the plan must provide for the same treatment of each claim in a particular class.

PROBLEM 8-7

After 12 years of marriage and four children, Jack Sprat fled his home and family obligations, and his wife Helen divorced him shortly thereafter. He never made a single payment of child support as ordered by the divorce court, and when he filed a Chapter 13 petition earlier this year he owed $32,000 support arrearages. Must his plan deal with this obligation? *See* Bankruptcy Code §§1322(a)(2), 507(a)(1), 1328(a)(2), and 523(a)(5). There is no way Jack's current income is sufficient to pay off this debt over the life of a Chapter 13 plan, even if the plan continues for five years, but Jack is certain he could pay it all off (including making the currently due payments) over ten years. Do you, as his attorney, have any advice for him?

The mandatory provisions generally are quite easy for debtors to meet, but if the debtor owes alimony or child support there could be trouble. Such claims are entitled to priority status under §507(a)(1), and thus have to be paid in full under the terms of the Chapter 13 plan. They are still also nondischargeable, even in Chapter 13 cases; §1328(a)(2).

If the debtor owes a significant amount of alimony and child support, he or she may not be able to obtain confirmation of a plan without the agreement of the ex-spouse to accept some lesser payment. However, this agreement might be more forthcoming than you would initially guess. A former spouse owed significant back alimony is not usually considered an ally of the debtor, but without confirmation of a Chapter 13 plan, the ex-spouse might have an even lesser chance of receiving any payment on those past-due amounts. Moreover, even when the payments are made under the plan, any remaining portion of the unpaid alimony or support obligation will still be excepted from the discharge. Therefore, putting the debtor in a position to make some payments over time and discharge other debts that would otherwise be competing for the debtor's assets could create a long-term net gain to the ex-spouse. In any event, the priority status for these claims combined with the requirement that all priority claims be paid in full in Chapter 13 cases significantly shifts the leverage available to those creditors in Chapter 13 cases.

B. Permissive Plan Provisions

Section 1322(b) contains a long list of provisions that debtors may include within their Chapter 13 plans. Moreover, the final item on the list provides that the debtor's plan may "include any other appropriate provision not inconsistent with this title." §1322(b)(11). This encourages creativity in plan drafting.

The remaining portions of §1322(b) authorize plan provisions setting out the classification of claims, the timing and amount of payments to creditors, the curing of prebankruptcy defaults and reinstatement of the terms of the obligation, the treatment of executory contracts, and the vesting of property in either the debtor or another entity.

The rules on confirmation in §1325 must also be considered during plan preparation. The court shall confirm a Chapter 13 plan if (1) it complies with the Bankruptcy Code, (2) appropriate fees have been paid, (3) it has been proposed in good faith, (4) it meets the "best interest of creditors test" (*see below*), (5) secured claims are properly paid or satisfied, and (6) the plan is feasible. Furthermore, if the Chapter 13 trustee or an unsecured creditor objects to the debtor's plan, the plan must provide either that the objecting creditor's claim will be paid in full or that the debtor will submit all of his or her disposable income into the plan for three years. Conspicuously absent from the confirmation standards is any requirement that creditors vote on the plan. We will consider the application of these provisions as they relate to general unsecured claims, secured claims, and a special category of secured claims — home mortgages.

C.   Treatment of General Unsecured Claims

Since creditors in Chapter 13 cases do not get to vote on a debtor's plan, §1325(a)(4) provides that the property to be distributed under the plan to those creditors must be at least as much as the creditors would receive in a Chapter 7 case. This is referred to as the best interest of creditors test. The notion is that since the creditors are receiving treatment that is equal to or better than that they would receive in a Chapter 7, they are essentially deemed to have accepted the plan. Since most consumer bankruptcy cases are either no asset or nominal asset cases, it is not very difficult to meet the best interest of creditors test in most Chapter 13 cases. In those cases in which the debtor has unencumbered nonexempt assets, the court must determine the value of those assets and must then compare that amount with the payments proposed to be made to unsecured creditors under the debtor's Chapter 13 plan. The present value of that stream of Chapter 13 payments must equal or exceed the value of the assets that would be distributed in a hypothetical Chapter 7 case.

PROBLEM 8-8

All parties in Alice's Chapter 13 bankruptcy proceeding agree that the unsecured creditors would have received $10,000 in a Chapter 7 liquidation. Alice's Chapter 13 plan therefore proposes to pay the creditors $2,000 once a year for five years. Can this plan be confirmed? What adjustments, if any, would be necessary to meet the "best interests" test?

Another significant hurdle for Chapter 13 debtors in obtaining confirmation of their plans is that the plan must be proposed in "good faith"; §1325(a)(3). A substantial body of law has arisen under this section, and we will consider that issue later in this chapter. More to the moment, if creditors object to the debtor's proposed Chapter 13 plan, the debtor must submit all of his or her disposable income into the plan in order to obtain confirmation. In defining "disposable income" the "means test" that we considered in Chapter 2 of this book is resurrected in the convoluted language of §1325(b)(2). If the debtor's current month income exceeds the state's median family income, the same calculations we did in Chapter 2 are used to define the amount that debtor must commit to funding the Chapter 13 plan.

The debtor can sidestep the requirement of paying all of his or her disposable income into the plan for three years by paying the claim of the objecting creditor *in full*; §1325(b)(1)(A). If the debtor does this, however, what's to keep the other creditors from raising the same objection? Presumably, any other wide-awake creditors will be heard from. Additionally, a plan that would pay the objecting creditor in full while other creditors with similar claims receive lesser payments arguably does not meet the antidiscrimination provision of §1322(b)(1).

PROBLEM 8-9

Rose Maybud's Chapter 13 plan put her creditors into different classes, as follows: (1) the priority claims would be placed in one class and paid in full; (2) Adam Finance, whose claim was guaranteed by Rose's Aunt Hannah, and this class will be paid in full; (3) her evil mother, to whom Rose owed $20,000, was placed in a separate class and the plan proposed to pay her 3 percent of that debt; and (4) all and the other creditors (unsecured) would be placed in the final class and paid 5 percent of the debts due them. A Chapter 7 liquidation would have paid unsecured creditors 3 percent. There are no secured creditors. Can this plan be confirmed?

Section 1322(a)(3) provides that if the debtor's plan classifies claims into different classes, all of the claims within a particular class must receive identical treatment. Note that the section does *not* require that all similar claims be placed in the same class. Instead, the provision is written only to address treatment within a class of claims. Section 1322(b)(1), however, provides that if the debtor's plan classifies claims, the plan "may not discriminate unfairly against any class." The section also provides that co-debtor claims can be treated "differently than other unsecured claims." This specific reference to codebtor claims has resulted in a authorization by some courts for their more favorable treatment vis-à-vis other unsecured claims, but the courts are not in agreement on this. *See* the extensive discussion of the possible meanings of the exact statutory language in the concurring of opinion of Judge Benavides in In re Ramirez, 204 F.3d 595, 596-601 (5th Cir. 2000).

Debtors also are interested in proposing more favorable treatment to claims that are otherwise nondischargeable in Chapter 13 — such as those for student loans — as compared to unsecured claims that will be discharged at the conclusion of the case. Alimony and support claims, which would also survive Chapter 13, *must* be paid in full as part of the plan since they are priority claims. The nondischargeable student loan, on the other hand, is not entitled to any particular priority under §507 of the Code. Thus, such a claim does not have to be paid in full in Chapter 13, though debtors would prefer to do that even if it will necessarily reduce the amounts other unsecured creditors will collect.

The courts have reached a variety of conclusions about the limits on the "special" treatment Chapter 13 debtors may give to "special" creditors. While one court stated that as long as the creditors were receiving at least what they would get in a Chapter 7 case the debtor could propose to pay creditors with "red headed secretaries" more than the other creditors — In re Sutherland, 3 B.R. 420 (Bankr. W.D. Ark. 1980) — most courts would refuse to allow such a classification.

PROBLEM 8-10

Ralph Rackstraw's Chapter 13 plan proposed to put his nondischargeable student loans into one class and pay that class in full, and his other unsecured creditors into a second class, and each would be paid 10 percent of their debts, the same amount they would have received in a Chapter 7 liquidation. Should the court confirm this plan? *See* Groves v. LaBarge (In re Groves), 39 F.3d 212 (8th Cir. 1994).

PROBLEM 8-11

Ralph has another idea. Since his student loans are his biggest worry, how about this: He'll file a Chapter 7 and discharge all his other debts, and then file a Chapter 13 and propose a plan that will pay off his student loans (this procedure is affectionately called a "Chapter 20" by the bankruptcy bar). Will this fly? *See* In re Tucker, 159 B.R. 325 (Bankr. D. Mont. 1993), and Johnson v. Home State Bank, 501 U.S. 78 (1990) (generally allowing good faith "Chapter 20s").

PROBLEM 8-12

Ralph has been told by you that §1325(b) requires that all of his disposable income be used to fund the plan for its first three years, so he asks about this possibility: His plan will pay all the unsecured creditors the same amount for the first three years (this amount will pay them even more than they would get in a Chapter 7 liquidation), and then the plan will continue for another two years, but it will pay only his student loan debt in this latter period. Is this one okay? *See* §1322(b)(10).

Some courts have approved more favorable treatment of student loan claims through the application of §1322(b)(5) of the Code. That section provides generally that the plan can cure past defaults and reinstate obligations that will outlast the plan. For example, according to its terms, a student loan debt may have eight years to run. The Chapter 13 plan may last only three years. The plan could provide for the payment of the past due amounts under the loan and the maintenance of current payments on the debt during the life of the plan. Since the debt would "outlast" the plan, it is excepted from the Chapter 13 discharge. §1328(a)(1). The decisions that authorize this treatment of student loan obligations do not address the impact of §502(b)(2) (the acceleration of unmatured claims) on the student loan claim. Certainly, §1322(b)(5), being a provision specific to Chapter 13, should override the acceleration of indebtedness rule of the more general provision in Chapter 5 of the Bankruptcy Code. Nevertheless, it does not follow that the full payment of current installments along with the curing of past defaults does not still constitute an unfair discrimination against the other creditors. Note also that §1322(b)(10) will not allow the payment of interest on such debts during the life of the plan unless all claims are paid in full.

PROBLEM 8-13

For the eight years that he has worked for the same company, Luke Kautz has regularly had an amount deducted from his paycheck and put in his pension plan to provide for his future retirement. From time to time he has borrowed money from this pension plan, and because of these borrowings currently owes the pension plan $4,000. The pension plan rules provide that if the employee does not repay borrowed sums, this amount is simply deducted from the amount to be paid at retirement. Now Luke has filed a Chapter 13 petition, and his plan proposes to pay the amount owed to the pension plan in full, while paying other creditors only 15 percent of the monies due them. Does this plan violate §1325(b)(1) and would you, as a bankruptcy judge, confirm it? *See* §1322(f).

D.   Disposable Income

PROBLEM 8-14

Sly Yates has amassed an enormous amount of unsecured debt due to the generosity of the issuers of credit cards, and he now wants to get rid of it in bankruptcy. A Chapter 7 liquidation would pay unsecured creditors nothing, so his Chapter 13 plan also proposes to pay them nothing (none of these debts would survive discharge). He recently obtained a well-paying job as a blackjack dealer in Las Vegas, and he wants to get on with his life. Will the court confirm this plan? *See* §1325(a)(3) and (b). Suppose Sly's income increases during the plan repayment period. Is the new excess income "disposable"? *Compare* In re Anderson, 21 F.3d 355 (9th Cir. 1994) (only *"projected"* disposable income must be submitted to fund plan), *with* In re Akin, 54 B.R. 700 (Bankr. D. Neb. 1985) (all increases in disposable income during the life of the plan must be used to fund the plan).

In 1984, Congress added the notion of disposable income to Chapter 13. Prior to that time, the primary focus of creditor efforts to prevent confirmation of Chapter 13 plans was the requirement that the plan be proposed in good faith. In particular, creditors objected on good faith grounds to plans that provided little or no payment to creditors. Those plans were otherwise confirmable because they met the best interest of creditors test given that the debtor had no nonexempt assets.

What does "disposable income" mean? Section 1325(b) gives two definitions for the term. If the debtor's annual income exceeds the median income of the same size family in the debtor's state, the means test of §707(b) determines the amount of the debtor's disposable income. Already the courts have noted that there are a number of interpretational questions about the determination of a debtor's "projected disposable income" in Chapter 13 cases. *See* Bankruptcy Code §1325(b)(1)(B). The amount of a debtor's disposable income also dictates the "applicable repayment period" for a Chapter 13 debtor. The following decision and problems highlight some of these issues.

In re Johnson

United State Bankruptcy Court, Northern District of Illinois, 2009
400 B.R. 639

EUGENE R. WEDOFF, Bankruptcy Judge.

This Chapter 13 case is before the court for ruling on the confirmation of the debtors' plan. The standing trustee has objected to confirmation, arguing that the plan fails to devote all of the debtors' "disposable income" received during the applicable commitment period to the payment of unsecured claims, as required by §1325(b) of the Bankruptcy Code (Title 11, U.S.C.). The dispositive issue is whether "disposable income" under §1325(b) must be calculated on the basis of the debtors' average income during the six months before bankruptcy, or whether debtors' post-bankruptcy income may be taken into consideration.

Many courts have addressed this issue with substantially conflicting results, but the best reading of the statutory language is that a debtor's post-bankruptcy income not only may be considered in determining disposable income, but should be the exclusive basis for doing so. Because the debtors' plan in this case devotes more than the required amount of their post-bankruptcy income to payments of unsecured debt, the plan complies with §1325(b) and will be confirmed over the trustee's objection. . . .

Factual Background

The relevant facts are not in dispute. Richard and Linda Johnson filed a Chapter 13 petition and plan on May 12, 2008. At the time, both of the Johnsons were working, and their combined gross monthly income was $13,500, which they reflected in Schedule I. (Docket No. 1.) In the Schedule J, the Johnsons calculated that after payroll deductions and their actual expenses, they had $3,705 per month in income that could be devoted to a Chapter 13 plan. (*Id.*) They submitted a plan that proposed monthly payments of almost all of this amount — $3,700 — for sixty months, a total of $220,000, of which $162,000 would be paid to general unsecured creditors. (Docket No. 9.)[2]

At the time they filed their petition, the Johnsons also filed Official Form 22C, the "means test" form, providing a different view of their income and expenses. (Docket No. 7.) Form 22C requires a statement of the average monthly income that debtors receive in the six calendar months before the filing of their bankruptcy cases. During the six calendar months before the Johnsons filed their case — November 2007 through April 2008 — Linda Johnson had received, in addition to her regular salary, workers compensation payments for a hand injury, but these payments stopped in April, before the bankruptcy filing. (*See* Debtors' Response to Trustee's Objection, Docket No. 35, at 2.) Including the workers compensation payments on Form 22C, as the form requires, the Johnsons reported average monthly income of $16,045. (Docket No. 7, Line 57.) The Johnsons then listed income deductions specified by Form 22C in a total amount of $11,505. (*Id.*, Line 52.) Finally, the Johnsons reported Form 22C "disposable income" (total income less deductions) as $4,540. (*Id.*, Line 57.)

The trustee relied on this $4,540 figure as the sole basis for her objection to confirmation. (Docket No. 24.) She argued that, under §1325(b) of the Code, the Johnsons must either make sixty payments of $4,540 — a total of $274,400 — toward allowed unsecured claims, or else pay those debts in full. Because the allowed general unsecured claims ($221,291) are less than that amount, the trustee contended that full payment of these claims is required, rather than the $162,000 that the Johnsons' plan proposes.

In response to the trustee's objection, the Johnsons amended Form 22C to reflect the income they were receiving when they filed their bankruptcy case, which did not include any workers compensation payments, instead of the six-month pre-filing average they originally reported. (Docket No. 35, Ex. E.) The amended form reflects disposable income of $1,995 monthly, substantially less than the $3,700 that the Johnsons' plan proposes to contribute. The amended monthly disposable income over sixty months would amount to $119,700.

The different calculations of available income can be set out in a table:

	Schedules I & J (post-filing income and actual expenses)	Original Form 22C (six-month pre-filing average income and means test expenses)	Amended Form 22C (post-filing income and means test expenses)
Income	$ 13,500	$ 16,045	$ 13,500
Deductions	9,795	11,505	11,505
Disposable income	3,705	4,540	1,995
60-month total	$222,300	$272,400	$119,700

2. Other portions of the funds contributed under the plan would pay secured and priority creditors. The allowed general unsecured claims in this case total $221,291. The trustee mistakenly asserts that the plan limits payments to 60% of this amount (less than $133,000). Paragraph E.8 of the plan actually states that general unsecured claims will be paid "to the extent possible" from the $220,000 contribution specified in Section D of the plan, "but *not less than* 60% of their allowed amount" (emphasis added). The 60% figure is thus a floor, not a ceiling, and the plan in fact provides for payment of $162,000 toward general unsecured claims.

The trustee has not contested the accuracy of any of the income or expense items reported by the Johnsons. She questions only their legal significance.

Legal Analysis

Section 1325 of the Bankruptcy Code sets out the requirements for confirmation of a Chapter 13 plan. Among these is §1325(b), a provision establishing minimum payments that a plan must make on account of unsecured claims if an unsecured creditor or the trustee objects. The text of §1325(b) was substantially amended by the Bankruptcy Abuse Prevention and Consumer Protection Act of 2005 ("BAPCPA"). As amended, §1325(b) is extensive, exceeding 600 words. Its basic operation, however, is simple:

(1) If an unsecured creditor or the trustee objects, then
(2) the plan must either provide for the claim of the objecting creditor to be paid in full [all claims if the trustee objects], or
(3) the plan must provide for unsecured claims to be paid with "all of the debtor's projected disposable income to be received in the applicable commitment period beginning on the date that the first payment is due under the plan."

The trustee has objected to the Johnsons' plan because, she asserts, it neither pays unsecured claims in full nor devotes to their payment "all of the debtor's projected disposable income to be received in the applicable commitment period."

The question raised by the objection is how much the Johnsons must propose to pay toward their unsecured claims under this requirement. Two terms of art are directly involved: "disposable income" and "applicable commitment period." Each depends to some extent on another term of art, "current monthly income," and so an understanding of current monthly income is a first step in assessing the payments toward unsecured debt required by §1325(b).

1. Determining Current Monthly Income

"Current monthly income" is defined in §101(10A) of the Code. Under the definition, "current monthly income" has three components: income inclusions, income exclusions, and a computation period.

- The income inclusions are
  (1) all income, both taxable and nontaxable, that the debtor receives;
  (2) in a joint case, all income, both taxable and nontaxable, that the debtor's spouse receives; and
  (3) all other amounts that are paid on a regular basis for the household expenses of the debtor, the debtor's dependents, and, in a joint case, the debtor's spouse if not otherwise a dependent.

- The income exclusions are
  (1) benefits received under the Social Security Act;
  (2) payments to victims of war crimes or crimes against humanity; and
  (3) payments to victims of international or domestic terrorism.

- The computation period is
  (1) the six calendar months before the bankruptcy filing if the debtor files a schedule of current income; or
  (2) if the debtor does not file the schedule, six months before the court determines the amount of current monthly income.[3]

The definition requires the computation of a monthly average of the included income, less the excluded income, "derived during" the computation period.

Several features of this definition are noteworthy. First, "current monthly income" is an artificial construct defined for a bankruptcy case rather than for an individual. It includes, for example, payments regularly made for the household expenses of the debtors' dependents even if these are gifts given directly to the dependents, and it includes the income of both debtors in a joint case. Thus, the income that an individual receives is only one element of the "current monthly income" for a bankruptcy case; "current monthly income" is not something that an individual can "have" or "receive." Second, the definition does not purport to measure the extent of the funds actually available to debtors. By excluding several sources of funding — such as social security benefits and irregular support payments — the definition assures that "current monthly income" in many bankruptcy cases will be substantially less than the funds actually available. Most notably, the definition departs from prior practice by excluding the income of a non-filing spouse to the extent that it is not regularly paid for the household expenses of the debtor or the debtor's dependents. Third, the definition's distinction between "debtor" and "debtor's spouse" in a joint case conflicts with other provisions of the Code that treat both joint filers interchangeably as "debtors." *See, e.g.,* 11 U.S.C. §302(b) ("After the commencement of a joint case, the court shall determine the extent, if any, to which the debtors' estates shall be consolidated.").

With this understanding of "current monthly income," the two specialized terms used in §1325(b) — "disposable income" received in the "applicable commitment period" — can be explored.

---

3. The second computation period will rarely, if ever, be applicable in Chapter 13. If the debtor does not file a schedule of current income (as required by §521(a)(1)(B)(ii) unless the court orders otherwise) during the first forty-five days of the case, the case is automatically dismissed under §521(i). *See In re Young*, No. 06-80397, 2006 WL 3524482, at *3 (Bankr. S.D. Tex. Dec. 6, 2006) (discussing the operation of §521). For practical purposes, then, the computation period in the definition of current monthly income for Chapter 13 cases is the six calendar months before the case filing.

2. Determining the Applicable Commitment Period

"Applicable commitment period" is defined in §1325(b) itself. Section 1325(b)(4)(A)(i) provides that the period is generally three years, but §1325(b)(4)(A)(ii) extends the period to five years if the "current monthly income of the debtor and the debtor's spouse combined, when multiplied by 12" is at least equal to a specified median income based on the debtor's household size and state of residence.

Section 1325(b)(4)'s use of current monthly income to determine the applicable commitment period creates a tension with the definition of current monthly income in §101(10A). Section 1325(b)(4)(A)(ii) requires that the current monthly income of the debtor and the debtor's spouse be "combined." However, as noted above, §101(10A) provides for only one "current monthly income" per case; under the definition, individuals do not have current monthly incomes that are capable of being combined. If a married debtor files individually, the only apparent way to combine current monthly incomes of the debtor and the debtor's spouse would be to calculate a current monthly income for each as though each had filed a separate bankruptcy case. That has the effect of including all of the income of each spouse for purposes of calculating the applicable commitment period, rather than only the income of the non-filing spouse regularly paid for the household expenses of the debtor and the debtor's dependents.

Because of the tension between §101(10A) and §1325(b)(4) with respect to spousal current monthly income, it is not possible to give complete effect to both provisions in calculating the applicable commitment period for a married debtor filing individually. Official Form 22C attempts to honor the "combining" mandated in §1325(b)(4) by requiring a statement of current monthly income from the non-filing spouse as though that spouse were in a separate bankruptcy case. Following the definition of current monthly income in §101(10A), however, the form also allows the debtor to subtract a non-filing spouse's income to the extent that it is not regularly paid for the household expenses of the debtor and the debtor's dependents.[4]

In joint cases, like the Johnsons' case, Form 22C requires that each spouse report separately the items included in the definition of current monthly income in §101(10A) and then combine the results, pursuant to §1325(b)(4)(A)(ii). This application of §1325(b) to joint cases does not appear to have been challenged, and the Johnsons completed Form 22C — in both their original and amended filings — by listing the income items applicable to each of them. The difference between the two

---

4. If the debtor makes this choice, the form will so indicate and a party in interest may argue that the full amount of the non-filing spouse's income is required to be counted under §1325(b)(4). Nearly all reported decisions on this issue have held that because a non-filing spouse has no current monthly income under the definition in §101(10A), only payments regularly made by the spouse for the household expenses of the debtor or the debtor's dependents should count as current monthly income for purposes of computing the applicable commitment period under §1325(b)(4). *See In re Stansell*, 395 B.R. 457, 461-62 (Bankr. D. Idaho 2008); *In re Dugan*, No. 07-40899-13, 2008 WL 3558217 (Bankr. D. Kan., Aug. 12, 2008); *In re Borders*, No. 07-12450, 2008 WL 1925190 (Bankr. S.D. Ala., April 30, 2008); *In re Grubbs*, No. 07-32822-KRH, 2007 WL 4418146 (Bankr. E.D. Va., Dec. 14, 2007); *In re Quarterman*, 342 B.R. 647 (Bankr. M.D. Fla. 2006). *But see In re Beasley*, 342 B.R. 280 (Bankr. C.D. Ill. 2006) (entire "current monthly income" of a non-filing spouse included in determining applicable commitment period).

submitted forms is the period for computation. Originally, the Johnsons reported their average income for the six calendar months preceding their bankruptcy case, as required by the form, consistent with the definition of current monthly income in §101(10A). In their amended filing, they reported the monthly income that they were receiving at the time of the bankruptcy case and expected to receive thereafter. (See Docket No. 1, Schedule I, Line 17.) For purposes of the applicable commitment period, however, there is no difference between the two forms — each produces a current monthly income in excess of the median family income in Illinois for a family the size of the Johnsons' household.[5] Their applicable commitment period is therefore five years, a conclusion not in dispute.

3.   Determining Disposable Income

The remaining term to be examined is "disposable income," which — to the extent that it is "projected . . . to be received in the applicable commitment period" — must be used to pay unsecured claims pursuant to §1325(b). "Disposable income" is defined in paragraphs (2)-(3) of §1325(b). The definition can be summarized as follows:

(1)   Disposable income is "current monthly income received by the debtor,"
(2)   subject to additional income exclusions for child support payments, foster care payments, and disability payments for a dependent child,
(3)   less expenditures necessary for the support of the debtor or a dependent of the debtor, for domestic support obligations, for charitable contributions, and for business operations,
(4)   with these necessary expenditures, except for charitable contributions, "determined in accordance with subparagraphs (A) and (B) of section 707(b)(2)" — the provisions defining the means test used in Chapter 7 bankruptcy cases — if the debtor's current monthly income is greater than the applicable median.

Most of the components of this definition can be applied to the Johnsons' case without dispute. Because the Johnsons' current monthly income is above the applicable median, their necessary expenditures are determined under the means test. And although §1325(b)(2) refers to current monthly income "received by the debtor," the Johnsons have not asserted that they can exclude income received by the debtor's spouse; in their reporting they included income that both of them received. There is no question that their income and expense items have been properly reported in conformity with the official form.

The sole dispute is over the period used to compute disposable income. Invoking the definition in §101(10A), the trustee argues that the Johnsons' currently monthly income is fixed at the monthly average for the six months before their bankruptcy

5. The Johnsons' original Form 22C declared current monthly income of $16,045, producing an annual income of $192,540. The amended Form 22C declared current monthly income of $13,500, or $162,000 annually. The Johnsons have a household of four. The annual median income for a family of four in Illinois at the time of the Johnsons' bankruptcy filing was $77,644. See Census Bureau Median Family Income by Family Size, reported at http://www.usdoj.gov/ust/eo/bapcpa/20080317/bci_data/median_income_table.htm (last visited January 23, 2009).

case, and that the disposable income their plan must devote to payments of unsecured debts is simply this current monthly income, multiplied by the sixty months of their applicable commitment period, less necessary expenditures under the means test. In other words, the trustee takes the computation period for disposable income to be the six months prior to bankruptcy. The Johnsons, on the other hand, contend that their disposable income must be based on the income that they actually anticipate receiving during the applicable commitment period, making the period for computing disposable income the five years after payments begin under their plan.

The question of how "disposable income" should be interpreted under the post-BAPCPA version of §1325(b) has been treated in scores of published decisions, including three by courts of appeals.[6] Most decisions adopt one of two approaches. Each of these approaches, however, accepts the six-month period before bankruptcy as at least the starting point for calculating projected disposable income.

a. The Conclusive Approach

One approach, adopted by the Ninth Circuit in *Maney v. Kagenveama (In re Kagenveama)*, 541 F.3d 868 (9th Cir. 2008), supports the trustee's position. This approach makes the six-month pre-bankruptcy period the conclusive basis for calculating disposable income under §1325(b), simply multiplying the average income from that period by the number of months in the applicable commitment period to generate the income from which necessary expenditures are subtracted to obtain disposable income.

The principal support for this "conclusive" application of the six-month pre-bankruptcy average income is the definition of disposable income in §1325(b), which applies deductions for necessary expenditures to "current monthly income" — defined in §101(10A) as income received during that six-month period. "Reading the statute as requiring 'disposable income,' as defined in subsection [1325](b)(2), to be projected out over the 'applicable commitment period' to derive the 'projected disposable income' amount is the most natural reading of the statute, and it is the one we adopt." *Id.* at 872.[7]

One difficulty with the conclusive approach is the unfortunate set of results it produces. Income received in the period *before* a bankruptcy filing will often be a poor measure of how much a debtor can pay to unsecured creditors *after* the bankruptcy filing. If a debtor's income has permanently declined as of the filing — like the Johnsons' income in the present case — it may be impossible for the debtor to make

---

6. *In re Wilson*, 397 B.R. 299, 307-18 (Bankr. M.D.N.C. 2008), presents a collection of over sixty decisions on the question. The question has also divided bankruptcy courts in the Seventh Circuit and in the Northern District of Illinois. *Compare In re Nance*, 371 B.R. 358 (Bankr. S.D. Ill. 2007), and *In re Ross*, 375 B.R. 437 (Bankr. N.D. Ill. 2007) (measuring disposable income based on income from the pre-filing period) *with In re Hilton*, 395 B.R. 433 (Bankr. E.D. Wis. 2008) and *In re Demonica*, 345 B.R. 895, 900 (Bankr. N.D. Ill. 2006) (post-filing income dispositive).

7. *In re Alexander*, 344 B.R. 742, 749 (Bankr. E.D.N.C. 2006), a leading case for the conclusive approach, set out its reasoning this way: "What is now considered 'disposable' is based upon historical data-current monthly income derived from the six-month period preceding the bankruptcy filing. 11 U.S.C. §§101(10A), 1325(b)(2). [I]n order to arrive at 'projected disposable income,' one simply takes the calculation mandated by §1325(b)(2) and does the math."

payments based on the pre-filing income. And if the debtor's income has permanently increased, payment based on the pre-filing income may be much lower than the debtor's actual income would allow. *See In re Hardacre*, 338 B.R. 718 (Bankr. N.D. Tex. 2006) (noting "the anomalous results that could occur by strictly adhering to section 101(10A)'s definition of 'current monthly income' "). Courts should be hesitant to accept statutory interpretations that seem to make no sense. *See Griffin v. Oceanic Contractors, Inc.*, 458 U.S. 564, 575, 102 S. Ct. 3245, 73 L. Ed. 2d 973 (1982) ("[I]nterpretations of a statute which would produce absurd results are to be avoided if alternative interpretations consistent with the legislative purpose are available.").

A more significant problem with the conclusive approach is that the language of §1325(b) itself does not align with a payment obligation based on pre-filing income. Section 1325(b) requires a debtor's plan to devote to payment of unsecured claims the "projected" disposable income "to be received during the applicable commitment period beginning on the first date payment is due under the plan." Several courts have noted that the word "projected" — which is not defined in the Bankruptcy Code — implies a prediction of what is likely to occur in the future, rather than a computation based on potentially outdated information from the past. *See, e.g., Hildebrand v. Petro (In re Petro)*, 395 B.R. 369, 377 (6th Cir. BAP 2008) (observing that "the word 'projected' is future oriented"); *In re Jass*, 340 B.R. 411, 415 (Bankr. D. Utah 2006) (noting the dictionary definition of "projected"). One cannot "project" what has already happened.

Even more awkward for the conclusive approach is the directive to pay the disposable income "to be received" during a particular future period — "the applicable commitment period beginning on the date that the first payment is due under the plan." If §1325(b) simply required the payment of a multiple of past monthly income, there would be no point in specifying a particular future period in which income was anticipated to be received. The date the case was filed, the date the plan was confirmed, or even the date of the debtor's next birthday would produce exactly the same result under the conclusive approach as would an applicable commitment period beginning on the date the first payment was to be made under the plan. Specifying a particular period only matters if events that occur during that period are relevant.

Finally, as noted above, "current monthly income" is only the starting point in determining "disposable income." Section 1325(b)(2) directs that the necessary expenses of maintaining the debtor's household, paying support obligations, making charitable contributions, and generating income must be deducted from "current monthly income" to derive the "disposable income" that a plan must pay out. Like income, these expense items are subject to change over time.[8] But nothing in §1325(b) or the definition of current monthly income suggests that expenses should

---

8. Perhaps most obviously, expenses change with the number of dependents for whom a debtor is responsible. A debtor will have higher expenses after the birth or adoption of a child; a debtor will have lower expenses after a formerly dependent child becomes self-sufficient. Similar changes in expenses will occur with fluctuations in the debtor's housing and transportation costs.

be assessed and averaged for a pre-filing period. To the contrary, §1325(b)(2)(A)(i) expressly provides for the deduction of a support obligation "that first becomes payable after the date the petition is filed," thus requiring that this expense item be measured on a post-filing basis and strongly suggesting that expenses generally are to be measured on that basis. Yet if the expenses that offset income are to be assessed post-filing, it is difficult to see how the income being offset would not likewise be assessed post-filing.

b. The Presumptive Approach

The other major approach to calculating disposable income under §1325(b), accepted by the Eighth and Tenth Circuits, responds to the practical difficulties caused by the use of prefiling income in the definition of current monthly income. *See Coop v. Frederickson (In re Frederickson)*, 545 F.3d 652 (8th Cir. 2008); *Hamilton v. Lanning (In re Lanning)*, 545 F.3d 1269, 1282 (10th Cir. 2008). Under this approach, the definition's six-month pre-filing average income is only "a starting point"; if a debtor's income has substantially changed, or if it is anticipated to change from the pre-filing average, a correction can be made. *See Frederickson*, 545 F.3d at 659 (adopting the view that "a debtor's 'disposable income' . . . is a starting point for determining the debtor's 'projected disposable income,' but that the final calculation can take into consideration changes that have occurred in the debtor's financial circumstances"); *Lanning*, 545 F.3d at 1282 (holding that "a Chapter 13 debtor's 'projected disposable income' is presumed to be the debtor's 'current monthly income,' as defined in . . . §101(10A)(A)(i), subject to a showing of a substantial change in circumstances").

The primary problem with the presumptive approach is the statutory language. Nothing in §1325(b) creates or implies a presumption of correctness in the average income from the six months before bankruptcy. This absence is particularly telling because the means test in §707(b)(2), which §1325(b) uses to determine the necessary-expenditure component of disposable income for higher income debtors, is itself an elaborate mechanism for determining a presumption of debt-paying ability, with the facts necessary to rebut the presumption specified in §707(b)(2)(B). For this reason, the Ninth Circuit observed that "Congress knows how to create a presumption" when one is intended. *Kagenveama*, 541 F.3d at 874.

Moreover, an approach making the definition of disposable income in §1325(b) merely presumptive necessarily expands judicial discretion regarding debtors' plan payments in Chapter 13. Discretion would be have to be exercised in deciding both the facts that would rebut the presumption and the rules (if any) that would replace the statutory definition when the presumption has been rebutted. A grant of such discretion, however, is not easily located in BAPCPA. The court in *Musselman v. eCast Settlement Corp.*, 394 B.R. 801, 812 (E.D.N.C. 2008), noted the difficulty:

> Beyond ensuring greater payouts by Chapter 13 debtors to their creditors, Congress, in its amendments to §1325(b), also sought to impose objective standards on Chapter 13 determinations, thereby removing a degree of judicial flexibility in bankruptcy proceedings.

Thus, . . . "[e]liminating flexibility was the point: the obligations of chapter 13 debtors would be subject to 'clear, defined standards,' no longer left 'to the whim of a judicial proceeding.' " *In re Farrar-Johnson*, 353 B.R. [224] at 231 [Bankr. N.D. Ill. 2006] (quoting Susan Jensen, A Legislative History of the Bankruptcy Abuse Prevention and Consumer Protection Act of 2005, 79 Am. Bankr. L.J. 485, 527 (2005)).

c. A Harmonizing Approach

Both the conclusive and presumptive approaches to disposable income in §1325(b) present substantial difficulties. To address these difficulties, it is helpful to point out their source: a conflict between part of the definition of "current monthly income" in §101(10A) and the use of "current monthly income" in §1325(b)'s definition of "disposable income." The definition in §101(10A) computes "current monthly income" during a six-month period before the bankruptcy filing. "Disposable income" in §1325(b), on the other hand, requires payment of disposable income (defined as "current monthly income" less specified expenses) "projected . . . to be received" during an "applicable commitment period" beginning after the bankruptcy filing. The two provisions are irreconcilable. *See Kibbe v. Sumski (In re Kibbe)*, 361 B.R. 302, 312 (1st Cir. BAP 2007) (finding an irreconcilable conflict between the definition of "disposable income" and the prospective implication of "projected").

When statutory provisions conflict, a court's task-to the extent it can — is to give effect to both. *Morton v. Mancari*, 417 U.S. 535, 550, 94 S. Ct. 2474, 41 L. Ed. 2d 290 (1974) (stating that "when two statutes are capable of coexistence, it is the duty of the courts, absent a clearly expressed congressional intention to the contrary, to regard each as effective"). Consistent with this rule, in calculating disposable income under §1325(b), most of the content of §101(10A) can be incorporated. Its income inclusions and exclusions can be given full effect. However, to the extent that two statutory provisions cannot be reconciled, the more specific governs the more general. *Busic v. United States*, 446 U.S. 398, 406, 100 S. Ct. 1747, 64 L. Ed. 2d 381 (1980) (holding that "a more specific statute will be given precedence over a more general one, regardless of their temporal sequence"). The specific provision of §1325(b)(1) regarding disposable income "to be received in the [post-filing] applicable commitment period" must therefore be given precedence over the general definition of current monthly income in §101(10A), which looks to income received pre-filing. The end result is a synthesis of §§101(10A) and 1325(b) that measures the "current monthly income" inclusions and exclusions of §101(10A) projected to be received by the debtor during the applicable commitment period defined by §1325(b), reduced by the necessary expenditures incurred by the debtor during that period.

This "harmonizing approach" honors the principle that statutory revisions should only result in changes to established practices to the extent that the revisions clearly provide for change. *See Finley v. United States*, 490 U.S. 545, 554, 109 S. Ct. 2003, 104 L. Ed. 2d 593 (1989) ("Under established canons of statutory construction, 'it will not be inferred that Congress, in revising and consolidating the laws, intended to change their effect unless such intention is clearly expressed.' ") (quoting *Anderson v. Pacific Coast S.S. Co.*, 225 U.S. 187, 199, 32 S. Ct. 626, 56 L. Ed. 1047 (1912)); *In re*

Wilson, 397 B.R. 299, 312 n. 20 (Bankr. M.D.N.C. 2008) (applying this principle to the interpretation of §1325(b)). Before the enactment of BAPCPA, it was the established practice to "project" disposable income under §1325(b) by looking to the income, net of necessary expenses, that the debtor actually anticipated receiving during the relevant post-filing period. *See In re Briscoe*, 374 B.R. 1, 15 (Bankr. D.C. 2007) (describing pre-BAPCPA practice). By measuring income and expenses anticipated to be received during the debtor's plan, the harmonizing approach continues this practice — one that BAPCPA does not clearly contradict — but also honors the changes in the income inclusions and exclusions that BAPCPA clearly specifies.

Other courts have adopted this harmonizing approach in interpreting §1325(b) as amended by BAPCPA. *See In re Kibbe*, 361 B.R. at 314 (holding that "the income component of 'projected disposable income' as set forth in §1325(b)(1)(B) is the anticipated actual income of the Debtor," as defined by the income inclusions and exclusions of §101(10A)); *In re Hardacre*, 338 B.R. 718, 723 (Bankr. N.D. Tex. 2006) (holding that "projected disposable income" under §1325(b)(1)(B) necessarily refers to income that the debtor reasonably expects to receive during the term of her plan, but that "Section 101(10A) continues to apply inasmuch as it describes the sources of revenue that constitute income, as well as those that do not").

Further precedent for the harmonizing approach can be found in the way Official Form 22A resolves another conflict presented by the definition of current monthly income in §101(10A). As noted above, neither a debtor nor the debtor's spouse has "current monthly income" under the definition, but §707(b)(7) requires a combination of "the current monthly income of the debtor . . . and the debtor's spouse." The form reconciles these conflicting provisions by requiring debtors to report the elements of the §101(10A) definition that can be applied to a non-filing spouse (the income inclusions and exclusions), while overriding the portions of the definition that contradict the substantive provision. See Official Form 22A, Lines 2c, 12-15.

Finally, the harmonizing approach avoids the problems inherent in both the conclusive and presumptive uses of the six-month average pre-filing income. In contrast to the presumptive approach, there is no undefined expansion of judicial discretion. In contrast to the conclusive approach, there is no attempt to force the square peg of §101(10A)'s computation period into the round hole of §1325(b)'s applicable commitment period.

4. Schedules and Forms

None of the forms and schedules that debtors are currently required to file provide the information needed to calculate disposable income received during the applicable commitment period. Official Form 22C provides for the reporting and calculation of current monthly income as defined in §101(10A). *See* Official Forms 22A-22C 2005-2008 committee note, Part A (2008). Accordingly, it directs debtors to report an average of income received during the six calendar months before the bankruptcy filing. *See* Official Form 22C, Lines 1-9. For the calculation of "necessary expenditures" prescribed by §707(b)(2) — which §1325(b)(3) employs to determine the disposable income of debtors with above-median income — Form 22C gives no explicit instruction as to the relevant time frame. However, its descriptions of each expense item are set out in present tense, indicating that current, rather than future expenses should be disclosed. *Id.*, Lines 24-58. The form makes no provision for reporting anticipated changes in either income or expenses during the applicable commitment period.

Schedules I and J (Official Forms 6I and 6J) — the schedules of current income and current expenditures required under §521(a)(1)(B)(ii) — do require a disclosure of changes in the reported information anticipated to occur after the schedule is filed. However, these schedules are designed to report the debtor's actual income and expenditures and therefore may vary substantially from the income and expense calculations used in determining disposable income under §1325(b). Schedule I requires an "[e]stimate of average or projected monthly income at time case filed," rather than during the six-month period before the case was filed, and it does not exclude from income either Social Security benefits or irregularly received support payments. Schedule J requires a statement of the debtor's actual expenses, rather than the allowances specified in §707(b)(2).

Accordingly, in order to report disposable income projected to be received during the applicable commitment period, a debtor must supplement Official Form 22C with a statement of any changes in the "current monthly income" as reported in the form, and any changes in the expenses allowed, anticipated to take place during the applicable commitment period. In many cases, of course, the information the form requires will not be anticipated to change, and no further disclosure would be required. But with debtors like the Johnsons, for whom a change in income from the six-month period before the bankruptcy filing has already occurred, an adjustment of disposable income as reported on the current form is essential.

5. The Johnsons' Plan

The amended Form 22C that the Johnsons submitted effectively reports the disposable income that they project to be received during their applicable commitment period. It properly omits the workers' compensation income that Mrs. Johnson received before the bankruptcy filing but will not receive during the applicable commitment period. The Johnsons' Schedules I and J report no anticipated changes in income or expenses for the year after these schedules were filed, and there is no basis for assuming any changes thereafter. Accordingly, $119,700, as reflected in the amended form, is the projected disposable income to be received in the applicable commitment period. The Johnsons' plan proposes to apply substantially more than this amount to make payments to unsecured creditors. The plan therefore satisfies the disposable income requirement of §1325(b), and the trustee's objection must be overruled.

Conclusion

For the reasons set out above, the Johnsons' Chapter 13 plan will be confirmed over the trustee's objection. A separate order will be entered to that effect.

PROBLEM 8-15

Richard and Lynne Yuppie happily rode the wave of high real estate values for a number of years. They refinanced the mortgage on their home four times from 2001 to 2007. After the latest refinancing, they owed $262,000 on a home that was appraised at $280,000. The housing market collapsed the next year, and the house is now realistically worth $175,000. They each have also suffered significantly reduced incomes, and jointly make approximately $65,000 per year, down from $95,000. The Yuppies also own a shoreline lot that is worth $100,000 subject to a mortgage in the amount of $125,000. Their monthly payment on the lake lot is $750. Assume that their income is close to the applicable state median income. If they plan to surrender the lake lot to the mortgage holder as a part of their Chapter 13 plan, can they still deduct the $750 monthly mortgage payment in determining the "applicable repayment period" for their plan? *See* Official Form 22C, line 42. *Compare* In re Marchionna, 393 B.R. 512 (Bankr. N.D. Oh. 2008), *with* In re Quigley, 391 B.R. 294 (Bankr. N.D. W.V. 2008).

PROBLEM 8-16

Bobby and Evon Smith's income exceeded the applicable state median income. They decided to file a Chapter 13 petition and completed all of the required documents. Their Official Form 22C showed that they had a negative disposable income. This was in contrast to the information set out on Schedules I and J which indicated that their actual income and expenses generated an actual net monthly income of $800. The Smiths filed a plan that provided for no payments to unsecured creditors arguing that they have no projected disposable income. Will the court confirm the plan over the objection of an unsecured creditor? *Compare* In re Kagenveama, 541 F.3d 868 (9th Cir. 2008) (current disposable income of $0 under means test calculation results in no projected disposable income), *with* In re Lanning, 545 F.3d 1269 (10th Cir. 2008) (court must consider potential for future increases in disposable income before confirmation of a Chapter 13 plan).

PROBLEM 8-17

Andrew Cooler owned and operated a service station/convenience store. The store had always made a small profit, but the fluctuation in gas prices caused the business to become unprofitable. In a typical month, the average cost of the goods purchased by the business was $100,000, and the gross sales were $140,000.

The other monthly operating expenses totaled $35,000. What is the current monthly income of the business? Bankruptcy Code §§101(10A); 1325(b)(2).

Most Chapter 13 debtors earn less than the state median income, so their disposable income is determined in the same way as it was prior to the 2005 amendments. In nonbusiness cases, the debtor's disposable income is the excess available after the payment of the ordinary living expenses of the debtor and the dependents of the debtor. This definition of disposable income essentially requires the bankruptcy judge to make lifestyle choices for debtors. The courts have considered whether haircut expenses are too extravagant and whether debtors should have cable TV, books and newspapers, luxury automobiles, and even country club memberships. Additionally, the bankruptcy courts have been forced to review debtors' tithing practices as well as their educational choices for their children. Consider the application of §1325(b) to the following case.

In re Cleary

United States Bankruptcy Court, District of South Carolina, 2006
357 B.R. 369

DAVID R. DUNCAN, Bankruptcy Judge.

THIS MATTER is before the Court for hearing on confirmation of the debtor's plan dated July 31, 2006. The chapter 13 trustee objects to confirmation on the basis that expenditures for private school tuition are not reasonable and necessary expenses and thus that the plan does not provide "that all of the debtor's projected disposable income to be received in the applicable commitment period . . . will be applied to make payments to unsecured creditors under the plan." 11 U.S.C. §1325(b)(1)(B).

Findings of Fact

1. Kevin Paul Cleary ("Debtor") filed a voluntary petition for relief under chapter 13 of the Bankruptcy Code on July 31, 2006.

2. Debtor is married, although his spouse did not join in the petition. Mr. and Mrs. Cleary have six children, the youngest age 7.

3. Debtor is employed as a driver for a nationwide parcel delivery service, and has been so employed for 21 years. His current net monthly take home pay, after deduction for taxes, union dues, and a 401k contribution, is $4,522.00.

4. Mrs. Cleary was not employed outside the home for approximately 15 years of the marriage. She has been employed as a teacher's aide at a parochial school for the past 2 years. Her net take home pay, after taxes and a small 401k contribution, is $918.50. An additional $813.00 is deducted from her pay check for tuition for three of the couple's children who attend the school. Mrs. Cleary's actual take home pay is $105.50.

5. The family's gross annual income is reported on Form B22C in the amount of $86,283.60.

6. The applicable median income for a South Carolina family of 8 is $86,918.00.

7. The family currently spends $1,165.00 for the mortgage payment, including taxes, insurance and home maintenance; $265.00 for utilities; $1,500.00 for food; $85.00 for automobile taxes and insurance; $465.00 for miscellaneous expenses (clothing, laundry, medical, recreation and personal); and $100.00 for transportation. The family spends $1,513.00 for private school (elementary and secondary) tuition each month.

8. Five of the six children attend private school. The sixth child attended private school until the current school year when he asked to attend public school for the experience. The testimony was that the sixth child would like to return to private school next year. Mr. and Mrs. Cleary receive assistance from the private high school in the form of reduced tuition because of their income and family size.

9. Mr. and Mrs. Cleary own an "$150,000" 3 bedroom ranch style home and modest furnishings. They also own three vehicles; a late model van, under lien, and two older cars. The home is subject to two mortgages and has little equity if Debtor's statements of the current market value and mortgage balances are correct.

10. In addition to the mortgages and automobile loan the Debtor has two purchase money furniture accounts, two loans secured by avoidable liens on household goods, and less than $18,000 in unsecured debt, mostly from credit cards.

11. The plan provides for monthly payments of $450 for 60 months. Trustee commission and expenses will be paid, an attorney fee of $1999 will be paid through the plan, the arrearage on the first mortgage will be cured through the plan (with ongoing payments made outside the plan), the indebtedness for the late model automobile will be paid in full under the plan, and unsecured creditors will receive a small dividend.

12. The plan and related motions also provide that the debt for the second mortgage on the home is current, that collateral for the two purchase money furniture loans will be surrendered, and that the non-purchase money liens on household goods will be avoided.

13. Mr. Cleary testified and was a credible witness. He testified that the family holds membership in the Catholic Church. Mrs. Cleary received a private Catholic school education as a child and teenager. She works outside the home only to fund the private school tuition for the children and otherwise would not do so. Mr. Cleary testified that the children are in private school so as to obtain a Catholic church based education and that this is very important to him and his wife.

14. Mr. Cleary credibly testified that his family has chosen to reduce expenditures in other categories in order to provide the funds for private school tuition. Given the family size, many of the expenses are well below reported averages and below that which the chapter 13 trustees in this district would deem objectionable in chapter 13 cases.

15. Mr. Cleary testified that the family lives in a school attendance zone with some of the better schools in a school district that does not enjoy a good reputation with many in the community and whose overall student population does not score well on standardized tests. Mr. Cleary testified that it is his belief that the children will receive a better education in private school.

16. Debtor's testimony, along with the sworn schedules of expense, sufficiently document the private school tuition.

17. The private school tuition expense of Debtor's family is not accounted for in the National Standards, Local Standards, or Other Necessary Expenses referred to in §707(b)(2)(A)(ii)(I).

Conclusions of Law

The Court is presented with the narrow issue of whether private school tuition is "an amount reasonably necessary to be expended for the maintenance or support of the debtor or a dependent of the debtor. . . ." §1325(b)(2)(A). The question is relevant because only such expense amounts as are reasonably necessary may be deducted from current monthly income to determine disposable income that must be paid to unsecured creditors. This analysis is necessary only if the trustee or holder of an allowed unsecured claim objects to confirmation. §1325(b)(1).

The determination of "disposable income" is a bifurcated process following the effective date of BAPCPA. " 'Disposable income' for above median income debtors is defined as a debtor's 'current monthly income', also a defined term under §101(10A), less amounts reasonably necessary 'to be expended' as determined by §707(b)(2)(A) and (B)." *In re Edmunds*, 350 B.R. 636 (Bankr. D.S.C. 2006). For below median income debtors, the majority of courts have used Schedules I and J to determine "projected disposable income." *See In re Dew*, 344 B.R. 655 (Bankr. N.D. Ala. 2006) (Schedules I and J, although there may be a second step); *In re Schanuth*, 342 B.R. 601 (Bankr. W.D. Mo. 2006) (current monthly income from Form B22C less Schedule J expenses); *In re Kibbe*, 342 B.R. 411 (Bankr. D.N.H. 2006) (Schedules I and J). Debtor is a below median income debtor. Here Debtor's Schedule I, line 3 gross income and Form B22C "current monthly income" is the same. Thus the Court need not navigate the path nor choose between §1325(b)(2) disposable income and §1325(b)(1)(B) projected disposable income as a starting point. *See In re Hardacre*, 338 B.R. 718 (Bankr. N.D. Tex. 2006); *In re Beasley*, 342 B.R. 280 (Bankr. C.D. Ill. 2006); *In re Dew*, at 660.

The expense calculation is also bifurcated. *See Schanuth* at 604. "Amounts reasonably necessary to be expended under paragraph (2) . . . [are] determined in accordance with subparagraphs (A) and (B) of section 707(b)(2), if the debtor has [annualized] current monthly income . . . greater than . . . [the applicable] median family income of the applicable State. . . ." §1325(b)(3). In sum, for an above median income debtor, the expenses are those supplied using the "means test" calculation with reference to standard Internal Revenue Service expenses recognized for debt collection purposes and to other defined expenses. For a below median income debtor, as we have here, the amounts reasonably necessary to be expended for the maintenance or support of the debtor or a dependent of the debtor are determined in the context of the estimated average monthly expenses reported on Schedule J. These expenses must undergo judicial analysis, in the face of an objection, as to reasonableness and necessity; or as some might say, "the old fashion way." This Court considers Schedules I and J in the confirmation process for both above and below median income debtors. *See In re Edmunds*, 350 B.R. 636 (Bankr. D.S.C. 2006).

The debtor bears the burden of showing that an expense is reasonable for confirmation purposes. *In re Watson*, 403 F.3d 1 (1st Cir. 2005); *Lynch v. Tate (In re Lynch)*, 299 B.R. 776, 779 (W.D.N.C. 2003). Prior to enactment of BAPCPA the courts were split on the subject of the reasonableness of private school tuition as a deduction from income to arrive at disposable income. The majority of the cases reject private school tuition as a reasonable and necessary expense; at least in the absence of educational necessity or special needs.[9] Earlier decisions expressed the "view that a debtor's creditors should not pay tuition for the debtor's children." *In re McNulty*, 142 B.R. 106 (Bankr. D.N.J. 1992); *See also In re Jones*, 55 B.R. 462 (Bankr. D. Minn. 1985) (Expressing the view, no longer held in many circles, that the public education was of high quality.). The fulcrum was to balance "creditor's rights against the appropriate basic needs of the debtors and their dependents." *Watson* at 8.

The public policy notion that private school tuition is a luxury expense for the purposes of calculating available income under either the chapter 7 means test or for the disposable income analysis in confirming a chapter 13 plan is swept aside by BAPCPA. An allowable expense is that for "each dependent child less than 18 years of age, not to exceed $1,500 per year per child, to attend a private or public elementary or secondary school if the debtor provides documentation of such expenses and a detailed explanation of why such expenses are reasonably necessary, and why such expenses are not already accounted for in the National Standards, Local Standards, or Other Necessary Expenses referred to in subclause (I)." §707(b)(2)(A)(ii)(IV). For some purposes at least, Congress has set forth the public policy that private school tuition can be a reasonable and necessary expense.

The Court then is faced with two issues. Is some expense for private school tuition reasonably necessary and, if so, in what amount? The pre-BAPCPA cases setting forth special circumstances are helpful in this analysis, although care must be shown to the public policy shift.

While the Debtor is retaining real estate, paying a 1% dividend to general unsecured creditors, and the children have no special education needs other than the fact that they are bright and need to be challenged; these factors are outweighed by others. The Debtor and his family have shown long term enrollment at parochial schools. All of the children attend private school, save one-who plans to return to private school next year. The Debtor's wife attended private school. The Debtor and his wife have strongly held religious convictions. The Debtor's wife would not work outside the

---

9. The majority cases are represented by *In re Watson*, 403 F.3d 1 (1st Cir. 2005); *In re Savage*, 311 B.R. 835 (1st Cir. BAP 2004); *In re Lynch*, 299 B.R. 776 (W.D.N.C. 2003); *In re Univest-Coppell Village, Ltd.*, 204 B.R. 497 (E.D. Tex. 1996). The cases approving private school tuition rest on special circumstances. *See In re Burgos*, 248 B.R. 446 (Bankr. M.D. Fla. 2000) (paying as much to unsecured creditors as expense of tuition, always attended parochial school, strong religious beliefs, debtors retained no real estate); *In re Nicola*, 244 B.R. 795 (Bankr. N.D. Ill. 2000) (some evidence of inadequate local schools and long term attendance of debtor's children at private school); *In re Webb*, 262 B.R. 685 (Bankr. E.D. Tex. 2001) (special needs child).

home (and did not do so for many years) except to provide additional income to pay for private school tuition. In fact, Mrs. Cleary's pay check is reduced by the amount of tuition for the couple's children who attend the elementary school where she works. The family's sacrifice of other basic expenses to fund private school tuition is note-worthy and, in this case, the deciding factor for the Court in approving the necessity and reasonableness of the expense for private school tuition. *See In re Grawey*, 2001 WL 34076376 (Bankr. C.D. Ill. 2001) (private school tuition and belt-tightening in the context of the dischargeability of student loans — sacrifices other basic necessities such as health care insurance). Debtor, if his testimony and schedules are truthful, could file a chapter 7 petition and it is very likely that he would lose no assets to administration for creditors. He is curing a small arrearage on his home loan through the chapter 13 plan, but the amount is *de minimis.* Debtor is giving up furniture secured by purchase money loans. For these reasons the Court finds that private school tuition is a reasonable and necessary expense of the debtor.

The final issue is whether Debtor is limited to a monthly expenditure of $125 per child in private school. If so he would be limited to $625 at present and $750 in the coming school year. The calculation of the means test in chapter 7 and of disposable income for above the median income debtors in chapter 13 limits the expenditure for private school tuition. This limit is presumptively reasonable. In the circumstances of this case the Court finds that the Debtor is not limited to this expense ceiling. This aspect of the decision is limited very narrowly to the facts of this case. Mrs. Cleary is not a co-debtor. Her income would likely not be available if the children withdrew from private school because she would not work outside the home. It is only because of her religious convictions that she works outside the home and sends her children to private school. Debtor and his family sacrifice significantly in the purchase of food and clothing and in the areas of recreation and transportation expense. The expense of $1,513.00 for private school tuition is a reasonable and necessary expense.

The objection of the trustee is overruled. The plan will be confirmed by separate order.

PROBLEM 8-18

Candace Kane is an architect who specializes in the design of smaller commercial buildings such as restaurants and retail outfits. She has been very successful in her profession. She has been less successful, however, in some of her own investments. As a result, Candace has sought Chapter 13 relief. While her income fluctuates, her creditors and the Chapter 13 trustee are relatively satisfied with the sufficiency and regularity of her income. They have questions, however, about some of her expenses. Candace leases a one-year old BMW for $525 per month. She uses the vehicle to visit job sites and meet with current and prospective clients. The trustee and her creditors have suggested that the car is an unnecessary expense, and her travel needs could be met just as well with a vehicle with a monthly cost of approximately half the current expense. Candace has responded that her car is important to the business because it presents the appropriate image for a successful architect. Furthermore, there would be additional costs beyond the basic monthly payment if Candace were required to purchase or lease a new car at this time. Is the BMW a reasonable expense? *Cf.* In re Lyall, 191 B.R. 78 (E.D. Va. 1996) (debtor/architect's luxury automobile is a tool of the trade for exemption purposes).

PROBLEM 8-19

Jim and Sue both had very good jobs and their combined annual income exceeded $100,000. Unfortunately, Jim's company "downsized" and Jim found himself unemployed for an extended period of time. Prior to the layoff, however, Jim and Sue had signed a long-term lease for a four-bedroom home in a very expensive part of town. They chose the location because of the reputation of the local schools that their three children would attend, as well as for the overall ambience of the neighborhood. The monthly rent is $1,800. The creditors have objected to the high monthly rent and suggested that acceptable housing can be obtained for $1,000 per month in other parts of town. They have argued that Jim and Sue do not have to move, at least not if they are willing to forgo bankruptcy relief under Chapter 13. Is the $1,800 per month rent a reasonable expense? If so, is $2,800 a reasonable expense? $1,100?

PROBLEM 8-20

Despite her name, Judy Christensen was not a particularly religious person until she began to experience some of life's rougher times. Among those hard times were financial problems. Just as her income was reduced and her expenses were increased, Judy concluded that she needed to become more actively involved in her church. She participated more regularly in the worship services and she began to donate $50 per week to the church. This $2,600 annual contribution represents 25 percent of her take-home pay after the required withholdings for taxes and the like. Judy has included this continuing weekly tithe in her Chapter 13 budget and creditors have objected. Is this a necessary and reasonable expense? Suppose the weekly tithe is $100? $10? Does your answer change if the payment is to cover the cost of private religious education for Judy's children? Is her plan confirmable if she had made *no* charitable contributions before her Chapter 13 petition was filed, but now plans to give ten percent of her disposable income to her church? *See* In re Cavanagh, 250 B.R. 107 (BAP 9th Cir. 2000).

E.   *Treatment of Secured Claims*

As you may recall, §506 of the Bankruptcy Code sets out the rules for determining the extent to which a claim is secured. A claim is secured to the extent of the lesser of the amount of the outstanding indebtedness or the value of the collateral. See Associates Commercial Corporation v. Rash, 520 U.S. 953 (1997) (when debtor proposes to retain collateral under a plan, the value of the collateral is the cost for the debtor to replace the property).

Section 1325(a)(5) affords the debtor three methods to obtain confirmation of a plan that provides for allowed secured claims. The holder of the secured claim may *accept* the plan, the debtor may *surrender* the collateral to the secured creditor, or the debtor may *distribute* to the secured claimant property that is equal in value to the allowed amount of the secured claim. Acceptance of a plan by a secured creditor requires an affirmative act and is the closest thing to voting in Chapter 13 cases. *But cf.* Andrews v. Loheit (In re Andrews), 49 F.3d 1404, 1409 (9th Cir. 1995) (in dicta, the court stated that the secured creditors' failure to object to the debtor's treatment of their claims under the plan constituted acceptance of the plan under §1325(a)(5)(A)).

The more likely means for a plan to provide appropriate treatment of secured claims is either through the surrender of the collateral to the secured creditor — in which case the secured claim is satisfied in full — or through the distribution of property to the secured creditor, which, as of the effective date of the Chapter 13 plan, is at least equal in value to the allowed amount of the secured claim. *See, e.g.,* In re Barnes, 32 F.3d 404 (9th Cir. 1994); In re Murphy, 175 B.R. 134 (Bankr. D. Mass. 1994). There are two primary components to the determination of the amount of payments required to meet the cram down standards of §1325(a)(5)(B): the value of the collateral and the interest rate to be charged on the deferred payments.

Even when the court arrives at a value for the collateral, it still must determine the appropriate interest rate to apply to the repayments. In 2004, the Supreme Court resolved the conflict in the courts of appeals as to the proper interest rate by holding that the courts should apply a "formula approach"; Till v. SCS Credit Corp., 541 U.S. 465 (2004). Under that approach, a court

> begins by looking to the national prime rate, reported daily in the press, which reflects the financial market's estimate of the amount a commercial bank should charge a creditworthy commercial borrower to compensate for the opportunity costs of the loan, the risk of inflation, and the relatively slight risk of default. Because bankrupt debtors typically pose a greater risk of nonpayment than solvent commercial borrowers, the approach then requires a bankruptcy court to adjust the prime rate accordingly. The appropriate size of that risk adjustment depends, of course, on such factors as the circumstances of the estate, the nature of the security, and the duration and feasibility of the reorganization plan. The court must therefore hold a hearing at which the debtor and any creditors may present evidence about the appropriate risk adjustment. Some of this evidence will be included in the debtor's bankruptcy filings, however, so the debtor and creditors may not incur significant additional expense. Moreover, starting from a concededly *low* estimate and adjusting *upward* places the evidentiary burden squarely on the creditors, who are likely to have readier access to any information absent from the debtor's filing (such as evidence about the "liquidity of the collateral market," *post,* at 1973 (SCALIA, J., dissenting)). Finally, many of the factors relevant to the adjustment fall squarely within the bankruptcy court's area of expertise.

541 U.S. at 478-79 (citations omitted). In actual practice, the value of the collateral and the interest rate applied to the repayment of the secured claim are both flexible.

To the extent a creditor is able to negotiate a higher value for the collateral, the debtor is likely to seek a lower interest rate on a repayment of the claim, and vice versa. *Till* now limits to some extent the parameters of those negotiations.

Sections 1322(b)(2) and (3) authorize the debtor to modify secured claims and to provide for the curing and waiving of any defaults. These rights, as limited by §1325(a)(5), provide opportunities for the debtor to deal with both oversecured and undersecured claims. If the value of the collateral is less than the amount of the outstanding indebtedness, then the claim is undersecured or partially secured. The remaining portion of the claim is an unsecured claim. Note that valuations of automobiles and other consumer goods are governed by §1325(a)(9).

PROBLEM 8-21

When she graduated from law school, Portia Moot bought a new car for $25,000, giving Nightflyer Loan Company a perfected security interest in the car when it financed its purchase price. One year later, when Portia filed a Chapter 13 petition, her law practice in ruins due to an ugly malpractice incident, the car was worth only $20,000, but she owed Nightflyer $24,000. What must her plan provide as to this debt? *See* §1325(a)(9). If the car is worth $20,000 but she has paid down the debt to $15,000, what can she do? The loan agreement has an acceleration clause providing that on missing a payment (and she has missed several) the entire loan amount comes due, and NLC is insisting on getting the entire $15,000 now, even though the original payment schedule would have extended her payments for another four years.

PROBLEM 8-22

The Walker-Thomas Furniture Company had sold Mrs. Williams many consumer items over the years, carefully taking a security interest in each and cross-collateralizing the debts so that each item stood as collateral for all other unpaid purchases. Her current balance due to the company is $5,800. Now Mrs. Williams has filed for protection under Chapter 13. Her plan proposes to surrender to it all the items she has purchased from the company except for the living room suite, which she loves dearly. She owes Walker-Thomas $1000 for this suite, but its current value is only $400, so her plan proposes to claim the suite as exempt property, paying Walker-Thomas $400 for the suite; *see* §522(f). Is this plan confirmable? *See* §1325(a)(5) and In re Williams, 168 F.3d 845 (5th Cir. 1999).

The addition of the "hanging paragraph" to Bankruptcy Code §1325(a)(9) in 2005 has generated significant litigation. It's called the "hanging paragraph" because, unlike most statutes, it is not identified by a number or letter. Following the regular style of the Bankruptcy Code, the paragraph that begins with "For purposes of paragraph (5) . . ." would normally be indented from the previous paragraph and designated as §1325(a)(9)(A). The hanging paragraph provides that the normal valuation process governed by §506 of the Code is inapplicable to a claim secured by a purchase money security interest that is less than one year old, or a purchase money security interest in a motor vehicle that was purchased within 910 days of the filing of the petition. Two issues in particular have occupied the courts. The first is the question of the definition of a purchase money security interest. As you should recall from your study of the avoidance of certain liens on otherwise exempt property (*see* §522(f)), purchase money security interests are defined by §9-103(a) of the Uniform Commercial Code. The Bankruptcy Code, however, contains no definition of a purchase money security interest. This has led to some disagreement among the courts, as you will see.

The second issue that the courts have faced in applying the hanging paragraph of §1325(a)(9) arises when the debtor proposes to surrender property governed by that section to the secured party in full satisfaction of the debt. In those situations, the debtor asserts that §1325(a)(9) means that the value of the collateral is equal to the debt secured by the collateral. Therefore, if the debtor surrenders the collateral to the creditor, it should satisfy the entire indebtedness secured by the property. The following cases illustrate the courts' reactions to these issues.

In re Hall

United States Bankruptcy Court, Southern District of West Virginia, 2008
400 B.R. 516

RONALD G. PEARSON, Bankruptcy Judge.

Pending before the Court is the objection of Ford Motor Credit Company, LLC, formerly Ford Motor Credit Company (hereinafter "Ford") to the Debtors' Chapter 13 plan. As a part of the plan, the Debtors assert that the financing by Ford of negative equity[10] on trade-in vehicle allows them to cramdown Ford's secured claim to the value of their 2007 Ford F150 pickup, despite the fact that the vehicle was purchased within 910 days of their bankruptcy filing. Ford contends that the full amount of its claim must be treated as secured regardless of the actual value of the collateral.

I. *Background*

On August 20, 2007, the Debtors entered into a contract with Moses Ford, Inc., of St. Albans, WV for the purchase of a 2007 Ford F150 pickup. The Debtors traded in a 2006 Chevrolet K2500 truck. The amount owing on the Debtors' trade-in was $34,599.00. Debtors were given a trade-in allowance of $27,239.18. In the common parlance of the automotive trade, the Debtors were "upside down" on their trade-in to the extent of this difference. Ford agreed to finance this "negative equity" totaling

---

10. When a vehicle's trade-in value is less than the amount of the debt secured by it, the excess debt is typically referred to as "negative equity" and is frequently "rolled into," or made part of, the financing package involving the purchase of a new vehicle.

$7,359.82. That sum was fully disclosed on the fact of the contract described as "Net Trade Payoff."

Approximately 7 months after purchasing the vehicle, the Debtors filed this Chapter 13 proceeding. In numbered paragraph 3 of their plan, the Debtors checked that there were no Class Three claims to be paid, which included motor vehicle claims within 910 days of the filing of the Chapter 13 petition. The plan proposed to pay Creditor's claim as a Class Four claim, listing the total claim at $40,500.00, with a secured value of $26,000. In essence the Debtors sought to bifurcate this claim pursuant to 11 U.S.C. §506 and Ford objected.

II. Discussion

The Debtors Chapter 13 plan proposes to bifurcate Ford's claim into a secured and unsecured portion. The unsecured portion is to be treated as an unsecured claim in the plan, and paid pro rata with other unsecured creditors. Ford objects to this treatment on the grounds that it holds a claim defined by the hanging paragraph following 11 U.S.C. §1325(a)(9) (commonly referred to as "910 car claims," or "the hanging paragraph" because it lacks an alphanumeric designation), and, therefore, holds a claim that cannot be bifurcated. While recognizing that Ford may otherwise hold a 910 car claim, the Debtors assert that the financing of negative equity removes Ford's claim from the protection of the hanging paragraph, which only protects "purchase money security interest securing the debt that is the subject of the claim":

> For purposes of paragraph (5), section 506 shall not apply to a claim described in that paragraph if the creditor has a purchase money security interest securing the debt that is the subject of the claim, the debt was incurred within the 910-day preceding the date of the filing of the petition, and the collateral for that debt consists of a motor vehicle . . . acquired for the personal use of the debtor. . . .

11 U.S.C. §1325(a).

The hanging paragraph is significant because, without the protection afforded by it, nothing prevents a debtor from using §506 (which ties the value of a creditor's security interest to the value of the secured collateral) to do exactly what the Debtor proposes: bifurcate Ford's claim against the purchased vehicle into secured and unsecured portions. Before being entitled to the protection of the hanging paragraph, a creditor must satisfy four conditions: (1) the creditor must have a purchase money security interest; (2) securing a debt that was incurred within 910 days before the filing of the bankruptcy petition; (3) the collateral for the debt must be a motor vehicle; and (4) the motor vehicle must have been acquired from the personal use of the debtor. *General Motors Acceptance Corp. v. Peaslee (In re Peaslee)*, 373 B.R. 252, 257 (W.D.N.Y. 2007). Here, there is essentially no dispute between the parties that elements two through four are present regarding Ford's claim. Therefore, the court must decide only whether (A) Ford holds a purchase money security interest, and (B) how to treat Ford's claim in the Debtor's bankruptcy.

A.   Purchase Money Security Interest & Negative Equity

The Debtors argue that Ford cannot have a purchase money security interest in a vehicle when a portion of the money loaned was not used for the purchase of the 2007 F150, but was used to payoff a pre-existing loan on the Debtor's trade-in vehicle.

The term "purchase money security interest" is not defined in the Bankruptcy Code. It is defined under State law. In West Virginia, §46-9-103(a)(*l*) of the Commercial Code states, "A security interest in goods is a purchase-money security interest to the extent that the goods are purchase-money collateral with respect to that security interest." In turn, "purchase-money collateral" is defined as "goods . . . that secure[ ] a purchase-money obligation incurred with respect to that collateral." §46-9-103(a)(1). The term "purchase-money obligation" is defined as "an obligation of an obligor incurred as all or part of the price of the collateral or for value given to enable the debtor to acquire rights in or the use of the collateral if the value is in fact so used." §46-9-103(a)(2). Thus, to be entitled to the protection of the hanging paragraph, a creditor must advance funds to the debtor for the purpose of purchasing an automobile.

Courts have reached two different outcomes in determining whether the financing of negative equity destroys a purchase money security interest in a consumer transaction. Some conclude that the financing for negative equity does not destroy the purchase money security interest because the financing of the negative equity is part of the price of the collateral, or value given to enable the debtor to acquire the collateral. *In re Conyers*, 379 B.R. 576, 579 (Bankr. M.D.N.C. 2007) (citing *GMAC v. Peaslee*, 373 B.R. 252 (W.D.N.Y. 2007)); *Graupner v. Nuvell Credit Corp.*, No. 4:07-CV-37CDL, 2007 WL 1858291, 2007 U.S. Dist. LEXIS 46144 (M.D. Ga. June 26, 2007); *In re Burt*, 378 B.R. 352 (Bankr. D. Utah 2007); *In re Bradlee*, No. 07-30527, 2007 Bankr. LEXIS 3863 (Bankr. W.D. La. Oct. 10, 2007); *In re Wall*, 376 B.R. 769 (Bankr. W.D.N.C. Sept.17, 2007); *In re Cohrs*, No. 07-21431A13G, 2007 WL 2050980, 2007 Bankr. LEXIS 2529 (Bankr. E.D. Cal. June 25, 2007); *In re Petrocci*, 370 B.R. 489 (Bankr. N.D.N.Y. 2007).

Others disagree on the basis that the finance of negative equity is not a component of the price of the collateral. *Conyers*, 379 B.R. at 580; *In re Westfall*, 376 B.R. 210 (Bankr. N.D. Ohio 2007); *In re Acaya*, 369 B.R. 564 (Bankr. N.D. Cal. 2007); *In re Price*, 363 B.R. 734 (Bankr. E.D. N.C. 2007)(affirmed in pertinent part by *Wells Fargo Financial North Carolina 1, Inc. v. Price*, 2007 WL 5297071 (E.D.N.C. 2007)); *In re Blakeslee*, 377 B.R. 724 (Bankr. M.D. Fla. 2007).

Importantly, Official Comment 3 to W. Va. Code §46A-9-103 states that "the 'price' of collateral or the 'value given to enable' [the purchase] includes obligations for expenses incurred in connection with acquiring rights in the collateral." Such expenses include sales taxes, finance charges, interest, costs of storage in transit, and administrative charges. *Id.* In *Peaslee*, 373 B.R. at 258, the district court included the finance of negative equity in this list. The ruling in *Peaslee* was based, in part, on New York's Motor Vehicle Retail Installment Sales Act, which contained a definition of "cash sale price." By statute, the sale price of a vehicle "include[s] the unpaid balance of any amount financed under an outstanding motor vehicle loan agreement. . .or the unpaid portion of the early termination obligation under an outstanding motor vehicle retail lease agreement." *Id.* at 261.

Unlike New York, West Virginia does not presently have a Motor Vehicle Retail Installment Sales Act. By analogy, the West Virginia Consumer Credit and Protection Act defines the term "cash price" as, "the price at which the goods, services or interest in land are offered for sale by the seller to cash buyers in the ordinary course of business, and may include: (a) applicable sales, use, privilege, and excise and documentary stamp taxes; (b) the cash price of accessories or related services such as delivery, installation, servicing, repairs, alterations and improvements; and (c) amounts actually paid or to be paid by the seller for registration, certificate of title or license fees." W. Va. Code §46A-1-102(6). Similarly, with regard to the assessment of a sales tax, the term "sales price" does not include consideration from "the exchange of other vehicles" §11-15-3c(b).

Apart from statutory definitions of what constitutes the "sales price" for a particular item, a hallmark of a purchase money security interest is that the creditor advance value "to enable the Debtor to acquire rights in or the use of the collateral. . . ." §46-9-103(a)(2). Logically, the financing of negative equity is not an integral component of the loan agreement to purchase a motor vehicle; it only serves as a convenience to the debtor. *E.g., Conyers*, 379 B.R. at 582 ("In this case, while the loan of additional money was a convenience and an accommodation to the Debtor, the court cannot find that it enabled the Debtor to acquire rights in or the use of the collateral."). No value is added to a vehicle when the creditor also finances the payoff of a trade-in's negative equity; negative equity financing is not necessary to purchase a motor vehicle. *E.g., Price*, 363 B.R. at 741 ("The funds loaned to satisfy the negative equity are not a component of the price of the collateral or the value given to enable the debtor to acquire rights in the collateral, and are significantly and qualitatively different from the fees, freight charges, storage costs, taxes, and similar expenses that are typically part of an automobiles sale."). The bankruptcy court in the Price case based its interpretation upon language under North Carolina law defining "purchase money obligation" that is identical to the language used in the West Virginia statute.

Therefore, the court finds that negative equity financing is not value given to enable the debtor to acquire rights in or the use of the collateral if the value is in fact so used. Negative equity is antecedent debt. If the Creditor had refinanced the Debtors' original car loan, there would be no question that the characterization of the security interest as purchase money would have been lost. It follows that refinancing negative equity by rolling it in to a new purchase money loan does not thereby create a purchase money obligation at least to the extent of the antecedent debt that was refinanced. Ford's financing of negative equity on the Debtors' trade-in is not a purchase money security interest.

B. Bifurcation into 910 and Non-910 Portions

Concluding that a creditor does not have a purchase money security interest in a motor vehicle when a creditor also finances negative equity, the court must determine whether that portion of the amount financed that actually went to purchase the vehicle is nonetheless entitled to the protection of the hanging paragraph.

Two clear lines of authority exist on this issue. The "dual status" rule holds that the non-purchase money security interest component of a claim does not destroy the purchase money security interest of the remainder of the claim. The "transformation" rule holds that the nonpurchase money component transforms the entire claim into a non-purchase money security interest. *E.g., In re Weiser*, 381 B.R. 263, 269 (Bankr. W.D. Mo. 2007) ("Courts have essentially adopted two lines of authority regarding treatment of combined purchase money and non-purchase money transactions, known as the 'dual status rule' and the 'transformation rule.' ")

For non-consumer transactions, §46-9-103(f)(1) of the West Virginia Commercial Code dictates that a purchase money security interest does not lose its status when the purchase money collateral also secures an obligation that is not a purchase money obligation. No corresponding provision exists for consumer transactions. Rather, by statute, the court is left to determine the proper rules, and the statute admonishes the court that it may not infer that the appropriate rule parallels those used for non-consumer transactions. §46-9-103(h). In other words, the statute requests that the court make up rules that are appropriate to the facts of the case before it.

Arguably, the application of the "dual status" rule would prevent debtors from incurring substantial debt secured by a vehicle prior to filing for bankruptcy and, subsequently, cramming down the debt to the value of the collateral. Whereas application of the "transformation" rule would render the hanging paragraph completely ineffective in situations involving the financing of negative equity. Rendering the hanging paragraph ineffective only means that creditors with 910 car claims are treated the same as a creditor that has a car claim that is 911 days old, which is the same treatment that the 910 creditor would have received before the enactment of the Bankruptcy Abuse Prevention and Consumer Protection Act of 2005.

Prior to BAPCPA, vehicle financers could be harmed by a debtor who acquired a vehicle in the months leading up to bankruptcy, then filed bankruptcy and crammed the creditor's claim down to the collateral value on the date of filing. Due to the rapid depreciation of motor vehicles the moment they leave the dealer's lot, debtors could often reap a benefit by cramming down the debt, only paying a secured claim equal to the depreciated value of the car. Home mortgages, while a traditionally appreciating asset, are protected from bifurcation and cramdown by 11 U.S.C. §1322(b). In enacting the hanging paragraph, Congress fixed this disparity to ensure that debtors could not load up on vehicle-secured debt pre-petition only to cram it down to the collateral value in bankruptcy. The Court finds that in adopting the dual status rule, the objectives of Congress in passing the hanging paragraph are best served. Accordingly, that is the rule to be applied in this case and in future cases in this district. With respect to payments made on pre-petition debts to which this rule is applied, the Court shall employ a presumption that payments on the two obligations were allocated proportionally.

III.   Conclusion

For the reasons set forth above, the Court concludes that with respect to the Debtors' treatment of Ford's claim in their Ch. 13 plan, Ford's objection is OVER-RULED in part, and SUSTAINED in part. The debtor is directed to modify the plan such that the negative equity in the trade-in vehicle is characterized as unsecured debt and the actual purchase money amount is treated as a 910 claim, with pre-petition payments made on the loan credited on a proportional basis to each part.

IT IS SO ORDERED.

Tidewater Finance Co. v. Kenney
United States Court of Appeals, Fourth Circuit, 2008
531 F.3d 312

ROTH, Senior Circuit Judge:

I.

This is a direct appeal by creditor Tidewater Finance Co. from the Bankruptcy Court's final order confirming debtor Jennifer Kenney's Chapter 13 bankruptcy plan. The narrow issue on appeal concerns a pure question of law and is a matter of first impression with this Court: Whether the "hanging paragraph" in 11 U.S.C. §1325(a), added by the Bankruptcy Abuse Prevention and Consumer Protection Act of 2005 (BAPCPA), prevents a creditor with a purchase money security interest in a "910 vehicle" from exercising his contractual right, under state law, to an unsecured claim for the portion of the debt not covered by the sale of such vehicle (i.e., the deficiency amount) after the vehicle is surrendered to the creditor by a Chapter 13 debtor pursuant to §1325(a)(5)(C).[11] We hold that the hanging paragraph does not operate to deprive such undersecured "910 creditors" of their deficiency claims because the parties are bound to their contractual rights and obligations under operative state law, and the Bankruptcy Code does not command otherwise. For this reason, we will reverse the decision of the Bankruptcy Court and remand the case for further proceedings consistent with this opinion.

---

11. The hanging paragraph applies to claims secured by a purchase money security interest in a motor vehicle purchased within 910 days of the bankruptcy filing. Such claims are referred to as "910 claims," the vehicles are called "910 vehicles," and the creditors are called "910 creditors." The hanging paragraph specifically excludes 910 claims from the bifurcation method prescribed under 11 U.S.C. §506.

II.

Kenney purchased a 2003 Chevrolet Impala from Calvary Cars & Service on September 29, 2006, under a Retail Installment Sales Contract. Pursuant to the sales contract, Kenney made a down payment of $700, financed with Calvary the payment of $12,102.24, which included the cost of the vehicle, taxes, and other required fees, and provided Calvary with a purchase money security interest in the vehicle securing the entire debt. Calvary perfected the security interest and then assigned the sales contract, including the perfected security interest to Tidewater. Tidewater's lien was noted on the vehicle's title.

On December 19, 2006, less than three months after purchasing the vehicle, Kenney filed for bankruptcy. On February 1, she filed an amended Chapter 13 reorganization plan which provided for the surrender of the vehicle in full satisfaction of the debt she owed to Tidewater even though the vehicle was worth less than the balance owed. On March 6, Tidewater filed an objection to the confirmation of the amended plan. On April 12, Tidewater filed a proof of claim listing the total amount of secured debt as $12,341.84. After obtaining relief from the automatic stay and disposing of the surrendered vehicle, Tidewater amended its proof of claim to change the status of the debt to unsecured and the total amount of debt to $5,271.34 — the deficiency amount due under the sales contract.

By order dated May 11, 2007, the Bankruptcy Court overruled Tidewater's objection to the plan's confirmation. Specifically, the Bankruptcy Court followed the approach taken by a majority of bankruptcy courts in other circuits, concluding that the hanging paragraph in 11 U.S.C. §1325(a) prevents a 910 creditor from bifurcating her claim and asserting an unsecured deficiency claim for any portion of the debt not covered by the sale of the vehicle. The Bankruptcy Court then entered its order confirming the plan on May 25, 2007.[12]

On June 5, 2007, the Bankruptcy Court certified, pursuant to Interim Rule 8001(f) of the Federal Rules of Bankruptcy Procedure and 28 U.S.C. §158(d)(2)(A), that a direct appeal from Tidewater presents, among other things, a question of law as to which there is no controlling decision of this Court or of the United States Supreme Court and which requires resolution of conflicting decisions among bankruptcy courts in various circuits. We granted Tidewater's timely petition for direct appeal.

III.

[1] We have subject matter jurisdiction over direct appeals from final orders of bankruptcy courts pursuant to 28 U.S.C. §158(d)(2). Because the narrow issue on appeal concerns the proper interpretation of the Bankruptcy Code, our review is plenary. *Butler v. David Shaw, Inc.*, 72 F.3d 437, 441 (4th Cir. 1996).

---

12. Kenney's Chapter 13 plan is funded at $210 per month for 36 months, a total of $7,560. It treats the surrender of the 910 vehicle to Tidewater as fully satisfying Kenney's entire indebtedness to Tidewater, including the $5,271.34 deficiency, and it promises a 15% dividend to all unsecured creditors, except Tidewater.

IV.

[2] Chapter 13 of the Bankruptcy Code affords a reorganization remedy for consumers and business owners with relatively small debts. *Johnson v. Home State Bank*, 501 U.S. 78, 82, 111 S. Ct. 2150, 115 L. Ed. 2d 66 (1991). A debtor who qualifies for Chapter 13 relief may submit a plan that modifies the rights of secured and unsecured creditors. The bankruptcy court will confirm the plan so long as it satisfies the requirements of 11 U.S.C. §1325(a). Under §1325(a)(5), a plan's proposed treatment of an "allowed secured claim" will be confirmed if the plan can provide that (1) the debtor and secured creditor agree on how the claim will be paid, *see id.* at §1325(a)(5)(A); or (2) the debtor retains the collateral securing the claim while the creditor retains the lien until either the debt is repaid under the plan or until the debtor receives a discharge, whichever occurs first, and the debtor pays adequate protection payments to the secured creditor, the total of which must not be less than the allowed amount of the claim as of the effective date of the plan, *see id.* at §1325(a)(5)(B); or (3) the debtor surrenders the secured collateral to the creditor holding the lien, *see id.* at §1325(a)(5)(C).

By enacting the BAPCPA in 2005, Congress revised §1325(a) by adding an unnumbered paragraph — commonly referred to as the hanging paragraph — at the end of that subsection. The hanging paragraph provides as follows:

> For purposes of paragraph (5), *section 506 shall not apply to a claim* described in that paragraph if the creditor has a *purchase money security interest* securing the debt that is the subject of the claim, the *debt was incurred within the 910-day preceding the date of the filing* of the petition, and the *collateral for that debt consists of a motor vehicle* (as defined in section 30102 of title 49) acquired for the personal use of the debtor, or if collateral for that debt consists of any other thing of value, if the debt was incurred during the 1-year period preceding that filing.

11 U.S.C. §1325(a) (emphasis added). Pertinent here, §506(a) specifies how an "allowed claim of a creditor secured by a lien on property" should be valued by providing a method of bifurcating, or dividing, a consumer's debt into secured and unsecured amounts, with the unsecured amount equaling the amount that the debt exceeds the current value of the collateral. *See* 11 U.S.C. §506(a). Under this bifurcation method, an undersecured creditor becomes an unsecured creditor for purposes of pursuing a deficiency claim.

Prior to the BAPCPA's enactment, if a Chapter 13 consumer debtor proposed a plan for confirmation which provided for the surrender of the 910 vehicle to the creditor pursuant to §1325(a)(5)(C), §506(a) supplied the creditor with a federal recourse remedy for a deficiency after the sale of the collateral.[13] However, since

---

13. Tidewater contends that the hanging paragraph does not apply to the surrender provision in §1325(a)(5)(C). To support this contention, Tidewater argues that prior to the BAPCPA's enactment, §506 was *only* applicable when the debtor retained collateral under §1325(a)(5)(B), and *not* applicable when the debtor surrendered the collateral under §1325(a)(5)(C). We do not agree. Rather, we conclude that, pre-BAPCPA, §506(a) applied to the surrender of collateral under §1325(a)(5)(C), especially given the Supreme Court's explicit recognition, in *Assocs. Commercial Corp. v. Rash*, 520 U.S. 953, 962, 117 S. Ct. 1879, 138 L. Ed. 2d 148 (1997), of the apparent applicability of §506(a) to the

the hanging paragraph was added to §1325(a), bankruptcy courts across the nation disagree as to the paragraph's effect on a 910 creditor's contractual right, under state law, to a deficiency judgment after the proceeds from the collateral's sale fail to satisfy the total debt owed. The majority of bankruptcy courts have concluded that, by eliminating the application of §506(a) to 910 claims, the hanging paragraph ensures that such creditors are without a remedy to bifurcate their loans into secured and unsecured portions, therefore rendering their loans non-recourse regardless of what the parties' contract allows. *See e.g, In re Kenney*, No. 06-71975-A, 2007 WL 1412921, at *5 (Bankr. E.D. Va. May 10, 2007) (listing cases in which bankruptcy courts have adopted the majority view). Conversely, a minority of bankruptcy courts have concluded that Article 9 of the Uniform Commercial Code (UCC) and contract law entitle 910 creditors to an unsecured deficiency judgment after surrender of the vehicle, unless the contract provides for a non-recourse loan. *Id.* at *4 (listing cases in which bankruptcy courts have adopted the minority view). Under this approach, the unsecured balance is treated in the same manner as other unsecured debts under a Chapter 13 reorganization plan.

More recently, a growing number of circuit courts have adopted the minority approach, thus recognizing a 910 creditor's right to assert an unsecured deficiency claim under state law when a Chapter 13 debtor surrenders her vehicle under §1325(a)(5)(c). *See DaimlerChrysler Financial Services Americas LLC v. Ballard*, 526 F.3d 634 (10th Cir. 2008); *Capital One Auto Fin. v. Osborn*, 515 F.3d 817 (8th Cir. 2008); *In the Matter of Wright*, 492 F.3d 829 (7th Cir. 2007); *cf. In re Long*, 519 F.3d 288 (6th Cir. 2008) (using the common law principle of interpretation known as "the equity of the statute" as a method of filling statutory gaps rather than resorting to non-bankruptcy law to preserve deficiency claims).

Based on a plain reading of the hanging paragraph, there is no question that Congress has unambiguously eliminated the 910 creditor's access to a federal remedy under §506(a). *See Ballard*, 526 F.3d at 638; *Osborn*, 515 F.3d at 821; *In re Wright*, 492 F.3d at 832. "Because the statutory language is clear, we need not look beyond it." *Ballard*, 526 F.3d at 638, *U.S. v. Ron Pair Enterprises, Inc.*, 489 U.S. 235, 241, 109 S. Ct. 1026, 103 L. Ed. 2d 290 (1989). However, in this case we are asked to decide whether a 910 creditor nevertheless has recourse against the debtor, under

---

surrender provision. Based on the language of §506(a) which specifies that valuation of collateral should be based upon its "disposition or use," Justice Ginsburg explained:

> As we comprehend §506(a), the "proposed disposition or use" of the collateral is of paramount importance to the valuation question. If a secured creditor does not accept a debtor's Chapter 13 plan, the debtor has two options for handling allowed secured claims: surrender the collateral to the creditor, *see* §1325(a)(5)(C); or, under the cram down option, keep the collateral over the creditor's objection and provide the creditor, over the life of the plan, with the equivalent of the present value of the collateral, *see* §1325(a)(5)(B). The "disposition or use" of the collateral thus turns on the alternative the debtor chooses—in one case the collateral will be surrendered to the creditor, and in the other, the collateral will be retained and used by the debtor.

Id. Accordingly, it is evident to this Court that §506 was applicable to the surrender provision in §1325(a)(5)(C) pre-BAPCPA and continues to be applicable post-BAPCPA.

another body of law, for the remainder of the debt owed. We join our sister courts in the Seventh, Eighth, and Tenth Circuits in holding that, after a debtor satisfies the requirements for plan confirmation under §1325(a)(5)(C) by surrendering his 910 vehicle, the parties are left to their contractual rights and obligations, and the creditor may pursue an unsecured deficiency claim under state law. *See Ballard*, 526 F.3d at 640-41; *Osborn*, 515 F.3d at 822-23; *Wright*, 492 F.3d at 832-33.

The principle that state law determines the rights and obligations of debtors and creditors when the Bankruptcy Code fails to supply a federal rule is well recognized. *See Butner v. United States*, 440 U.S. 48, 55, 99 S. Ct. 914, 59 L. Ed. 2d 136 (1979); *see also Travelers Cas. & Sur. Co. v. Pac. Gas & Elec. Co.*, ____ U.S. ____, 127 S. Ct. 1199, 1204-05, 167 L. Ed. 2d 178 (2007) (explaining the settled principle that "[c]reditors' entitlements in bankruptcy arise in the first instance from the underlying substantive law creating the debtor's obligation, subject to any qualifying or contrary provisions of the Bankruptcy Code") (citations omitted); *Am. Bankers Ins. Co. of Florida v. Maness*, 101 F.3d 358, 365 (4th Cir. 1996) ("[W]hen Congress has not provided an explicit alternative to state law, we are mindful that the Bankruptcy Code was written in the shadow of state law and conclude that Congress intended state law to fill the interstices.") (quoting *In re Estate of Medcare HMO*, 998 F.2d 436, 441 (7th Cir. 1993)). The Supreme Court in *Butner* explained the logic behind this principle as follows:

> *Property interests are created and defined by state law. Unless some federal interest requires a different result, there is no reason why such interests should be analyzed differently simply because an interested party is involved in a bankruptcy proceeding.* Uniform treatment of property interests by both state and federal courts within a State serves to reduce uncertainty, to discourage forum shopping, and to prevent a party from receiving "a windfall merely by reason of the happenstance of bankruptcy." *Lewis v. Manufacturers National Bank*, 364 U.S. 603, 609, 81 S. Ct. 347, 350, 5 L. Ed. 2d 323. The justifications for application of state law are not limited to ownership interests; they apply with equal force to security interests, including the interest of a mortgagee in rents earned by mortgaged property.

440 U.S. at 55, 99 S. Ct. 914 (emphasis added). Accordingly, *Butner* confirms that, as with property interests, state law creates and defines security interests at issue in bankruptcy proceedings if no federal law requires a different result.

The Seventh Circuit Court of Appeals was the first court to resolve the split among bankruptcy courts regarding the hanging paragraph's effect on 910 claims when a vehicle is surrendered under §1325(a)(5)(C). *See Wright*, 492 F.3d 829. In *Wright*, the court relied on the principle of *Butner* to affirm the decision of a bankruptcy judge who declined to approve a debtor's reorganization plan which proposed the surrender of a 910 vehicle to a creditor in full satisfaction of a debt owed. 492 F.3d at 832-33. Applying *Butner*, the *Wright* court held that, with §506 no longer applicable to 910 claims, state law, in conjunction with the parties' underlying contract, created and defined a 910 creditor's entitlement to an unsecured deficiency judgment upon surrender (and subsequent sale) of the vehicle. *Id.*

The *Wright* court made clear that "it is a mistake to assume . . . that §506 is the *only* source of authority for a deficiency judgment when the collateral is deficient."

Id. at 832. Rather, the court recognized the principle in *Butner* that "state law determines rights and obligations when the [Bankruptcy] Code does not supply a federal rule." *Id.* (*citing Butner*, 440 U.S. 48, 99 S. Ct. 914, 59 L. Ed. 2d 136 (1979)). Following this principle, the court concluded that (1) nothing in the Bankruptcy Code prohibits or qualifies an unsecured deficiency claim under state law following the surrender of collateral pursuant to §1325(a)(5)(C); (2) "[c]reditors don't need §506 to create, allow, or recognize security interests, which rest on contracts (and the UCC) rather than federal law"; and (3) rather, "[s]ection 502 tells bankruptcy courts to allow claims that stem from contractual debts" and "nothing in §502 disfavors or curtails secured claims." *Id.* at 832-33. Accordingly, the *Wright* court concluded that the "fallback under *Butner* is the parties' contract (to the extent the deal is enforceable under state law)[,]" and any deficiency after surrender and sale of the collateral "must be treated as an unsecured debt." *Id.* at 833.

We are persuaded by the *Wright* court's reasoning and join the Seventh, Eighth, and Tenth Circuit Courts of Appeals in holding that, when a Chapter 13 debtor surrenders a 910 vehicle in accordance with §1325(a)(5)(C), the hanging paragraph does not extinguish a 910 creditor's unsecured deficiency claim so long as state law, in conjunction with the parties' contract, allows for such claim. Specifically, we agree that §506 is not the exclusive method for separating out the deficiency as an unsecured portion of a 910 claim. Pre-BAPCPA, the bifurcation method articulated in §506 presented an undersecured 910 creditor with a federal recourse remedy against a Chapter 13 debtor who surrendered a vehicle with a market value less than the debt owed. Post-BAPCPA, we recognize that §506 is no longer applicable to 910 claims, and we find no other bifurcation method in the Bankruptcy Code nor a rule in the Code which qualifies or eliminates a 910 creditor's contractual entitlement to a deficiency claim under state law. Thus, we conclude that such a deficiency claim may be pursued by a 910 creditor as an unsecured claim in a bankruptcy proceeding. In this regard, we recognize that, before the hanging paragraph was added, §506(a), as applied to 910 claims, merely provided "a method for the judicial valuation of an allowed secured claim; it [did] not provide a definition of the phrase 'allowed secured claim' applicable to other provisions of the Bankruptcy Code" which might be interpreted to preclude an unsecured claim for a deficiency. *Ballard*, 526 F.3d at 640 (*citing Dewsnup v. Timm*, 502 U.S. 410, 417, 112 S. Ct. 773, 116 L. Ed. 2d 903 (1992)). As the Seventh Circuit Court of Appeals recognized, "§502 rather than §506 determines whether a claim should be allowed. . . ." *Wright*, 492 F.3d at 832. Because §502 directs bankruptcy courts to allow claims stemming from contractual debts and neither diminishes nor disapproves of secured claims, it is evident to us that such deficiency claims must be permitted to the extent that state law allows for them. *See* 11 U.S.C. §§502(a), 502(b)(1), 502(k); *see also Travelers Cas. & Sur. Co.*, 127 S. Ct. at 1206 ("[W]e generally presume that claims enforceable under applicable state law will be allowed in bankruptcy unless they are expressly disallowed."); *Osborn*, 515 F.3d at 822 (recognizing that "nothing in §502 or §1325 denies a creditor an unsecured deficiency claim").

Here, Tidewater is entitled, under state law and the parties' underlying contract, to a deficiency judgment against Kenney. The parties' sales contract provides Tidewater with a security interest in the vehicle, and such interest *"secures payment of all [Kenney] owe[s] on this contract"* and "secures [all] other agreements in this contract." *App.* 140-43 (emphasis added). The contract further provides that, upon Tidewater's sale of the vehicle, Tidewater "will apply the money from the sale, less allowed expenses, to the amount [Kenney] owe[s,]" and, *"[i]f money from the sale is not enough to pay the amount [Kenney] owe[s,] [she] must pay the rest to [Tidewater]."* *Id.* (emphasis added). Moreover, the sales contract specifies that "[f]ederal law and the law of the state of [Virginia] apply to this contract." *Id.* Given the explicit language in the parties' contract, there is no dispute that the contract provides Tidewater with a right to pursue a deficiency claim, and such contract is enforceable under Virginia law, particularly that state's version of Article 9 of the UCC. *See* VA. CODE ANN. §§8.9A-607-626; U.C.C. §§9-607-626.

Accordingly, we hold that, by surrendering the 910 vehicle, Kenney gave Tidewater the full market value of the collateral, and any deficiency after the sale of the vehicle is an unsecured debt that must be treated as an unsecured claim in the bankruptcy reorganization plan. *See Ballard*, 526 F.3d at 640-41; *Osborn*, 515 F.3d at 822-33; *Wright*, 492 F.3d at 833. We join the Seventh Circuit Court of Appeals in further recognizing that "[such unsecured debt] need not be paid in full, any more than [Kenney's] other unsecured debts, but it can't be written off *in toto* while other unsecured creditors are paid some fraction of their entitlements." *Wright*, 492 F.3d at 833.

V.

For the foregoing reasons, we vacate the judgment of the Bankruptcy Court and remand this case for further proceedings in accordance with this opinion.

F.   Treatment of Home Mortgages

The most important asset for many Chapter 13 debtors is their home. It is also generally their largest obligation. In fact, the failure to maintain current payments on a mortgage frequently leads to the creditor initiating foreclosure proceedings, and the debtor's response is the commencement of the Chapter 13 case. Claims secured by a mortgage on the debtor's principal residence are treated specially in Chapter 13.[14] While §1322(b)(2) generally authorizes the modification of secured claims, claims "secured only by a security interest in real property that is the debtor's principal

---

14. This treatment is also given to residential mortgage holders in Chapter 11. Bankruptcy Code §1123(b)(5).

residence" may not be modified. For definitions of the relevant terms, see §§101(13A) and 101(27B).

PROBLEM 8-23

Nero Wolfe's New York townhouse was worth $220,000, but his mortgage on it was for $350,000. His Chapter 13 plan proposed to engage in lien-stripping, here meaning that he would pay the mortgagee $220,000 (plus interest) during the life of the plan, and deal with the $130,000 shortage as an unsecured claim (as to which the plan proposed only a 5 percent payment). Can he do this, or does §1322(b)(2) forbid it?

Nobelman v. American Savings Bank
United States Supreme Court, 1993
508 U.S. 324

Justice THOMAS delivered the opinion of the Court.

This case focuses on the interplay between two provisions of the Bankruptcy Code. The question is whether §1322(b)(2) prohibits a Chapter 13 debtor from relying on §506(a) to reduce an undersecured homestead mortgage to the fair market value of the mortgaged residence. We conclude that it does and therefore affirm the judgment of the Court of Appeals.

I.

In 1984, respondent American Savings Bank loaned petitioners Leonard and Harriet Nobelman $68,250 for the purchase of their principal residence, a condominium in Dallas, Texas. In exchange, petitioners executed an adjustable rate note payable to the bank and secured by a deed of trust on the residence. In 1990, after falling behind in their mortgage payments, petitioners sought relief under Chapter 13 of the Bankruptcy Code. The bank filed a proof of claim with the Bankruptcy Court for $71,335 in principal, interest, and fees owed on the note. Petitioners' modified Chapter 13 plan valued the residence at a mere $23,500 — an uncontroverted valuation — and proposed to make payments pursuant to the mortgage contract only up to that amount (plus prepetition arrearages). Relying on §506(a) of the Bankruptcy Code, petitioners proposed to treat the remainder of the bank's claim as unsecured. Under the plan, unsecured creditors would receive nothing.

The bank and the Chapter 13 trustee, also a respondent here, objected to petitioners' plan. They argued that the proposed bifurcation of the bank's claim into a secured claim for $23,500 and an effectively worthless unsecured claim modified the bank's rights as a homestead mortgagee, in violation of 11 U.S.C. §1322(b)(2). The Bankruptcy Court agreed with respondents and denied confirmation of the plan. The District Court affirmed, In re Nobelman, 129 B.R. 98 (N.D. Tex. 1991), as did the Court of Appeals, 968 F.2d 483 (1992). We granted certiorari to resolve a conflict among the Courts of Appeals, 506 U.S. 1020, 113 S. Ct. 654, 121 L. Ed. 2d 580 (1992).

II.

Under Chapter 13 of the Bankruptcy Code, individual debtors may obtain adjustment of their indebtedness through a flexible repayment plan approved by a bankruptcy court. Section 1322 sets forth the elements of a confirmable Chapter 13 plan. The plan must provide, inter alia, for the submission of a portion of the debtor's future earnings and income to the control of a trustee and for supervised payments to creditors over a period not exceeding five years. See 11 U.S.C. §§1322(a)(1) and 1322(c). Section 1322(b)(2), the provision at issue here, allows modification of the rights of both secured and unsecured creditors, subject to special protection for creditors whose claims are secured only by a lien on the debtor's home. It provides that the plan may "modify the rights of holders of secured claims, other than a claim secured only by a security interest in real property that is the debtor's principal residence, or of holders of unsecured claims, or leave unaffected the rights of holders of any class of claims." 11 U.S.C. §1322(b)(2) (emphasis added).

The parties agree that the "other than" exception in §1322(b)(2) proscribes modification of the rights of a homestead mortgagee. Petitioners maintain, however, that their Chapter 13 plan proposes no such modification. They argue that the protection of §1322(b)(2) applies only to the extent the mortgagee holds a "secured claim" in the debtor's residence and that we must look first to §506(a) to determine the value of the mortgagee's "secured claim." Section 506(a) provides that an allowed claim secured by a lien on the debtor's property "is a secured claim to the extent of the value of [the] property"; to the extent the claim exceeds the value of the property, it "is an unsecured claim." Petitioners contend that the valuation provided for in §506(a) operates automatically to adjust downward the amount of a lender's undersecured home mortgage before any disposition proposed in the debtor's Chapter 13 plan. Under this view, the bank is the holder of a "secured claim" only in the amount of $23,500 — the value of the collateral property. Because the plan proposes to make $23,500 worth of payments pursuant to the monthly payment terms of the mortgage contract, petitioners argue, the plan effects no alteration of the bank's rights as the holder of that claim. Section 1322(b)(2), they assert, allows unconditional modification of the bank's leftover "unsecured claim."

This interpretation fails to take adequate account of §1322(b)(2)'s focus on "rights." That provision does not state that a plan may modify "claims" or that the plan may not modify "a claim secured only by" a home mortgage. Rather, it focuses on the modification of the *"rights of holders"* of such claims. By virtue of its mortgage contract with petitioners, the bank is indisputably the holder of a claim secured by a lien on petitioners' home. Petitioners were correct in looking to §506(a) for a judicial valuation of the collateral to determine the status of the bank's secured claim. It was permissible for petitioners to seek a valuation in proposing their Chapter 13 plan, since §506(a) states that "[s]uch value shall be determined . . . in conjunction with any hearing . . . on a plan affecting such creditor's interest." But even if we accept petitioners' valuation, the bank is still the "holder" of a "secured claim," because petitioners' home retains $23,500 of value as collateral. The portion of the bank's claim that exceeds $23,500 is an "unsecured claim componen[t]" under §506(a), United States v. Ron Pair Enterprises, Inc., 489 U.S. 235, 239 n.3, 109 S. Ct. 1026, 1030 n.3, 103 L. Ed. 2d 290 (1989) (internal quotation marks omitted); however, that determination does not necessarily mean that the "rights" the bank enjoys as a mortgagee, which are protected by §1322(b)(2), are limited by the valuation of its secured claim.

The term "rights" is nowhere defined in the Bankruptcy Code. In the absence of a controlling federal rule, we generally assume that Congress has "left the determination of property rights in the assets of a bankrupt's estate to state law," since such "[p]roperty interests are created and defined by state law." Butner v. United States, 440 U.S. 48, 54-55, 99 S. Ct. 914, 918, 59 L. Ed. 2d 136 (1979). *See also* Barnhill v. Johnson, 503 U.S. 393, 398, 112 S. Ct. 1386, 1389, 118 L. Ed. 2d 39 (1992). Moreover, we have specifically recognized that "[t]he justifications for application of state law are not limited to ownership interests," but "apply with equal force to security interests, including the interest of a mortgagee." *Butner, supra*, at 55, 99 S. Ct., at 918. The bank's "rights," therefore, are reflected in the relevant mortgage instruments, which are enforceable under Texas law. They include the right to repayment of the principal in monthly installments over a fixed term at specified adjustable rates of interest, the right to retain the lien until the debt is paid off, the right to accelerate the loan upon default and to proceed against petitioners' residence by foreclosure and public sale, and the right to bring an action to recover any deficiency remaining after foreclosure. *See* Record 135-140 (deed of trust), 147-151 (promissory note); 3 Tex. Prop. Code Ann. §§51.002-51.005 (Supp. 1993). These are the rights that were "bargained for by the mortgagor and the mortgagee," Dewsnup v. Timm, 502 U.S. 410, 417, 112 S. Ct. 773, 778, 116 L. Ed. 2d 903 (1992), and are rights protected from modification by §1322(b)(2).

This is not to say, of course, that the contractual rights of a home mortgage lender are unaffected by the mortgagor's Chapter 13 bankruptcy. The lender's power to enforce its rights — and, in particular, its right to foreclose on the property in the event of default — is checked by the Bankruptcy Code's automatic stay provision. 11 U.S.C. §362. *See* United Savings Assn. of Texas v. Timbers of Inwood Forest Associates, Ltd., 484 U.S. 365, 369-370, 108 S. Ct. 626, 629-630, 98 L. Ed. 2d 740 (1988). In addition, §1322(b)(5) permits the debtor to cure prepetition defaults on a home mortgage by paying off arrearages over the life of the plan "notwithstanding" the exception in §1322(b)(2). These statutory limitations on the lender's rights, however, are independent of the debtor's plan or otherwise outside §1322(b)(2)'s prohibition.

Petitioners urge us to apply the so-called "rule of the last antecedent," which has been relied upon by some Courts of Appeals to interpret §1322(b)(2) the way petitioners favor. *E.g.*, In re Bellamy, 962 F.2d 176, 180 (CA2 1992); In re Hougland, 886 F.2d 1182, 1184 (CA9 1989). According to this argument, the operative clause "other than a claim secured only by a security interest in . . . the debtor's principal residence" must be read to refer to and modify its immediate antecedent, "secured claims." Thus, §1322(b)(2)'s protection would then apply only to that subset of allowed "secured claims," determined by application of §506(a), that are secured by a lien on the debtor's home — including, with respect to the mortgage involved here, the bank's secured claim for $23,500. We acknowledge that this reading of the clause is quite sensible as a matter of grammar. But it is not compelled. Congress chose to use the phrase "claim secured . . . by" in §1322(b)(2)'s exception, rather than repeating the term of art "secured claim." The unqualified word "claim" is broadly defined under the Code to encompass any "right to payment, whether . . . secure[d] or unsecured" or any "right to an equitable remedy for breach of performance if such breach gives rise to a right to payment, whether . . . secure[d] or unsecured." 11 U.S.C. §101(5) (1988 ed., Supp. III). It is also plausible, therefore, to read "a claim secured only by a [homestead lien]" as referring to the lienholder's entire claim, including both the secured and the unsecured components of the claim. Indeed, §506(a) itself uses the phrase "claim . . . secured by a lien" to encompass both portions of an undersecured claim.

This latter interpretation is the more reasonable one, since we cannot discern how §1322(b)(2) could be administered under petitioners' interpretation. Petitioners propose to reduce the outstanding mortgage principal to the fair market value of the collateral, and, at the same time, they insist that they can do so without modifying the bank's rights "as to interest rates, payment amounts, and [other] contract terms." Brief for Petitioners 7. That appears to be impossible. The bank's contractual rights are contained in a unitary note that applies at once to the bank's overall claim, including both the secured and unsecured components. Petitioners cannot modify the payment and interest terms for the unsecured component, as they propose to do, without also modifying the terms of the secured component. Thus, to preserve the interest rate and the amount of each monthly payment specified in the note after having reduced the principal to $23,500, the plan would also have to reduce the term of the note dramatically. That would be a significant modification of a contractual right. Furthermore, the bank holds an adjustable rate mortgage, and the principal and interest payments on the loan must be recalculated with each adjustment in the interest rate. There is nothing in the mortgage contract or the Code that suggests any basis for recalculating the amortization schedule — whether by reference to the face value of the remaining principal or by reference to the unamortized value of the collateral. This conundrum alone indicates that §1322(b)(2) cannot operate in combination with §506(a) in the manner theorized by petitioners.

In other words, to give effect to §506(a)'s valuation and bifurcation of secured claims through a Chapter 13 plan in the manner petitioners propose would require a modification of the rights of the holder of the security interest. Section 1322(b)(2) prohibits such a modification where, as here, the lender's claim is secured only by a lien on the debtor's principal residence.

The judgment of the Court of Appeals is therefore

Affirmed.

[The concurring opinion of Justice Stevens is omitted.]

QUESTIONS

Note the "rights" that Justice Thomas identifies as those protected against modification. Does that mean that mortgage holders retain their rights to collect deficiencies in those states in which deficiencies are allowed notwithstanding the debtor's Chapter 13 discharge? Is §524(a)(2) relevant to this issue?

PROBLEM 8-24

Steffi Graph is a mathematics professor. She is generally quite good with numbers but she miscalculated some of her financial dealings, and is now seeking Chapter 13 relief. Her house is worth $75,000. She owes First Bank $80,000, an amount that is secured by a first mortgage on the property. She also owes Nightflyer Finance Co. $10,000. That loan is secured by a second mortgage on the house. Can Steffi strip the lien of Nightflyer off the residence? See In re McDonald, 205 F.3d 606 (3rd Cir. 2000), and In re Mann, 249 B.R. 831 (BAP 1st Cir. 2000).

PROBLEM 8-25

Ricky and Lucy bought their house from Fred and Ethel. They paid $100,000 for the house. To obtain the funds, they borrowed $80,000 from Octopus National Bank and gave a first mortgage on the residence to ONB. Fred and Ethel took back a note secured by a second mortgage on the property for the remaining $20,000. The first mortgage was payable in equal monthly installments for 30 years. The second mortgage was payable in 36 monthly payments of $100 each, with the balance due with a balloon payment at the end of the period. One year later, Ricky and Lucy are three months behind on both mortgages, and the house is now worth only $87,000. Can they keep the house? How much will they have to pay ONB and Fred and Ethel? See §1322(b)(2) and (c)(2); In re Witt, 113 F. 3d 508 (4th Cir. 1997); In re Young, 199 B.R. 643 (Bankr. E.D. Tenn. 1996).

The protection given to home mortgages is also limited by the requirement that the residence be the *only* collateral held by the creditor. Additionally, the property must be the debtor's principal residence. Each of these limitations has created some opportunity for interpretation.

PROBLEM 8-26

Harry Flashman's home was subject to an $80,000 mortgage in favor of Fraser State Bank, where he also had checking and savings accounts. At the time Harry filed his Chapter 13 petition he owed the bank $67,000 on his home loan, but he had $4,300 in his two accounts with the bank. Remembering that a bank's right of setoff is a secured claim per §506(a), can Harry's Chapter 13 plan modify the bank's rights as mortgagee?

Suppose instead that when Harry first took out his mortgage Fraser State Bank had required him to maintain an escrow account with it to insure the payment of hazard insurance on the property as well as real estate taxes. The agreement between Harry and the bank provided that Fraser State had an interest in those "escrow" funds. Does §1322(b)(2) prevent the modification of the mortgage? See §101(27B) which defines "incidental property," which in turn is part of the "debtor's principal residence" as defined in §101(13A).

Not only must the mortgage not be secured by additional security, it must attach solely to the debtor's *principal* residence. On occasion, debtors have a mixed use for their residence. Some debtors may conduct a business out of their home, and others may use the home itself as a business, such as by operating a bed and breakfast. To what extent are these mortgages subject to modifications?

In re Guilbert

United States District Court, Rhode Island, 1995
176 B.R. 302

LAGUEUX, Chief Judge.

This matter is before the Court as a bankruptcy court appeal. Jurisdiction has been conferred by 28 U.S.C. §158(a). The appellant, Jeannette R. Guilbert, has sought review of the bankruptcy court's order declining confirmation of her Chapter 13 plan. 165 B.R. 88. The bankruptcy court ruled that Guilbert's proposed plan was unconfirmable because it contemplated an improper bifurcation of a secured interest in real estate, in contravention of 11 U.S.C. §1322(b)(2). For the following reasons, the order of the bankruptcy court is reversed.

I.   Facts

The dispute in this case arises out of a loan transaction that occurred on November 30, 1988, between the creditor, Marquette Credit Union ("Marquette"), and the debtors, Jeannette R. Guilbert ("Guilbert") and Leo E. Dufresne ("Dufresne"). The loan was in the amount of $125,500, and it was secured by a mortgage ("Mortgage") encumbering a three unit dwelling located at 215-217 Burnside Avenue, Woonsocket, Rhode Island ("Property").

Guilbert and Dufresne are mother and son. They live in separate units of the Property. The third unit of the Property is, from time to time, rented to third parties in consideration for the payment of rent to Guilbert. Family members have resided in the third unit in the past.

On September 19, 1988, both Guilbert and Dufresne completed a Marquette Consumer Credit Application. According to their applications, the Property was encumbered at that time by mortgages in favor of Bank of New England in the amount of approximately $25,500 and in favor of Fleet Bank in the amount of approximately $75,000. The purpose of the loan for which the applications were submitted was to refinance the Property and to provide approximately $25,000 in startup capital for Dufresne's new business involving security information services.

On November 30, 1988, the closing for the loan transaction occurred. At that time, Dufresne and Guilbert completed and signed a HUD-1A Settlement Statement, which set forth how the Loan proceeds were to be disbursed. Of the total proceeds of $125,500, $25,127.23 was applied to pay off the mortgage to Bank of New England, $76,327.03 was applied to pay off the mortgage to Fleet, and $22,491.74 was disbursed to Guilbert and/or Dufresne. As consideration for the loan, Guilbert and Dufresne executed and delivered a demand promissory note ("Note") in the amount of $125,500 as well as the Mortgage encumbering the Property to Marquette.

Three years later, in October, 1991, Dufresne and Guilbert defaulted on the Note. After the default, in both February and June, 1992, Marquette, by now in Receivership, accelerated the indebtedness pursuant to the Note and made demand upon Guilbert and Dufresne for payment in full. Guilbert and Dufresne failed to pay.

Shortly thereafter, the Receiver for Marquette assigned the loan, the Note and the Mortgage to the Rhode Island Depositors' Economic Protection Corporation ("DEPCO"). DEPCO, now standing in the shoes of Marquette, made demand upon Guilbert and Dufresne for payment of the unpaid balance of the Note in full in May, 1993. When Guilbert and Dufresne failed to pay, DEPCO scheduled a foreclosure sale of the Property for September 30, 1993.

Six days before the foreclosure sale, on September 24, 1993, Guilbert filed her petition for protection pursuant to Chapter 13 of the United States Bankruptcy Code. As part of the plan submitted to the Bankruptcy Court, Guilbert proposed to bifurcate DEPCO's claim into a secured claim and an unsecured claim, a power conferred on Chapter 13 debtors pursuant to §506(a). Guilbert sought this bifurcation in part because the estimated or appraised value of the Property was less than the value of the Mortgage. The Property had been appraised on September 30, 1993, by Albert G. Brian, IFA, who estimated that the then fair market value of the property was $69,000. Guilbert's plan was that she would honor the entirety of the secured portion of DEPCO's claim ($69,000) and that she would pay the unsecured portion ($53,555.07) pursuant to a 36 percent plan over 60 months.

DEPCO objected to this bifurcation in the bankruptcy court. DEPCO argued that the Chapter 13 plan proposed by Guilbert could not be confirmed since the plan did not comply with 11 U.S.C. §1322(b)(2), which precludes the modification of a mortgagee's interest in property used only as the primary residence of the debtor. Bankruptcy Judge Votolato agreed, and, on March 23, 1994, he issued an order that the proposed plan was an impermissible modification of the Mortgage in violation of 11 U.S.C. §1322 and Nobelman v. American Savings Bank, 508 U.S. 324, 113 S. Ct. 2106, 124 L. Ed. 2d 228 (1993). This Court granted Guilbert's motion for leave to appeal on May 3, 1994, and oral argument was heard on July 13, 1994. The matter is now in order for decision. . . .

III. Analysis

The principal argument advanced by appellant Guilbert for reversal is that bifurcation of the mortgage rights held by DEPCO is not prohibited by 11 U.S.C. §1322(b)(2). Section 1322(b)(2) allows a Chapter 13 repayment plan to

> modify the rights of holders of secured claims, *other than a claim secured only by a security interest in real property that is the debtor's primary residence*, or of the holders of unsecured claims, or leave unaffected the rights of holders of any class of claims.

11 U.S.C. §1322(b)(2) (emphasis added). Guilbert argues that DEPCO's mortgage claim may be modified both (1) because the Property is not the debtor's primary residence and (2) because DEPCO's security interest attaches to more property than "only . . . the debtor's primary residence." These arguments will be considered *seriatim.*

Appellant's first argument seeks to invalidate the protections of DEPCO's rights conferred by §1322(b)(2) by stating that the Property in this case is not her primary residence. The basis for this argument is the design of the Property: it contains three units, of which Guilbert occupies only one. Another unit is occupied by her son, and the remaining unit has been rented in the past, with the income paid to Guilbert. Appellant offers these facts to prove that the Property is "something other than a residence." Appellant's Brief, at 5.

This argument, however, is not persuasive. That the residence in which the debtor primarily resides is also a source of income to the debtor does not render it "something other than a [primary] residence." Regardless of its income-earning functions or its residents, the Property is, has been, and will continue to be Guilbert's primary residence. As Judge Votolato wrote below, the language of §1322(b)(2) "does not say, nor does it in any way imply that if the debtor's principal residence is also used to house other tenants, paying or otherwise, that [the mortgagee's claim] may be open to modification by the home owner." Indeed, if that were the case, homeowners poised to file for protection under Chapter 13 would, as a matter of course, seek temporary tenants prior to their filing, in order to modify the rights that their secured creditors have in their home. Such an apparent loophole is contrary to the spirit of Nobelman v. American Savings Bank, *supra*, as well as §1322(b)(2), which protects creditors who lend to debtors seeking to purchase their principal residence. *See Nobelman*, 508 U.S. at 332, 113 S. Ct. at 2111 (Stevens, J., concurring).

Guilbert has never argued that she does not primarily reside at the Property. Rather, her contention is that she does not occupy the whole Property and therefore the Property is not her primary residence. While some courts have found this line of argument persuasive, *see e.g.*, In re Zablonski, 153 B.R. 604, 605 (Bankr. D. Mass. 1993), this Court does not. Had Congress meant to except creditors holding liens on multi-unit dwellings or dwellings not exclusively occupied by the debtor from the protections of §1322(b)(2), it could have easily done so. However, given the procreditor history of this portion of the statute, *see Nobelman*, 508 U.S. at 332, 113 S. Ct. at 2111 (Stevens, J., concurring), such an intent seems unlikely. As a result, this Court finds appellant's argument misplaced. Accord In re Glenn, 760 F.2d 1428 (6th Cir. 1985); In re Ballard, 4 B.R. 271 (Bankr. E.D. Va. 1980).

Moreover, as a matter of fact, the Property has essentially been a home to Guilbert's family. Dufresne, her son and a so-called rent-paying tenant of another unit, is also a co-owner of the Property. His "rent" amounts to payment of the property taxes each year, an obligation he would already have as co-owner of the house anyway. Furthermore, when it has been rented, the third unit has at times been occupied by family members. These facts weaken appellant's position that the Property is an income producing property in which Guilbert lives incidentally. It is clearly her primary residence.

Therefore, this Court concludes that the Property is Guilbert's primary residence. As a result, appellant's first argument fails to remove DEPCO's claim from the protections available under §1322(b)(2) to creditors holding a lien on a debtor's primary residence.

Appellant's second argument attempts to illustrate that DEPCO is not entitled to the protections accorded by §1322(b)(2) by focusing on the scope of the Mortgage. Appellant argues that since the Mortgage held by DEPCO attaches to personalty as well as to the primary residence of Guilbert, that Guilbert may bifurcate DEPCO's claims pursuant to §506(a). DEPCO's additional security interest in the personalty of Guilbert and Dufresne, appellant argues, effectively prevents DEPCO from asserting the protections of §1322(b)(2). . . .

To support her argument that DEPCO's lien attaches to more property than simply her primary residence, Guilbert relies on several paragraphs of the Mortgage agreement. In particular, Guilbert cites the following portions: (1) P II., which gives DEPCO a mortgage in "buildings and improvements. . . . , together with all fixtures and tangible personal property now or hereafter owned by [Guilbert and Dufresne] or in which [Guilbert and Dufresne have] an interest (but only to the extent of the interest) and placed in or upon the [Property] or the buildings or improvements thereon"; (2) P IV., which gives DEPCO an interest in "equipment and fixtures of every kind and description now or hereafter owned by [Guilbert and Dufresne] or in which [Guilbert and Dufresne have] any interest (but only to the extent of the interest) and situated or to be situated upon or in, or used in connection with the operation of, the [Property] . . . , together with any renewals, replacements, or additions thereto, substitutions therefore [sic] and proceeds thereof; and (3) Covenant 9, in which Guilbert and Dufresne "assign to [DEPCO] all rents due or to become due in the future from the occupants of the [Property], or any part thereof, on any existing or future lease or tenancy. . . ."

DEPCO has responded by arguing that the sum of the above-cited language is nothing more than "boilerplate language" and that, as such, the language cannot be used to remove DEPCO's claims from the protections of §1322(b)(2). As support, they rely on In re Davis, 989 F.2d 208 (6th Cir. 1993). In that case, the Sixth Circuit considered the question of whether a mortgage contract that mentioned "rents, royalties, profits, and fixtures" should be removed from the prohibition against bifurcation. In holding that the mortgage could not be bifurcated, the Court stated that the language "did not extend the security interest beyond items which are inextricably bound to the real property itself as part of the possessory bundle of rights." Id., at 212.

The Mortgage in this case can be distinguished on its face from the one in *Davis*. The mortgage contract in Davis only applied to "rents, royalties, profits, and fixtures"; it made no mention of personalty at all. In this case, however, the Mortgage specifically mentions both "equipment" and, more importantly, "tangible personal property," and it contains no provisions to modify or restrict this interest. While it is true, as DEPCO argues, that the original mortgagee did not file any UCC statements to perfect the security interest in the personalty, perfection does not relate to the validity of the agreement between the appellant and Marquette and now its successor DEPCO. *See* James J. White, et al., Uniform Commercial Code, §22-3 (3d ed. 1988). The only relevant question is whether a security interest in personalty has been created by the Mortgage. The plain language of the Mortgage agreement here clearly does that, both by using the word "secures," a so-called "magic word," In re Penn Housing Corp., 367 F. Supp. 661 (W.D. Pa. 1973), and by adequately describing the collateral, In re Genuario, 109 B.R. 550 (Bankr. D.R.I. 1989) (holding that "general intangibles" was a sufficient description of a liquor license).

The nature of the loan in this case also strongly suggests that the language in the Mortgage creating a security interest in personalty was clearly intended and was not merely a "boilerplate provision." The Marquette applications filed out by Dufresne and Guilbert noted that not only was the loan to be used to refinance the Property, but also was to be used to provide the startup capital for a business that Dufresne intended to develop in security information services. The inference is compelling that the security interest in the personal property on the premises was meant to secure, at least in part, the business portion of the loan.

The Mortgage in this case is similar to the mortgage considered in In re Hammond, 27 F.3d 52 (3d Cir. 1994). In that post-*Nobelman* case, the Third Circuit considered the issue of whether bifurcation of a claim held by a mortgagee was appropriate under §506(a) in a case where the mortgage security was not only an interest in the primary residence of the debtor, but also an interest in "appliances, machinery, furniture and equipment (whether fixtures or not) of any nature whatsoever." Id., at 57. In deciding that bifurcation was permissible, the Third Circuit held that the additional personalty named in the *Hammond* mortgage created a broader claim than one "secured only by a security interest in the real property that is the debtor's principal residence." As a result, the protections of §1322(b)(2) were unavailable to the mortgagee.

Those observations are fairly applied to the facts of this case. In this Mortgage, where the language "tangible personal property" refers to a category of property significantly broader than the one considered in *Hammond*, the Mortgage clearly creates a claim in property other than the debtor's primary residence, and, like the mortgage in *Hammond*, it cannot enjoy the protections of §1322(b)(2). At no time was the Mortgage modified so that it would apply only to the real property serving as Guilbert's primary residence.

Since DEPCO, as mortgagee, cannot claim the protections of §1322(b)(2), bifurcation of the Mortgage is permissible. Therefore, the order of the bankruptcy court is reversed and the matter is remanded for reconsideration of the debtor's plan in light of this Opinion.

PROBLEM 8-27

When lawyer Sam Ambulance bought his home, he financed its purchase price by a loan from Octopus National Bank. He originally used it only as his residence, but when he separated from his wife he moved his law offices to the ground floor, and now 46 percent of the building is used for professional purposes. Although the mortgage amount is currently $90,000, the value of the house is only $75,000, and Sam's Chapter 13 plan proposes to modify ONB's claim by reducing the secured claim to $75,000, decreasing the interest rate, reducing the monthly payment schedule, and releasing his wife from any further liability on the house. The remaining debt to the bank would be deemed unsecured and paid the same 5 percent the other unsecured creditors are getting under the plan. The bank, of course, objects to this, claiming protection from modification under §1322(b)(2). How will this come out? *See* Parker v. Federal Home Loan Mortgage Corp., 179 B.R. 492 (E.D. La. 1995).

PROBLEM 8-28

As a new lawyer, you are especially pleased to have convinced the president of Statewide Mortgage Company to hire you to handle the company's legal needs. One of the first issues the company asks you to address is the protection available to its mortgage claims in Chapter 13 cases. You have described generally to the company the protection for home mortgages in Chapter 13 cases, and the president was relieved by your repeated reference to the special treatment given to home mortgage lenders in Chapter 13. Two weeks later, the president forwarded a notice of bankruptcy from a Chapter 13 debtor on whose real estate the company held the mortgage. Statewide had made a loan to enable to debtor to purchase the residence four years earlier. Eighteen months ago the debtor moved out of that property and into another home. He retained title to the property and is renting the property to a third party. Is the mortgage company's mortgage subject to modification under the Chapter 13 plan? In re Saglio, 153 B.R. 4 (Bankr. D.R.I. 1993); In re Boisvert, 156 B.R. 357 (Bankr. D. Mass. 1993).

Home mortgages are fully secured. There are two reasons for this. First, most lenders require a significant down payment by the debtor as a condition to making the mortgage loan. This creates a cushion for the creditor's interest. Second, most residences do not decrease significantly in value. Some depreciation in residential real estate markets has occurred (for example, in Texas, California, and New England), but by and large residential real estate prices have held steady or increased over time. Therefore, debtors are not usually in the position of stripping down or stripping off home mortgages in Chapter 13 cases. Instead, debtors are more likely to be seeking Chapter 13 relief in order to retain a home that is more valuable than the outstanding mortgage balance.

PROBLEM 8-29

I.M. Seised and his wife, Ellen, made an appointment to see you, a bankruptcy attorney, at 2:00 P.M. They arrived on time, only to tell you that their major problem is that Last National Bank is foreclosing on their home and planning to sell it. "When?" you ask. "At 4:00 P.M. today," they reply. You get very busy and file a Chapter 13 petition (sans schedules — that can be done later), as fast as you can. Are you too late if the petition is filed (a) one minute before the sale was finalized; (b) one minute after the sale was completed by awarding the property to Last National Bank itself, the only bidder; or (c) one minute after Steve Innocent bought the property at the foreclosure sale (you should know that state law permits the debtor to redeem the property for one year from the date of the foreclosure sale by paying the buyer the amount he or she paid at that sale, plus interest). *See* Bankruptcy Code §1322(c)(1).

PROBLEM 8-30

Actors Alfred and Lynn were "on location" for an extended period of time. This was good news for their acting careers, because they were working. Unfortunately, it kept them away from their normal routine, and they neglected to pay their mortgage. Eventually, the mortgage holder foreclosed on the property, and the property was sold at a properly conducted foreclosure sale on March 11. Under the applicable state law, the owners of the property have one year to redeem the property, from the purchaser at the foreclosure sale. To redeem the property, they must pay the amount paid by the purchaser at the foreclosure sale plus 10 percent. The foreclosure sale price was $64,000. It is now 11 months after the foreclosure sale, and Alfred and Lynn have filed a Chapter 13 petition. Can they still cure the default under their mortgage and recover their property? *See, e.g.,* In re Brown, 282 B.R. 880 (Bankr. E.D. Ark. 2002); In re Stephens, 221 B.R. 290 (Bankr. D. Me. 2002); Krawczyk v. U.S., 201 B.R. 589 (Bankr. N.D. Ga. 1996).

IV.   Modification

Confirmation of a Chapter 13 plan binds the debtor and each creditor to its terms. Bankruptcy Code §1327(a). Creditors must accept what the debtor has agreed to pay under the plan. This applies to both secured and unsecured creditors. Another consequence of confirmation of Chapter 13 plans is that the property of the estate (*see* §1306) vests in the debtor unless the plan or the order confirming the plan provides otherwise. Bankruptcy Code §1327(b). This can have a significant effect, as follows.

PROBLEM 8-31

When Donald Hotel was creating his Chapter 13 plan, he knew that his ex-wife Ivana, to whom he owed much in the way of past-due alimony, would be very interested in its terms. The plan proposed paying her the alimony debt over a period of five years, but he suspected she would like to have it all immediately. Should his plan provide that the property of the *estate* does not vest in the debtor until the conclusion of payments under the plan, or should it become property of the *debtor* at the moment of the confirmation of the plan? *See* Bankruptcy Code §362(b)(2)(B).

Confirmation of a Chapter 13 also has a "near" res judicata effect. It is not a complete res judicata effect because the plan may be modified even after confirmation. Section 1329 modifications can be proposed by either the debtor, the trustee, or the holder of an allowed unsecured claim. Typically, debtors would propose modifications to reduce payments or shorten the time for payments, while the trustee and creditors in particular would seek increases in the payments called for by the plan. Modifications are unlikely to be allowed in the absence of a significant change in circumstances. Nonetheless, those changes do occur and in appropriate instances courts will approve a creditor's proposed modifications to a debtor's Chapter 13 plan.

PROBLEM 8-32

You represent Yeomen National Bank, an unsecured creditor in the Chapter 13 bankruptcy of Leonard Meryll, whose confirmed plan is currently paying 10 percent to unsecured creditors over a three-year period. Leonard, a novelist, has just sold his latest book for a record advance of $1,000,000, and he is suddenly swimming in money. Do you have any suggestions for your client? *See* In re Arnold, 869 F.2d 240 (4th Cir. 1989); In re Solis, 172 B.R. 530 (Bankr. S.D.N.Y. 1994).

The 2005 amendments to the Code contain an important reporting requirement that will provide the trustee and Chapter 13 creditors with information about changes in the debtor's financial situation. *See* §521(f).

While an argument can be made that permitting creditors to propose postconfirmation modifications of Chapter 13 plans is inconsistent with the voluntary nature of the Chapter, debtors do not have to accept the proposals. Even if the court finds the modification appropriate and confirms the plan as modified, the debtor can simply dismiss the proceedings on his or her own motion. Generally speaking, however, modification of plans after confirmation is not the norm. Therefore, creditors should not rely on the ability to propose postconfirmation modifications in evaluating the response they might offer to a debtor's initially proposed Chapter 13 plan.

In re Szostek
United States Court of Appeals, Third Circuit, 1989
886 F.2d 1405

MANSMANN, Circuit Judge.

Debtors in bankruptcy here appeal from the decision of the district court which granted a creditor's motion to revoke confirmation of a Chapter 13 plan. We are asked to determine whether the secured creditor may be deemed to have accepted the plan by failing to object to it timely or, if the bankruptcy court's failure to apply provisions of 11 U.S.C.A. §1325(a) (5)(B)(ii) (West 1979), relating to present value constitutes grounds for vacating the plan. In addition, we must determine whether the trustee in bankruptcy and the bankruptcy court are independently required to verify that a Chapter 13 plan meets all statutory requirements or whether they may rely on the lack of objection thereto.

We conclude that the district court erred by reversing the bankruptcy court's confirmed action of the debtor's plan. Although the present value provision found in §1325(a)(5)(B)(ii) was not applied by the bankruptcy court in determining the amount of the creditor's claim, this does not constitute grounds for vacating a confirmed plan where the creditor has not timely objected to the plan. We further conclude that, although prior to confirmation the bankruptcy court and trustee do have a responsibility to verify that a Chapter 13 plan complies with the Bankruptcy Code provisions, after the plan is confirmed the policy favoring the finality of confirmation is stronger than the bankruptcy court's and the trustee's obligations to verify a plan's compliance with the Code. Therefore, we will reverse the order of the district court and remand for the issuance of an appropriate order reinstating the judgment of the bankruptcy court.

I.

On July 7, 1987, Fred and Denise Szostek filed a Chapter 13 bankruptcy petition. On August 3, 1987, the bankruptcy court issued an order scheduling the meeting of creditors, establishing a deadline for objections to the Szosteks' Chapter 13 plan and scheduling a hearing on confirmation of the plan for December 15, 1987. Pursuant to Bankr. Rules 3020(b) and 9014, the court's order stated that any objections to the confirmation of the debtor's plan shall be filed no later than ten days before the confirmation hearing. The filing deadline was thus December 5, 1987. The Kissell Company ("Kissell"), creditor and appellee, received notice of the deadline for filing objections. On August 18, 1987, Kissell filed a secured claim, based on a purchase money mortgage in the amount of $29,242.41. A few weeks later, on September 8, 1987, the Szosteks filed an objection to Kissell's claim on the ground that Kissell had violated the Truth in Lending Act ("TILA"), 15 U.S.C.A. §1601 et seq., in the course of the residential loan transaction and, therefore, claimed they were entitled to a $1,000 recoupment.

On the same day, the Szosteks also filed their First Amended Chapter 13 Plan, which proposed payments totalling approximately $40,000.00. The plan did not, however, provide for interest to be paid on allowed secured claims, i.e., present value.[15] A hearing on the Szosteks' objection to Kissell's claim was scheduled for December 15, 1987, the same date as the confirmation hearing.

On October 14, 1987, Kissell filed an amended proof of claim which was in the same amount as previously requested, $29,242.41. The Szosteks subsequently filed an amended objection to Kissell's claim on the ground that the value of the mortgage exceeded the value of the home and that the secured claim had to be bifurcated into two portions, secured and unsecured. The Szosteks sought both a determination of the amount of Kissell's security interest pursuant to 11 U.S.C.A. §506(a), (d), as well as the relief pursuant to the TILA.

Szosteks' counsel served a copy of Szosteks' First Amended Plan upon Kissell's counsel on November 16, 1987. Sometime prior to December 15, 1987, the attorneys for the Szosteks and for Kissell had a conversation in which Kissell's counsel requested a continuance of the hearing on Szosteks' objection to Kissell's claim so that an appraisal of Szosteks' property could be obtained. During this conversation, Kissell's counsel did not request a continuance of the confirmation hearing on the plan, which was also scheduled for December 15, 1987.

Kissell's counsel later testified that he assumed that Szosteks' counsel had agreed to both postponement of the hearing on Szosteks' objection to Kissell's claim and to postponement of the confirmation hearing. Szosteks' counsel later testified that he understood the continuance request was only for the hearing on Szosteks' objection to Kissell's proof of claim.

On December 15, 1987, the bankruptcy court held the confirmation hearing as scheduled at which the Szosteks appeared, but Kissell did not. Since no objections to the plan had been filed, upon recommendation of the standing Chapter 13 trustee, the Szosteks' First Amended Plan was confirmed by the court on December 15, 1987. The confirmed plan provided for payments as follows: (1) $4,003.00 to the trustee; (2) payment in full on Kissell's allowed secured claim; and (3) the balance to the holders of allowed unsecured claims. . . .

The hearing on Szosteks' objections to Kissell's proof of claim was held on January 25, 1988. It was at this hearing that Kissell's attorney first learned that the

---

15. The meaning of present value was explained by the bankruptcy court in In re Fisher, 29 B.R. 542 (Bkrtcy. D. Kan. 1983) as follows:

"Present value" or the "time value of money" is not a legal concept, but rather it is a term of art in the financial community. It simply means that a dollar received today is worth more than a dollar to be received in the future. To compensate the creditor for not receiving its money today, the debtor is charged an additional amount of money. The charge is based on a rate of interest called a "discount rate." The discount rate is used to calculate how much the creditor should be paid so it will have the same amount of money in the future as it would have had if it did not have to wait to be paid. 29 B.R. at 543.

Szosteks' plan had been confirmed. It appears from the record that Kissell's attorney took no action to challenge confirmation of the plan at that time. Consequently, no appeal was filed within ten days of the plan confirmation as required by Bankr. Rule 8002(a), nor did Kissell's attorney seek to file any appeal after learning of the confirmed plan on January 25, 1988.

On March 21, 1988, the bankruptcy court issued a memorandum and order determining Kissell's secured claim to be $25,110.00 and its unsecured claim to be $3,132.41. The March 21, 1988, order was, in part, based upon the parties' agreement that Kissell had violated the TILA and that a $1,000.00 recoupment was appropriate. The court apportioned the recoupment between Kissell's secured and unsecured claims. As part of its order, the bankruptcy court specifically noted that any challenge to the December 15, 1987, confirmation of the Szosteks' plan was not an issue before the court.

As a result of prevailing on the TILA objection, Szosteks' counsel filed a motion for attorneys fees pursuant to 15 U.S.C.A. §1640. Kissell opposed the motion on the ground that, as part of the parties' agreement that there was a TILA violation, Szosteks' counsel had agreed to waive attorneys fees.

On May 20, 1988, four months after learning of the plan's confirmation, Kissell filed a motion seeking dismissal of the debtors' petition, revocation of confirmation under 11 U.S.C.A. §1330, and alternatively, modification of the plan or relief from the automatic stay. Kissell's motion was based on alleged fraud by the Szosteks in obtaining confirmation of the plan and the contention that the plan should not have been confirmed because it did not provide for paying Kissell interest on its secured claim, i.e., present value.

The bankruptcy court held two hearings in June of 1988 on Szosteks' motion for attorneys fees and on Kissell's motion to dismiss, revoke confirmation, and modify the plan. On December 6, 1988, the bankruptcy court awarded attorneys fees and costs under TILA in the amount of $1,009.50 and denied Kissell's motion to dismiss, revoke confirmation, and modify the plan, 93 B.R. 399 (Bkrtcy. E.D. Pa. 1988). The bankruptcy court held that Kissell's allegation that confirmation of the plan was procured by fraud was not supported by the evidence and thus, the plan was not revocable under §1330(a).

A timely appeal was taken to the United States District Court for the Eastern District of Pennsylvania where, although the district court affirmed the finding that there was no fraud, the court reversed the bankruptcy court's order denying Kissell's motion to dismiss, revoke confirmation and modify the plan. The district court vacated confirmation of Szosteks' Chapter 13 plan and remanded the case on the basis that neither the bankruptcy court nor the trustee had fulfilled its independent obligation of insuring that the Szosteks' plan complied with 11 U.S.C.A. §1325(a)(5). However, the district court affirmed the bankruptcy court's award of attorneys fees. The Szosteks appeal. Since the district court sits as an appellate court in reviewing cases from the bankruptcy court, the district court is neither a finder of fact, nor is any more qualified than the court of appeals to evaluate the decision of the bankruptcy court. Consequently, our review on appeal from the district court in a bankruptcy case is plenary. Universal Minerals, Inc. v. C.A. Hughes & Co., 669 F.2d 98, 101-02 (3d Cir. 1981).

II.

We are faced here with a clash between two seemingly divergent policies involved in the Bankruptcy Code. On the one hand is the policy of finality, as evidenced by §1327, which provides that, absent fraud, confirmation of a debtor's plan binds both the debtor and the creditors. Under §1327, a confirmation order is res judicata as to all issues decided or which could have been decided at the hearing on confirmation. On the other hand is the language of §1325(a) which provides that a court shall confirm a plan which meets the conditions listed in that section. The conflict resulted here when a confirmation order was entered for a plan which did not provide for the calculation of present value of the creditor's claim, a requirement of §1325(a)(5)(B)(ii). Thus, we must determine whether, in the absence of fraud, the failure of a creditor to attend the confirmation hearing, object timely to the plan, or appeal the order of confirmation, regardless of the reason, precludes the creditor from obtaining full recovery of the present value of its claim when such was not provided for in the confirmed plan.

A.

To understand the tension between the code sections, we must first look at one of the relevant portions of the Bankruptcy Code. We find that 11 U.S.C.A. §1327(a) provides as follows:

> Effect of confirmation. (a) The provisions of a confirmed plan bind the debtor and each creditor, whether or not the claim of such creditor is provided for by the plan, and whether or not such creditor has objected to, has accepted or has rejected the plan.

11 U.S.C.A. §1327 (West 1979).

One leading commentator has recently interpreted this section as follows:

> It is quite clear that the binding effect of a Chapter 13 plan extends to any issue actually litigated by the parties and any issue necessarily determined by the confirmation order, including whether the plan complies with sections 1322 and 1325 of the Bankruptcy Code. For example, a creditor may not after confirmation assert that the plan was not filed in good faith, . . . that the creditor should have been paid interest; that the debtor is ineligible for Chapter 13 relief; or that the plan is otherwise inconsistent with the Code in violation of section 1322(b)(10) or section 1325(a)(1).

5 Collier on Bankruptcy, §1327.01 (5th ed. 1988).

Both the bankruptcy court and the district court held that there was no fraud in securing the confirmation of the Szosteks' plan. We note that Kissell has abandoned its claim that the Szosteks' confirmed plan was procured by fraud. Clearly, there can be no revocation of the plan based on §1330(a).

The finality of confirmed plans was discussed by the Supreme Court in Stoll v. Gottlieb, 305 U.S. 165, 59 S. Ct. 134, 83 L. Ed. 104 (1938). At issue in *Stoll* was a corporate debtor's plan which included cancellation of a guaranty to pay a bond. Prior to confirmation, there had been no objections to the plan. After confirmation, however, the creditor filed an action in state court to recover on the guaranty. The Supreme Court held that the finality of the bankruptcy confirmation order barred the creditor from litigating its claim. . . .

Similarly, in Matter of Gregory, 705 F.2d 1118 (9th Cir. 1983), the Court of Appeals for the Ninth Circuit held that the failure to raise an objection at the confirmation hearing, or to appeal from the confirmation order, should preclude an attack on the plan or any provision therein as being illegal in a subsequent proceeding. The court of appeals noted that the creditor's treatment seemed "grossly unfair" because of a zero-payment plan provision where the debtor, a convicted embezzler, owed $17,000 to his employer. Nonetheless, the court concluded, if a creditor ignores the bankruptcy proceedings, he does so at his peril. 705 F.2d at 1123. . . .

B.

We must examine the provisions of 11 U.S.C.A. §1325(a), which directs the handling of secured claims, against this policy of finality. The Bankruptcy Code's criteria for treatment of secured claims in Chapter 13 plans are set forth in 11 U.S.C.A. §1325(a)(5). According to §1325(a)(5), in order for a plan to be confirmed, with respect to each allowed secured claim provided for by the plan, one of the following three conditions must be met:

    (A)   the holder of such claim has accepted the plan;

    (B)   (i) the plan provides that the holder of such claim retain the lien securing such claim; and
             (ii) the value, as of the effective date of the plan, of property to be distributed under the plan on account of such claim is not less than the allowed amount of such claim; or

    (C)   the debtor surrenders the property securing such claim to such holder. . . .

11 U.S.C.A. §1325(a)(5)(A)-(C).

The district court determined that surrendering the property in question was not a consideration in this case. Therefore, the subpart (C) condition of 11 U.S.C.A. §1325(a)(5) was not an issue. The question then becomes whether the Szosteks' plan met either the conditions of subparts (A) or (B). Kissell reasons that since the Szosteks' plan does not provide for present value on his secured claim pursuant to subpart (B)(ii), the plan should not have been confirmed and, consequently, must be revoked. Thus, Kissell interprets the Code to require that only if the plan meets the conditions of §1325(a)(5) can it be confirmed.

If the provisions of §1325(a)(5) are mandatory, as Kissell contends, then a plan cannot be confirmed if it does not meet the requirements of that section. We must determine whether §1325(a)(5)(B)(ii) is mandatory, as Kissell contends, or whether the section is discretionary, i.e., it guarantees confirmation if a plan comports with the statutory provisions, but does not mandate that the provisions be met in order for confirmation to occur. We note at the outset that the Code section which explicitly contains mandatory requirements for confirmation of a debtor's Chapter 13 plan is 11 U.S.C.A. §1322, which unequivocally states "the plan shall" do three things. [The court quoted §1322.]

By comparison, the language of §1325(a) states that a "court shall confirm a plan if" certain things occur. However, it does not state "only if" the described events occur. Thus, the logical interpretation is that if the conditions of §1325(a) occur, the court must confirm the plan. On the other hand, if the conditions of §1325(a) are not met, although the requirements of §1322 are fulfilled, the court has the discretion to confirm the plan. If Congress had intended for §1325(a) to be mandatory, it could have included that requirement with the requirements already listed in §1322. Review of a comparable bankruptcy section, one dealing with the confirmation of Chapter 11 plans, supports the conclusion that §1325(a) is not mandatory. . . .

III.

Kissell's final argument, the one which was accepted by the district court resulting in the revocation of the confirmation order, is that the bankruptcy court and the trustee did not fulfill their obligations when they approved a plan which was not in compliance with 11 U.S.C.A. §1325(a)(5). The role of the court in this context was discussed in In re Bowles, 48 B.R. 502 (Bkrtcy. E.D. Va. 1985), where the bankruptcy court held that it had an independent duty to examine a plan for compliance with the code even though no objections by creditors were made. In agreement are In re Steinhorn, 27 B.R. 43 (Bkrtcy. S.D. Fla. 1983), and In re Lucas, 3 B.R. 252 (Bkrtcy. S.D. Cal. 1980), where the bankruptcy courts held that the court itself has a responsibility to determine whether a debtor's plan meets code requirements. However, these cases involved the court questioning the provisions of the plan prior to confirmation, not afterward. Moreover, in both Bowles and Steinhorn, the court found that the creditors' plans were not proposed in good faith. . . .

While we do not understate the importance of the obligation of the bankruptcy court or the trustee to determine that a plan complies with the appropriate sections of the Bankruptcy Code prior to confirmation of the plan, we nonetheless recognize that the affirmative obligation to object to the Szosteks' plan rested with Kissell, not with the bankruptcy court or the trustee. As noted by the Court of Appeals for the Tenth Circuit in In re Ruti-Sweetwater, Inc., 836 F.2d 1263 (10th Cir. 1988), creditors are obligated to take an active role in protecting their claims. *See also* In re Record Club of America, 38 B.R. 691, 696 (M.D. Pa. 1983) (the Bankruptcy Code contemplates that concerned creditors will take an active role in protecting their claims). Otherwise, Rules 3017 and 3020(b), which set a deadline for filing objections to a plan, would have no substance. Kissell's position that, even in the absence of fraud, a confirmed plan which does not comply with the present value provision in §1325(a)(5)(B)(ii) can be vacated is inconsistent with the general policy favoring the finality of confirmed plans as evidenced by the Supreme Court's decision in *Stoll.*

IV.

We hold that the Szosteks' plan was accepted by the Kissell Corporation since Kissell failed to object timely to the plan's confirmation. Moreover, we find that the provisions in 11 U.S.C.A. §1325(a)(5) are not mandatory and do not require the revocation of the confirmed plan under the facts of this case. Because the district court based its determination that the bankruptcy court and trustee had failed to fulfill their obligations on an improper construction of §1325, we will reverse the order of the district court which vacated the bankruptcy court's order confirming the reorganization plan and remand for the entry of an appropriate order reinstating the order of the bankruptcy court.

QUESTION

If the plan did not provide for the payment of the administrative expenses or for the payment of taxes, both entitled to priority under §507(a), but it was nonetheless confirmed and all payments made under it, when these omissions come to light can the creditors at issue (who did receive notice of the hearing confirming the plan, but did not attend) reopen everything and require payment of the debts due to them? *See* Bankruptcy Code §1322(a)(2) and In re Escobedo, 28 F.3d 34 (7th Cir. 1994).

V.   Discharge

In the original version of Bankruptcy Code Chapter 13, a significant feature was the "super discharge," freeing the debtor from many obligations that would have survived a Chapter 7 discharge (and thus encouraging debtors to use Chapter 13). However, Congress chipped away at this idea year after year, and with the adoption of the 2005 amendments to the Code it has become what members of the bankruptcy bar call the "super-light discharge." Section 1328(a) formerly provided that debts of the kind specified under §523(a)(5), (8), and (9) were nondishcargeable in Chapter 13 cases, but the other categories of debts set out in §523(a) could be discharged through the completion of all Chapter 13 plan payments. Under the 2005 version of the Code, however, many more of the §523 (a) categories are nondischargeable in Chapter 13 cases. The §1328(a) discharge still frees the debtor from claims for property settlements that are not in the nature of alimony, §523(a)(15), as well as *some* claims for willful and malicious injuries to another person or the property of another person under §523(a)(6). Section 1328(a)(4) provides that damages for willful *or* malicious injuries to an individual (but not their property) are nondischargeable in Chapter 13, thus limiting the discharge of §523 (a)(6) claims in Chapter 13.

Hardship discharge. In the event that the debtor is unable to make all the payments called for by the plan, he or she may be eligible for a *hardship discharge* in appropriate circumstances. Those circumstances are:

(1) The debtor's failure to complete such payments is due to circumstances for which the debtor should not justly be held accountable;
(2) [The payments made under the plan already meet or exceed the best interest of creditors test]; and
(3) Modification of the plan . . . is not practicable.

Hardship discharges are relatively rare. More likely the case would be converted to Chapter 7 or dismissed when the debtor is unable to complete payments called for by the plan. Additionally, debtors who are unable to meet the payment obligation for reasons they cannot control would seem likely candidates for postconfirmation modification of the plan, to reduce the payments called for in the plan to those that have already been made. The courts, however, have not generally permitted debtors to propose modifications of this nature, recognizing that allowing such a modification would essentially read the hardship discharge out of Chapter 13.

PROBLEM 8-33

Tom Brown completed an expensive education with massive help from student loans. When repaying these loans became troublesome, Tom filed a Chapter 13 petitition, and in his plan he proposed to pay only 25 percent to the student loan creditors, with the plan providing that this would discharge these debts, adding that "pursuant to §523(a)(8), excepting said loans from discharge will impose an undue hardship on the debtor and debtor's dependents." The student loan creditors, due to malpractice by their busy attorneys failed to file an objection to this, and the plan was confirmed. Tom made all payments under the plan and was granted a discharge. When the student loan creditors nonetheless tried to collect the debts allegedly still due them, Tom reopened his bankruptcy case to get a court order declaring these debts discharged. Will he prevail? *See* In re Andersen, 179 F.3d 1253 (10th Cir. 1999). If you are an attorney representing debtors in Chapter 13 proceedings, is the addition of language like this a good idea? *See* In re Evans, 242 B.R. 407 (Bankr. S.D. Ohio 1999), and In re Hensley, 249 B.R. 318 (Bankr. W.D. Okla. 2000).

VI. Conversion and Dismissal of Chapter 13 Cases

If the debtor no longer wishes to continue a Chapter 13 case, he or she may dismiss the case or convert it to another Chapter of the Code. Under §1307(b), the court is directed to dismiss the case on the debtor's request unless the pending Chapter 13 case was previously converted from another Chapter of the Code. The language of §1307(b) is unqualified, but some courts have converted Chapter 13 cases, rather than dismiss them at the debtor's request. For example, when motions filed by the trustee or creditors to convert a Chapter 13 to a Chapter 7 case are pending, courts frequently will deny a debtor's motion to dismiss the proceedings, pending a resolution of the conversion motions. *See, e.g.*, In re Viewig, 80 B.R. 838 (Bankr. E.D. Mich. 1987); In re Tatsis, 72 B.R. 908 (Bankr. W.D.N.C. 1987). *But see* In re Beatty, 162 B.R. 853 (Bankr. 9th Cir. 1994) (court held that debtor could dismiss Chapter 13 case even after Bankruptcy Court had orally ordered conversion to Chapter 7 as long as no written order effecting conversion had been entered prior to debtor's dismissal request). Additionally, §105 of the Bankruptcy Code may provide the court with additional power to prevent the dismissal of a case in appropriate circumstances. *See* In re McCraney, 172 B.R. 868 (N.D. Ohio 1993) (case held open to permit investigation of debtor's allegedly fraudulent actions in the bankruptcy case).

There is another way in which a Chapter 13 case may be dismissed. The 2005 amendments to the Bankruptcy Code added §1308, which requires the debtor to file income tax returns with the court, or face dismissal or conversion of the case to Chapter 7. §1309(e). The amendments also provide that if the debtor fails to file all of the information required by §521(a)(1), the case will be dismissed 46 days after the date of the filing of the petition.

In many instances, Chapter 13 plans are unsuccessful, and the case is then converted to Chapter 7. Conversion of the case has several consequences. First, conversion constitutes an order for relief under the new Chapter. §348(a). Furthermore, the conversion does not "effect a change in the date of the filing of the petition, the commencement of the case, or the order for relief." Id. Therefore, timing matters such as preference periods, fraudulent conveyance recovery periods, and the like are not changed by the conversion of the case.

Section 348(f) explicitly provides that property of the Chapter 7 estate is not enhanced by the property acquired by the debtor during the Chapter 13 case that would not have been property of the estate, had the case been a Chapter 7 proceeding from the beginning. In addition, reevaluations of property and allowed secured claims in the original Chapter 13 case continue to apply in the subsequent Chapter 7 proceeding. Thus, when the debtor's plan crams down a secured creditor's claim, the value set for that property in the Chapter 13 case continues through to the Chapter 7 case, and payments made on the secured claim during the Chapter 13 proceeding reduce the secured claim pro tanto.

PROBLEM 8-34

The court confirmed Dave Detter's Chapter 13 plan, which provided that the claim of Auto Finance Corp. would be bifurcated into an $8,000 secured claim and a $4,000 unsecured claim. Under the plan, Dave was to make 36 payments of $250 in order to pay the secured claim in full. Eighteen months into the plan, Dave had paid $4,500 to Auto Finance under the terms of the plan, but he was forced to convert the case to

Chapter 7. What are Dave's options with respect to the vehicle? Bankruptcy Code §§348(f)(1); 722; In re Hargis, 103 B.R. 912 (Bankr. E.D. Tenn. 1989).

PROBLEM 8-35

Donna Detter was struggling along in her Chapter 13 case. She was barely able to make her payments under the plan, but had tightened her belt sufficiently so that she had completed a year's worth of payments. Two months later, she was fortunate enough to inherit a substantial amount of money from her grandparents' estate. She became entitled to this inheritance more than 180 days after the commencement of the case, and so she moved to convert the case to Chapter 7. She argued that the conversion of the case did not change the date of the filing of the petition, and that in a Chapter 7 case this inheritance would not be property of the estate under §541(a)(5). Her creditors, on the other hand, are understandably upset by Donna's actions. Do they have any grounds to reach the inheritance? Bankruptcy Code §348(f)(1)(A), (2); In re Lybrook, 951 F.2d 136 (7th Cir. 1991).

Sometimes conversion of Chapter 13 cases occurs before confirmation of the debtor's plan. Even in the absence of confirmation, however, the debtor may have been making payments to the Chapter 13 trustee in anticipation of confirmation of the plan. When confirmation is not forthcoming and the case is converted to Chapter 7, there may be a significant amount of funds in the possession and control of the Chapter 13 trustee. Section 1326(a)(1) directs the debtor to make payments proposed by the plan soon after the plan is filed. Section 1326(a)(2) instructs the trustee to return those payments to the debtor (after the payment of administrative expenses) if the plan is not confirmed. Since most payments in Chapter 13 cases are taken from the debtor's wages, those funds would not be property of a Chapter 7 estate. §541(a)(6). Therefore, distributing those amounts back to the debtor in the absence of a confirmed plan is appropriate.

Conversion of a case may not only be *from* Chapter 13, but it may also be *to* Chapter 13. A debtor may file a Chapter 7 petition and shortly thereafter decide that he or she would rather proceed under Chapter 13. For example, such a conversion may be sought because the debtor could not reach an agreement with a creditor to reaffirm a debt and retain the collateral for that debt. So the debtor converts the case to Chapter 13 and retains the collateral by paying for it through the Chapter 13 plan. Conversion might also occur because the debtor played a bit fast and loose with the provisions of Chapter 7, and when the Chapter 7 trustee challenged this misbehavior, the debtor responded by converting the case to Chapter 13. Section 706(a) seems to provide the debtor with an absolute right to convert the case, but, in the case that follows, the Supreme Court concludes that there are limits. Bankruptcy professionals were largely surprised by the decision. They expected that the court would simply note that while the debtor has an unqualified right to convert a Chapter 7 case to Chapter 13, the debtor has no right to stay in Chapter 13 if grounds for "reconversion" or dismissal exist. What does the Court's holding and analysis say about the power of bankruptcy courts to monitor debtor behavior, and can its decision be reconciled with the oft-recited plain meaning rule?

Marrama v. Citizens Bank of Massachusetts
United States Supreme Court, 2007
549 U.S. 365

Justice STEVENS delivered the opinion of the Court.

The principal purpose of the Bankruptcy Code is to grant a " 'fresh start' " to the " 'honest but unfortunate debtor.' " *Grogan v. Garner*, 498 U.S. 279, 286, 287, 111 S. Ct. 654, 112 L. Ed. 2d 755 (1991). Both Chapter 7 and Chapter 13 of the Code permit an insolvent individual to discharge certain unpaid debts toward that end. Chapter 7 authorizes a discharge of prepetition debts following the liquidation of the debtor's assets by a bankruptcy trustee, who then distributes the proceeds to creditors. Chapter 13 authorizes an individual with regular income to obtain a discharge after the successful completion of a payment plan approved by the bankruptcy court. Under Chapter 7 the debtor's non-exempt assets are controlled by the bankruptcy trustee; under Chapter 13 the debtor retains possession of his property. A proceeding that is commenced under Chapter 7 may be converted to a Chapter 13 proceeding and vice versa. 11 U.S.C. §§706(a), 1307(a) and (c).

An issue that has arisen with disturbing frequency is whether a debtor who acts in bad faith prior to, or in the course of, filing a Chapter 13 petition by, for example, fraudulently concealing significant assets, thereby forfeits his right to obtain Chapter 13 relief. The issue may arise at the outset of a Chapter 13 case in response to a motion by creditors or by the United States trustee either to dismiss the case or to convert it to Chapter 7, see §1307(c). It also may arise in a Chapter 7 case when a debtor files a motion under §706(a) to convert to Chapter 13. In the former context, despite the absence of any statutory provision specifically addressing the issue, the federal courts are virtually unanimous that prepetition bad-faith conduct may cause a forfeiture of any right to proceed with a Chapter 13 case. In the latter context, however, some courts have suggested that even a bad-faith debtor has an absolute right to convert at least one Chapter 7 proceeding into a Chapter 13 case even though the case will thereafter be dismissed or immediately returned to Chapter 7. We granted certiorari to decide whether the Code mandates that procedural anomaly. 547 U.S. 1191, 126 S. Ct. 2859, 165 L. Ed. 2d 894 (2006).

I

On March 11, 2003, petitioner, Robert Marrama, filed a voluntary petition under Chapter 7, thereby creating an estate consisting of all his property "wherever located and by whomever held." 11 U.S.C. §541(a). Respondent Mark DeGiacomo is the trustee of that estate. Respondent Citizens Bank of Massachusetts (hereinafter Bank) is the principal creditor.

In verified schedules attached to his petition, Marrama made a number of statements about his principal asset, a house in Maine, that were misleading or inaccurate. For instance, while he disclosed that he was the sole beneficiary of the trust that owned the property, he listed its value as zero. He also denied that he had transferred any property other than in the ordinary course of business during the year preceding the filing of his petition. Neither statement was true. In fact, the Maine property had substantial value, and Marrama had transferred it into the newly created trust for no consideration seven months prior to filing his Chapter 13 petition. Marrama later admitted that the purpose of the transfer was to protect the property from his creditors.

After Marrama's examination at the meeting of creditors, see 11 U.S.C. §341, the trustee advised Marrama's counsel that he intended to recover the Maine property as an asset of the estate. Thereafter, Marrama filed a "Verified Notice of Conversion to Chapter 13." Pursuant to Federal Rule of Bankruptcy Procedure 1017(c)(2), the notice of conversion was treated as a motion to convert, to which both the trustee and the Bank filed objections. Relying primarily on Marrama's attempt to conceal the Maine property from his creditors,[16] the trustee contended that the request to convert was made in bad faith and would constitute an abuse of the bankruptcy process. The Bank opposed the conversion on similar grounds.

At the hearing on the conversion issue, Marrama explained through counsel that his misstatements about the Maine property were attributable to "scrivener's error," that he had originally filed under Chapter 7 rather than Chapter 13 because he was then unemployed, and that he had recently become employed and was therefore eligible to proceed under Chapter 13. The Bankruptcy Judge rejected these arguments, ruling that there is no "Oops" defense to the concealment of assets and that the facts established a "bad faith" case. App. 34a-35a. The judge denied the request for conversion.

Marrama's principal argument on appeal to the Bankruptcy Appellate Panel for the First Circuit was that he had an absolute right to convert his case from Chapter 7 to Chapter 13 under the plain language of §706(a) of the Code. The panel affirmed the decision of the Bankruptcy Court. It construed §706(a), when read in connection with other provisions of the Code and the Bankruptcy Rules, as creating a right to convert a case from Chapter 7 to Chapter 13 that "is absolute only in the absence of extreme circumstances." *In re Marrama*, 313 B.R. 525, 531 (1st Cir. BAP 2004). In concluding that the record disclosed such circumstances, the panel relied on Marrama's failure to describe the transfer of the Maine residence into the revocable trust, his

---

16. The trustee also noted that in his original verified schedules Marrama had claimed a property in Gloucester, Mass., as a homestead exemption, see 11 U.S.C. §522(b)(2); Mass. Gen. Laws, ch. 188, §1 (West 2005), but testified at the meeting of creditors that he did not reside at the property and was receiving rental income from it, App. 71a-72a. Moreover, when asked at the meeting whether anyone owed him any money, Marrama responded "No," *id.*, at 50a, and in response to a similar question on Schedule B to his petition, which specifically requested a description of any "tax refunds," Marrama indicated that he had "none." Supp. App. 6. In fact, Marrama had filed an amended tax return in July 2002 in which he claimed the right to a refund, and shortly before the hearing on the motion to convert, the Internal Revenue Service informed the trustee that Marrama was entitled to a refund of $8,745.86, App. 30a-31a.

attempt to obtain a homestead exemption on rental property in Massachusetts, and his nondisclosure of an anticipated tax refund.

On appeal from the panel, the Court of Appeals for the First Circuit also rejected the argument that §706(a) gives a Chapter 7 debtor an absolute right to convert to Chapter 13. In addition to emphasizing that the statute uses the word "may" rather than "shall," the court added:

> "In construing subsection 706(a), it is important to bear in mind that the bankruptcy court has unquestioned authority to dismiss a chapter 13 petition — as distinguished from converting the case to chapter 13 — based upon a showing of 'bad faith' on the part of the debtor. We can discern neither a theoretical nor a practical reason that Congress would have chosen to treat a first time motion to convert a chapter 7 case to chapter 13 under subsection 706(a) differently from the filing of a chapter 13 petition in the first instance." *In re Marrama*, 430 F.3d 474, 479 (2005) (citations omitted).

While other Courts of Appeals and bankruptcy appellate panels have refused to recognize any "bad faith" exception to the conversion right created by §706(a), see n. 2, *supra*, we conclude that the courts in this case correctly held that Marrama forfeited his right to proceed under Chapter 13.

II

The two provisions of the Bankruptcy Code most relevant to our resolution of the issue are subsections (a) and (d) of 11 U.S.C. §706, which provide:

> "(a) The debtor may convert a case under this chapter to a case under chapter 11, 12, or 13 of this title at any time, if the case has not been converted under section 1112, 1208, or 1307 of this title. Any waiver of the right to convert a case under this subsection is unenforceable."

> "(d) Notwithstanding any other provision of this section, a case may not be converted to a case under another chapter of this title unless the debtor may be a debtor under such chapter."

Petitioner contends that subsection (a) creates an unqualified right of conversion. He seeks support from language in both the House and Senate Committee Reports on the provision. The Senate Report stated:

> "Subsection (a) of this section gives the debtor the one-time absolute right of conversion of a liquidation case to a reorganization or individual repayment plan case. If the case has already once been converted from chapter 11 or 13 to chapter 7, then the debtor does not have that right. The policy of the provision is that the debtor should always be given the opportunity to repay his debts, and a waiver of the right to convert a case is unenforceable." S. Rep. No. 95-989, p. 94 (1978); see also H.R. Rep. No. 95-595, p. 380 (1977) (using nearly identical language).

The Committee Reports' reference to an "absolute right" of conversion is more equivocal than petitioner suggests. Assuming that the described debtor's "opportunity to repay his debts" is a short-hand reference to a right to proceed under Chapter 13, the statement that he should "always" have that right is inconsistent with the earlier recognition that it is only a one-time right that does not survive a previous conversion to, or filing under, Chapter 13. More importantly, the broad description of the right as "absolute" fails to give full effect to the express limitation in subsection (d). The words "unless the debtor may be a debtor under such chapter" expressly conditioned Marrama's right to convert on his ability to qualify as a "debtor" under Chapter 13.

There are at least two possible reasons why Marrama may not qualify as such a debtor, one arising under §109(e) of the Code, and the other turning on the construction of the word "cause" in §1307(c). The former provision imposes a limit on the amount of indebtedness that an individual may have in order to qualify for Chapter 13 relief. More pertinently, the latter provision, §1307(c), provides that a Chapter 13 proceeding may be either dismissed or converted to a Chapter 7 proceeding "for cause" and includes a nonexclusive list of 10 causes justifying that relief. None of the specified causes mentions prepetition bad-faith conduct (although subparagraph 10 does identify one form of Chapter 7 error — which is necessarily prepetition conduct — that would justify dismissal of a Chapter 13 case). Bankruptcy courts nevertheless routinely treat dismissal for prepetition bad-faith conduct as implicitly authorized by the words "for cause." See n. 1, *supra*. In practical effect, a ruling that an individual's Chapter 13 case should be dismissed or converted to Chapter 7 because of prepetition bad-faith conduct, including fraudulent acts committed in an earlier Chapter 7 proceeding, is tantamount to a ruling that the individual does not qualify as a debtor under Chapter 13. That individual, in other words, is not a member of the class of " 'honest but unfortunate debtor[s]' " that the bankruptcy laws were enacted to protect. See *Grogan v. Garner*, 498 U.S., at 287, 111 S. Ct. 654. The text of §706(d) therefore provides adequate authority for the denial of his motion to convert.

The class of honest but unfortunate debtors who do possess an absolute right to convert their cases from Chapter 7 to Chapter 13 includes the vast majority of the hundreds of thousands of individuals who file Chapter 7 petitions each year. Congress sought to give these individuals the chance to repay their debts should they acquire the means to do so. Moreover, as the Court of Appeals observed, the reference in §706(a) to the unenforceability of a waiver of the right to convert functions "as a consumer protection provision against adhesion contracts, whereby a debtor's creditors might be precluded from attempting to prescribe a waiver of the debtor's right to convert to chapter 13 as a non-negotiable condition of its contractual agreements." 430 F.3d, at 479.

A statutory provision protecting a borrower from waiver is not a shield against forfeiture. Nothing in the text of either §706 or §1307(c) (or the legislative history of either provision) limits the authority of the court to take appropriate action in response to fraudulent conduct by the atypical litigant who has demonstrated that he is not entitled to the relief available to the typical debtor. On the contrary, the broad authority granted to bankruptcy judges to take any action that is necessary or appropriate "to prevent an abuse of process" described in §105(a) of the Code, is surely adequate to authorize an immediate denial of a motion to convert filed under §706 in lieu of a conversion order that merely postpones the allowance of equivalent relief and may provide a debtor with an opportunity to take action prejudicial to creditors.

Indeed, as the Solicitor General has argued in his brief *amicus curiae*, even if §105(a) had not been enacted, the inherent power of every federal court to sanction "abusive litigation practices," see *Roadway Express, Inc. v. Piper*, 447 U.S. 752, 765, 100 S. Ct. 2455, 65 L. Ed. 2d 488 (1980), might well provide an adequate justification for a prompt, rather than a delayed, ruling on an unmeritorious attempt to qualify as a debtor under Chapter 13.

Accordingly, the judgment of the Court of Appeals is affirmed.

It is so ordered.

Justice ALITO, with whom THE CHIEF JUSTICE, Justice SCALIA, and Justice THOMAS join, dissenting.

Under the clear terms of the Bankruptcy Code, a debtor who initially files a petition under Chapter 7 has the right to convert the case to another chapter under which the case is eligible to proceed. The Court, however, holds that a debtor's conversion right is conditioned upon a bankruptcy judge's finding of "good faith." Because the imposition of this condition is inconsistent with the Bankruptcy Code, I respectfully dissent.

I

The Bankruptcy Code unambiguously provides that a debtor who has filed a bankruptcy petition under Chapter 7 has a broad right to convert the case to another chapter. Title 11 §706(a) states:

> "[A] debtor may convert a case under this chapter to a case under chapter 11, 12, or 13 of this title at any time, if the case has not been converted under section 1112, 1208, or 1307 of this title."

The Code restricts a Chapter 7 debtor's conversion right in two-and only two-ways. First, §706(a) makes clear that the right to convert is available only once: A debtor may convert so long as "the case has not been converted [to Chapter 7] under section 1112, 1208, or 1307 of this title." Second, §706(d) provides that a debtor wishing to convert to another chapter must meet the conditions that are needed in order to "be a debtor under such chapter." Nothing in §706(a) or any other provision of the Code suggests that a bankruptcy judge has the discretion to override a debtor's exercise of the §706(a) conversion right on a ground not set out in the Code. Thus, a straightforward reading of the Code suggests that a Chapter 7 debtor has the right to convert the debtor's case to Chapter 13 (or another chapter) provided that the two express statutory conditions contained in §706 are satisfied.

This reading of the Code is buttressed by the contrast between the terms of §706 and the language employed in other Code provisions that give bankruptcy judges the discretion to deny conversion requests. As noted, §706(a) says that a Chapter 7 debtor "may convert" the debtor's case to another chapter. Chapters 11, 12, and 13 contain similar provisions stating that debtors under those chapters "may convert" their cases to other chapters. See §§1112(a), 1208(a), and 1307(a) (2000 ed. and Supp. IV). Chapters 11, 12, and 13 also contain separate provisions governing conversion requests by other parties in interest. For example, the applicable provision in Chapter 11 provides:

> "On request of a party in interest and after notice and a hearing, *the court may convert* a case under this chapter to a case under chapter 11 of this title at any time." §706(b) (emphasis added).

See also §§1112(b), 1208(b), (d), and 1307(c).

In these sections, parties in interest are not given a right to convert. Rather, parties in interest are authorized to request conversion. And the authority to convert, after notice and a hearing, is expressly left to the discretion of the bankruptcy court, which "may convert" the case if the general standard of "cause" is found to have been met. If the Code had been meant to give a bankruptcy court similar authority when a Chapter 7 debtor wishes to convert, the Code would have used language similar to that in §§1112(b), 1208(b), (d), and 1307(c). Congress knew how to limit conversion authority in this way, and it did not do so in §706(a).

In Chapter 7, Congress did directly address the consequences of the sort of conduct complained of in this case. In §727(a)(3), Congress specified that a debtor may be denied a discharge of debts if "the debtor has concealed . . . records, and papers, from which the debtor's financial condition or business transactions might be ascertained." The Code further provides that discharge may be denied if the debtor has "made a false oath or account" or "presented or used a false claim." §727(a)(4). In addition to blocking discharge, Congress could easily have deemed such conduct sufficient to bar conversion to another chapter, but Congress did not do so.

Instead of taking that approach, Congress included in the statutory scheme several express means to redress a debtor's bad faith. First, if a bankruptcy court finds that there is "cause," the court may convert or reconvert a Chapter 11 or Chapter 13 restructuring to a Chapter 7 liquidation. §§1112(b), 1307(c). Second, a Chapter 13 debtor must propose a repayment plan to satisfy the debtor's creditors — a plan that is subject to court approval and must be proposed in good faith. §§1325(a)(3), (4); accord, §1328(b)(2). Third, a debtor's asset schedules are filed under penalty of perjury. 28 U.S.C. §1746; Fed. Rule Bkrtcy. Proc. 1008. Fourth, a Chapter 13 case is overseen by a trustee who is empowered to investigate the debtor's financial affairs, to furnish information regarding the bankruptcy estate to parties in interest, and to oppose discharge if necessary. 11 U.S.C. §§704(4), (6) and (9). See also §1302(b) (defining the powers of a Chapter 13 trustee in part by reference to the powers of a Chapter 7 trustee). These measures, as opposed to the "good faith" requirement crafted by the Court, represent the Code's strategy for dealing with debtors who engage in the type of abusive tactics that the Court's opinion targets.

In sum, the Code expressly gives a debtor who initially files under Chapter 7 the right to convert the case to another chapter so long as the debtor satisfies the requirements of the destination chapter. By contrast, the Code pointedly does not give the bankruptcy courts the authority to deny conversion based on a finding of "bad faith." There is no justification for disregarding the Code's scheme.

II

In reaching the conclusion that a bankruptcy judge may override a Chapter 7 debtor's conversion right based on a finding of "bad faith," the Court reasons as follows. Under §706(d), a Chapter 7 debtor may not convert to another chapter "unless the debtor may be a debtor under such chapter." Under §1307(c), a Chapter 13 proceeding may be dismissed or converted to Chapter 7 "for cause." One such "cause" recognized by bankruptcy courts is "bad faith." Therefore, a Chapter 7 debtor who has proceeded in "bad faith" and wishes to convert his or her case to Chapter 13 is not eligible to "be a debtor" under Chapter 13 because the debtor's case would be subject to dismissal or reconversion to Chapter 7 pursuant to §1307(c). I cannot agree with this strained reading of the Code.

The requirements that must be met in order to "be a debtor" under Chapter 13 are set forth in 11 U.S.C.A. §109 (main ed. and Supp. 2006), which is appropriately titled "Who may be a debtor." The two requirements that are specific to Chapter 13 appear in subsection (e). First, Chapter 13 is restricted to individuals, with or without their spouses, with regular income. Second, a debtor may not proceed under Chapter 13 if specified debt limits are exceeded.

As the Court of Appeals below correctly understood, §706(d)'s requirement that a debtor may convert only if "the debtor may be a debtor under such chapter" obviously refers to the chapter-specific requirements of §109. *In re Marrama*, 430 F.3d 474, 479, n. 3 (C.A.1 2005).

Rather than reading §§109(e) and 706(d) together, the Court puts §109(e) aside and treats §706(d) as a separate repository of additional requirements (namely, the absence of the grounds for dismissal or reconversion under §1307(c)) that a Chapter 7 debtor must satisfy *before* conversion to Chapter 13. But §1307(c) plainly does not set out requirements that an individual must meet in order to "be a debtor" under Chapter 13. Instead, §1307(c) sets out the standard ("cause") that a bankruptcy court must apply in deciding whether, in its discretion, an already filed Chapter 13 case should be dismissed or converted to Chapter 7. Thus, the Court's holding in this case finds no support in the terms of the Bankruptcy Code.

In holding that a bankruptcy judge may deny conversion based on "bad faith," the Court of Appeals appears to have been influenced by the belief that following the literal terms of the Code would be pointless. *Id.*, at 479-481. Specifically, the Court of Appeals observed that if a debtor who wishes to convert from Chapter 7 to Chapter 13 has exhibited such "bad faith" that the bankruptcy court would immediately convert the case back to Chapter 7 under §1307(c), then no purpose would be served by requiring the parties and the court to go through the process of conversion and prompt reconversion. *Id.*, at 481.

It is by no means clear, however, that conversion under §706(a) followed by a reconversion proceeding under §1307(c) would be an empty exercise. The immediate practical effect of following the statutory scheme is compliance with Bankruptcy Rule 1017(f), which applies Bankruptcy Rule 9014 to the reconversion. Fed. Rule Bkrtcy. Proc. 1017(e)(1). Rule 9014(a), in turn, requires that the request be made by motion and that "reasonable notice and opportunity for hearing . . . be afforded the party against whom relief is sought." The Court's decision circumvents this process and forecloses the right that a Chapter 13 debtor would otherwise possess to file a Chapter 13 repayment and reorganization plan, 11 U.S.C. §1321, which must be filed in good faith and which must demonstrate that creditors will receive no less than they would under an immediate Chapter 7 liquidation, §§1325(a)(3) and (4); accord, §1328(b)(2). While the plan must be filed no later than 15 days after filing the petition or conversion, the debtor may file the plan at the time of conversion, *i.e.*, before the reconversion hearing. Fed. Rule Bkrtcy. Proc. 3015(b).

Moreover, it is not clear whether, in converting a case "for cause" under §1307(c), a bankruptcy court must consider the debtor's plan (if already filed) and, if the plan must be considered, whether the court must take into account whether the plan was filed in good faith, whether it honestly discloses the debtor's assets, whether it demonstrates that creditors would in fact fare better under the plan than under a liquidation, and whether the plan in some sense "cures" prior bad faith. Today's opinion renders these questions academic, and little is left to guide what a bankruptcy court must consider, or may disregard, in blocking a §706(a) conversion.

The Court notes that the Bankruptcy Code is intended to give a "fresh start" to the "honest but unfortunate debtor." *Ante*, at 1107, 1111 (quoting *Grogan v. Garner*, 498 U.S. 279, 286, 287, 111 S. Ct. 654, 112 L. Ed. 2d 755 (1991)). But compliance with the statutory scheme-conversion to Chapter 13 followed by notice and a hearing on the question of reconversion would at least provide some structure to the process of identifying those debtors whose " 'bad faith' " meets the Court's standard for consignment to liquidation, *i.e.*, " 'bad faith' " conduct that is "atypical" and "extraordinary." *Ante*, at 1111-1112, n. 11.

III

Finally, the Court notes two alternative bases for its holding. First, the Court points to 11 U.S.C. §105(a), which governs a bankruptcy court's general powers. Second, the Court suggests that even without a textual basis, a bankruptcy court's inherent power may empower it to deny a §706(a) conversion request for bad faith. Obviously, however, neither of these sources of authority authorizes a bankruptcy court to contravene the Code. On the contrary, a bankruptcy court's general and equitable powers "must and can only be exercised within the confines of the Bankruptcy Code." *Norwest Bank Worthington v. Ahlers*, 485 U.S. 197, 206, 108 S. Ct. 963, 99 L. Ed. 2d 169 (1988); accord, *SEC v. United States Realty & Improvement*

Co., 310 U.S. 434, 455, 60 S. Ct. 1044, 84 L. Ed. 1293 (1940) ("A bankruptcy court . . . is guided by equitable doctrines and principles except in so far as they are inconsistent with the Act").

Ultimately, §105(a) and a bankruptcy court's inherent powers may have a role to play in a case such as this. The problem the Court identifies is a real one. A debtor who is convinced that he or she can successfully conceal assets has a significant incentive to pursue Chapter 7 liquidation in lieu of a Chapter 13 restructuring. If successful, the debtor preserves wealth; if unsuccessful, the debtor can convert to Chapter 13 and land largely where the debtor would have been if he or she had fully disclosed all assets and proceeded in Chapter 13 in the first instance.

Bankruptcy courts have used their statutory and equitable authority to craft various remedies for a range of bad faith conduct: requiring accountings or reporting of assets; enjoining debtors from alienating estate property; penalizing counsel; assessing costs and fees; or holding the debtor in contempt. But whatever steps a bankruptcy court may take pursuant to §105(a) or its general equitable powers, a bankruptcy court cannot contravene the provisions of the Code.

Because the provisions of the Code rule out the procedure that was followed in this case by the bankruptcy court, I would reverse the judgment of the Court of Appeals.

Marrama addressed the application of §706(a) to a debtor's motion to convert a case to Chapter 13. Does *Marrama* also govern the application of §1307(b) when a debtor seeks to dismiss a Chapter 13 case? Note that while §706(a) provides that a debtor "may" convert a case from Chapter 7 to Chapter 13, §1307(b) directs that the court "shall" dismiss a case upon the request of a debtor. *Compare* In re Rosson, 545 F.3d 764 (9th Cir. 2008) (*Marrama* means that the debtor's right to dismiss a Chapter 13 case is not absolute), *with* In re Polly, 392 B.R. 236 (Bankr. N.D. Tex. 2008) (debtor's right to dismiss Chapter 13 case is absolute).

VII.   The "Involuntary" Chapter 13

We have noted on several occasions that Chapter 13 is an entirely voluntary Chapter of the Bankruptcy Code. Only the debtor may commence a Chapter 13 case, and only the debtor may file a Chapter 13 plan. Nevertheless, some debtors who seek Chapter 7 relief can be "forced" into Chapter 13.

Section 707(b) is the chief battleground here. It allows for a motion to dismiss a Chapter 7 petition filed by a consumer if "abuse" of that Chapter would otherwise occur. The "means test" that we discussed in detail in Chapter 2 of this book comes into play here, keeping comparatively wealthy debtors from discharging their consumer debts in a Chapter 7, and thus urging them to file a Chapter 13 petition and pay some or all of those debts. Over and above the mechanics of the means test, abuse can be shown in other ways, as the cases below demonstrate, though the 2005 amendments to §707(b)(3) added this guidance to resolving the matter:

> (3) In considering under paragraph (1) whether the granting of relief would be an abuse of the provisions of this chapter in a case in which the presumption in subpragraph (A)(i) of such paragraph does not arise or is rebutted, the court shall consider
>> (A) whether the debtor filed the petition in good faith; or
>> (B) the totality of the circumstances (including whether the debtor seeks to reject a personal services contract and the financial need for such rejection as sought by the debtor) of the debtor's financial situation demonstrates abuse.

This 2005 revision of §707(b) raises the question of whether debtors who "pass" the means test can nevertheless face dismissal of their Chapter 7 cases. Certainly, if a court finds that the debtor has filed the case in bad faith, the case can be dismissed under §707(b)(3)(A). This provision protects the integrity of the court and the bankruptcy process. More difficult, however, is the question of the dismissal of a case under §707(b)(3)(B) when the debtor has already passed the means test. On the one hand, the debtor can argue that he or she has passed the repayment test that Congress has established and should therefore not be subject to a second test of essentially the same kind. In response, trustees and creditors are likely to argue that consideration of dismissal under §707(b)(2) is entirely separate from consideration of dismissal under the totality of the circumstances test of §707(b)(3). The courts have taken slightly different views on the issue as you can see in the cases that follow. How should the courts evaluate the debtor's financial condition for the totality of the circumstances test of §707(b)(3)? *See also* Eugene R. Wedoff, Means Testing in the New §707(b), 79 Am. Bankr. L.J. 231, 246-47 (2005); Ned W. Waxman & Justin H. Rucki, Chapter 7 Bankruptcy Abuse: Means Testing Is Presumptive, But "Totality" Is Determinative, 47 Hous. L. Rev. 901 (2008).

In re Baeza
United States Bankruptcy Court, Eastern District of California, 2008
398 B.R. 692

W. RICHARD LEE, Bankruptcy Judge.

The United States Trustee ("UST") disputes certain deductions claimed by the Debtors on Form 22A (the "Means Test"). Based thereon, the UST moves to dismiss this case as a presumed abuse of chapter 7 pursuant to 11 U.S.C. §707(b)(2). In the alternative, the UST contends that the Debtors have the ability to repay a substantial portion of their debts through a chapter 13 plan. The UST asks that the case be dismissed as an abuse of chapter 7 based on the totality of the circumstances of the Debtors' financial situation pursuant to §707(b)(3) (the "Motion"). In response, the Debtors contend that they would not be required to pay anything to their unsecured creditors in a chapter 13. For the reasons set forth below, the UST's Motion will be granted.

This memorandum decision contains the court's findings of fact and conclusions of law required by Federal Rule of Civil Procedure 52(a), made applicable to this contested matter by Federal Rule of Bankruptcy Procedure 7052. The court has jurisdiction over this matter pursuant to 28 U.S.C. §1334, 11 U.S.C. §707, and General Orders 182 and 330 of the U.S. District Court for the Eastern District of California. This is a core proceeding as defined in 28 U.S.C. §157(b)(2)(A).

Findings of Fact

The Debtors filed a voluntary petition for relief under chapter 7 of the Bankruptcy Code on July 31, 2008. The Debtors are individuals with primarily consumer debts. Their scheduled unsecured debts total $53,889 and their scheduled secured debts total $436,777. Based on the statement of intention filed with the petition, the Debtors intend to surrender the collateral for almost all of their secured debt, approximately $433,876, including their home, one vehicle, an ATV, and a travel trailer. Consequently, the Debtors' only remaining secured debt will be $2,900 for an automobile.

The Debtors' combined current monthly income ("CMI") as stated in their amended Means Test is $10,348. Their annualized income (CMI x 12) is $124,176, which exceeds the median income for a family of five in California. The Debtors claim deductions in the Means Test totaling $11,466 per month. The resulting "monthly disposable income" is stated to be a negative $1,118.18.

The Debtors' amended schedules I and J give a different picture of their current financial situation. Schedule I lists a combined average monthly gross income in the amount of $7,616. Their average monthly net income is $5,883. Schedule J lists monthly expenses in the amount of $5,404, which include: $525 for utilities; $300 for home maintenance; $800 for food; $400 for clothing, laundry and dry-cleaning; $500 for transportation; $200 for recreation; $50 for charitable contributions; $480 for auto and other insurance costs; a car payment of $110; education expenses for their children of $100; and $59 for a membership in "George Brown Gym." After deducting these expenses from the available net income, the Debtors are left with $479 each month. The UST contends that this is enough money to pay a substantial portion of the scheduled unsecured debts through a 60-month chapter 13 plan.

Issues Presented

The first issue is whether this case is presumptively abusive under §707(b)(2). Second, the court is asked to decide if the case is an abuse of chapter 7 based on the totality of the circumstances of the debtor's financial situation under §707(b)(3). A threshold question to the second issue is whether the "totality of the circumstances" test requires the court to look forward and decide if the Debtors would actually be required to pay anything to their unsecured creditors through a chapter 13 plan.

Overview of §707(b)

The chapter 7 case of an individual debtor whose debts are primarily consumer debts may be dismissed under §707(b)(1) if the court finds, after notice and a hearing, that the granting of a discharge would be an abuse of chapter 7. BAPCPA offers two standards for determining the "abuse" issue. Abuse may be presumed under the objective test prescribed in §707(b)(2), the Means Test. The function of the Means Test is to estimate the ability of chapter 7 debtors to repay their debts. If the debtor's annualized income exceeds the applicable median family income, and the Means Test shows that the debtor has the ability to repay the lesser of 25% of the nonpriority unsecured claims, or $10,950, over a period of five years, then a presumption of abuse arises. Section 707(b)(2)(A) prescribes a comprehensive list of allowable expenses for making that determination.

Section 707(b)(3) offers a more subjective test for abuse based on the debtor's good faith and the "totality of the circumstances . . . of the debtor's financial situation. . . ." Unlike the Means Test, the Bankruptcy Code does not define "totality of the circumstances." In addition, there is little case law interpreting the phrase under BAPCPA. Prior to BAPCPA, the Ninth Circuit looked to the "totality of the circumstances" to interpret the term "substantial abuse" in former §707(b). *In re Price*, 353 F.3d 1135, 1139-40 (9th Cir. 2004). Because Congress retained the phrase "totality of the circumstances" in BAPCPA, the court may look to pre-BAPCPA case law to construe the meaning of that phrase under §707(b)(3).

Analysis

Presumption of Abuse

The UST contends that the Debtors' case is presumed to be an abuse of chapter 7 because the Debtors' annualized income greatly exceeds the median family income and they have enough "disposable income" to pay at least $10,950 over 60 months. §707(b)(2). The Debtors' disposable income is in dispute here because they claimed an enormous deduction on their Means Test, $3,969 per month, based on contractual payments to secured creditors pursuant to §707(b)(2)(A)(iii). However, the collateral for most of this secured debt has been or will be for surrendered in the bankruptcy.

The Debtors respond that the presumption of abuse does not apply because the monthly deduction for secured debts should be based upon the contracts in effect as of the commencement of the bankruptcy case. They argue that they are entitled to deduct the contractual payments to secured creditors even though they have stopped making the payments and are in the process of surrendering the collateral. There appears to be no dispute that if the contractual payments are considered, then the Debtors will "pass" the Means Test, meaning that their disposable income will be below the threshold for "presumed abuse" as set forth in §707(b)(2). Conversely, if the payments for surrendered collateral are not considered, then the Debtors will have disposable income well in excess of the threshold which triggers the presumption of abuse.

Alternatively, the UST argues that the Debtors' case is an abuse of chapter 7 based on the totality of the circumstances of the Debtors' financial situation under §707(b)(3). Subsections 707(b)(2) and (b)(3) are mutually exclusive. The court need not address the §707(b)(2) argument summarized above, if it otherwise finds an abuse of chapter 7 under §707(b)(3). Even if the court were to conclude that the Debtors pass the Means Test without creating a presumption of abuse, it is inconsequential if the case is otherwise "abusive" under §707(b)(3).

Section 707(b)(3) clearly states that the court shall consider whether the totality of the circumstances of the debtor's financial situation demonstrates abuse when the presumption *does not* arise. *See In re Paret*, 3A7 B.R. 12 (Bankr. D. Del. 2006) (the term "shall" in §707(b)(3) "explicitly mandates" consideration of the totality of the circumstances to determine whether abuse exists if the presumption of abuse under §707(b)(2) does not arise or is rebutted); *see also* Eugene R. Wedoff, *Means Testing in the New §707(B)*, 79 Am. Bankr. L.J. 231, 236 (2005) ("[B]ecause the general abuse provisions of §707(b)(3) expressly apply when the means test has been rebutted, 'passing' the means test does not preclude a discretionary finding of abuse by the court. . . . [I]f a debtor's overall financial circumstances would easily allow the debtor to repay debts . . . the court may find abuse.").

Abuse Under the Totality of the Circumstances

In *Price*, the Ninth Circuit prescribed some nonexclusive factors for courts to consider when reviewing the "totality of the circumstances" under §707(b):

(1)   Whether the debtor has a likelihood of sufficient future income to fund a Chapter 11, 12, or 13 plan which would pay a substantial portion of the unsecured claims;
(2)   Whether the debtor's petition was filed as a consequence of illness, disability, unemployment, or some other calamity;
(3)   Whether the schedules suggest the debtor obtained cash advancements and consumer goods on credit exceeding his or her ability to repay them;
(4)   Whether the debtor's proposed family budget is excessive or extravagant;
(5)   Whether the debtor's statement of income and expenses is misrepresentative of the debtor's financial condition; and
(6)   Whether the debtor has engaged in eve-of-bankruptcy purchases.

In re Price, 353 F.3d at 1139-40.

The court in *Price* went on to state that the debtor's *ability* to repay his debts is the primary factor in determining substantial abuse; "The primary factor defining substantial abuse is the debtor's *ability* to pay his debts *as determined by the ability to fund a Chapter 13 plan.* Thus, we have concluded that a 'debtor's *ability to pay his debts* will, standing alone, justify a section 707(b) dismissal.' " *Id.* at 1140 (quoting *Zolg v. Kelly, III (In re Kelly)*, 841 F.2d 908, 914 (9th Cir. 1988)) (emphasis added).

The Debtors contend that their ability to pay creditors should not be part of the "totality of the circumstances" inquiry. This issue has been addressed, on similar facts, in a post-BAPCPA chapter 7 decision, *In re Pak*, 343 B.R. 239 (Bankr. N.D. Cal. 2006). The chapter 7 debtor was unemployed for the six months prior to his bankruptcy and, consequently, was not subject to the chapter 7 Means Test and the presumption of abuse standard. After the period of unemployment, the debtor returned to work and was earning an annualized income of more than $100,000. The United States Trustee moved to dismiss the case as an abuse of chapter 7 pursuant to §707(b)(3). Because the Means Test formula did not apply to the debtor, he argued that his ability to pay debts was not a part of the "totality of the circumstances" test for abuse. The court rejected that argument and granted the United States Trustee's motion stating:

> The Court also finds instructive section 707(b)(3)'s use of the phrase "the totality of the circumstances." Prior to BAPCPA, courts considered whether to dismiss a consumer case for "substantial abuse" under section 707(b)(1) based on the "totality of the circumstances." All courts considered the debtor's ability to pay to be an important factor in this context. It would be counterintuitive to construe this same phrase, as used in BAPCPA, to exclude a consideration of the debtor's ability to pay.

Id. at 243 (internal citation omitted).

Turning now to the facts of this case, it appears that at least two of the *Price* factors, the first and second, are relevant. The Debtors have enjoyed an annual income that is substantially more than the applicable median family income in California. While their income may have recently decreased, they also are no longer burdened with oppressive payments to secured creditors which consumed a large percentage of their income. There is no showing that the Debtors filed this joint petition as a result of illness, disability, unemployment, or calamity. The Debtors' own schedules show that the Debtors have *the ability to repay* a substantial portion of their unsecured debts based on their current financial situation. In the case of *Hebbring v. U.S. Trustee*, 463 F.3d 902 (9th Cir.2006), the Ninth Circuit affirmed the dismissal of a chapter 7 case for *substantial* abuse where the debtor could afford to pay as little as 27% to her unsecured creditors over three years. *Id.* at 908-09.

Predicting Payments in a Hypothetical Chapter 13

The Debtors argue that the "totality of the circumstances" inquiry compels the court to predict what would be required of the Debtors in a hypothetical chapter 13. They contend, based on the Ninth Circuit's recent decision in *In re Kagenveama, supra* 541 F.3d at 868, that they could confirm a "zero payment" chapter 13 plan because the chapter 13 Means Test, Form 22C, would show that they do not have any disposable income. If the Debtors would not have to pay anything to their creditors through a chapter 13 plan, they contend that a discharge in this case would not be an "abuse" of chapter 7.

The Debtors' argument mischaracterizes the issue and misstates the law. The question before the court is not whether the Debtors *would be required* to pay anything to their unsecured creditors in a chapter 13, but rather, whether they have the *ability to pay* something substantial to their unsecured creditors. The answer to that question is unequivocally yes. The Debtors focus on the first half of the operative language in §707(b)(3)(B), the "totality of the circumstances" phrase without addressing the phrase, "of the debtor's financial situation." By the plain meaning of

§707(b)(3)(B), the court must consider the Debtors' actual financial situation. The test under §707(b)(3) is not tied to or limited by the statutory Means Test formula that drives §707(b)(2). For that reason alone, the Debtors' argument should be rejected.

This is not the time or the place to determine what the Debtors would be required to pay in a hypothetical chapter 13. This is not a chapter 13 case and the person to ask the "confirmation" questions in a chapter 13 would be the chapter 13 trustee who is not a party in this case. The Debtors do not deny that they have the *ability to repay* a substantial amount to their unsecured creditors without placing an undue burden on the Debtors or their dependants. Based on the Debtors' schedules, they have the *ability to pay* approximately $479 per month to fund a chapter 13 plan for the benefit of those creditors.

The Debtors' reliance on *In re Kagenveama* is misplaced. *Kagenveama* deals with confirmation of a plan under §1325. There is nothing in *Kagenveama* to suggest that its holding should be applied to §707(b). Indeed, even the *Kagenveama* court recognized that the Means Test may not be the end of the inquiry in a chapter 13, "[w]e stress that nothing in our opinion prevents the debtor, the trustee, or the holder of an allowed unsecured claim to request modification of the [chapter 13] plan after confirmation pursuant to §1329." 541 F.3d at 877. Further, *Kagenveama* only dealt with one element of chapter 13 plan confirmation, the "disposable income" test under §1325(b)(1)(B). There are other factors which a chapter 13 trustee is entitled to examine and which a debtor must satisfy to confirm a plan in chapter 13. Most notable of these are the "good faith" inquiries under §§1325(a)(3) and (a)(7),[17] and the chapter 7 liquidation test under §1325(a)(4).

Conclusion

Based on the foregoing, the court finds and concludes, based on the totality of the circumstances, that the Debtors have the ability to pay a substantial portion of the debts for which they seek a discharge and that the granting of a discharge in this case would be an abuse of chapter 7. Accordingly, the UST's motion to dismiss will

---

17. The court is aware of the pre-BAPCPA case law which held that "good faith" under §1325(a)(3) does not require a substantial repayment to unsecured creditors. (*Goeb v. Heid (In re Goeb)*, 675 F.2d 1386 (9th Cir. 1982)). However, prior to BAPCPA, the "good faith" inquiry bore some relationship to the debtor's actual financial condition. The debtors in *Goeb* did not have enough disposable income to make a substantial payment to their unsecured creditors. Congress changed the definition of "disposable income" with the enactment of BAPCPA to a formula which, as here, may bear no relationship to the debtor's financial situation. Accordingly, it is not clear that the holding in *Goeb* would still apply when the debtors can actually afford to pay a substantial dividend to their unsecured creditors. Even the *Goeb* court recognized that the debtors must act equitably in proposing their chapter 13 plan. "[T]he court must make its good-faith determination in the light of *all* militating factors." *Id.* at 1390 (emphasis in original). The Debtors refer the court to a recent unpublished bankruptcy court decision, *In re Smith*, 2008 WL 4964720 (Bankr. W.D. Wash.), in which the court concluded, on facts similar to this case, that the chapter 13 plan was filed in good faith so long as it meets the statutory disposable income requirement. At least one other bankruptcy court has found that the "good faith" test was not satisfied when a debtor with no "disposable income" could actually pay his creditors in full. *In re Marti*, 393 B.R. 697 (Bankr. D. Neb. 2008). The court in *Marti* found that the Means Test is meaningless when the debtor had no income prior to filing and a substantial income immediately after filing. 393 B.R. at 701. The "good faith" issue appears to be unsettled on these facts in the Ninth Circuit.

be granted unless the Debtors voluntarily convert their case to chapter 13 and file a chapter 13 plan within 10 days from service of this ruling. If the case is not so converted, then the UST shall submit an order dismissing this case.

In re Nockerts

United States Bankruptcy Court, Eastern District of Wisconsin, 2006
357 B.R. 497

SUSAN V. KELLEY, Bankruptcy Judge.

The U.S. Trustee has moved to dismiss this case based on a presumption of abuse under Bankruptcy Code §707(b)(2) or as an abuse under §707(b)(3). This chapter 7 case was filed on August 15, 2006, and is governed by the Bankruptcy Abuse Prevention and Consumer Protection Act of 2005 (BAPCPA). The parties have stipulated to most of the facts.

The Debtors are "above-median" debtors; their annualized current monthly income is $82,131, which exceeds the Wisconsin median of $60,106 for a family of three. Accordingly, in BAPCPA jargon, the Debtors must pass the "means test" in order to qualify for chapter 7 relief. The means test is codified in the provisions of §707(b)(2) and the calculations are performed on Official Form B22A. Under §707(b)(2)(A), the case will be presumed an abuse unless the debtor passes the means test or successfully rebuts the presumption of abuse by showing special circumstances, and then only to the extent that those circumstances are proven to justify additional expenses or adjustments.

[The court concluded that the monthly payments on secured claims for property that was to be surrendered to the secured creditors could be deducted from the debtors' current monthly income in applying the means test. As a result of these deductions, the debtors passed the means test.]

* * * *

The U.S. Trustee alternatively contends that the Debtors' case should be dismissed as an abuse under the "totality of circumstances" test of §707(b)(3). That section of the Bankruptcy Code states:

> In considering under paragraph (1) whether the granting of relief would be an abuse of the provisions of this chapter in a case in which the presumption in subparagraph (A)(i) of such paragraph does not arise or is rebutted, the court shall consider —
>   (A) whether the debtor filed the petition in bad faith; or
>   (B) the totality of the circumstances (including whether the debtor seeks to reject a personal services contract and the financial need for such rejection as sought by the debtor) of the debtor's financial situation demonstrates abuse.

Unlike when proceeding under §707(b)(2), the U.S. Trustee does not enjoy the benefit of a presumption of abuse when pursuing a §707(b)(3) motion. To succeed, the U.S. Trustee must prove that the debtor filed the case in bad faith or that the totality of the circumstances of the debtor's financial situation demonstrates abuse.

The "totality of circumstances" test has its roots in pre-BAPCPA law. Although the Seventh Circuit Court of Appeals had not weighed in on the issue, a District Court in this Circuit analyzed the case law in *In re Ontiveros*, 198 B.R. 284 (C.D. Ill. 1996). The court explained that in ruling on "substantial abuse" motions under the prior version of §707(b), the circuit courts devised three main approaches: (1) the *per se* rule of the Eighth and Ninth Circuits under which the debtor's ability to pay his debts, standing alone, justified dismissal; (2) the totality of the circumstances test of the Fourth Circuit which required a showing of more than an ability to pay; and (3) the hybrid approach of the Sixth Circuit which permitted the dismissal based on ability to pay alone, but also allowed the debtor to demonstrate mitigating circumstances. *Id.* at 287.

The means test of §707(b)(2) appears to be a codification of the *per se* rule, with its presumption of abuse for debtors who have the ability to pay based on application of the means test formula. The Fourth Circuit's "totality of the circumstances" test was adopted by name in BAPCPA §707(b)(3)(B), suggesting that *something other* than an ability to pay is required to succeed on a Motion to Dismiss under this section. Further, as illustrated in *Ontiveros*, examining the "totality" of the circumstances suggests considering more than one factor (i.e., ability to pay).

In *Green v. Staples (In re Green)*, the Fourth Circuit Court of Appeals held that other factors must be considered in addition to the debtor's ability to fund a chapter 13 plan:

> The "totality of the circumstances" approach involves an evaluation of factors such as the following:
>
> (1)   Whether the bankruptcy petition was filed because of sudden illness, calamity, disability, or unemployment;
> (2)   Whether the debtor incurred cash advances and made consumer purchases far in excess of his ability to repay;
> (3)   Whether the debtor's proposed family budget is excessive or unreasonable;
> (4)   Whether the debtor's schedules and statement of current income and expenses reasonably and accurately reflect the true financial condition; and
> (5)   Whether the petition was filed in good faith.

934 F.2d 568, 572 (4th Cir. 1991). The Fourth Circuit rejected the notion that ability to pay alone is cause for dismissal as a substantial abuse of chapter 7. *Id.*

Interpreting the §707(b)(3) test as requiring proof of more than the ability to fund a chapter 13 plan gives appropriate weight to the statutory means test, which is, after all, the Congressional formula for determining ability to pay. To apply the means test, dislike the result, and then examine the debtor's ability to fund a chapter 13 plan under §707(b)(3), renders the means test "surplusage." For example, line 22 of Form B22A allows a debtor to deduct local standards for transportation, vehicle operation or public transportation. According to Form B22A, these expenses are deductible regardless of whether the debtor pays the expenses of operating a vehicle and regardless of whether the debtor uses public transportation. Debtors in this area can deduct $358 for operating two or more vehicles. If the Schedule J discloses that the debtor was paying significantly less to operate the vehicles (for example, if the debtor was a little old above-median income lady who only drove the vehicles to church on Sunday), it would not appear appropriate for the U.S. Trustee to move for dismissal under §707(b)(3) solely because the debtor had the ability to use the excess income to fund a chapter 13 plan. To perform the means test and then perform another means test that is more to the U.S. Trustee's liking ignores the plain language of the statute and would be a waste of judicial resources. In *In re Deaton*, discussing why the "totality of circumstances" test must include more than a simple calculation of the debtor's ability to fund a chapter 13 plan, the court reviewed the legislative history of the "substantial abuse" provision and stated:

> If Congress had intended to institute a system of mandatory Chapter 13, it would have had no difficulty in saying so in direct, explicit language. Congress rejected this proposal, at least in part, because its adoption would have laid an unbearable burden on the bankruptcy court system as presently constituted. That system depends for its viability upon the administrative disposition without significant intervention by the bankruptcy judge, of the great bulk of consumer Chapter 7 cases. To require that official to review every Chapter 7 consumer case and make the kind of careful determination required in determining whether a successful Chapter 13 case could be maintained by the debtor, would call for a great expansion of manpower, and consequent expense, in the bankruptcy court system.

65 B.R. 663, 665 (Bankr. S.D. Ohio 1986).

This Court is not suggesting that the debtor's ability to pay should not be considered as a factor in the "totality of the circumstances" test, or that passing the means test ends the inquiry. For example, where debtors have "manipulated" the means test, the case should be dismissed under §707(b)(3). As Judge Wedoff explained in *Means Testing in the New §707(b)*:

> Thus, for purposes of the means test, debt secured even by such items as luxury vehicles, pleasure boats, and vacation homes would be deductible. Moreover, under a plain language analysis, the balance of a balloon mortgage that became contractually due during the five years after the bankruptcy filing-and perhaps even the total balance due on a defaulted mortgage that had been contractually accelerated-would be entirely deductible. However, if deductions of this sort allowed a wealthy debtor to avoid the presumption of abuse under the means test, an abuse might still be found in consideration of the "the totality of the circumstances . . . of the debtor's financial situation" pursuant to 707(b)(3).

79 Am. Bankr. L.J. 231, 273 (Spring 2005).

Moreover, the cases that have granted §707(b)(3) "totality of the circumstances" motions based on a debtor's ability to pay are distinguishable from this one. *In re Paret*, 347 B.R. 12 (Bankr. D. Del. 2006), *In re Pennington*, 348 B.R. 647 (Bankr. D. Del. 2006), and *In re Pak*, 343 B.R. 239 (Bankr. N.D. Cal. 2006), all involved below-median income debtors. Accordingly, the courts in those cases, limited by §707(b)(7), were prohibited from subjecting those debtors to the means test under §707(b)(2). Since no means test was performed, an inquiry into the debtors' ability to pay was rightly conducted, *for the first time.* Here, the Debtors have already undergone — and passed — the means test. As §707(b)(3) states, the court shall consider the totality of the circumstances "in a case in which the presumption . . . does not arise [(i.e., the debtor passed the means test)] or is rebutted [(i.e., the debtor failed the means test, but provided a sufficient explanation)]." This language suggests that an inquiry into a debtor's financial situation requires an inquiry into *more than* what is tested in the means test.

Under the pre-BAPCPA totality of the circumstances test, proof of more than just an ability to fund a chapter 13 plan was needed to demonstrate "substantial abuse." *Green,* 934 F.2d at 572. Stated another way, while ability to pay is a factor in the totality of circumstances test, and may even be the primary factor to be considered, if it is the only indicia of abuse, the case should not be dismissed under that test. Given the detailed nature of the means test in §707(b)(2), this Court holds that similar to the old totality of the circumstances test, more than an ability to pay (as shown on the debtor's Schedule I and J) must be shown to demonstrate abuse under §707(b)(3)(B). This additional evidence may include the *Green* factors, or may point to a manipulation of the means test as illustrated by Judge Wedoff's article.

In this case, the parties focused almost exclusively on §707(b)(2), and very little evidence was introduced at the hearing relating to the totality of the circumstances test under §707(b)(3). Before the Court can decide whether the totality of the circumstances illustrates abuse and warrants dismissal of the Debtors' case, the parties must improve the record and support their §707(b)(3) arguments. The Court will schedule a hearing at which the U.S. Trustee will be allowed to establish that additional factors warrant dismissal, and the Debtors will be allowed to establish any mitigating factors that would suggest this case is not an abuse of chapter 7 under the totality of the circumstances.

CHAPTER *9*

Reorganization in Chapter 11

I.   Getting Started

In recent years it has seemed as though every time you open the newspaper or listen to the news some corporation[1] is filing for protection under Chapter 11 of the Bankruptcy Code. Reorganization is an attractive way for an ailing business to stave off the collection efforts of its creditors while getting time to formulate a plan that will turn the business around and return it to being a profit-making enterprise. On the other hand, it is estimated that more than 50 percent of all filings in Chapter 11 are made by debtors who have no real chance of creating a confirmable plan of reorganization, so that the filing is made either in bad faith or by an exhausted debtor who is clutching at straws or indulging in ridiculous optimism ("terminal euphoria," as it is sometimes characterized). In the meantime, the creditors look aghast as the assets of the debtor leak away, hurting secured and unsecured creditors alike to the good of no one, with everything sacrificed to the egos of managers and owners who don't know when to quit.

Only rarely are Chapter 11 cases filed unexpectedly. Usually, the debtor has been in an economic slide for some time. There may be a precipitating event (foreclosure, repossession, acceleration of indebtedness, and the like), but it is usually the accumulation of losses over time that results in a Chapter 11 filing. In fact, in many instances, the debtor files the petition only after attempts at nonbankruptcy workouts have failed. For most businesses, the lenders are monitoring the debtor's financial progress, and the lender and borrower each would prefer that the business be successful. Successful businesses repay their debts. So, the parties frequently negotiate repayment adjustments and other provisions (for example, the lender may require the borrower to retain a turnaround expert or other consultant to oversee or recommend restructuring of the business) to get the business back on its feet and profitable again.

---

1. Chapter 11, though usually used by business debtors, is in no way so limited, and even individuals are eligible for Chapter 11 relief; *see* Toibb v. Radloff, 501 U.S. 157 (1991). The 2005 amendments to the Code have some specific rules for individuals in Chapter 11. They must do credit counseling ("Um, Mr. Trump, you seem to be spending quite a bit of money on hair spray each month") under §109(h), but they don't seem to have to complete the usual financial management course. They must pay all disposable income for the longer of five years or the period for which payments are called for under the plan; §1128(a)(15). Some plan payments on restructured secured claims could cover 20 years or more. This is a significant possible glitch in the statute.

These efforts might ripen into nonbankruptcy plans in which the debtor and its creditors adjust the debts. Other possibilities include assignments for the benefit of creditors, and sales of the debtor's encumbered assets under Article 9 of the UCC. Of course, the lender's interest and the borrower's interest diverge when the lender decides that the risk of nonpayment of the debt is too great. At that point, if not sooner, the debtor looks very closely at Chapter 11 as a solution.

Chapter 11 cases are as varied as the businesses that file them. The same chapter governs both Chrysler LLC (and 24 of its affiliates) and Mom & Pop's, Inc., a restaurant that seats 40 and employs eleven people. Other than residing in the same chapter, these cases are quite different. When Chrysler filed its Chapter 11 petition, it also filed dozens of motions and declarations on the same day (not surprisingly, these are commonly referred to as "first day motions"). You can take a look at many of these documents as well as the petitions themselves at this website: <www.chryslerrestructuring.com>. Mom & Pop's is unlikely to have a website for its Chapter 11 case, and it probably will have only the petition and perhaps a very small number of other filings on the first day of its case. Nevertheless, the same principles and provisions apply to each case. As you study those provisions, consider how well they might work for each kind of case.

PROBLEM 9-1

The owner of Medical Supplies, Inc., calls you for advice. His company sells medical items to hospitals, and one of its buyers, Quality Heart Care, a nursing home for those with cardiology problems, yesterday filed a Chapter 11 petition while owing Medical Supplies $80,000, unsecured, for goods delivered over the past eight months. Quality Heart Care, the owner tells you, is headed by complete imbeciles who never had a clue how a business is run. The president of the company is Howard Care, who is a splendid doctor but whose business sense is so bad that the company's records do not exist, taxes have not been paid for the last two years, the regular employees have all quit and been replaced by temps with no experience, and most assets were repossessed by secured creditors months ago. Apparently there is no cash to run the business. The owner of Medical Supplies has these questions for you:

(a)   Will Howard Care still be in charge? *See* §§1107 and 1101(1). For how long? *See* §1121(b).

(b)   Can anything be done to stop this madness? *See* §§1104, 1108, 1112(b).

(c)   Will Medical Supplies, Inc., have any voice in the Chapter 11 proceeding? The owner tells you that his company is probably the largest unsecured trade creditor. *See* §§1102 and 1103. Will Medical Supplies get paid for any work it does in the bankruptcy? *See* §503(b)(3)(F).

Chapter 11 anticipates that the debtor's business will continue. Of course, the debtor has the advantage of the automatic stay, and interest is no longer running on unsecured claims. While these advantages are substantial, the filing of a bankruptcy petition does not free the debtor from all restrictions on the operation of the business. Section 959(b) of Title 28 provides that trustees and debtors in possession "shall manage and operate the property in [their possession] according to the valid laws of the State in which such property is situated, in the same manner that the owner or possessor thereof would be bound to do if in possession thereof." This section prevents debtors from paying their employees less than minimum wages, from discharging hazardous wastes, and from otherwise gaining advantages over competing businesses that are not in bankruptcy.

In recent years, there has been a vigorous debate about the efficacy of Chapter 11. For the most telling of the attacks, calling for outright repeal of Chapter 11, *see* M. Bradley & M. Rosenzweig, The Untenable Case for Chapter 11, 101 Yale L.J. 1043 (1992). Chapter 11, of course, has its defenders; *see* L. LoPucki, Strange Visions in a Strange World: A Reply to Professors Bradley and Rosenzweig, 91 Mich. L. Rev. 79 (1992), and E. Warren, The Untenable Case for Repeal of Chapter 11, 102 Yale L.J. 437 (1992). The controversy over Chapter 11 has continued, and much has been written about the significance of the lure of large cases. In 2004, Prof. Lynn M. LoPucki published a book provocatively titled *How Competition for Big Cases Is Corrupting the Bankruptcy Courts*. The University of Buffalo Law Review then published a symposium on the book in July 2006. Prof. LoPucki argues that the disproportional filing of large Chapter 11 cases in Delaware and the Southern District of New York supports his conclusion that bankruptcy courts improperly encourage filing in their districts. Of course, his arguments are much more elaborate than can be set out here, as are the responses to his claims. They demonstrate quite clearly, however, that the debate on the efficacy of Chapter 11 is ongoing and unlikely to abate. For another recent discussion of the same issue, see Elizabeth Warren & Jay Lawrence Westbrook, The Success of Chapter 11: A Challenge to the Critics, 107 Mich. L. Rev. 603 (2009).

As Problem 9-1 suggests, there are limits on the ability of the debtor to control its future in Chapter 11. The sections cited in the Problem demonstrate that on the filing of the petition the debtor is now called the "debtor in possession" and given the powers usually reserved for the trustee in bankruptcy. During the first 120 days of the bankruptcy proceeding, the debtor in possession (or DIP) is given the exclusive right to file a plan of reorganization. However, the DIP is subject to certain controls. Committees of creditors and equity security holders (i.e., the stockholders) may be appointed to oversee what is going on; if they don't like it they can file various motions to dismiss the Chapter 11, convert it to Chapter 7, have a trustee appointed, and so forth.

Another possibility is the appointment of an *examiner*. Read §§1104(c) and 1106(b). This official is, in effect, a detective who investigates what is going on and makes recommendations to the bankruptcy judge. These recommendations could include the appointment of a trustee, but note that under §§321(b) and 327(f), the examiner is disqualified from thereafter serving as either the trustee or an employee of the trustee. Why would Congress have imposed this bar? For a case demonstrating what an angry bankruptcy judge can do when the DIP is mismanaging the business, *see* In re Bonneville Pacific Corp., 196 B.R. 868, (Bankr. D. Utah 1996).

PROBLEM 9-2

Quality Heart Care filed its Chapter 11 on Tuesday and on the following Friday it filed a proposed plan that would slowly sell off the company's assets over a two-year period, at the end of which time the company would dissolve, having distributed all of its assets and leaving its stockholders with worthless sheets of paper in their portfolios. Medical Supplies, Inc., its largest trade creditor, calls you, its attorney, for advice. Can Chapter 11 be used for liquidation in this fashion? *See* §1123(a)(5)(D) and (b)(4). Why would Quality Heart — or any debtor — file in Chapter 11 rather than Chapter 7 if this is what is intended? Is this use of Chapter 11 in the best interest of Medical Supplies, Inc.? In the best interests of the patients? *See* §333.

PROBLEM 9-3

You have been the attorney for Luddite Technologies for the past five years and, in spite of your excellent legal advice, LT has slid steadily toward the jurisdiction of the bankruptcy courts. Last week you filed LT's Chapter 11 bankruptcy petition. Must you now cease your representation of the company or can you become the attorney for the debtor in possession? *See* §§1107 and 327.

(a)   Suppose LT owes your firm $10,000 for prebankruptcy services. Is the outstanding debt a disqualifying characteristic? *See* §101(14)(A). What if LT paid your long overdue bill two weeks before the petition was filed? Are you now allowed to represent it in the Chapter 11? *See* Diamond Lumber v. Unsecured Creditors' Committee, 88 B.R. 773 (N.D. Tex. 1988). Can your firm take a security interest in LT's assets to collateralize the fee agreement without creating a conflict? *See* In re Martin, 817 F.2d 175 (1st Cir. 1987).

(b)   Attorneys who provide general representation to corporations often serve as the corporate secretary and prepare and retain the corporate books. If your partner has held this position until she resigned last month, can your firm represent the debtor? *See* §101(14)(D).

If all of these rules are meticulously observed, isn't the debtor being deprived of the counsel it desires? Won't it cost the debtor (and therefore the creditors) a lot more to bring in an attorney who is unfamiliar with the debtor's history and operations?

In re The Leslie Fay Companies, Inc.

United States Bankruptcy Court, Southern District of New York, 1994
175 B.R. 525

TINA L. BROZMAN, Bankruptcy Judge.

Rarely am I faced with a motion as troubling as this one, the United States Trustee's motion to disqualify Weil, Gotshal & Manges ("Weil Gotshal"), the debtors' counsel, from further representation of its clients and to deny the firm fees because of its failure to disclose what the United States Trustee ("U.S. Trustee") dubs disabling conflicts. The motion is predicated upon the report of an examiner who had concluded that Weil Gotshal was not disinterested when retained and had failed to reveal to the court the connections which led to his conclusion. I am in accord with the examiner's assessment, although I do not share his view that the appropriate sanction is limited to imposition on Weil Gotshal of a portion of the costs which he incurred investigating Weil Gotshal's status. Indeed, it is the nature of the sanction which is the troubling element here for, as the examiner found, Weil Gotshal has rendered services competently and loyally to the debtors, notwithstanding its derelictions in the area of disclosure, and the debtors undoubtedly will be harmed by Weil Gotshal's complete removal from the case some twenty months into the reorganization effort. This fear of harm to the debtors is shared by both official committees as well as the examiner.

I.

A. Background

The Leslie Fay Companies, Inc. ("Leslie Fay") is a large, publicly-owned corporation primarily engaged in designing, manufacturing, and selling women's dresses, suits, and sportswear. It is one of the few large American clothing manufacturers which still manufactures in the United States.

On January 29, 1993, Leslie Fay's controller, Donald Kenia, disclosed to senior management that he had been making unsupported entries into Leslie Fay's general ledger, resulting in a significant misstatement of its financial standing. Two days later, senior management informed Leslie Fay's board of directors (the "Board" or "Board of Directors") which in turn disclosed the existence of the false entries to the general public.

The Board directed its audit committee (the "Audit Committee") to conduct an investigation into the facts and circumstances surrounding the accounting irregularities. At the time, the Audit Committee was composed of three independent, non-management directors: Ira J. Hechler, a private investor; Ralph Destino, Chairman of Cartier, Inc.; and Michael L. Tarnopol, a senior officer at Bear Stearns & Co. ("Bear Stearns"). The Board then appointed Steven Friedman, the only other outside director of Leslie Fay, to join Hechler, Destino, and Tarnopol on the Audit Committee and in their investigation of the accounting irregularities. Friedman is a senior manager of Odyssey Partners L.P. ("Odyssey"), a large partnership that acts principally as a merchant bank.

Included in the Audit Committee's charter were the identification of all parties who may have been involved in the accounting irregularities and the consideration of possible legal claims that could be asserted on behalf of Leslie Fay. Toward those ends, the Audit Committee retained the accounting firm of Arthur Andersen & Co. and Weil Gotshal. Prior to its retention by the Audit Committee, Weil Gotshal had not done any work for Leslie Fay, whose general outside counsel was the law firm of Parker, Chapin, Flattau & Klimpl ("Parker Chapin").

In late February, 1993, the Audit Committee issued preliminary results of its work, announcing that Leslie Fay's 1991 profits had been overstated by over $12 million. Accordingly, the accounting firm of BDO Seidman ("Seidman"), Leslie

Fay's independent auditors, officially withdrew its signature from Leslie Fay's 1991 financial statements. The Audit Committee had also learned by this point that Kenia's initial representation that he alone was responsible for the false entries was not true. As was later confirmed, the fraud reached to Leslie Fay's chief financial officer, Paul Polishan.

B.   Weil Gotshal's Court-Approved Retention and the Subsequent Questions

The consequences of this burgeoning scandal were calamitous to Leslie Fay. Lenders and suppliers froze its credit lines, and Leslie Fay was unable to secure the financing necessary for the continued operation of its business. This led to an expansion of Weil Gotshal's role to include advice on financial restructuring. On April 5, 1993, nine weeks into the Audit Committee's investigation, Weil Gotshal filed chapter 11 petitions on behalf of Leslie Fay and its affiliates (the group referred to for convenience as "Leslie Fay"). The same day, Weil Gotshal submitted an application for retention as counsel for the debtors in possession, which was approved by the Hon. Cornelius Blackshear of this court. The order contemplated that Weil Gotshal would continue in its work for the Audit Committee as part and parcel of its representation of the debtors. The U.S. Trustee, the only party in interest to receive notice, had indicated that he did not object to the retention.

By late September, the Audit Committee completed its investigation, and on September 27, 1993, it disclosed its findings to the Board of Directors. The Audit Committee concluded that there was no evidence that any member of the debtors' current senior management or the Board of Directors knew of or participated in the fraudulent entries, which it estimated totalled some $160 million. The Audit Committee also discovered, contrary to what was originally believed, that the accounting irregularities dated back to at least 1990. These findings were made public on September 29, 1993.

At just about this time, questions regarding Weil Gotshal's disinterestedness were raised by the official committee of unsecured creditors (the "Creditors' Committee"). A hearing on first interim fee applications had been set for November 4, 1993. Both the Creditors' Committee and the U.S. Trustee filed objections to Weil Gotshal's request for fees on the grounds that Weil Gotshal was not disinterested as required by 11 U.S.C. §327(a) (title 11 of the United States Code hereafter referred to as the "Code") and had failed to file a full and complete disclosure as required by Fed. R. Bankr. P. 2014.[2]

Weil Gotshal responded to the objections by asserting that it had met the Code's disinterestedness requirement and had fully satisfied its disclosure obligations in its retention affidavit. In addition, Weil Gotshal submitted a supplemental affidavit

---

2. Rule 2014 deals with applications for professional employment in bankruptcy cases and requires "a verified statement of the person to be employed setting forth the person's connections with the debtor, creditors, or any other party in interest, their respective attorneys and accountants, the United States trustee, or any person employed in the office of the United States trustee."

containing information regarding certain of its previously-undisclosed relationships that had been questioned by the Creditors' Committee.

C. Appointment of the Examiner

On December 2, 1993, in response to the cloud hovering over Weil Gotshal's representation of the debtors, Leslie Fay moved for the appointment of an examiner to look into Weil Gotshal's disclosure and disinterestedness and the veracity of the Audit Committee's report in light of those issues. The Creditors' Committee agreed that I should appoint an examiner, but asked that the scope of the examiner's retention be expanded beyond that proposed by Leslie Fay. On December 16, 1993, I ordered the appointment of an examiner who would be charged with two tasks, the first of which was undertak[ing] such investigation and analyses as are necessary to formulate a recommendation to the Court as to whether the law firm of Weil, Gotshal & Manges, in its capacity as attorneys for the Debtors in Possession herein, under the circumstances of these Chapter 11 cases and in accordance with section 327 of the Bankruptcy Code and Rule 2014 of the Federal Rules of Bankruptcy Procedure, is disinterested or holds or represents an interest adverse to the Debtors' estates or made adequate disclosure. The second task assigned to the examiner was to evaluate whether (i) there were any viable claims that could be asserted against any other parties in connection with the accounting irregularities that could increase the size of the chapter 11 estate; and (ii) whether the Audit Committee's work in that regard had been acceptable or if further investigating was necessary. I approved the appointment of Charles A. Stillman as examiner on January 18, 1994. Over the next six months, the examiner conducted a thorough investigation into Weil Gotshal's alleged conflicts and into the Audit Committee's investigation of the accounting irregularities.

D. What the Examiner Found

1. The Audit Committee Membership

The disclosure of the accounting irregularities in early 1993 prompted a flurry of litigation. Weil Gotshal represented the Audit Committee members with respect to some of these matters. Class actions were filed charging certain officers and directors, including members of the Audit Committee, with securities fraud (the "Securities Fraud Litigation"), on the grounds that, as members of the Audit Committee, they knew or should have known of the irregularities, and that the irregularities caused a precipitous drop in the price of Leslie Fay stock. Weil Gotshal represented the Audit Committee in these actions, negotiating an agreement to drop the members' names from the litigation, subject to certain conditions. In addition, a shareholder's derivative suit was commenced in state court (the "Derivative Suit"), charging the Audit Committee with essentially the same impropriety that the Securities Fraud Litigation alleged. Weil Gotshal accepted service of process on behalf of the Audit Committee members, but had done nothing more with regard to this lawsuit prior to Weil Gotshal's retention in the Chapter 11 cases.[3]

2.   Weil Gotshal's Relationships with the Potential Targets of Its Investigation

Whereas prior to Weil Gotshal's retention by the Audit Committee it had never represented Leslie Fay, it did maintain professional and personal relationships with parties that had an interest in the outcome of the Audit Committee investigation. Yet none of these relationships was disclosed to the court.

a.   Tarnopol/Bear Stearns

Michael L. Tarnopol is a director of Leslie Fay and was a member of the Audit Committee throughout the period when the accounting irregularities were taking place. He is also a senior officer at Bear Stearns. Bear Stearns, a large investment bank, is a valuable client of Weil Gotshal, and was so at the time of Weil Gotshal's retention by Leslie Fay. Weil Gotshal admitted to the examiner that it would not initiate a lawsuit against Bear Stearns on behalf of another client without Bear Stearns' consent.

Bear Stearns was the lead underwriter in a secondary public offering of 2.1 million shares of Leslie Fay stock, then valued at approximately $40 million (the "Stock Sale") in June, 1991, well after the accounting irregularities began.

The examiner concluded that Tarnopol was a potential target of the Audit Committee's investigation.

b.   Friedman/Odyssey

Steven Friedman is a director of Leslie Fay who was appointed to the Audit Committee when the accounting irregularities came to light. At the time of Weil Gotshal's retention, he was also a general partner of Odyssey. Odyssey is another longstanding client of Weil Gotshal, one against whom Weil Gotshal also would not initiate suit absent the client's consent. Additionally, Odyssey and Friedman were the owners of the 2.1 million shares that were the subject of the Stock Sale.

Weil Gotshal also represented Friedman personally, providing him with estate planning services in 1988 and 1989. It has done the same for other Odyssey partners. Moreover, two other Odyssey partners had served on Leslie Fay's Board of Directors during the period of the accounting irregularities.

The examiner found that Friedman, like Tarnopol, was a potential target of the Audit Committee's investigation.

---

3. The Justice Department got into the act as well, commencing an investigation into the accounting fraud at Leslie Fay. The Audit Committee assured the United States Attorney of its intent to fully cooperate with the investigation. Typically, Weil Gotshal was responsible for responding to information requests by the U.S. Attorney on behalf of the Audit Committee.

c. BDO Seidman

Seidman was Leslie Fay's independent auditor during the period of the accounting irregularities. It was Seidman that had certified Leslie Fay's false financial statements. That Seidman was a natural target of the Audit Committee's investigation is obvious. Not surprisingly, Seidman was a party to both the Securities Fraud Litigation and the Derivative Suit. Seidman is also a Weil Gotshal client, albeit on a much smaller scale than Bear Stearns or Odyssey. Weil Gotshal has represented Seidman in two matters. One matter involved the nonpublic investigation of a former Seidman client by a federal regulatory agency. Weil Gotshal assisted Seidman in furnishing documents requested by that agency. That matter was inactive at the time of Weil Gotshal's retention by Leslie Fay. Weil Gotshal also represented Seidman in a malpractice lawsuit commenced against Seidman in June, 1992. As of the date of Weil Gotshal's retention by court order, the case was still active, although the amount of fees involved in that case was relatively small.

3. Weil Gotshal's Undisclosed Representation of Leslie Fay's Seventh Largest Creditor

At the time of Weil Gotshal's retention, Forstmann & Co. ("Forstmann") was Leslie Fay's seventh largest creditor, with a claim of approximately $700,000. It subsequently sold its claim and resigned from the Creditors' Committee. Weil Gotshal was general outside counsel to Forstmann through 1991 and since then has served Forstmann in a more limited role, nonetheless continuing to represent Forstmann on a variety of matters.

E. The Extent of Weil Gotshal's Disclosure

In connection with Weil Gotshal's retention application of April 5, 1993, Alan B. Miller, a partner of the firm, submitted an affidavit of retention to the court in which he professed that, to the best of his knowledge, Weil Gotshal did not "hold[] or represent[] any interest adverse to the debtors or their estates in the matters upon which [Weil Gotshal] was to be employed." The affidavit disclosed that Weil Gotshal had been working for the Audit Committee, had counseled Leslie Fay with regard to its efforts to restructure its debt, and had assisted it in the filing of the Chapter 11 petitions. The affidavit also disclosed generally that Weil Gotshal represented entities that were "claimants of the Debtors in matters totally unrelated to the Debtors' cases." Some examples of those claimants were listed, although Forstmann was not one of them. (Even after the Creditors' Committee was formed and Forstmann was made a member, Weil Gotshal did not disclose its representation of Forstmann.) In addition, the affidavit contained the boilerplate statement that Weil Gotshal was involved in numerous unrelated matters with attorneys and accountants that represented parties-in-interest in the Chapter 11 cases, but that none of those relationships was adverse to Leslie Fay.

Weil Gotshal did not disclose, however, that it had professional relationships with individual Audit Committee members. It did not disclose that it represented Bear

Stearns and Odyssey, and that those companies were connected to Friedman and Tarnopol, respectively. It did not disclose Bear Stearns' and Odyssey's relationship to the Stock Sale. Similarly, Weil Gotshal did not disclose its relationship with Seidman, despite the fact that, even at the time, Weil Gotshal recognized that Leslie Fay might have claims against Seidman.

F.   The Examiner's Conclusions

The examiner concluded that "Weil Gotshal was not disinterested in the matter, and did not make proper disclosure, as mandated by the Bankruptcy Code and related provisions." (Ex. Report at 3). Specifically, he found that Weil Gotshal had failed to disclose its relationship to two of the members of the Audit Committee and the firms of which they were partners, to Seidman and to one of the debtors' largest unsecured creditors. And he concluded that these undisclosed relationships, if known, would have cast substantial doubt on whether Weil Gotshal could conduct a fair and impartial investigation for the Audit Committee. However, he also found that "[t]he conflict presented [was] principally one of perception: under all the circumstances, there [was] a fair perception that because of multiple representations and client relationships, Weil Gotshal would be unable to act solely in the debtors' best interests." (Ex. Report at 3). According to the examiner, Weil Gotshal caused the debtors no actual injury, and represented them in an exemplary fashion. Thus, he concluded, the appropriate sanction would be the disallowance out of future fees of some of the cost of his investigation into Weil Gotshal's disinterestedness and disclosure, but he recommended that "disqualifying Weil Gotshal, or imposing a sanction beyond such limited allowance of fees, [was] not warranted." Id.

II.

The U.S. Trustee took a different view of things and on October 19, 1994, moved to disqualify Weil Gotshal from serving as counsel to the debtor in possession and for the imposition of economic sanctions. The U.S. Trustee bases his motion upon the findings of the examiner, disagreeing, however, with his conclusion that no actual harm accrued to Leslie Fay. Although the U.S. Trustee does not question the examiner's opinion that Weil Gotshal vigorously represented Leslie Fay, he believes that Weil Gotshal's asserted lack of disinterestedness called the integrity of the Audit Committee's investigation into question, regardless of how thoroughly the investigation was actually performed. According to the U.S. Trustee, "when the credibility of an action by the Debtors' counsel is an integral element of the very task to be performed — as it was in this case — any 'conflict' which exists in performing that function causes actual harm." (U.S. Trustee Mot. to Disqualify at 20).

In response to the U.S. Trustee's motion, Weil Gotshal vigorously denies that it ever had any conflict of interest or that it did not meet its disclosure obligations.

In Weil Gotshal's view, "the U.S. Trustee's allegations are simply wrong as a matter of fact and law." (Weil Gotshal Memorandum of Law at 2). Trying to turn the defense of its actions into an attack on the motives of those who have raised any question, Weil Gotshal has labeled the initial Creditors' Committee challenge as a pressure tactic and the U.S. Trustee's motion as a vindictive action prompted by certain newspaper articles which must have been unsettling to the Trustee. This is somewhat startling given the existence of a report by an independent examiner which concluded that there was substance to the concerns first voiced by the Creditors' Committee.

Perhaps ironically, the Creditors' Committee now opposes the U.S. Trustee's motion, at least to the extent that it seeks to disqualify Weil Gotshal. As mentioned earlier, the Creditors' Committee fears grave harm to Leslie Fay, and, by extension, its creditors, stockholders and employees, should Weil Gotshal be disqualified. The Committee's preferred remedy is an economic sanction. The Official Committee of Equity Security Holders (the "Equity Committee") essentially concurs with the Creditors' Committee, admitting that disclosure was not complete but recommending that disqualification is unwarranted.

III.

There are two grounds upon which the U.S. Trustee bases his motion, first, that Weil Gotshal did not make the complete disclosure mandated by Fed. R. Bankr. P. 2014 and second, that Weil Gotshal was in fact not disinterested at the time of its retention in the Chapter 11 cases, in violation of section 327(a) of the Code. The legal standards governing each theory are distinct and deserve separate attention. The facts to which the law must be applied will follow the discussion of the legal standards.

A. Legal Standards Governing Retention

Section 327(a) of the Code, quoted earlier in this decision, seemingly imposes two requirements on a trustee or debtor in possession seeking to employ counsel: (i) that the attorney does not hold or represent an interest adverse to the estate and (ii) that the attorney is disinterested. The word "disinterested" is a term of art, defined in section 101(14) of the Code as, among other things, not having "an *interest materially adverse* to the interest of the estate . . ." (emphasis added). It is from this immediately apparent that the statutory definition of "disinterested" includes the first prong of the requirements for retention under section 327(a) (although the definition of "disinterested" includes the concept of materiality, which is not mentioned in section 327). Thus, the First Circuit has noted that "the twin requirements of disinterestedness and lack of adversity telescope into a single hallmark." In re Martin, 817 F.2d 175, 181 (1st Cir. 1987); *see also* In re BH & P, Inc., 949 F.2d 1300, 1314 (3d Cir. 1991).

The requirements of section 327 cannot be taken lightly, for they "serve the important policy of ensuring that all professionals appointed pursuant to [the section] tender undivided loyalty and provide untainted advice and assistance in furtherance of their fiduciary responsibilities." Rome v. Braunstein, 19 F.3d 54, 58 (1st Cir. 1994). "Once counsel is employed, 'a lawyer owes his allegiance to the entity and not to the stockholder, director, officer, employee, representative or other person connected with the entity.'" In re Grabill Corp., 113 B.R. 966, 970 (Bankr. N.D. Ill. 1990) quoting In re King Resources Co., 20 B.R. 191, 200 (D. Colo. 1982). Concern with the proper attention to fiduciary obligation has prompted a major treatise on bankruptcy to observe that section 327's standards "are to be rigidly applied." 2 L. King, Collier on Bankruptcy, ¶327.03 (15th ed. 1994).

The Code does not attempt to define what constitutes an adverse interest. However, interests are not considered "adverse" merely because it is possible to conceive a set of circumstances under which they might clash. *See* TWI International, Inc. v. Vanguard Oil and Service Co., 162 B.R. 672, 675 (S.D.N.Y. 1994) (conflicts that are "hypothetical or theoretical" not a basis for disqualification); In re Kelton Motors, Inc., 109 B.R. 641, 650 (Bankr. D. Vt. 1989). The more difficult area is when a live conflict of interest has not quite emerged, yet the factual scenario is sufficiently susceptible to that possibility so as to make the conflict more than merely "hypothetical or theoretical." The courts have been far from uniform in the way they have formulated tests for dealing with this type of situation.

A handful of courts has held or implied that only "actual," and not "potential," conflicts of interest are disabling. (Citations omitted.) A greater number of courts, including some in this district, have concluded that even "potential" conflicts of interest are disabling. (Citations omitted.) Yet other courts have been critical of the very distinction between actual and potential conflicts. *See, e.g.*, In re Kendavis Indus. International, Inc., 91 B.R. 742, 744, 755-56 (Bankr. N.D. Tex. 1988). Recently, in *TWI International*, decided in the Southern District of New York, 162 B.R. at 675, the district court stated that "'disqualification should be mandated when an actual, as opposed to hypothetical or theoretical, conflict is present. This in no way precludes disqualification for a potential conflict. The test is merely one of a *potential actual conflict*.'" Id., quoting In re Wm. J. O'Connor, 52 B.R. 892, 897 (Bankr. W.D. Okla. 1985).

The debate over this issue may be more semantic than substantive, for a close review of the cited cases indicates that the results were largely driven by the facts of each case. And indeed, in the context of section 327, that is precisely the way it should be. (Citations omitted.) Potential conflicts, no less than actual ones, can provide motives for attorneys to act in ways contrary to the best interests of their clients. Rather than worry about the potential/actual dichotomy it is more productive to ask whether a professional has "either a meaningful incentive to act contrary to the best interests of the estate and its sundry creditors — an incentive sufficient to place those parties at more than acceptable risk — or the reasonable perception of one." In re Martin, 817 F.2d at 180-81. In other words, if it is plausible that the representation of another interest may cause the debtor's attorneys to act any differently than they would without that other representation, then they have a conflict and an interest adverse to the estate. . . .

C. The Application of the Law to the Facts

1. Weil Gotshal Represented Interests that Were Materially Adverse to the Debtors at the Time of Its Retention

Leslie Fay's bankruptcy, while certainly not unique, was at least unusual in that it was a direct consequence of fraud that had been perpetrated against the company, its shareholders, and its creditors. When the petitions were filed on April 5, 1993, the Audit Committee was far from completing the investigation it had undertaken; thus there was no way to be sure of the extent of the irregularities, or whether others besides Kenia and Polishan may have been involved. The Justice Department had already begun a criminal investigation into the fraud, and private party civil suits had also been commenced naming, among others, Leslie Fay's directors and its accountants. Because Weil Gotshal was requesting retention not only as Leslie Fay's general bankruptcy counsel but also to complete an investigation into a fraud which may have reached into senior management or even the board of directors, it was especially important that the court ensure that counsel was completely disinterested. Thus, it was incumbent upon Weil Gotshal to be particularly thorough in its retention affidavit. Unfortunately, Weil Gotshal failed to give the court the ability to consider whether the firm had disabling conflicts. At the time of its retention, Weil Gotshal had significant ties to three potential targets of investigation, and yet told neither the court nor the U.S. Trustee.

Weil Gotshal's connections to Tarnopol and Friedman were not insignificant, as Weil Gotshal would have this court find. Both held positions in the highest tiers of Bear Stearns and Odyssey, respectively, which were large and valuable clients of Weil Gotshal. Thus, Weil Gotshal had a perceptible economic incentive not to pursue the possibility of claims against Tarnopol and Friedman with the same vigor and intensity it might have otherwise applied.

Weil Gotshal does not deny that it would not have been disinterested had there been viable claims against Tarnopol and Friedman, but rather contends that by the time it had been retained on April 5, it was clear that no such claims existed. This is said to be so for a number of reasons. First, the Audit Committee was already nine weeks into its investigation, and no evidence had turned up to implicate the Audit Committee or the Board of Directors. Second, according to Weil Gotshal, the scope of liability for outside directors under Delaware law is so narrow that any claims against them were "speculative and hypothetical." I disagree on both counts.

Weil Gotshal relies heavily on the fact that,

> [d]uring the interviews conducted prior to the commencement of Chapter 11 proceedings, Mr. Kenia admitted that the adjustments to Leslie Fay's financial records were made at his direction. He also stated that the adjustments were made without the knowledge or participation of the independent auditors or the Board of Directors.

(Weil Gotshal Memo. of Law in Opposition to U.S. Trustee's Motion at 34). It is amazing that Weil Gotshal would give so much weight to the "admission" of a man who had committed wholesale fraud upon the company whose finances it was his job to protect, and who had already lied at least once by denying Polishan's involvement in the fraud. As it so happens, it was later discovered "that the adjustments had taken place over a longer time than previously asserted by Mr. Kenia," (Weil Gotshal Memo. of Law at 14) further confirmation that Kenia was not to be taken at his word.[4] Moreover, I am unpersuaded that Weil Gotshal could have been certain of the outcome of the Audit Committee's investigation in April, when that investigation would not be completed until September. By its own admission, Weil Gotshal did not realize the full scope of the accounting irregularities until the middle of May. Id. In light of all this, Weil Gotshal's claim that it knew at the time of its court-approved retention that the outside directors could not have been liable rings hollow.

It is true that the outside directors had significant protections under Delaware law, *see generally*, Donald E. Pease, Outside Directors: Their Importance to the Corporation and Protection from Liability, 12 Del. J. Corp. L. 25 (1987), but that is a far cry from saying that they could under no circumstances have been found liable. For example, because the investigation was not nearly completed as of the petition date, it is impossible to say for certain that the directors had not been "reckless," which, as the examiner pointed out and Weil Gotshal did not deny, might provide a basis of liability under Delaware law. *See, e.g.*, Bell Atlantic Corp. v. Bolger, 2 F.3d 1304, 1312 (3d Cir. 1993); Solash v. Telex Corp., 1988 WL 3587, *8 (Del. Ch. Jan. 19, 1988). Apparently, the outside directors thought enough of their potential liability to file indemnification claims against Leslie Fay in this court. At any rate, I do not deny that Weil Gotshal may have had an honest belief in the likely immunity of Leslie Fay's outside directors. "The point, however, is that such a determination must be made by the counsel who is in a position to make an independent judgment." *Bohack*, 607 F.2d at 263. And here, the attorneys with the entanglements were the ones who were determining whether Leslie Fay would have claims against the outside directors. . . .

I also find that Weil Gotshal was not disinterested relative to Seidman. Seidman was Leslie Fay's independent auditor throughout the period of the irregularities, and was therefore a very obvious target of potential plaintiffs. Indeed, Seidman was named in both the Derivative Suit and the Securities Fraud Litigation. Weil Gotshal does not deny this, nor does it deny that Leslie Fay may still have claims against Seidman. Rather, it defends its disinterestedness by pointing to the relative insignificance of Seidman as a client to Weil Gotshal. (At the time of Leslie Fay's Chapter 11 filing, Weil Gotshal was representing Seidman with regard to two matters, one of which was already inactive and one which subsequently became so, and the total fees in those cases approximated $40,000.) The short answer to this is that Weil Gotshal should be presumed to be loyal to its client. That the client may not be a major client is no reason to think that Weil Gotshal would ignore the relationship.

In any event, the size of the billing is irrelevant for another reason as well. Dennis J. Block, a Weil Gotshal partner, admitted in a deposition conducted by the examiner that Weil Gotshal would not have sued Seidman even if the facts warranted it.

---

4. This means, too, that Weil Gotshal could not and did not know when it was retained by court order whether Leslie Fay might have any claims against Bear Stearns, Odyssey and Friedman arising out of the Stock Sale, another area in which Weil Gotshal had entanglements.

This, stated Block, was because Weil Gotshal represented accountants and "as a matter of Weil Gotshal policy," would therefore "not sue an accounting firm, period." (Dep. of Dennis J. Block at 126-27). Block testified that Weil Gotshal "told the audit committee and the board" of this policy, and had further told them:

> [I]f in fact it turned out that there would be a reason to take action against Seidman we would look at the facts, we'd tell them what the facts are but that would be something, ultimately, one, [sic] we'd be unwilling to handle because we don't sue accounting firms and that would be something that the company would have to deal with other counsel on.

Id. at 127. Although Weil Gotshal told the Audit Committee about its policy, it elected not to impart this important information to either myself or the U.S. Trustee, an omission that is simply inexcusable. There are two problems with Weil Gotshal's nondisclosure. Certainly that information was relevant to whether Weil Gotshal's retention was in the best interest of the estate given that it would not sue Seidman and retention of special counsel might have entailed additional cost to the estate. But in addition, this undisclosed condition of employment particularly when coupled with a client relationship with Seidman cast doubt on whether Weil Gotshal was the proper independent counsel to conduct the investigation into Seidman's conduct and possible liability. An unbiased investigation of the facts is no less crucial than an unbiased evaluation of the law in assessing potential claims. By unilaterally reserving the role of investigating Seidman to itself, Weil Gotshal created the "opportunity for the exercise of [its] conflicting interests," by projecting the facts in a light more favorable to Seidman than it should have. In re Codesco, 18 B.R. at 999. I do not say that Weil Gotshal actually did that, nor do I mean to disparage Weil Gotshal's integrity by suggesting that it probably would have. But when evaluating conflicts of interest, I must do so objectively, "irrespective of the integrity of the person under consideration." In re Martin, 817 F.2d at 181.

As Judge Friendly noted in In re Ira Haupt & Co., 361 F.2d 164, 168 (2d Cir. 1966), quoted with approval in *Bohack*, 607 F.2d at 263, "[t]he conduct of bankruptcy proceedings not only should be right but must seem right." And here, Weil Gotshal's conduct of an investigation where it had undisclosed ties to three of the targets just does not seem right. The better solution, as I will expand upon shortly, would have been for Weil Gotshal to decline the Audit Committee's representation. But in any case, once Leslie Fay filed for Chapter 11 relief, it was no longer Weil Gotshal's decision to make. It was for the court, and not Weil Gotshal, to determine whether in fact a conflict existed and, if so, what the remedy should be. The "decision should not be left to counsel, whose judgment may be clouded by the benefits of potential employment." Rome v. Braunstein, 19 F.3d at 59. . . .

2. Weil Gotshal Did Not Make a Complete and Candid Disclosure as Required by Rule 2014, Thereby Causing Actual Injury to Leslie Fay

As I have explained, the requirements of Fed. R. Bankr. P. 2014 are more encompassing than those governing the disinterestedness inquiry under section 327.

For while retention under section 327 is only limited by interests that are "materially adverse," under Rule 2014, "all connections" that are not so remote as to be de minimus must be disclosed. Consequently, there is "no merit to the . . . argument that [a party] did not have to disclose its connections . . . because its attorneys did not feel that a conflict existed." In re Rusty Jones, Inc., 134 B.R. 321, 345 (Bankr. N.D. Ill. 1991). Weil Gotshal had no right to "make a unilateral determination regarding the relevance of a connection." Arlan's, 615 F.2d at 470.

Weil Gotshal urges that it is not necessary to disclose connections to companies with which the members of the debtor's board of directors are affiliated. As a general statement, that may have some validity. But where counsel is being retained to conduct an investigation into the actions of, among others, senior management and the members of the board of directors, most assuredly connections with entities affiliated with board members that could cause pressure on investigating counsel must be disclosed. It is by the same rationale that the connection with Seidman had to be disclosed.

Not only did Weil Gotshal violate Rule 2014 by not disclosing its connections to Friedman, Tarnopol and Seidman, it also violated the rule by not disclosing its connection to Forstmann, one of the largest creditors which served for a short while on the Creditors' Committee. Forstmann had employed Weil Gotshal as its regular counsel through 1991 and was still using Weil Gotshal on a more limited scale at the time of the April 5 filing. This was not merely a *de minimus* connection. The boilerplate language to the effect that Weil Gotshal may have in the past represented, currently represents, and may in the future represent entities which are claimants of the debtors was insufficient to alert the court to Weil Gotshal's representation of a creditor which was high on the list of the debtors' twenty largest creditors (from which list a creditors' committee is normally selected). The boilerplate is reasonable to cover inadvertent failures to disclose insignificant connections; it is not an adequate substitute for disclosure of representation of known and significant creditors. To rule any other way would be to eviscerate the disclosure requirements of Rule 2014(a). At a minimum, the order retaining Weil Gotshal should have carved out from the firm's role the responsibility for considering the *bona fides* of the Forstmann claim and Forstmann's prepetition course of dealing with Leslie Fay. By not disclosing its connection with Forstmann, Weil Gotshal caused the court to skip over an area which deserved some attention.

Weil Gotshal's nondisclosure caused Leslie Fay very real harm. The Creditors' Committee spent time and energy examining Weil Gotshal's relationships to determine if it should request some form of relief. Leslie Fay itself felt compelled to ask for the appointment of an examiner to inquire into Weil Gotshal's compliance with the law. Not only was this examination necessary, but because of Weil Gotshal's undisclosed relationships it was necessary as well for the examiner to insure that Weil Gotshal's work for the Audit Committee was free from reproach. In other words, the examiner had to investigate the investigation. This entailed duplication of much of what Weil Gotshal had already done, at considerable expense to the estate. Weil Gotshal suggests that the Audit Committee's retention of Arthur Andersen was sufficient to "sanitize" the investigation without the necessity of the examiner reviewing the work product. I cannot agree. Whereas the accountants are competent and diligent, their role was to uncover what was wrong with the debtors' books and records, not to determine liability therefor. It was simply beyond their expertise to render any opinion on what claims Leslie Fay might possess arising out of the fraud, and whether it was worthwhile to pursue such claims. At further expense to the estate, the Equity Committee was required to respond to the motion for sanctions so as to protect its constituency. These are tangible costs which Weil Gotshal foisted upon the estate by virtue of its nondisclosure. Thus, we are not faced solely with upholding the integrity of the bankruptcy process, although, of course, that is an important concern as well.

The shame in all of this is that the heavy financial and emotional toll in this matter could have been avoided completely. For had Weil Gotshal revealed its connections at the time it requested court approval of its retention, an examiner could have been appointed early on to review and then complete the Audit Committee's investigation, and, if warranted, special counsel could have been thereafter appointed to institute suit. This arrangement might even have permitted Weil Gotshal's retention, albeit in a narrower role. Unfortunately, Weil Gotshal's silence prevented that from happening. I do not mean to suggest that I believe Weil Gotshal to have been venal. The examiner's report shows that not to have been so. Harvey Miller, the partner from Weil Gotshal who argued this motion, reminded me that he had spent the last 30 years upholding the integrity of this court. I believe him to have been truthful in that statement. But that does not excuse the firm's arrogating to itself the decision as to whether it had a conflict of interest with the case in general or with the Audit Committee investigation in particular. Weil Gotshal was mandated to reveal any connections which might cast any doubt on the wisdom of its retention and leave for the court the determination of whether a conflict existed. It did not comply with that obligation.

D. The Sanctions To Be Granted

The foregoing discussion brings us right back to where I began, with the troubling aspects of this motion. I have wide discretion in my selection of an appropriate remedy. . . .

There is no question but that here the facts, if disclosed, would have led to a legitimate worry that Weil Gotshal could not impartially represent the debtors in their investigation of the financial irregularities and the decisions whether and whom to sue. Because the court was not armed with the facts, there was no meaningful opportunity provided for the court to determine whether to approve or disapprove Weil Gotshal's retention. Plainly, this implicates the integrity of the judicial process by which disinterested counsel is selected. On the other hand, by virtue of the reports prepared by the examiner, we know that Weil Gotshal actually performed the investigation competently and consistent with its fiduciary obligations to the estates. This suggests that the harm to Leslie Fay, which has been a victim first of an accounting scandal and then of a legal one, should assume some importance in the equation by which an appropriate sanction is selected.

Admittedly, in every bankruptcy case the replacement of counsel causes disruption. And to refuse to replace counsel simply because the facts become known only late into the process could perversely encourage professionals to hold back information from the court. But this is a special case, in more ways than one. Unfortunately, only ten days or so ago I reluctantly signed an order authorizing Leslie Fay to pay its debtor-in-possession lender a fee of $500,000 for a one-month amendment to the loan. This was necessitated by Leslie Fay's failure by a substantial margin to meet its projections, in violation of covenants contained in the loan. The information regarding Leslie Fay's financial performance became available only in September and Leslie Fay is now revising its projections and negotiating with the lender for an amendment to the debtor-in-possession financing agreement. Simultaneously, and as part and parcel of the interim agreement with the lender, Leslie Fay is preparing a term sheet for a plan of reorganization which it has committed to present to the Committees by January 15, 1995. Put differently, Leslie Fay is at a critical juncture in its reorganization efforts.

The cases have been here some 20 months. During that time Leslie Fay has endured the forced departure of its financial staff, which is a blow no debtor in possession would willingly suffer; a crippling strike this past summer; and now, financial results which are far from those targeted, necessitating an expensive reevaluation of its business strategy. The financial burdens to Leslie Fay of remaining in chapter 11 are enormous. It may not be able to withstand the great delay and cost occasioned by the departure of the counsel with whom it has worked so long. It must begin the process of emerging from this court.

In an effort to reconcile the twin concerns of preserving the integrity of the bankruptcy process and the viability of the reorganization case, I have determined that I will permit Weil Gotshal to remain in the case to complete what it has begun. That is, Weil Gotshal may see the case through to reorganization and may finish those contested matters and adversary proceedings in which it is presently engaged. New counsel is to be brought in, however, to handle new matters such as litigation regarding claims, any avoidance actions and suits for relief arising out of the accounting irregularities. (To the extent that some of these matters could be handled more efficiently by counsel to one or the other of the committees, rather than special counsel to the debtors, I would consider that as well.) . . . To the extent that Weil Gotshal may be called upon in a limited fashion to provide background to new counsel, I trust that it will not seek to charge this expense to its client, an expense caused solely by Weil Gotshal's conduct.

With respect to the economic sanction which is sought by the U.S. Trustee, relief is plainly warranted there, too, both for nondisclosure and pursuant to section 328 of the Code, which permits the court to deny compensation for services and reimbursement of expenses of a professional person retained pursuant to section 327 if, at any time during that employment, the professional person is not disinterested or holds an adverse interest to the interest of the estate with respect to the matter on which the professional person is employed. Given that I am disqualifying Weil Gotshal from handling new matters, I am limiting the economic sanction to disgorgement of the costs, direct and indirect, of both of the examiner's investigations and of the failure to disclose. This should relieve Leslie Fay of the burden imposed by its counsel. I have insufficient information to fix that number now. The costs are to include, however, not only the approximately $800,000 in fees and expenses incurred by the examiner and his professionals, but also those incurred by the Committees in dealing with Weil Gotshal's relationships and its disqualification or retention, because Leslie Fay would not otherwise have had to bear that expense. I decline to require Weil Gotshal to disgorge the fees paid it in connection with the Audit Committee investigation because that would foist upon Weil Gotshal the cost of not one, but two, investigations. One investigation would have been necessary in any event and was therefore an expense that is not related to Weil Gotshal's nondisclosure. In the event that Weil Gotshal, the Committees and the U.S. Trustee are unable to agree on the sum to be disgorged, they may schedule a further hearing to fix that number.

Conclusion

The motion of the U.S. Trustee is granted in part and denied in part. SETTLE ORDER consistent with this decision.

Section 330, stating rules governing the compensation of those providing services to the bankruptcy estate, was enacted to "guard against a recurrence of the 'sordid chapters' in the history of fees in corporate reorganizations." S. Rep. No. 989, 96th Cong., 2d Sess. 40, reprinted in 1978 U.S. Code Cong. & Admin. News 5787, 5826 (quoting Dickinson Industrial Site, Inc. v. Cowan, 309 U.S. 382, 388, 60 S. Ct. 595, 599, 84 L. Ed. 819 (1940)). The 75th Congress in 1937 had this to say:

> The record of corporate reorganizations . . . is not pleasant. It shows the absolute control exercised over reorganizations by the inside few; it shows the financial well-being of investors and the public sacrificed to the insiders' desire for protection and for profit. . . . It shows that these delays, these futile prolongations of the agony of reorganizations were frequently due to deliberate sabotage by a group which had something to gain and was unwilling to compromise. . . . The record also shows, with overwhelming proof, that plans of reorganization were frequently dictated by a single interest — by a closely knit inside group; primarily in the interests of that group and of dubious wisdom so far as interests outside the inner circle were concerned.

H.R. Rep. No. 1409, 75th Cong., 1st Sess., at 38 (1937) (statement of Justice William O. Douglas).

The courts have not been kind to lawyers and accountants employed in situations in which they clearly could not pass the disinterestedness tests of the Bankruptcy Code. In In re Federated Department Stores, Inc., 44 F.3d 1310 (6th Cir. 1995), the Sixth Circuit completely denied fees to a financial advisor that had been hired to straighten out the fiscal mess of the debtor company. The bankruptcy court had noted that the proposed financial advisor was technically not qualified to serve since it had many past contacts with the debtor in multiple capacities, but had nonetheless allowed the appointment because the proposed advisor was arguably the best in its field and, given that many of the other candidates would have similar conflicts, the bankruptcy court felt that a literal reading of §§101(14) and 327(a) was not required. The Sixth Circuit, pointing to its own earlier ruling against such a reading of these sections, required the financial advisor to disgorge all fees paid after the earlier ruling was handed down.

So, future lawyers, pay attention to the following from Judge Harold C. Abramson in a case in which he required bankruptcy counsel to disgorge 50 percent of the fees already paid:

> To make the Court's holding more concrete, the Court holds that whenever counsel for a debtor corporation has any agreement, express or implied, with management or a director of the debtor, or with a shareholder, or with any control party, to protect the interest of that party, counsel holds a conflict. That conflict is not potential, it is actual, and it arises the date that representation commences. This holding would apply equally to partnerships. An attorney who claims to represent a partnership, but also has some agreement, whether express or implied, with the general or limited partners, or with any control person, to protect its interest, that attorney has an actual conflict of interest, and is subject to disqualification and a disallowance of fees. The concept of *potential* conflicts is a contradiction in terms. Once there is a conflict, it is *actual — not potential.*

In re Kendavis Indus. International, Inc., 91 B.R. 742, 754 (Bankr. N.D. Tex. 1988). Suppose that the relationship is disclosed, and the benefit to the estate outweighs the costs? *See* In re Pittsfield Weaving Co., 355 B.R. 404 (Bankr. D.N.H. 2006) (court permits continued representation of debtor by counsel who represents related parties, but the court also emphasizes that the attorney had not received any retainer).

Finally it should be noted that the 2005 amendments to the Code placed severe new limits on retention bonuses and severance pay for corporate executives trying to fatten their purses in Chapter 11; *see* §503(c). Read that section and the following problem carefully and consider whether Congress has sufficiently closed the loophole or whether the statute simply provides another opportunity for creative drafting of employment agreements.

PROBLEM 9-4

Grandstand Industries, Inc. manufactured heavy equipment for the construction industry. When the economy soured, building projects were abandoned, and Grandstand's sales dropped dramatically. It thinks it can turn the business around, but it wants to make sure that it doesn't lose its best executives to competitors in the industry and to other companies. Can it keep these important employees on hand? Does it matter if the employee is an officer of the corporation? What's the difference between an "incentive bonus" and a "retention bonus"? *See* In re Nellson Neutraceutical, Inc., 369 B.R. 787 (Bankr. D. Del. 2007); Rebecca Revich, The KERP Revolution, 81 Am. Bankr. L.J. 81 (2007).

II. Running the Show

A Chapter 11 filing gives a business breathing room in which to rethink its place in the business world while prepetition creditors furiously twiddle their thumbs. The automatic stay slams down, freezing all creditor action, interest stops accruing on unsecured debts,[5] and the debtor in possession — legally a new entity, though in reality the same folks who were running the company at the moment the petition was filed — embarks on the task of creating a confirmable plan of reorganization. During this period the business will keep on operating, meaning both business as usual (but with all income devoted to the daily expenses of the enterprise, instead of servicing debt), and the making of various choices allowed by the Bankruptcy Code about which practices to continue and which to drop. The text below focuses on this period: postpetition to plan confirmation.

PROBLEM 9-5

Celfones Unchained purchased 80 cases of cellphone covers on credit from Coverall Plastics on May 1. It owes Coverall Plastics $20,000 for this purchase, but Celfones has run out of money. It is considering filing a Chapter 11 bankruptcy petition. The Uniform Commercial Code gives sellers a right to demand return of goods ordered on credit if demand is made within ten days of delivery to the insolvent buyer; UCC §2-702. Can Coverall (which will need the covers to keep the business going in Chapter 11) avoid this by waiting to file until May 15th? *See* Bankruptcy Code §546(c); cf. §503(b)(9).

PROBLEM 9-6

The leveraged buyout of Luddite Technologies so looted the company that it was forced to file a Chapter 11 petition two months after the buyout was completed. The same management that had engineered the leveraged buyout is still in charge of the company in Chapter 11, and now the company president comes to you, the corporate attorney, with this question: can Luddite attack as fraudulent transfers the security interests in the company's assets that were given to the bank that financed the leveraged buyout, or is Luddite estopped from doing so because it voluntarily granted these security interests prior to the filing of the bankruptcy petition?

---

5. For years there was a major battle in the courts as to whether undersecured creditors should be allowed interest during the plan creation and approval period. The argument as to why this should be done was that otherwise the creditor was not getting the value out of the collateral that could have been realized on its immediate foreclosure, sale, and investment of the proceeds. The argument against was based on the language of §506, which has always been read to deny the awarding of postpetition interest on unsecured claims. The United States Supreme Court, in an opinion by Justice "Read the Plain Language of the Statute" Scalia, adopted the latter position in United States Assn. of Texas v. Timbers of Inwood Forest Assn., 484 U.S. 108 (1988). Since that opinion was handed down Congress has allowed interest to undersecured creditors having an interest in single asset real estate where the debtor has filed for reorganization but has not filed a confirmable plan within 90 days; *see* §362(d)(3).

A.   Use, Sale, or Lease of Property of the Estate; Cash Collateral

Stopping creditor collection activity through the operation of the automatic stay gives the debtor a breathing spell. It does not, however, create income. To do that the debtor must continue to operate its business, whatever that may be. Generally, that involves the sale of goods or services. Section 363 of the Bankruptcy Code governs the use, sale, or lease of property of the estate. It provides, among other things, that the debtor[6] may use, sell, or lease property of the estate other than in the ordinary course of business after notice and a hearing. A Chapter 11 debtor in possession operating its business may enter into these transactions in the ordinary course of business without any court approval or notice to creditors. This is true even if creditors have a security interest in or mortgage on the property that the debtor intends to use. There is, however, a significant limitation on this power. If the property that the debtor intends to use is "cash collateral," then the use, sale, or lease of the property is permissible only if the secured creditor consents to the treatment, or the court, after notice and hearing, authorizes the transaction; §363(c)(2).

Cash collateral is "cash, negotiable instruments, documents of title, securities, deposit accounts, or other cash equivalents in which the estate and an entity other than the estate have an interest and includes the proceeds, products, offspring, rents, or profits of property [including hotel fees]. . . ." Given this definition, a debtor whose inventory is subject to a security interest in favor of a lender must be prepared to deal with that creditor's claim under §363(c). Even though the inventory is not cash collateral, it will soon be transmuted into cash collateral.

If the debtor is able to sell its inventory for cash and collect its accounts receivable the debtor is obligated to "segregate and account" for that cash collateral. §363(c)(4). The Code recognizes that a creditor's claim that is secured by cash collateral is much more vulnerable than a claim that is secured by "hard assets." Consequently, the Code requires first that the cash collateral be segregated, and second that the debtor obtain court authorization prior to its use. Debtors obtain approval to use cash collateral generally by entering into agreements with the creditor permitting that use. The following case provides a fairly detailed description of the kinds of provisions that the debtor and a creditor might agree upon to permit the use of cash collateral.

In re JKJ Chevrolet, Inc.

United States Bankruptcy Court, Eastern District of Virginia, 1995
190 B.R. 542

Martin V.B. Bostetter, Jr., Chief Judge.

On July 8, 1992, this Court entered an order authorizing the debtor, JKJ Chevrolet, Inc., to use Ford Motor Credit Corporation's ("Ford Credit") cash collateral to

---

6. Section 363(b)(1) refers to the trustee, but the debtor in possession in Chapter 11 cases has the powers of a trustee including the power to use, sell, or lease property under §363.

pay its employees for work performed prior to the sale of the debtor's business on March 10, 1992. Ford Credit appealed the July 8th order to the United States District Court for the Eastern District of Virginia. The District Court remanded the matter instructing this Court to make a finding as to whether Ford Credit received adequate protection for its security interest.

For the reasons set forth below, we find that Ford Credit was adequately protected to enable the debtor to use cash collateral pursuant to section 363 of the Bankruptcy Code.

I. Facts

The debtor, JKJ Chevrolet, Inc., was an automobile dealership located in Northern Virginia which was formerly controlled by John W. Koons, Jr. On October 21, 1991, the debtor filed a voluntary petition under Chapter 11 of the Bankruptcy Code. The debtor continued operating its business pursuant to §§1107 and 1108 of the Code. The schedules listed Ford Credit as having a secured claim in the amount of $14,541,372.40. Ford Credit is the primary secured creditor of the debtor by virtue of various security and other agreements under which Ford Credit provided floorplan financing to the debtor for its motor vehicle inventory. Under the terms of the security agreements, Ford Credit held a first priority security interest in virtually all the debtors' assets. In order to continue operating its business, the debtor required the use of Ford Credit's cash collateral. During the course of the debtor's Chapter 11 case, Ford Credit and the debtor entered into three consent orders that authorized the debtor to use Ford Credit's cash collateral, subject to certain restrictions.[7]

The final consent order granted Ford Credit relief from the stay effective March 10, 1992, the same date that this Court approved the sale of the assets of the debtor to James E. Koons. Following the sale, Ford Credit took control of the debtor's funds, and in particular, "seized" the paychecks of the debtor's employees. On April 16, 1992, the debtor filed a motion seeking permission to use the funds seized by Ford Credit to pay its employees approximately $297,525.60 in post-petition wages, commissions, employee benefits and payroll taxes for work performed through March 10, 1992.

Ford Credit opposed the debtor's motion. Following an evidentiary hearing on June 2, 1992, this Court granted the debtor's motion and authorized the debtor to pay its employees' salaries and commissions, employee benefits and payroll taxes aggregating $209,179.51. On September 29, 1992, we denied Ford Credit's motion to alter and amend the judgment. Ford Credit appealed to the United States District Court for the Eastern District of Virginia. On September 17, 1993, the District Court remanded the matter, instructing this Court to make a finding as to whether Ford Credit was

---

7. The consent orders were made final by order dated February 18, 1992 (the "final consent order"). The final consent order authorized the debtor to operate its business in the ordinary course, subject to the terms and conditions specified in the order. Specifically, the final consent order provided that the debtor "shall pay, but only from Available Cash Collateral, all post-petition wages, employee benefits and employer contributions to employee benefit plans when due." Final Order P 14(f). Thus, payment of employee wages was explicitly authorized by order of this Court.

adequately protected. On February 28, 1994, Ford Credit filed a motion to reopen the record on remand. The debtor opposed the motion, and a hearing was held on April 12, 1994. Following oral argument on April 12th, we ruled from the bench that it was not necessary to reopen the record and took the matter under advisement.

II. Discussion

In order to protect the interests of secured creditors, the Bankruptcy Code imposes limitations on a debtor's use of property in attempting to reorganize. Section 363 of the Code limits the debtor's ability to use "cash collateral." Section 363 of the Code states in relevant part:

> (2) The trustee may not use . . . cash collateral . . . unless — (A) each entity that has an interest in such cash collateral consents; or (B) the court, after notice and a hearing, authorizes such use . . . in accordance with the provisions of this section.

11 U.S.C. §363.

Ford Credit withdrew its consent to the debtor's use of cash collateral under the terms of the final consent order when it seized the employees' paychecks on March 10, 1992. Alternatively, Ford Credit's consent expired upon the termination of the final consent order by its own terms on March 10th. The final consent order expressly provides that "[a]ny extension of debtor's right to use cash collateral beyond [the] termination date, [i.e., March 10, 1992] without Ford Credit's consent shall be subject to (a) approval by this Court upon request by Debtor for continued use of cash collateral after notice to Ford Credit and an opportunity to be heard." Final Order at ¶22. Therefore, the only means by which the debtor would be allowed to use cash collateral is with this Court's authorization. Our authority to permit the use of cash collateral is governed by §363(c) which requires a finding of adequate protection under §363(e).

At the outset, we note that we reject Ford Credit's argument that because the cash collateral order expired on March 10, 1992, the debtors could not subsequently seek authority to use funds to pay operating expenses incurred prior to March 10th, but not due until after March 10th. Moreover, as noted above, the express terms of the final consent order addressed the debtor's right to seek court authority to use cash collateral beyond the termination date. This Court is not inclined to implement such a rigid approach to the reorganization process. Ford Credit benefitted from the work performed by the debtor's employees up to and including March 10, 1992. The happenstance of the expiration of the cash collateral order before the wages were actually paid should not preclude payment of wages due employees. *See* In re Phoenix Pipe and Tube, L.P., 174 B.R. 688, 689-90 (E.D. Pa. 1994) (secured creditor prohibited from objecting to expenses to which they expressly consented; debtor authorized to use cash collateral to pay employees for work performed through date of expiration of cash collateral order).

In our order of July 8, 1992, we authorized the debtor to use Ford Credit's cash collateral in the amount of $209,179.51 for wages, employee benefits and payroll taxes incurred through March 10, 1992. In ruling from the bench, we specifically found that there was sufficient evidence that on March 10, 1992, approximately $240,000 was available cash collateral. Further, the evidence revealed that Ford Credit benefitted from the work performed by the employees in that the business continued to operate as a going concern through March 10th, and therefore, the value of Ford Credit's all-encompassing security interest was, at the very least, maintained. Accordingly, we concluded that the debtor was authorized to use cash collateral to pay the employees who had worked to keep the business operating.

The question remains, however, was Ford Credit "adequately protected"? Ford Credit asserts that the evidence adduced at the June 2nd hearing indicates that a "collateral shortfall" existed as of February 22, 1992, and therefore, it was not "adequately protected." Paragraph 7(b) of the final consent order defines "collateral shortfall" as follows:

> b. If at any time the value of the Debtor's cash, cash equivalents, inventory, Eligible Accounts Receivable (defined below) and other collateral subject to Ford Credit's liens and security interest is less than the value of the same categories of collateral as of October 21, 1991 (a "Collateral Shortfall"), the Debtor's authority to use Available Cash Collateral shall immediately cease. . . .

At the June 2nd trial, Ford Credit put on evidence prepared by Coopers & Lybrand that between October 22, 1991 (the petition date) and February 22, 1992, its collateral position dropped by $432,983. We decline to equate Ford Credit's definition of "collateral shortfall" with lack of "adequate protection" as required by §363(e).

Adequate protection is a flexible concept that is determined by considering the facts of each case. *See* In re O'Connor, 808 F.2d 1393, 1396-97 (10th Cir. 1987) (" 'adequate protection' [is] a concept which is to be decided flexibly on the proverbial 'case-by-case' basis"). While section 361 does not itself address the issue of the date of valuation of a creditor's collateral for purposes of determining whether adequate protection exists, the House Report discussion of the language of section 361 explains:

> The section does not specify how value is to be determined, nor does it specify when it is to be determined. These matters are left to case-by-case interpretation and development. It is expected that the courts will apply the concept in light of the facts of each case and general equitable principles.
>
> It is not intended that the courts will develop a hard and fast rule that will apply in every case. The time and method of valuation is not specified precisely, in order to avoid that result. . . . [F]lexibility is important to permit the courts to adapt to varying circumstances and changing modes of financing.

H.R. Rep. No. 95-595, 95th Cong., 1st Sess. 339 (1978), reprinted in 1978 U.S.C.C.A.N. 5963, 6295; *see also* Paccom Leasing Co. v. Deico Electronics (In re Deico Electronics, Inc.), 139 B.R. 945, 947 (9th Cir. BAP 1992). Thus, "the protection afforded a creditor whose cash collateral is permitted by the Court to be used by a debtor in possession is whatever condition is deemed necessary to provide adequate protection of the creditor's interest." In re Quality Beverage Co., Inc., 181 B.R. 887, 896 (Bankr. S.D. Tex. 1995).

Section 361 of the Code provides three non-exclusive means of providing adequate protection. These alternatives include requiring the debtor to make a cash payment or periodic cash payments to the extent of a decrease in the value of the property. 11 U.S.C. §361(1). Alternatively, the debtor may provide an additional or replacement lien to the extent of a decrease in the value of the property. 11 U.S.C. §361(2). Lastly, adequate protection may be provided by granting other relief that will result in the indubitable equivalent of the interest in the property. 11 U.S.C. §361(3).

As adequate protection to Ford Credit for allowing the debtor to use its cash collateral, the debtor provided all three forms of adequate protection expressly provided for under §361. The final consent order required the debtor to make adequate protection payments, grant adequate protection liens, and imposed significant terms and conditions on the debtor's ability to use its cash collateral. Some of those terms and conditions included the following:

1. The order required the debtor to maintain a segregated bank account and deposit into the account on a daily basis all cash, checks, and cash equivalents from any source. Final Order ¶2.
2. The order required the debtor to remit to Ford Credit all proceeds from the sales of floorplan vehicles within 2 business days after the sale. Final Order ¶4.
3. The order required the debtor to maintain a second segregated bank account for all proceeds from the sale of non-floorplan vehicles. The debtor could use Ford Credit's cash collateral from this account only to the extent that the cash collateral did not exceed the debtor's profits from sales of vehicles, sales of parts and services, operation of the finance and insurance sections, and operation of the rental vehicle division (defined in the order as "Available Cash Collateral"). Final Order ¶¶4(d), 6.
4. Ford Credit claimed all "certificates of origin" and "certificates of title" relating to vehicles that remained on the debtor's lot after October 22, 1991. Final Order ¶5.
5. The order provided for a Ford Credit representative to remain on the debtor's premises to observe all sales transactions and to inspect its collateral. Additionally, the order required the debtor to keep Ford Credit informed of all business transactions occurring after normal business hours, and to make its books, records, and financial information available to Ford Credit representatives and its accountants. Final Order ¶9.
6. "As further adequate protection," the order granted Ford Credit a "valid first security interest in all of [the] debtor's post-petition accounts, accounts receivable . . . , inventory, parts, motor vehicles of all kinds, . . . rebates from manufacturers, contract rights, profits and proceeds from the sale of vehicles, parts and performance of labor . . . and also any value in vehicle trade-ins and all products and proceeds thereof. . . ." Final Order ¶15.
7. Finally, the debtor was required to provide weekly collateral summaries to Ford Credit which included a statement of the debtor's cash and cash equivalents, an inventory of vehicles and parts and an aging report on all outstanding accounts receivable. Final Order ¶7.

Ford Credit correctly asserts that the ultimate burden of proof on the issue of adequate protection lies with the debtor. 11 U.S.C. §363(o)(1). We find that the debtor has met its burden. The testimony at the June 2nd hearing indicated that the debtor was at all times in compliance with the terms and conditions outlined above. There has been no suggestion that the debtor was uncooperative, that payments were not timely made or that the debtor failed to operate its business in a commercially reasonable manner. Moreover, a representative of Ford Credit was present at the dealership every day overseeing the debtor's business operations. It was not until after the sale of the business that Ford Credit asserted that notwithstanding that all of its requirements were in place, at some point during the course of the reorganization its collateral position fell. Ford Credit further contends that although they drafted the "adequate protection" requirements of the final consent order, the debtor is somehow now required to prove some "additional" adequate protection existed. We find Ford Credit's position disingenuous.

At the June 2nd hearing, the debtor adduced sufficient evidence to show that it was complying with the conditions of the final consent order as required by Ford Credit. John Koons, III, debtor's general manager, testified that to the best of his knowledge, the debtor was complying with the terms and conditions set forth in the cash collateral orders. Tr. at 25, 27, 66. He testified that there was a representative from Ford Credit at the dealership during the entire time the cash collateral orders were in effect monitoring the day to day operations and making sure that they were in compliance with the cash collateral orders. Tr. at 25-28. Further, Mr. Koons testified that at no time before March 10th did a Ford Credit representative inform him that the debtor was not in compliance with the cash collateral orders. Tr. at 66. Harry Moore, branch manager for Ford Motor Credit, confirmed Mr. Koons' testimony that a representative from Ford Credit was present at the dealership every day monitoring the operations in accordance with the cash collateral order. Tr. at 75.

The only evidence that the debtor was not in conformity with the cash collateral orders was the testimony of Frederick Miller, an accountant with Coopers & Lybrand. Mr. Miller testified for Ford Credit that the weekly financial reports required to be submitted to Ford Credit by the debtor under paragraph 9 of the final consent order were not accurate. Tr. at 84. However, Mr. Koons testified that he prepared the collateral summaries with the assistance of the debtor's comptroller and that the figures were accurate. Tr. at 63-64, 107. Thus, the only evidence that the debtor was not in compliance with the final consent order is disputed evidence that the weekly collateral summaries provided to Ford Credit were not accurate.

Additionally, the evidence as to Ford Credit's collateral position was unsubstantiated. The parties adduced conflicting evidence as to Ford Credit's collateral position during the course of the reorganization. Mr. Miller prepared a report on the financial status of the debtor which indicated a collateral shortfall in the amount of $432,983 as of February 22, 1992. Tr. at 93. Mr. Koons disagreed with Mr. Miller's conclusion because the numbers Mr. Miller used to determine the debtor's collateral position on the petition date were incorrect. Tr. at 108-09. In fact, the debtor's reports showed that there had been no collateral shortfall. Tr. at 90. Mr. Miller and Mr. Koons met to discuss the differences in their figures, and they simply could not agree. Tr. at 90-91. Neither party presented evidence as to Ford Credit's collateral position as of March 10, 1992. Consequently, the evidence as to Ford Credit's collateral position was at best unclear.

Notwithstanding the conflicting testimony as to Ford Credit's collateral position, we reject Ford Credit's contention that it was not adequately protected. The evidence indicates, and we conclude therefrom, that sufficient adequate protection existed to enable the debtor to use Ford Credit's cash collateral to pay its employees $209,179.51 for work performed through March 10, 1992. Disputed evidence of inaccurate weekly financial summaries does not amount to lack of adequate protection. Furthermore, the "potential" decline in Ford's collateral position of $432,983 as of February 22, 1992, standing alone, is insufficient to rebut the debtor's undisputed testimony that it was in all other respects complying with Ford Credit's adequate protection requirements under the final consent order on March 10th.

The situation here is not a general request to use cash collateral for ongoing business operations, but a specific request to use a specific amount of cash collateral for specific expenses incurred in the ordinary course of business. In In re Dynaco Corporation, 158 B.R. 552 (Bankr. D.N.H. 1993), the Court allowed the debtor to use the secured creditor's cash collateral to pay employee wage claims that became due post-petition for work performed pre-petition. As adequate protection, the Court required that the secured creditor be given a replacement lien to cover the use of cash collateral for that purpose. Id. at 553. In support of its holding, the *Dynaco* Court stated:

> The secured claimant has benefitted from the work performed by the employees of these debtors prior to the bankruptcy filing and therefore the secured claimant will not be heard in opposition to payment for the wages due those employees for services which benefitted and created additional collateral for the secured claimant.

Id. at 552; *cf.* In re Phoenix Pipe and Tube, L.P., 174 B.R. 688, 690 (Bankr. E.D. Pa. 1994) ("§506(c) provides that the collateral of a secured creditor may be charged for expenses which are necessary, reasonable and benefit the creditor. Included in recoverable expenses is the labor in creating collateral. Here, employee expenses were clearly necessary.").

In this case, the work performed by the debtor's employees in good faith benefitted Ford Credit to the extent that the debtor's business continued and that its going concern value was preserved. Ford Credit was receiving adequate protection payments and replacements liens. There is no evidence that these requirements were insufficient to allow the debtor to use $209,179.51 of Ford Credit's cash collateral to pay its employees. Although Ford Credit was concerned about its collateral position as early as December, 1991, they literally stood by and watched the employees work through the date of the sale of the business and now refuse to pay them just compensation. Ford Credit cannot now say that in hindsight the adequate protection payments, replacement liens and other conditions placed on the debtor did not adequately protect its interest to allow the use of its cash collateral to pay employee wages.

Accordingly, for the reasons set forth above, we find that Ford Credit was adequately protected to enable the debtor to use $209,179.51 of Ford Credit's cash collateral to pay its employees. The Court shall enter an appropriate order.

Order

For the reasons set forth in the Memorandum Opinion dated the 12th day of December, 1995, and entered herein, IT IS HEREBY ORDERED that the upon remand from the United States District Court for the Eastern District of Virginia for a finding of adequate protection, we find that Ford Motor Credit Corporation was adequately protected to enable the debtor to use $209,179.51 of Ford Credit's cash collateral to pay its employees.

As the court noted in the above case, a debtor seeking court authority to use cash collateral has the burden of proof on the issue of providing adequate protection of the creditor's interest. Not surprisingly, the creditor has the burden of proof on the "validity, priority, or extent of [the creditor's] interest." §363(o). The interest that the creditor has includes the setoff rights of a bank in the debtor's deposit accounts at that bank. The limited access to these accounts under §363(c)(2) leads many debtors to withdraw any funds on deposit in banks to which the debtor is indebted and redeposit those amounts in other banks to which the debtor is not indebted.

Having cash available at the outset of the case is usually vital to the debtor. Suppliers may be unwilling to sell to the debtor other than on a COD basis, and some employees' wages may be past due. Frequently, debtors will seek permission to pay those prepetition wage claims out of cash collateral or postpetition financing (which we will discuss later). These factors provide some of the background against which the debtor and secured creditor negotiate the use of the cash collateral.

B.   *Executory Contracts*

Not only in Chapter 11, but in all other Chapters as well, the trustee or debtor in possession is given the chance to decide which prepetition contracts are good and should therefore be honored ("assumed"), and which are too burdensome to the estate and should thus be rejected, meaning that the debtor breaches the contract, turning it into a monetary claim that will be paid the same as other creditors having claims. Read §365(a) and (g).

PROBLEM 9-7

When Circus of Animals, a traveling entertainment, filed its Chapter 7 bankruptcy petition, the trustee, Charity Hallett, immediately took over running its operation until the assets could be sold off in an orderly fashion; *see* §721. She examined the circus's current contracts and discovered the following:

(a)   Animal Eats, Inc., a seller of food for animals of all kinds, had a contract with the circus by which it agreed to provide all the foods the various animals would eat for the next two years at a very competitive price. In fact, Hallett is sure she can't find such a good deal anywhere else.

(b)   A major reason for the circus's going under was an employment contract with its major animal handler, John Stay, who had been hired away from a competing circus at double his former salary and, it is rumored by the other members of the staff, more than twice what he is worth.

What should the trustee do about these contracts? How long does she have to think it over? *See* §365(d)(1). If this were a Chapter 11 proceeding, how long would the debtor in possession have? *See* §365(d)(2). If she assumes the Animal Eats contract, what priority will the seller enjoy as to food ordered postpetition? *See* §§364(a), 503(b)(1), and 507(a)(1).

In re Pioneer Ford Sales, Inc.

United States Court of Appeals, First Circuit, 1984
729 F.2d 27

BREYER, Circuit Judge.

The Ford Motor Company appeals a federal district court decision, 30 B.R. 458, allowing a bankrupt Ford dealer (Pioneer Ford Sales, Inc.) to assign its Ford franchise over Ford's objection to a Toyota dealer (Toyota Village, Inc.). The district court decided the case on the basis of a record developed in the bankruptcy court. The bankruptcy court, 26 B.R. 116, had approved the transfer, which ran from Pioneer to Fleet National Bank (Pioneer's principal secured creditor) and then to Toyota Village. Fleet sought authorization for the assignment because Toyota Village will pay $10,000 for the franchise and buy all parts and accessories in Pioneer's inventory at fair market value (about $75,000); if the franchise is not assigned, Ford will buy only some of the parts for between $45,000 and $55,000. Thus, the assignment will increase the value of the estate. Fleet is the appellee here.

The issue that the case raises is the proper application of 11 U.S.C. §365(c)(1)(A), an exception to a more general provision, 11 U.S.C. §365(f)(1), that allows a trustee in bankruptcy (or a debtor in possession) to assign many of the debtor's executory contracts even if the contract itself says that it forbids assignment. The exception at issue reads as follows:

> (c) The trustee [or debtor in possession] may not assume or assign an executory contract . . . of the debtor, whether or not such contract . . . prohibits assignment if—

(1)(A) applicable law excuses [the other party to the contract] from accepting performance
from . . . an assignee . . . whether or not [the] . . . contract . . . prohibits . . . assignment.

The words "applicable law" in this section mean "applicable non-bankruptcy
law." *See* H.R. Rep. No. 95-595, 95th Cong., 1st Sess. 348 (1977), reprinted in
[1978] U.S. Code Cong. & Ad. News 5787, 5963, 6304; S. Rep. No. 95-989, 95th
Cong., 2d Sess. 59 (1978), reprinted in [1978] U.S. Code Cong. & Ad. News 5787,
5845. Evidently, the theory of this section is to prevent the trustee from assigning (over
objection) contracts of the sort that contract law ordinarily makes nonassignable, i.e.,
contracts that cannot be assigned when the contract itself is silent about assignment. At
the same time, by using the words in (1)(A) "whether or not the contract prohibits
assignment," the section prevents parties from using contractual language to prevent the
trustee from assigning contracts that (when the contract is silent) contract law typically
makes assignable. Id. Thus, we must look to see whether relevant nonbankruptcy law
would allow Ford to veto the assignment of its basic franchise contract "whether or not"
that basic franchise contract itself specifically "prohibits assignment."

The nonbankruptcy law to which both sides point us is contained in Rhode
Island's "Regulation of Business Practices Among Motor Vehicle Manufacturers,
Distributors and Dealers" Act, R.I. Gen. Laws §31-5.1-4(C)(7). It states that

[N]o dealer . . . shall have the right to . . . assign the franchise . . . without the consent of the
manufacturer, except that such consent shall not be unreasonably withheld.

The statute by its terms allows a manufacturer to veto an assignment where the
veto is reasonable but not otherwise. The statute's language also indicates that it
applies "whether or not" the franchise contract itself restricts assignment. Thus,
the basic question that the case presents is whether Ford's veto was reasonable in
terms of the Rhode Island law.

Neither the district court nor the bankruptcy court specifically addressed this
question. Their failure apparently arose out of their belief that 11 U.S.C.
§365(c)(1)(A) refers only to traditional personal service contracts. But in our view
they were mistaken. The language of the section does not limit its effect to personal
service contracts. It refers *generally* to contracts that are not assignable under nonbankruptcy law. State laws typically make contracts for personal services nonassignable (where the contract itself is silent); but they make other sorts of contracts
nonassignable as well. *See, e.g.*, N.Y. State Finance Law §138 (1974) (making certain
government contracts unassignable); N.Y. General Municipal Law §109 (1977)
(same); N.C. Gen. Stat. §147-62 (1978) (same). The legislative history of §365(c)
says nothing about "personal services." To the contrary, it speaks of letters of credit,
personal loans, and leases — instances in which assigning a contract may place the
other party at a significant disadvantage. The history thereby suggests that (c)(1)(A)
has a broader reach.

The source of the "personal services" limitation apparently is a bankruptcy court
case, In re Taylor Manufacturing, Inc., 6 B.R. 370 (Bkrtcy. N.D. Ga. 1980), which

other bankruptcy courts have followed. The Taylor court wrote that (c)(1)(A) should be interpreted narrowly, in part because it believed that (c)(1)(A) conflicted with another section, (f)(1), which states in relevant part:

> Except as provided in subsection (c) . . . , notwithstanding a provision . . . in applicable law that prohibits . . . the assignment of [an executory] contract . . . the trustee may assign [it]. . . .

As a matter of logic, however, we see no conflict, for (c)(1)(A) refers to state laws that prohibit assignment "whether or not" the contract is silent, while (f)(1) contains no such limitation. Apparently (f)(1) includes state laws that prohibit assignment only when the contract is not silent about assignment; that is to say, state laws that enforce contract provisions prohibiting assignment. *See* 1 Norton, Bankruptcy Law and Practice §23.14. These state laws are to be ignored. The section specifically excepts (c)(1)(A)'s state laws that forbid assignment even when the contract is silent; they are to be heeded. Regardless, we fail to see why a "conflict" suggests that (c)(1)(A) is limited to "personal services."

The *Taylor* court cites 2 Collier on Bankruptcy §365.05 and the Commission Report, H.R. Doc. No. 93-137, 93rd Cong., 1st Sess. 199 (1973), in support. Both of these sources speak of personal services. However, they do not say that (c)(1)(A) was intended to be limited to personal services. Indeed, since it often is difficult to decide whether or not a particular duty can be characterized by the label "personal service," it makes sense to avoid this question and simply look to see whether state law would, or would not, make the duty assignable where the contract is silent. Thus, the Fifth Circuit has found no reason for limiting the scope of (c)(1)(A) to personal service contracts. In re Braniff Airways, Inc., 700 F.2d 935, 943 (5th Cir. 1983). Fleet concedes in its brief that "the exception to assignment [of §365(c)(1)(A)] is not limited to personal services contracts." We therefore reject the district court's conclusion in this respect.

Although the district court did not explicitly decide whether Ford's veto was reasonable, it decided a closely related question. Under other provisions of §365 a bankruptcy court cannot authorize assignment of an executory contract if (1) the debtor is in default, unless (2) there is "adequate assurance of future performance." §365(b)(1)(C). Pioneer is in default, but the bankruptcy and district courts found "adequate assurance." For the sake of argument, we shall assume that this finding is equivalent to a finding that Ford's veto of the assignment was unreasonable. And, we shall apply a "clearly erroneous" standard in reviewing the factual element in this lower court finding. Fed. R. Civ. P. 52. On these assumptions, favorable to Fleet, we nonetheless must reverse the district court, for, in our view, any finding of unreasonableness, based on this record, is clearly erroneous.

Our review of the record reveals the following critical facts. First, in accordance with its ordinary business practice and dealer guidelines incorporated into the franchise agreement, Ford would have required Toyota Village, as a dealer, to have a working capital of at least $172,000, of which no more than half could be debt. Toyota Village, however, had a working capital at the end of 1981 of $37,610; and its net worth was $31,747. Although the attorney for Fleet at one point in the bankruptcy proceedings said Toyota Village could borrow some of the necessary capital from a bank, he made no later reference to the point, nor did he ever specifically state how much Toyota Village could borrow. Since the tax returns of Toyota Village's owner showed gross income of $27,500 for 1981, there is no reason to believe that the owner could readily find the necessary equity capital.

Second, at a time when Japanese cars have sold well throughout the United States, Toyota Village has consistently lost money. The financial statements in the record show the following operating losses:

	1977	1978	1979	1980	1981
Loss	($7,522)	($7,552)	($13,938)	($12,684)	($21,317)

At the same time, the record contains no significant evidence tending to refute the natural inference arising from these facts. The bankruptcy court mentioned five factors that it said showed that Toyota Village gave "adequate assurance" that it could do the job. (1) Toyota Village was an established dealership. (2) Toyota Village was "located within 500 yards of the present Ford dealership." (3) Toyota Village had a proven track record for selling cars. (4) Toyota Village was willing and able to pay $15,000 that Pioneer still owed Ford. (5) The owner and sole stockholder of Toyota Village testified that he was willing and able to fulfill the franchise agreement. The first of these factors (dealer experience), while favoring Toyota Village, is weak, given the record of continuous dealership losses. The second (location) proves little, considering that Pioneer went bankrupt at the very spot. The third (track record) cuts against Toyota Village, not in its favor, for its track record is one of financial loss. The fourth (willingness to pay a $15,000 debt that Pioneer owed Ford) is relevant, but it shows, at most, that Toyota Village believed it could make a success of the franchise. The fifth (ability to act as franchisee) is supported by no more than a simple statement by the owner of Toyota Village that he could do the job.

We do not see how the few positive features about Toyota Village that the record reveals can overcome the problem of a history of losses and failure to meet Ford's capital requirements. In these circumstances, Ford would seem perfectly reasonable in withholding its consent to the transfer. Thus, Rhode Island law would make the franchise unassignable.

The Rhode Island authority we have found supports this conclusion. In Dunne Leases Cars & Trucks v. Kenworth Truck Co., 466 A.2d 1153 (R.I. 1983) the Supreme Court of Rhode Island held that failure to meet a condition in the franchise agreement requiring a leasing business to be removed from the dealership site provided due cause for the manufacturer's decision to terminate the dealership agreement. In Scuncio Motors, Inc. v. Subaru of New England, Inc., 555 F. Supp. 1121 (D.R.I. 1982), *aff'd*, 715 F.2d 10 (1st Cir. 1983), the federal district court for the District of Rhode Island wrote that failure to meet a franchise requirement to provide additional selling space provided cause to terminate a dealer contract. Inability to meet capital requirements, as revealed here, would seem to provide reasonable grounds for objecting to a franchise transfer *a fortiori*. If not, a manufacturer would have to allow the transfer of its franchise to virtually any auto dealer.

One might still argue that under Rhode Island law the only "reasonable" course of action for Ford is to allow the transfer and then simply terminate Toyota Village if it fails to perform adequately. This suggestion, however, overlooks the legal difficulties that Ford would have in proving cause for termination under the Rhode Island "Regulation of Business Practices Among Motor Vehicle Manufacturers, Distributors and Dealers" Act. R.I. Gen. Laws §31-5.1-4(D)(2). The very purpose of the statute — protecting dealer reliance — suggests that it ought to be more difficult for a manufacturer to terminate a dealer who has invested in a franchise than to oppose the grant of a franchise to one who has not. In any event, the law does not suggest a manufacturer is "unreasonable" in objecting to a transfer unless he would have "good cause" to terminate the transferee. And, to equate the two standards would tend to make the "unreasonable" provision superfluous. Thus, we conclude that the Rhode Island law would make the franchise unassignable on the facts here revealed. Therefore, neither the bankruptcy court nor the district court had the power to authorize the transfer. . . .

For these reasons, the judgment of the district court is Reversed.

PROBLEM 9-8

Mega Motors Manufacturing Co. filed a Chapter 11 petition. Among the business practices it intended to change was its relationship with its automobile dealers throughout the country. Foreign automobile manufacturers had a much more favorable contractual arrangement with their dealers, and, to copy that, Mega Motors wants to reject existing contracts with its dealers and to negotiate new contracts with selected ones. If the applicable nonbankruptcy law is the same as the Rhode Island law described in *Pioneer Ford*, can Mega Motors reject those contracts?

PROBLEM 9-9

When the famous rock band The Body Bags had a series of financial difficulties stemming from very high people signing all the wrong contracts, the band filed for protection under Chapter 11, and since no one appeared sufficiently coherent to run things, a trustee was appointed. While the lead singer of the band was undergoing very special treatment at a drug clinic, the trustee, who had played the bass guitar in a high school band, decided to go on in his place and notified the organizer of the group's upcoming nationwide tour that the tour contract was hereby assumed and that the trustee would be singing in the spot of its missing member. The tour operator phones you for legal advice. This is going to be a financial disaster for everyone. What can be done to avoid it? See §365(c)(1).

PROBLEM 9-10

Suppose the opposite happens: It is the tour operator who files in Chapter 11, and The Body Bags wants out of the contract it has signed for an upcoming nationwide tour. Personal service contracts are not assignable as a matter of common law, and The Body Bags has heard that the debtor in possession is a different legal entity from the entity with whom it signed the original contract. Can it now dump this contract and accept a similar (but more lucrative) one with another tour operator? Read §365(c)(1) again and also the following case.

In re Catapult Entertainment, Inc.

United States Court of Appeals, Ninth Circuit, 1999
165 F.3d 747

FLETCHER, Circuit Judge:

Appellant Stephen Perlman ("Perlman") licensed certain patents to appellee Catapult Entertainment, Inc. ("Catapult"). He now seeks to bar Catapult, which has since become a Chapter 11 debtor in possession, from assuming the patent licenses as part of its reorganization plan. Notwithstanding Perlman's objections, the bankruptcy court approved the assumption of the licenses and confirmed the reorganization plan. The district court affirmed the bankruptcy court on intermediate appeal. Perlman appeals that decision. We are called upon to determine whether, in light of §365(c)(1) of the Bankruptcy Code, a Chapter 11 debtor in possession may assume certain nonexclusive patent licenses over a licensor's objection. We conclude that the bankruptcy court erred in permitting the debtor in possession to assume the patent licenses in question.

I.

Catapult, a California corporation, was formed in 1994 to create an online gaming network for 16-bit console videogames. That same year, Catapult entered into two license agreements with Perlman, wherein Perlman granted to Catapult the right to exploit certain relevant technologies, including patents and patent applications.

In October 1996, Catapult filed for reorganization under Chapter 11 of the Bankruptcy Code. Shortly before the filing of the bankruptcy petition, Catapult entered into a merger agreement with Mpath Interactive, Inc. ("Mpath"). This agreement contemplated the filing of the bankruptcy petition, followed by a reorganization via a "reverse triangular merger" involving Mpath, MPCAT Acquisition Corporation ("MPCAT"), and Catapult. Under the terms of the merger agreement, MPCAT (a wholly-owned subsidiary of Mpath created for this transaction) would merge into Catapult, leaving Catapult as the surviving entity. When the dust cleared, Catapult's creditors and equity holders would have received approximately $14 million in cash, notes, and securities; Catapult, in turn, would have become a wholly-owned subsidiary of Mpath. The relevant third party creditors and equity holders accepted Catapult's reorganization plan by the majorities required by the Bankruptcy Code.

On October 24, 1996, as part of the reorganization plan, Catapult filed a motion with the bankruptcy court seeking to assume some 140 executory contracts and leases, including the Perlman licenses. Over Perlman's objection, the bankruptcy court granted Catapult's motion and approved the reorganization plan. The district court subsequently affirmed the bankruptcy court. This appeal followed. We have jurisdiction pursuant to 28 U.S.C. §158(d) and, because the relevant facts are undisputed, review the orders below *de novo*. *See* Everex Sys. v. Cadtrak Corp. (In re CFLC, Inc.), 89 F.3d 673, 675 (9th Cir. 1996).

II.

Section 365 of the Bankruptcy Code gives a trustee in bankruptcy (or, in a Chapter 11 case, the debtor in possession) the authority to assume, assign, or reject the executory contracts and unexpired leases of the debtor, notwithstanding any contrary provisions appearing in such contracts or leases. See 11 U.S.C. §365(a) & (f). This extraordinary authority, however, is not absolute. Section 365(c)(1) provides that, notwithstanding the general policy set out in §365(a):

> (c) The trustee may not assume or assign any executory contract or unexpired lease of the debtor, whether or not such contract or lease prohibits or restricts assignment of rights or delegation of duties, if
>
> > (1)(A) applicable law excuses a party, other than the debtor, to such contract or lease from accepting performance from or rendering performance to an entity other than the debtor or the debtor in possession, whether or not such contract or lease prohibits or restricts assignment of rights or delegation of duties; and
>
> > > (B) such party does not consent to such assumption or assignment. . . .

11 U.S.C. §365(c). Our task, simply put, is to apply this statutory language to the facts at hand and determine whether it prohibits Catapult, as the debtor in possession, from assuming the Perlman licenses without Perlman's consent.[8]

While simply put, our task is not so easily resolved; the proper interpretation of §365(c)(1) has been the subject of considerable disagreement among courts and commentators. On one side are those who adhere to the plain statutory language, which establishes a so-called "hypothetical test" to govern the assumption of executory contracts. *See* In re James Cable Partners, 27 F.3d 534, 537 (11th Cir. 1994) (characterizing §365(c)(1)(A) as posing "a hypothetical question"); In re West Elec., Inc., 852 F.2d 79, 83 (3d Cir. 1988) (same); In re Catron, 158 B.R. 629, 633-38 (E.D.

---

8. Perlman also contends that, even if Catapult were entitled to assume the Perlman licenses, §365(c)(1) also prohibits the assignment of the Perlman licenses to Mpath, accomplished by Catapult here through the contemplated Catapult-MPCAT-Mpath reverse triangular merger. Because we conclude that §365(c)(1) bars Catapult from assuming the Perlman licenses, we express no opinion regarding whether the merger transaction contemplated by Catapult would have resulted in a prohibited "assignment" within the meaning of §365(c)(1).

Va. 1993) (same), *aff'd without op.*, 25 F.3d 1038 (4th Cir. 1994). On the other side are those that forsake the statutory language in favor of an "actual test" that, in their view, better accomplishes the intent of Congress. *See* Institut Pasteur v. Cambridge Biotech Corp., 104 F.3d 489, 493 (1st Cir.) (rejecting the hypothetical test in favor of the actual test), *cert. denied*, 521 U.S. 1120, 117 S. Ct. 2511, 138 L. Ed. 2d 1014 (1997).[9] Although we have on two occasions declined to choose between these competing visions, *see* Worthington v. General Motors Corp. (In re Claremont Acquisition Corp.), 113 F.3d 1029, 1032 (9th Cir. 1997); *Everex*, 89 F.3d at 676-77, today we hold that we are bound by the plain terms of the statute and join the Third and Eleventh Circuits in adopting the "hypothetical test."

III.

We begin, as we must, with the statutory language. See Connecticut Nat'l Bank v. Germain, 503 U.S. 249, 253-54, 112 S. Ct. 1146, 117 L. Ed. 2d 391 (1992) (noting that the statutory language is the "cardinal canon" to be addressed "before all others"); Jeffries v. Wood, 114 F.3d 1484, 1495 (9th Cir.) (en banc) ("In statutory interpretation, the starting point is always the language of the statute itself."), cert. denied, 522 U.S. 1008, 118 S. Ct. 586, 139 L. Ed. 2d 423 (1997). The plain language of §365(c)(1) "link[s] nonassignability under 'applicable law' together with a prohibition on assumption in bankruptcy." 1 DAVID G. EPSTEIN, STEVE H. NICKLES & JAMES J. WHITE, BANKRUPTCY §5-15 at 474 (1992). In other words, the statute by its terms bars a debtor in possession from assuming an executory contract without the nondebtor's consent where applicable law precludes assignment of the contract to a third party. The literal language of §365(c)(1) is thus said to establish a "hypothetical test": a debtor in possession may not assume an executory contract over the nondebtor's objection if applicable law would bar assignment to a hypothetical third party, even where the debtor in possession has no intention of assigning the contract in question to any such third party. See In re James Cable, 27 F.3d at 537 (characterizing §365(c)(1)(A) as presenting "a hypothetical question"); In re West Elecs., 852 F.2d at 3 (same).

Before applying the statutory language to the case at hand, we first resolve a number of preliminary issues that are either not disputed by the parties, or are so clearly established as to deserve no more than passing reference. First, we follow the lead of the parties in assuming that the Perlman licenses are executory agreements within the meaning of §365. Second, it is well-established that §365(c)'s use of the term "trustee" includes Chapter 11 debtors in possession. *See* Institut Pasteur, 104 F.3d at 492 n. 7; In re James Cable Partners, 27 F.3d at 537; In re West Elecs., 852

---

9. The weight of lower court authority appears to favor the "actual test." *See, e.g.*, Texaco Inc. v. Louisiana Land and Expl. Co., 136 B.R. 658, 668-71 (M.D. La. 1992); In re GP Express Airlines, Inc., 200 B.R. 222, 231-33 (Bankr. D. Neb. 1996); In re Am. Ship Bldg. Co., 164 B.R. 358, 362-63 (Bankr. M. D. Fla. 1994); In re Fastrax, 129 B.R. 274, 277 (Bankr. M. D. Fla. 1991); In re Hartec Enters., Inc., 117 B.R. 865, 871-73 (Bankr. W.D. Tex. 1990), *vacated on other grounds*, 130 B.R. 929 (W.D. Tex. 1991); In re Cardinal Indus., Inc., 116 B.R. 964, 976-82 (Bankr. S.D. Ohio 1990) (rejecting hypothetical test in connection with similar statutory language of §365(e)(2)(A)).

F.2d at 82. Third, our precedents make it clear that federal patent law constitutes "applicable law" within the meaning of §365(c), and that nonexclusive[10] patent licenses are "personal and assignable only with the consent of the licensor." *Everex*, 89 F.3d at 680.

When we have cleared away these preliminary matters, application of the statute to the facts of this case becomes relatively straightforward:

> (c) *Catapult* may not assume . . . the *Perlman licenses*, . . . if
>
> (1)(A) *federal patent law* excuses *Perlman* from accepting performance from or rendering performance to an entity other than *Catapult* . . . and
>
> (B) *Perlman* does not consent to such assumption . . .

11 U.S.C. §365(c) (substitutions in italics). Since federal patent law makes nonexclusive patent licenses personal and nondelegable, §365(c)(1)(A) is satisfied. Perlman has withheld his consent, thus satisfying 365(c)(1)(B). Accordingly, the plain language of §365(c)(1) bars Catapult from assuming the Perlman licenses.

IV.

Catapult urges us to abandon the literal language of §365(c)(1) in favor of an alternative approach, reasoning that Congress did not intend to bar debtors in possession from assuming their own contracts where no assignment is contemplated. In Catapult's view, §365(c)(1) should be interpreted as embodying an "actual test": the statute bars assumption by the debtor in possession only where the reorganization in question results in the nondebtor actually having to accept performance from a third party. Under this reading of §365(c), the debtor in possession would be permitted to assume any executory contract, so long as no assignment was contemplated. Put another way, Catapult suggests that, as to a debtor in possession, §365(c)(1) should be read to prohibit assumption and assignment, rather than assumption or assignment.

Catapult has marshalled considerable authority to support this reading. The arguments supporting Catapult's position can be divided into three categories: (1) the literal reading creates inconsistencies within §365; (2) the literal reading is incompatible with the legislative history; and (3) the literal reading flies in the face of sound bankruptcy policy. Nonetheless, we find that none of these considerations justifies departing from the plain language of §365(c)(1).

---

10. One of the two Perlman licenses began its life as an exclusive license. Perlman in a sworn declaration stated that, pursuant to its terms, the license has since become nonexclusive. Because Catapult has not offered any rebuttal evidence, and because neither party raised the issue in connection with the issues raised in this appeal, we will assume that the Perlman licenses are nonexclusive. Accordingly, we express no opinion regarding the assignability of exclusive patent licenses under federal law, and note that we expressed no opinion on this subject in Everex. *See* Everex, 89 F.3d at 679 ("Federal law holds a nonexclusive patent license to be personal and nonassignable . . .") (emphasis added).

A.

Catapult first argues that a literal reading of §365(c)(1) sets the statute at war with itself and its neighboring provisions. Deviation from the plain language, contends Catapult, is necessary if internal consistency is to be achieved. We agree with Catapult that a court should interpret a statute, if possible, so as to minimize discord among related provisions. *See* 2A NORMAN J. SINGER, SUTHERLAND STATUTORY CONSTRUCTION §46.06 (5th ed. 1992) ("A statute should be construed so that effect is given to all its provisions, so that no part will be inoperative or superfluous, void or insignificant, and so that one section will not destroy another unless the provision is the result of obvious mistake or error."). However, the dire inconsistencies cited by Catapult turn out, on closer analysis, to be no such thing.

Catapult, for example, singles out the interaction between §365(c)(1) and §365(f)(1) as a statutory trouble spot. *See* In re Catron, 158 B.R. at 636 (exploring apparent conflict between subsections (c)(1) and (f)(1)); In re Cardinal Indus., 116 B.R. at 976-77 (same). Subsection (f)(1) provides that executory contracts, once assumed, may be assigned notwithstanding any contrary provisions contained in the contract *or applicable law:*

> (f)(1) Except as provided in subsection (c) of this section, notwithstanding a provision in an executory contract or unexpired lease of the debtor, or in applicable law, that prohibits, restricts, or conditions the assignment of such contract or lease, the trustee may assign such contract or lease under paragraph (2) of this subsection . . .

11 U.S.C. §365(f)(1) (emphasis added).

The potential conflict between subsections (c)(1) and (f)(1) arises from their respective treatments of "applicable law." The plain language of subsection (c)(1) bars assumption (absent consent) whenever "applicable law" would bar assignment. Subsection (f)(1) states that, contrary provisions in applicable law notwithstanding, executory contracts may be assigned. Since assumption is a necessary prerequisite to assignment under §365, *see* 11 U.S.C. §365(f)(2)(A), a literal reading of subsection (c)(1) appears to render subsection (f)(1) superfluous. In the words of the Sixth Circuit, "[S]ection 365(c), the recognized exception to 365(f), appears at first to resuscitate in full the very anti-assignment 'applicable law' which 365(f) nullifies." In re Magness, 972 F.2d 689, 695 (6th Cir.1992) (Guy, J., concurring). Faced with this dilemma, one district court reluctantly concluded that the "[c]onflict between subsections (c) and (f) of §365 is inescapable." *See* In re Catron, 158 B.R. at 636.

Subsequent authority, however, suggests that this conclusion may have been unduly pessimistic. The Sixth Circuit has credibly reconciled the warring provisions by noting that "each subsection recognizes an 'applicable law' of markedly different scope." In re Magness, 972 F.2d at 695; accord In re James Cable, 27 F.3d at 537-38; In re Lil' Things, Inc., 220 B.R. 583, 590-91 (Bankr. N. D. Tex. 1998); In re Antonelli, 148 B.R. 443, 448 (D. Md. 1992), *aff'd without op.*, 4 F.3d 984 (4th Cir. 1993). Subsection (f)(1) states the broad rule — a law that, as a general matter, "prohibits, restricts, or conditions the assignment" of executory contracts is trumped by the provisions of subsection (f)(1). *See* In re James Cable, 27 F.3d at 538; *Magness*, 972 F.2d at 695. Subsection (c)(1), however, states a carefully crafted exception to the broad rule — where applicable law does not merely recite a general ban on assignment, but instead more specifically "excuses a party . . . from accepting performance from or rendering performance to an entity" different from the one with which the party originally contracted, the applicable law prevails over subsection (f)(1). *See* id. In other words, in determining whether an "applicable law" stands or falls under §365(f)(1), a court must ask why the "applicable law" prohibits assignment. *See* In re Magness, 972 F.2d at 700 (J. Guy, concurring); In re Antonelli, 148 B.R. at 448. Only if the law prohibits assignment on the rationale that the identity of the contracting party is material to the agreement will subsection (c)(1) rescue it.[11] *See* id. We agree with the Sixth and Eleventh Circuits that a literal reading of subsection (c)(1) does not inevitably set it at odds with subsection (f)(1).

Catapult next focuses on the internal structure of §365(c)(1) itself. According to Catapult, the literal approach to subsection (c)(1) renders the phrase "or the debtor in possession" contained in §365(c)(1)(A) superfluous.[12] In the words of one bankruptcy court, "[i]f the directive of Section 365(c)(1) is to prohibit assumption whenever applicable law excuses performance relative to any entity other than the debtor, why add the words 'or debtor in possession?' The [hypothetical] test renders this phrase surplusage." In re Hartec, 117 B.R. at 871-72; *accord* In re Fastrax, Inc., 129 B.R. at 277; In re Cardinal Indus., 116 B.R. at 979.

A close reading of §365(c)(1), however, dispels this notion. By its terms, subsection (c)(1) addresses two conceptually distinct events: assumption and assignment. The plain language of the provision makes it clear that each of these events is contingent on the nondebtor's separate consent. Consequently, where a nondebtor consents to the *assumption* of an executory contract, subsection (c)(1) will have to be applied a second time if the debtor in possession wishes to assign the contract in question. On that second application, the relevant question would be whether "applicable law excuses a party from accepting performance from or rendering performance to an entity other than . . . *the debtor in possession.*" 11 U.S.C. §365(c)(1)(A) (emphasis added). Consequently, the phrase "debtor in possession," far from being rendered superfluous by a literal reading of subsection (c)(1), dovetails neatly with the disjunctive language that opens subsection (c)(1): "The trustee may not assume or assign. . . ." 11 U.S.C. §365(c) (emphasis added); *cf.* In re Catron, 158

---

11. We note that, in the instant case, the federal law principle against the assignability of nonexclusive patent licenses is rooted in the personal nature of a nonexclusive license — the identity of a licensee may matter a great deal to a licensor. *See* In re CFLC, 89 F.3d at 679 (explaining rationale behind federal law rule against assignability).

12. The phrase in question was added by Congress in 1984, replacing an earlier formulation focusing on the "trustee or an assignee":

(1)(A) applicable law excuses a party, other than the debtor, to such contract or lease from accepting performance from or rendering performance to an entity other than the trustee or an assignee of such contract or lease whether or not such contract or lease prohibits or restricts assignment of rights or delegation of duties.

11 U.S.C. §365(c)(1)(A) (prior language stricken through).

B.R. at 636 (rejecting argument that literal reading of §365(c) makes "or assign" superfluous insofar as assumption is a prerequisite to assignment).

A third potential inconsistency identified by Catapult relates to §365(c)(2). According to Catapult, a literal reading of subsection (c)(1) renders subsection (c)(2) a dead letter. *See* In re Cardinal Indus., 116 B.R. at 980 (explicating this argument). Subsection (c)(2) provides:

> (c) The trustee may not assume or assign any executory contract or unexpired lease of the debtor, whether or not such contract or lease prohibits or restricts assignment of rights or delegation of duties, if . . .
>
> (2) such contract is a contract to make a loan, or extend other debt financing or financial accommodations, to or for the benefit of the debtor, or to issue a security of the debtor . . .

11 U.S.C. §365(c)(2). According to Catapult, the contracts encompassed by subsection (c)(2) are all nonassignable as a matter of applicable state law. As a result, a literal reading of subsection (c)(1) would seem to snare and dispose of every executory contract within subsection (c)(2)'s scope. Perlman, however, persuasively rebuts this argument, noting that even if the state law governing the assignability of loan agreements and financing contracts is relatively uniform today, Congress by enacting subsection (c)(2) cemented nationwide uniformity in the bankruptcy context, effectively ensuring creditors that these particular contracts would not be assumable in bankruptcy. Put another way, it is the national uniformity of applicable state law that has rendered subsection (c)(2) superfluous, not the terms of subsection (c)(1).

In any event, subsection (c)(1) does not completely swallow up subsection (c)(2). Subsection (c)(1) by its terms permits assumption and assignment of executory loan agreements so long as the nondebtor consents. *See* 11 U.S.C. §365(c)(1)(B). Subsection (c)(2), in contrast, bans assumption and assignment of such agreements, consent of the nondebtor notwithstanding. *See* Transamerica Commercial Fin. Corp. v. Citibank, N.A. (In re Sun Runner Marine, Inc.), 945 F.2d 1089, 1093 (9th Cir. 1991) ("Section 365(c)(2) unambiguously prohibits the assumption of financial accommodation contracts, regardless of the consent of the non-debtor party."); 2 WILLIAM L. NORTON, JR., NORTON BANKRUPTCY LAW and PRACTICE 2D §39:19 ("[T]he correct view is that executory credit contracts may not be assumed in bankruptcy regardless of the desires of the parties."). Accordingly, contrary to Catapult's assertion, subsection (c)(1) does not necessarily catch upriver all the fish that would otherwise be netted by subsection (c)(2). Once again, the "inconsistency" identified by Catapult proves evanescent under close scrutiny. We see no reason why these two provisions cannot happily coexist.[13]

---

13. Catapult also advances what it claims is a fourth inconsistency by contrasting the plain language of §365(c)(1) with the provisions of §365(e)(1), which nullifies "ipso facto" clauses. In rejecting this contention, it is enough to note that §365(e)(2)(A) expressly revives "ipso facto" clauses in precisely the same executory contracts that fall within the scope of §365(c)(1).

We conclude that the claimed inconsistencies are not actual and that the plain language of §365(c)(1) compels the result Perlman urges: Catapult may not assume the Perlman licenses over Perlman's objection. Catapult has not demonstrated that, in according the words of subsection (c)(1) their plain meaning, we do violence to subsection (c)(1) or the provisions that accompany it.

B.

Catapult next urges that legislative history requires disregard of the plain language of §365(c)(1). First off, because we discern no ambiguity in the plain statutory language, we need not resort to legislative history. *See* Davis v. Michigan Dep't of Treasury, 489 U.S. 803, 808-09 n.3, 109 S. Ct. 1500, 103 L. Ed. 2d 891 (1989) ("Legislative history is irrelevant to the interpretation of an unambiguous statute."); Gumport v. Sterling Press (In re Transcon Lines), 58 F.3d 1432, 1437 (9th Cir. 1995); Brooker v. Desert Hosp. Corp., 947 F.2d 412, 414 (9th Cir. 1991).

We will depart from this rule, if at all, only where the legislative history clearly indicates that Congress meant something other than what it said. *See* City of Auburn v. United States, 154 F.3d 1025, 1029 (9th Cir. 1998); California v. Montrose Chem. Corp., 104 F.3d 1507, 1515 (9th Cir. 1997). Here, the legislative history unearthed by Catapult falls far short of this mark. The legislative history behind §365(c) was exhaustively analyzed by the bankruptcy court in In re Cardinal Industries, 116 B.R. at 978-80. Its discussion makes it clear that there exists no contemporaneous legislative history regarding the current formulation of subsection (c)(1). Id. at 978 ("[T]here is no authoritative legislative history for BAFJA as enacted in 1984."). Catapult, however, argues that the language as ultimately enacted in 1984 had its genesis in a 1980 House amendment to an earlier Senate technical corrections bill. The amendment was accompanied by "a relatively obscure committee report." 1 David G. Epstein, Steve H. Nickles & James J. White, Bankruptcy §5-15 (1992). In explaining the amendment, the report stated:

> This amendment makes it clear that the prohibition against a trustee's power to assume an executory contract does not apply where it is the debtor that is in possession and the performance to be given or received under a personal service contract will be the same as if no petition had been filed because of the personal service nature of the contract.

In re Cardinal Indus., 116 B.R. at 979 (quoting H.R. Rep. No. 1195, 96th Cong., 2d Sess. §27(b) (1980)).[14] However, since the report relates to a different proposed bill, predates enactment of §365(c)(1) by several years, and expresses at most the thoughts of only one committee in the House, we are not inclined to view it as the sort

---

14. We note that several courts have relied on this legislative history in rejecting the "hypothetical test" in favor of the "actual test." *See, e.g.,* Summit Invest. and Dev. Corp. v. Leroux, 69 F.3d 608, 613 (1st Cir. 1995); In re Fastrax, 129 B.R. at 277. For the reasons set forth herein, we respectfully disagree with their analysis.

of clear indication of contrary intent that would overcome the unambiguous language of subsection (c)(1).[15]

C.

Catapult makes the appealing argument that, as a leading bankruptcy commentator has pointed out, there are policy reasons to prefer the "actual test." *See* 3 LAWRENCE P. KING, COLLIER ON BANKRUPTCY §365.06[1][d][iii] (15th ed. revised) (arguing that sound bankruptcy policy supports the actual test). That may be so, but Congress is the policy maker, not the courts.

Policy arguments cannot displace the plain language of the statute; that the plain language of §365(c)(1) may be bad policy does not justify a judicial rewrite. And a rewrite is precisely what the actual test requires. The statute expressly provides that a debtor in possession "may not assume or assign" an executory contract where applicable law bars assignment and the nondebtor objects. 11 U.S.C. §365(c)(1) (emphasis added). The actual test effectively engrafts a narrow exception onto §365(c)(1) for debtors in possession, providing that, as to them, the statute only prohibits assumption and assignment, as opposed to assumption or assignment. *See* In re Fastrax, 129 B.R. at 277 (admitting that, by adopting the actual test, the court reads the word "assume" out of subsection (c) with respect to debtors in possession).

V.

Because the statute speaks clearly, and its plain language does not produce a patently absurd result or contravene any clear legislative history, we must "hold Congress to its words." Brooker, 947 F.2d at 414-15. Accordingly, we hold that, where applicable nonbankruptcy law makes an executory contract nonassignable because the identity of the nondebtor party is material, a debtor in possession may not assume the contract absent consent of the nondebtor party. A straightforward application of §365(c)(1) to the circumstances of this case precludes Catapult from assuming the Perlman licenses over Perlman's objection. Consequently, the bankruptcy court erred when it approved Catapult's motion to assume the Perlman licenses, and the district court erred in affirming the bankruptcy court.

REVERSED.

———————

Before §365 can be applied to any given contract that contract must be "executory," a word undefined in the Bankruptcy Code. What does it mean? In the common

---

15. Catapult also would find favorable legislative history in the enactment of §365(c)(2). Its argument draws an inference against the hypothetical test from Congress' enactment of subsection (c)(2) in the face of statements in the House report implying that (c)(2) is unnecessary in light of (c)(1). As noted above, subsection (c)(2) is not inconsistent with the literal reading of subsection (c)(1), and thus its adoption does not undermine the hypothetical test.

law of contracts, it means "unperformed," but the bankruptcy courts have been persuaded by a famous law review article that the term is more complicated than that. Professor Vern Countryman proposed this in his article Executory Contracts in Bankruptcy: Part I, 57 Minn. L. Rev. 439, 460 (1973), where he defined an executory contract as one in which "the obligation of both the bankrupt and the other party to the contract are so far unperformed that the failure of either to complete performance would constitute a material breach excusing the performance of the other." While some courts have rejected this "material breach" test — *see* In re Norquist, 43 B.R. 224 (Bankr. E.D. Wash. 1984) — most have accepted it and required a finding that both parties to the contract still have substantial obligations to perform before the contract is subject to §365 treatment.

In re Rovine Corporation

United States Bankruptcy Court, Western District of Tennessee, 1980
6 B.R. 661

WILLIAM B. LEFFLER, Chief Bankruptcy Judge.

I.

This cause came on to be heard upon a Motion for New Trial or to Amend Judgment filed by the plaintiff, Burger King Corporation, pursuant to Rule 923 of the Rules of Bankruptcy Procedure.

On May 2, 1980, the defendant filed a petition under Chapter 11 of the Bankruptcy Code. Since that time the debtor has continued in possession of its property and has continued to operate its business without the intervention of a trustee. At the time of the filing, the defendant was a franchisee of the plaintiff, Burger King Corporation. On May 13, 1980, the plaintiff filed an application with the Court asking that the defendant be compelled to adopt or reject the franchise agreement as an executory contract under §365(d) of the Bankruptcy Code. On July 18, 1980, the defendant rejected the franchise agreement. On July 28, 1980, the plaintiff filed a complaint with the Court seeking to enforce a covenant not to compete contained in the rejected franchise agreement. The covenant not to compete provided that upon termination of the franchise agreement and for a period of 18 months thereafter, the defendant would not engage in any business which was the same or similar to the plaintiff's business in a location within a 5-mile radius of the franchise premises.

On August 4, 1980, the Court entered a Memorandum Opinion holding that: (1) the covenant not to compete was executory in nature; (2) said covenant was rejected as a part of the defendant's prior rejection of the franchise agreement; and (3) the effect of rejection was to relieve the defendant and its estate of the obligations imposed via the covenant not to compete. The Court therefore refused the plaintiff's request for a temporary injunction. *See* In re Rovine Corporation, Bkrtcy., 5 B.R. 402 (1980). The plaintiff filed its instant motion on August 12, 1980, asking that the Court amend its prior judgment in this cause and grant the plaintiff's request for a temporary injunction enforcing the covenant not to compete.

II.

The plaintiff notes that the rejection of an executory contract not previously assumed gives rise to a claim against a debtor's estate under §502(g) of the Bankruptcy Code. However, the plaintiff also notes that the definition of "claim" under §101(4) of the Code excludes a right to an equitable remedy for breach of performance if such breach does not give rise to a right of payment. The plaintiff alleges that its remedy against the defendant is that of injunction and that the franchise agreement does not provide for monetary damages. Therefore, there is no right to payment that is a necessary element of the Code's definition of "claim." From these observations the plaintiff contends that Congress intended to retain the right of a nonbankrupt party to enforce covenants not to compete.

The plaintiff further contends that the covenant not to compete is fully executed in that it constituted an obligation of the defendant which immediately followed the termination of the franchise agreement. As such, the plaintiff contends that the covenant in question is a divisible part of the franchise agreement and may still be enforced via injunction notwithstanding the defendant's previous rejection under §365 of the Code.

Finally, the plaintiff proposes an alternative argument. Despite the fact that it was the plaintiff's motion which brought about the defendant's rejection of the franchise agreement as an executory contract, the plaintiff now contends that the franchise agreement taken in its entirety is not an executory contract in the bankruptcy sense. As a basis for this alternative contention the plaintiff argues that the grant of a franchise is comparable to a license. The plaintiff would have this Court hold that as a license the franchise agreement was performed in material part by the plaintiff upon the granting of the franchise to the defendant and the agreement was, therefore, fully executed on the part of the plaintiff at that point, except for certain duties the plaintiff describes as administrative and therefore nonmaterial.

III.

This Court's decision to reconsider the instant case is further evidence of problems various courts have encountered in their struggle to define the term "executory contract" as used in the bankruptcy context. In this Court's prior decision, the Court considered only the covenant not to compete and the question of whether it was an executory provision of the franchise agreement. The question of the executory nature of the remaining provisions of the franchise agreement was not an issue. Now upon further reflection and in light of the plaintiff's contention that the agreement was fully executed on its part, the Court feels that the franchise agreement must be viewed in its entirety in order to decide the question of its executory nature.

IV.

The primary issues to be considered by the Court are as follows:

(1) Was the franchise agreement an executory contract within the meaning of §365 of the Bankruptcy Code, and therefore subject to rejection by the defendant?

(2) If the franchise agreement was an executory contract under §365, did the rejection of said agreement relieve the defendant and its estate of the obligations of the covenant not to compete, or may the plaintiff still enforce said covenant notwithstanding rejection?

V.

Probably the most comprehensive analysis of the term "executory contract" as used in the bankruptcy context is found in Professor Vern Countryman's two-part article appearing in 47 Minn. L. Rev. 436 (1973) and 58 Minn. L. Rev. 479 (1974). This article concerns executory contracts under §70(b) of the Bankruptcy Act, the statutory predecessor to §365 of the Bankruptcy Code.

Professor Williston in his work on contracts has stated that, "all contracts to a greater or lesser extent are executory. When they cease to be so, they cease to be contracts." 1 S. Williston, Contracts §14 (3d ed. 1957). However, Professor Countryman notes that such an "expansive meaning can hardly be given to the term (executory contract) as used in the bankruptcy sense. Rather the term "executory contract" should be defined "in the light of the purpose for which the trustee is given the option to assume or reject." 57 Minn. L. Rev. 439, 450 (1973). Or in the words of the 6th Circuit Court of Appeals: "The key, it seems, to deciphering the meaning of the executory contract rejection provisions, is to work backward, proceeding from an examination of the purposes rejection is expected to accomplish. If those objectives have already been accomplished, or if they can't be accomplished through rejection, then the contract is not executory within the meaning of the Bankruptcy Act." In re Jolly, 574 F.2d 349, 351 (1978).

Professor Countryman goes on to analyze relevant court decisions on the subject of executory contracts in bankruptcy and states that that term does not encompass contracts fully performed by the nonbankrupt party, where the bankrupt party has only partially performed or not performed at all. 57 Minn. L. Rev. 439, 451 (1973). Nor does the term encompass contracts fully performed by the bankrupt party, but not fully performed by the nonbankrupt party. 57 Minn. L. Rev. 439, 458 (1973). The term *executory contracts*, however, does cover contracts where the obligations of both parties remain at least partially and materially unperformed at the time of bankruptcy. 57 Minn. L. Rev. 439, 460-461 (1973). The definition of executory contract offered by Professor Countryman and adopted by many courts is as follows: "A contract under which the obligation of both the bankrupt and the other party to the contract are so far unperformed that the failure of either to complete performance would constitute a material breach excusing the performance of the other." 57 Minn. L. Rev. 460 (1973).

As an example of a case involving an executory contract under §70(b) of the Bankruptcy Act, Professor Countryman cites Wagstaff v. Peters, 203 Kan. 108, 453 P.2d 120 (1969). This case involved a contract for the sale of a bankrupt's business. At the time of bankruptcy the buyer remained liable for a part of the purchase price and the bankrupt sellers remained obligated: (1) to pay certain accounts payable; (2) to advise and consult with the buyers; and, as in the instant case, (3) not to enter into a competing business. The trustee had failed to assume this contract within the time specified in §70 of the Act. When the trustee subsequently brought an action against the buyers on the contract, the court in *Wagstaff* held that: (1) the contract was executory in nature because it involved future performance on both the buyer's and seller's part and (2) the entire contract was conclusively presumed to be rejected due to the trustee's failure to affirm within the allotted time.

As noted previously the plaintiff compares the instant franchise agreement to a license and contends that as a license the agreement was fully performed by it at the time of the execution or the agreement. A franchise agreement is in many respects similar to a license. In the typical franchise agreement a company (the franchisor) owns a trademark or trade name which it licenses to others (the franchisees) to use upon the condition that the franchisees conform their business to standards established by the franchisor. Evans v. S. S. Kresge Co., 394 F. Supp. 817, 844 (W.D. Pa. 1975). The franchise agreement between the plaintiff and defendant conforms to this general description. The plaintiff licensed the use of its systems, service marks, and trade marks to the defendant in return for the payment of a franchise fee. These mutual obligations were fully performed by both parties at the time of the Chapter 11 filing. During the term of the agreement the defendant agreed inter alia to make specified royalty payments to the plaintiff and also agreed not to compete with the plaintiff during the term of the agreement and for a specified time thereafter. These obligations remained to be performed by the defendant at the time of the filing. If there remained no other obligations or promises to be performed by the plaintiff under the term of the agreement, the contract in question would probably be executed in that the plaintiff would have fully performed prior to the filing date. However, this is not the case. The plaintiff agreed during the term of the franchise agreement to "use its best efforts to maintain the high reputation of Burger King Restaurants and in connection therewith to make available to franchisee" other services of the company. (Pages 2 and 3 of the Franchise Agreement.) The promise to make available these additional services was an obligation of the plaintiff that remained to be performed as of the filing date. In general these services included advising and consulting with the defendant in regards to merchandising, marketing, advertising research, special recipe techniques, food preparation, new restaurant services and other operational developments subsequently devised by the plaintiff. In essence the plaintiff agreed to continue to advise and consult with the defendant concerning the operation of its franchise and to afford said defendant the benefit of its expertise in the restaurant field as such aid was needed by the defendant. As is the case of most franchise agreements, the instant agreement required a continuing cooperative effort between franchisor and franchisee. *See* Evans v. S. S. Kresge Co., *supra.*

Returning to the plaintiff's license analogy, Professor Countryman in part two of his article discusses the executory nature of patent licenses and states:

> The usual patent license, by which the patentee-licensor authorizes the licensee to exercise some part of the patentee's exclusive right to make, use and vend the patented item in return for payment of royalties, ordinarily takes the form of an executory contract. A license simply to use patented equipment is typically a part of an agreement by which the equipment is leased to the licensee in return for royalty payments. Such an agreement is clearly within the Bankruptcy Act's concept of an executory contract. A license merely to use a consumable patented product necessarily provides for the supplying of the product to the licensee. If the patentee-licensor is in any way responsible for supplying the product, the contract is executory. The same is true of a license to sell patented products manufactured by the patentee-licensor.
>
> Where there is no express undertaking by the licensor, the agreement with the licensee may not be executory because the licensor may have fully performed merely by executing the license agreement. Thus a close question may be presented by a license to make and sell a patented product where another licensee undertakes to apply the product. Even in these close cases, however, there may be an implied undertaking by the licensor which brings all patent licenses within the ambit of an executory contract. It has been held in a patentee-licensor's infringement action against a third party that a final judgment adjudicating the patent invalid constitutes a "complete failure of consideration" amounting to an "eviction" which releases the licensee from any further obligation to pay royalties. Moreover, since the death of the doctrine of "licensee estoppel," the licensee can set up the invalidity of the patent as a defense when sued by the licensor for royalties due under the license. Hence, all patentee-licensors are now substantially in the position of having warranted to their licensees the validity of their patents. Although the sanction for the breach of such a warranty is only forfeiture of royalties rather than liability for damages, *this continuing undertaking by the licensor is enough to justify the treatment of all unexpired patent licenses as executory contracts.*

(Emphasis added) 58 Minn. L. Rev. 479, 501-502 (1974).

The Court is of the opinion that Professor Countryman's comments regarding patent licenses are applicable to the instant franchise agreement. The aforesaid comments recognize the interests of a licensee or franchisee in the continuing undertaking of the licensor or franchisor to cooperate in the operation of the franchised business and to insure that the license or franchise will not be infringed upon by third parties. These undertakings on the part of the instant plaintiff remained unperformed after the Chapter 11 filing and constituted a part of the consideration for the defendant's obligations under the franchise agreement. In other words, the franchise agreement in question was unperformed in material part by both the plaintiff and defendant as of the filing date of the defendant's Chapter 11. Therefore, the Court holds that said agreement was an executory contract within the meaning of §365 of the Code and as such was subject to rejection by the defendant.

VI.

The remaining issue to be decided concerns the survivability of the covenant not to compete. The precise question may be phrased as follows: May a party to an executory contract, rejected by a debtor-in-possession pursuant to §365 of the

Bankruptcy Code, compel enforcement of a provision of that contract which restrains said debtor from competing with that party? The Court must answer this question in the negative. An executory contract must be rejected in its entirety or not at all. In re Klaber Bros., Inc., 173 F. Supp. 83 (S.D.N.Y. 1959). It must be remembered that the purpose of both §70(b) of the Act and §365 of the Code is to allow the rejection of executory contracts which are burdensome to the estate and the assumption of executory contracts which would benefit the estate. These sections were intended to solve the problem of assumption of liabilities, i.e., excusing or requiring future specific performance by the debtor depending upon assumption or rejection. 4A, Collier on Bankruptcy, Par. 70.43(2), page 523 (14th ed.); 2 Collier on Bankruptcy, Par. 365.01 pages 365-9 through 365-10 (15th ed. 1979). The effect of rejection is to relieve a debtor and its estate of the obligation imposed under an executory contract. In re Middleton 3 B.R. 610, 613 (B. Ct. E.D. Pa. 1980). In the instant case the covenant not to compete was a part of the franchise agreement. Since the franchise agreement has been rejected by the defendant as an executory contract, the covenant not to compete must also be deemed rejected. The Court, therefore, must deny the plaintiff's request that the Court's prior judgment in this case be amended and must also refuse the plaintiff's request for a temporary injunction.

VII.

The Court must also disagree with the plaintiff's contention that it has no claim against the defendant's estate as that term is defined in §101(4) of the Code. §502(g) specifically grants the plaintiff a nonadministrative claim based upon the rejection of the franchise agreement. Any damages incurred by the plaintiff as a result of the rejection would constitute a "right to payment" sufficient under §101(4). In fact the plaintiff has filed a proof of claim in the amount of $528,295.02.

VIII.

The above constitutes this Court's findings of fact and conclusions of law pursuant to Bankruptcy Rule 752.

Counsel for the defendant is instructed to enter an order consistent with the Court's Memorandum Opinion.

PROBLEM 9-11

World-famous daredevil Hector Gasp made his money by performing death-defying stunts in front of large crowds. His chief rival, Carl Tightrope, signed a contract with Gasp by which Tightrope agreed to pay Gasp $100,000 if on December 25, 2008, Gasp would ride his motorcycle from one cliff to another over Purple Gulch (which Tightrope had failed to clear when he tried it last year, resulting in serious injuries that still trouble him—he entered into this contract because he was sure Gasp would not be able to jump Purple Gulch, thus returning their reputations to the same level). Tightrope paid the $100,000 to Gasp that September with the understanding that it would be returned if Gasp did not make the jump successfully. On November 1, 2008, Gasp filed a Chapter 11 petition. If he wants to reject this contract, may he do so? What if he decides that he wants to assume it, make the jump successfully, and thereby enhance his reputation? Is the contract assumable under the Countryman test?

The Countryman test has come under major criticism in recent years as scholars have contended that it creates unnecessary complications that common sense would resolve without it, so that there is less here than meets the eye. In a much-cited law review article Professor Jay Lawrence Westbrook attacked the whole concept of "executoriness" as "pernicious." *See* J. Westbrook, A Functional Analysis of Executory Contracts, 74 Minn. L. Rev. 227, 282 (1989). In another influential article Michael Andrew commented that "the clothes have no emperor." M. Andrew, Executory Contracts in Bankruptcy: Understanding "Rejection," 59 U. Colo. L. Rev. 845, 932 (1988); *see also* M. Andrew, Executory Contracts Revisited: A Reply to Professor Westbrook, 62 U. Colo. L. Rev. 1 (1991). It is expected that this debate will continue in the case law, particularly where the Countryman test would produce absurd results.

PROBLEM 9-12

COR and Penn Traffic entered into a "Project Agreement" providing for, *inter alia*, the exchange of certain parcels of land, the site preparation and construction of a modern supermarket, reimbursement by COR to Penn Traffic of a specified portion of the construction costs, Penn Traffic's conveyance to COR of the parcel of land on which the supermarket is situated, and Penn Traffic's leaseback of the improved supermarket parcel from COR. At the time of Penn Traffic's bankruptcy filing, COR had performed all of its obligations under the Project Agreement except for the reimbursement of the construction costs (amounting to approximately $3.5 million) and the tender of a lease to Penn Traffic. Penn Traffic had not conveyed the supermarket parcel to COR. COR tendered reimbursement of the $3.5 million in construction costs, as well as a signed lease, as called for by the Project Agreement. Penn Traffic declined to accept COR's tender and, several months thereafter, moved to reject the Project Agreement. Does COR's tender of its remaining obligations under the agreement mean that there is no executory contract for the debtor to assume or reject? In re Penn Traffic Co., 524 F. 3d 373 (2d Cir. 2008).

PROBLEM 9-13

Soap opera star Melody Tears had a contract to appear in the popular daytime drama All My Coffee on a major network, and her contract ran for two more years. She has just received an offer to go to Europe to make a motion picture, and she is sure that if she does this the movie will Catapult her onto bigger entertainment projects than she has had in the past. If she files a Chapter 11 or Chapter 13 petition, can she reject the All

My Coffee contract and get out from under it? *See* In re Carrere, 64 B.R. 156 (Bankr. C.D. Cal. 1986).

PROBLEM 9-14

Oops Moving Company had a contract with Vans of North America to purchase four new moving vans and pay for them over a three-year period. Two of the vans were delivered, and Oops Moving loved how they handled, but had trouble making the payments, missing several in a row. When Vans of North America threatened to repossess the vans, Oops filed a Chapter 11 petition. Now, as the debtor in possession Oops wants to assume this contract, but Vans points to a clause that provides for acceleration of the entire purchase price in the event any payments were missed and demands that amount. What can Oops do here? *See* §§365(b)(1), 1123(d). What does "adequate assurance of future performance" mean? *See* Uniform Commercial Code §2-609, from which the phrase is taken. Vans of North America also highlights another clause in the contract under which it claims the right to repossess its vans; this clause provides that if the buyer becomes insolvent or files a petition in bankruptcy, the contract is at an end and the vans revert to the seller. How can Oops cure this default? *See* §365(b)(2) and (e).

PROBLEM 9-15

Owl Bookstore had established a revolving credit line with Octopus National Bank by which the bank agreed to loan Owl Bookstore sums of money every month in return for a promise of repayment and a security interest in the store's inventory of books. The amount loaned varied as a percentage of the current value of the inventory, and the loan commitment ran for a two-year period. After the first year of this arrangement Owl Bookstore filed a Chapter 11 petition and notified ONB that it was assuming this contract. ONB has no intention of loaning money to a company in bankruptcy. Must it do so? *See* §365(c)(2). Is §365(c)(2) limited to loans or does it extend to trade creditors?

PROBLEM 9-16

Bill Glasses was a computer nerd par excellence, in love with the Internet and all the possibilities it created. He devised a revolutionary computer program for surfing the Net called Net Master, and he promptly patented it under the name of his company, Bill Glasses, Inc. The computer world sang the program's praises, and Glasses signed a contract with Web World by which his company would grant a license to Web World, which would develop Net Master and have the exclusive right for ten years to market this new product in return for a set monthly royalty fee. The contract also provided that Glasses and his company would provide consultation services to Web World so that the product could constantly be made better. Things went well for the first two years of the contract, but then a series of bad investments forced Bill Glasses, Inc., into Chapter 11. The debtor in possession promptly rejected this contract with Web World and has announced that it plans to sell the rights to market Net Master to one of Web World's competitors. The president of Web World calls you, the company's attorney, for advice.

(a)   Can Glasses do this to Web World? *See* §365(n).

(b)   If Glasses refuses to provide the consultation services called for under the contract, can Web World deduct the damages this causes from the royalty payments?

(c)   If the original contract contains a clause giving Web World the option to extend its exclusive right to market the product for an additional five years at the end of the first ten-year period, can Web World still do this once Glasses's bankruptcy has occurred?

PROBLEM 9-17

Portia Moot's law practice thrived, and eventually she employed 20 people. She became very fond of the little office building that housed her practice, and after renting space there for five years she made an offer to buy the entire building from its owner, Garden Properties, Inc., which accepted the offer and signed a contract allowing Portia to purchase the property over a ten-year period, during which Garden Properties would maintain the property by keeping it clean, painting various parts of it according to a schedule, policing the grounds, and so forth. Portia commenced making her payments on the purchase price, but was annoyed when Garden Properties, Inc., filed a Chapter 11 petition and rejected the contract with Portia. You are the associate in her firm who handles her bankruptcy practice, so she turns this over to you. Can they evict her? If she wants out, can she do so? Can she get her payments back? If they sell the property to someone else, what are her rights? If she wants to keep the contract going, can she deduct from her payments the damages the seller causes her when it fails to do the agreed-on maintenance work? Can she file a claim in the bankruptcy proceeding for the damages Garden Properties is causing her? As to all of this, *see* §365(i) and (j). The Bankruptcy Code contains similar rules protecting those purchasing timeshares in realty; *see* §365(h)(2).

PROBLEM 9-18

When contract negotiations between management and labor for renewing an existing agreement broke down to the point where someone actually pulled out a gun and had to be subdued, workers declared a wildcat strike, which the company countered with a wildcat bankruptcy, a same-day Chapter 11 petition. You are the chief negotiator for the union. Is the company going to be able to reject its current collective bargaining agreement and force the union to start over from scratch? *See* §1113.

PROBLEM 9-19

The horror novels of author Nick Fear were popular worldwide. His publisher was Trade Books, Inc., a large New York concern, and his contract with Trade Books gave it the exclusive rights to publish and market his next five novels. The contract also provided that Trade Books could not assign this contract to any other entity. When

Trade Books filed its Chapter 11 petition, the debtor in possession assumed this contract and promptly proposed selling it to Bargain Books of Pennsylvania for a large sum. The latter would then become the publisher of Fear's next five novels. Bargain Books has a reputation for cutting corners and treating its authors shabbily. Fear hires you as his attorney. Is he protected by the nonassignment clause? Must he entrust his reputation to Bargain Books? Can he sue Trade Books if Bargain Books does not adequately perform its part of the deal? *See* §365(f) and (k).

In re Joshua Slocum, Ltd.

United States Court of Appeals, Third Circuit, 1990
922 F.2d 1081

A. LEON HIGGINBOTHAM, JR., Chief Judge.

This case concerns the power of the bankruptcy court to excise a paragraph from a shopping center lease. On November 21, 1988 (the "Filing Date"), Joshua Slocum, Ltd., a Pennsylvania corporation (the "Debtor"), filed a voluntary petition for relief under Chapter 11 of the United States Code with the bankruptcy court. On February 16, 1989, the bankruptcy court appointed Melvin Lashner (the "Trustee") to act as trustee in the case pursuant to 11 U.S.C. §1104. Appellant George Denney ("Denney") contends that the bankruptcy court erred in entering its orders excising paragraph 20 of the lease in question, and then authorizing the assumption and assignment of that lease, without paragraph 20, over his objections. He also maintains that the district court erred in affirming the bankruptcy court's decision. We agree with the appellant and therefore will reverse the district court's summary affirmance of the bankruptcy court's judgment.

I. Facts and Procedural History

The Debtor, Joshua Slocum, Ltd., d/b/a J.S. Acquisition Corporation, began its relationship with Landlord, George Denney, in May of 1983 when Debtor signed a ten year lease for retail space at the Denney Block in Freeport, Maine. The Denney Block, which consisted of three buildings containing seven stores, was developed in two phases commencing in 1982 and completed in 1983. The first phase was undertaken by Cole Haan, a manufacturer and retailer of fine men's and women's shoes, of which Denney is the President. Cole Haan purchased and renovated a building on Main Street in Freeport, Maine, and gave Denney the option to purchase the building in the event that the stock of Cole Haan was acquired by a third person. When the capital stock of Cole Haan was purchased by Nike, George Denney exercised his option to purchase the Cole Haan building.

Shortly thereafter, Denney purchased the building immediately adjoining the Cole Haan building and a third building separated from the second building by a courtyard. Architectural plans to develop the two new buildings in a manner consistent with the Cole Haan building as a common scheme were commissioned by Denney and presented to the Freeport, Maine planning board for approval.

The buildings comprising Denney Block front on Main Street and are part of the downtown shopping district in Freeport. The shopping district consists of a number of streets lined with stores. In addition to the Landlord's three buildings, the Denney Block has a courtyard located between two of its buildings and a parking lot behind the stores. George Denney owns the parking lot which is primarily for the use of patrons of the Denney Block, although according to local ordinance it is also open to the public (thus, it can be used by all persons who shop in the stores along Main Street, Freeport).

Debtor's lease, signed in 1983, along with the leases of some or all of the other Denney Block tenants, contains an average sales clause. This clause allows for Debtor or Landlord to terminate the lease if, after six years, Debtor's average yearly sales are below $711,245. A similar option also existed after the third year of the lease. At that point, either party held the power to terminate the lease if the tenant's average yearly sales were below $602,750.

The lease also contains a percentage rent clause. For the years currently remaining in the lease, this clause requires the tenant to pay additional rent in the amount of four percent of gross sales in excess of $1,175,362. Otherwise, the base rent due in the final five years of the lease is $3,917.88 per month. The leases also require the tenants to provide Landlord with financial information concerning their business so that these lease provisions can be implemented.

Joshua Slocum, Ltd. filed a voluntary petition for relief under Chapter 11 of the United States Bankruptcy Code with the bankruptcy court. By application to the bankruptcy court dated February 2, 1989 (the "Application"), the Trustee requested authorization to assume and assign the Lease pursuant to 11 U.S.C. §365. In March 1989, Denney filed written objections and a memorandum of law in opposition to the application with the bankruptcy court.

By opinion (the "opinion") and order both dated March 29, 1989 (the "interim order"), 99 B.R. 250, the bankruptcy court granted the relief requested in the Application and authorized the Trustee to assume and assign the Lease to European Collections, Inc. (the "assignee"). The bankruptcy court entered another Order on April 11, 1989 (the "final order"), setting forth fully the rights and obligations of the parties. In the opinion and the final order, the bankruptcy court held unenforceable and excised paragraph 20 of the Lease ("paragraph 20"), which provides that "in the event that Tenant's gross sales for the first six (6) lease-years of the term of this Lease do not average Seven Hundred Eleven Thousand Two Hundred Forty Five and 00/100 Dollars ($711,245.00) per lease-year either Landlord or Tenant may elect to terminate this Lease."

The court approved the assignment of the lease without paragraph 20 to European Collections. European Collection has begun occupancy and operation of a store in George Denney's premises in Freeport, Maine. Denney's consolidated appeals followed.

On May 31, 1989, the Trustee filed a motion to dismiss George Denney's appeal as moot. By Order dated December 21, 1989 the district court affirmed without opinion the bankruptcy court's opinion and final order and denied Trustee's motion to dismiss. On January 22, 1990, Denney appealed the district court order.

II. Discussion . . .

B. Shopping Center

The Bankruptcy Code imposes heightened restrictions on the assumption and assignment of leases for shopping centers. *See* 11 U.S.C. §365(b)(3). A debtor in a bankruptcy proceeding can raise working capital by assuming and assigning executory leases and contracts. *See* 11 U.S.C. §365. Ordinarily to obtain the bankruptcy court's permission to assign a lease a debtor need only provide assurance that the assignee will perform under the lease's terms. *See* 11 U.S.C. §365(f)(2)(B). However, Congress in 1978 and again in 1984 placed additional restrictions on assignment of shopping center leases in order to protect the rights of the lessors and the center's other tenants. *See* S. Rep. Nos. 98-70, 98th Cong. 1st Sess. (1983). Congress recognized that unlike the usual situation where a lease assignment affects only the lessor, an assignment of a shopping center lease to an outside party can have a significant detrimental impact on others, in particular, the center's other tenants. Id. However, the Bankruptcy Code does not define "shopping center." Rather, the proper definition of this term "is left to case-by-case interpretation." In re Goldblatt Brothers, Inc., 766 F.2d 1136, 1140 (7th Cir. 1985).

George Denney, the landlord of the Denney Block, wishes to take advantage of these heightened restrictions in order to block the assignment of the lease to European Collections. Thus, appellant Denney contends that the Denney Block is a "shopping center" within the meaning of 11 U.S.C. §365(b)(3). We agree.

However, the bankruptcy court agreed with the appellee, Trustee, and found that Denney Block was not a "shopping center" within the meaning of 11 U.S.C. §365(b)(3). The court looked to *Collier* on Bankruptcy and two cases addressing the question of whether a particular arrangement of stores constitutes a "shopping center" for purposes of §365(b)(3). *See* In re Goldblatt Bros., Inc., 766 F.2d 1136, 1140-41 (7th Cir. 1985); In re 905 Int'l Stores, Inc., 57 B.R. 786, 788-89 (E.D. Mo. 1985). Both of these appellate decisions affirm bankruptcy court determinations that the respective premises in question were not in "shopping centers."

In *Goldblatt*, although the court found the common ownership of contiguous parcels, the presence of an "anchor tenant" (Goldblatt) and joint off street parking adjacent to all stores was significant in deciding whether the arrangement at issue was a shopping center, those factors were not determinative. The court was persuaded by the absence of other typical indicia of shopping centers, i.e., a master lease, fixed hours during which the stores are all open, common areas and joint advertising, and particularly whether the stores were developed to be a shopping center. *See* 766 F.2d at 1141.

In *905 Int'l*, the court, in finding that the arrangement at issue in that case was not a "shopping center," was impressed with "the absence of contractual interdependence among tenants." 57 B.R. at 788. That case, like *Goldblatt*, also sets out several objective criteria in determining whether an arrangement is a "shopping center." In addition to contractual interdependence, these factors include the existence of percentage rent clauses, anchor tenant clauses, joint contribution to trash and maintenance needs, contiguous grouping of stores, a tenant mix, and restrictive clauses. Relying on the indicia pointed to in *Goldblatt*, the court found that only one of the four, joint advertising, was satisfied, and concluded the stores did not comprise a shopping center.

The bankruptcy court utilized the correct criteria for determining what constitutes a "shopping center." The court's focus on the physical attributes of the Denney Block, however, i.e., the fact that it was located on a typical "Main St." in a downtown district, is not a factor laid out as dispositive in the Bankruptcy Code, Collier's treatise, or either of the above cited cases. Nor is there any intrinsic sense to the bankruptcy court's conclusion that the Denney Block's location makes it fall outside the purview of the definition of "shopping center." The court noted that "a shopping center brings to mind a configuration of stores which are not free-standing or detached in the sense that stores appear in a typical 'Main St.' downtown shopping district. Such a downtown shopping district is usually considered in many communities, as the *alternative* (emphasis in original) to the archetypal 'shopping center,' i.e., the large enclosed shopping mall." Bankruptcy Court Opinion (Appendix at 218). While it is true that the mall is the archetypal "shopping center," all shopping centers do not necessarily take the form of shopping malls.

Location is only one element in the determination of whether a group of stores can properly be described as a "shopping center." However, more significant are the following criteria sketched in *Collier, Goldblatt* and *905 Int'l*:

(a)   A combination of leases;
(b)   All leases held by a single landlord;
(c)   All tenants engaged in the commercial retail distribution of goods;
(d)   The presence of a common parking area;
(e)   The purposeful development of the premises as a shopping center;
(f)   The existence of a master lease;
(g)   The existence of fixed hours during which all stores are open;
(h)   The existence of joint advertising;
(i)   Contractual interdependence of the tenants as evidenced by restrictive use provisions in their leases;
(j)   The existence of percentage rent provisions in the leases;
(k)   The right of the tenants to terminate their leases if the anchor tenant terminates its lease;
(l)   Joint participation by tenants in trash removal and other maintenance;
(m)   The existence of a tenant mix; and
(n)   The contiguity of the stores.

We do not think that the bankruptcy court gave adequate consideration to all of the factors described above and gave undue weight to the testimony that the Denney Block does not look like a shopping center. *See* Appendix at 98,219. The bankruptcy court placed what it termed "the physical configuration" of the Denney Block at the center of its analysis, *see* id. at 219-20: "we find that the physical characteristics of the

Denney Block preclude its characterization as a 'shopping center.'" Id. at 218. We are not convinced that the physical configuration of the property plays such a prominent role. Indeed, Collier notes that "the most important characteristic will be a combination of leases held by a single landlord, leased to commercial retail distributors of goods, with the presence of a common parking area." 2 Collier on Bankruptcy ¶365.04[3]. Except for contiguity of stores criterion listed above, the appearance of premises or their location within a downtown shopping district has not been cited as a factor in the determination of whether a group of stores is a "shopping center." All of the stores of Denney Block, except to the extent that they are separated by common areas, are contiguous.

Moreover, George Denney is the sole landlord of all the stores in the Denney Block. Those stores share and provide support for the maintenance of common areas. The stores are all retail distributors of goods subject to substantially similar leases which include both percentage rent provisions and clauses for the benefit of other tenants that restrict the type of goods that a tenant may sell. There is a mix of tenants at Denney Block. Cole Haan primarily sells footwear, Laura Ashley sells a variety of goods including clothing, wall paper and linens, Jones New York sells men's and women's clothing, Benneton [sic] sells sports wear, Class Perfume sells perfume and Christmas Magic sells Christmas decorations and ornaments. The plot plan for Denney Block was presented to the Freeport planning board as a common scheme.

The bankruptcy court found that there was no common parking because customers of stores other than those shops in the Denney Block also use parking lot located directly behind it. That common parking is available at the Denney Block is not obviated by the fact that according to local ordinance the public must also have access to that lot. Hence, the Denney Block satisfies, with the exception of joint advertising, the existence of a master lease and the right of a tenant to terminate the lease if the anchor tenant does so, all of the criteria for determining what constitutes a "shopping center," and all of the "most important" characteristics listed by Collier. Because the bankruptcy court did not adequately consider each of the factors enumerated above its reading of the Act was overly restrictive.

The provisions of Section 365 are intended to remedy three "serious problems caused shopping centers and their solvent tenants by the administration of the bankruptcy code." 130 Cong. Rec. S8891 (statement by the Hon. Orrin G. Hatch, a ranking majority member of the Senate Committee on the Judiciary and a Senate conferee), reprinted in 1984 U.S. Code Cong. & Admin. News 590, 598. Congress wished to alleviate the hardship caused landlord and tenant resulting from vacancy or partial operation of the debtor's space in the shopping center. Section 365 also insures that the landlord will continue to receive payments due under the lease. Finally, the statute guarantees to the landlord and remaining tenants that the tenant mix will not be substantially disrupted. Each of these serious problems was faced by Denney and the remaining shops after Joshua Slocum, Ltd. went bankrupt. We conclude that in light of the harms Section 365 was intended to remedy, and after application of all relevant criteria, denying Denney and his tenants the protections of Section 365 would not further the congressional will.

Additionally, the legislative history of the Bankruptcy Reform Act of 1978 briefly addresses the definition of a "shopping center."

> A shopping center is often a carefully planned enterprise, and though it consists of numerous individual tenants, the center is planned as a single unit, often subject to a master lease or financing agreement. Under these agreements, the tenant mix in a shopping center may be as important to the lessor as the actual promised rental payments, because certain mixes will attract higher patronage of the stores in the center, and thus, a higher rental for the landlord from those stores that are subject to a percentage of gross receipts rental agreement.

H.R. Rep. No. 95-595, 95th Cong., 1st Sess. 348 (1977), reprinted in 1978 U.S. Code Cong. & Admin. News 5787, 6305 (emphasis added).

We think that the Denney Block fits within Congress' conceptualization of a shopping center. The use of the term "often" in the above quoted passage indicates that the existence of a master lease should not be determinative in this court's analysis. We also note that a "single unit" as described above does not have to be an enclosed mall as the bankruptcy court would have it, but rather could be properly conceived of as a cluster of three relatively contiguous buildings as with the Denney Block.

We conclude that Denney Block is a "shopping center" within the meaning of 11 U.S.C. §365(b)(3) and should be entitled to its special protections.

C.   Bankruptcy Court's Power to Excise Paragraph 20 of the Lease

The bankruptcy court, in considering the motion of the Trustee, Melvin Lashner to allow the Debtor, Joshua Slocum, Ltd. to assume and assign its store lease with the Denney Block (*see* 11 U.S.C. §365(a)), held that the average sales clause in paragraph 20 of that lease unenforceable because it is not material or economically significant to the landlord and/or landlord's other tenants. The bankruptcy court granted Trustee's motion to assume and assign the lease and deleted the average sales clause. Appellant, George Denney takes issue with the court's authority to excise paragraph 20 of his leasehold with Joshua Slocum, Ltd. We shall defer the issue of whether that clause was material until later in our discussion. However, we now turn our attention to the question of the bankruptcy court's authority to delete paragraph 20.

Paragraph 20 of Joshua Slocum, Ltd.'s lease at the Denney Block provides as follows:

> Paragraph 20 ("average sales"):
>   Option to Terminate. In the event that Tenant's gross sales for the first three (3) lease-years of the term of this Lease do not average at lease Six Hundred Thousand Seven Hundred Fifty and 00/100 Dollars ($602,750.00) per lease-year, either Landlord or Tenant may elect to terminate this Lease; and in the event that Tenant's gross sales for the first six (6) lease-years of the term of this lease do not average Seven Hundred Eleven Thousand Two Hundred Forty Five Dollars and 00/100 Dollars ($711,245.00) per lease-year, either Landlord or Tenant may elect to terminate this Lease. Such election must be made, if at all, by written notice to the other party received within thirty (30) days from the date of receipt by Landlord of the accountant's statement described in Paragraph 4(b) hereinabove; and termination shall become effective ninety (90) days after receipt of such notice. . . .

Appendix at 15-16.

The bankruptcy court viewed this average sales provision as a cleverly disguised anti-assignment clause. The court stated:

> Perhaps the most novel issue raised by this motion is the enforceability of the "minimum sales" provision which, if enforced, would probably allow Denney to terminate the Lease in July, 1989. If this provision were enforced, with EC having to incorporate the Debtor's sales record through February 20, 1989, the value of the Lease would obviously be nominal. EC's offer to pay $77,000 for the right to obtain an assignment of the Lessee was expressly predicated on its receiving the right to utilize the Debtor's former Freeport store for at least the remaining four years of the lease. It is certainly questionable whether, in the short time before EC could open the store and July, 1989, it could attain a sales volume, when combined with the Debtor's interrupted sales record, sufficient to meet that required as the minimum in the first six lease-years of the Debtor's lease.

Appendix at 227 (Bankruptcy Court Opinion). Working from the premise that Denney Block is not a "shopping center," the bankruptcy court held that the heightened protection accorded to non-debtor contractual rights under §365(b)(3) of the Bankruptcy Code does not apply and turned its attention to §365(f) dealing with assumptions and assignments of lease in non-shopping center cases. However, as discussed above, Denney Block is a "shopping center" and thus, §365(f) does not apply.

The bankruptcy court does have some latitude in waiving contractual provisions when authorizing a trustee to assume and assign an unexpired lease. Section 365(b)(2) on its face permits the court to ignore so-called ipso facto and forfeiture clauses. *See* In re TSW Stores of Nanuet, Inc., 34 B.R. 299, 305 (Bankr. S.D.N.Y. 1983); In re U.L. Radio Corp., 19 B.R. 537 (Bankr. S.D.N.Y. 1982). However, the court's authority to waive the strict enforcement of lease provisions in the context of shopping center cases like this one is further qualified by §365(b)(3) of the Bankruptcy Code. Even under the tightly drawn definition of "adequate assurance" in the shopping center context, Congress did not envision literal compliance with all lease provisions; insubstantial disruptions in, inter alia, tenant mix, and insubstantial breaches in other leases or agreements were contemplated and allowed.[16] 11 U.S.C. §365(b)(3)(C), (D); *see also* U.L. Radio Corp., 19 B.R. 537, 544; TSW Stores, 34 B.R. 299.

In this case, however, the bankruptcy court did not have the authority to excise paragraph 20 of the shopping center lease which addresses the landlord and/or tenant's option to terminate dependent upon the average sales generated by the tenant. We note that even if the Denney Block were not a shopping center, the bankruptcy court's authority to excise paragraph 20 of the lease is questionable. That paragraph must be read in conjunction with paragraph 4, the percent rent clause of the lease

---

16. The court's authority to waive strict enforcement of lease provision in the non-shopping center cases will permit deviations which exceed those permitted in shopping center cases. U.L. Radio, 19 B.R. 537, 544. *See also* In re Peterson's Ltd., Inc., 31 B.R. 524 (Bankr. S.D.N.Y. 1983) (a change in use was authorized to permit an assignment of a so-called high class tobacco shop to an assignee who sold discounted cigars); In re Fifth Avenue Originals, 32 B.R. 648 (Bankr. S.D.N.Y.1983) (a lease assumption and assignment from a high-class boutique selling clothing and accessories for both sexes to Diane von Furstenberg, a designer offering women's clothing and accessories, was approved).

which provides a formula requiring Joshua Slocum, Ltd. to pay a percentage of the lease as specified on any amount in excess of the designated gross sales threshold for a given lease-year (*See* Appendix at pp. 3-4). These two clauses taken together clearly indicate that a bargained for element in this contract was that tenant, Joshua Slocum, Ltd., average a certain volume of sales as specified in paragraph 20 of the lease so that the Landlord could accurately calculate the minimum total rent expected pursuant to paragraph 4 of the lease. Even standing alone, paragraph 20 is an essential bargained for element of this lease agreement because it governs occupancy. We also note that paragraph 20 of the lease falls within the statutory meaning of "other consideration due" under the lease, and without this clause the trustee could not give adequate assurance as to its future performance.

Congress has suggested that the modification of a contracting party's rights is not to be taken lightly. Rather, a bankruptcy court in authorizing assumptions and assignment of unexpired leases must be sensitive to the rights of the non-debtor contracting party (here, George Denney) and the policy requiring that the non-debtor receive the full benefit of his or her bargain. *See* U.L. Radio Corp., 19 B.R. 537; TSW Stores of Nanuet, 34 B.R. 299. Congress' solicitous attitudes toward shopping centers is reflected in the legislative history regarding §365(b)(3), which states:

> A shopping center is often a carefully planned enterprise, and though it consists of numerous individual tenants, the center is planned as a single unit, often subject to a master lease or financing agreement. Under these agreements, the tenant mix in a shopping center may be as important to the lessor as the actual promised rental payments, because certain mixes will attract higher patronage of the stores in the center, and thus a higher rental for the landlord from those stores that are subject to a percentage of gross receipts rental agreement. Thus, in order to assure a landlord of his bargained for exchange, the court would have to consider such factors as the nature of the business to be conducted by the trustee or his assignee, whether that business complies with the requirements of any master agreement, whether the kind of business proposed will generate gross sales in an amount such that the percentage rent specified in the lease is substantially the same as what would have been provided by the debtor, and whether the business proposed to be conducted would result in a breach of other causes in master agreements relating, for example to tenant mix and location.

H.R. Rep. No. 595, 95th Cong., 1st Session 348-49, reprinted in 1978 U.S. Code Cong. & Admin. News 5963, 6305; *see also* S.R. Rep. No. 95-989, reprinted in id. at 5787, 5845.

In excising paragraph 20, the bankruptcy court undermined both the Congressional policy and the statutory requirement under §365(b)(3)(A) that the trustee give adequate assurance of "other consideration due" under an unexpired lease. We find that the bankruptcy court did not have the authority to excise paragraph 20 of the lease. . . .

III. Conclusion

In conclusion, having satisfied ourselves that we have appellate jurisdiction, we hold that the Denney Block, a contiguous grouping of stores, is subject to the heightened restrictions on the assumption and assignment of leases of real property in shopping centers. See 11 U.S.C. §365(b)(3). We find that the district court erred in affirming the bankruptcy court's approval of the assignment of the leasehold at issue without paragraph 20, an average sales clause, to European Collections. The bankruptcy court did not have authority to excise paragraph 20, a material provision governing the terms of occupancy under the lease. Therefore, we will vacate the judgment of the district court and remand to the district court for further proceedings consistent with this opinion.

C.   Leases

The last case, dealing as it does with a lease, might more properly belong in this section of the book, but let's leave it where it is since its major point is not about leases but about the ability of the debtor in possession to use the assume and assign power of §365. It should be noted that where the lease involves a shopping center, §365 has a number of special rules preventing assumption and assignment if this would violate provisions such as tenant mixes, use, location, radius, and so on. See §365(b)(3) and (h)(1)(D). Since a huge percentage of retail business in the United States is done in shopping centers, this is worth remembering.

That aside, leases cause a number of legal problems in bankruptcy proceedings under all of the Chapters of Title 11. The following Problems and cases explore such problems while also reviewing matters briefly addressed in earlier chapters.

PROBLEM 9-20

The law firm of Factory, Factory & Money, a partnership, fell on hard times after a series of ugly headlines in the press using words such as "bribery," "misappropriations," and "fraud," and was forced to file a Chapter 11 petition. Skyscraper, Inc., was the landlord from whom it rented an entire floor near the top of the largest building in the state. When the firm missed six months of rental payments in a row, Skyscraper, Inc., initiated eviction proceedings. F, F & M responded with a Chapter 11 petition.

(a)   Is the lease property of the estate at all, given that the landlord had declared a default for failure to pay rent and had taken steps toward eviction? *See* §§541(b)(2) and 365(b)(1) and (c)(3).

(b)   Skyscraper, Inc., filed a claim in the bankruptcy proceeding for the past due rent and for all future rent. Can it get this much? *See* §502((b)(6). May it claim the status of a secured creditor for the amount due it since state law gives landlords a lien on the property of their tenants for the amount of past due rent? *See* §545(3).

(c)   If the original terms of F, F & M's lease provided that the lease would last until March 1, 2009, and the bankruptcy had been filed on February 4 of that year, would the filing prevent Skyscraper from evicting the law firm on March 1? *See* the sections cited at the end of a, above, and §362(b)(10).

(d)   Once the petition was filed, F, F & M stopped paying rent. Can they do this? *See* §365(d)(3). How long does the debtor in possession have to decide whether to assume or reject the lease? *See* §365(d)(4).

(e)   If Skyscraper, Inc., the landlord, had been the one to file a bankruptcy petition, does the law firm have the right to move, or may it stay and keep making rental payments, or can it refuse to make payments if the landlord stops furnishing the usual services (cleanup, security, etc.)? *See* §365(h)(1).

(f)   If F, F & M had leased a number of copiers from B.I.G. Machines, Inc., prior to the filing of its bankruptcy petition, how quickly must it act in deciding to assume or reject this lease, and must it continue to make lease payments in the period before it makes up its mind as to this? *See* §365(d)(1), (2), and (10).

(g)   F, F & M's lease with Skyscraper, Inc. had a clause allowing the landlord to terminate the lease if the tenant ceased to be open to the public for more than two days. If F, F & M had been forced to close its doors for a week before filing its petition, is this clause going to cause it trouble? *See* §365(b)(1)(A).

The above rules apply to business leases. What happens if the debtor/tenants are consumers?

PROBLEM 9-21

Mimi and Roger, married artists, rented a luxury apartment in a ritzy part of town, paying an exorbitant amount of rent each month. When they filed their joint bankruptcy petition, they had missed paying any rent for the past six months, so the landlord, Larsen Management, initiated foreclosure proceedings after Mimi and Roger had failed to respond to a series of dunning letters and phone calls. Will the automatic stay protect them here? Can they assume the lease under §365? Can their trustee? *See* §365(d)(1) and (2).

D.   Obtaining Credit

In Chapter 11, the debtor in possession must keep a business running, and this means paying all the bills as they come due: employees, trade creditors, and the like, although the automatic stay frees the debtor from having to make payments that service outstanding debt. Understandably, new entities dealing with the debtor or old entities asked to extend credit to the debtor would be hesitant to do so unless given some protection in the Chapter 11 proceeding. Let's deal with the issues this raises.

PROBLEM 9-22

Rural Radio, Inc., was a mom-and-pop operation that played country and western music in a small community. It had always borrowed money from Last National Bank to finance its existence, and it was deep in debt to LNB and many others when it filed its Chapter 11 petition. As debtor in possession, what can Rural Radio do to obtain new credit?

(a) If LNB or any other lender is willing to loan Rural Radio a small amount of money unsecured (granted, that is *unlikely*), must this loan agreement be approved by the bankruptcy court? *See* §364(a) and (b).

(b) If LNB is unwilling to make an unsecured loan to the station, what incentives can the station offer the bank? *See* §364(c). Suppose Towers of Tennessee, a manufacturer of radio towers, had sold Rural Radio a new broadcasting tower on credit two years ago and had taken a purchase money security interest in the tower. Does §364(d) authorize the court to give LNB a lien that is *senior* to that of Towers of Tennessee? If the court does this, can Towers of Tennessee appeal, and, if successful, wipe out the lien the bankruptcy court gave to LNB? *See* §364(e). Why in the world would Congress have enacted this last subsection?

(c) When Rural Radio filed its Chapter 11 petition, Towers of Tennessee made a motion to lift the automatic stay so that it could foreclose the purchase money security interest it had in the broadcasting tower, but the court denied this motion, holding that T of T's security interest in the tower was sufficient to afford it adequate protection. This proved to be wrong when the tower was struck by lightning and destroyed, and it turned out that no insurance covered the loss. At this point the bankruptcy judge granted T of T a §507(b) super priority over all other administrative expenses and other priority claims; *see* §507(b). Shortly thereafter, when Rural Radio needed financing, it proposed borrowing money from Last National Bank and giving LNB top priority over all other priority claims, including that of T of T. You are the attorney for T of T, and the company president asks you if its priority position can be trumped in this fashion. *See* §364(c)(1).

(d) Can LNB demand that any lien it is given protect not only future credit but also that it had extended before the petition was filed? See the next case.

In re Saybrook Manufacturing Co., Inc.

United States Court of Appeals, Eleventh Circuit, 1992
963 F.2d 1490

Cox, Circuit Judge:

Seymour and Jeffrey Shapiro, unsecured creditors, objected to the bankruptcy court's authorization for the Chapter 11 debtors to "cross-collateralize" their prepetition debt with unencumbered property from the bankruptcy estate. The bankruptcy court overruled the objection and also refused to grant a stay of its order pending appeal. The Shapiros appealed to the district court, which dismissed the case as moot under section 364(e) of the Bankruptcy Code because the Shapiros had failed to obtain a stay. We conclude that this appeal is not moot and that cross-collateralization is not authorized under the Bankruptcy Code. Accordingly, we reverse and remand.

I. Facts and Procedural History

Saybrook Manufacturing Co., Inc., and related companies (the "debtors"), initiated proceedings seeking relief under Chapter 11 of the Bankruptcy Code on December 22, 1988. On December 23, 1988, the debtors filed a motion for the use of cash collateral and for authorization to incur secured debt. The bankruptcy court entered an emergency financing order that same day. At the time the bankruptcy petition was filed, the debtors owed Manufacturers Hanover approximately $34 million. The value of the collateral for this debt, however, was less than $10 million. Pursuant to the order, Manufacturers Hanover agreed to lend the debtors an additional $3 million to facilitate their reorganization. In exchange, Manufacturers Hanover received a security interest in all of the debtors' property — both property owned prior to filing the bankruptcy petition and that which was acquired subsequently. This security interest not only protected the $3 million of post-petition credit but also secured Manufacturers Hanover's $34 million pre-petition debt.

This arrangement enhanced Manufacturers Hanover's position vis-à-vis other unsecured creditors, such as the Shapiros, in the event of liquidation. Because Manufacturers Hanover's pre-petition debt was undersecured by approximately $24 million, it originally would have shared in a pro rata distribution of the debtors' unencumbered assets along with the other unsecured creditors. Under the financing order, however, Manufacturers Hanover's pre-petition debt became fully secured by all of the debtors' assets. If the bankruptcy estate were liquidated, Manufacturers Hanover's entire debt — $34 million pre-petition and $3 million post-petition — would have to be paid in full before any funds could be distributed to the remaining unsecured creditors.

Securing pre-petition debt with pre- and post-petition collateral as part of a post-petition financing arrangement is known as cross-collateralization. The Second Circuit aptly defined cross-collateralization as follows:

> [I]n return for making new loans to a debtor in possession under Chapter XI, a financing institution obtains a security interest on all assets of the debtor, both those existing at the date of the order and those created in the course of the Chapter XI proceeding, not only for the new loans, the propriety of which is not contested, but [also] for existing indebtedness to it.

Otte v. Manufacturers Hanover Commercial Corp. (In re Texlon Corp.), 596 F.2d 1092, 1094 (2d Cir. 1979).

The Shapiros filed a number of objections to the bankruptcy court's order on January 13, 1989. After a hearing, the bankruptcy court overruled the objections. The Shapiros then filed a notice of appeal and a request for the bankruptcy court to stay its financing order pending appeal. The bankruptcy court denied the request for a stay on February 23, 1989.

The Shapiros subsequently moved the district court to stay the bankruptcy court's financing order pending appeal; the court denied the motion on March 7, 1989. On May 20, 1989, the district court dismissed the Shapiros' appeal as moot under 11 U.S.C. §364(e) because the Shapiros had failed to obtain a stay of the financing order pending appeal, rejecting the argument that cross-collateralization is contrary to the Code. Shapiro v. Saybrook Mfg. Co. (In re Saybrook Mfg. Co.), 127 B.R. 494 (M.D. Ga. 1991). The Shapiros then appealed to this court.

II. *Issues on Appeal*

1. Whether the appeal to the district court and the appeal to this court are moot under section 364(e) of the Bankruptcy Code because the Shapiros failed to obtain a stay of the bankruptcy court's financing order.
2. Whether cross-collateralization is authorized under the Bankruptcy Code.

III. *Contentions of the Parties*

The lenders argue that this appeal is moot under section 364(e) of the Bankruptcy Code. That section provides that a lien or priority granted under section 364 may not be overturned unless it is stayed pending appeal. Even if this appeal were not moot, the Shapiros are not entitled to relief. Cross-collateralization is a legitimate means for debtors to obtain necessary financing and is not prohibited by the Bankruptcy Code.

The Shapiros contend that their appeal is not moot. Because cross-collateralization is not authorized under bankruptcy law, section 364(e) is inapplicable. Permitting cross-collateralization would undermine the entire structure of the Bankruptcy Code by allowing one unsecured creditor to gain priority over all other unsecured creditors simply by extending additional credit to a debtor. . . .

V. *Discussion*

A. Mootness

We begin by addressing the lenders' claim that this appeal is moot under section 364(e) of the Bankruptcy Code. Section 364(e) provides that:

> The reversal or modification on appeal of an authorization under this section to obtain credit or incur debt, or of a grant under this section of a priority or a lien, does not affect the validity of any debt so incurred, or any priority or lien so granted, to an entity that extended such credit in good faith, whether or not such entity knew of the pendency of the appeal, unless such authorization and the incurring of such debt, or the granting of such priority or lien, were stayed pending appeal.

11 U.S.C. §364(e). The purpose of this provision is to encourage the extension of credit to debtors in bankruptcy by eliminating the risk that any lien securing the loan will be modified on appeal.

The lenders suggest that we assume cross-collateralization is authorized under section 364 and then conclude the Shapiros' appeal is moot under section 364(e). This is similar to the approach adopted by the Ninth Circuit in Burchinal v. Central Washington Bank (In re Adams Apple, Inc.), 829 F.2d 1484 (9th Cir. 1987). That court held that cross-collateralization was "authorized" under section 364 for the purposes of section 364(e) mootness but declined to decide whether cross-collateralization was illegal per se under the Bankruptcy Code. Id. at 1488 n.6. *See also* Unsecured Creditors' Committee v. First National Bank & Trust Co. (In re Ellingsen MacLean Oil Co.), 834 F.2d 599 (6th Cir. 1987), *cert. denied*, 488 U.S. 817, 109 S. Ct. 55, 102 L. Ed. 2d 33 (1988).

We reject the reasoning of In re Adams Apple and In re Ellingsen because they "put the cart before the horse." By its own terms, section 364(e) is only applicable if the challenged lien or priority was authorized under section 364. *See* Charles J. Tabb, Lender Preference Clauses and the Destruction of Appealability and Finality: Resolving a Chapter 11 Dilemma, 50 Ohio St. L.J. 109, 116-35 (1989) (criticizing In re Adams Apple, In re Ellingsen, and the practice of shielding cross-collateralization from appellate review via mootness under section 364(e)); *see also* In re Ellingsen, 834 F.2d at 607 (Merritt, dissenting) (arguing that section 364(e) was not designed to prohibit creditors from challenging pre-petition matters and that "[l]enders should not be permitted to use their leverage in making emergency loans in order to insulate their prepetition claims from attack"). We cannot determine if this appeal is moot under section 364(e) until we decide the central issue in this appeal — whether cross-collateralization is authorized under section 364. Accordingly, we now turn to that question.

B.   Cross-Collateralization and Section 364

Cross-collateralization is an extremely controversial form of Chapter 11 financing. Nevertheless, the practice has been approved by several bankruptcy courts. *See, e.g.*, In re Vanguard Diversified, Inc., 31 B.R. 364 (Bankr. E.D.N.Y. 1983); In re Roblin Indus., Inc., 52 B.R. 241 (Bankr. W.D.N.Y. 1985); In re Beker Indus. Corp., 58 B.R. 725 (Bankr. S.D.N.Y. 1986). *Contra* In re Monach Circuit Indus., Inc., 41 B.R. 859 (Bankr. E.D. Pa. 1984). Even the courts that have allowed cross-collateralization, however, were generally reluctant to do so. *See* McLemore v. Citizens Bank (In re Tom McCormick Enterprises, Inc.), 26 B.R. 437, 439-40 (Bankr. M.D. Tenn. 1983).

In In re Vanguard, for example, the bankruptcy court noted that cross-collateralization is "a disfavored means of financing" that should only be used as a last resort. In re Vanguard, 31 B.R. at 366. In order to obtain a financing order including cross-collateralization, the court required the debtor to demonstrate (1) that its business operations would fail absent the proposed financing, (2) that it is unable to obtain alternative financing on acceptable terms, (3) that the proposed lender will not accept less preferential terms, and (4) that the proposed financing is in the general creditor body's best interest. Id. This four-part test has since been adopted by other bankruptcy courts which permit cross-collateralization. *See, e.g.*, In re Roblin, 52 B.R. at 244-45.

The issue of whether the Bankruptcy Code authorizes cross-collateralization is a question of first impression in this court. Indeed, it is essentially a question of first impression before any court of appeals. Neither the lenders' brief nor our own research has produced a single appellate decision which either authorizes or prohibits the practice. . . .

Cross-collateralization is not specifically mentioned in the Bankruptcy Code. *See, e.g.,* In re Beker, 58 B.R. at 741 (conceding that cross-collateralization is not expressly permitted by the Code). We conclude that cross-collateralization is inconsistent with bankruptcy law for two reasons. First, cross-collateralization is not authorized as a method of post-petition financing under section 364. Second, cross-collateralization is beyond the scope of the bankruptcy court's inherent equitable power because it is directly contrary to the fundamental priority scheme of the Bankruptcy Code. *See generally* Charles J. Tabb, A Critical Reappraisal of Cross-Collateralization in Bankruptcy, 60 S. Cal. L. Rev. 109 (1986).

Section 364 authorizes Chapter 11 debtors to obtain secured credit and incur secured debt as part of their reorganization. It provides, in relevant part, that:

> (c) If the trustee is unable to obtain unsecured credit allowable under section 503(b)(1) of this title as an administrative expense, the court, after notice and a hearing, may authorize the obtaining of credit or the incurring of debt —
>> (1) with priority over any or all administrative expenses of the kind specified in section 503(b) or 507(b) of this title;
>> (2) secured by a lien on property of the estate that is not otherwise subject to a lien; or
>> (3) secured by a junior lien on property of the estate that is subject to a lien.
>
> (d)(1) The court, after notice and a hearing, may authorize the obtaining of credit or incurring of debt secured by a senior or equal lien on property of the estate that is subject to a lien only if —
>> (A) the trustee is unable to obtain such credit otherwise; and
>> (B) there is adequate protection of the interest of the holder of the lien on the property of the estate on which such senior or equal lien is proposed to be granted.
>
>> (2) In any hearing under this subsection, the trustee has the burden of proof on the issue of adequate protection.

11 U.S.C. §364(c) & (d) (emphasis added). By their express terms, sections 364(c) & (d) apply only to future — i.e., post-petition — extensions of credit. They do not authorize the granting of liens to secure pre-petition loans.

The bankruptcy court for the Eastern District of Pennsylvania reached this same conclusion regarding section 364(c) in In re Monach. "[T]he terms of §364(c) appear to limit the extent of the priority or lien to the amount of the credit obtained or debt incurred *after* court approval." In re Monach, 41 B.R. at 862 (emphasis in original). *See also* In re Ellingsen, 834 F.2d at 601 (noting that "the express language of [section 364(c)] suggests that the priority or lien granted thereunder is limited to securing the newly incurred debt authorized by that provision"). Similarly, the bankruptcy court for the District of New Hampshire held that section 364(d) was limited to future credit or debt. "Section 364(d) speaks only of the granting of liens as security for *new credit* authorized by the Court." In re Tenney Village Co., 104 B.R. 562, 570 (D.N.H. 1989) (emphasis added).

Given that cross-collateralization is not authorized by section 364, we now turn to the lenders' argument that bankruptcy courts may permit the practice under their general equitable power. Bankruptcy courts are indeed courts of equity, *see, e.g.,* Young v. Higbee Co., 324 U.S. 204, 65 S. Ct. 594, 89 L. Ed. 890 (1945); 11 U.S.C. §105(a), and they have the power to adjust claims to avoid injustice or unfairness. Pepper v. Litton, 308 U.S. 295, 60 S. Ct. 238, 84 L. Ed. 281 (1939). This equitable power, however, is not unlimited.

> [T]he bankruptcy court has the ability to deviate from the rules of priority and distribution set forth in the Code in the interest of justice and equity. The Court cannot use this flexibility, however, merely to establish a ranking of priorities within priorities. Furthermore, absent the existence of some type of inequitable conduct on the part of the claimant, which results in injury to the creditors of the bankrupt or an unfair advantage to the claimant, the court cannot subordinate a claim to claims within the same class.

In re FCX, Inc., 60 B.R. 405, 409 (E.D.N.C. 1986) (citations omitted).

Section 507 of the Bankruptcy Code fixes the priority order of claims and expenses against the bankruptcy estate. 11 U.S.C. §507. Creditors within a given class are to be treated equally, and bankruptcy courts may not create their own rules of superpriority within a single class. 3 Collier on Bankruptcy §507.02[2] (15th ed. 1992). Cross-collateralization, however, does exactly that. *See, e.g.,* In re FCX, 60 B.R. at 410. As a result of this practice, post-petition lenders' unsecured pre-petition claims are given priority over all other unsecured pre-petition claims. The Ninth Circuit recognized that "[t]here is no . . . applicable provision in the Bank-ruptcy Code authorizing the debtor to pay certain pre-petition unsecured claims in full while others remain unpaid. To do so would impermissibly violate the priority scheme of the Bankruptcy Code." In re Sun Runner, 945 F.2d at 1094 (citations omitted). *See also* In re Tenney Village, 104 B.R. at 570 (holding that §364 does not authorize bankruptcy courts to change the priorities set forth in §507.)

The Second Circuit has noted that, if cross-collateralization were initiated by the bankrupt while insolvent and shortly before filing a petition, the arrangement "would have constituted a voidable preference." In re Texlon, 596 F.2d at 1097. The fundamental nature of this practice is not changed by the fact that it is sanctioned by the bankruptcy court. We disagree with the district court's conclusion that, while cross-collateralization may violate some policies of bankruptcy law, it is consistent with the general purpose of Chapter 11 to help businesses reorganize and become profitable. In re Saybrook, 127 B.R. at 499. Rehabilitation is certainly the primary purpose of Chapter 11. This end, however, does not justify the use of any means. Cross-collateralization is directly inconsistent with the priority scheme of the Bankruptcy Code. Accordingly, the practice may not be approved by the bankruptcy court under its equitable authority.

VI.   *Conclusion*

Cross-collateralization is not authorized by section 364. Section 364(e), therefore, is not applicable and this appeal is not moot. Because Texlon-type cross-collateralization is not explicitly authorized by the Bankruptcy Code and is contrary to the basic priority structure of the Code, we hold that it is an impermissible means of obtaining post-petition financing. The judgment of the district court is REVERSED and the case is REMANDED for proceedings not inconsistent with this opinion.

REVERSED and REMANDED.

QUESTION

The bankruptcy bar raised its collective eyebrows when this case was handed down. Isn't the rule of *Saybrook* a rather obvious end-run around §364(e)? How would it cause you, attorney for a postpetition lender being approached for a loan, to couch your advice if the transaction were extraordinary?

PROBLEM 9-23

Octopus National Bank had long been the bank of Luddite Technologies and during this history had always covered Luddite's overdrafts in its bank account. Luddite came to rely on this, so that almost every day it overdrew the account in the amount of $10,000 or more, but each time made up the shortfall the following day when it was made aware of the exact figures of its various transactions. Four months after Luddite filed its Chapter 11 petition, the bank was sent a copy of an order of the bankruptcy court granting Abacus, Inc., a major trade creditor of the debtor that had agreed to ship products on credit, a priority security interest in all monies generated by the sale of its products. The bank was well aware that these monies were being routinely deposited into Luddite's account with it. Nonetheless, for the first year of the bankruptcy, ONB kept covering Luddite's overdrawals and reimbursing itself out of the subsequent deposits, though the amount of the overdrafts kept increasing. By the time the bankruptcy court was alerted to the whole procedure, ONB was covering overdrafts of $90,000 before it suddenly stopped paying any of Luddite's checks. Has the bank violated the automatic stay? Must it reimburse the estate for all the credit it has extended since the bankruptcy petition was filed? *See* §364(a) and In re Garofalo's Finer Foods, Inc., 186 B.R. 414 (Bankr. N.D. Ill. 1995).

E.   *Selling Assets*

PROBLEM 9-24

Octopus National Bank had a perfected security interest in any rental payments generated by those renting rooms from the Happy Earwig Motel. If the motel files a Chapter 11 bankruptcy petition, will this priority be effective in bankruptcy also?

See §552. If the debtor in possession proposes using these rental amounts to finance its day-to-day operations, does the bank have standing to object? *See* §363(a) through (e).

In re Lionel Corporation

United States Court of Appeals, Second Circuit, 1983
722 F.2d 1063

CARDAMONE, Circuit Judge:

This expedited appeal is from an order of United States District Judge Dudley B. Bonsal dated September 7, 1983, approving an order entered earlier that day by the United States Bankruptcy Court for the Southern District of New York (Ryan, J.). The order authorized the sale by Lionel Corporation, a Chapter 11 debtor in possession, of its 82 percent common stock holding in Dale Electronics, Inc. to Peabody International Corporation for $50 million.

I. Facts

On February 19, 1982, the Lionel Corporation — toy train manufacturer of childhood memory — and two of its subsidiaries, Lionel Leisure, Inc., and Consolidated Toy Company, filed joint petitions for reorganization under Chapter 11 of the Bankruptcy Code. Resort to Chapter 11 was precipitated by losses totalling $22.5 million that Lionel incurred in its toy retailing operation during the two-year period ending December 1982.

There are 7.1 million shares of common stock of Lionel held by 10,000 investors. Its consolidated assets and liabilities as of March 31, 1983, were $168.7 million and $191.5 million, respectively, reflecting a negative net worth of nearly $23 million. Total sales for 1981 and 1982 were $295.1 million and $338.6 million. Lionel's creditors hold approximately $135.6 million in pre-petition claims, and they are represented in the ongoing bankruptcy proceedings by an Official Creditors' Committee whose 13 members hold $80 million of those claims. The remaining $55 million is scattered among thousands of small creditors.

Lionel continues to operate its businesses and manage its properties pursuant to 11 U.S.C. §§1107-1108, primarily through its wholly-owned subsidiary, Leisure. Leisure operates Lionel's presently owned 56 specialty retail stores, which include a number of stores formerly managed by Lionel's other subsidiary, Consolidated Toy. In addition to the stock of Leisure and Consolidated Toy, Lionel has other assets such as the right to receive royalty payments relating to the manufacture of toy trains.

Lionel's most important asset and the subject of this proceeding is its ownership of 82 percent of the common stock of Dale, a corporation engaged in the manufacture of electronic components. Dale is not a party to the Lionel bankruptcy proceeding. Public investors own the remaining 18 percent of Dale's common stock, which is listed on the American Stock Exchange. Its balance sheet reflects assets and liabilities as of March 31, 1983, of $57.8 million and $29.8 million, respectively, resulting in shareholders equity of approximately $28.0 million. Lionel's stock investment in Dale represents approximately 34 percent of Lionel's consolidated assets, and its interest in Dale is Lionel's most valuable single asset. Unlike Lionel's toy retailing operation, Dale is profitable. For the same two-year period ending in December 1982 during which Lionel had incurred its substantial losses, Dale had an aggregate operating profit of $18.8 million.

On June 14, 1983, Lionel filed an application under section 363(b) seeking bankruptcy court authorization to sell its 82 percent interest in Dale to Acme-Cleveland Corporation for $43 million in cash. Four days later the debtor filed a plan of reorganization conditioned upon a sale of Dale with the proceeds to be distributed to creditors. Certain issues of the reorganization remain unresolved, and negotiations are continuing; however, a solicitation of votes on the plan has not yet begun. On September 7, 1983, following the Securities and Exchange Commission's July 15 filing of objections to the sale, Bankruptcy Judge Ryan held a hearing on Lionel's application. At the hearing, Peabody emerged as the successful of three bidders with an offer of $50 million for Lionel's interest in Dale.

The Chief Executive Officer of Lionel and a Vice-President of Salomon Brothers were the only witnesses produced and both testified in support of the application. Their testimony established that while the price paid for the stock was "fair," Dale is not an asset "that is wasting away in any sense." Lionel's Chief Executive Officer stated that there was no reason why the sale of Dale stock could not be accomplished as part of the reorganization plan, and that the sole reason for Lionel's application to sell was the Creditors' Committee's insistence upon it. The creditors wanted to turn this asset of Lionel into a "pot of cash," to provide the bulk of the $70 million required to repay creditors under the proposed plan of reorganization.

In confirming the sale, Judge Ryan made no formal findings of fact. He simply noted that cause to sell was sufficiently shown by the Creditors' Committee's insistence upon it. Judge Ryan further found cause — presumably from long experience — based upon his own opinion that a present failure to confirm would set the entire reorganization process back a year or longer while the parties attempted to restructure it.

The Committee of Equity Security Holders, statutory representatives of the 10,000 public shareholders of Lionel, appealed this order claiming that the sale, prior to approval of a reorganization plan, deprives the equity holders of the Bankruptcy Code's safeguards of disclosure, solicitation and acceptance and divests the debtor of a dominant and profitable asset which could serve as a cornerstone for a sound plan. The SEC also appeared and objected to the sale in the bankruptcy court and supports the Equity Committee's appeal, claiming that approval of the sale side-steps the Code's requirement for informed suffrage which is at the heart of Chapter 11.

The Creditors' Committee favors the sale because it believes it is in the best interests of Lionel and because the sale is expressly authorized by §363(b) of the Code. Lionel tells us that its ownership of Dale, a non-operating asset, is held for

investment purposes only and that its sale will provide the estate with the large block
of the cash needed to fund its plan of reorganization.

From the oral arguments and briefs we gather that the Equity Committee believes
that Chapter 11 has cleared the reorganization field of major pre-plan sales —
somewhat like the way Minerva routed Mars — relegating §363(b) to be used only
in emergencies. The Creditors' Committee counters that a bankruptcy judge should
have absolute freedom under §363(b) to do as he thinks best. Neither of these arguments is wholly persuasive. Here, as in so many similar cases, we must avoid the
extremes, for the policies underlying the Bankruptcy Reform Act of 1978 support a
middle ground — one which gives the bankruptcy judge considerable discretion yet
requires him to articulate sound business justifications for his decisions.

II. Discussion

The issue now before this Court is to what extent Chapter 11 permits a bankruptcy
judge to authorize the sale of an important asset of the bankrupt's estate, out of the
ordinary course of business and prior to acceptance and outside of any plan of reorganization. Section 363(b), the focal point of our analysis, provides that "[t]he trustee,
after notice and a hearing, may use, sell, or lease, other than in the ordinary course of
business, property of the estate." 11 U.S.C. §363(b) (Supp. V 1981).

On its face, section 363(b) appears to permit disposition of any property of the
estate of a corporate debtor without resort to the statutory safeguards embodied in
Chapter 11 of the Bankruptcy Code, 11 U.S.C. §1101 et seq. (Supp. V 1981). Yet,
analysis of the statute's history and over seven decades of case law convinces us that
such a literal reading of section 363(b) would unnecessarily violate the congressional
scheme for corporate reorganizations.

A.   Bankruptcy Act of 1867 — The "Perishable" Standard

An early statutory reference providing for the sale of a debtor's property prior to
final liquidation of the estate in limited circumstances was Section 25 of the Bankruptcy Act of 1867 (As of March 2, 1967, 14 Stat. 517). Congress there stated:

> "*And be it further enacted*, That when it appears to the satisfaction of the court that the estate
> of the debtor, or any part thereof, is of *a perishable nature, or liable to deteriorate in value*, the
> court may order the same to be sold, in such manner as may be deemed most expedient, under the
> direction of the messenger or assignee, as the case may be, who shall hold the funds received in
> place of the estate disposed of. . . ." (emphasis added and in original).

The 1867 Act did not provide for reorganizations; nevertheless, the requirements that
the property be of a perishable nature or liable to deteriorate in value and that there be
loss if the same is not sold immediately were also found in General Bankruptcy Order
No. XVIII(3), adopted by the Supreme Court in 1898. General Order in Bankruptcy
No. XVIII, 89 F. viii (November 28, 1898).

From 1898 through 1937, the Bankruptcy Act did not contain a specific provision permitting pre-adjudication sales of a debtor's property. But, pursuant to General Order XVIII, this Circuit over fifty years ago upheld an order that approved a private, pre-adjudication sale of a bankrupt's stock of handkerchiefs. Not only was merchandise sold at a price above its appraised value, but Christmas sales had commenced and the sale of handkerchiefs would decline greatly after the holidays. Our court held that the concept of "perishable" was not limited to its physical meaning, but also included property liable to deteriorate in price and value. In re Pedlow, 209 F. 841, 842 (2d Cir. 1913). *See* Hill v. Douglass, 78 F.2d 851, 853-54 (9th Cir. 1935) (sale of road-making equipment of a contractor to prevent its repossession approved).

B.   Chandler Act of 1938 — The "Upon Cause Shown" Standard

Section 116(3) of the 1938 Act, which was the immediate predecessor of §363(b), was originally enacted as section 77B(c) in 1937. Section 116(3) provided: "Upon the approval of a petition, the judge may, in addition to the jurisdiction, powers and duties hereinabove and elsewhere in this chapter conferred and imposed upon him and the court . . . (3) authorize a receiver or a trustee or a debtor in possession, upon such notice as the judge may prescribe and upon cause shown, to lease or sell any property of the debtor, whether real or personal, upon such terms and conditions as the judge may approve." This section applied in Chapter X proceedings, and a similar provision, §313(2), pertained to Chapter XI cases. Thus, when reorganization became part of the bankruptcy law, the long established administrative powers of the court to sell a debtor's property prior to adjudication were extended to cover reorganizations with a debtor in possession under Chapter XI pursuant to §313(2), 11 U.S.C. §§701 et seq., as well as a trustee in control under Chapter X pursuant to §116(3), 11 U.S.C. §§501 et seq. These sections, as their predecessors, were designed to handle leases or sales required during the time lag between the filing of a petition for reorganization and the date when the plan was approved.[17]

The Rules of Bankruptcy Procedure applicable in Chapters X and XI, the Act's reorganization procedures, provided for a sale of all or part of a bankrupt's property after application to the court and "upon cause shown." Rules 10-607(b), 11-54. Despite the provisions of this Rule, the "perishable" concept, expressed in the view that a pre-confirmation or pre-adjudication sale was the exception and not the rule, persisted. As one commentator stated, "[o]rdinarily, in the absence of perishable goods, or depreciation of assets, or actual jeopardy of the estate, a sale

---

17. A letter from a district judge in California addressed to the House Committee holding hearings on these sections illustrates one of the reasons for the addition in 1937 of rules permitting pre-confirmation sales. The letter recounted the difficulty the writer had in a reorganization involving a California land company whose business consisted of selling real property. Because of the lack of clear authority to sell, title companies refused to certify title to the land during the time interval after a petition had been filed and prior to plan approval. The writer therefore recommended adoption of legislation that would grant the bankruptcy judge authority to issue orders during the time from filing to approval permitting the sale or lease of the debtor's property. Letter of United States District Judge Leon R. Yankwich to Reuben G. Hunt, April 16, 1937. Hearing on H.R. 6439 and H.R. 8046, 75th Cong., 1st Sess. (1937) at 222.

will not be ordered, particularly prior to adjudication." 1 Collier on Bankruptcy ¶2.28(3) (14th ed. 1978) (footnotes omitted).

Thirty years after In re Pedlow, *supra*, in Frank v. Drinc-O-Matic, Inc., 136 F.2d 906 (2d Cir. 1943), we upheld the sale of a debtor's 19 vending machines that were subject to a vendor's lien and in the possession of their manufacturer. We noted that the trustee had no funds with which to redeem the machines and that six months had passed from the filing of the petition without proposal of a reorganization plan. Finally, we stated that appellate review of the power exercised by a lower court in directing a sale pursuant to §116(3) was limited to whether the district court had abused its discretion. Id. at 906.

Citing §116(3) of the Act, we next affirmed an order of a sale of vats, kettles and other brewing machinery which, with "'the approach of warm weather . . . will, because of lack of use and refrigeration, deteriorate rapidly and lose substantially all their value.'" In re V. Loewer's Gambrinus Brewery Co., 141 F.2d 747, 748 (2d Cir. 1944). While the court acknowledged the viability of the "perishable" property concept, it upheld the sale even though virtually all of the income producing assets of the debtor were involved. The same proceeding, then entitled Patent Cereals v. Flynn, 149 F.2d 711 (2d Cir. 1945), came before us the following year. We said it made no difference whether sale of a debtor's property preceded or was made part of a plan of reorganization. Id. at 712. Nothing, we continued, in former section 216 (providing for the sale of a reorganizing debtor's property pursuant to a plan) precluded approval of a plan after a sale of all or a substantial part of the debtor's property. Section 216 merely permitted a plan providing for such sale and did not forbid a plan after such a sale has already taken place. Id. at 713. . . .

C.   The Bankruptcy Reform Act of 1978

Section 363(b) of the Code seems on its face to confer upon the bankruptcy judge virtually unfettered discretion to authorize the use, sale or lease, other than in the ordinary course of business, of property of the estate. Of course, the statute requires that notice be given and a hearing conducted, but no reference is made to an "emergency" or "perishability" requirement nor is there an indication that a debtor in possession or trustee contemplating sale must show "cause." Thus, the language of §363(b) clearly is different from the terms of its statutory predecessors. And, while Congress never expressly stated why it abandoned the "upon cause shown" terminology of §116(3), arguably that omission permits easier access to §363(b). *See* In re Brookfield Clothes, Inc., 31 B.R. 978, 984 (S.D.N.Y. 1983). Various policy considerations lend some support to this view.

First and foremost is the notion that a bankruptcy judge must not be shackled with unnecessarily rigid rules when exercising the undoubtedly broad administrative power granted him under the Code. As Justice Holmes once said in a different context, "[s]ome play must be allowed for the joints of the machine . . ." Missouri, Kansas & Texas Ry. Co. v. May, 194 U.S. 267, 270, 24 S. Ct. 638, 639, 48 L. Ed. 971 (1904). To further the purposes of Chapter 11 reorganization, a bankruptcy judge must have substantial freedom to tailor his orders to meet differing circumstances. This is exactly the result a liberal reading of §363(b) will achieve.

Support for this policy is found in the rationale underlying a number of earlier cases that had applied §116(3) of the Act. In particular, this Court's decision in *Sire Plan* was not hinged on an "emergency" or "perishability" concept. Lip service was paid to the argument that a partially constructed building is a "wasting asset," but the real justification for authorizing the sale was the belief that the property's value depended on whether a hotel could be built in time for the World's Fair and that an advantageous sale after the opening of the World's Fair seemed unlikely. Thus, the reason was not solely that a steel skeleton was deteriorating, but rather that a good business opportunity was presently available, so long as the parties could act quickly. In such cases therefore the bankruptcy machinery should not straightjacket the bankruptcy judge so as to prevent him from doing what is best for the estate.

Just as we reject the requirement that only an emergency permits the use of §363(b), we also reject the view that §363(b) grants the bankruptcy judge carte blanche. Several reasons lead us to this conclusion: the statute requires notice and a hearing, and these procedural safeguards would be meaningless absent a further requirement that reasons be given for whatever determination is made; similarly, appellate review would effectively be precluded by an irreversible order, and, finally, such construction of §363(b) swallows up Chapter 11's safeguards. In fact, the legislative history surrounding the enactment of Chapter 11 makes evident Congress' concern with rights of equity interests as well as those of creditors.

Chapter 5 of the House bill dealing with reorganizations states that the purpose of a business reorganization is to restructure a business' finances to enable it to operate productively, provide jobs for its employees, pay its creditors and produce a return for its stockholders. The automatic stay upon filing a petition prevents creditors from acting unilaterally or pressuring the debtor. Report of the Committee on the Judiciary, House of Representatives, to accompany H.R. 8200, H.R. Rep. No. 95-595, 95th Cong. 1st Sess. (1977) at 16, U.S. Code Cong. & Admin. News, 1978, p. 5787, reprinted in 2 Collier on Bankruptcy (appendix) (15th ed. 1983) (hereinafter H.R. Rep. No. 95-595). The plan of reorganization determines how much and in what form creditors will be paid, whether stockholders will continue to retain any interests, and in what form the business will continue. Requiring acceptance by a percentage of creditors and stockholders for confirmation forces negotiation among the debtor, its creditors and its stockholders. Id. at 221. A fair analysis of the House bill reveals that reorganization under the 1938 Chandler Act, though designed to protect creditors, had, over the years, often worked to their detriment and to the detriment of shareholders as well. Id. at 221. The primary reason reorganization under the Act had not served well was that disclosure was minimal and reorganization under the Act was designed to deal with trade debt, not secured or public debt or equity. The present bill, it was believed, provides some form of investor protection to make it a "fairer reorganization vehicle." Id. at 226. The key to the reorganization Chapter, therefore, is disclosure. Id. To make disclosure effective, a provision was included that there be a disclosure statement and a hearing on the adequacy of the information it contains. Id.

at 227. The essential purpose served by disclosure is to ensure that public investors are not left entirely at the mercy of the debtor and its creditors. For that reason the Securities and Exchange Commission, for example, has an absolute right to appear and be heard on behalf of the public interest in an orderly securities market. Id. at 228.

The Senate hearings similarly reflect a concern as to how losses are to be apportioned between creditors and stockholders in the reorganization of a public company. S. Rep. No. 95-989, 95th Cong. 2d Sess. 9 (1978), reprinted in 3 Collier on Bankruptcy (appendix) (15th ed. 1983) (hereinafter S. Rep. No. 95-989). Noting that "the most vulnerable today are public investors," the Senate Judiciary Committee Report states that the bill is designed to counteract "the natural tendency of a debtor in distress to pacify large creditors with whom the debtor would expect to do business, at the expense of small and scattered public investors." S. Rep. No. 95-989 at 10, U.S. Code Cong. & Admin. News p. 5796. The Committee believed that investor protection is most critical when the public company is in such financial distress as to cause it to seek aid under the bankruptcy laws. Id. The need for this protection was plain. Reorganization under the 1938 Act was often unfair to public investors who lacked bargaining power, and these conditions continued. Echoing the conclusion of the House Committee, the Senate Committee believed that the bill would promote fairer and more equitable reorganizations granting to public investors the last chance to conserve values that corporate insolvency has jeopardized. Id. at 10-11.

III.   *Conclusion*

The history surrounding the enactment in 1978 of current Chapter 11 and the logic underlying it buttress our conclusion that there must be some articulated business justification, other than appeasement of major creditors, for using, selling or leasing property out of the ordinary course of business before the bankruptcy judge may order such disposition under section 363(b).

The case law under section 363's statutory predecessors used terms like "perishable," "deteriorating," and "emergency" as guides in deciding whether a debtor's property could be sold outside the ordinary course of business. The use of such words persisted long after their omission from newer statutes and rules. The administrative power to sell or lease property in a reorganization continued to be the exception, not the rule. Collier on Bankruptcy ¶2.28(b) (*supra*). In enacting the 1978 Code Congress was aware of existing case law and clearly indicated as one of its purposes that equity interests have a greater voice in reorganization plans — hence, the safeguards of disclosure, voting, acceptance and confirmation in present Chapter 11.

Resolving the apparent conflict between Chapter 11 and §363(b) does not require an all or nothing approach. Every sale under §363(b) does not automatically short-circuit or side-step Chapter 11; nor are these two statutory provisions to be read as mutually exclusive. Instead, if a bankruptcy judge is to administer a business reorganization successfully under the Code, then — like the related yet independent tasks performed in modern production techniques to ensure good results — some play for the operation of both §363(b) and Chapter 11 must be allowed for.

The rule we adopt requires that a judge determining a §363(b) application expressly find from the evidence presented before him at the hearing a good business reason to grant such an application. In this case the only reason advanced for granting the request to sell Lionel's 82 percent stock interest in Dale was the Creditors' Committee's insistence on it. Such is insufficient as a matter of fact because it is not a sound business reason and insufficient as a matter of law because it ignores the equity interests required to be weighed and considered under Chapter 11. The court also expressed its concern that a present failure to approve the sale would result in a long delay. As the Supreme Court has noted, it is easy to sympathize with the desire of a bankruptcy court to expedite bankruptcy reorganization proceedings for they are frequently protracted. "The need for expedition, however, is not a justification for abandoning proper standards." Protective Committee for Independent Stockholders of TMT Trailer Ferry, Inc. v. Anderson, 390 U.S. 414, 450, 88 S. Ct. 1157, 1176, 20 L. Ed. 2d 1 (1968). Thus, the approval of the sale of Lionel's 82 percent interest in Dale was an abuse of the trial court's discretion.

In fashioning its findings, a bankruptcy judge must not blindly follow the hue and cry of the most vocal special interest groups; rather, he should consider all salient factors pertaining to the proceeding and, accordingly, act to further the diverse interests of the debtor, creditors and equity holders, alike. He might, for example, look to such relevant factors as the proportionate value of the asset to the estate as a whole, the amount of elapsed time since the filing, the likelihood that a plan of reorganization will be proposed and confirmed in the near future, the effect of the proposed disposition on future plans of reorganization, the proceeds to be obtained from the disposition vis-à-vis any appraisals of the property, which of the alternatives of use, sale or lease the proposal envisions and, most importantly perhaps, whether the asset is increasing or decreasing in value. This list is not intended to be exclusive, but merely to provide guidance to the bankruptcy judge.

Finally, we must consider whether appellants opposing the sale produced evidence before the bankruptcy court that such sale was not justified. While a debtor applying under §363(b) carries the burden of demonstrating that a use, sale or lease out of the ordinary course of business will aid the debtor's reorganization, an objectant, such as the Equity Committee here, is required to produce some evidence respecting its objections. Appellants made three objections below: First, the sale was premature because Dale is not a wasting asset and there is no emergency; second, there was no justifiable cause present since Dale, if anything, is improving; and third, the price was inadequate. No proof was required as to the first objection because it was stipulated as conceded. The second and third objections are interrelated. Following Judge Ryan's suggestion that objections could as a practical matter be developed on cross-examination, Equity's counsel elicited testimony from the financial expert produced by Lionel that Dale is less subject than other companies to wide market fluctuations. The same witness also conceded that he knew of no reason why those interested in Dale's stock at the September 7, 1983 hearing would not be just as interested six months from then.[18]

The only other witness who testified was the Chief Executive Officer of Lionel, who stated that it was only at the insistence of the Creditors' Committee that Dale stock was being sold and that Lionel "would very much like to retain its interest in Dale." These uncontroverted statements of the two witnesses elicited by the Equity Committee on cross-examination were sufficient proof to support its objections to the present sale of Dale because this evidence demonstrated that there was no good business reason for the present sale. Hence, appellants satisfied their burden.

Accordingly, the order appealed from is reversed and the matter remanded to the district court with directions to remand to the bankruptcy court for further proceedings consistent with this opinion.

WINTER, Circuit Judge, dissenting:

In order to expedite the decision in this matter, I set forth my dissenting views in summary fashion.

The following facts are undisputed as the record presently stands: (i) Lionel sought a buyer for the Dale stock willing to condition its purchase upon confirmation of a reorganization plan. It was unsuccessful since, in the words of the bankruptcy judge, "the confirmation of any plan is usually somewhat iffy," and few purchasers are willing to commit upwards of $50 million for an extended period without a contract binding on the other party; (ii) every feasible reorganization plan contemplates the sale of the Dale stock for cash; (iii) a reorganization plan may be approved fairly soon if the Dale stock is sold now. If the sale is prohibited, renewed negotiations between the creditors and the equity holders will be necessary, and the submission of a plan, if any, will be put off well into the future; and (iv) the Dale stock can be sold now at or near the same price as it can be sold later.

The effect of the present decision is thus to leave the debtor in possession powerless as a legal matter to sell the Dale stock outside a reorganization plan and unable as an economic matter to sell it within one. This, of course, pleases the equity holders who, having introduced no evidence demonstrating a disadvantage to the bankrupt estate from the sale of the Dale stock, are now given a veto over it to be used as leverage in negotiating a better deal for themselves in a reorganization.

The likely results of today's decision are twofold: (i) The creditors will at some point during the renewed protracted negotiations refuse to extend more credit to Lionel, thus thwarting a reorganization entirely; and (ii) notwithstanding the majority decision, the Dale stock will be sold under Section 363(b) for exactly the same reasons offered in support of the present proposed sale. However, the ultimate reorganization plan will be more favorable to the equity holders, and they will not veto the sale.

It seems reasonably obvious that result (i) is something that the statutory provisions governing reorganizations, including Section 363(b), are designed to avoid.

---

18. As noted, the bidding for Dale started with a $43 million offer from Acme-Cleveland and has since jumped to $50 million. There is no indication that this trend will reverse itself.

Result (ii) not only is contrary to the purpose of the reorganization provisions in causing delay and further economic risk but also suffers from the legal infirmity which led the majority to reject the proposed sale, the only difference between the two sales being the agreement of the equity holders.

The equity holders offered no evidence whatsoever that the sale of Dale now will harm Lionel or that Dale can in fact be sold at a reasonable price as part of a reorganization plan. The courts below were quite right in not treating their arguments seriously for they are the legal equivalent of the "Hail Mary pass" in football.[19]

Simply obtaining authority to sell a debtor's assets does not ensure that it will generate a high return. The debtor's business may have created substantial obligations both to current and future creditors. Potential purchasers of the assets would be most interested in being sure that they would not be saddled with the debtor's obligations. Section 363(f) permits the sale of assets free and clear of claims.

The full range of §363(f) has recently come into question. The section has long been used to strip mortgages and security interests from property with those liens then attaching to the proceeds of the sale. Moreover, §363(k) provides that the lienholder can credit bid at the sale, meaning the creditor bids in the amount of the debt owed without having to produce new funding. In most instances, state law allows a sale of property by a secured creditor that will result in the removal of the lien of the selling creditor and the liens of all properly noticed junior lienors. *See, e.g.,* UCC §9-617. The case reprinted below surprised many in the bankruptcy community. It raises serious questions about the efficacy of many §363 sales. The court relies on a California decision, Nguyen v. Calhoun, 105 Cal. App. 4th 428, 438, 129 Cal. Rptr. 2d 436, 445 (Cal. Ct. App. 2003), to conclude that the property was not subject to any applicable nonbankruptcy law that would permit the sale of the property free and clear of liens. In *Nguyen*, the owner of property was facing a foreclosure, and he sold the property to a third party. The foreclosure was thereafter concluded, and a battle ensued between the third party who had purchased the property from the original owner, and the person who purchased the property at the foreclosure sale. In finding in favor of the person who purchased the property at the foreclosure sale, the court noted that the sale of the

---

19. With due respect to my colleagues, the problem of statutory interpretation is entirely straightforward and not deserving of a lengthy exegesis into legal history. The language of Section 363(b) is about as plain as it could be and surely does not permit a judicial grafting of stringent conditions on the power of trustees. As for its legislative history, the words "upon cause shown" were dropped by the Congress from the predecessor to Section 363(b) in 1978, a signal clearly dictating that Congress meant what it said. The equity holders argue that Chapter 11's provisions for disclosure, hearing and a vote before confirmation of a reorganization plan stringently limit the authority of trustees under 11 U.S.C. §363(b). However, a reorganization plan affects the rights of the parties as well as the disposition of assets, and there is no inconsistency in allowing the disposition of property outside the confirmation proceedings. Arguably, some transactions proposed under Section 363(b) would, if carried out, eliminate a number of options available for reorganization plans and thereby pre-ordain a particular kind of plan or preclude a reorganization entirely. In such a case, a colorable claim can be made for a limitation on a trustee's power under Section 363(b) narrowly tailored to prevent such a result in order to effectuate the core purposes of Chapter 11. However, it is not disputed that in the present case the final reorganization plan will include a sale of Dale stock. A sale now thus does not preclude any feasible reorganization plan.

property by the original owner to the third party did not extinguish the lien that was being foreclosed. Does this case support the court's conclusion in *In re PW, LLC*?

In re PW, LLC

Bankruptcy Appellate Panel for the Ninth Circuit, 2008
391 B.R. 25

MARKELL, Bankruptcy Judge.

This appeal presents a simple issue: outside a plan of reorganization, does §363(f) of the Bankruptcy Code permit a secured creditor to credit bid its debt and purchase estate property, taking title free and clear of valid, nonconsenting junior liens? We hold that it does not.

In reaching this conclusion, we reject the contention that once the sale is consummated, the appeal from the order stripping the junior creditor's liens is moot and immune from scrutiny, and we hold that, in the circumstances of this case, the junior lienholder's rights are preserved.

The debtor in this case, PW, LLC ("PW"), owned prime real estate in Burbank, California. DB Burbank, LLC ("DB"), an affiliate of a large public hedge fund, held a claim of more than $40 million secured by PW's property. But problems large and small plagued PW's development plan. These problems ultimately led to PW's chapter 11 bankruptcy and to the appointment of Nancy Knupfer as PW's chapter 11 trustee ("Trustee").

DB, working with the Trustee, organized a campaign to consolidate all of PW's property and development rights and to sell this package, free and clear of all claims and encumbrances, at a sale supervised by the bankruptcy court. At the sale, DB was the highest bidder, paying its consideration by credit-bidding the entire amount of its debt.

The only problem was the existence of a consensual lien securing a claim of approximately $2.5 million in favor of a junior creditor, Clear Channel Outdoor, Inc. ("Clear Channel"). Relying solely on §363(f)(5), the bankruptcy court confirmed the sale to DB free and clear of Clear Channel's lien. The bankruptcy court then denied a stay of the sale pending appeal, as did our motions panel.

The first issue presented is whether the appeal is moot. We conclude that while any relief related to the transfer of title to DB is moot, stripping Clear Channel's lien and related state law rights present an issue that is discrete and separable from title transfer. That part of Clear Channel's appeal is not moot.

After reviewing applicable law, we conclude that §363(f)(5) cannot support transfer of PW's property free and clear of Clear Channel's lien based on the existing record. We thus reverse that portion of the bankruptcy court's order authorizing the sale to DB free and clear of Clear Channel's lien, and we remand the matter to the bankruptcy court for further proceedings.

Finally, Clear Channel contends that a separate payment obligation from DB to the Trustee was subject to Clear Channel's lien, and that the bankruptcy court improperly stripped its lien rights in that payment obligation. We hold that the payment obligation was not subject to Clear Channel's lien, and we affirm on this point.

I. Facts

Before filing for bankruptcy, PW owned and was attempting to develop real property in Burbank, California. It had a development agreement with the City of Burbank ("Development Agreement") that provided entitlements for a mixed-use complex of luxury condominiums and retail space. In order to realize the value of the entitlements, however, PW had to acquire an assemblage of eighteen parcels of real estate by February 2009. When it filed bankruptcy, PW owned only fourteen of the necessary parcels. It had, however, entered into an agreement to acquire the final four parcels, which were occupied by a church ("Church Property"). Closing this agreement and the final purchase of the Church Property was conditioned on the church's finding another suitable location for its activities.

DB held a first-priority lien on substantially all of PW's assets. It began foreclosure proceedings in July 2006 and sought the appointment of a state court receiver. After the receiver was appointed, DB lent the receiver more money to buy additional parcels.

During this time, DB and PW tried to negotiate a chapter 11 plan. They had not reached an agreement when, on November 20, 2006, on the eve of a scheduled foreclosure sale, PW filed a chapter 11 case. DB immediately moved for, and the bankruptcy court granted, the appointment of a trustee, which was done on December 27. The receiver turned over all of PW's assets to the Trustee in January 2007.

The Trustee faced several immediate problems. These included obtaining and paying the cure amounts related to the contract to acquire the Church Property, and otherwise implementing the terms of the Development Agreement. In addition, as a "single asset real estate" case, *see* 11 U.S.C. §101(51B), it was likely that DB would be granted relief from stay under §362(d)(3).

In response, the Trustee proposed to sell PW's property and began discussions with DB to that end. With bankruptcy court authorization, the Trustee hired a real estate broker to market PW's property to others. In addition, to facilitate acquisition of the Church Property, the broker agreed to help the Trustee find a new location for the church.

After negotiation, the Trustee and DB entered into an agreement they called a "Binding Term Sheet," which established detailed sale procedures for an auction and sale of PW's assets. Under its terms, the Trustee gained time to market and sell PW's property and to resolve disputes that had arisen regarding the Church Property.

The Binding Term Sheet also provided that DB would serve as a stalking horse bidder for a sale of PW's property. If there were no qualified overbidders, DB would buy PW's property for $41,434,465, which the parties called the "Strike Price." In addition, DB agreed to pay the Trustee a "Carve-Out Amount" of up to $800,000 for certain administrative fees and other expenses. DB also agreed not to seek relief from the automatic stay and to refrain from communicating with third parties regarding the sale of PW's assets.

On March 20, 2007, the bankruptcy court entered an order establishing a procedure for the sale of PW's property. Two days later, the Trustee moved to approve the sale free and clear of liens under §363(f)(3) and (f)(5).

Clear Channel opposed the motion, asserting that §363(f) was not applicable. Over Clear Channel's objection, on April 26, 2007, the bankruptcy court entered a separate order authorizing the sale free and clear of Clear Channel's lien under §363(f)(5) ("Sale Order").

The March 20 order set May 7 as the deadline for submitting written bids, and the same order set the minimum overbid at $43,618,048, plus whatever amount was necessary to cure defaults related to acquiring the Church Property. Only three bids were timely received, and none qualified. The highest was a nonconforming contingent bid of only $25.25 million.

With no qualified overbidders, the Binding Term Sheet required the Trustee to sell PW's property to DB at the Strike Price, DB to pay the Trustee the Carve-Out Amount, and DB to pay certain administrative fees, including the receiver's fees and other expenses.

On May 31, 2007, the bankruptcy court confirmed the sale to DB and found that DB was a purchaser in good faith. The court entered an order to this effect ("Confirmation Order"), and declined to stay that order pending appeal, as did a prior motions panel of this court.

The sale closed on June 15, 2007. Clear Channel received no payment under the terms of the sale because DB's credit bid meant that there were no proceeds to which Clear Channel's lien could attach. Since closing, DB has paid out more than $1.5 million, including $250,000 in final payment to the receiver for fees and expenses, $550,000 to the estate as the remaining Carve-Out Amount, $750,000 to a senior lienholder, and other amounts necessary to pay outstanding real estate taxes and other costs of closing. For her part, the Trustee has made payments out of the Carve-Out Amount to herself and her professionals on an interim basis.

Clear Channel filed a timely appeal on May 1, 2007, and seeks reversal of both the Sale Order and the Confirmation Order. Clear Channel also asserts that its lien extends to the Carve-Out Amount and seeks reversal of the bankruptcy court's order that it does not. . . .

3.   Statutory Mootness Under §363(m)

Sales of property of the estate under §363(b) and (c) are protected by §363(m), which states:

> The reversal or modification on appeal of an authorization under subsection (b) or (c) of this section of a sale or lease of property does not affect the validity of a sale or lease under such authorization to an entity that purchased or leased such property in good faith, whether or not such entity knew of the pendency of the appeal, unless such authorization and such sale or lease were stayed pending appeal.

11 U.S.C. §363(m).

Section 363(m) is a codification of some aspects of equitable mootness with respect to sales. Unlike equitable mootness, however, §363(m) provides for specific procedures and findings in order to provide certainty for sales.

DB contends that this section deprives this court of the ability to affect the sale. It argues that Clear Channel did not obtain a stay pending appeal, and the bankruptcy court made findings that DB acted in good faith. These facts reinforce our decision not to tamper with transfer of title to DB. The appeal for that part of the transaction is equitably moot, as we noted above, and the facts establish that it is also protected by §363(m).

But the Confirmation Order authorized both a sale of PW's property and lien-stripping. While the lack of a stay and a transfer of the property would be relevant to whether §363(m) applies to a sale authorized by §363(b), these facts continue to be relevant only if §363(m) applies to lien-stripping authorizations under §363(f). We do not consider these facts, however, because we conclude that §363(m) does not apply to lien-stripping under §363(f).

First, §363(m) by its terms applies only to "an authorization under subsection (b) or (c) of this section. . . ." Here, the remaining challenge is to the authorization under subsection (f) to sell the property free of Clear Channel's lien. Section 363(m) thus cleaves a distinction between authorizations to "use, sell or lease . . . property of the estate" as set forth in §363(b) and authorizations under §363(f) to "sell property under subsection (b) or (c) of this section free and clear of any interest in such property. . . ." Section 363(m) thus protects the court's authorization of a sale, in this case, out of the ordinary course of business, again making a distinction between the authorization of a sale and the terms under which the sale is to be made.

Second, the subsection limits only the ability to "affect the validity of a sale or lease under such authorization. . . ." Here, the telling locution is the limitation of §363(m) to "sale[s] or lease[s]" authorized under §363(b) or (c). Omitted is the "use" prong of authorization. As a result, a plain-language reading of the section would not give §363(m) protection to an out-of-the-ordinary-course use approved by a bankruptcy court. . . .

This limitation leads us to conclude that Congress intended that §363(m) address only changes of title or other essential attributes of a sale, together with the changes of authorized possession that occur with leases. The terms of those sales, including the "free and clear" term at issue here, are not protected.

Indeed, Congress could easily have broadened the protection of §363(m) to include lien-stripping. As an example, it could have stated that all "transfers" were to be protected, as that term is broadly defined in §101(54). It did not. Instead, it restricted the protection of §363(m) to sales and leases.

That §363(m) is so limited can also be seen by comparing the language chosen- sales or leases-with Congress's efforts to protect liens and security interests granted by the estate in §364. Section 364 permits the estate to grant liens and security interests similar to those sought to be stripped here. To protect lenders' reliance of on such grants, Congress added §364(e) to the Code. It states:

(e) The reversal or modification on appeal of an authorization under this section to obtain credit or incur debt, or of a grant under this section of a priority or a lien, does not affect the validity of any debt so incurred, or any priority or lien so granted, to an entity that extended such credit in good faith, whether or not such entity knew of the pendency of the appeal, unless such authorization and the incurring of such debt, or the granting of such priority or lien, were stayed pending appeal.

In §364(e), Congress chose words specific to the task — "debt," "lien," and "priority." That these types of words are absent from §363(m) underscores congressional intent not to insulate and immunize lien-stripping actions from appellate review.

Not surprisingly, DB argues that its agreement to purchase the property was conditioned on receiving a free and clear title. For that reason, the Confirmation Order contained language both of sale and of lien-stripping. In DB's view, the sale language cannot be separated from the lien-stripping language because both sale and lien-stripping were integral to its decision to purchase the property. *See, e.g., Official Committee of Unsecured Creditors v. Trism, Inc. (In re Trism, Inc.)*, 328 F.3d 1003, 1007 (8th Cir. 2003). In short, DB contends that authorization for the sale also authorized the lien-stripping, and that one cannot be affected without necessarily affecting the other.

In response, we observe that in choosing the words it did in §363(m), Congress did not intend the two types of actions to receive the same level of protection. That is, divesting the estate of property and vesting it in another is treated differently from stripping a lien. Put another way, stripping a lien is not a sale or a lease protected by the language of §363(m), either directly or indirectly.

A more nuanced response is that a sophisticated lender such as DB knew of the risks inherent in relying solely on §363(f)(5) to strip Clear Channel's lien. It could not have avoided these risks by, for example, insisting that the Confirmation Order contain an explicit contractual condition that there be no appellate review. That would have been rejected out of hand, as any other express condition that similarly violated law or public policy would have been. But a party ought not be able to do indirectly what it cannot do directly, and we are reluctant to interpret §363(m) to give DB indirectly a review-free stripping of Clear Channel's non-bankruptcy property rights. DB cannot mask an improper condition of the transfer — avoiding appellate review — by cloaking it as an essential and inseparable part of a sale.

The response to this argument is that all that the Code and Rules provide for creditors such as Clear Channel is the ability to seek a stay pending appeal. But in these circumstances, when a bond staying the consummation of the deal would have been far in excess of the lien that Clear Channel is trying to protect, we question whether that remedy is exclusive.

In short, DB knew or should have known all along that lien-stripping might not work. So its assertion that the sale was inseparable from the lien-stripping rings hollow, as does its argument that a stay was required to avoid mootness. *See Suter*, 504 F.3d at 990 (failure to obtain stay not always fatal to mootness defense). We conclude that, on these facts, lien-stripping under §363(f)(5) is not protected under §363(m).

B. Statutory Interpretation of §363(f)

Our holding that the appeal is not moot requires us to consider whether §363(f) permits the stripping of Clear Channel's lien. Sales free and clear of interests are authorized under §363(f). That subsection provides:

> (f) The trustee may sell property under subsection (b) or (c) of this section free and clear of any interest in such property of an entity other than the estate, only if—
>> (1) applicable nonbankruptcy law permits sale of such property free and clear of such interest;
>> (2) such entity consents;
>> (3) such interest is a lien and the price at which such property is to be sold is greater than the aggregate value of all liens on such property;
>> (4) such interest is in bona fide dispute; or
>> (5) such entity could be compelled, in a legal or equitable proceeding, to accept a money satisfaction of such interest.

11 U.S.C. §363(f).

Of the five paragraphs that authorize a sale free and clear, three do not apply to this appeal. Paragraph (1) does not apply because applicable law—California real property law—does not permit a sale free and clear, and indeed would preserve Clear Channel's lien despite the transfer. *Nguyen v. Calhoun*, 105 Cal. App. 4th 428, 438, 129 Cal. Rptr. 2d 436, 445 (Cal. Ct. App. 2003) ("Real property is transferable even though the title is subject to a mortgage or deed of trust, but the transfer will not eliminate the existence of that encumbrance. Thus, the grantee takes title to the property subject to all deeds of trust and other encumbrances, whether or not the deed so provides.") (citations omitted). Paragraph (2) is inapplicable as Clear Channel did not consent to the transfer free of its interest. Paragraph (4) applies only if the interest is in bona fide dispute, and no one disputes the validity of Clear Channel's lien. As a result, we need only analyze the bankruptcy court's ability to authorize a sale free and clear of Clear Channel's lien under paragraphs (3) and (5).

1. Guidance on Interpretation

We first review case law on statutory interpretation because paragraphs (3) and (5) of §363(f) present legitimate and difficult questions of statutory interpretation. Paragraph (3), for example, uses a nonstandard term to refer to the claims held by creditors secured by the property being sold. It refers to the "aggregate value of all liens" on the property. The Code, however, tends to refer not to the economic value of the property secured by liens but to the value of claims secured by those liens. *See, e.g.*, 11 U.S.C. §§506(a); 1129(b)(2). If §363(f)(3) had been worded to refer to the "aggregate value of all claims secured by liens on such property," it would have been in the mainstream of other provisions of the Code, and no real question would be presented. But it was not. This variant locution requires us to decide whether the unusual construction should be given special interpretive significance.

Paragraph (5) presents an even greater conundrum: the competing constructions seem either to render it so specialized as never to be invoked, or all-powerful, subsuming all the other paragraphs of §363(f). Before launching into the task of interpreting these two paragraphs, we should first review applicable rules of construction for federal statutes. *See* Thomas F. Waldron & Neil M. Berman, *Principled Principles of Statutory Interpretation: A Judicial Perspective after Two Years of BAPCPA*, 81 Am. Bankr. L.J. 195, 202-11 (2007).

When construing any federal statute, the presumption is that the accepted and plain meaning of the words used reflects the sense in which Congress used them. As the Supreme Court has stated:

> The starting point in discerning congressional intent is the existing statutory text . . . and not the predecessor statutes. It is well established that "when the statute's language is plain, the sole function of the courts — at least where the disposition required by the text is not absurd — is to enforce it according to its terms."

Lamie v. United States Trustee, 540 U.S. 526, 534, 124 S. Ct. 1023, 157 L. Ed. 2d 1024 (2004), quoting *Hartford Underwriters Ins. Co. v. Union Planters Bank, N.A.*, 530 U.S. 1, 6, 120 S. Ct. 1942, 147 L. Ed. 2d 1 (2000) (in turn quoting *United States v. Ron Pair Enters., Inc.*, 489 U.S. 235, 241, 109 S. Ct. 1026, 103 L. Ed. 2d 290 (1989)).

But there is more. Because the words of a statute are meant to be law, the legal background of the words used, as well as a lawyer's understanding of them, are also important. Part of the background relevant to this appeal is Congress's promulgation of federal bankruptcy law as a separate title of the United States Code. This separate title is organized as a cohesive code. For example, it groups similar topics together through the use of chapters, and it uses common, defined terms throughout. *See* 11 U.S.C. §101. To aid in consistent application, the Code's terms are sometimes defined in ways that vary from standard English. A "custodian," for example, is not a janitor or building superintendent, but rather a receiver or trustee for the debtor's property. *See* 11 U.S.C. §101(11).

Further, the Supreme Court has acknowledged that even undefined words and phrases in the Bankruptcy Code should presumptively receive the same construction, even if found in different parts of the code. *See Rousey v. Jacoway*, 544 U.S. 320, 326-27, 125 S. Ct. 1561, 161 L. Ed. 2d 563 (2005) (looking at use of "on account of" in provisions of the Bankruptcy Code other than the one at issue). *See also Davis v. Mich. Dep't of Treasury*, 489 U.S. 803, 809, 109 S. Ct. 1500, 103 L. Ed. 2d 891 (1989) ("[S]tatutory language cannot be construed in a vacuum. It is a fundamental canon of statutory construction that the words of a statute must be read in their context and with a view to their place in the overall statutory scheme."); *Am. Bankers Ass'n v. Gould*, 412 F.3d 1081, 1086 (9th Cir. 2005) ("Our goal in interpreting a statute is to understand the statute 'as a symmetrical and coherent regulatory scheme' and to 'fit, if possible, all parts into a . . . harmonious whole.'") (quoting *Food & Drug Admin. v. Brown & Williamson Tobacco Corp.*, 529 U.S. 120, 133, 120 S. Ct. 1291, 146 L. Ed. 2d 121 (2000).

That brings us to §363(f), and its proper interpretation.

2. Paragraph (3) and Sales for Less Than the Amount of All Claims Secured by the Property

PW's property sold for less than the amount of claims secured by PW's property. DB and the Trustee contend that §363(f)(3) authorizes the sale free and clear of the liens in this situation. The bankruptcy court found, and we agree, that §363(f)(3) cannot be so used.

The actual text of paragraph (3) permits a sale free and clear of an interest only if:

> (3) such interest is a lien and the price at which such property is to be sold is greater than the aggregate value of all liens on such property; . . .

The Trustee asserts that the "aggregate value of all liens" in this paragraph means the economic value of such liens, rather than their face value. This argument arises from §363(f)(3)'s variance from general Code usage; that is, whether its reference to "value of all liens" is simply an unfortunate deviation from the Code's general preference to refer to claims, and not liens, or whether it has some other significance.

The Trustee and DB assert that, under conventional bankruptcy wisdom, supported by §506(a), the amount of an allowed secured claim can never exceed the value of the property securing the claim. Since a secured claim is a form of "lien," *see* 11 U.S.C. §101(37), some courts have found that an estate representative may use §363(f)(3) to sell free and clear of the property rights of junior lienholders whose nonbankruptcy liens are not supported by the collateral's value. That is, there may be a sale free and clear of "out-of-the-money" liens. *See, e.g., In re Beker Indus. Corp.*, 63 B.R. 474, 476-77 (Bankr. S.D.N.Y. 1986); *In re Terrace Gardens Park P'ship*, 96 B.R. 707 (Bankr. W.D. Tex. 1989); *In re Oneida Lake Dev., Inc.*, 114 B.R. 352 (Bankr. N.D.N.Y. 1990); *In re WPRV-TV, Inc.*, 143 B.R. 315, 320 (D.P.R. 1991); *Milford Group, Inc. v. Concrete Step Units, Inc. (In re Milford Group, Inc.)*, 150 B.R. 904, 906 (Bankr. M.D. Pa. 1992); *In re Collins*, 180 B.R. 447, 450-51 (Bankr. E.D. Va. 1995).

We disagree. This reading expands §363(f)(3) too far. It would essentially mean that an estate representative could sell estate property free and clear of any lien, regardless of whether the lienholder held an allowed secured claim. We think the context of paragraph (3) is inconsistent with this reading. If Congress had intended such a broad construction, it would have worded the paragraph very differently. *See Ron Pair Enters.*, 489 U.S. at 242 n.5, 109 S. Ct. 1026 (Congress knows distinction between types of liens, and language of the Bankruptcy Code should be interpreted in a way that acknowledges that knowledge). For this reason, many courts and commentators have rejected this approach. *See, e.g., Richardson v. Pitt County (In re Stroud Wholesale, Inc.)*, 47 B.R. 999, 1002 (E.D.N.C. 1985), *aff'd mem.*, 983 F.2d 1057 (4th Cir. 1986); *Scherer v. Fed. Nat'l Mortgage Ass'n (In re Terrace Chalet Apartments, Ltd.)*, 159 B.R. 821 (N.D. Ill. 1993); *In re Perroncello*, 170 B.R. 189 (Bankr. D. Mass. 1994); *In re Feinstein Family P'ship*, 247 B.R. 502 (Bankr. M.D. Fla. 2000); *In re Canonigo*, 276 B.R. 257 (Bankr. N.D. Cal. 2002); *Criimi Mae Servs.*

Ltd. P'ship v. WDH Howell, LLC (In re WDH Howell, LLC), 298 B.R. 527 (D.N.J. 2003); *see also In re Healthco Int'l, Inc.,* 174 B.R. 174 (Bankr. D. Mass. 1994); 3 Collier on Bankruptcy ¶363.06[4][a] (Alan N. Resnick & Henry J. Sommer eds., 15th ed. rev. 2008).

But another reason, rooted in the text of the paragraph, exists to reject such an expansive reading. Paragraph (3) permits the sale free and clear only when "the price at which such property is to be sold *is greater than* the aggregate value of all liens. . . ." 11 U.S.C. §363(f)(3) (emphasis added). If, as DB and the Trustee assert, "aggregate value of all liens" means the aggregate amount of all allowed secured claims as used in §506(a), then the paragraph could *never* be used to authorize a sale free and clear in circumstances like those present here; that is, when the claims exceed the value of the collateral that secures them. In any case in which the value of the property being sold is less than the total amount of claims held by secured creditors, the total of all allowed secured claims will *equal,* not exceed, the sales price, and the statute requires the price to be "greater than" the "value of all liens." *See, e.g., In re Gen. Bearing Corp.,* 136 B.R. 361, 366 (Bankr. S.D.N.Y. 1992).

As a result, we join those courts cited above that hold that §363(f)(3) does not authorize the sale free and clear of a lienholder's interest if the price of the estate property is equal to or less than the aggregate amount of all claims held by creditors who hold a lien or security interest in the property being sold.

3.   Paragraph (5) and Sales for Less Than the Lienholder's Claim

The parties' main dispute lies over the proper application of §363(f)(5). The bankruptcy court, supported by the Trustee and DB, found that the plain meaning of that paragraph permitted a sale free and clear of Clear Channel's lien. On appeal, Clear Channel argues that the paragraph's plain meaning does not support the bankruptcy court's construction. Clear Channel has the best of this argument. We thus reverse on this point. Because the meaning of paragraph (5) is anything but plain, we must carefully consider the statute's wording and the competing interpretations.

We start with the text of the statute. Section 363(f)(5) permits an estate representative, such as the Trustee, to sell free of an entity's interest in estate property if:

> (5) such entity could be compelled, in a legal or equitable proceeding, to accept a money satisfaction of such interest.

We parse this paragraph to contain at least three elements: that (1) a proceeding exists or could be brought, in which (2) the nondebtor could be compelled to accept a money satisfaction of (3) its interest.

Courts are divided over the interpretation of each of these elements. We analyze these components in reverse order. We start first with an analysis of what Congress meant by an "interest," then move to the proper construction of a money satisfaction, and conclude with an examination of appropriate legal and equitable proceedings.

a.   Lien as Interest

Clear Channel's primary contention is that the term "interest" must be read narrowly to exclude liens such as the one it holds. So read, §363(f)(5) would be inapplicable, as a matter of law, to authorize the sale free and clear of Clear Channel's lien. *See, e.g., In re Canonigo*, 276 B.R. at 266. Clear Channel asserts that to do otherwise renders the other subsections under §363(f) mere surplusage.

We reject Clear Channel's argument. We believe that Congress intended "interest" to have an expansive scope, as shown by *United States v. Knox-Schillinger (In re Trans World Airlines, Inc.)*, 322 F.3d 283 (3d Cir. 2003). In *TWA*, the Third Circuit held that there were two "interests" subject to §363(f)(5): 1) travel vouchers issued in connection with settlement of a discrimination action and 2) discrimination claims made by the EEOC. The court reasoned that, if the debtor-airline had liquidated its assets under Chapter 7 of the Bankruptcy Code, the claims at issue would have been converted to dollar amounts, and the claimants would have received the distribution provided to other general unsecured creditors on account of their claims. Similarly, the EEOC discrimination claims were reducible to, and could have been satisfied by, monetary awards even if injunctive relief was sought. *Id.* at 290-91. *See also P.K.R. Convalescent Ctrs., Inc. v. Virginia (In re P.K.R. Convalescent Ctrs., Inc.)*, 189 B.R. 90, 94 (Bankr. E.D. Va. 1995) (statutory right to recapture depreciation on sale of health facility an interest within meaning of §363(f)(5)). *See also* Kuney, 76 Am. Bankr. L.J. at 257 (lien is a subset of interests).

Some cases, however, have adopted a restricted construction of "interest" in order to prevent needless overlap. In particular, cases such as *In re Canonigo* reason that the term "interest" must be read differently in (f)(5) from every other use of the term in §363(f). *In re Canonigo*, 276 B.R. at 265.

But the distinctions drawn by *Canonigo* are not supported by the plain reading we are required to give to the statute. It is telling that the introductory sentence to §363(f) broadly refers to "any interest," and that four of the following paragraphs then refer back to "such interest." Within this group is §363(f)(3), which explicitly states that it applies only if "such interest is a lien," making it apparent that Congress intended a lien to be a type of interest. Congress would not have used the language it did in paragraph (f)(3), or at least would have included additional language in paragraph (5), if it had intended to exclude liens from paragraph (f)(5).

In addition, though the Code does not define "interest," it does define "lien." Clear Channel's reading contradicts that definition in which lien "means charge against or *interest* in property." 11 U.S.C. §101(37) (emphasis added). The definition of lien provides another inference consistent with the interpretation that a lien is but one type of interest. Clear Channel asserts that *Canonigo*'s interpretation promotes the statutory purpose of avoiding the use of §363(f) as a means of escaping the rigors of the chapter 11 plan confirmation process. Daniel J. Carragher, *Sales Free and Clear: Limits on §363(f) Sales*, Am. Bankr. Inst. L.J., at 16 (July/August 2007).

Consistent with the plain reading of §363(f) generally, and §363(f)(5) in particular, we construe "interest" to include the type of lien at issue in this appeal.

b. *Compelling Money Satisfaction*

Clear Channel's alternative position is that if §363(f)(5) does apply to authorize a sale free and clear of liens, then the bankruptcy court erred in holding that Clear Channel "could be compelled . . . to accept a money satisfaction" of its interest.

i. Compelling Satisfaction for Less Than Full Payment

The bankruptcy court found paragraph(f)(5) applicable whenever a claim or interest can be paid with money. We do not think that §363(f)(5) is so simply analyzed. Although it is tautological that liens securing payment obligations can be satisfied by paying the money owed, it does not necessarily follow that such liens can be satisfied by paying *any* sum, however large or small. We assume that paragraph (5) refers to a legal and equitable proceeding in which the nondebtor could be compelled to take *less* than the value of the claim secured by the interest. *See In re Gulf States Steel, Inc. of Ala.*, 285 B.R. 497, 508 (Bankr. N.D. Ala. 2002).

Other courts agree and hold that it is not the type of interest that matters, but whether monetary satisfaction may be compelled for less than full payment of the debt related to, or secured by, that interest. *In re Terrace Chalet Apts.*, 159 B.R. at 829 ("By its express terms, Section 363(f)(5) permits lien extinguishment if the trustee can demonstrate the existence of another legal mechanism by which a lien could be extinguished without full satisfaction of the secured debt."); *In re Stroud Wholesale, Inc.*, 47 B.R. at 1002; *WBQ P'ship v. Virginia Dep't of Med. Assistance Servs. (In re WBQ P'ship)*, 189 B.R. 97, 107 (Bankr. E.D. Va. 1995). If full payment were required, §363(f)(5) would merely mirror §363(f)(3) and render it superfluous. *In re Terrace Chalet Apts.*, 159 B.R. at 829.

Under the view that full payment is not necessary, it is not the amount of the payment that is at issue, but whether a "mechanism exists to address extinguishing the lien or interest without paying such interest in full." *In re Gulf States Steel*, 285 B.R. at 508. Other courts have required a showing of the basis that could be used to compel acceptance of less than full monetary satisfaction. *See, e.g., id.; In re Terrace Chalet Apts.*, 159 B.R. at 829.

Although this view leads to a relatively small role for paragraph (5), we are not effectively writing it out of the Code. Paragraph (5) remains one of five different justifications for selling free and clear of interests, and its scope need not be expansive or all-encompassing. So long as its breadth complements the other four paragraphs consistent with congressional intent, without overlap, our narrow view is justified.

Examples can be formulated that demonstrate this complementary aspect of a narrow view of paragraph (5). One might be a buy-out arrangement among partners, in which the controlling partnership agreement provides for a valuation procedure that yields something less than market value of the interest being bought out. *See, e.g., De Anza Enters. v. Johnson*, 104 Cal. App. 4th 1307, 128 Cal. Rptr. 2d 749 (2002) (joint venturer may compel specific performance of buyout of other venturer's interest pursuant to joint venture agreement); *Oliker v. Gershunoff*, 195 Cal. App.

3d 1288, 241 Cal. Rptr. 415 (1987) (statute provided that partnership could compel buyout of withdrawing partner for a fair price to be determined by several factors). Another might be a case in which specific performance might normally be granted, but the presence of a liquidated-damages clause allows a court to satisfy the claim of a nonbreaching party in cash instead of a forced transfer of property. *See, e.g., O'Shield v. Lakeside Bank,* 335 Ill. App. 3d 834, 269 Ill. Dec. 924, 781 N.E.2d 1114 (2002). Yet another might be satisfaction of obligations related to a conveyance of real estate that normally would be specifically performed but for which the parties have agreed to a damage remedy. *S. Motor Co. v. Carter-Pritchett-Hodges, Inc. (In re MMH Automotive Group, LLC),* 385 B.R. 347 (Bankr. S.D. Fla. 2008). In these cases, a court could arguably compel the holders of the interest to take less than what their interest is worth.

Of course, if the interest is such that it may be vindicated only by compelling or restraining some action, it does not qualify under this aspect of §363(f)(5), and the estate cannot sell free and clear of that interest. *See, e.g., Gouveia v. Tazbir,* 37 F.3d 295 (7th Cir. 1994) (landowners whose land bordered on estate's land could not be compelled to accept money damages in lieu of equitable relief for violation of a reciprocal land covenant restricting the neighborhood to single-story, residential property; estate could therefore not sell the property free of the covenant under §363(f)(5)). *See also In re WBQ P'ship,* 189 B.R. at 106 (finding §363(f)(5) inapplicable to restrictive covenants without reference to specific state law governing monetary versus equitable satisfaction) (dicta); *In re 523 E. Fifth Street Hous. Pres. Dev. Fund Corp.,* 79 B.R. 568, 576 (Bankr. S.D.N.Y. 1987) (court may not sell free and clear of covenant to provide low-income housing).

ii. Construction Consistent with §§363(f)(3) and 1206

While the bankruptcy court's reading is plausible if paragraph (5) is read in isolation, statutory interpretation requires a more detailed examination of the context of the statute. *See, e.g., Davis v. Michigan Dep't of Treasury,* 489 U.S. 803, 809, 109 S. Ct. 1500, 103 L. Ed. 2d 891 (1989) ("[S]tatutory language cannot be construed in a vacuum. It is a fundamental canon of statutory construction that the words of a statute must be read in their context and with a view to their place in the overall statutory scheme."). Put another way, any interpretation of paragraph (5) must satisfy the requirement that the various paragraphs of subsection (f) work harmoniously and with little overlap. The bankruptcy court's broad interpretation does not do this.

Initially, if the Trustee's and DB's interpretation were accepted, paragraph (5) would swallow and render superfluous paragraph (3), a provision directed specifically at liens. The specific provisions of paragraph (3) would never need to be used, since all liens would be covered, regardless of any negative or positive relationship between the value of a creditor's collateral and the amount of its claim. A result that makes one of five paragraphs redundant should be avoided.

A more narrow reading is also suggested by Congress's addition of §1206 to the Code in 1986. Pre-BAPCPA section 1206 provided that:

> [a]fter notice and a hearing, *in addition to the authorization contained in section 363(f),* the trustee in a case under this chapter may sell property under section 363(b) and (c) free and clear of any interest in such property of an entity other than the estate if the property is farmland or farm equipment, except that the proceeds of such sale shall be subject to such interest.

11 U.S.C.A §1206 (West 2004) (emphasis added). Congress thus intended §1206 to supplement an estate's rights. 8 Collier on Bankruptcy, *supra,* at ¶1206.01[2] ("The rights granted to the trustee under §1206 supplement rather than replace a similar right provided by §363(f)."). As a result, both §363(f)(5) and §1206 apply to sales of estate property in chapter 12.

The interpretive challenge is to construe §363(f)(5) in a way that complements §1206. In this regard, the first difference between the two provisions is that, unlike §363(f), §1206 grants an absolute right to sell free and clear of an interest so long as the interest attaches to the proceeds. This absolute right does not exist in §363(f)(5), requiring a more narrow interpretation.

Congress added §1206 in 1986. Its purpose was "to allow family farmers to sell assets not needed for the reorganization prior to confirmation without the consent of the secured creditor subject to the approval of the court." H.R. Rep. No. 958, 99th Cong., 2nd Sess. 50 (1986), U.S. Code Cong. & Admin. News 1986, pp. 5246, 5251. Significantly, Congress explicitly made it clear that an interest includes a lien. *Id.* But §1206 would be unnecessary with respect to liens if §363(f)(5) already permitted a sale. *See In re Brileya,* 108 B.R. 444, 447 (Bankr. D. Vt. 1989) ("Section 1206 modifies §363(f) so the debtor can sell assets not necessary to the reorganization without the secured creditor's consent.").

We follow this reasoning and hold that the bankruptcy court must make a finding of the existence of such a mechanism and the trustee must demonstrate how satisfaction of the lien "could be compelled." *In re Terrace Chalet Apts.,* 159 B.R. at 829-30. Here the bankruptcy court should not have explicitly dismissed the argument that any such finding or showing is required.

c. *Legal or Equitable Proceeding*

Paragraph (5) requires that there be, or that there be the possibility of, some proceeding, either at law or at equity, in which the nondebtor could be forced to accept money in satisfaction of its interest. The bankruptcy court reasoned that there was no need to prove the existence or possibility of a qualifying legal or equitable proceeding when the interest at issue was a lien because all liens, by definition, are capable of being satisfied by money.

The language of §363(f)(5) indicates that compelling a nondebtor to accept a monetary satisfaction cannot be the sole focus of the inquiry under that paragraph. The statute additionally requires that "such entity could be compelled, *in a legal or equitable proceeding,* to accept" such a monetary satisfaction. 11 U.S.C. §363(f)(5) (emphasis added). The question is thus whether there is an available type or form of legal or equitable proceeding in which a court could compel Clear Channel to release its lien for payment of an amount that was less than full value of Clear Channel's claim. Neither the Trustee nor DB has directed us to any such proceeding under nonbankruptcy law, and the bankruptcy court made no such finding.

The Trustee points out that courts have found that cramdown under §1129(b)(2) is a qualifying legal or equitable proceeding. *See, e.g., In re Gulf States Steel*, 285 B.R. at 508; *In re Grand Slam USA, Inc.*, 178 B.R. 460, 462 (E.D. Mich. 1995); *In re Healthco*, 174 B.R. at 176; *In re Terrace Chalet Apts.*, 159 B.R. at 829.

We disagree with the reasoning of these courts. As a leading treatise recognizes, use of the cramdown mechanism to allow a sale free and clear under §363(f)(5) uses circular reasoning-it sanctions the effect of cramdown without requiring any of §1129(b)'s substantive and procedural protections. 3 Collier on Bankruptcy, *supra*, at ¶363.06[6]. If the proceeding authorizing the satisfaction was found elsewhere in the Bankruptcy Code, then an estate would not need §363(f)(5) at all; it could simply use the other Code provision.

In addition, this reasoning undercuts the required showing of a separate proceeding. For example, it is correct that §1129(b)(2) permits a cramdown of a lien to the value of the collateral, but it does so only in the context of plan confirmation. To isolate and separate the cramdown from the checks and balances inherent in the plan process undermines the entire confirmation process, and courts have been leery of using §363(b) to gut plan confirmation or render it superfluous.

We thus hold that Congress did not intend under §363(f)(5) that nonconsensual confirmation be a type of legal or equitable proceeding to which that paragraph refers. As a result, the availability of cramdown under §1129(b)(2) is not a legal or equitable proceeding to which §363(f)(5) is applicable.

In short, for the reasons outlined above, §363(f)(5) does not apply to the circumstances of this case.

C. Were Payments Made Pursuant to the "Carve-Out" Free and Clear of Clear Channel's Lien?

Clear Channel asserts that the removal of its lien from the Carve-Out Amount was an abuse of discretion both procedurally and substantively. We think this misperceives the nature of the Carve-Out Amount, and we thus affirm on this point.

Implicit in Clear Channel's argument is that the Carve-Out Amount was "sold" and that it constitutes proceeds of the sale of PW's property. The structure of the transaction, however, does not fit Clear Channel's characterization. The governing documents do not provide that the Carve-Out Amount was part of the Strike Price paid by DB, which DB was then obligated to rebate to the Trustee. Rather, DB's obligation to pay the Carve-Out Amount "to [PW's] estate upon the Sale" was a separate obligation.

The statement of the obligation was physically and logically isolated from DB's obligation to pay the Strike Price. Its source is in a separate part of the Binding Term Sheet, and the ultimate calculation of the amount payable incorporated factors separate from the sale. Thus, while the Sale Order expressly attached Clear Channel's lien to the proceeds of the sale, the Carve-Out Amount was not proceeds. As a result, no procedural or substantive rights of Clear Channel were violated, as Clear Channel cannot claim an interest in DB's nonpurchase obligations to the Trustee.

IV. *Conclusion*

1. Considerations of equitable mootness and §363(m) render moot Clear Channel's appeal of the validity of the sale of PW's property to DB. But Clear Channel's appeal of the lien-stripping is not equitably moot because we can fashion effective relief, and it is not statutorily moot because §363(m) is inapplicable.

2. The bankruptcy court did not apply the correct legal standard under §363(f)(5), and it therefore did not make the findings required by that paragraph. We therefore reverse that part of the bankruptcy court's order that held that, under §363(f)(5), the sale was free and clear of Clear Channel's lien.

3. Further, because of the bankruptcy court's incorrect interpretation of the statute, we remand this case for further proceedings consistent with this disposition. This will allow the parties to attempt to identify a qualifying proceeding under nonbankruptcy law (if one exists) that would enable them to strip Clear Channel's lien and make the sale of PW's property to DB free and clear under §363(f)(5).

4. We affirm the bankruptcy court's holding that Clear Channel's lien did not attach to the Carve-Out payment that DB made to the Trustee.

There is another situation in which the purchaser of a debtor's assets may be liable for the seller's debts. Successor liability (the purchaser's liability to the seller's creditors) arises generally either when the transfer essentially continued the seller's business, when the transfer basically constituted a merger of the seller and the buyer, and when the sale is viewed as a fraudulent attempt to evade the seller's creditors' claims. Additionally, the purchaser could, of course, assume the seller's obligations. If this liability might be imposed on the assets after the purchase, the price that would be paid for those assets would be reduced to reflect this risk.

The courts thus far have split over whether a sale under §363(f) of the Bankruptcy Code can override the state law principles of successor liability. For example, since the liability attaches as a result of the application of state law, the Seventh Circuit has held that the happenstance of bankruptcy as "location" of the sale does not shelter the sale from this doctrine. Chicago Truck Drivers, Helpers and Warehouse Workers Union Pension Fund v. Tasemkin, Inc., 59 F.3d 48 (7th Cir. 1995). Other courts have held to the contrary that the bankruptcy courts can protect the purchasers of the assets from the bankruptcy estate. WBQ Partnership v. Virginia Dept. of Medical Assistance Servs., 189 B.R. 97 (Bankr. E.D. Va. 1995). To the extent that the case in which the sale takes place involves liability for injuries suffered from asbestos, §524(g), added to the Code in 1994, permits transfers without liability continuing to attach to the assets as long as the requirements of that section are met. This section essentially codifies the result reached in Kane v. Johns-Manville Corp., 843 F.2d 636

(2d Cir. 1988). Whether this protection will be granted in other cases must await the test of time.

III.   The Plan of Reorganization

A.   *Exclusivity*

During the first 120 days following the filing of the Chapter 11 petition only the debtor in possession may file a plan, see §1121(b), a significant advantage that gives the debtor leverage to negotiate with the creditors and secure their acceptance of any proposed plan. If the debtor in possession does file a plan within the initial 120 days, §1121(c)(3) allows the debtor more breathing room: another 60 days of exclusivity in which to solicit acceptance of the plan. These periods may, for cause, be shortened or lengthened by the court, but in no event may the period be extended more than 18 months from the filing of the petition; §1121(d). This is still a considerable period of time in which no interest is running on unsecured debt, and administrative expenses — which must be paid in full in cash at the moment of the confirmation of the plan, see §1129(a)(9)(A) — are escalating, creating pressures on all parties involved.

Small business debtors. Congress created special rules for small entities in Chapter 11, designed to expedite the process. Small businesses, defined in §101(51)(D), are business entities not involved in owning or operating real estate whose debts do not exceed $2,000,000 and for whom there is no active committee of unsecured creditors. For such debtors the exclusivity period is 180 days, and §1121(e) requires that all plans be filed within the 300 days after the petition is filed. Section 1129(e) also provides that confirmation of a plan in a small business case must occur within 45 days of the filing of the plan unless the court grants an extension for an additional reasonable time. Small business debtors also have special filing requirements under §308(b), and must comply with certain other duties under §1116.

Sometimes the debtor files the Chapter 11 petition with a prepackaged plan all ready to go, thus speeding up the process greatly, but often the debtor files the petition in order to create the breathing room in which to create the plan and sell it to the creditors who must vote on it.

Section 1125 forbids the debtor in possession or anyone proposing a plan from soliciting acceptance of the proposal until those who will vote are given a court-approved disclosure statement containing adequate information about the information and either the plan itself or a summary thereof. Read §1125(a) and (b).

PROBLEM 9-25

Because Luddite Technology had many different kinds of creditors (secured lenders, trade creditors, employees, tort claimants, the union, stock and bond holders) it is worried that the disclosure statement will be so complicated and long that it will confuse many readers. It will also be very costly to print and distribute a huge disclosure statement to all these entities. Can Luddite, with the court's approval, give each type of creditor a short version of the disclosure statement containing only the information that that particular creditor needs to know? *See* §1125(c). Suppose Luddite is a small business debtor. Could its plan of reorganization also serve as a disclosure statement? *See* §1125(f).

In re Century Glove, Inc.
United States Court of Appeals, Third Circuit, 1988
860 F.2d 94

JAMES HUNTER, III, Circuit Judge:

Century Glove, Inc. ("Century Glove"), a debtor seeking reorganization under the federal bankruptcy laws, seeks review of a district court order dismissing sanctions imposed on its creditors. Century Glove claims that one of its creditors, First American Bank ("FAB"), unlawfully solicited the votes of other creditors, in violation of 11 U.S.C. §1125. The bankruptcy court agreed, imposing sanctions against FAB and invalidating another creditor's rejection of Century Glove's plan. On appeal, the district court reversed, holding FAB's action lawful. Century Glove now appeals to this court. We will affirm the order of the district court.

I.

Century Glove filed its petition seeking reorganization in bankruptcy on November 14, 1985. On August 1, 1986, Century Glove filed its reorganization plan, along with a draft of the disclosure statement to be presented along with the plan. Arguing that Century Glove's largest claimed assets are speculative lawsuits (including one against FAB), FAB presented a copy of an alternative plan to the unsecured creditors' committee. FAB advised that it would seek court approval to present its plan as soon as possible. The committee ultimately rejected the plan in favor of that of the debtor. On December 2, 1986, the bankruptcy court approved Century Glove's disclosure statement. A copy of the plan, the statement, and a sample ballot were then sent to Century Glove's creditors entitled to vote on the plan's acceptance.

Between December 12 and December 17, 1986, an attorney for FAB, John M. Bloxom, telephoned attorneys representing several of Century Glove's creditors. Among these creditors were Latham Four Partnerships ("Latham Four") and Bankers Trust New York Corporation ("BTNY"). Bloxom sought to find out what these creditors thought of the proposed reorganization, and to convince them to vote against the plan. He said that, while there was no other plan approved for presentation, and thus no other plan "on the table," FAB had drafted a plan and had tried to file it. The creditors' attorneys then asked for a copy of the plan, which FAB provided. The copies were marked "draft" and covering letters stated that they were submitted to the creditors for their comments. The draft did not contain certain information necessary for a proper disclosure statement, such as who would manage Century Glove after reorganization.

With a copy of its draft plan, FAB also sent to Latham Four a copy of a letter written to the unsecured creditors' committee by its counsel. In the letter, dated August 26, 1986, counsel questioned the committee's endorsement of the Century Glove plan, arguing that the lawsuits which Century Glove claims as assets are too speculative. As stated, the committee endorsed the plan anyway. Upset with this decision, one of its members sent a copy of the letter to a former officer of Century Glove. The officer then sent a copy, unsolicited, to FAB. Uncertain whether the letter was protected by an attorney-client privilege, FAB asked the committee member whether he had disclosed the letter voluntarily. He said that he had, and furnished a second copy directly to FAB. FAB attached this letter to a motion before the bankruptcy court seeking to have the committee replaced. The bankruptcy court later held the letter a privileged communication.

BTNY had made a preliminary decision on September 12, 1986, to reject Century Glove's plan. It reaffirmed this decision on December 15, when it received a copy of the plan and disclosure. Counsel for BTNY spoke with Bloxom the next day, December 16, 1986, and Bloxom mailed a letter confirming the call, but by mistake Bloxom did not send a draft of the alternate plan until December 17. On that day, counsel for BTNY prepared its ballot rejecting Century Glove's plan, and informed Bloxom of its vote.

After receiving the several rejections, Century Glove petitioned the bankruptcy court to designate, or invalidate, the votes of FAB, Latham Four and BTNY. Century Glove argued that FAB had acted in bad faith in procuring these rejections.

II.

The bankruptcy court held that FAB had violated 11 U.S.C. §1125(b), which allows solicitation of acceptance or rejections only after an approved disclosure statement has been provided the creditor. Though a statement had been filed and provided, the bankruptcy court stated that:

> solicitations . . . must be limited by the contents of the plan, the disclosure statement, and any other court-approved solicitation material. The solicitee may not be given information outside of these approved documents.

The bankruptcy court found that FAB violated the section by providing additional materials such as copies of its draft plan. 74 B.R. 952.

The bankruptcy court also concluded that FAB had violated "the spirit of §1121(b), since FAB was apparently seeking approval of a plan which was not yet filed and which it could not file. . . ." This "impropriety" was "heightened" by the absence from the FAB plan of such information as "who will manage the debtor." The bankruptcy court also found "improper" the disclosure by FAB of the August 26, 1986, letter to the creditors' committee. The court found that FAB's "machinations" in procuring a second copy of the letter showed that it was "obviously wary" that the letter might be privileged.

The bankruptcy court held invalid Latham Four's vote. It allowed the vote of BTNY, however, finding that the creditor had proved it had not relied on FAB's statements in deciding to reject Century Glove's plan. The court declined to bar FAB from participating further in the reorganization, finding such a sanction "too harsh," but instead, ordered FAB to pay for "all costs incurred by [Century Glove] in prosecuting" its motions. The amount of these damages was not specified. Both parties appealed the decision to the district court.

In a decision dated January 5, 1988, the district court affirmed the bankruptcy court rulings allowing BTNY's vote, but reversed the designation of Latham Four and the imposition of money sanctions against FAB. 81 B.R. 274. The district court disagreed that §1125(b) requires approval for all materials accompanying a solicitation, and found such a reading in conflict with the bankruptcy code's policy of fostering free negotiation among creditors. The district court held that merely supplying additional information does not constitute "bad faith" or a violation of the bankruptcy rules. Therefore, the court concluded, the bankruptcy court had erred in finding that FAB had improperly solicited rejections of the Century Glove plan.

The district court next considered whether FAB had improperly sought acceptance of its own plan. The court found that, in order to facilitate negotiations, communications between creditors should not easily be read as solicitations. Because Bloxom did not make a "specific request for an official vote," In re Synder, 51 B.R. 432, 437 (Bankr. D. Utah 1985), FAB's action "may only be fairly characterized as part of FAB's negotiations." Because FAB did not unlawfully solicit rejections, and did not solicit acceptances, the designation and sanction orders of the bankruptcy court were reversed. Century Glove appeals to this court. . . .

IV.

Century Glove argues that the district court erred in holding FAB did not improperly solicit rejections of Century Glove's reorganization plan. . . .

Section 1125(b) states, in pertinent part, that:

> An acceptance or rejection of a plan may not be solicited after the commencement of the case under this title from a holder of a claim or interest with respect to such claim or interest, unless, at the time of or before such solicitation, there is transmitted to such holder the plan or summary of the plan, and a written disclosure statement approved, after notice and a hearing, by the court as containing adequate information.

There is no question that, at the time of FAB's solicitations, the solicitees had received a summary of the plan and a court-approved statement disclosing adequate information. Also, the bankruptcy court's factual conclusion that FAB was seeking rejections of Century Glove's plan is not clearly erroneous, and so must be assumed. Century

Glove argues that FAB also was required to get court approval before it could disclose additional materials in seeking rejections.

Century Glove's interpretation of the section cannot stand. Century Glove argues, and the bankruptcy court assumed, that only approved statements may be communicated to creditors. The statute, however, never limits the facts which a creditor may receive, but only the time when a creditor may be solicited. Congress was concerned not that creditors' votes were based on misinformation, but that they were based on no information at all. *See* H.R. 95-595, at pp. 225-25, 95th Cong., 2d Sess., 124 Cong. Rec. __, reprinted in, 1978 U.S.C.C.A.A.N. 5963, 6185 (House Report). Rather than limiting the information available to a creditor, §1125 seeks to guarantee a minimum amount of information to the creditor asked for its vote. *See* S.R. 95-989, at p. 121, 95th Cong., 2d Sess., 124 Cong. Rec. __, reprinted in, 1978 U.S.C.C.A.A.N. 5787, 5907 ("A plan is necessarily predicated on knowledge of the assets and liabilities being dealt with and on factually supported expectations as to the future course of the business. . . .") (Senate Report). The provision sets a floor, not a ceiling. Thus, we find that §1125 does not on its face empower the bankruptcy court to require that all communications between creditors be approved by the court.

As the district court pointed out, allowing a bankruptcy court to regulate communications between creditors conflicts with the language of the statute. A creditor may receive information from sources other than the disclosure statement. Section 1125 itself defines "typical investor" of a particular class in part, as one having "such ability to obtain such information from sources other than the disclosure required by this section. . . ." 11 U.S.C. §1125(a)(2)(C). In enacting the bankruptcy code, Congress contemplated that the creditors would be in active negotiations with the debtor over the plan. *See infra*, part V. The necessity of "adequate information" was intended to help creditors in their negotiations. *See* In re Gulph Woods, 83 B.R. 339 (Bankr. E.D. Pa. 1988). Allowing the bankruptcy court to regulate communications between creditors under the guise of "adequate information" undercuts the very purpose of the statutory requirement.

Lastly, Century Glove's reading of §1125 creates procedural difficulties. Century Glove provides this court no means to distinguish predictably between mere interpretations of the approved information, and additional information requiring separate approvals. Therefore, to be safe, the creditor must seek prior court approval for every communication with another creditor (or refrain from communication), whether soliciting a rejection or an acceptance. Congress can hardly have intended such a result. It would multiply hearings, hence expense and delay, at a time when efficiency is greatly needed.[20] We also note that, as expressed in the House Report, Congress

---

20. Expense was a prime reason Congress suspended the applicability of the laws to reorganizations. *See* House Report 1978 U.S.C.C.A.A.N. at 6186. The costs of delay was a prime reason the debtor was given a limited "exclusivity period" to present its reorganization plan. *See infra*, Part V.

evidently contemplated a single hearing on the adequacy of the disclosure statement. *See* House Report, 1978 U.S.C.C.A.A.N. at 6186.[21]

Century Glove argues that two additional instances show that FAB violated §1125(b). First, it claims that FAB's draft plan contained material misrepresentations, mostly omissions. Second, it claims that FAB improperly disclosed to Latham Four a letter the bankruptcy court later found privileged. The bankruptcy court found both "improper" in support of its finding under §1125(b), and Century Glove argues that the bankruptcy court's decision can be affirmed on these grounds. The problem with the argument is that it rests on an erroneous interpretation of the law. Once adequate information has been provided a creditor, §1125(b) does not limit communication between creditors. It is not an antifraud device. Thus, the bankruptcy court erred in holding that FAB had violated §1125(b) by communicating with other materials. The district court therefore properly reversed the bankruptcy court on this issue.

V.

Though FAB was not limited in its solicitation of rejections, §1125 did prevent FAB from soliciting acceptances of its own plan. The bankruptcy court held that, "since FAB was apparently seeking approval of a plan which was not yet filed," FAB violated §1125. The court also found that FAB's actions violated the spirit of §1121, which provides the debtor with a limited, exclusive right to present a plan. Reversing, the district court held that solicitations barred by §1125(b) include only the "specific request for an official vote," and not discussions of and negotiations over a plan leading up to its presentation. In re Snyder, 51 B.R. 432, 437 (Bankr. D. Utah 1985). Because Bloxom explained that he was sending the draft only for discussion purposes, the district court found that the transmittal "may only be fairly characterized as part of FAB's negotiations." We exercise plenary review over the proper interpretation of the legal term "solicitation."

We agree with the district court that "solicitation" must be read narrowly. A broad reading of §1125 can seriously inhibit free creditor negotiations. All parties agree that FAB is not barred from honestly negotiating with other creditors about its unfiled plan. "Solicitations with respect to a plan do not involve mere requests for opinions." Senate Report, 1978 U.S.C.C.A.A.N. at 5907. The purpose of negotiations between creditors is to reach a compromise over the terms of a tentative plan. The purpose of compromise is to win acceptance for the plan. We find no principled, predictable difference between negotiation and solicitation of future acceptances.

---

21. Century Glove relies for its interpretation of §1125 entirely on statements in a bankruptcy treatise. *See* 5 Collier on Bankruptcy §1125.03, at 1125-39 ff. (15th ed. 1987). The author found the provision ambiguous, and states only that a creditor "should" seek approval. As argued above, strong policy and administrative reasons — not to mention the likely intent of Congress — argue that this court should not impose any additional requirements on communications between creditors.

We therefore reject any definition of solicitation which might cause creditors to limit their negotiations.[22]

A narrow definition of "solicitation" does not offend the language or policy of 11 U.S.C. §1121(b). The section provides only that the debtor temporarily has the exclusive right to file a plan (and thus have it voted on). It does not state that the debtor has a right to have its plan considered exclusively. A right of exclusive consideration is not warranted in the policy of the section. Congress believed that debtors often delay confirmation of a plan, while creditors want quick confirmation. Therefore, unlimited exclusivity gave a debtor "undue bargaining leverage," because it could use the threat of delay to force unfair concessions. House Report, 1978 U.S.C.C.A.A.N. at 6191. On the other hand, Congress evidently felt that creditors might not seek the plan fairest to the debtor. Therefore, Congress allowed a limited period of exclusivity, giving the debtor "adequate time to negotiate a settlement, without unduly delaying creditors." Id. Section 1121 allows a debtor the threat of limited delay to offset the creditors' voting power of approval. FAB did nothing to reduce Century's threat of limited delay, and so did not offend the balance of bargaining powers created by §1121 or the "spirit" of the law.

On the contrary, Century Glove's reading of §1121(b) would in fact give the debtor powers not contemplated by Congress. The ability of a creditor to compare the debtor's proposals against other possibilities is a powerful tool by which to judge the reasonableness of the proposals. A broad exclusivity provision, holding that only the debtor's plan may be "on the table," takes this tool from creditors. Other creditors will not have comparisons with which to judge the proposals of the debtor's plan, to the benefit of the debtor proposing a reorganization plan. The history of §1121 gives no indication that Congress intended to benefit the debtor in this way. The legislative history counsels a narrow reading of the section, one which FAB's actions do not violate.

We recognize that §1125(b) bars the untimely solicitation of an "acceptance or rejection," indicating that the same definition applies to both. A narrow definition might allow a debtor to send materials seeking to prepare support for the plan, "for the consideration of the creditors," without adequate information approved by the court. Though such preparatory materials may undermine the purpose of adequate disclosure, the potential harm is limited in several ways. First, a creditor still must receive adequate information before casting a final vote, giving the creditor a chance to reconsider its preliminary decision. The harm is further limited by free and open negotiations between creditors. Last, because they are not "solicitations," pre-disclosure communications may still be subject to the stricter limitations of the securities laws. 11 U.S.C. §1125(e). Where, as here, the creditors are counselled and already have received disclosure about the debtor's business, there seems little need for additional procedural formalities. *See, e.g.,* In re Northwest Recreational Activities, Inc., 4 B.R. 43 (Bankr. N.D. Ga. 1980) (negotiations between debtor and creditor precede §1125(b) approvals).

---

22. Barring negotiations also would provide an unwarranted boon for the debtor: creditors wholly unable to be sure that an alternative plan can be agreed are more likely to vote for the debtor's proposal rather than risk unknown delay.

Therefore, we hold that a party does not solicit acceptances when it presents a draft plan for the consideration of another creditor, but does not request that creditor's vote. Applying this definition, FAB did not solicit acceptances of its plan. Century Glove does not dispute that FAB never asked for a vote, and clearly stated that the plan was not yet available for approval. Bloxom communicated with lawyers for the creditors, and there is no suggestion by Century that these lawyers did not understand the limitations. Also as Century argues, FAB never sent its plan to Hartford Insurance because Hartford firmly opposed Century's plan. Contrary to Century's conclusion, though, this fact argues that FAB sent copies of its plan because it was interested in obtaining rejections, not acceptances. (An opponent of Century's plan would be an ideal person to solicit for acceptances.) These undisputed facts require a finding that FAB did not "solicit" acceptances within the meaning of §1125(b).

VI.

We hold that the district court correctly determined that Century Glove failed to show that FAB violated 11 U.S.C. §1125 by soliciting acceptances or improperly soliciting rejections. We therefore will affirm the district court's order reversing the imposition of costs against FAB. We do not decide, however, whether the circumstances merit designation of the votes of any creditors.

Because the plan frequently contemplates the issuance of stock in the newly reorganized company, Congress made the deliberate decision not to apply the usual securities laws to the solicitation of the plan, and §1125(d) and (e) therefore makes the application of those rules irrelevant, though the Securities and Exchange Commission is allowed to be heard on the issue of whether the disclosure statement contains adequate information; *see also* §1145.

B. Absolute Priority Rule

The debtor in possession is permitted to divide the creditors into classes under rules we will discuss later and then have the classes of creditors vote to accept or reject the plan. If all of the classes of creditors vote to accept the plan it will be confirmed (assuming it meets certain other statutory requirements, which we shall also explore). But what happens if one or more classes of creditors vote to reject the plan? According to §1129(b), the plan can still be confirmed (the so-called "cram down") by the bankruptcy court if it is "fair and equitable," but what does this mean? First of all, the phrase permits the court to police what is going on and stop the debtor in possession from dealing with its creditors in bad faith. Remember that bankruptcy is an equitable proceeding, and its overarching maxim is that "equity is equality." It has always been a truism of insolvency law that creditors should be paid before equity interests (the stockholders) get anything, and this idea is the guiding spirit behind what is commonly called the "absolute priority" rule, reflected in §1129(b)(2), which gives a partial definition (note the word "includes") of the meaning of "fair and equitable." Under that subsection, secured creditors must be given the present value of their security over the life of the plan, and unsecured creditors must either be paid in full as of the effective date of the plan or junior interests (the stockholders) can receive nothing under the plan. Subsection (2)(C) goes even further with this concept of absolute priority: if the unsecured creditors are paid in full, the equity interests must be similarly prioritized; thus holders of preferred stock must be paid in full before holders of common stock can get anything.

The upshot of all this can be devastating.

PROBLEM 9-26

Rural Radio, Inc., is a small radio station that has been run by the McCoy family since the 1930s, and Ma and Pa McCoy own 100 percent of the stock in the company. Their largest creditor is Hatfield County Bank, which has a security interest in all of the station's assets. Those assets are worth approximately $500,000, but the current debt due the bank is $650,000. Other creditors are owed $80,000. The president of the bank has taken a personal dislike to the McCoys, and when they come to your office, they tell you that if they file for bankruptcy there is no way the bank will vote in favor of the plan. They calculate that they could pay the secured debt in full, but could only pay the unsecured creditors about 40 percent of what is outstanding. You tell the McCoys about the absolute priority rule and explain that this means they will have to surrender any interest they have in the station (unless the new owners hire them on as paid employees). They break down in tears and ask if there is anything they can do to stay in control. You explain that the Chapter 11 plan might provide for dissolving all the old stock and the issuance of new stock, and that they could buy the new stock if they have any money. They don't. However, they have an idea: how about in return for the new stock they contribute their considerable talents in running the radio station and promise to work tirelessly in the future to make the station profitable so that it could pay much of its debt (this is sometimes called "sweat equity")? Will this contribution allow them to remain in control?

In re Ahlers
United States Supreme Court, 1988
485 U.S. 197

Justice WHITE delivered the opinion of the Court.

In this case, the Court of Appeals found that respondents' promise of future "labor, experience, and expertise" permitted confirmation of their Chapter 11 reorganization plan over the objections of their creditors, even though the plan violated the "absolute priority rule" of the Bankruptcy Code. Because we find this conclusion at odds with the Code and our cases, we reverse.

I.

Respondents operate a failing family farm in Nobles County, Minnesota. Between 1965 and 1984 they obtained loans from petitioners, securing the loans with their farmland, machinery, crops, livestock, and farm proceeds. In November 1984, respondents defaulted on their loan payments to petitioner Norwest Bank Worthington; at the time, the aggregate loan balance owed the petitioners exceeded $1 million.

Following the default, Norwest filed a replevin action in Minnesota state court seeking possession of the farm equipment respondents had pledged as security. However, two weeks later respondents obtained an automatic stay of the replevin proceedings, when they filed a petition for reorganization under Chapter 11 of the Bankruptcy Code. *See* 11 U.S.C. §362(a) (1982 ed. and Supp. IV).

Petitioners filed motions in the Bankruptcy Court for relief from the automatic stay. 11 U.S.C. §362(d) (1982 ed., Supp. IV). After decisions by the Bankruptcy and the District Courts, these motions were ultimately considered by the Court of Appeals, which prohibited petitioners from repossessing any equipment, pending a determination by the District Court of the probability of success of a reorganization plan to be filed by respondents. App. to Pet. for Cert. A-76-A-77. On remand, the District Court found respondents' reorganization plan to be "utter[ly] unfeasibl[e]." Id., at A-86. It therefore affirmed the Bankruptcy Court's initial decision to grant petitioners relief from the automatic stay.

On appeal, the Court of Appeals reversed. It found that respondents could file a feasible reorganization plan. 794 F.2d 388, 399 (CA8 1986). Consequently, the Court of Appeals remanded the case with instructions that the Bankruptcy Court entertain and confirm a reorganization plan which comported with an outline suggested in a lengthy appendix to the Eighth Circuit's opinion. Id., at 408-414.

In reaching this conclusion, the Court of Appeals rejected petitioners' contention that, because of the "absolute priority rule" in the Bankruptcy Code, 11 U.S.C. §1129(b)(2)(B)(ii) (1982 ed. and Supp. IV), their legitimate objections to any reorganization plan which allowed respondents to retain an interest in the farm property was sufficient to bar confirmation of such a plan. Petitioners contended that the absolute priority rule prohibited respondents from retaining their equity interest in the farm, which is junior to the creditors' unsecured claims. But the Court of Appeals, relying on this Court's decision in Case v. Los Angeles Lumber Products Co., 308 U.S. 106, 60 S. Ct. 1, 84 L. Ed. 110 (1939), held that the absolute priority rule did not bar respondents from retaining their equity interest in the farm if they contributed "money or money's worth" to the reorganized enterprise. It further concluded that respondents' "yearly contributions of labor, experience, and expertise" would constitute a contribution of "money or money's worth," and therefore would permit confirmation of a reorganization plan over petitioners' objections. 794 F.2d, at 402-403. Judge John Gibson, in dissent, criticized the majority's application of the absolute priority rule and its reading of *Los Angeles Lumber* as "unprecedented, illogical, and unfair." 794 F.2d, at 406. He concluded that the absolute priority rule barred respondents' retention of an equity interest in the farm over petitioners' legitimate objections.

After the Eighth Circuit — sharply divided — denied rehearing en banc, id., at 414-415, petitioners sought review by this Court. We granted certiorari to consider the Court of Appeals' application of the absolute priority rule, 483 U.S. 1004, 107 S. Ct. 3227, 97 L. Ed. 2d 733 (1987), and now reverse.

II.

As the Court of Appeals stated, the absolute priority rule "provides that a dissenting class of unsecured creditors must be provided for in full before any junior class can receive or retain any property [under a reorganization] plan." 794 F.2d, at 401. The rule had its genesis in judicial construction of the undefined requirement of the early bankruptcy statute that reorganization plans be "fair and equitable." See Northern Pacific R. Co. v. Boyd, 228 U.S. 482, 504-505, 33 S. Ct. 554, 560, 57 L. Ed. 931 (1913); Louisville Trust Co. v. Louisville, N.A. & C.R. Co., 174 U.S. 674, 684, 19 S. Ct. 827, 830, 43 L. Ed. 1130 (1899). The rule has since gained express statutory force, and was incorporated into Chapter 11 of the Bankruptcy Code adopted in 1978. See 11 U.S.C. §1129(b)(2)(B)(ii) (1982 ed., Supp. IV). Under current law, no Chapter 11 reorganization plan can be confirmed over the creditors' legitimate objections (absent certain conditions not relevant here) if it fails to comply with the absolute priority rule.

There is little doubt that a reorganization plan in which respondents retain an equity interest in the farm is contrary to the absolute priority rule. The Court of Appeals did not suggest otherwise in ruling for respondents, but found that such a plan could be confirmed over petitioners' objections because of an "exception" or "modification" to the absolute priority rule recognized in this Court's cases.

The Court of Appeals relied on the following dicta in Case v. Los Angeles Lumber Products Co., supra, 308 U.S., at 121-122, 60 S. Ct., at 10:

> It is, of course, clear that there are circumstances under which stockholders may participate in a plan of reorganization of an insolvent debtor. . . .
> [W]e believe that to accord "the creditor of his full right of priority against the corporate assets" where the debtor is insolvent, the stockholder's participation must be based on a contribution in money or money's worth, reasonably equivalent in view of all the circumstances to the participation of the stockholder.

The Court of Appeals found this language applicable to this case, concluding that respondents' future contributions of "labor, experience, and expertise" in running the farm — because they have "value" and are "measurable" — are "money or money's worth" within the meaning of *Los Angeles Lumber*. 794 F.2d, at 402. We disagree.[23]

---

23. The United States, as *amicus curiae*, urges us to reverse the Court of Appeals ruling and hold that codification of the absolute priority rule has eliminated any "exception" to that rule suggested by *Los Angeles Lumber*. *See* Brief for United States as Amicus Curiae 17-23. Relying on the statutory language and the legislative history, the United States argues that the 1978 Bankruptcy Code "dropped the infusion-of-new-capital exception to the absolute priority rule." Id., at 22.

Los Angeles Lumber itself rejected an analogous proposition, finding that the promise of the existing shareholders to pledge their "financial standing and influence in the community" and their "continuity of management" to the reorganized enterprise was "[in]adequate consideration" that could not possibly be deemed "money's worth." 308 U.S., at 122, 60 S. Ct., at 10. No doubt, the efforts promised by the Los Angeles Lumber equity holders — like those of respondents — had "value" and would have been of some benefit to any reorganized enterprise. But ultimately, as the Court said in *Los Angeles Lumber,* "[t]hey reflect merely vague hopes or possibilities." Id., at 122-123, 60 S. Ct., at 11. The same is true of respondents' pledge of future labor and management skills.

Viewed from the time of approval of the plan, respondents' promise of future services is intangible, inalienable, and, in all likelihood, unenforceable. It "has no place in the asset column of the balance sheet of the new [entity]." *Los Angeles Lumber*, 308 U.S., at 122-123, 60 S. Ct., at 11. Unlike "money or money's worth," a promise of future services cannot be exchanged in any market for something of value to the creditors today. In fact, no decision of this Court or any Court of Appeals, other than the decision below, has ever found a promise to contribute future labor, management, or expertise sufficient to qualify for the *Los Angeles Lumber* exception to the absolute priority rule. In short, there is no way to distinguish between the promises respondents proffer here and those of the shareholders in Los Angeles Lumber; neither is an adequate contribution to escape the absolute priority rule.

Respondents suggest that, even if their proposed contributions to the reorganized farm do not fit within the *Los Angeles Lumber* dicta, they do satisfy some broader exception to the absolute priority rule. Brief for Respondents 23-24. But no such broader exception exists. Even if Congress meant to retain the *Los Angeles Lumber* exception to the absolute priority rule when it codified the rule in Chapter 11 — a proposition that can be debated, *see* n.3, supra — it is clear that Congress had no intention to expand that exception any further. When considering adoption of the current Code, Congress received a proposal by the Bankruptcy Commission to modify the absolute priority rule to permit equity holders to participate in a reorganized enterprise based on their contribution of "continued management . . . essential to the business" or other participation beyond "money or money's worth." *See* H.R. Doc. No. 93-137, pt. 1, pp. 258-259 (1973). This proposal — quite similar to the Court of Appeals' holding in this case — prompted adverse reactions from numerous

---

We need not reach this question to resolve the instant dispute. As we discuss *infra*, at 104-106, we think it clear that even if the *Los Angeles Lumber* exception to the absolute priority rule has survived enactment of the Bankruptcy Code, this exception does not encompass respondents' promise to contribute their "labor, experience, and expertise" to the reorganized enterprise.

Thus, our decision today should not be taken as any comment on the continuing vitality of the *Los Angeles Lumber* exception — a question which has divided the lower courts since passage of the Code in 1978. *Compare, e.g.,* In re Sawmill Hydraulics, Inc., 72 B.R. 454, 456, and n.1 (Bkrtcy. Ct. C.D. Ill. 1987), *with, e.g.,* In re Pine Lake Village Apartment Co., 19 B.R. 819, 833 (Bkrtcy. Ct. S.D.N.Y. 1982). Rather, we simply conclude that even if an "infusion-of-'money-or-money's-worth'" exception to the absolute priority rule has survived the enactment of §1129(b), respondents' proposed contribution to the reorganization plan is inadequate to gain the benefit of this exception.

sources. Congress ultimately rejected the proposed liberalization of the absolute priority rule and adopted the codification of the rule now found in 11 U.S.C. §1129(b)(2)(B)(ii) (1982 ed. and Supp. IV). "This [section] codifies the absolute priority rule from the dissenting class on down." *See* H.R. Rep. No. 95-595, p. 413 (1977), U.S. Code Cong. & Admin. News 1978, pp. 5787, 6369. We think the statutory language and the legislative history of §1129(b) clearly bar any expansion of any exception to the absolute priority rule beyond that recognized in our cases at the time Congress enacted the 1978 Bankruptcy Code.

In sum, we find no support in the Code or our previous decisions for the Court of Appeals' application of the absolute priority rule in this case. We conclude that the rule applies here, and respondents' promise of future labor warrants no exception to its operation.

III.

Respondents advance two additional arguments seeking to obviate the conclusion mandated by the absolute priority rule.

A.

Respondents first advance a variety of "equitable arguments" which, they say, prevent the result we reach today. Respondents contend that the nature of bankruptcy proceedings — namely, their status as proceedings in "equity" — prevents petitioners from inequitably voting in the class of unsecured creditors, and requires that a "fair and equitable" reorganization plan in the best interests of all creditors and debtors be confirmed. *See* Brief for Respondents 14-16, 23-24. Similarly, the Court of Appeals found it significant that — in its view — respondents' wholly unsecured creditors (as opposed to petitioners, who have partially secured claims) would fare better under the proposed reorganization plan than if the farm was liquidated. 794 F.2d, at 402.

The short answer to these arguments is that whatever equitable powers remain in the bankruptcy courts must and can only be exercised within the confines of the Bankruptcy Code. The Code provides that undersecured creditors can vote in the class of unsecured creditors, 11 U.S.C. §506(a), the Code provides that a "fair and equitable" reorganization plan is one which complies with the absolute priority rule, 11 U.S.C. §1129(b)(2)(B)(ii) (1982 ed. and Supp. IV), and the Code provides that it is up to the creditors — and not the courts — to accept or reject a reorganization plan which fails to provide them adequate protection or fails to honor the absolute priority rule, 11 U.S.C. §1126 (1982 ed. and Supp. IV).

The Court of Appeals may well have believed that petitioners or other unsecured creditors would be better off if respondents' reorganization plan was confirmed. But that determination is for the creditors to make in the manner specified by the Code. 11 U.S.C. §1126(c). Here, the principal creditors entitled to vote in the class of unsecured creditors (i.e., petitioners) objected to the proposed reorganization. This was their prerogative under the Code, and courts applying the Code must effectuate their decision.

B.

Respondents further argue that the absolute priority rule has no application in this case, where the property which the junior interest holders wish to retain has no value to the senior unsecured creditors. In such a case, respondents argue, "the creditors are deprived of nothing if such a so-called 'interest' continues in the possession of the reorganized debtor." Brief for Respondents 19. Here, respondents contend, because the farm has no "going concern" value (apart from their own labor on it), any equity interest they retain in a reorganization of the farm is worthless, and therefore is not "property" under 11 U.S.C. §1129(b)(2)(B)(ii) (1982 ed. and Supp. IV).

We join with the consensus of authority which has rejected this "no value" theory. Even where debts far exceed the current value of assets, a debtor who retains his equity interest in the enterprise retains "property." Whether the value is "present or prospective, for dividends or only for purposes of control" a retained equity interest is a property interest to "which the creditors [are] entitled . . . before the stockholders [can] retain it for any purpose whatever." Northern Pacific R. Co. v. Boyd, 228 U.S., at 508, 33 S. Ct., at 561. Indeed, even in a sole proprietorship, where "going concern" value may be minimal, there may still be some value in the control of the enterprise; obviously, also at issue is the interest in potential future profits of a now-insolvent business. See SEC v. Canandaigua Enterprises Corp., 339 F.2d 14, 21 (CA2 1964) (Friendly, J.). And while the Code itself does not define what "property" means as the term is used in §1129(b), the relevant legislative history suggests that Congress' meaning was quite broad. " '[P]roperty' includes both tangible and intangible property." See H.R. Rep. No. 95-595, at 413, U.S. Code Cong. & Admin. News 1978, at 6369.

Moreover, respondents' "no value" theory is particularly inapposite in this case. This argument appears not to have been presented to the Eighth Circuit, which implicitly concluded — to the contrary of respondents' position here — that the equity interest respondents desire to retain has some value. See 794 F.2d, at 402-403. Even cursory consideration reveals that the respondents' retained interest under the plan might be "valuable" for one of several reasons. For example, the Court of Appeals provided that respondents would be entitled to a share of any profits earned by the sale of secured property during the reorganization period, id., at 403, and n.18 — an interest which can hardly be considered "worthless." And there is great common sense in petitioners' contention that "obviously, there is some going concern value here, or the parties would not have been litigating over it for the last three years." Tr. of Oral Arg. 15-16.

Consequently, we think that the interest respondents would retain under any reorganization must be considered "property" under §1129(b)(2)(B)(ii), and therefore can only be retained pursuant to a plan accepted by their creditors or formulated in compliance with the absolute priority rule. Since neither is true in this case, the Court of Appeals' judgment for respondents cannot stand.

IV.

In rejecting respondents' position, we do not take lightly the concerns which militated the Eighth Circuit towards its result. As a Bankruptcy Judge commented on the Court of Appeals' decision in this case: "We understand the motivation behind the majority opinion in [In re] Ahlers [794 F.2d 388 (CA8 1986)]. Farm bankruptcies are in a state of crisis and we, too, sympathize with the plight of the American farmer. Nevertheless, the solution proposed by the Ahlers majority is contrary to the Bankruptcy Code and a long line of case law." In re Stegall, 64 B.R. 296, 300 (Bkrtcy. Ct. C.D. Ill. 1986).

Family farms hold a special place in our Nation's history and folklore. Respondents and amici paint a grim picture of the problems facing farm families today, and present an eloquent appeal for action on their behalf. Yet relief from current farm woes cannot come from a misconstruction of the applicable bankruptcy laws, but rather, only from action by Congress.

The error of the Court of Appeals' approach is further revealed by an examination of a measure Congress has recently enacted to cope with these very same concerns, the Family Farmers Bankruptcy Act of 1986, Pub. L. 99-554, §255, 100 Stat. 3105-3114. The Act creates a new Chapter 12 bankruptcy proceeding, under which family farmers can retain an equity interest in their farms while making loan repayments under a reorganization plan. *See* 11 U.S.C. §1201 *et seq.* (1982 ed., Supp. IV).

The legislative history of the Act makes it clear that one of Congress' principal concerns in adopting Chapter 12 was the difficulties farmers encountered in seeking to reorganize under Chapter 11. And yet, as respondents concede, the Court of Appeals' decision here creates a method of proceeding under Chapter 11 which is far more advantageous to farmers than is Chapter 12. *See* Brief for Respondents 6-9; Tr. of Oral Arg. 23-25. Thus, given respondents' reading of Chapter 11, Congress enacted a relief provision in Chapter 12 which is less favorable to its intended beneficiaries than is current law. But in adopting Chapter 12, Congress thought it was doing just the opposite. "[W]here, as here, Congress adopts a new law . . . [it] normally can be presumed to have had knowledge of the interpretation given to the [old] law." Lorillard v. Pons, 434 U.S. 575, 581, 98 S. Ct. 866, 870, 55 L. Ed. 2d 40 (1978). We think Congress' understanding of Chapter 11 and its absolute priority rule — and not respondents' — is the correct one. We do not believe that Congress created, in Chapter 12, an option for farm reorganizations less accessible to most farmers than current Chapter 11 proceedings.

V.

In sum, because we find the decision below to be contrary to the Bankruptcy Code and this Court's previous cases, the judgment of the Court of Appeals is reversed, and the case is remanded for further proceedings consistent with this opinion.

It is so ordered.

———————————

In a footnote the court specifically avoided the question of whether the new value exception to the absolute priority rule survives at all, a question that has divided the lower courts in subsequent opinions, as we shall see when we return to this issue in the discussion of claims classification.

In a remarkable study of actual Chapter 11 reorganizations, Professors Lynn LoPucki and William Whitford found that cram down under §1129(b) did not often occur. Instead, the debtor in possession and its creditors typically reached agreement on a plan that the court then confirmed. *See* L. LoPucki & W. Whitford, Bargaining over Equity's Share in the Bankruptcy Reorganization of Large, Publicly Held Companies, 139 U. Pa. L. Rev. 125 (1990). This does not mean, however, that the *threat* of cram down or the loss of equity interest demanded by the absolute priority rule had no effect on the negotiations. The article concluded that in small business reorganizations, where the continued presence of an interested management/equity ownership was important, the absolute priority rule had little effect, since the business would die if that management quit working. But the authors also found that even in big business reorganizations, the creditors usually voted to allow equity to emerge from the process with some continued ownership rights.

It should also be noted that the bargaining leverage can arise from the threat, always looming in the background, to convert the Chapter 11 to a Chapter 7. The debtor in possession will argue that voting for a plan that will pay the unsecured creditors a lot more than they will get in a Chapter 7 liquidation is the sensible thing to do, even if it means the stockholders hang on to their ownership interests. Conversely, the creditors can bargain for a bigger chunk of the pie by saying they will vote against the proposed plan if they don't get paid more, and if this means a liquidation, so be it. Many times the creditors rightly believe that the Chapter 11 plan is an unrealistic dream that will siphon off the debtors' current assets to the advantage of no one, so that they would be better off with an immediate sale of those assets in Chapter 7.

These issues come up in the cases that follow, but an understanding of some of them depends on appreciating the §1111(b) election, so let's address that next.

C. The §1111(b) Election

Section 1111(b) gives certain creditors rights they might want to exercise depending on the situation. It is, however, one of those statutes that you had better know what it is about *before* you read it, or you will exit from its language as confused as ever. The Problems that follow are designed to give it context. For a splendid article on point, *see* S. Haydon, S. Owens, T. Salerno & C. Hansen, The 1111(b)(2) Election: A Primer, 13 Bankr. Dev. J. 99 (1996).

PROBLEM 9-27

At a time when the real estate market was very, very good, Octopus National Bank loaned Barbara Speculator's company $2,000,000 to buy the biggest office building in town, agreeing to take a mortgage on the building and not requiring her or her company to enter into any personal liability to repay the loan. ONB entered into this "nonre-course" arrangement, which had a very nice interest rate, because it was clear that the building was easily worth more than the debt and was appreciating in value every day as the market rose. Ten years later the real estate market has collapsed; the building is worth only $900,000, but the bank is still owed $1,500,000. If Speculator's company files a Chapter 11 petition that proposes to pay the bank only $900,000, must the bank write off the rest of the debt as a bad loan? *See* §1111 (b)(1)(A).

There are two elections in §1111(b), and it is important to keep them apart, since they deal with separate issues. The first permits a creditor like ONB to participate in the Chapter 11 proceeding not only as a secured creditor but also as an unsecured creditor, even though it had agreed that it would have no rights against the debtor outside of bankruptcy. Why did Congress do this? Consider that if bankruptcy had not intervened ONB could have repossessed the building and kept it for itself. If the real estate market improved and the building regained some or all of its former worth, the bank could recapture a portion of the unsecured debt that would otherwise have been lost. Without the rule of §1111(b), Speculator could cash the bank out at $900,000 and herself get the benefit of any future appreciation of the building's worth.

PROBLEM 9-28

In Problem 9-27, ONB saw the wisdom of participating in the Chapter 11 as both a secured and an unsecured creditor, but Speculator's plan proposed to sell the building on the open market. Does §1111(b) allow the bank a vote as an unsecured creditor? *See* §1111(b)(1)(A)(ii). Why or why not? How can the bank protect its interests? *See* §363(k).

PROBLEM 9-29

Same facts as Problem 9-27, but ONB comes to you, its attorney, with the following additional information. The plan that Speculator has filed proposes to pay unsecured creditors 10 percent of their claims and ONB $900,000 (plus interest) over the 10-year life of the plan. Thus ONB will get the current value of the building plus 10 percent of the unsecured portion of its claim. What bothers ONB about this is that the real estate market is improving and the building might be worth more than $2,000,000 in 10 years. What can it do? *See* §1111(b)(2).

Here the bank would be well advised to make the second elections in §1111(b) (assuming it can get the class into which it is placed to do so — note that the election must be made by the *class* per §1111(b)(1)(A)(i)). Under §1111(b) this means the bank will give up any rights to participate in the Chapter 11 proceeding as an unsecured creditor, *but the plan must pay the entire debt owed to the bank as if it were all secured!* There is a catch, however, and it is that if not all classes accept the plan, so that cram down is proposed under §1129(b)(2)(A)(i)(ii), the secured claim need only be paid "deferred cash payments totaling at least the allowed amount of such claim . . . of at least the value of such holder's interest in the estate's interest in such property." This refers one back to §1129(a)(7)(B), which addresses what the creditor making the §1129(b) election must receive: the "value of such holder's interest in the estate's interest in the property that secures" the claim. What all this convoluted language means is this: The plan must pay ONB enough over the years that the plan lasts so that the bank gets both the present value of the collateral ($900,000 plus interest) and the total of the payments to the bank must pay the entire debt owed to ONB ($1,500,000) but *without interest* on the unsecured portion.

PROBLEM 9-30

Barbara Speculator comes to you, her attorney, for advice. ONB has made the §1111(b) election and demands that the plan be amended to pay the bank $1,500,000 over the life of the plan. What are her options?

PROBLEM 9-31

If Speculator's company had had personal liability on the original debt, could ONB still have made the §1111(b) election to protect the undersecured portion of the amount owed to it? Read §1111(b) carefully.

PROBLEM 9-32

Suppose that ONB has the first mortgage on the office building in the last few Problems and that Speculator's company had later taken out a second mortgage on the building in favor of Nightflyer Finance Company, which had made the company a loan of $100,000. The building is now worth $900,000, and ONB is still owed $1,500,000. None of the debt due Nightflyer has been paid. Can Nightflyer make the §1111(b) election? *See* §1111(b)(1)(B)(i).

D. Classification of Claims

The debtor in possession must get all classes of creditors to vote for the plan in order to get it confirmed without a cram down. If that is not possible, the rules on cram down still require that at least one of the impaired classes vote for the plan or cram down is not possible, see §1129(a)(10), which carries over to §1129(b)(1) (why could Congress have imposed such a requirement?). This can lead to some creative classifications in the proposed plan.

PROBLEM 9-33

Your client is Abacus, Inc., to whom Luddite Technologies owes $80,000 unsecured for abacuses it purchased. Luddite has filed a Chapter 11 petition, and its proposed plan places Abacus in a class of trade creditors who will be paid 10 percent of the amounts due them. There are 30 other trade creditors in this class, but the combined amounts Luddite owes them is $50,000. How important will the vote of Abacus, Inc., be to Luddite? See §1126(c).

In re U.S. Truck Company, Inc.

United States Court of Appeals, Sixth Circuit, 1986
800 F.2d 581

CORNELIA G. KENNEDY, Circuit Judge.

The Teamsters National Freight Industry Negotiating Committee (the Teamsters Committee), a creditor of U.S. Truck Company, Inc. (U.S. Truck) — the debtor-in-possession in this Chapter 11 bankruptcy proceeding — appeals the District Court's order confirming U.S. Truck's Fifth Amended Plan of Reorganization. The Teamsters Committee complains that the plan does not satisfy three of the requirements of 11 U.S.C. §1129. The District Court, which presided over the matter after the resignation of Bankruptcy Judge Stanley B. Bernstein, held that the requirements of section 1129 had been satisfied. We agree.

I.

Underlying this appeal is the Teamsters Committee's claim that U.S. Truck is liable to its employees for rejecting a collective bargaining agreement between the local union and U.S. Truck. After filing its petition for relief under Chapter 11 of the Bankruptcy Code on June 11, 1982, U.S. Truck, a trucking company primarily engaged in intrastate shipping of parts and supplies for the automotive industry, sought to reject the collective bargaining agreement. U.S. Truck rejected the agreement with the approval of then-Bankruptcy Judge Woods, in December 1982. Judge Woods found that rejection of the agreement was "absolutely necessary to save the debtor from collapse." Memorandum Opinion and Order, December 6, 1982, at page 8. New agreements have been negotiated to the satisfaction of each participating local union. Such agreements have been implemented over the lone dissent of the Teamsters Joint Area Rider Committee. Under the most recently mentioned agreement in the record (due to have expired in March 1985), U.S. Truck was able to record monthly profits in the range of $125,000 to $250,000. These new agreements achieved such results by reducing wages and requiring employees to buy their own trucking equipment, which the employees then leased to the company. . . .

II.

Section 1129 contains two means by which a reorganization plan can be confirmed. The first way is to meet all eleven of the requirements of subsection (a), including (a)(8), which requires all impaired classes of claims or interests to accept the plan. The other way is to meet the requirements of subsection (b), which, first, incorporates all of the requirements of subsection (a), except for that contained in subsection (a)(8), and, second, imposes two additional requirements. Confirmation under subsection (b) is commonly referred to as a "cram down" because it permits a reorganization plan to go into effect over the objections of one or more impaired classes of creditors. In this case, U.S. Truck sought approval of its plan under this "cram down" provision.

III.

The Teamsters Committee's first objection is that the plan does not meet the requirement that at least one class of impaired claims accept the plan, see 11 U.S.C. §1129(a)(10), because U.S. Truck impermissibly gerrymandered the classes in order to neutralize the Teamsters Committee's dissenting vote. The reorganization plan contains twelve classes. The plan purports to impair five of these classes — Class VI (the unsecured claim of Manufacturer's National Bank of Detroit based on a mortgage); Class VII (the secured claim of John Graham, Trustee of Transportation Services, Inc., based on a loan); Class IX (the Teamsters Committee's claim based on rejection of the collective bargaining agreement); Class XI (all secured claims in excess of $200.00 including those arising from the rejection of executory contracts); and Class XII (the equity interest of the stockholder of the debtor). As noted above, section 1129(a)(10), as incorporated into subsection (b)(1), requires at least one of these classes of impaired claims to approve the reorganization plan before it can be confirmed. The parties agree that approval by Class XII would not count because acceptance must be determined without including the acceptance of the plan by any insider. See 11 U.S.C. §1129(a)(10). The Code's definition of "insider" clearly includes McKinlay Transport, Inc. See 11 U.S.C. §101(28)(B)(iii), (30). Thus, compliance with subsection (a)(10) depends on whether either of the other three classes that approved the plan — Class VI, Class VII, or Class XI — was a properly constructed impaired class. The Teamsters Committee argues that Classes VI and VII were not truly impaired classes and that Class XI should have included Class IX, and hence was an improperly constructed class.[24] Because we find that Class XI was a

---

24. Had the debtor included the Teamsters Committee's claim in Class XI, the Committee's vote to reject the plan would have swung the results of the Class XI vote from an acceptance to a rejection. *See* 11 U.S.C. §1126(c) (setting forth the requirement that creditors holding at least two-thirds in amount of allowed claims of a class accept).

properly constructed class of impaired claims, we hold that the plan complies with subsection (a)(10).

The issue raised by the Teamsters Committee's challenge is under what circumstances does the Bankruptcy Code permit a debtor to keep a creditor out of a class of impaired claims which are of a similar legal nature and are against the same property as those of the "isolated" creditor. The District Court held that the Code permits such action here because of the following circumstances: (1) the employees represented by the Teamsters Committee have a unique continued interest in the ongoing business of the debtor; (2) the mechanics of the Teamsters Committee's claim differ substantially from those of the Class XI claims; and (3) the Teamsters Committee's claim is likely to become part of the agenda of future collective bargaining sessions between the union and the reorganized company. *See* 47 B.R. at 939-40. Thus, according to the court, the interests of the Teamsters Committee are substantially dissimilar from those of the creditors in Class XI. We must decide whether the Code permits separate classification under such circumstances.

Congress has sent mixed signals on the issue that we must decide. Our starting point is 11 U.S.C. §1122.

§1122. Classification of Claims or Interests

(a)   Except as provided in subsection (b) of this section, a plan may place a claim or interest in a particular class only if such claim or interest is substantially similar to the other claims or interests of such class.

(b)   A plan may designate a separate class of claims consisting only of every unsecured claim that is less than or reduced to an amount that the court approves as reasonable and necessary for administrative convenience.

The statute, by its express language, only addresses the problem of dissimilar claims being included in the same class. It does not address the correlative problem — the one we face here — of similar claims being put in different classes. Some courts have seized upon this omission, and have held that the Code does not require a debtor to put similar claims in the same class. We think the courts erred in holding that section 1122(a) prohibits classification based on the presence of a co-debtor. Section 1122(a) specifies that only claims which are "substantially similar" may be placed in the same class.

It does not require that similar claims *must* be grouped together, but merely that any group created must be homogenous. *See* 5 Collier on Bankruptcy ¶1122.03[1][b] at 1122-6 (15th ed. 1982); *accord*, In re Gay, 3 B.R. 336 (Bkrtcy. D. Colo. 1980); In re Kovich, 4 B.R. 403 (Bkrtcy. W.D. Mich. 1980). Although some courts have held that section 1122(a) prohibits classification based on any criterion other than legal right to the debtor's assets, *see, e.g.*, In re Iacovoni, 2 B.R. 256, 260-61 (Bkrtcy. D. Utah), the plain language of the statute contradicts such a construction. Moreover, section 1122(a) so interpreted would conflict with section 1322(b)(1), which specifically authorizes designation of more than one class of unsecured creditor, each presumably with equal legal rights to the debtor's estate. Barnes v. Whelan, 689 F.2d 193, 201

(D.C. Cir. 1982) (emphasis in original) (holding that Chapter 13 debtor may group his unsecured debtors according to whether or not a co-debtor is present); *see also* In re Planes, 48 B.R. 698, 701 (Bkrtcy. N.D. Ga. 1985); In re Moore, 31 B.R. 12, 16 (Bkrtcy. D.S.C. 1983).

Further evidence that Congress intentionally failed to impose a requirement that similar claims be classified together is found by examining the "classification" sections of the former Bankruptcy Act. The applicable former provisions were 11 U.S.C., sections 597 (from former Chapter X) and 751 (from former Chapter XI).

> §597. Classification of creditors and stockholders. For the purposes of the plan and its acceptance, the judge shall fix the division of creditors and stockholders into classes according to the nature of their respective claims and stock. For the purposes of such classification, the judge shall, if necessary, upon the application of the trustee, the debtor, any creditor, or an indenture trustee, fix a hearing upon notice to the holders of secured claims, the debtor, the trustee, and such other persons as the judge may designate, to determine summarily the value of the security and classify as unsecured the amount in excess of such value.
>
> §751. Classification of creditors. For the purposes of the arrangement and its acceptance, the court may fix the division of creditors into classes and, in the event of controversy, the court shall after hearing upon notice summarily determine such controversy.

Section 597 was interpreted to require all creditors of equal rank with claims against the same property to be placed in the same class. *See* In re Los Angeles Land and Investments, Ltd., 282 F. Supp. 448, 453 (D. Hawaii 1968) (quoting In re Scherk v. Newton, 152 F.2d 747 (10th Cir. 1945), *aff'd,* 447 F.2d 1366 (9th Cir. 1971)). Congress' switch to less restrictive language in section 1122 of the Code seems to warrant a conclusion that Congress no longer intended to impose the now-omitted requirement that similar claims be classified together. *See* Matter of Huckabee Auto Co., 33 B.R. 132, 137 (Bkrtcy. M.D. Ga. 1981). However, the legislative history indicates that Congress may not have intended to change the prior rule. The Notes of the Senate Committee on the Judiciary state:

> This section [1122] codifies current case law surrounding the classification of claims and equity securities. It requires classification based on the nature of the claims or interests classified, and permits inclusion of claims or interests in a particular class only if the claim or interest being included is substantially similar to the other claims or interests of the class.

S. Rep. No. 989, 95th Cong., 2d Sess. 118, reprinted in 1978 U.S. Code Cong. & Ad. News 5787, 5904. . . .

In this case, U.S. Truck is using its classification powers to segregate dissenting (impaired) creditors from assenting (impaired) creditors (by putting the dissenters into a class or classes by themselves) and, thus, it is assured that at least one class of impaired creditors will vote for the plan and make it eligible for cram down consideration by the court. We agree with the Teamsters Committee that there must be some limit on a debtor's power to classify creditors in such a manner. The potential for abuse would be significant otherwise. Unless there is some requirement of keeping similar claims together, nothing would stand in the way of a debtor seeking out a few impaired creditors (or even one such creditor) who will vote for the plan and placing them in their own class.[25] . . .

The District Court noted three important ways in which the interests of the Teamsters Committee differ substantially from those of the other impaired creditors. Because of these differences, the Teamsters Committee has a different stake in the future viability of the reorganized company and has alternative means at its disposal for protecting its claim. The Teamsters Committee's claim is connected with the collective bargaining process. In the words of the Committee's counsel, the union employees have a "virtually unique interest." *See* 47 B.R. at 939. These differences put the Teamsters Committee's claim in a different posture than the Class XI claims. The Teamsters Committee may choose to reject the plan not because the plan is less than optimal to it as a creditor, but because the Teamsters Committee has a noncreditor interest — e.g., rejection will benefit its members in the ongoing employment relationship. Although the Teamsters Committee certainly is not intimately connected with the debtor, to allow the Committee to vote with the other impaired creditors would be to allow it to prevent a court from considering confirmation of a plan that a significant group of creditors with similar interests have accepted. Permitting separate classification of the Teamsters Committee's claim does not automatically result in adoption of the plan. The Teamsters Committee is still protected by the provisions of subsections (a) and (b), particularly the requirements of subsection (b) that the plan not discriminate unfairly and that it be fair and equitable with respect to the Teamsters Committee's claim. In fact, the Teamsters Committee invokes those requirements, but as we note in the following sections, the plan does not violate them.

IV.

The Teamsters Committee's second objection is that the plan is not fair and equitable. This objection focuses on the provision of the plan that allows McKinlay Transport, Inc., to purchase all 100,000 shares of common stock from U.S. Truck for $100,000. The Teamsters Committee notes that McKinlay currently owns all of the existing common stock in U.S. Truck, and thus the plan impermissibly permits an equity security holder (whose interest is junior to other creditors) to retain its ownership interest in the reorganized company. . . .

If McKinlay were retaining an interest without contributing any capital, the plan would clearly violate the Code. *See* In re Genesee Cement, Inc., 31 B.R. 442, 443 (Bkrtcy. E.D. Mich. 1983). But McKinlay is giving up its prior interest and participating in the reorganized company by making a $100,000 contribution. The question, put in terms of the Code's language, is whether McKinlay is receiving its interest in the reorganized company "on account of" its junior claim. This involves looking

---

25. We need not speculate in this case whether the purpose of separate classification was to line up the votes in favor of the plan. The debtor admitted that to the District Court. *See* Debtor's Response to Objections to Confirmation Filed by the Teamsters National Freight Negotiating Committee, at 6 (Jan. 23, 1985).

at the need for the contribution and whether McKinlay paid a fair price for its interest.

In Case v. Los Angeles Lumber Prods. Co., 308 U.S. 106, 60 S. Ct. 1, 84 L. Ed. 110, *reh'g denied*, 308 U.S. 637, 60 S. Ct. 258, 84 L. Ed. 529 (1939), the Court validated stockholder participation in a plan of reorganization of an insolvent debtor. Especially in [Kansas City Terminal Ry. v. Central Union Trust Co., 271 U.S. 445, 46 S. Ct. 549, 70 L. Ed. 1028 (1926)] did this Court stress the necessity, at times, of seeking new money "essential to the success of the undertaking" from the old stockholders. Where that necessity exists and the old stockholders make a fresh contribution and receive in return a participation reasonably equivalent to their contribution, no objection can be made. Id., 308 U.S. at 121, 60 S. Ct. at 10. Applying the Supreme Court's standard to this case, we must decide whether the District Court was clearly erroneous in its findings supporting its conclusion that the contribution was substantial and "essential."

The relevant evidence on this issue is set forth in the District Court's opinion. 47 B.R. at 942-43. The Teamsters Committee argues that $100,000 cannot possibly be essential or substantial when the debtor is reporting monthly profits of over $100,000. Considered alone, the monthly profit statistics make a strong argument for the Teamsters Committee's position. However, the District Court relied on other probative evidence that minimizes the relevance of those statistics. Significantly, the Teamsters Committee presented no independent evidence to support its objection. It relied solely on its ability to cross-examine U.S. Truck's witnesses.

The District Court heard testimony that investment in the reorganized company would be a risky proposition. There was no labor stability in light of the imminent expiration of a collective bargaining agreement that had been negotiated shortly after U.S. Truck filed for bankruptcy. As the Teamsters Committee points out, the then-current agreement was acceptable to the employees only because of the dire circumstances. Furthermore, the Teamsters Committee's own claim against the debtor is a substantial one and has not been resolved. The debtor's expert witness, Van Conway, testified that U.S. Truck was in a risky industry and that the other problems unique to it rendered income figures unreliable. Conway concluded that in light of all the facts, the contribution was essential. Again, the Teamsters Committee offered no refuting evidence. Under such circumstances, we conclude that the District Court's findings were not clearly erroneous.

V.

The Teamsters Committee's final objection is that the plan does not satisfy subsection 1129(a)(11). That subsection states that the confirmation is permitted only if it is "not likely to be followed by the liquidation, or the need for further financial reorganization, of the debtor or any successor to the debtor under the plan. . . ." The Teamsters Committee contends that because the debtor is under the control of a competitor, and will continue to be under such control as a reorganized company, the District Court erred in finding that it is not likely that the company will be liquidated.

The lines of corporate control indicate that U.S. Truck was, and will be, in the hands of a competing company. Agnes Anne Moroun will have sole ownership of the reorganized company. Moroun also holds 15 percent of the outstanding stock of Cen Tra, Incorporated, which in turn owns all the outstanding stock of Central Transport Company, Central Cartage and GLS Leasco. McKinlay acquired all of the stock of U.S. Truck immediately after U.S. Truck filed its Chapter 11 petition. Since then, U.S. Truck has vacated its terminals and relocated its freight operations to terminals owned by the Central Group. The Central Group has also leased new trailers, tractors and high-lows to U.S. Truck. The Teamsters Committee complains that the Central Group can divert U.S. Truck business to itself and thus leave the reorganized company high and dry. The Teamsters Committee also noted that U.S. Truck's leases with the Central Group were oral and of unfixed duration, exposing the reorganized company to the risk that its favorable lease terms could be cancelled on a whim.

In light of the evidence available to the District Court, we conclude that the court's finding that the reorganized company is unlikely to liquidate is not clearly erroneous. The following factors are relevant to such a finding: (1) the adequacy of the capital structure; (2) the earning power of the business; (3) economic conditions; (4) the ability of management; (5) the probability of the continuation of the same management; and (6) any other related matter which determines the prospects of a sufficiently successful operation to enable performance of the provisions of the plan. *See* In re Landmark at Plaza Park, Ltd., 7 B.R. 653, 659 (Bkrtcy. D.N.J. 1980). Neither party presented evidence or argument about the adequacy of the capital structure, although the Teamsters Committee has noted that U.S. Truck has resorted primarily to leasing of its equipment and machinery. The earning power, as discussed earlier, is a poor indicator of feasibility in this case. Management's ability has not been impugned, except in connection with the Teamsters Committee's argument that the Central Group will exert its control to the detriment of the reorganized company. . . .

The District Court noted that there is an inherent tension in determining that a capital contribution by current shareholders is necessary (because of the precarious position of the reorganized company) and then determining that that plan is not likely to fail. In the context of this case, that tension is resolved by the court's finding that the capital contribution is both necessary and sufficient to make the plan work. Neither that finding, nor any one of those mentioned above, is clearly erroneous.

The District Court's judgment is affirmed.

———————

The classification of creditors can arise indirectly even before a plan is proposed. For example, the debtor and creditor may be engaged in litigation over the claim, and in the course of that litigation they may propose a settlement of the matter in such a way that it not only establishes the validity of the claim, but it may provide for some payment of the claim. Unless all claims are likely to be paid in full, other similarly situated creditors may object to the apparently special treatment being given to the creditor whose claim is the subject of the settlement. Is this a way around the prohibition on unfair discrimination? The case that follows explores the problem.

In re Tower Automotive, Inc.
United States Bankruptcy Court, Southern District of New York, 2006
342 B.R. 158

ALLAN L. GROPPER, Bankruptcy Judge.

Before the Court is a motion by the Debtors to approve two settlements modifying retiree benefits pursuant to 11 U.S.C. §1114(e)(1)(B). One settlement was reached with the Milwaukee Unions, while the other settlement was reached with an Official Committee of Retired Employees (the "Retiree Committee"). The settlements were reached in connection with the Debtors' motion, filed on January 4, 2006, to reject collective bargaining agreements pursuant to 11 U.S.C. §1113(c) and to modify retiree benefits pursuant to 11 U.S.C. §1114(g) (the "1113/1114 Motion"). After extensive discovery and briefing, the 1113/1114 Motion came before the Court for a five-day trial commencing on February 27, 2006. The settlement with the Milwaukee Unions (the "Milwaukee Settlement") was announced in open court at the outset of the trial and the Milwaukee Unions did not participate in the trial. The Retiree Committee actively participated in the trial and reached a settlement with the Debtors before a decision on the 1113/1114 Motion was rendered by the Court (the "Retiree Settlement" and collectively with the Milwaukee Settlement, the "Settlements"). The Official Committee of Unsecured Creditors (the "Creditors Committee") participated fully in the briefing and trial and in subsequent conferences.

By motion dated April 5, 2006, the Debtors moved for approval of the Settlements (the "Settlement Approval Motion"). In brief, the Settlements provide that (i) VEBA trusts will be established to provide future benefits for the retirees represented by the Milwaukee Unions and the Retiree Committee, respectively; (ii) cash payments will be made to start up the trusts; and (iii) the trusts will principally be funded by unsecured claims that are designed to compromise and liquidate the future benefits that would have otherwise been received by the retirees. In addition, since it is not known at this point in the cases what an unsecured claim will be worth, the Milwaukee Unions and the Retiree Committee each receive a guaranteed minimum recovery, which, in the case of the Milwaukee Unions, is increased in the event certain bondholders, who potentially represent a class of general unsecured creditors, receive a recovery of more than 85% on their claims. The Settlements also resolve a host of complicated grievance, NLRB, arbitration and litigation proceedings between the Debtors and the Milwaukee Unions. The Debtors, in turn, receive what they have consistently represented they most need-relief from burdensome legacy costs that would otherwise be a cash drain on their treasuries for decades. The cash impact of the Settlements is immediate. Among other things, upon approval of the Milwaukee and Retiree

Settlements, the Debtors will no longer be obligated to pay approximately $20 million at the end of this year.[26]

The Creditors Committee was the only party to object to the approval of the Settlements and objected to the Settlements on three grounds: (i) the Settlements violate the Bankruptcy Code because they guarantee a level of recovery for certain creditors, while other allegedly similarly situated creditors do not, as of yet, have any assurance as to their recovery; (ii) the Settlements comprise a *sub rosa* plan of reorganization; and (iii) the Settlements do not satisfy Fed. R. Bankr. P. 9019. The Settlement Approval Motion came on for a hearing on April 26, 2006, and the Court took the testimony of Jeffrey Kersten, the Debtors' senior vice president for strategy and business development, in support thereof. For the reasons stated below, the Settlements are approved.

Discussion

I. The Statute

11 U.S.C. §1114(e)(1) provides:

> Notwithstanding any other provision of this title, the debtor in possession, or the trustee if one has been appointed under the provisions of this chapter (hereinafter in this section "trustee" shall include a debtor in possession), shall timely pay and shall not modify any retiree benefits, except that —
>
>> (A) the court, on motion of the trustee or authorized representative, and after notice and a hearing, may order modification of such payments, pursuant to the provisions of subsections (g) and (h) of this section; or
>>
>> (B) the trustee and the authorized representative of the recipients of those benefits may agree to modification of such payments, after which such benefits as modified shall continue to be paid by the trustee.

Section 1114 was added to the Bankruptcy Code by the Retiree Benefits Bankruptcy Protection Act of 1988. It provides for appointment of a committee of retired employees to serve as the authorized representative of those persons receiving retiree benefits not covered by a collective bargaining agreement. See 11 U.S.C. §1114(d). Patterned after §1113, it then both protects and sets out a procedure for the modification of retiree benefits, providing for modification of retiree benefits only if the court finds that

> (i) prior to the hearing, the trustee has made a proposal to the authorized representative of the retirees
>
>> (a) the proposal is based on the most complete and reliable information available at the time of such proposal;

---

26. Section 1114 requires that retiree benefit payments be continued during the course of a Chapter 11 case unless a court order is obtained or unless there is an agreement otherwise with the authorized representative of the retirees. 11 U.S.C. §1114(e)(1).

(b) the proposal provides for the modifications in the retiree benefits that are necessary to permit the reorganization of the debtor; and

(c) the proposal assures that all creditors, the debtor and the affected parties are treated fairly and equitably;

(ii) the trustee has provided the representative of the retirees with relevant information as is necessary to evaluate the proposal;

(iii) the trustee has met, at reasonable times, with the authorized representative of the retirees to confer in good faith while attempting to reach mutually satisfactory modifications of the retiree benefits

(a) these meetings must take place in the period between the making of the proposal and the date of the hearing;

(iv) the authorized representative of the retirees has refused to accept such proposal without good cause; and

(v) the proposed modification is necessary to permit the reorganization of the debtor, assures that all creditors, the debtor and all of the affected parties are treated fairly and equitably, and is clearly favored by the balance of the equities.

11 U.S.C. §§1114(f)-(g).

II.   The Settlements do not unfairly discriminate in favor of the retirees and against the general unsecured creditors

The Creditors Committee's first objection is that the Settlements prefer retirees by giving them a "guaranteed recovery" while the remaining general, "similarly situated" unsecured creditors do not know how they will be treated under a plan of reorganization. This refrain is not a viable objection to most settlements during the course of a bankruptcy case and prior to confirmation of a plan. Debtors routinely settle matters during a case, as "compromises are a normal part of the process of reorganization." *Barry v. Smith (In re New York, New Haven and Hartford Railroad Co.)*, 632 F.2d 955, 959 (2d Cir. 1980). Even the Creditors Committee conceded, at the hearing, that if the Debtors had paid only cash in the Settlements, it would not have objected on a "guaranteed recovery" theory. The form of a settlement, however, is only one factor to be considered in connection with a ruling on the reasonableness of a settlement. In this case, the Debtors have no excess cash and a principal purpose of the 1113/1114 Motion was to achieve cash savings now and in the future. The Creditors Committee has never satisfactorily explained why, under the circumstances, the Debtors could not provide retirees with a guaranteed proof of claim amount and use currency other than cash to effect the Settlements.

In any event, the Creditors Committee ignores the plain language of §1114 in asserting that general unsecured creditors are situated similarly to retirees. Section 1114 requires a good faith course of negotiation before benefits can be modified, and it allows a debtor to modify retiree benefits without the agreement of the authorized representative only if it can show (among other things) that (i) the authorized representative refused to accept a proposal without good cause, and (ii) "such modification is necessary to permit the reorganization of the debtor and assures that all creditors, the debtor, and all of the affected parties are treated fairly and equitably, and is clearly favored by the balance of the equities." See 11 U.S.C. §1114(g)(3).

The statute requires the parties to attempt to come to an agreement on terms. General unsecured creditors have no such specific protection in Chapter 11, either with respect to the process of bargaining or the substantive provisions of a plan. Despite the importance of good faith negotiation in connection with the Chapter 11 process, the Bankruptcy Code gives a debtor broad authority to alter the rights of unsecured creditors in a plan of reorganization. 11 U.S.C. §§1123, 1129. By contrast, unless the Court approves a modification in accordance with §1114 standards and procedures, a plan must provide for the continuation of retiree benefits "for the duration of the period the debtor has obligated itself to provide such benefits" at an unmodified level. 11 U.S.C. §1129(a)(13).

The Committee's alternative contention is that if benefits are modified under §1114, retirees are entitled to receive only general unsecured claims that must be treated in the same fashion as other general unsecured claims in a subsequent plan. This argument suggests that the only permissible outcome in a §1114 proceeding is either a victory for the retirees or the complete elimination of all retiree benefits, either by trial or settlement, in return for a general unsecured claim. As discussed above, however, §1114 requires a course of negotiations "to reach mutually satisfactory modifications of such retiree benefits," if possible. Agreement is one of the two ways retiree benefits can be modified under §1114. *Hourly Employees/Retirees of Debtor v. Erie Forge & Steel, Inc.*, 2004 WL 385023 (W.D. Pa. Feb.2, 2004), *aff'd on other grounds*, 418 F.3d 270 (3d Cir. 2005). The possibility of an agreement would be greatly impeded if the only legally permissible offer the Debtors could make was to give retirees a general unsecured claim at the end of the day. No court has so held, and cases have approved settlements in §1114 proceedings that provide retirees with consideration in a form that does not exclusively comprise an unsecured claim. See, e.g., *In re GF Corp.*, 120 B.R. 421 (Bankr. N.D. Ohio 1990); *Hourly Employees/Retirees of Debtor*, 2004 WL 385023, at *4.

The fact that Congress intended §1114 to allow a modification of benefits that includes recovery in a form other than an unsecured claim is confirmed by the following passage from the legislative history of §1114, providing an example of how the statute would work:

> If the present value of the health insurance benefits of retirees is $100 million at the time the petition is filed and the court orders a modification reducing benefit payments by $25 million, the retirees have an unsecured claim for the full $25 million. If every unsecured creditor receives 50 cents on every dollar, retirees would receive $12.5 million in addition to the continuation of 75 percent of their original health benefit.

S.Rep. No. 119, 100th Cong., 1st Sess. 1, 6 n. 2, reprinted in 1988 U.S. Code Cong. & Admin. News 683, 688 n.2. The hypothetical illustrates one outcome where retiree benefits are not treated like unsecured claims. The Committee cites *In re Ionosphere Clubs, Inc.*, 134 B.R. 515 (Bankr. S.D.N.Y. 1991), for the proposition that an order providing for modification of retiree benefits gives rise only to a general unsecured claim. However, the issue there was whether the retirees would have a priority administrative claim if benefits were modified by court order (not agreement), and the *Ionosphere* court relied on the passage from the Legislative History, quoted above, as confirmation of the fact that modifications required by court order do not automatically create administrative claims. 134 B.R. at 526.

III.   The Settlements do not constitute a *sub rosa* plan

The Creditors Committee's second argument is that the Settlements constitute a *sub rosa* plan of reorganization because they dictate terms with which the Debtors will have to comply in the future. In extreme circumstances, courts have refused to approve settlements or other transactions by a debtor, such as the sale of all or substantially all assets, without the benefit of a confirmed plan or court-approved disclosure statement and without an adequate business justification. See *In re Decora Indus., Inc.*, 2002 WL 32332749, at *8 (D. Del. May 20, 2002); *Official Comm. of Unsecured Creditors v. Raytech Corp. (In re Raytech Corp.)*, 190 B.R. 149, 151 (Bankr. D. Conn. 1995); see also, *Comm. of Equity Sec. Holders v. Lionel Corp. (In re Lionel Corp.)*, 722 F.2d 1063 (2d Cir. 1983) (sale of most important asset without articulated business justification); *Institutional Creditors of Continental Air Lines, Inc. v. Continental Air Lines, Inc. (In re Continental Air Lines, Inc.)*, 780 F.2d 1223 (5th Cir. 1986) (new lease transactions after bankruptcy). Such settlements encroached "on a right afforded creditors or equity holders in the chapter 11 plan process." *In re Crowthers McCall Pattern, Inc.*, 114 B.R. 877, 885 (Bankr. S.D.N.Y. 1990).

On the other hand, courts have approved even large and important settlements prior to confirmation of a plan, notwithstanding a "*sub rosa* plan" objection, where the settlements did not dispose of all of the debtor's assets, restrict creditors' rights to vote as they deemed fit on a plan of reorganization, or dictate the terms of a plan of reorganization. See *Official Comm. of Unsecured Creditors v. Cajun Elec. Power Coop., Inc. (In re Cajun Elec. Power Coop., Inc.)*, 119 F.3d 349, 354 (5th Cir. 1997); *In re Allegheny Int'l, Inc.*, 117 B.R. 171 (W.D. Pa. 1990); *In re Dow Corning Corp.*, 192 B.R. 415 (Bankr. E.D. Mich. 1996). As the Court stated in the *Cajun Electric Power* case, rejecting a *sub rosa* plan argument, the settlement there did "not dispose of all claims against [the debtor], nor does it restrict creditors' rights to vote as they deem fit on a proposed reorganization plan [nor does it] dispose of virtually all of [the debtor's] assets. . . ." 119 F.3d at 355.

The Settlements here do not dictate any of the terms of a future plan of reorganization, do not restructure the Debtors' business or finances generally, and do not restrict any rights afforded to creditors in the chapter 11 process, such as the right to vote on a proposed plan of reorganization in the manner they see fit. The Settlements merely provide additional consideration to retirees in exchange for modifying their benefits. Although this consideration may be different from the consideration to be given general unsecured creditors, the difference (as discussed above) is expressly permitted under §1114. Moreover, §1114(f) requires that a debtor seeking to modify retiree benefits make "a proposal to the authorized representative of the retirees, based on the most complete and reliable information available at the time of such proposal. . . ." No party argued that it was unfair for the retirees to have to negotiate before their representatives knew the treatment of other general unsecured creditors in a plan of reorganization. There similarly is no basis for the Creditors Committee to argue that a settlement cannot now be approved that fixes the Debtors' obligation to the retirees.

IV. The Settlements meet the standards of Bankruptcy Rule 9019

The Creditors Committee's third argument is that the Settlements do not meet the standards of Bankruptcy Rule 9019, which provides, in relevant part, "[o]n motion by the trustee and after notice and a hearing, the court may approve a compromise or settlement." Fed. R. Bankr. P. 9019(a). A court assesses a settlement by determining whether it "fall[s] below the lowest point in the range of reasonableness." *Anaconda-Ericsson, Inc. v. Hessen (In re Teltronics Servs., Inc.),* 762 F.2d 185, 189 (2d Cir. 1985). In making this assessment, there is a general presumption in favor of settlements, *Fogel v. Zell,* 221 F.3d 955, 960 (7th Cir. 2000), as "compromises are favored in bankruptcy." *Myers v. Martin (In re Martin),* 91 F.3d 389, 393 (3d Cir. 1996), quoting 9 Collier, *Bankruptcy* ¶9019.03[1] (15th ed. 1993); see also *Fishell v. Soltow (In re Fishell),* 1995 WL 66622, at *2 (6th Cir. Feb. 16, 1995).

Although the Creditors Committee invoked the Bankruptcy Rule 9019 standards, it adduced nothing of substance to support the contention that the Settlements are unreasonable. Indeed, the Creditors Committee conceded, at the hearing, that its 9019 objection rested on the proposition, which the Court has rejected, that the Debtors as a matter of law cannot give the Milwaukee Unions and the Retiree Committee more than a general, unsecured claim if the retiree benefits are modified. Under these circumstances, the Court summarily rejects the Committee's contentions under Bankruptcy Rule 9019. Moreover, having heard five days of testimony on the 1113/1114 Motions, the Court has no reason not to endorse a settlement that satisfies the Debtors' principal goal, saving cash, while affording significant protection for the rights that Congress required be preserved for the retirees. The litigation posed significant risks for both sides. Despite the Committee's contentions, it is in the interests of all parties to go forward with these Settlements so that the Debtors and the Committee can proceed to negotiate a plan and an end to these cases.

The Debtors are directed to submit orders approving the Settlements.

As you can well imagine there is a great deal of litigation over both the classification of claims and the new value exception to the absolute priority rule. Let's look at each in turn.

Some courts have read §1122(a) literally: it only addresses who can be placed in a class and says nothing about whether similar claims must be in the same class. *See, e.g.,* In re AG Consultants Grain Div., Inc., 77 B.R. 665 (Bankr. N.D. Ind. 1987) (similar claims allowed in different classes). Others have required all similar claims in the same class; Hanson v. First Bank of South Dakota, 828 F.2d 1310 (8th Cir. 1987) (all unsecured creditors must be in the same class).

The bankruptcy courts in recent decades have been clogged with single asset realty cases in which the debtor owns one major asset (a building) and has one major creditor (the mortgagee). In the depressed real estate market of the 1980s, these bankruptcies hit the courts and the mortgagee struggled in case after case to get to the collateral, only to be stymied by the debtor's maneuvers in Chapter 11. Keeping the major creditor out of a class of unsecured creditors permitted that class to vote for the plan, even though impaired, and as we shall see, doing so permits cram down. If the major creditor is required to be in the same class as the unsecured creditors, it can outvote them and reject the plan, blocking cram down. Particularly where the mortgagee could make the §1111(b) election have there been a series of cases in which the propriety of putting the undersecured mortgagee in the same class as the unsecured creditors has been at issue. In one leading case on point Judge Edith Jones, tired of debtors stalling their major creditors in single asset realty cases, required that the undersecured mortgagee be placed in the same class as other unsecured creditors, thundering in a now-famous quotation: *"Thou shalt not classify similar claims differently in order to gerrymander an affirmative vote on a reorganization plan!"* In re Greystone III Joint Venture, 995 F.2d 1274, 1279 (5th Cir. 1991). Other courts have found that a creditor with a §1111(b) election has such different rights that a separate class from the unsecured creditors is mandated; see In re Woodbrook Associates, 19 F.3d 312 (7th Cir. 1994). The Supreme Court weighed in on the problem of single asset real estate cases in Bank of America National Trust and Savings Association v. 203 North LaSalle Street Partnership, 526 U.S. 434 (1999).

In *203 North LaSalle*, the debtor was a limited partnership that owned 15 floors of a downtown Chicago office building. It owed over $90 million which was secured by a non-recourse mortgage on the real estate. A non-recourse mortgage is one in which the borrower has no personal liability and the mortgagee's protection is limited to collecting its claim from the property. The debtor filed a plan of reorganization that would have resulted in the debtor retaining ownership of the property, the secured claim was to be reduced to $54.5 million and paid within 10 years, the unsecured deficiency of $38.5 million would be paid approximately $6 million while the $90,000 owed to trade creditors would be paid in full, without interest. The limited partners would contribute approximately $5 to the business. One side effect of the plan was to avoid approximately $20 million in personal tax liabilities that the partners would have incurred if the property were sold. The Seventh Circuit had held that the partners' contributions under the plan were sufficient to overcome the absolute priority rule. The Court of Appeals concluded that the post-confirmation ownership of the property by the partners was on account of their new contribution and not "on account" of their prior ownership interest.

The Supreme Court reversed. It noted that only the debtor had the right to propose a plan because of the exclusivity provisions of §1121. This exclusivity operated in the case to prevent any independent valuation of the underlying property. The debtor set the value of the property through the terms of the plan, with only the bankruptcy court's determination of the value of the property based on testimony presented at a hearing as a protection of the creditor's interest. Instead, the Court suggested that some more reliable market test should be used in these cases. Among the possibilities are permitting the creditor to credit bid on the property or having some other public form of auction. The Court, however, did not indicate specifically how the standard can be met. Clearly though, the Court concluded that the exclusive right of the debtor to file a plan provides too great an opportunity for the debtor to manage the process to the detriment of the secured creditor. It stated that

> Given that the opportunity is property of some value, the question arises why old equity alone should obtain it, not to mention at no cost whatever. The closest thing to an answer favorable to the Debtor is that the old equity partners would be given the opportunity in the expectation that in taking advantage of it they would add the stated purchase price to the estate. *See* Brief for Respondent 40-41. But this just begs the question why the opportunity should be exclusive to the old equity holders. If the price to be paid for the equity interest is the best obtainable, old equity does not need the protection of exclusiveness (unless to trump an equal offer from someone else); if it is not the best, there is no apparent reason for giving old equity a bargain. There is no reason, that is, unless the very purpose of the whole transaction is, at least in part, to do old equity a favor. And that, of course, is to say that old equity would obtain its opportunity, and the resulting benefit, because of old equity's prior interest within the meaning of subsection (b)(2)(B)(ii). Hence it is that the exclusiveness of the opportunity, with its protection against the market's scrutiny of the purchase price by means of competing bids or even competing plan proposals, renders the partners' right a property interest extended "on account of" the old equity position and therefore subject to an unpaid senior creditor class's objection.

526 U.S. at 456.

PROBLEM 9-34

The largest television network company in the United States, DEF, Inc., had four disastrous seasons in a row and ended up filing a Chapter 11 petition to give it room in which to stave off creditors and rethink its position in the industry. It filed a plan of reorganization that was very generous to the creditors, proposing to pay them all in full over the eight-year life of the plan. GHI, Inc., a rival network sensing blood, contacted all the members of one of the proposed classes, bought out their claims at full value, and took over those claims. It now wants to exercise the right of the class to vote against the plan. Can it do this? *See* §1126(c) and (e); In re MacLeod Co., 63 B.R. 654 (Bankr. S.D. Ohio 1986).

E. *Impairment of Claims*

Before a class is allowed to vote on the proposed plan, that class must be "impaired." A class that is unimpaired is conclusively presumed to have accepted the plan. What does "impaired" mean? Read §1124.

PROBLEM 9-35

Octopus National Bank has a first mortgage on the newest casino in Las Vegas, WYNN BIG, and the property is worth a great deal more than the amount ONB has loaned WYNN BIG. You are the attorney for ONB, and your client asks you this question: If the country suddenly becomes more puritanical and repudiates gambling, sending WYNN BIG into Chapter 11, and ONB is then put in a separate class as to which the debtor in possession proposes payments that will pay the entire debt plus postpetition interest, will it be impaired (and thus have a vote)? The ONB executive who asks you this question has just been to a seminar concerning problems businesses have in bankruptcy, and he points out that the filing of the petition invoked the automatic stay, which kept the bank from exercising a clause in the loan agreement by which it could call the loan at any moment and demand full payment. Surely that is an impairment — or is it?

In re Atlanta-Stewart Partners

United States Bankruptcy Court, Northern District of Georgia, Atlanta Division, 1996
193 B.R. 79

ARMAND DAVID KAHN, Bankruptcy Judge.

The above-styled Chapter 11 bankruptcy case is before the Court on consideration of approval of the Debtor's Disclosure Statement. A hearing was held on December 5, 1995. Objections to the Disclosure Statement were filed by Equitable Life Insurance Company of Iowa ("Equitable") and the United States Trustee. At the hearing, the issue of the implications of the 1994 Amendments to the Bankruptcy Code dealing with §1124 arose. The Court took the matter of the approval of the Debtor's Disclosure Statement under advisement and directed the Parties to file briefs. After consideration of argument of counsel and the briefs filed, the Court finds that it will approve the Debtor's Disclosure Statement for the following reasons.

In its proposed Plan of Reorganization, the Debtor classifies its creditors into five (5) separate classes. The dispute surrounds Class 4, which is "an administrative convenience class consisting of those unsecured creditors whose individual allowed claims are less than $1,000." Debtor's Plan of Reorganization at 5. The Debtor proposes to pay Class 4 creditors 95 percent of their allowed claims. Equitable objects to the Disclosure Statement, *inter alia*, on the ground that the Debtor's proposed Plan of Reorganization is unconfirmable on its face because the Debtor cannot obtain the favorable vote from at least one impaired class of creditors. It charges that the Debtor has artificially impaired Class 4 by not paying this class 100 percent of their claims. In its Response, the United States Trustee has calculated that paying Class 4 creditors the additional 5 percent of their claims would only cost the Debtor $154.33. United States Trustee's Response to Debtor's Disclosure Statement at 2.

The Debtor counters that Class 4 has not been artificially impaired and that, even if it were to amend its Plan of Reorganization to pay Class 4 creditors 100 percent of their allowed claims, that class would still be impaired according to the Bankruptcy

Code, as amended by the 1994 Amendments. Therefore, if Class 4 votes in favor of the Debtor's Plan of Reorganization, it would satisfy §1129(a)(10), which requires that "[i]f a class of claims is impaired under the plan, at least one class of claims that is impaired under the plan has accepted the plan, determined without including any acceptance of the plan by any insider."

Prior to the 1994 Amendments, §1124 read as follows:

Except as provided in section 1123(a)(4) of this title, a class of claims or interest is impaired under a plan unless, with respect to each claim or interests of such class, the plan —

(1) leaves unaltered the legal, equitable, and contractual rights to which such claim or interest entitles the holder of such claim or interest;

(2) notwithstanding any contractual provision or applicable law that entitles the holder of such claim or interest to demand or receive accelerated payment of such claim or interest after the occurrence of a default —

(A) cures any such default that occurred before or after the commencement of the case under this title, other than a default of a kind specified in section 365(b)(2) of this title;

(B) reinstates the maturity of such claim or interest as such maturity existed before such default;

(C) compensates the holder of such claim or interest for any damages incurred as a result of any reasonable reliance by such holder on such contractual provision or such applicable law; and

(D) does not otherwise alter the legal, equitable, or contractual rights to which such claim or interest entitles the holder of such claim or interest; or

(3) provides that, on the effective date of the plan, the holder of such claim or interest receives, on account of such claim or interest, cash equal to —

(A) with respect to a claim, the allowed amount of such claim; or

(B) with respect to an interest, if applicable, the greater of —

(i) any fixed liquidation preference to which the terms of any security representing such interest entitle the holder of such interest; or

(ii) any fixed price at which the debtor, under the terms of such security, may redeem such security from such holder.

11 U.S.C. §1124. The 1994 Amendments deleted subsection (3) in its entirety. The Debtor contends that, with the deletion of §1124(3), a class of creditors which is paid in full is now impaired, because there is nothing remaining in §1124 which would define such a class as unimpaired.

Equitable argues a class receiving payment in full from an insolvent debtor should still be considered an unimpaired class under §1124(1), which provides that a class of claims is unimpaired if the plan "leaves unaltered the legal, equitable, and contractual rights to which such claim or interest entitles the holder of such claim or interest." However, the common sense reading of this subsection would not include payment in full. Obviously, a creditor who receives payment of its claim in its entirety does not retain any legal, equitable, or contractual rights. In addition, the suggested reading of §1124(1) would have rendered the former §1124(3) superfluous.

In deleting §1124(3), Congress was responding to the result reached in the case of In re New Valley, 168 B.R. 73 (Bankr. D.N.J. 1994). In *New Valley*, the court determined that, where a solvent debtor's plan proposed to pay a class of creditors in full, but without postpetition interest, the class was unimpaired pursuant to §1124(3).

While deleting §1124(3) in its entirety seems an extreme remedy for the problem arising in New Valley (for example, Congress could have amended §1124(3) to distinguish between solvent and insolvent debtors), the legislative history demonstrates that Congress intended to do away with the concept that a creditor receiving payment in full is unimpaired.

> As a result of this change, if a plan proposed to pay a class of claims in cash in the full allowed amount of the claims, the class would be impaired entitling creditors to vote for or against the plan of reorganization. If creditors vote for the plan or reorganization, it can be confirmed over the vote of a dissenting class of creditors only if it complies with the "fair and equitable" test under section 1129(b)(2) of the Bankruptcy Code and it can be confirmed over the vote of dissenting individual creditors only if it complies with the "best interests of creditors" test under section 1129(a)(7) of the Bankruptcy Code.

140 Cong. Rec. H10752 (Oct. 4, 1994).

Although treating a class of creditors receiving payment in full as impaired seems contrary to the way we have traditionally thought of impairment under the Code, it does have some advantages. For example, litigation over artificial impairment will now be avoided, because debtors will not be forced to contrive an impaired class by placing certain creditors in a separate class and paying that class less than 100 cents on the dollar. In addition, the fight over confirmation will now focus on the heart of the plan and whether the plan is "fair and equitable" and in the "best interest of creditors."

The Court notes that this is a case of first impression. It appears that no other court has published an opinion discussing the ramifications of the deletion of §1124(3). The Court must rely on the language of §1124, without subsection (3), and the legislative history. After much thought, the Court must agree with the Debtor's position that, under §1124 as amended, a class of creditors which will receive payment in full upon the effective date of the plan is impaired within the meaning of the Bankruptcy Code.

Therefore, in the case sub judice, the Court finds that the Debtor's Disclosure Statement should be approved. The issue of whether the Debtor's Plan of Reorganization should be amended to increase the payment to Class 4 creditors to 100 percent may be renewed by objection in the context of the hearing on confirmation.

Order

Thus, in accordance with the reasoning above, IT IS THE ORDER OF THE COURT that the objections to the Debtor's Disclosure Statement filed by Equitable Life Insurance Company of Iowa and the United States Trustee be, and the same hereby are, OVERRULED.

IT IS THE FURTHER ORDER OF THE COURT that the Debtor's Disclosure Statement filed on October 31, 1995, be, and the same hereby is, APPROVED.

The Clerk is hereby directed to serve a copy of this Order on the Debtor, Debtor's attorney, the Movant's attorney, and the United States Trustee.

IT IS SO ORDERED.

QUESTION

If the entire amount of the allowed claim is paid in full, in what way is the claim impaired? *See* §502(b)(2).

F.   Contents of the Plan

PROBLEM 9-36

Ozymandias, Inc. once had a vast empire, but having since fallen on hard times, it has been forced to file a Chapter 11 petition. You are the bankruptcy judge on this one, and all of the impaired classes of creditors have voted for the proposed plan. Will you confirm the plan under §1129(a) if there are the following possibilities?

(a)   There is not enough money to immediately pay the administrative expenses that have been piling up during the two-year period since the filing of the petition, but the plan proposes to pay this debt over the six-year life of the plan. *See* §1129(a)(9)(A).

(b)   The plan proposes to pay the employees their §507(a)(3) wage claims (with appropriate interest) over the six years that the plan will last. *See* §1129(a)(9)(B).

(c)   The plan put Shelley National Bank into a class in which its claim got outvoted when the class accepted the plan, but the plan does not propose to pay the bank as much as it would get if Ozymandias were liquidated in a Chapter 7 proceeding. *See* §1129(a)(7).

(d)   As you examine the evidence it becomes obvious to you that there is no chance that Ozymandias, Inc., will be able to generate the income that will be necessary to fund the plan, although, since all the creditors voted for it, the debtor was somehow able to talk the creditors into entering the same fantasy world the debtor inhabits. *See* §1129(a)(11) (the bankruptcy bar calls this the "feasibility" requirement).

(e)   If not all the classes of impaired creditors have voted for the plan, can you, the judge, nonetheless confirm the plan under the cram down provisions if the other requirements of §1129(b) are met and one impaired class did vote for the plan, although this pro-plan class was entirely composed of stockholders who had loaned Ozymandias, Inc. money? *See* §1129(a)(10) and (b)(1).

G.   Postconfirmation

In Chapter 11, confirmation has a dramatic effect. It releases the debtor immediately from all debts,[27] vests the property of the estate in the debtor, and sweeps

---

27. However, an individual debtor cannot use Chapter 11 to escape from debts that would not be discharged in a Chapter 7 bankruptcy; see §1141(d)(2). The 2005 amendments to the Code imposed Chapter 13 types of restrictions on individuals in Chapter 11, providing, for example, require that all the debtor's disposable income be devoted to funding the plan. *See* §1129(a)(15).

away all liens not protected by the plan; *see* In re Penrod, 50 F.3d 459 (7th Cir. 1995) (liens not mentioned in the plan are nonetheless discharged by confirmation); *but see* Reliable Electric Co. v. Olson Constr. Co., 726 F.2d 620 (10th Cir. 1984) (debt of creditor who had no notice of confirmation hearing not discharged).

PROBLEM 9-37

Ozymandias, Inc.'s plan was confirmed by you, the bankruptcy judge, but four months into the plan the downturn in the national economy caused the company to stop making all the payments called for under the plan. The creditors are now upset that they are not getting paid and motions are being filed, some of which contend that Ozymandias lied to everyone in its disclosure statement. What are your options? Read §§1144; 1127(b); 1112.

CHAPTER 10

Family Farmer Reorganizations

In 1986, Congress enacted Chapter 12 of the Bankruptcy Code in reaction to a perceived financial crisis among small farmers. Declining agricultural land values had put the squeeze on farmers who had borrowed against the previously higher land values. The existing bankruptcy law — particularly Chapter 11 — was viewed as too costly and too complicated to provide adequate relief for many small farm bankruptcies. Thus Chapter 12 came into being, and since its inception Congress has expanded Chapter 12 to include family fishermen, defined in §101(19A).

In a sense, Chapter 12 is a "Chapter 11 in Chapter 13 clothing." That is, these proceedings are intended to reorganize the business of a family farmer, but the reorganization is accomplished under provisions that are quite similar to Chapter 13. Among other things, creditors do not vote in Chapter 12 cases, and there is a codebtor stay. As in Chapter 13, the Chapter 12 debtor's postpetition income is property of the estate. The provisions governing plans and confirmation of plans also are substantially alike in Chapters 12 and 13.

I. Eligibility

With the exception of Chapter 9 (Municipal Bankruptcy), Chapter 12 has the most restrictive eligibility requirements for relief. Not just any farmer can obtain relief under Chapter 12. Such a farmer must be a "family farmer." *See* §101(18). The rules for a "family fisherman," are similar to those discussed below, though the numbers differ is some respects — *see* §101(19A).

Section 109(f) states, in deceptively simple terms, that "only a family farmer with regular annual income may be a debtor under Chapter 12." The language is deceptively simple because the definition of "family farmer" set out in §101(18) is a great deal more complicated. Under that section, family farmers are defined in terms of both income and liabilities. The aggregate debts of the family farmers may not exceed $3,544,525, and at least 50 percent of the noncontingent liquidated debts of those debtors must arise out of a farming operation. Similarly, at least 50 percent of the debtor's gross income must also arise out of a farming operation. Unlike Chapter 13, Chapter 12 allows corporate and partnership entities to qualify for relief. If the debtor is a corporation or a partnership, more than 50 percent of the outstanding stock or equity must be held by a single family (and its relatives), and the family must conduct the farming operation. Additionally, more than 80 percent of the value of the assets must relate to the farming operation. As with individual Chapter 12 debtors, the debt limit is $3,544,525, and at least 80 percent of the debt must be farm debt.

Determining Chapter 12 eligibility requires an evaluation of income and debts with respect to the debtor's *farming operations*. Section 101(21) defines a farming operation as including "farming, tillage of the soil, dairy farming, ranching, production or raising of crops, poultry, or livestock, and production of poultry or livestock products in an unmanufactured state." Because the term "includes" is not limiting, other activities may constitute farming operations. *See* §102(3). Apply the forgoing sections to the following Problems and decide whether any or all of these entities are eligible for Chapter 12 relief.

PROBLEM 10-1

Farmer Brown raises crops on 100 acres of land. He sells most of the crops to area grocery stores and restaurants, but he also sells directly to the public at a roadside stand. In 2010, Farmer Brown made a profit of $26,000 from the sale of his crops. He also made $12,500 as a bus driver for the local school system, a job he needs to make ends meet. In 2011, he sold $50,000 worth of crops, but his farming expenses totaled $41,000, leaving a net profit of only $9,000. That year, he earned $13,000 as a bus driver. In 2012, his crops sold for $72,000 with expenses of only $31,000, for a net profit of $41,000. Once again his bus driving income was $13,000. Unfortunately, a customer of Brown's roadside vegetable stand obtained a judgment against Brown for injuries the customer suffered when the wooden sign on top of the vegetable stand came loose and struck the customer. The customer obtained a judgment in the amount of $175,000 against Brown and has aggressively sought to enforce the judgment. Is Farmer Brown eligible for Chapter 12 relief if he files a petition on November 15, 2012? Is he eligible if he postpones the filing until January 2, 2013?

PROBLEM 10-2

Aero Bug Juice Corp. operates a crop dusting service. It owns a small plane and has contracts with approximately 20 local farmers to dust their crops each year. The company's income fluctuates greatly based on the success of the farmers it serves. If crop yields are down or weather problems intervene, Aero's income suffers accordingly. Is the company eligible for Chapter 12 relief? *See* In re Van Air Flying Service, Inc., 146 B.R. 816 (Bankr. E.D. Ark. 1992).

PROBLEM 10-3

John Chapman owns and operates a 60-acre fruit farm. He tends the orchards and runs a "pick your own" service. In addition, he harvests a portion of the crop and sells both fruit and cider to local grocery stores. Forty-five percent of his annual income is derived from this operation. Another 45 percent of his income comes from his financial consulting business. The remaining 10 percent of his income is derived from the rental of 10 acres of his farm to another farmer. Is Chapman eligible for Chapter 12 relief? *Compare* In re Edwards, 924 F.2d 798 (8th Cir. 1991), *with* In re Coulston, 98 B.R. 280 (Bankr. E.D. Mich. 1989). Does it make any difference if Chapman rents out the farmland on a cash basis or if the rent is payable by transfer of a share of the crop grown on the parcel?

PROBLEM 10-4

Overwhelmed by the increasing bureaucracy connected with the practice of medicine, Dr. Kildare "retired" to a 200-acre ranch to raise thoroughbred horses. He had always specialized in high-risk surgery, so the substantial risks involved in horse racing were nothing new to him. He experienced some early success, and one of his first racehorses, Angie-O-Plasty, won several races. The horse was then retired to stud, and other horse owners brought their mares to Dr. Kildare's ranch for breeding with Angie-O-Plasty. The mares would remain at the ranch until their foals were four months old, at which time mare and foal would be transported back to their owners. The net fees received by Dr. Kildare for this breeding service represented 90 percent of his annual income. Is Dr. Kildare eligible for Chapter 12 relief? In re Cluck, 101 B.R. 691 (Bankr. E.D. Okla. 1989); In re McKillips, 72 B.R. 565 (Bankr. N.D. Ill. 1987); In re Maike, 77 B.R. 832 (Bankr. D. Kan. 1987).

II.   Effect of Commencement of the Case

As with the filing of a Chapter 13 petition, commencing a Chapter 12 case creates a codebtor stay in addition to the automatic stay of §362. Under §1201 of the Code, creditors may not take any action to collect consumer debts of the Chapter 12 debtor from any individual who is liable with the Chapter 12 debtor for the debt. The language of §1201 mirrors that of §1301, and decisions under that section obviously will guide the courts in Chapter 12 cases. The bulk of the debt in a Chapter 12 case, however, is not consumer debt. Therefore, the impact of the codebtor stay in such cases is minimal.

Another consequence of the commencement of a Chapter 12 case is that an estate is created. Again, like Chapter 13, the estate is broader in those chapters than in cases under Chapter 7 or Chapter 11. Section 541 applies to Chapter 12 cases, but the property of the estate is enhanced by the property described in §1207 of the

Bankruptcy Code. All of the postpetition property that the debtor acquires becomes property of the Chapter 12 estate if that property would have been covered by §541 of the Bankruptcy Code. Similarly, the earnings from postpetition services performed by the debtor are also property of the bankruptcy estate. §1207(a)(2).

III.   The Chapter 12 Plan

Continuing the parallels to Chapter 13, in Chapter 12 only the debtor may file a plan. Section 1221 gives the debtor 90 days after the order for relief to file a plan unless the court extends that period "if the need for an extension is attributable to circumstances for which the debtor should not justly be held accountable." Furthermore, the mandatory provisions of Chapter 12 plans are the same as those required in Chapter 13. *Compare* §1222(a) *with* §1322(a). Generally speaking, this requires the debtor to fund the plan and to pay all priority claims in full unless the creditor agrees to some other treatment. Finally, if the plan classifies claims, all claims must receive the same treatment in a particular class.

Chapter 12 plans also may include provisions similar to those allowed in Chapter 13 plans. There are, however, significant differences between the permissive plan provisions under Chapter 12 as compared to Chapter 13. First, §1222(b) allows the modification of all claims, even those secured only by an interest in the debtor's residence. Second, §1222(b)(8) authorizes the sale of property of the estate pursuant to the plan. Finally, §1222(b)(9) permits the payment of allowed secured claims over a period that exceeds the repayment period allowed under §1222(c), which is the same three-year/five-year repayment period found in Chapter 13 cases. *See* §1322(d). This last distinction from Chapter 13 is perhaps the most important difference. We will consider it in more detail as we evaluate the impact of Chapter 12 on secured claims.

IV.   Confirmation of the Plan

Confirmation of the plan is governed by §1225. Once again, the language of this section essentially parallels that of §1325 of the Bankruptcy Code, so that decisions on confirmation of Chapter 13 plans will guide courts considering Chapter 12 plans. Since unsecured creditors do not vote on Chapter 12 plans, the Bankruptcy Code provides three fundamental protections for their claims. First, the debtor's plan must meet the best interest of creditors test. §1225(a)(4). Second, the plan must be proposed in good faith. §1225(a)(3). Finally, if the holder of an unsecured claim or the trustee objects, the debtor's plan must provide for the submission of all of the debtor's projected disposable income for at least three years to fund the plan.

Determining a Chapter 12 debtor's expenses is often more difficult than determining a Chapter 13 debtor's expenses. In addition to the living expenses of the debtor and the debtor's dependents, Chapter 12 debtors have business expenses that need to be considered. Section 1225(b)(2)(B) requires the projection of the debtor's business expenses over the life of the plan. These expenses could include the purchase of additional equipment and perhaps even land if necessary for the successful operation of the debtor's farm. In this sense, the presentation of a debtor's plan begins to resemble the Chapter 11 process. Business justifications need to be offered for the incurring of the expenses projected by the debtor.

A. Cram Down of Secured Claims

Chapter 12 departs sharply from Chapter 13 with respect to the cram down of secured claims. In Chapter 13 cases the debtor's plan may not extend beyond five years. If the debtor proposes any modification of his secured claim under the plan, then the secured claim must be paid in full during the life of the plan. In Chapter 12, however, the plan may provide for the payment of allowed secured claims the period exceeding the three- or five-year limits set out in §1222(c). §1222(b)(9). Since these payments will continue for a period greater than the period of the plan, these debts are not discharged at the conclusion of payments under the plan. Section 1228(a)(1) specifically excepts from the discharge both long-term debts that are cured under §1222(b)(5) and the modified secured claims that are payable for a period longer than the plan. Consequently, those modified secured claims are excepted from the discharge.

The ability to stretch out payments on secured claims for an extended period is vital in Chapter 12. The debtor often carries substantial debts secured by the farmland. If these amounts had to be paid within three to five years, the plan would not be feasible. Determining the proper repayment terms on modified secured claims often is the primary issue in the cases.

In re Fortney
United States Court of Appeals, Seventh Circuit, 1994
36 F.3d 701

ENGEL, Circuit Judge.

In this farm bankruptcy case, we must determine if Chapter 12 of the Bankruptcy Code, 11 U.S.C. §§1201-1231, compels a bankruptcy judge to extend the repayment of a secured tax debt beyond the three year duration of the debtors' reorganization plan. The bankruptcy judge below determined that the debtors, Thomas and LaVonna Fortney, should satisfy their $18,569.76 tax obligation to Vernon County within three years. The Chapter 12 Trustee, Daniel Freund, objects to confirmation of the Fortneys' plan, arguing that the taxes should be repaid at a much slower pace, so that more farm income will be available to satisfy the claims of unsecured creditors. The district court approved the plan over the Trustee's objections, concluding that Chapter 12 vests the bankruptcy court with discretion to structure an appropriate repayment schedule for secured debts. For the following reasons, we AFFIRM the judgment of the district court.

I. *Background*

Chapter 12 of the bankruptcy code governs reorganization of family farms. "Congress created Chapter 12 in 1986 in order to give family farmers facing bankruptcy a fighting chance to reorganize their debts and keep their land." In re Kerns, 111 B.R. 777, 788 (S.D. Ind. 1990) (citation omitted); In re Bowlby, 113 B.R. 983, 988 (Bankr. S.D. Ill. 1990).

The Fortneys own a farm in Viroqua, Wisconsin, near La Crosse. The Fortneys filed for bankruptcy relief on September 4, 1992, and the bankruptcy court for the Western District of Wisconsin approved their reorganization plan on June 2, 1993. On January 11, 1994, the district court affirmed the decision of the bankruptcy court over the objections of the Chapter 12 Trustee.

The Fortneys have two secured real estate obligations: a tax lien of $18,569.76 held by Vernon County, and a mortgage of $140,430.24 held by AgriBank. Their plan provides for repayment of their tax debt over a span of three years, while the mortgage is scheduled for repayment over a twenty year period.

The Fortneys have more than $90,000 in unsecured debt. During the three years that the plan will be in effect, the unsecured creditors are to receive: (1) a minimum payment of $7,200, and (2) 40 percent of the Fortneys' gross annual farm income in excess of $150,000. If the Fortneys successfully complete the payments scheduled under the plan, the remaining unsecured debts will be discharged.

II. *Confirmation of a Chapter 12 Plan*

Chapter 12 contains two confirmation requirements designed to protect unsecured creditors. Section 1225(a)(4) sets out the well-known "best interests of the creditors" test, which denies confirmation to any plan which provides unsecured creditors with less compensation than they would receive upon liquidation of the farm. See 5 Collier on Bankruptcy ¶1225.02[4] (15th ed. 1993). Liquidation of the Fortneys' farm would provide their unsecured creditors with a total of $6,584.42. By offering the unsecured creditors a minimum payment of $7,200, the Fortneys' plan satisfies the best interests test.

Chapter 12 contains a second protection for those unsecured farm creditors who object to confirmation of a reorganization plan: the "disposable income" test. Under this test, unsecured creditors who object to confirmation of the debtors' plan are guaranteed to receive at a minimum all of the disposable income earned by the farm while the plan is in effect:

> If the trustee or the holder of an allowed unsecured claim objects to the confirmation of the plan, then the court may not approve the plan unless . . . the plan provides that all of the debtor's projected disposable income to be received [during the pendency of the plan] . . . will be applied to make payments under the plan. ¶11 U.S.C. §1225(b)(1)(B). *See, e.g.,* In re Fleshman, 123 B.R.

842, 843-44 (Bankr. W.D. Mo. 1990); In re Wobig, 73 B.R. 292, 293 (Bankr. D. Neb. 1987); In re Citrowske, 72 B.R. 613, 616 (Bankr. D. Minn. 1987).

The Fortneys' plan "shall run for thirty-six (36) months." During this period, unsecured creditors are entitled to receive all of the Fortneys' "disposable income" — that portion of the farm income "which is not reasonably necessary . . . for the[ir] maintenance or support" or "for the continuation, preservation, and operation of the[ir] business." 11 U.S.C. §1225(b)(2).

The disposable income test allows the debtor to retain a sufficient but not extravagant level of income. As one court explained:

> A fundamental purpose of the disposable income provision is to prevent large expenditures by debtors for non-essential items which ultimately reduce the sum available to pay holders of unsecured claims. . . . This Court . . . will not permit [the debtor] to acquire goods or services not reasonably necessary for support at the expense of the unpaid, unsecured creditors. The purposes of [the disposable income test] would be ill-served if the Court were to allow the debtor in the instant case to [finance] purely recreational property not reasonably necessary for maintenance or support of the debtor . . . while his general unsecured creditors are to receive, over an extended period of time, less than half of the total amount of their claims.

In re Hedges, 68 B.R. 18, 20-21 (Bankr. E.D. Va. 1986).

Unfortunately, the disposable income test cannot provide all unsecured creditors with compensation, because not all debtors will be able to generate disposable income. By definition, disposable income represents "left overs" — that portion of the farm income remaining after the deduction of those payments "necessary" for the farmer's subsistence and for operation of the farm. *See* 11 U.S.C. §1225(b)(2), *supra.* If the bankruptcy court determines that all of a farmer's income is needed to satisfy secured obligations, a plan which generates no disposable income may be confirmed — despite providing little compensation to the unsecured creditors. As a result, the impact of the disposable income test in any particular case depends to a large extent upon the margin by which the debtor's income exceeds his or her expenses. A debtor whose income greatly exceeds expenses may provide unsecured creditors with a substantial amount of disposable income, while a debtor with a slim profit margin may generate hardly any disposable income at all.

III. The Proper Amortization of Secured Debts

The Trustee objects to the repayment of Vernon County's secured tax claim within three years. Pointing to the twenty year amortization of the Fortneys' mortgage obligation, the Trustee would have the bankruptcy court prolong the tax payments in a similar fashion. Stretching such payments out over a longer period would substantially reduce the size of the Fortneys' monthly payments to the county. The Trustee's motivation in reducing the size of the Fortneys' monthly secured debt payments is to increase the amount of disposable income available for unsecured creditors.

The Trustee argues that there is no basis in the Code for amortization of the secured tax claim over a shorter period than the mortgage claim. The Trustee concedes that the Code grants unsecured tax claims higher priority than ordinary *unsecured* claims, 11 U.S.C. §507(a)(7), but he insists that all secured claims (including secured tax claims) have equal priority under the Code. Furthermore, the Trustee suggests that the Code requires the bankruptcy court to amortize secured debts over the longest possible time span, in order to maximize the amount of disposable farm income available for unsecured creditors.

The district court concluded that the bankruptcy court was permitted to amortize the tax claim and the mortgage claim over different time periods. However, the district court did not — as the Trustee suggests — justify the three year repayment of the taxes on the ground that secured tax claims deserve preferential treatment. In fact, the district court explicitly rejected any such notion:

> The Trustee is correct in his contention that Chapter 12 does not establish a category of secured claims requiring priority status over other secured claims. There is no provision in the Code which *requires* that real estate tax liens be amortized within the three to five year pendency of a plan.

In the district court's view, the Fortneys are permitted to repay the taxes over three years and the mortgage over twenty years because Chapter 12 provides the bankruptcy court with discretion to fashion appropriate secured debt repayment schedules. Given such discretion, the district court concluded that the bankruptcy court's approach sought to accommodate important differences between a tax lien and a mortgage:

> [N]othing in the Code requires that all secured claims be paid within the same time period. Here the real estate tax lien is to be paid within three years and the AgriBank claim is to be paid within twenty years. There are valid reasons for differentiating between these claims. Counties, unlike mortgage holders, are not in the business of long term financing. Amortizing the $140,430 AgriBank claim over three years would make the payments prohibitive.

Within this framework, the question on appeal narrows to whether Chapter 12 dictates any particular amortization schedule for the repayment of secured debts. Because the Trustee challenges the district court's interpretation of the Bankruptcy Code, we review *de novo* the legal conclusions drawn below. In re West, 22 F.3d 775, 777 (7th Cir. 1994) ("we review . . . conclusions of law *de novo*").

Looking first to the text of Chapter 12, we find a general rule that all payments under a reorganization plan must be made within three years. 11 U.S.C. §1222(c). The three year repayment of the Fortneys' overdue taxes certainly adheres to this statutory directive.

As the Trustee enthusiastically notes, an exception to the three year repayment rule can be found in 11 U.S.C. §1222(b)(9). Under that section, the bankruptcy court may approve plans which "provide for payment of secured claims . . . over a period exceeding the period permitted under section 1222(c)." The court's "[d]iscretionary" power to prolong secured debt repayment has been described as Chapter 12's "most significant provision affecting the rights of secured claimants." 5 Collier on Bankruptcy ¶1222.04.

Although section 1222(b)(9) clearly authorizes the bankruptcy court to extend secured debt repayment in certain circumstances, the text of this section does not indicate when such extension is appropriate or desirable, nor does it indicate that such extension is ever mandatory. Thus, the district court interpreted section 1222(b)(9) as *permitting* prolonged amortization of secured debts, but not *requiring* deviation from the three year repayment rule in any particular case. The Trustee, in contrast, argues that by permitting long-term amortization of secured debts, section 1222(b)(9) implicitly repeals section 1222(c)'s three year repayment rule. In place of the three year repayment rule found in the Code, the Trustee implores us to require slow repayment of secured debts whenever unsecured creditors face a risk of receiving inadequate compensation.

We find no merit in the Trustee's argument that Chapter 12 prohibits repayment of the Fortneys' overdue taxes within three years. No statutory language suggests that amortization over a longer period is compulsory. The only text on point is the general three year repayment rule found in section 1222(c) . . . which clearly undermines any suggestion that the Code requires slow repayment of secured claims.

Although section 1222(b)(9) permits the repayment of secured debts over a period exceeding three years, there is no requirement of such extension in any particular circumstance. A popular bankruptcy treatise characterizes section 1222(b)(9) as a discretionary provision. 5 Collier on Bankruptcy ¶1222.04. Certainly Congress could have made such extensions mandatory if it so chose, but we refuse to write such a substantial provision into the statute in the absence of any textual or historical support.

The Trustee insists that a requirement of long-term amortization can be found in section 1225(b)(1)(B), the disposable income test. As the Trustee notes, this statutory provision prevents the Fortneys from using disposable income to repay secured obligations. *See, e.g., Fleshman, supra*, 123 B.R. at 846-47; *Wobig, supra*, 73 B.R. at 293; *Citrowske, supra*, 72 B.R. at 616. According to the Trustee, the unsecured creditors' right to receive disposable income carries with it a corresponding right to restructure the Fortneys' secured debts in a fashion which maximizes the amount of disposable income flowing to unsecured creditors.

We cannot agree with the Trustee that the disposable income test implicitly grants unsecured creditors the right to insist upon any particular amortization of secured debts. Congress has given unsecured creditors two specific protections: the best interests test and the disposable income test. The federal courts have no power to add novel protections to this precise list, especially at the expense of creditors with secured interests. The disposable income test guarantees that unsecured creditors will receive any farm income remaining after necessary expenses are paid. The Fortneys' plan, which allocates 40 percent of the gross annual farm income over $150,000 to the unsecured creditors, obeys this command. The Fortneys' payments to Vernon County, upon which the Trustee fixates, do not even implicate the disposable income test, because the income used to make these payments *is not disposable.* The statutory definition of disposable income excludes all "expenditures necessary for the continuation, preservation, and operation of the debtor's business." 11 U.S.C. §1225(b)(2)(B), *supra.* Because payments to the county scheduled under the Fortneys' plan are "necessary" to prevent foreclosure, the unsecured creditors have no claim to this income.

Finally, we reject the Trustee's suggestion that all secured debts must be extended if the bankruptcy court permits the debtor to extend the repayment of any one particular secured obligation. No Code provision requires the amortization of all secured debts on a uniform schedule. Chapter 12 of the Bankruptcy Code generally requires that all payments due under a plan must be made within three years. 11 U.S.C. §1222(c). An exception to this rule, 11 U.S.C. §1222(b)(9), vests the bankruptcy court with discretionary authority to extend repayment when appropriate. Where the Bankruptcy Code "commits [such a] decision ... to the discretion of the court," the bankruptcy court's exercise of that discretion will only be reviewed on appeal for abuse. In re Leventhal & Co., 19 F.3d 1174, 1177 (7th Cir. 1994). We find no abuse of discretion in this case. The bankruptcy court articulated valid and meaningful reasons for extending the repayment of the Fortneys' mortgage, but for not extending the repayment of their overdue taxes. Any shorter term for repayment of the mortgage would burden the farm with intolerable monthly obligations. In contrast, the bankruptcy court determined that the Fortneys could manage to pay the tax debt while the plan was in effect, so no extension of time was necessary. Furthermore, the county — unlike the bank — is not a voluntary creditor and not in the lending business. The citizens, schools, police, and parks of Vernon County need not wait for their payments like some stockholders in a financial venture. The important differences between the two debts provide ample justification for amortizing them differently. Accordingly, we agree with the district court that no Code provision prohibits the repayment of the Fortneys' secured tax debt within three years.

IV.   Lack of Good Faith

The Trustee argues that the Fortneys' plan was not offered in good faith, as required by 11 U.S.C. §1225(a)(3), because slower repayment of the tax debt would provide unsecured creditors with more disposable income. Because it is possible under section 1222(b)(9) for the Fortneys to repay their taxes more slowly, and therefore increase the disposable income flowing to the unsecured creditors, the Trustee argues that the Fortneys' proposal to pay the county in three years exhibits bad faith. The Trustee complains that such prompt repayment — and the resulting reduced level of disposable income — unfairly and unnecessarily increases the amount of unsecured debt which will ultimately be discharged.

In evaluating whether a plan was proposed in good faith, this court has declined "to adopt a specific test" because "good faith is a term incapable of precise definition." Instead, we prefer to "look to the totality of the circumstances and, thereby, make good faith determinations on a case-by-case basis." In re Love, 957 F.2d 1350, 1355 (7th Cir. 1992). "[W]e will not overturn" the finding of good faith made by the bankruptcy court below "unless it is clearly erroneous." In re Andreuccetti, 975 F.2d 413, 420 (7th Cir. 1992). . . .

Accordingly, the judgment below is AFFIRMED.

PROBLEM 10-5

Fred Cluck runs a poultry farm. He borrowed $125,000 from Rural State Bank to construct poultry houses where the chickens are raised. The repayment term of the original loan was eight years with payments to be made on a quarterly basis and interest accruing at 11 percent per year. The life expectancy of poultry houses is 10 years. Cluck filed this Chapter 12 proceeding two years after the houses were built. He has proposed to pay the allowed secured claim of RSB in full, through quarterly payments made over the next 15 years, with an interest rate of 8 percent on the outstanding balance of the claim. RSB has objected to the treatment it would receive under the plan. Is the plan confirmable? In re Rice, 171 B.R. 399 (Bankr. N.D. Ala. 1994).

As with Chapter 13 plans, a prerequisite to confirmation of a Chapter 12 plan is that it be feasible; §1225(a)(6). The debtor has the burden of showing an ability to make all the payments called for by the plan. The court must scrutinize the debtor's projections as to the liability of the farming operation.

In re Gough

United States Bankruptcy Court, Middle District of Florida, 1995
190 B.R. 455

GEORGE L. PROCTOR, Bankruptcy Judge.

This case came before the Court for confirmation of debtors' Chapter 12 plan. C. Victor Butler, Jr. (Butler), a secured creditor, objected to the plan. The Court heard the objection and received evidence regarding confirmation at a hearing held on November 7, 1995, and the Court now enters the following findings of fact and conclusions of law:

Findings of Fact

1. Debtors own and operate a citrus growing operation on an 80-acre parcel in Marion County, Florida, and a 20-acre parcel in Lake County, Florida. Of the 100 acres, 68 are planted and harvested. Both groves were severally damaged by freezes in 1984 and 1986. Both groves were replanted in 1987 and damaged again by freezes in 1989. (Debtors' Brief p. 1).
2. Debtors filed for relief under Chapter 12 of the Bankruptcy Code on June 14, 1995, and filed their plan on September 20, 1995.
3. Debtors grow in excess of 10 varieties of citrus and have staggered harvest times to spread the risk of weather-related loss. (Debtors' Brief p. 1).
4. Debtors' crop yield for 1994-95 was 3,869 boxes. Debtors' plan projects production for the next three seasons as follows:
   1995-96   6,125 boxes
   1996-97   9,465 boxes
   1997-98   11,815 boxes
   (Debtors' Plan, File Doc. 13).

5. Debtors estimate their production income at $4 per box. (Debtors' Plan, File Doc. 13).
6. Debtors and their son perform all manual labor associated with the citrus production. Debtors' estimate their annual maintenance costs at $12,240. Debtors do not maintain crop insurance. (Butler Brief p. 5).
7. Based on their projected crop yield, debtors propose to fund the plan in three annual installments as follows:
    $12,000 payment due May 1, 1996
    $24,000 payment due May 1, 1997
    $30,000 payment due May 1, 1998
    (Debtors' Plan, File Doc. 13).
8. Debtors' anticipated income and expenses during the plan are as follows:

	1995-96	1996-97	1997-98
Income:			
Social Security	$ 5,500	$ 5,500	$ 5,500
Citrus Crops	$24,500	$37,860	$47,260
Expenses:			
Living	$ 5,760	$ 5,760	$ 5,760
Crop Maintenance	$12,240	$13,600	$17,000

(Debtors' Plan, File Doc. 13).
9. On May 30, 1995, Butler obtained a Summary Final Judgment For Foreclosure against the debtors in the Circuit Court for Marion County, Florida. On July 17, 1995, Butler filed a proof of claim in the amount of $132,748.04. Debtors listed Butler as a secured creditor in the same amount.
10. Debtors' plan provides that Butler will be paid in full with interest at 10 percent per annum. The plan provides that Butler's claim will be negatively amortized during the first year of the plan with Butler receiving only a partial interest payment of $9,072. (Debtors' Brief p. 4). Thereafter, the principal and interest which accrues in the first year under the plan is reamortized with Butler receiving $18,144 each year until May 1, 2007, when a balloon of the remaining balance is due. The plan requires the debtors to make payments directly to Butler beyond the life of the plan.
11. Butler filed an objection to confirmation, claiming that the plan is not feasible. Butler also argues that the value he will receive under the plan is less than the amount of his allowed claim.

Conclusions of Law

Chapter 12 plans are confirmed if they meet the following requirements of 11 U.S.C. §1225: [the court quoted §1225(a)].

Butler objects to confirmation of debtors' plan pursuant to 11 U.S.C. §1225(a)(5) and (a)(6).

Butler's Objection Pursuant to §1225(a)(5)

Butler objects to confirmation of debtors' plan pursuant to 11 U.S.C. §1225(a)(5), claiming that his claim will not receive full value under the plan. The plan, however, provides that Butler will retain his lien and that his claim will be paid in full. The plan also utilizes a provision of 11 U.S.C. §1222(c) which allows debtors to pay a secured creditor beyond the life of the plan. The Court rejects Butler's argument that his claim would not be paid in full and finds that the plan meets the requirements of §1225(a)(5).

Feasibility — 11 U.S.C. §1225(a)(6)

Feasibility is fundamentally a fact question which requires the Court to determine the debtors' reasonable probability of payment. In re Rape, 104 B.R. 741, 748 (W.D.N.C. 1989) (quoting In re Crowley, 85 B.R. 76, 78-79 (W.D. Wis. 1988)). To meet the feasibility standard of §1225(a)(6), the debtors must prove the likelihood that they can make all payments required under the plan and comply with the plan.

To promote reorganization attempts of family farmers, the Court gives the debtors the benefit of the doubt on the issue of feasibility. In re Snider Farms, Inc., 83 B.R. 1003, 1013 (Bankr. N.D. Ind. 1988). Thus, the Court does not require the debtors to "guarantee the ultimate success of [their] plan, but only to provide a reasonable assurance that the plan can be effectuated." In re Butler, 101 B.R. 566, 567 (Bankr. E.D. Ark. 1989).

The law, however, requires the debtors to prove the feasibility of their plan based on objective facts. "The test is whether the things which are to be done after confirmation can be done as a practical matter under the facts." In re Rape, 104 B.R. 741, 749 (W.D.N.C. 1989) (quoting In re Clarkson, 767 F.2d 417, 420 (8th Cir. 1985)). Especially important for Chapter 12 debtors is the feasibility of their market projections. Other courts have cautioned, however, that "[m]arket projections must be supported by some factual basis in order for them to be regarded by the Court as anything more than wishful thinking." In re Snider Farms, Inc., 83 B.R. 1003, 1013 (Bankr. N.D. Ind. 1988).

Thus, to be feasible, a Chapter 12 plan must be more than "technically possible." In re Foertsch, 167 B.R. 555, 566 (Bankr. D.N.D. 1994). "[I]f 'the most optimistic view of the debtors' economic future, based on debtors' own projections, shows that the debtors' projected income would be insufficient to make all of the plan payments in the first year, confirmation of the plan must be denied.' " In re Rape, 104 B.R. 741, 749 (W.D.N.C. 1989) (quoting In re Bartlett, 92 B.R. 142, 144 (E.D.N.C. 1988)).

If debtors' crop yield projections and anticipated social security income meet their expectations, the debtors could technically afford to fund their plan. The feasibility of the plan, however, remains suspect. Butler asserts several facts to support his argument that the debtors' plan is not feasible. First, the debtors' groves only produced a little over 4,000 boxes of fruit in the 1994-95 season. Butler argues that based on their production history, it is unlikely that debtors will be able to triple their crop yield in a three year period as required by the plan. Secondly, Butler argues that the market price relied on by the debtor is speculative and cannot provide an objective basis for projecting future income. Butler next argues that the debtors failure to maintain crop insurance and their failure to properly maintain their groves is an indication that the debtors' crop yield will decrease rather than increase over the life of the plan.

Butler also argues that the debtors cannot reasonably expect to increase their crop yield when the only labor performed in the planting, maintenance, and harvesting is by the debtors and their son. Finally, Butler argues that the debtors' plan is not feasible because it would require the debtors to survive on $480 a month without increase for the next three years.

In attempts to prove the feasibility of their plan, the debtors produced evidence showing that they have planted an additional 20 acres to be harvested next season. Debtors also testified that they have allotted more money in the plan to be spent on grove maintenance. Debtors further testified that they can survive on $480 per month.

The Court, however, is unpersuaded by debtors' evidence. The facts of this case make it clear that the debtors' projected crop yield for the next three seasons is overly optimistic. The Court finds that debtors' groves are not capable of producing the projected crop yield income needed to fund the plan. Although the debtors testified that the yield from the additional 20 acres and the increased maintenance on the other planted areas would ensure an increasing crop yield, an adverse expert witness testified that the debtors' groves are in poor condition, and that the young trees on the newly planted parcel will not be capable of producing fruit in time to meet the first projected increase.

The Court also finds that it is not feasible for the debtors to expect a larger production when they perform all of the manual labor themselves. A large citrus production necessitates more manpower or mechanized capability to plant, maintain, and harvest the fruit.

Finally, the Court finds that it is highly impractical to assume debtors can support themselves, two residences, and two automobiles on $480 a month for the next three years. Debtors' plan leaves them no flexibility for health or other emergencies and erroneously assumes that the cost of living will not increase over the next three years. The Court finds that the plan is not feasible and cannot be confirmed pursuant to 11 U.S.C. §1225(a)(6).

Conclusion

Butler's objection to confirmation pursuant to 11 U.S.C. §1225(a)(5) is overruled because Butler will retain his lien and the plan provided that Butler would have received the full value of his claim. Butler's objection to confirmation pursuant to 11 U.S.C. §1225(a)(6) is sustained because the plan is not feasible. By separate order, the Court will sustain Butler's objection to confirmation, deny confirmation of the plan, and dismiss the case.

In *Gough*, the court denied confirmation of the plan and dismissed the case, but it also rejected the creditor's objection to the plan provision that would have negatively amortized the secured claim. Negative amortization results when the payments to the creditor are insufficient to cover all of the accruing interest. See Findings of Fact ¶10. Other courts have refused to confirm such plans on the grounds that they do not adequately protect the secured creditor's property interest. *See, e.g.,* In re Howard, 272 B.R. 864 (Bankr. E.D. Tenn. 1997).

V. Discharge

The provisions governing the discharge in Chapter 12 cases continue both the parallels and the discrepancies with Chapter 13. As in Chapter 13, the discharge in Chapter 12 is entered at the conclusion of the payments being made under the plan. §1228(a). Similarly, there is provision for a hardship discharge if the debtor is unable to make all of the payments called for by the plan. §1228(b). The scope of the discharge in Chapters 12 and 13 are very similar. In Chapter 12, the exceptions to discharge set out in §523(a) are fully applicable in Chapter 12 without regard to the type of discharge entered in the case. *See* §1228(a)(2), (c)(2). The Chapter 13 full payment discharge is nearly identical, but it continues to permit the discharge of debts covered by §523(a)(6).

Recall that the exceptions to discharge set out in §523(a)(2), (4), (6), and (15) are not self-executing. That is, the creditors must act in a timely fashion to have these types of claims declared nondischargeable. If they fail to file a complaint in the bankruptcy court within 60 days after the §341 meeting of creditors then they are barred from raising the issue. Bankruptcy Rule 4007(c).

This time limit is particularly significant when comparing the timing requirement for the filing of a Chapter 12 debtor's plan. Under §1221, the debtor has 90 days from the commencement of the case to file a plan. Thus, the debtor could file a plan that provides for a substantial repayment of the debts. This could lead creditors to ignore the need to file a nondischargeability complaint, relying instead on an anticipated substantial recovery under the plan. If the debtor then modifies the plan to reduce the payments called for under the original plan, the completion of those payments under the confirmed plan will discharge the debts, and the creditor will be barred from asserting the nondischargeability claim at this later date.

CHAPTER *11*

Jurisdiction

I. Basic Issues

One issue of constitutional law has made jurisdiction in the bankruptcy courts more complicated than it should be. The problem arises from the fact that Article III of the United States Constitution vests the judicial power of the United States in courts whose judges must be appointed for life and whose salaries cannot be diminished during their time in office. Bankruptcy judges do not fit within Article III since they are appointed (by the United States Courts of Appeals) to 14-year terms; 28 U.S.C. §152. Bankruptcy judgeships are created under Article I of the Constitution as a corollary to the right of Congress to enact bankruptcy laws.

The Bankruptcy Code of 1978 (the "Title 11" referred to in the jurisdictional statutes we are about to examine) nonetheless gave the bankruptcy courts broad jurisdiction to hear any and all matters having to do with bankruptcy, and in *Northern Pipeline Constr. Co. v. Marathon Pipe Line Co.*, 458 U.S. 50 (1982), the United States Supreme Court held that doing so was unconstitutional since Article I judges were exercising Article III powers. Congress then had a choice: turn all the bankruptcy judges into Article III judges (which was politically dicey) or limit the matters that could be heard in the bankruptcy courts, the eventual decision.

Your statute book will have in it the relevant statute: Title 28 of the United States Code (Judiciary and Judicial Procedure). Two of its sections are most important to the issue of jurisdiction: §§157 and 1334. Hunt them up and examine them carefully to understand the material that follows.

Look first at 28 U.S.C. §1334. Subsection (a) gives the federal district courts original and exclusive jurisdiction over all bankruptcy cases, so that a bankruptcy petition can only be filed in these courts. The bankruptcy courts are units of the federal district courts,[1] so it is in these subservient courts that the petition is actually filed.

---

1. *See* 28 U.S.C. §151.

PROBLEM 11-1

When Ozymandias, Inc. filed its Chapter 11 petition in the Southern District of Ohio, where its corporate headquarters were located, it had assets in 35 different states across the country. Can the bankruptcy court exercise jurisdiction over assets that are not in southern Ohio? *See* 28 U.S.C. §1334(e).

PROBLEM 11-2

The dominant reason that Ozymandias, Inc. filed its bankruptcy petition was that it feared the outcome of a class action fraud suit that had been brought against it in a state court in Illinois. The case had gone to trial, which had taken three months, and had been sent to the jury on the day the bankruptcy petition was filed, thus stopping the trial. The attorney for the plaintiffs immediately made a motion to lift the stay so the jury could resume its deliberations. If you were the federal district judge in whose district the bankruptcy had been filed, would you grant this motion? *See* 28 U.S.C. §1334(c).[2] If you would not, could the disappointed party appeal? *See* 28 U.S.C. §1334(d).

Subsection (b) of §1334 gives the federal district courts "original but not exclusive jurisdiction of all civil proceedings arising under title 11, or arising in or related to cases under title 11." What does this mean? The phrase is used again in 28 U.S.C. §157(a), which says that such cases are "referred" to the bankruptcy judges of the district, meaning that the judges, in effect, act as federal magistrates when hearing bankruptcy matters. Section 157(b) allows bankruptcy judges to hear "core proceedings" in the bankruptcy court and enter appropriate orders and judgments, but for noncore proceedings the bankruptcy court can only submit proposed findings of fact and conclusions of law to the district court for final judgment; *see* §157(c)(1). The idea here is this: there can be no constitutional objection to having bankruptcy judges rule on issues that are purely bankruptcy matters, but as soon as the bankruptcy judge is faced with nonbankruptcy issues, Article III of the Constitution requires that the life-tenured, salary-protected federal district judge take over.

In re Wood

United States Court of Appeals, Fifth Circuit, 1987
825 F.2d 90

WISDOM, Circuit Judge:

This appeal calls upon us to decipher the jurisdictional provisions of the Bankruptcy Amendments and Federal Judgeship Act of 1984. A brief history of the Act may cast some light on the nature of our task.

Years of effort to reform the bankruptcy laws culminated with the enactment of the Bankruptcy Reform Act of 1978. As part of its overall goal to create a more efficient procedure for administering bankruptcies, the 1978 Act vested broad powers

---

2. Subsection (c)(2) refers to what is called "mandatory abstention."

in the bankruptcy courts. This reform was short-lived. In 1982 the Supreme Court decided Marathon v. Northern Pipelines. The Court declared the jurisdictional provision of the 1978 Act unconstitutional because, in short, it vested Article III judicial power in Article I judges. Courts were left to their own devices while Congress deliberated a response to *Marathon*. With prompting from bench, bar, and law professors with expertise in bankruptcy, Congress responded with the Bankruptcy Amendments and Federal Judgeship Act of 1984. Essentially, Congress reenacted the 1978 Act, but divided its jurisdictional grant into "core" proceedings, over which the bankruptcy courts exercise full judicial power — and "otherwise related" or "non-core" proceedings — over which the bankruptcy courts exercise only limited power. In this case, we must decide two issues: first, whether bankruptcy jurisdiction exists; second, if jurisdiction does exist, whether the bankruptcy court may proceed over this matter as a "core" or a "non-core" proceeding.

I.

This case results from a dispute among the directors/stockholders of a medical clinic. In 1981, Dr. James Wood and Dr. Arthur Wood, III, formed the Wayne Clinic, P.A., each becoming the owner of 1000 shares of stock. In March of 1984, Dr. James Wood and his wife, Carol Wood, filed a Chapter 11 bankruptcy petition in the Southern District Court of Mississippi. In May of 1985, Dr. Arthur Wood filed a complaint in the same court alleging that in November of 1984, Dr. and Mrs. James Wood and Woodrow Barham, acting together as directors of the clinic, wrongfully issued additional stock to Dr. James Wood. The complaint stated that in the Spring of 1985, Dr. James Wood received a disproportionate distribution from the clinic as the result of the wrongful stock issuance in violation of the agreement between Dr. James Wood and Dr. Arthur Wood that they were to be equal partners in the clinic. The complaint seeks damages and declaratory relief.

The bankruptcy judge of the district denied the defendants' motion to dismiss for lack of subject-matter jurisdiction and held that the matter was a core proceeding. On appeal to the district court, the court held that the matter was neither a "core" proceeding, over which the bankruptcy judge had full judicial power, nor an "otherwise related" or "non-core" proceeding, over which the bankruptcy judge has limited judicial power. The court dismissed the complaint for lack of subject-matter jurisdiction. The plaintiffs appealed to this Court.

II.

The starting point in our analysis is 28 U.S.C. §1334. In relevant part this provision provides:

(a) Except as provided in subsection (b) of this section, the district court shall have original and exclusive jurisdiction of all cases under title 11.

(b) Notwithstanding any Act of Congress that confers exclusive jurisdiction on a court or courts other than the district courts, the district courts shall have original but not exclusive jurisdiction of all civil proceedings arising under title 11, or arising in or related to cases under title 11.

Section 1334 lists four types of matters over which the district court has jurisdiction:

1. "Cases under title 11,"
2. "Proceedings arising under title 11,"
3. Proceedings "arising in" a case under title 11, and
4. Proceedings "related to" a case under title 11.

The first category refers merely to the bankruptcy petition itself, over which district courts (and their bankruptcy units) have original and exclusive jurisdiction. Our concern, however, is with the other proceedings listed in subsection 1334(b), over which the district courts have original, but not exclusive, jurisdiction.

There is almost no legislative history to guide us in interpreting the 1984 Act. Subsection 1334(b), however, was taken verbatim from subsection 1471(b) of the 1978 Act. The legislative history and judicial interpretations of that Act therefore are instructive.

Legislative history indicates that the phrase "arising under title 11, or arising in or related to cases under title 11" was meant, not to distinguish between different matters, but to identify collectively a broad range of matters subject to the bankruptcy jurisdiction of federal courts. Congress was concerned with the inefficiencies of piecemeal adjudication of matters affecting the administration of bankruptcies and intended to give federal courts the power to adjudicate all matters having an effect on the bankruptcy. Courts have recognized that the grant of jurisdiction under the 1978 Act was broad.

Nothing in *Marathon* suggests that we should read the corresponding provisions of the 1984 Act differently. The jurisdictional provision of the 1978 Act, section 1471, accomplished two things. First, subsection (b) vested an expansive bankruptcy jurisdiction in the district courts. Second, subsection (c) conferred the power to exercise that jurisdictional grant in the bankruptcy courts. The issue in *Marathon* was not the constitutionality of subsection (b), but the constitutionality of subsection (c). *Marathon* held that Congress could not vest the whole of bankruptcy jurisdiction in bankruptcy courts because the jurisdictional grant encompassed proceedings too far removed from the "core" of traditional bankruptcy powers to allow them to be adjudicated by non-Article III judges.[3] The holding in *Marathon* suggests no concern over the constitutionality of the scope of bankruptcy jurisdiction defined by Congress; its concern is with the placement of that jurisdiction in non-Article III courts. In response to *Marathon*, Congress altered the placement of bankruptcy jurisdiction by creating a statutory distinction between core and non-core proceedings and restricting the power of bankruptcy courts to adjudicate the latter. Because *Marathon* did not compel Congress to reduce the scope of bankruptcy jurisdiction, it seems plain that Congress intended no change in the scope of jurisdiction set forth in the 1978 Act when it later enacted section 1334 of the 1984 Act.

The district court expressed its concern that an overbroad interpretation of section 1334 would bring into federal court matters that should be left to state courts to decide. . . . There is no necessary reason why that concern must be met by restrictive interpretations of the statutory grant of jurisdiction under section 1334.

3. *See Marathon*, 458 U.S. at 71, 102 S. Ct. at 2871, 73 L. Ed. 2d at 615.

The Act grants the district court broad power to abstain whenever appropriate "in the interest of justice, or in the interest of comity with State courts or respect for State law." The abstention provisions of the Act demonstrate the intent of Congress that concerns of comity and judicial convenience should be met, not by rigid limitations on the jurisdiction of federal courts, but by the discretionary exercise of abstention when appropriate in a particular case. Here, the possibility of abstention was not raised in the district court.

For the purpose of determining whether a particular matter falls within bankruptcy jurisdiction, it is not necessary to distinguish between proceedings "arising under," "arising in a case under," or "related to a case under," title 11. These references operate conjunctively to define the scope of jurisdiction. Therefore, it is necessary only to determine whether a matter is at least "related to" the bankruptcy. The Act does not define "related" matters. Courts have articulated various definitions of "related," but the definition of the Court of Appeals for the Third Circuit appears to have the most support: "whether the outcome of that proceeding could *conceivably* have any effect on the estate being administered in bankruptcy."[4] This definition comports with the legislative history of the statutory predecessor to section 1334. Neither *Marathon* nor general concerns of comity counsel against its use. We adopt it as our own.

Applying this test to the case before us, we find that the complaint is sufficiently related to the pending bankruptcy to allow the district court to exercise jurisdiction under section 1334. The complaint against the bankruptcy debtors could have a conceivable effect on their bankruptcy. The plaintiff seeks to recover stock and monies that the debtors allegedly appropriated from the clinic. They seek to resolve the disputed allocation of interest in the clinic. To the extent that the debtors' interest in the clinic, their stock holdings, or their withdrawals are now property of the estate, the complaint against them has a potential effect on their estate.

The debtors argue that the complaint raises a post-petition claim that will not affect their bankruptcy. Generally, post-petition claims are not dischargeable in bankruptcy and, therefore, do not affect the estate. To fall within the court's jurisdiction, the plaintiffs' claims must affect the estate, not just the debtor. Although we acknowledge the possibility that this suit may ultimately have no effect on the bankruptcy, we cannot conclude, on the facts before us, that it will have no conceivable effect. First, the complaint raises a dispute over the division of ownership of the clinic. Because the debtors held their stock in the clinic before filing for bankruptcy, the disputed share is now part of the estate. Second, the complaint seeks to recover stock and cash withdrawals made after the filing of the petition. Although post-petition acquisitions of the debtor are generally not part of the estate, they may be estate property in this case if considered income from pre-petition property. We raise these possibilities, not to

---

4. Pacor, Inc. v. Higgins, 743 F.2d 984, 994 (3d Cir. 1984) (emphasis added); *accord* In re Dogpatch U.S.A., Inc., 810 F.2d 782, 786 (8th Cir. 1987); In re Salem Mortgage Co., 783 F.2d 626, 634 (6th Cir. 1986); In re Globe Parcel Service, 71 B.R. 323, 326 (E.D. Pa. 1987); In re World Financial Services Center, Inc., 64 B.R. 980, 988 (Bankr. S.D. Cal. 1986); In re Cemetery Development Corp., 59 B.R. 115, 121 (Bankr. M.D. La. 1986).

resolve them, for that matter is left to the district and bankruptcy courts to decide under federal law, but to illustrate the conceivable effect of the complaint on the administration of the bankruptcy. . . .

III.

We have decided that subject-matter jurisdiction exists over this proceeding. We must now determine the placement of that jurisdiction. Our analysis turns to 28 U.S.C. §157, the response of Congress to Marathon and its replacement for subsection 1471(c) of the 1978 Act. In contrast to subsection 1471(c), section 157 does not give bankruptcy courts full judicial power over all matters over which the district courts have jurisdiction under section 1334. With respect to proceedings other than the bankruptcy petition itself, section 157 divides all proceedings into two categories. Subsection 157(b)(1) gives bankruptcy judges the power to determine "all core proceedings arising under title 11, or arising in a case under title 11" and to enter appropriate orders and judgments. Subsection 157(c)(2) gives the bankruptcy judge the limited power to hear "a proceeding that is not a core proceeding but that is otherwise related to a case under title 11" and to submit proposed findings of fact and conclusions of law to the district court, subject to de novo review. The essential distinction that must be made, therefore, is whether this action is a core or non-core proceeding.

The statute does not define core proceedings. Subsection (b)(2) does provide a nonexclusive list of examples, three of which are arguably relevant here:

(A)   matters concerning the administration of the estate;
(B)   allowance or disallowance of claims against the estate . . . ; and
(C)   other proceedings affecting the liquidation of the assets of the estate or the adjustment of the debtor-creditor or the equity security holder relationship. . . .

We note that the last example is broadly worded; indeed, "proceedings affecting . . . the estate" is similar in scope to the test of jurisdiction: proceedings having a "conceivable effect on the estate." We decline, however, to give such a broad reading to subsection 157(b)(2)(O); otherwise, the entire range of proceedings under bankruptcy jurisdiction would fall within the scope of core proceedings, a result contrary to the ostensible purpose of the 1984 Act. That purpose is to conform the bankruptcy statute to the dictates of Marathon.

Specifically, Marathon involved an adversarial proceeding brought by the debtor-in-bankruptcy on a pre-petition claim arising under state substantive law against a defendant who had not filed a claim in bankruptcy. A plurality of the Supreme Court held that the proceeding could not be adjudicated by the bankruptcy court. The exact extent of Marathon's holding is subject to debate. Certain principles can be extracted from its opinions, principles that apparently have been incorporated into the 1984 Act.

Justice Brennan, writing for the plurality, held that only controversies involving "public rights," rights provided to an individual by Congress under one of its exceptional powers under the Constitution, may be removed from Article III courts and delegated to non-Article III tribunals. Justice Brennan implicitly recognized that the exceptional powers of Congress under the bankruptcy clause may sometimes allow for such delegations of judicial power:

> But the restructuring of debtor-creditor relations, which is at the core of the federal bank-ruptcy power, must be distinguished from the adjudication of state-created private rights, such as the right to recover contract damages that is at issue in this case. The former may well be a "public right," but the latter obviously is not.[5]

Concerning the latter controversy, he noted:

> This claim may be adjudicated in federal court on the basis of its relationship to the petition for reorganization. But this relationship does not transform the state-created right into a matter between the Government and the petitioner for reorganization. Even in the absence of the federal scheme, the plaintiff would be able to proceed against the defendant on the state-law contractual claims.[6]

Two points are suggested by this language. First, bankruptcy judges may exercise full judicial power over only those controversies that implicate the peculiar rights and powers of bankruptcy or, in Justice Brennan's words, controversies "at the core of the federal bankruptcy power." Second, controversies that do not depend on the bankruptcy laws for their existence — suits that could proceed in another court even in the absence of bankruptcy — are not core proceedings. These points are echoed by Chief Justice Burger in his dissent in which he characterized the plurality opinion as follows:

> the Court's holding is limited to the proposition . . . that a "traditional" state common-law action, not made subject to a federal rule of decision, and related only peripherally to an adjudication of bankruptcy under federal law, must, absent the consent of the litigants, be heard by an "Article III court."[7]

Justice White expressed concern, however, that the plurality's holding placed too much emphasis on the existence of state law issues in the proceeding before the bankruptcy court:

> Second, the distinction between claims based on state law and those based on federal law disregards the real character of bankruptcy proceedings. . . . The crucial point to be made is that in the ordinary bankruptcy proceeding the great bulk of creditor claims are claims that have accrued under state law prior to bankruptcy — claims for goods sold, wages, rent, utilities, and the like. . . . Every such claim must be filed and its validity is subject to adjudication by the bankruptcy court. The existence and validity of such claims recurringly depend on state law. Hence, the bankruptcy judge is constantly enmeshed in state-law issues.[8]

---

5. 458 U.S. 71, 102 S. Ct. at 2871, 73 L. Ed. 2d at 615 (emphasis added).
6. Id. at 72 n.26, 102 S. Ct. at 2872 n.26, 73 L. Ed. 2d at 615 n.26.
7. Id. at 92, 102 S. Ct. at 2882, 73 L. Ed. 2d at 628 (Burger, C.J., dissenting).
8. Id. at 96-97, 102 S. Ct. at 2884-85, 73 L. Ed. 2d at 631 (White, J., dissenting).

Section 157 of the 1984 Act incorporates the principles suggested in the language of the *Marathon* opinions. The reference in the Act to "core" proceedings is taken directly from Justice Brennan's description of matters that involve the peculiar powers of bankruptcy courts. The Act describes non-core proceedings as "otherwise related," an apparent reference to Chief Justice Burger's description of the *Marathon* proceeding as "related only peripherally to an adjudication of bankruptcy." Mindful of the limitations of the plurality's holding and of Justice White's observations concerning state law, Congress added: "A determination that a proceeding is not a core proceeding shall not be made solely on the basis that its resolution may be affected by State law."[9]

The meaning of core proceedings is illuminated also by the textual context in which it appears. Subsection 157(b)(1) vests full judicial power in bankruptcy courts over "*core proceedings arising under title 11, or arising in a case under title 11.*" The prepositional qualifications of core proceedings are taken from two of the three categories of jurisdiction set forth in section 1334(b): proceedings "arising under" title 11, "arising in" title 11 cases, and "related to" title 11 cases. Although the purpose of this language in section 1334(b) is to define conjunctively the scope of jurisdiction, each category has a distinguishable meaning. These meanings become relevant because section 157 apparently equates core proceedings with the categories of "arising under" and "arising in" proceedings.

Congress used the phrase "arising under title 11" to describe those proceedings that involve a cause of action created or determined by a statutory provision of title 11. Apparently, the phrase was taken from 28 U.S.C. §1331, conferring federal question jurisdiction in which it carries a similar and well-accepted meaning. The meaning of "arising in" proceedings is less clear, but seems to be a reference to those "administrative" matters that arise *only* in bankruptcy cases. In other words, "arising in" proceedings are those that are not based on any right expressly created by title 11, but nevertheless, would have no existence outside of the bankruptcy.

As defined above, the phrases "arising under" and "arising in" are helpful indicators of the meaning of core proceedings. If the proceeding involves a right created by the federal bankruptcy law, it is a core proceeding; for example, an action by the trustee to avoid a preference. If the proceeding is one that would arise only in bankruptcy, it is also a core proceeding; for example, the filing of a proof of claim or an objection to the discharge of a particular debt. If the proceeding does not invoke a substantive right created by the federal bankruptcy law and is one that could exist outside of bankruptcy it is not a core proceeding; it may be *related* to the bankruptcy because of its potential effect, but under section 157(c)(1) it is an "otherwise related" or non-core proceeding.

Finally, the interpretation of core proceeding based on its equation with "arising under" and "arising in" proceedings comports with the interpretation suggested by *Marathon*. Justice Brennan's description of "core" matters parallels that of matters "arising under" title 11 — matters invoking a substantive right created by federal bankruptcy law. Moreover, his comment that the matter could have proceeded absent

9. 28 U.S.C. §157(b)(3).

the bankruptcy suggests a contrast with "arising in" proceedings — matters that could arise only in bankruptcy.

We hold, therefore, that a proceeding is core under section 157 if it invokes a substantive right provided by title 11 or if it is a proceeding that, by its nature, could arise only in the context of a bankruptcy case. The proceeding before us does not meet this test and, accordingly, is a non-core proceeding. The plaintiff's suit is not based on any right created by the federal bankruptcy law. It is based on state created rights. Moreover, this suit is not a proceeding that could arise only in the context of a bankruptcy. It is simply a state contract action that, had there been no bankruptcy, could have proceeded in state court.

The plaintiff argues that his action is literally a claim against the estate, which is expressly defined as a core proceeding by section 157(b)(2)(B). We disagree. In determining the nature of a proceeding for purposes of determining core status, the court must look to both the form and the substance of the proceeding. The form of this action is not that of a "claim" as that term is used in bankruptcy law. A claim against the estate is instituted by filing a proof of claim as provided by the bankruptcy rules. The filing of the proof invokes the special rules of bankruptcy concerning objections to the claim, estimation of the claim for allowance purposes, and the rights of the claimant to vote on the proposed distribution. Understood in this sense, a claim filed against the estate is a core proceeding because it could arise only in the context of bankruptcy. Of course, the state-law right underlying the claim could be enforced in a state court proceeding absent the bankruptcy, but the nature of the state proceeding would be different from the nature of the proceeding following the filing of a proof of claim. Here, the plaintiff has not filed a proof of claim and has not invoked the peculiar powers of the bankruptcy court.

The substance of this action does not support a finding of core status. The essential issue in the proceeding is whether the defendants are liable to the plaintiff under state law. The suit does not raise as primary issues such matters as dischargeability, allowance of the claim, or other bankruptcy matters. Conceivably, a final judgment in this proceeding in the plaintiff's favor may lead to proceedings to allow the claim or to discharge the debt. At this juncture, however, these concerns are speculative and insubstantial issues in the proceeding. The plaintiff's suit is not a core proceeding.

The judgment of the district court is VACATED and the case is remanded to the district court for further proceedings consistent with this opinion.

The "related to a case under title 11" test the court quotes from Pacor, Inc. v. Higgins, 743 F.2d 984, 994 (3d Cir. 1984), "whether the outcome of that proceeding could conceivably have any effect on the estate being administered in bankruptcy," has been cited with approval by the United States Supreme Court in Celotex Corp. v. Edwards, 514 U.S. 300, 115 S. Ct., 131 L. Ed. 2d 403 (1995). The test has also proved popular with other Circuit Courts of Appeal; *see* In re Canion, 196 F.3d 579 (5th Cir. 1999).

PROBLEM 11-3

You are a bankruptcy judge handling the Ozymandias, Inc. bankruptcy. Determine which of the following are core proceedings under 28 U.S.C. §157(b) so you can issue appropriate orders and final judgments, and which are not, so that your findings must be submitted to the district court for approval.

(a) A motion to lift the automatic stay so that a creditor can repossess Ozymandias's inventory.

(b) An action to recover a dividend paid to stockholders on the eve of bankruptcy.

(c) Ozymandias's president, Percy Sand, supposedly agreed to sell the company's Nevada plant to Traveler Company, but the agreement was only partially in writing and, since it involves the sale of realty, this triggers issues of the Statute of Frauds and the parol evidence rule. The Traveler Company has filed a claim based on this alleged agreement.

(d) In return for a loan, Shelley National Bank took a security interest in Ozymandias's accounts receivable, but the debtor in possession argues that the financing statement covering this transaction does not meet the statutory requirements of §9-402 of the Uniform Commercial Code, so the bank's security interest is unperfected.

(e) A sex discrimination suit alleging that the company's hiring practices have kept women out of meaningful positions in management. Note 28 U.S.C. §157(d) and the following case.

In re Vicars Insurance Agency, Inc.

United States Court of Appeals, Seventh Circuit, 1996
96 F.3d 949

HARLINGTON WOOD, Jr., Circuit Judge.

These consolidated cases require us to consider the scope of the mandatory "withdrawal of reference" provision of the Bankruptcy Code, 28 U.S.C. §157(d). This statute requires district courts to reassume primary authority over a proceeding formerly delegated to the bankruptcy court when confronted with certain interpretive circumstances. While the statutory language in question is seemingly straightforward, the many and varied interpretations of this provision by bankruptcy and district courts demonstrate that its "plain meaning" has been somewhat difficult to discern. Despite the varied approaches, the question has received little attention from the courts of appeals and is a matter of first impression in this circuit.

I. *Background*

Appellants United National Insurance Company, Diamond State Insurance Company, and Hallmark Insurance Company are all part of the same corporate "family" called the United National Group ("UNG"). In late 1991 these companies concluded an agreement with Transportation Underwriters, Inc. ("TUI"), a firm controlled by James K. Culley, allowing TUI to underwrite physical damage insurance for commercial vehicles according to certain terms. One term of particular relevance required TUI to write only policies limited to one month's duration, with renewal possible but subject to the same limited time basis. The agreement also permitted "continuous" policies, but required that these too be subject to monthly premium charges.

Soon after the agreement with TUI was concluded, Culley delegated the obligations of TUI to Vicars Insurance and E&S Facilities ("Vicars," "E&S," or "debtors"), other entities under his control. UNG alleges that these companies then intentionally violated the agreement by selling policies and collecting premiums on an annual rather than a monthly basis. UNG claims that Vicars and E & S falsely reported the policy terms to UNG as monthly (not annual) and improperly retained or diverted to other uses all but a small fraction of the premiums, all further violations of the agreement. Such practices allegedly occurred over about a year and involved more than 4800 insurance policies.

This alleged financial scheme was eventually discovered or otherwise went awry. The record is unclear as to the next events, but these specifics need not detain us. UNG soon demanded various payments in accordance with the agreement. When these demands went unsatisfied, UNG filed a civil action in the United States District Court for the Eastern District of Pennsylvania in June, 1994 against Vicars, E & S, and one Richard Trakimas, an officer of Vicars. Based on the policy and premium irregularities described above, the complaint alleged five counts including violations of the Racketeer Influenced and Corrupt Organizations Act ("RICO"), 18 U.S.C. §1961 et seq., common law fraud, civil conspiracy, and unjust enrichment. This suit forced Vicars and E & S into bankruptcy; both companies filed voluntary petitions for reorganization under Chapter 11 of the Bankruptcy Code in the Bankruptcy Court for the Southern District of Indiana.

UNG responded to these filings with a motion requesting the district court in Indianapolis to withdraw the reference of their civil claims from the bankruptcy court in each case. Some of the companies within UNG then filed proofs of claims for recovery of premiums due and treble damages amounting to several million dollars. The debtors answered with objections to these claims on various grounds and a counterclaim for tortious interference with contract. Both district judges denied the motions to withdraw the reference, with Judge McKinney joining the views of Judge Barker. Thereafter the district court judges certified each order of denial for an interlocutory appeal. This court granted permission for the same and ordered consolidation of the two appeals for argument.

II. *Discussion*

As it is a question of law, we will review the denial of a motion to withdraw the reference to a bankruptcy court on a plenary basis.

Statutory language often finds its way into our law books by a tortuous path, and the mandatory withdrawal provision at issue here is no exception. Its immediate source, the Bankruptcy Amendments and Federal Judgeship Act of 1984 ("the Amendments Act" or "Act"), was enacted by Congress in response to the Supreme Court's decision in Northern Pipeline Constr. Co. v. Marathon Pipe Line Co., 458

U.S. 50, 102 S. Ct. 2858, 73 L. Ed. 2d 598 (1982). The Court's plurality opinion in *Marathon* has been the subject of much academic speculation and commentary, and its precise contours remain open to debate. It will suffice here to note that in general terms the decision limited the power of Congress to assign adjudicative authority to federal bankruptcy judges.[10] Much bankruptcy law was thus rendered open to attack on constitutional grounds. Attempting to rectify this problem and abide by the constitutional constraints of *Marathon*, Congress passed the Amendments Act. The Act gave the district courts original jurisdiction over all cases arising under title 11 of the Bankruptcy Code, *see* 28 U.S.C. §1334(b), but also allowed federal courts to "refer" bankruptcy cases to the bankruptcy judges for the district automatically. *See* 28 U.S.C. §157(a). This authority to refer was tempered, however, with a provision that the reference may or shall be withdrawn in certain situations:

> The district court may withdraw, in whole or in part, any case or proceeding referred under this section, on its own motion or on timely motion of a party, for cause shown. The district court shall, on timely motion of a party, so withdraw a proceeding if the court determines that resolution of the proceeding requires consideration of both title 11 and other laws of the United States regulating organizations or activities affecting interstate commerce.

28 U.S.C. §157(d).

The second sentence quoted above, the so-called mandatory withdrawal provision at issue here, has spawned several cases and generated a variety of readings. This is perhaps not surprising considering its several ambiguous phrases, which combine lower court discretion with flexible terms such as "resolution," "consideration," and "affecting."

Appellants argue that the mandatory withdrawal provision should be interpreted almost literally, but concede that the "consideration" required of at least the non-title 11 law must be "material." This expansive view of the term "consideration" has commanded little support. Overwhelmingly courts and commentators agree that the mandatory withdrawal provision cannot be given its broadest literal reading, for sending every proceeding that required passing "consideration" of non-bankruptcy law back to the district court would "eviscerate much of the work of the bankruptcy courts," In re Adelphi Institute, Inc., 112 B.R. 534, 536 (S.D.N.Y. 1990) (quoting 1 Collier on Bankruptcy para. 3.01 (15th ed. 1987)).[11] From a litigant's perspective, such a reading would also create an "escape hatch" by which bankruptcy matters could easily be removed to the district court. *See* Note, Closing the Escape Hatch in the Mandatory Withdrawal Provision of 28 U.S.C. §157(d), 36 U.C.L.A. L. Rev. 417 (1988). This might in turn encourage delaying tactics (perhaps further draining the

---

10. "The Court's holding in that case establishes only that Congress may not vest in a non-Article III court the power to adjudicate, render final judgment, and issue binding orders in a traditional contract action arising under state law, without consent of the litigants, and subject only to ordinary appellate review." Thomas v. Union Carbide Agric. Prods. Co., 473 U.S. 568, 584, 105 S. Ct. 3325, 3334, 87 L. Ed. 2d 409 (1985) (citations omitted).

11. "[A]ny reading of §157(d) which limits bankruptcy court jurisdiction to questions arising solely under the [Bankruptcy] Code would strip the court of much of its authority to resolve debtor-creditor disputes, since numerous Code provisions themselves require reference to other state and federal law." In re White Motor Corp., 42 B.R. at 703.

resources of the debtor), forum shopping, and generally unnecessary litigation. The legislative history of the Act reveals that this concern was recognized by Congress (the term "escape hatch" comes from the congressional debates) and that the measure's author and proponents denied any such effect, stressing that they intended the provision to be read narrowly. *See* 130 Cong. Rec. H1849-50 (daily ed. Mar. 21, 1984) (remarks of Rep. Kastenmeier); S. Rep. No. 55, 98th Cong., 1st Sess. 16 (1983) ("the Committee intends . . . mandatory recall [to] be construed narrowly.").

As we indicated, courts have uniformly agreed that a narrow interpretation is indeed required. To achieve this, however, several avenues have been taken. The first court to consider §157(d) relied on the wording of the section, which requires withdrawal only when "consideration" of both title 11 and non-Code federal statutes is necessary for the "resolution" of a case or proceeding, together with "the congressional goal of having expert bankruptcy judges determine complex Code matters to the greatest extent possible," and concluded that withdrawal should be granted only if the current proceeding could not be resolved without "substantial and material consideration" of the non-Code federal law. In re White Motor Corp., 42 B.R. at 704. This "substantial and material" gloss has been accepted as an appropriate reading of the statute and effectuation of Congress' intent by most courts, including the Second Circuit. *See* Shugrue v. Air Line Pilots Assn., Intl. (In re Ionosphere Clubs, Inc.), 922 F.2d 984 (2d Cir. 1990), *cert. denied*, 502 U.S. 808, 112 S. Ct. 50, 116 L. Ed. 2d 28 (1991). We join that view today.

Some courts and commentators have attempted to narrow the statute by focusing on other elements of the provision, including the usage of the words "both" and "and" ("*both* title 11 . . . *and* other laws") to determine whether "substantial and material consideration" is required of title 11 law in addition to non-Code federal law. *See* American Freight Sys. v. I.C.C. (In re American Freight System), 150 B.R. 790, 793 (D. Kan. 1993) (and citations therein). Still others have analyzed whether or how the non-Code law in question "affects" interstate commerce. *See, e.g.*, In re Blackman, 55 B.R. 437, 450 (Bankr. D.D.C. 1985); In re Rubin Bros. Footwear, Inc., 73 B.R. 346, 351 (S.D.N.Y. 1987). Neither party to this appeal questions the fact that this proceeding requires consideration of title 11 law, nor do they contest the proposition that the RICO statute "affects" interstate commerce. We will thus leave these finer issues of interpretation for another day. We do note, however, that whatever one considers the rationale for the mandatory withdrawal provision to be — constitutional concerns, legislative preference, expertise of the respective courts, etc — it would be somewhat anomalous to require withdrawal of a proceeding that contains, say, both title 11 and complex antitrust interpretation issues, but leaves to the bankruptcy court those cases or proceedings that require complex analysis of the antitrust statutes alone.

Thus we return to the "substantial and material consideration" test. A helpful adjective has been added, but this too is imprecise and has generated several readings. What constitutes "substantial" consideration of a non-title 11 statute? Answers to this question have a broad range. At the least restrictive end of the spectrum, one court has held that this requirement is met if a proceeding merely "presents a non-Title 11 federal question which will affect the outcome of the proceeding." Contemporary Lithographers, Inc. v. Hibbert (In re Contemporary Lithographers), 127 B.R. 122, 127 (M.D.N.C. 1991).

The majority of courts have taken a narrower view, however, examining a variety of factors. These generally require that the issues in question require more than the mere application of well-settled or "hornbook" non-bankruptcy law; "significant interpretation" of the non-Code statute must be required.[12] United States v. Johns-Manville Corp. (In re Johns-Manville Corp.), 63 B.R. 600, 603 (S.D.N.Y. 1986); City of New York v. Exxon Corp., 932 F.2d 1020, 1026 (2d Cir. 1991) (also using term "substantial interpretation").

The most restrictive interpretations have identified particular contexts as the only situations appropriate for mandatory withdrawal. These have included proceedings where non-title 11 issues "dominated" bankruptcy issues, see In re Lenard, 124 B.R. 101, 102 (D. Colo. 1991), or where the proceeding presented a conflict between statutes, a question of first impression, or a constitutional challenge. See In re Adelphi Institute, 112 B.R. 534, 537 (S.D.N.Y. 1990).

We believe the proper approach to mandatory withdrawal analysis lies in the middle of this spectrum. Given the discretion granted to district courts by §157(d), there is little reason to assume that withdrawal is required by the mere presence of a non-title 11 issue, even if that issue is outcome determinative. This reading, which makes withdrawal virtually automatic, reads out of the statute both district court discretion and any "consideration" whatsoever.

Delimiting specific contexts where mandatory withdrawal is required is also a problematic approach. Such identification is useful only to the extent that the context in question will always require a court to devote substantial consideration to the issues involved. This may or may not be true in every particular instance. In any event the specifics of the particular context or posture should be fleshed out by the moving party to demonstrate that the grounds for withdrawal are satisfied (i.e., substantial and material consideration is required). That party ultimately bears the risk of nonpersuasion. In re Michigan Real Estate Ins. Trust, 87 B.R. 447, 459 (E.D. Mich. 1988) (citations omitted).

In accordance with the statute's terms, then, the guiding question must be whether consideration is required, not merely the context in which the issue is presented. Here unfortunately no bright line can be drawn. Courts have defined "consideration" to mean "something more than the mere process of examining, thinking about, or taking into account." In re McCrory Corp., 160 B.R. 502, 505 (S.D.N.Y. 1993); American Freight Sys., 150 B.R. at 792. This definition is similar to the application/interpretation distinction first drawn in *Johns-Manville*, which we believe identifies the heart

---

12. The court in *Johns-Manville* stated that:

> It would seem incompatible with congressional intent to provide a rational structure for the assertion of bankruptcy claims to withdraw each case involving the straightforward application of a federal statute to a particular set of facts. It is issues requiring a significant interpretation of federal laws that Congress would have intended to have decided by a district judge rather than a bankruptcy judge.

In re Johns-Manville Corp., 63 B.R. 600, 602 (S.D.N.Y. 1986).

of the matter. This approach is in accordance with the terms of §157(d), Congress' intent, and the practicalities of litigation. We therefore hold that as far as non-title 11 issues are presented, mandatory withdrawal is required only when those issues require the interpretation, as opposed to mere application, of the non-title 11 statute, or when the court must undertake analysis of significant open and unresolved issues regarding the non-title 11 law. The legal questions involved need not be of "cosmic proportions," In re Rimsat, Ltd., 196 B.R. 791, 799 (N.D. Ind. 1995), but must involve more than mere application of existing law to new facts.

We also note a decision regarding mandatory withdrawal does not prevent district court involvement. Indeed, a safety device is provided by the other sentence of §157(d). This "permissive" withdrawal provision allows a district court to withdraw, at any time, even a part of a case or proceeding on its own motion or that of a party, for cause shown. See 28 U.S.C. §157(d). Thus even if the court determines that mandatory withdrawal does not apply, it may prefer to withdraw or limit the reference nonetheless. Some bankruptcy courts, even though they are without jurisdiction to hear a motion for withdrawal, see 28 U.S.C. §157(d), make recommendations to the district court as to whether this should be done. See, e.g., In re Golden Gulf, Ltd., 73 B.R. 685, 686 (Bankr. E.D. Ark. 1987) (recommendation regarding mandatory withdrawal); In re Michigan Real Estate Ins. Trust, 87 B.R. at 465 (recommendation regarding discretionary withdrawal).

This brings us to the application of these principles to this particular case. UNG claims that even under a narrow interpretation of §157(d) withdrawal is required because of the RICO violations alleged in its civil complaint. These violations are based in part upon theories of aiding and abetting liability. While this circuit has not commented on the possibility of aiding and abetting liability in civil RICO actions, others have approved the theory. See Jaguar Cars, Inc. v. Royal Oaks Motor Car Co., 46 F.3d 258, 270 (3d Cir. 1995) (aiding and abetting liability appropriate where defendant knew of substantive act and acted with intent to facilitate it); Armco Indus. Credit Corp. v. SLT Warehouse Co., 782 F.2d 475, 485 (5th Cir. 1986) ("mere negative acquiescence" is not enough to establish aiding and abetting civil liability under RICO; defendant must have affirmatively acted in a way that facilitated success of illegal action).

Since UNG filed its civil complaint in the Third Circuit, it contends that it is unclear whether the law of that circuit or this one (the circuit in which the bankruptcy claim is adjudicated) should apply. Thus UNG argued to the district court that:

> issues may arise in the consideration of [UNG]'s RICO claims which, although settled in favor of [UNG] in those jurisdictions in which such issues have been entertained, may be questions of first impression should the law of the Seventh Circuit rather than the Third Circuit be found to apply in this case.

The district court found that the possibility that RICO claims "might involve novel issues" was not enough to trigger mandatory withdrawal. The court characterized UNG's concerns as at most "speculative" and at worst "completely hypothetical." Furthermore, the court stressed that the bankruptcy court was not without guidance on the issue from other courts, including district court holdings within this circuit. The court concluded that "[e]ither way, UNG falls far short of establishing 'that this case involves anything more than a routine application of RICO law.'" In re E & S Facilities, 181 B.R. 369, 373 (S.D. Ind. 1995) (quoting In re Laventhol & Horwath, 139 B.R. 109, 116 (S.D.N.Y. 1992)).

We agree with this conclusion. UNG may be without guidance as to which circuit's law will definitively apply to the claim, but this conjectural concern by itself (for UNG offered little else to the district courts) does not necessarily trigger "substantial and material consideration" of a non-title 11 statute. Similarly, neither is it enough that an issue simply has not been considered at the circuit court level. As the district court recognized, law from lower courts exists in both circuits (and others) for a bankruptcy judge's guidance and application. . . .

For these reasons we agree that UNG failed to satisfy its burden of persuasion on the issue of mandatory withdrawal, and the decisions of the district courts are accordingly AFFIRMED.

PROBLEM 11-4

In the month immediately before it filed its Chapter 11 petition, Oops Moving Co. lost control of one of its loaded moving vans on one of the steepest slopes in San Francisco, and the van careened into the crowd at a Chinese New Year celebration, killing and wounding 34 people. Where should the claims of these hapless people be heard? See 28 U.S.C. §§157(b)(2), (4), (5), and 1334(c)(2). If all concerned agreed that the bankruptcy court would be the best forum in which to settle these tort claims, would the bankruptcy court then have jurisdiction? See §157(c)(2). In such a case, could the bankruptcy court empanel a jury? See §157(e) and the materials that follow.

II.   Jury Trials

Historically, jury trials were very much the exception in bankruptcy proceedings. As courts of equity, bankruptcy courts generally operated without juries. Prior to the enactment of the Bankruptcy Code in 1978, bankruptcy court jurisdiction was broken down into "summary" proceedings and "plenary" proceedings. Summary proceedings (held in the bankruptcy courts) involved those issues that were most central to the bankruptcy case such as the granting or denial of a discharge and the allowance of claims. Plenary matters concerned issues that were more peripheral to the case, but they had to be brought in forums outside the bankruptcy courts. An example would be an action to recover property that was in the possession of a third party and was not subject to the control of the debtor. Plenary cases were treated as comparable to civil actions outside of bankruptcy. Therefore, the parties' right to a jury trial under the Seventh Amendment was recognized in those plenary actions.

The Bankruptcy Code discarded the notions of summary and plenary jurisdiction. Furthermore, bankruptcy court jurisdiction was expanded so that many actions that previously would have been heard by the district courts were brought within the jurisdiction of the bankruptcy courts. This created a need to reconsider the reach of the Seventh Amendment's right to jury trial in bankruptcy proceedings.

In 1989, the Supreme Court held that a creditor who had not filed a claim in a bankruptcy case was entitled to a jury trial in an action commenced by the trustee to recover fraudulent conveyances. Granfinanciera v. Nordberg, 492 U.S. 33, 109 S. Ct. 2782, 106 L. Ed. 2d 26 (1989). The Supreme Court noted the lack of clarity in the statutory scheme creating jurisdiction in the bankruptcy courts and addressing the right to a jury trial, and found that nothing in those provisions limited or expanded the reach of the Seventh Amendment. The Seventh Amendment preserves the right to jury trial in suits at common law as that right existed in 1791 when the amendment was ratified. The court then conducted an extensive historical analysis of fraudulent conveyance actions and determined that these cases would be brought at law in England in 1791. Therefore, the Constitution protected the creditors' right to a jury trial in 1989.

Prior to the enactment of the Bankruptcy Code, the impact of the distinction between summary and plenary jurisdiction caused many creditors to refrain from filing proof of their claims in order to avoid a finding that they had submitted to the summary jurisdiction of the court. A number of changes effected by the Bankruptcy Code were intended to bring more claims into the process and to diminish the significance of a creditor's decision whether to file proof of a claim. The reemergence of the availability of a jury trial in some cases has reinserted into the mix the consideration of whether a creditor should file proof of a claim in a particular case. Subsequent to *Granfinanciera*, the Court held in Langencamp v. Culp, 498 U.S. 42 (1990), that a creditor who files proof of a claim has waived the right to a jury trial in an action commenced by the trustee to recover a preference allegedly received by the creditor. The Court referred back to *Granfinanciera* and reiterated that by filing a claim, the creditor has submitted to the equitable jurisdiction of the bankruptcy court in its larger efforts to complete the claims allowance process. Obviously, the decision whether to file a claim is now again an important one for creditors to make.

The courts have continued to address issues at the edges of whether a party has a right to a jury trial.

In re Worldcom, Inc.

United States Bankruptcy Court, Southern District of New York, 2007
378 B.R. 745

ARTHUR J. GONZALEZ, Bankruptcy Judge.

Before the Court is the motion of WorldCom Communications, Inc. and its subsidiaries (the "Debtors" or "WorldCom") to strike Communications Network International, Ltd.'s ("CNI") demand for a jury trial. WorldCom argues that CNI does not have a right to a jury trial because it subjected itself to the jurisdiction of the bankruptcy court upon filing its proof of claim and that WorldCom's objections and claim bear directly on the claims-allowance process. CNI argues that WorldCom's claim does not bear directly on the allowance of the proof of claim, therefore, it is entitled to a jury trial.

Upon consideration of the pleadings and the hearing on this matter on October 24, 2007, the Court grants WorldCom's motion to strike CNI's demand for a jury trial. The Court finds that CNI subjected itself to the equitable jurisdiction of the Court when it filed its proof of claim and WorldCom's breach of contract claim bears directly on the claims-allowance process, thus converting WorldCom's contract claim, a traditionally legal action, into an equitable action for which there is no Seventh Amendment right to a jury trial.

I.   *Jurisdiction*

The Court has subject matter jurisdiction over this proceeding under sections 157 and 1334 of title 28 of the United States Code and under the July 10, 1984 "Standing Order of Referral of Cases to Bankruptcy Judges" of the United States District Court for the Southern District of New York (Ward, Acting C.J.). This matter is a core proceeding under section 157 of title 28 of the United States Code. Venue is proper before the Court under sections 1408 and 1409 of title 28 of the United States Code.

II.   *Background*

A.   Background Information About the Debtors

Debtors provided a broad range of communications services in over 200 countries on six continents. Through their core communications service business, which included voice, data, internet, and international services, the Debtors carried more data over their networks than any other telecommunications entity. The Debtors were the second largest carrier of consumer and small business long distance telecommunications services in the United States and provided a wide range of retail and wholesale communications services.

On July 21, 2002 and November 8, 2002, the Debtors commenced cases under chapter 11 of title 11 of the United States Code (the "Bankruptcy Code"). By orders dated July 22, 2002 and November 12, 2002, the Debtors' chapter 11 cases were consolidated for procedural purposes only and were jointly administered.

On October 29, 2002, the Court entered an order establishing January 23, 2003 as the deadline for the filing of proofs of claim against the Debtors (the "Bar Date"). On October 31, 2003, the Court entered an order confirming the Debtors' Modified Second Amended Joint Plan of Reorganization (the "Plan"). The Plan became effective on April 20, 2004 (the "Effective Date"). Upon the Effective Date, WorldCom changed its name to MCI, Inc. On January 6, 2006, Verizon Communications, Inc. and MCI, Inc. merged. Under the relevant agreement, MCI, Inc. merged with and into Eli Acquisition, LLC, as a direct, wholly owned subsidiary of Verizon Communications, Inc. Eli Acquisition, LLC, as the surviving entity, was immediately renamed MCI, LLC. MCI, LLC is now doing business as Verizon Business Global, LLC.

B.   Business Relationship Between WorldCom and CNI

The background information about WorldCom and its business relationship and litigation with CNI are set out in detail in the Court's earlier opinion denying CNI's proof of claim. *See MCI WorldCom Commc'ns, Inc. v. Commc'ns Network Int'l, Ltd. (In re WorldCom, Inc.),* No. 02-13533 (AJG), Adv. Proc. No. 04-04338 (AJG), 2006 WL 693370, at *1-3 (Bankr. S.D.N.Y. Mar. 13, 2006), *leave to appeal denied,* 358 B.R. 76 (S.D.N.Y. Dec. 6, 2006).

In brief, CNI resells telecommunications services from common carriers like WorldCom to its own customers. In December 1997, WorldCom and CNI entered into a written agreement, the "Intelenet Agreement," which, according to CNI, WorldCom eventually deemed inappropriate for the parties' relationship. In November 1998, CNI provided WorldCom with a copy of the WorldCom Rebiller Service Agreement (the "Rebiller Agreement") that was signed only by CNI. On January 29, 1999, WorldCom gave a copy of the Rebiller Agreement signed by both parties to CNI. On that same day, CNI signed an amendment to the Rebiller Agreement that WorldCom signed on February 4, 1999. WorldCom invoiced CNI monthly for services provided under the Rebiller Agreement.

C.   Procedural History

Prior to filing for bankruptcy, on February 14, 2001, WorldCom filed a lawsuit against CNI in the United States District Court for the Eastern District of Pennsylvania to recover unpaid amounts for telecommunications services WorldCom provided to CNI (the "Pennsylvania Action"). WorldCom based its claims on theories of contract, negotiable instrument, *quantum meruit,* and unjust enrichment. In its complaint, WorldCom alleges that, on or about March 1, 1999, CNI gave WorldCom a check for $20,000 that was dishonored and returned due to insufficient funds. WorldCom states that on or about April 15, 1999, it received a $20,000 payment from CNI. WorldCom also alleges that, on or about April 16, 1999, CNI remitted a check to WorldCom for $66,398.45 that was dishonored and returned due to insufficient funds. WorldCom asserts that CNI did not make any further payments after April 1999. Shortly thereafter, WorldCom states that it terminated CNI's service due to nonpayment. (Compl. ¶¶7-18.)

CNI answered only the contract count of the complaint and counterclaimed for fraud, intentional nondisclosure, breach of contract, defamation, and punitive damages. In its breach of contract counterclaim, CNI argues that WorldCom improperly billed CNI by failing to provide Retex rebates and to reimburse CNI for switching telephone numbers and by charging CNI taxes. CNI asserts that WorldCom overcharged it for usage and improperly charged it for non-usage related charges (PIC-C charges). (Answer and Counterclaims ¶¶26-28.) Further, CNI contends that if WorldCom properly credited and charged CNI's account, WorldCom actually owes CNI money. (Answer and Counterclaims ¶40.) CNI's answer included a demand for a jury trial.

WorldCom moved to dismiss CNI's counterclaims, arguing that most of the claims were barred by the filed-rate doctrine. In August 2001, the district court, pursuant to the doctrine of primary jurisdiction, denied the motion, stayed the Pennsylvania Action, and referred it to the Federal Communications Commission ("FCC"). However, neither party pursued the matter with the FCC. In May 2002, CNI moved to lift the stay in the Pennsylvania Action. The motion was granted and the Pennsylvania Action resumed until WorldCom filed for bankruptcy.

On January 22, 2003, CNI filed a timely proof of claim of $17,701,534, which was assigned claim no. 22183. The proof of claim reasserted its counterclaims in the Pennsylvania Action. On October 12, 2004, WorldCom initiated an adversary proceeding against CNI, objecting to the proof of claim and reasserting the issues in WorldCom's complaint in the Pennsylvania Action. On October 22, 2004, CNI filed an answer, again responding only to the contract count of the complaint. CNI's answer included a demand for a jury trial. On February 22, 2005, WorldCom moved for judgment on the pleadings seeking dismissal of all the claims in CNI's proof of claim. WorldCom also moved for judgment on the issue of CNI's liability regarding its claims based on negotiable instrument, *quantum meruit,* and unjust enrichment, all of which CNI had failed to answer. CNI moved to file responses *nunc pro tunc* to the negotiable instrument, *quantum meruit,* and unjust enrichment counts in the adversary proceeding and also cross-moved for judgment on the pleadings.

On March 13, 2006, the Court granted WorldCom's motion for judgment on the pleadings to the extent that CNI's claims were dismissed. *See In re WorldCom, Inc.,* 2006 WL 693370, at *12. WorldCom's motion was denied, however, as to CNI's liability for unpaid services. *See id.* The Court also granted CNI's motion to file responses *nunc pro tunc* to WorldCom's negotiable instrument, *quantum meruit,* and unjust enrichment claims and denied CNI's cross-motion for judgment on the pleadings. *Id.* In that opinion, the Court stated that the parties' written agreements superseded any alleged oral agreement and that CNI cannot enforce discounts promised outside of the filed tariff. *Id.* at *7-8.

On April 26, 2006, CNI filed an amended answer responding to WorldCom's non-contract claims. On May 1, 2006, CNI filed a motion for leave to appeal. That motion was denied on December 6, 2006 by the United States District Court for the Southern District of New York. On January 1, 2007, WorldCom filed a summary judgment motion. CNI moved for leave to file a sur-reply memorandum in opposition to WorldCom's summary judgment motion. On July 9, 2007, the Court granted CNI's motion for leave to file a sur-reply memorandum in part, only to the extent that it addressed WorldCom's contention regarding CNI's failure to timely dispute its charges, and denied CNI's motion in part regarding any remaining issues. On that same day, the Court granted WorldCom's summary judgment motion in part as to the issue of CNI's breach of the Rebiller Agreement and denied the summary judgment motion in part on the grounds that there is a genuine issue of material fact regarding WorldCom's claim for damages. *See MCI WorldCom Commc'ns, Inc. v. Commc'ns Network Int'l, Ltd. (In re WorldCom, Inc.),* No. 02-13533 (AJG), Adv. Proc. No. 04-04338 (AJG), 2007 WL 1989262 (Bankr. S.D.N.Y. July 9, 2007).

On October 5, 2007, WorldCom filed a motion to strike CNI's jury trial demand. On October 17, 2007, CNI filed its reply to that motion. On October 24, 2007, the Court heard oral argument on the motion.

III. Parties' Contentions

A. WorldCom's Contentions

WorldCom argues that CNI does not have a right to a jury trial because CNI submitted itself to the jurisdiction of the bankruptcy court upon filing its proof of claim. WorldCom contends that a creditor who files a proof of claim is not entitled to a jury trial if the dispute at issue affects the claims-allowance process as the dispute is thereby inextricably intertwined with a public right. (Mem. Supp. Mot. Strike 3-4, 7-8; Mot. Strike Hr'g, Oct. 24, 2007.) WorldCom also argues that its objections and claim arise out of the same contracts, tariffs, and transactions as the facts asserted in CNI's proof of claim and are, therefore, core proceedings under section 157 of title 28. Further, WorldCom argues that CNI's proof of claim and WorldCom's objections and claim implicate the restructuring of the debtor-creditor relationship between CNI and WorldCom as to which entity owes money and how much it owes. WorldCom asserts that if CNI had prevailed on its proof of claim that WorldCom owed it for improper charges, fraud, and breach of contract, the Court would have had to resolve the issue of how much CNI owed World-Com for services WorldCom provided to CNI in order to determine the amount payable on CNI's proof of claim against WorldCom. Consequently, WorldCom contends that CNI waived its jury trial right as to any issue integrally related to its proof of claim when CNI filed its proof of claim. (Mem. Supp. Mot. Strike 7-8.)

In addition, WorldCom argues that a claimant's right to a jury trial is determined based upon the circumstances that existed when the jury trial was demanded, not where the parties are in the litigation process at the time the Court determines the jury demand. (Mot. Strike Hr'g, Oct. 24, 2007.) Lastly, WorldCom asserts that the issues in the instant case are not the type of issues that are split between the bench and a jury as CNI contends and that under CNI's rationale, whenever a debtor had an offset and asserted it in a counterclaim, there would always be a jury trial. (Mot. Strike Hr'g, Oct. 24, 2007.)

B. CNI's Contentions

CNI argues that when it filed its proof of claim, it did not waive its right to a jury trial because WorldCom's claim does not bear directly on the allowance of the claim. CNI contends that resolving WorldCom's claim is not vital to the bankruptcy process; instead, it is only incidentally related to the bankruptcy process. CNI asserts that WorldCom is asking for money damages to compensate the estate and that if World-Com prevails, the estate is enlarged and the dispute does not affect the claims-allowance process. CNI contends that this is evidenced by the fact that the Court disallowed the proof of claim prior to resolving WorldCom's breach of contract claim. (Mem. Opp'n Mot. Strike 3-4.)

Further, CNI argues that a claimant's right to a jury trial is determined based upon the circumstances that exist at the time of trial, meaning at the time the Court rules on the jury demand, thus, the Court must consider the fact that it disallowed the proof of claim in determining whether WorldCom's claim implicates the claims-allowance process. (Mot. Strike Hr'g, Oct. 24, 2007.) In addition, CNI argues that a determination as to whether a claimant is entitled to a jury trial is determined on an issue-by-issue basis. CNI asserts that since the Court has already ruled on the proof of claim, WorldCom's claim is a separate and independent issue, thus, it has the right to a jury trial. (Mot. Strike Hr'g, Oct. 24, 2007.)

IV.   Discussion

A.   Jury Trial Right

1.   Seventh Amendment

The right to a jury trial in an action commenced in federal court is determined as a matter of federal law. *Ernst & Young v. Bankruptcy Services, Inc. (In re CBI Holding Co.)*, 311 B.R. 350, 365 n.8 (S.D.N.Y. 2004) (citation omitted). The Seventh Amendment of the United States Constitution preserves the right to a jury trial for actions at common law, where the value in controversy exceeds twenty dollars and concerns a private right. *Granfinanciera, S.A. v. Nordberg*, 492 U.S. 33, 41, 109 S. Ct. 2782, 2790, 106 L. Ed. 2d 26 (1989) (citations omitted); *see also McClelland v. Braverman Kaskey & Caprara, P.C. (In re McClelland)*, 332 B.R. 90, 94 (Bankr. S.D.N.Y. 2005) (citation omitted). In determining whether a claimant is entitled to a jury trial, the Court must first determine whether the action is legal or equitable by comparing it to actions brought in the English courts during the 18th century prior to the merger of law and equity courts. Second, the Court must determine whether the remedy sought is legal or equitable. The second line of inquiry should be given greater weight. *Granfinanciera*, 492 U.S. at 42, 109 S. Ct at 2790; *Germain v. Conn. Nat'l Bank*, 988 F.2d 1323, 1328 (2d Cir. 1993).

However, a party does not have a right to a jury trial "for cases 'involving statutory rights that are integral parts of a public regulatory scheme and whose adjudication Congress has assigned to . . . a specialized court of equity,' " because those rights are deemed " 'public.' " *Germain*, 988 F.2d at 1331 (quoting *Granfinanciera*, 492 U.S. at 55 n.10, 109 S. Ct. at 2797 n.10). The *Germain* court further explained that the action "must be inextricably intertwined with a public right; the 'involvement' may not be casual or vague." *Id.* In *Germain*, the Second Circuit held that the trustee's action did not "bear[ ] a close nexus to any statutory public right" because it did not affect "the essence of the bankruptcy regulatory scheme of allowing or reordering claims." *Id.* However, if a party's action is inextricably intertwined with a statutory public right, such as the bankruptcy regulatory scheme of allowing or reordering claims, then the party does not have a Seventh Amendment right to a jury trial. *Id.*

Neither WorldCom nor CNI dispute that a contract claim was historically tried in a court of law and that the monetary relief WorldCom seeks is legal in nature, which is ordinarily triable by a jury.[13] Therefore, in order to determine whether CNI has a jury trial right, the Court must determine whether WorldCom's breach of contract claim is inextricably intertwined with a public right — the claims-allowance process. If so, CNI would not have a jury trial right as to WorldCom's breach of contract claim.

2.   Effect of the Claims-Allowance Process

A creditor's right to a jury trial depends upon whether that creditor filed a proof of claim *and* if the dispute in which it requested a jury trial implicates the claims-allowance process. *See Germain,* 988 F.2d at 1329 ("[T]he *Katchen, Granfinanciera,* and *Langenkamp* line of Supreme Court cases stands for the proposition that by filing a proof of claim a creditor forsakes its right to adjudicate before a jury any issue *that bears directly on the allowance* of that claim. . . ."). There is no right to a jury trial as to any issue bearing directly on the claims-allowance process, such as a determination as to the validity of a creditor and the creditor hierarchy, because the legal issue has been converted into an equitable issue. *Id.* at 1329-30 (right to a jury trial waived as to disputes bearing directly on the claims-allowance process "on the theory that the legal issue has been converted to an issue of equity"); *see also Langenkamp v. Culp,* 498 U.S. 42, 44, 111 S. Ct. 330, 331, 112 L. Ed. 2d 343 (1990) (per curiam) ("In *Granfinanciera* we recognized that by filing a claim against a bankruptcy estate the creditor triggers the process of 'allowance and disallowance of claims,' thereby subjecting himself to the bankruptcy court's equitable power." (quoting *Granfinanciera,* 492 U.S. at 58-59, 59 n.14, 109 S. Ct. at 2799-2800, 2799 n.14)).

Actions that are legal in nature, entitling a claimant to a jury trial, are not " 'magically converted into equitable issues' " simply because the actions are connected to a bankruptcy proceeding, which is an equitable proceeding. *Germain,* 988 F.2d at 1329 (quoting *Ross v. Bernhard,* 396 U.S. 531, 538, 90 S. Ct. 733, 738, 24 L. Ed. 2d 729 (1970)). In a bankruptcy proceeding, however, a legal action converts into an equitable action if that action becomes part of the claims-allowance process "because determining pro rata distribution is characteristically equitable." *Id.* An action becomes part of the claims-allowance process if it "is integrally related to the equitable reordering of debtor-creditor and creditor-creditor relations. If an equitable reordering cannot be accomplished without resolution of what would otherwise be a legal dispute, then that dispute becomes an essential element of the broader equitable controversy." *Id.*

If a creditor's proof of claim is met with an adversary proceeding and the determination of that adversary proceeding affects the claims-allowance process, the creditor does not have a right to a jury trial, even if the adversary proceeding involves claims historically tried in a court of law. *In re CBI Holding Co.,* 311 B.R. at 365 (citing *Langenkamp,* 498 U.S. at 44, 111 S. Ct. at 331; *Granfinanciera,* 492 U.S. at

---

13. Since the parties do not dispute that a contract claim and monetary relief are traditionally legal in nature and there is ordinarily a right to a jury trial, the Court does not have to conduct the analysis set forth in *Granfinanciera* to determine whether the action is legal or equitable.

58-59, 59 n.14, 109 S. Ct. at 2799-2800, 2799 n.14). However, a determination that an action is "core" is given "minimal weight." *Germain,* 988 F.2d at 1327-28.

The Second Circuit's discussion of *Frost, Inc. v. Miller, Canfield, Paddock & Stone, P.C. (In re Frost),* 145 B.R. 878 (Bankr. W.D. Mich.1992)[14] in *Germain* implies that if a debtor's counterclaims in response to a creditor's proof of claim are found to be integrally related to the claims-allowance process — meaning that the debtor does not have a Seventh Amendment right to a jury trial — then the creditor does not have a jury trial right as to any of the counterclaims either. *Germain,* 988 F.2d at 1330 n.9 ("To the extent that [*Frost*] is suggesting that the debtor was essentially objecting to the allowance of the attorney's claim and that the debtor's success meant the disallowance of the attorney's claim, we agree that the debtor's objection was part of the claims-allowance process."). *See also McClelland v. Braverman Kaskey & Caprara, P.C. (In re McClelland),* 332 B.R. 90, 96 (Bankr. S.D.N.Y. 2005).

Here, WorldCom's adversary proceeding, which includes its objections to CNI's proof of claim and breach of contract claim, is inextricably intertwined with CNI's proof of claim. It arises out of the same underlying contracts as CNI's proof of claim and both are logically related. If the Court had determined that CNI had any amount due to it under the contracts forming the basis of its assertions in the proof of claim, the Court would have had to resolve WorldCom's breach of contract claim at that time in order to determine the amount of CNI's proof of claim. The Court finds that the resolution of WorldCom's claim bears directly on the claims-allowance process for which there is no Seventh Amendment right to a jury trial because WorldCom's claim and objections to CNI's proof of claim are factually and legally intertwined with CNI's proof of claim — all are based on the same operative facts and contracts. The jury trial right is waived as to any matter that the Court would be required to resolve in order to determine the proof of claim's validity or amount, including offsets against a creditor's claim due to a debtor's counterclaim. *See In re Frost,* 145 B.R. 878; *see also In re CBI Holding Co.,* 311 B.R. at 355-366; *In re McClelland,* 332 B.R. at 91-93, 97-98.

3.   Timing of Jury Trial Waiver

CNI argues that since the Court previously determined the proof of claim, World-Com's claim is a separate and independent issue, thus, CNI has a right to a jury trial. However, it is the filing of the proof of claim that invokes the waiver, even though the scope and breadth of the waiver of the jury trial right may not be ascertained until analyzed in the context of the claim asserted against the creditor. It is immaterial whether the creditor filed its proof of claim prior or subsequent to the commencement

---

14. In *Frost,* the debtor filed an adversary proceeding that objected to a proof of claim for unpaid legal fees and included counterclaims for negligence and breach of contract. The debtor demanded a jury trial. The bankruptcy court denied the request. The bankruptcy court found that the counterclaims asserted by the debtor arose from the same conduct as the proof of claim and "require[d] examination of the overall debtor-creditor relationship." Therefore, the bankruptcy court concluded that the counterclaims were an inextricable part of the claims-allowance process. *In re Frost,* 145 B.R. at 879, 882.

of the adversary proceeding or whether the jury trial demand preceded or followed the filing of the proof of claim. Additionally, it is immaterial whether the proof of claim has been disallowed prior to the Court's determination of the jury trial demand. In each situation, the filing of the proof of claim invokes the claims-allowance process and the creditor subjects itself to the equitable jurisdiction of the Court thereby waiving its right to a jury trial as to any issue that bears directly on the claims-allowance process. *See SNA Nut Co. v. The Häagen-Dazs Co.*, 302 F.3d 725, 730 (7th Cir. 2002) (" 'nothing in [the relevant Supreme Court precedent] suggests that it makes any difference whether the filing of the adversary proceeding precede[d] or follow[ed] the submission of a claim against the bankruptcy estate . . . submission of the claim still would trigger the process of allowance and disallowance of claims. . . . ' ") (alterations in original) (quoting *In re Peachtree Lane, Assocs.*, 150 F.3d 788, 798 (7th Cir. 1998)).

In *SNA Nut Co.*, the bankruptcy court disallowed the proof of claim prior to determining the jury trial demand. SNA Nut Co. ("SNA") commenced two adversary proceedings against Häagen-Dazs. The first alleged Häagen-Dazs owed SNA money for nuts SNA delivered to Häagen-Dazs, the second alleged that Häagen-Dazs breached five supply contracts. Subsequent to the commencement of the adversary proceeding, Häagen-Dazs filed a proof of claim against SNA and a jury trial demand in the second action. The bankruptcy court disallowed the proof of claim when it approved a settlement agreement in the first action. Prior to the trial in the second action, SNA filed a motion to strike the jury trial demand. The bankruptcy court granted SNA's motion and the district court affirmed that decision. On appeal, the Seventh Circuit held that when Häagen-Dazs filed its proof of claim against the bankruptcy estate, it triggered the process of allowing and disallowing claims thereby consenting to the bankruptcy court's equitable jurisdiction and thus, it no longer had a right to a jury trial. *See SNA Nut Co.*, 302 F.3d at 728-31.

The Court's determination that no amount is due to CNI under its proof of claim does not affect the analysis the Court must conduct under *Germain* or the scope or breadth of the waiver at issue. When CNI filed its proof of claim against the bankruptcy estate, it triggered the claims-allowance process, thereby subjecting itself to the equitable jurisdiction of the bankruptcy court. It is the filing of the proof of claim, not its validity, that invokes the waiver of a jury trial right. Hence, the timing of any determination of the validity of the proof of claim is irrelevant to the waiver of a jury trial right. The disallowance of CNI's claim simply resolved CNI's part of the claims-allowance process, it did not end the process. Since the claims-allowance process is still implicated, CNI does not have a right to a jury trial. To hold otherwise would have the anomalous result that a creditor waives its jury trial right *only* if all or a portion of its proof of claim is allowed, yet retains the right if its proof of claim is disallowed in its entirety. In other words, the conversion of the contract dispute from a legal issue to an equitable issue would be temporary and would become permanent only if the proof of claim were allowed in order to offset the contract issue affirmatively raised by the debtor. If not, the creditor would have a right to a jury trial. There is no support for such a finding.

B. Retention of Jury Trial Right

The Court notes that the only cases supporting the retention of the jury trial right for a creditor who files a proof of claim that is met with an adversary proceeding in response to the proof of claim, which is integrally related to that proof of claim, are cases where that creditor properly withdrew its proof of claim such that it was treated as a legal nullity — as if it had never been filed. As a result, that creditor would be deemed not to have submitted itself to the equitable jurisdiction of the bankruptcy court and, therefore, the adversary proceeding asserted against it would not implicate the claims-allowance process. The Seventh Circuit suggested this outcome in *SNA Nut Co.* when it stated that if a creditor properly withdrew its proof of claim, it "retained" its right to a jury trial. *SNA Nut Co.,* 302 F.3d at 731 (distinguishing *Smith v. Dowden,* 47 F.3d 940, 943 (8th Cir. 1995) and *In re 20/20 Sport, Inc.,* 200 B.R. 972, 979-80 (Bankr. S.D.N.Y. 1996) on the basis that the creditors properly withdrew their proof of claim in *Dowden* and *20/20 Sport*); *see, e.g., Dowden,* 47 F.3d at 943 (creditor retains jury trial right if proof of claim is properly withdrawn; the withdrawn claim thereby becomes a legal nullity and the creditor is treated as if the proof of claim had never been filed, therefore, the creditor has not submitted itself to the equitable jurisdiction of the court and the adversarial proceeding is not integrally related to the claims-allowance process). This is not the situation before the Court.

V. *Conclusion*

WorldCom's motion to strike CNI's jury demand is granted. When CNI filed its proof of claim, it subjected itself to the equitable jurisdiction of the Court and CNI does not have a jury trial right as to any issue implicating the claims-allowance process. The Court finds that WorldCom's breach of contract claim arises from the same contracts, tariffs, and transactions as CNI's proof of claim. The contracts that CNI alleges that WorldCom breached in its proof of claim are the very same contracts that WorldCom alleges CNI breached. Therefore, World-Com's breach of contract claim is inextricably intertwined with the claims-allowance process and as a result the contract dispute, a traditionally legal issue, has been converted into an equitable issue for which there is no Seventh Amendment right to a jury trial.

The Debtor is to settle an order consistent with this opinion.

QUESTIONS

Does the question of the availability of a jury trial bring notions of "jurisdiction by ambush" back into the bankruptcy process? Which party wants a jury trial? What leverage does the availability of a jury trial provide to the parties? How does the 1994 enactment of 28 U.S.C. §157(e) affect these issues?

PROBLEM 11-5

Willie Wonka Corp. filed for Chapter 11 relief and actually had a plan confirmed in the case. As a part of its plan of reorganization, the debtor retained the right to collect preferences from creditors. One of the preference actions was brought against Mairzy Doats. The debtor had paid Mairzy $100,000 within 60 days of the commencement of the case in partial settlement of a wrongful death action stemming from the death of Mairzy's husband after eating a very bad piece of chocolate. Another $150,000 was due under the settlement at the time of the commencement of the case, but it has not been paid. In response to the preference action, Mairzy filed a compulsory counterclaim to have the court enforce the settlement. Mairzy demanded a jury trial, and Wonka has moved to strike the jury demand. What result? In re Schwinn Bicycle Co., 184 B.R. 195 (Bankr. N.D. Ill. 1995).

The issues relating to bankruptcy court jurisdiction and the availability of jury trials would all go away if bankruptcy judges were appointed under Article III of the Constitution. Proposals to that effect have been made for nearly 30 years. Nevertheless, Congress has never seen fit to put bankruptcy judges in life tenure positions. A significant stumbling block to those efforts is the fact that the creation of Article III bankruptcy judges would put the President in the position of making several hundred judicial appointments with the advice and consent of the Senate, a politically dicey matter. Should this ever happen, however, many of the questions that arise over the jurisdiction of the bankruptcy courts will be removed, and the costs attended to resolving those matters would likewise be saved by the estate and other parties in interest.

III. Appeals

Reflecting the status of bankruptcy judges as Article I judges, appeals from their decisions historically go first to the district court, where an Article III judge can decide the matter. The 2005 amendments to the Code authorize lower courts to certify "a question of law as to which there is no controlling decision of the court of appeals for the circuit or of the Supreme Court of the United States, or involves a matter of public importance" for direct appeal to the relevant Court of Appeals; 28 U.S.C. §158(d). Even if the court or all of the appellants and appellees certify the matter, the Court of Appeals itself still must decide to accept the appeal.

The Bankruptcy Code also authorizes the creation of Bankruptcy Appellate Panels (BAPs). These are panels comprised of three bankruptcy judges who hear appeals from the bankruptcy courts. The circuits have begun to create BAPs, but their right to hear appeals is significantly restricted by the ability of the district judges in a particular district to vote to prohibit the appeal of bankruptcy court decisions to a BAP. Appeals in those districts will continue to be made to the district court. Whether the appeal is to the district court or to a BAP, appeals from those decisions are made to the Courts of Appeals and thereafter to the Supreme Court.

Part VIII of the Rules of Bankruptcy Procedure governs appellate matters. Most importantly, Rule 8002(a) provides that "[t]he notice of appeal shall be filed with the clerk within ten days of the date of the entry of the judgment, order, or decree appealed from." This time for filing a notice of appeal is significantly shorter than the rules applicable in most other courts. Therefore, you should be especially vigilant in taking action to appeal decisions of bankruptcy courts. *See, e.g.*, In re Arbuckle, 988 F.2d 29 (5th Cir. 1993) (bankruptcy court order entered on February 28, 1992 [a leap year] was received by mail by debtors' attorney on March 6, and notice of appeal sent by "overnight mail" on Saturday March 7 filed by the bankruptcy clerk on March 10, 1992, was filed one day late and appeal was dismissed).

TABLE OF CASES

TABLE OF STATUTES
AND REGULATIONS

INDEX